TEXTS & MATERIALS ON INTERNATIONAL HUMAN RIGHTS

What constitutes a fair trial for Saddam Hussein? What rights do survivors of Hurricane Katrina have to food and water? How does international law try to regulate trafficking of women and children into Europe? When can a State legitimately avoid complying with human rights due to a perceived terrorist threat?

International human rights, now more than ever, is at the forefront of global politics and encompasses a broad and diverse range of subjects, issues and geographical jurisdictions. This new textbook takes a thematic approach to the subject by collecting material around concepts and frameworks rather than specific rights making it the ideal companion for most courses in international human rights.

Cases and materials are clearly separated from the main body of the text so that extracted material is immediately recognisable. The surrounding text contextualises each extract and explains the relevant issues, while questions throughout the book encourage students to analyse and debate the material they are reading. This book is ideal for students seeking to truly engage with and understand the key issues concerning the study of international human rights.

Dr Rhona K. M. Smith is Reader in Law at Northumbria University.

TEXTS & MATERIALS ON INTERNATIONAL HUMAN RIGHTS

Rhona K. M. Smith

Routledge·Cavendish
Taylor & Francis Group
LONDON AND NEW YORK

First published 2007 by Routledge-Cavendish
2 Park Square, Milton Park, Abingdon, Oxon OX14 4RN

Simultaneously published in the USA and Canada
by Routledge-Cavendish
270 Madison Ave, New York, NY 10016

Routledge-Cavendish is an imprint of the Taylor & Francis Group, an informa business

Typeset in Palatino and Gill Sans by
RefineCatch Limited, Bungay, Suffolk
Printed and bound in Great Britain by
Antony Rowe Ltd, Chippenham, Wiltshire

British Library Cataloguing in Publication Data
A catalogue record for this book is available from the British Library

Library of Congress Cataloging in Publication Data
A catalog record for this book has been requested

ISBN 10: 1–85941–938–0 (pbk)
ISBN 13: 978–1–85941–938–0 (pbk)

This book seeks to provide an introduction to international human rights law, particularly those primary sources (treaties, other instruments and jurisprudence) which elaborate the fundamental rights and freedoms to which we are all entitled. International human rights benefits remarkably from the world wide web. Indeed, it is possible to access almost all the primary materials through the official websites of the key organisations: the United Nations; Council of Europe; International Labour Organisation; Organisation of American States; African Union. A wealth of non-governmental organisations, charities, governments and individuals add to this their own views, guidelines and materials. Never in history have we, wherever we are in the world, been able to freely and easily access as much information on our 'common birthright' of human rights as we can today. Although a remarkable resource, the sheer volume of information available can appear daunting. Thus this text provides an entry into the maze of material, introducing the key topics and the key materials. It is neither a substitute for reading the primary resources nor is it intended to compare with the esteemed monographs, other books and commentaries already on the market. In the space available, it cannot cover the entire range of rights and freedoms. Rather it takes a thematic approach, attempting to draw together the main areas of activity under umbrella headings, demonstrating the interdependence and indivisibility of international human rights. Inevitably there are repetitions and omissions, as well as different approaches to the materials selected.

The chapters cover the fundamentals of international human rights (ie what they are, where to find them, how to enforce them), then the rights accorded to key vulnerable groups, reflecting those areas which appear to be of most interest to students (hence also including a chapter (15) on international humanitarian and criminal laws). As the book is targeted at undergraduates and those new to the area, the principal problem in selecting materials was anticipating what will be taught in introductory courses and be of most interest to intending students. Inevitably, the final product cannot satisfy everyone so any and all constructive comments are welcomed.

With a focus on primary materials, almost all the extracts are in the public domain and freely available. However, I sought the consent of the relevant bodies for reproduction of extracted materials. To this end, I am grateful to the international and regional organisations for permission to reproduce jurisprudence and documents. In particular my gratitude to Bianka Ochs of the OHCHR in Geneva for ploughing through lists of documents to ensure permission was granted. I have, for reasons of copyright, limited the use of secondary sources. In its place, I have provided indicative further reading lists at the conclusion of each chapter to assist with further research.

As far as possible, the text and materials were accurate as at 4 December 2005. However, as Cavendish became Routledge-Cavendish thereafter, it took some eight months for the proofs to be produced. I have thus attempted to rewrite and update the text of the proofs to be accurate on 8 September 2006 with a few minor 'tweaks' at third proofs, November 2006.

In accordance with the old Scottish saying, 'the best laid schemes o' Mice an' Men gang aft agley'. As external circumstances seemed to thwart the compilation of this text at every turn, inevitably friends and family deserve acknowledgement and heartfelt gratitude for their support and understanding as yet again I retreated from normality and resorted to working almost every evening and weekend. Zoe Botterill (who left just before the manuscript was submitted) and Madeleine Langford proved most helpful when this project was eventually reallocated to them by Cavendish after Ruth Massey's departure for pastures new. I also benefitted from the assistance of Gareth Codd who agreed (and managed) to bring some order to the manuscript at very short notice. Finally my International Human Rights students at Strathclyde and Northumbria Universities have, over the years, enlightened me as to what students find most useful and interesting.

Til Far, Mor og Lorna, mange tak.
RKMS

CONTENTS

TABLE OF CASES

TABLE OF LEGISLATION

TABLE OF TREATIES AND INSTRUMENTS

CHAPTER I

SOURCES OF INTERNATIONAL HUMAN RIGHTS

To many, human rights have their origins in the mists of time. Undoubtedly, human rights are bound up in philosophical thought and religious tenets. The very idea of governance involves some elements of delineation of rights and obligations on the part of the governors and the governed. A degree of reciprocity underpins this: loyalty of the people in return for protection from external harm. Such early history retains echoes today and such a concept of the rule of law is entwined with many elements of human rights.

Respect for the right to life finds expression in almost all religious texts and faiths. Religions such as Buddhism demand a high level of respect for the life of all creatures (even to the extent of advocating vegetarianism), while religions permitting the taking of life for food (e.g. Islam) prescribe clearly the methods for killing animals. Those beliefs in earlier times which evinced ritual sacrifice included specific instructions to precede the taking of life. Similar examples from other religious tenets can easily be located. Most faiths include a guide to the rules for the operation of civil society; whether in the Koran, the Bible, the Torah or other texts, the similarities are clear. Respect for elements of human dignity, family life and rules concerning combat have early origins. Indeed many religious texts also contain rules on justice.

As for philosophy, some elements of human rights are bound up in the evolution of the rule of law; other elements find early expression in the revolution of political theory in the eighteenth century, primarily in Europe. However, earlier philosophical writings exhibit concepts now identifiable as human rights: Confucius and Tao are two examples from Asia.

As Tomuschat notes, 'international protection of human rights is a chapter of legal history that has begun at a relatively late stage in the history of humankind' (Tomuschat, C, *Human Rights between Idealism and Realism*, 2003, Oxford: OUP, p 7). As a reflection of this, for the purposes of these materials, the principal sources of human rights are taken in the modern context and are drawn from the principal human rights instruments. Human rights are thus viewed herein as creatures of international law, norms created according to international law and traditions. It is thus appropriate to first outline the mechanisms for creating such norms under international law. Legal force ascribes to international human rights through treaties and customary international law. Today international legal instruments form the basis of human rights in the new world order. This does not diminish the importance of developing an understanding of philosophical and theoretical traditions. Rather the approach of this text is practical and the emphasis must be on legal norms from here on in.

The following diagram illustrates the main sources of international human rights. Note that they all overlap to a certain (not necessarily quantifiable) extent.

For the purpose of this chapter, international laws are addressed under treaties, States' custom and practice is considered under customary international law and national tradition is omitted from detailed discussion as obviously it varies from State to State. The most significant impact it has concerns national legal theory and whether a State adheres to, for example, a liberal or socialist theory of rights. National mechanisms for realising the protection of human rights are discussed in Chapter 7.

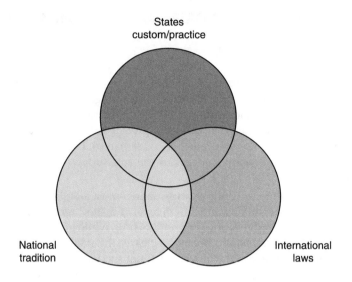

States
custom/practice

National
tradition

International
laws

1.1 TREATIES

Treaties are those binding instruments adopted by States which enshrine the fundamental rights and freedoms to which the State ascribes, and to which its nationals are
entitled. These instruments take many forms and a plethora have emerged on a number of diverse topics over the last 50 years. Treaties are legally binding on the States
which sign up and ratify them. The Vienna Convention on the Law of Treaties 1969 is
a key international agreement which governs the creation, operation and legal effect
of most treaties in effect today. It includes the major rules and regulations concerning
treaties and, although not all States have ratified it, many elements represent common
State practice and thus it will be used as indicative of the law of treaties throughout.

1.1.1 What are Treaties?

Vienna Convention on the Law of Treaties 1969 Art 2(1)(a)

"treaty" means an international agreement concluded between States in written form and governed by international law, whether embodied in a single instrument or in two or more related
instruments and whatever its particular designation.

Treaties are formal sources of international law and very common in international
human rights law. Simply put, treaties are contracts concluded under international
law and thus they are legally binding on States which have agreed to them. As indicated by the Vienna Convention, terminology varies—treaties, conventions, covenants, protocols, charters and statutes are the most common terms—but irrespective of
what the instrument is called, certain common features can be identified. Primarily,
most are written (although oral treaties can exist, no relevant examples pertain to
international human rights) and thus the content of the rights and freedoms can easily
be identified. Treaties can be bilateral (between two parties) or multilateral (between
many States) although international human rights treaties are usually multilateral
instruments open to any State to sign up to at any time. This is in accordance with the
goal of achieving universal human rights.

Treaties are commonly drafted by representatives of States, the 'umbrella' organisation (United Nations; Council of Europe, etc.) and even representatives of non-governmental organisations and thus the beneficiaries of the treaty are the peoples of the world/region. Often an international conference will be convened to allow a wide number of States to debate the proposed terms of the treaty and decide which clauses are and are not acceptable. Such conferences may launch or conclude declared international decades or years, thereby providing greater impetus to the achievement of international consensus on the matter. The Convention on the Rights of the Child is a prime example; it was adopted at the end of the International Decade on the Rights of the Child. The recent International Decade on the World's Indigenous Peoples, in contrast, did not succeed in producing an agreed text on the rights of indigenous peoples (see Chapter 12), although one of the first acts of the Human Rights Council in June 2006 ameliorated the position.

Treaties may be given a formal name (or title) but are frequently referred to by the city in which the text was agreed by the drafting States. Common examples are the Banjul Charter on Human and Peoples' Rights of the African Union; the San Salvador Protocol to the American Convention on Human Rights and the Geneva Conventions on the Laws of War. Note that several treaties on different subjects may be concluded in the one city, thus designating treaties solely on the basis of the city (even with the date) is not necessarily definitive. The full title of the treaty may be required for identification purposes.

1.1.2 How do States agree to Treaties?

All States possess the capacity to conclude treaties (Vienna Convention on the Law of Treaties Art 6). Membership of the United Nations is not necessarily required but recognition by other States as a State is. There is normally a two part process to be followed by States wishing to be bound by the terms of treaties: signature and ratification. States joining a treaty after it has entered into force usually accede to it (whether a State accedes or ratifies can also depend on the nature of the State and its approach to treaty law). These terms are explained in the Vienna Convention.

Vienna Convention on the Law of Treaties 1969

Article 11

The consent of a State to be bound by a treaty may be expressed by signature, exchange of instruments constituting a treaty, ratification, acceptance, approval or accession, or by any other means if so agreed.

Article 12

1. The consent of a State to be bound by a treaty is expressed by the signature of its representative when:

   (a) the treaty provides that signature shall have that effect;

   (b) it is otherwise established that the negotiating States were agreed that signature should have that effect; or

   (c) the intention of the State to give that effect to the signature appears from the full powers of its representative or was expressed during the negotiation.

2. For the purposes of paragraph 1:

   (a) the initialing of a text constitutes a signature of the treaty when it is established that the negotiating States so agreed;

(b) the signature *ad referendum* of a treaty by a representative, if confirmed by his State, constitutes a full signature of the treaty.

Article 14

1. The consent of a State to be bound by a treaty is expressed by ratification when:

   (a) the treaty provides for such consent to be expressed by means of ratification;

   (b) it is otherwise established that the negotiating States were agreed that ratification should be required;

   (c) the representative of the State has signed the treaty subject to ratification; or

   (d) the intention of the State to sign the treaty subject to ratification appears from the full powers of its representative or was expressed during the negotiation.

2. The consent of a State to be bound by a treaty is expressed by acceptance or approval under conditions similar to those which apply to ratification.

Article 15

The consent of a State to be bound by a treaty is expressed by accession when:

(a) the treaty provides that such consent may be expressed by that State by means of accession;

(b) it is otherwise established that the negotiating States were agreed that such consent may be expressed by that State by means of accession; or

(c) all the parties have subsequently agreed that such consent may be expressed by that State by means of accession.

Once a State has indicated its intention to be bound by a treaty, such as at a major international conference launching the treaty, the State representatives will usually be required to return to their respective States and seek national approval and ratification for the terms of the treaty.

Treaties are generally signed by a prominent and authorised State official (see Vienna Convention Art 7 for who has powers to conclude treaties on behalf of States) to indicate political will to accede to its terms. At this time, the treaty is politically and morally binding on the State. Such a signature is then ratified after the relevant national procedures are followed. National law, particularly the constitutional provisions, determine whether a referendum is required or what steps are necessary to obtain parliamentary or governmental approval of a treaty. Only once an instrument is ratified will it become legally binding on States and thus enforceable. Some treaties do not require ratification, becoming binding solely on signature. In order that the list of States who are bound by an instrument is contemporary, it is normal for States to submit ratification documents to a central body (often the United Nations Secretary-General) for dissemination to other States who are already bound by the instrument.

The following is an example of a signature and ratification clause.

Convention on the Political Rights of Women 1952 Art IV

1. This Convention shall be open for signature on behalf of any Member of the United Nations and also on behalf of any other State to which an invitation has been addressed by the General Assembly.

2. This Convention shall be ratified and the instruments of ratification shall be deposited with the Secretary-General of the United Nations.

Question

In terms of national constitutional law, why are signature and ratification treated separately and why may both be required before a state is bound?

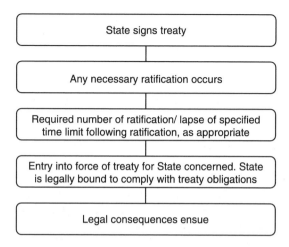

When ratifying an instrument, a State may also elect to indicate whether it wishes to avoid legal liability for certain clauses. This is called a reservation. Reservations and declarations can have a significant effect on the legal impact of an instrument and are discussed in more detail in Chapter 3.

1.1.3   When do treaties become legally binding?

In terms of international law, treaties become legally binding when they enter into force. In other words, they become applicable and enforceable law on that date. Note that treaties only apply to those States which have agreed to be bound by the provisions of the treaty in question. States cannot be forced to comply with a treaty which has not entered into force or not been ratified by them. Obviously, political pressure can be, and is, exerted to secure compliance with certain human rights, for example through trade and aid agreements. However, this is distinct from the legal enforcement of treaties.

Vienna Convention on the Law of Treaties 1969 Art 24

(1) A treaty enters into force in such a manner and upon such a date as it may provide or as the negotiating States may agree.

(2) Failing any such provision or agreement, a treaty enters into force as soon as consent to be bound by the treaty has been established for all the negotiating States.

(3) When the consent of a State to be bound by a treaty is established on a date after the treaty has come into force, the treaty enters into force for that State on that date, unless the treaty provides otherwise.

Usually a clause near the end of the treaty will specify when the treaty becomes legally binding on contracting parties, that is, when it enters into force. This clause in the International Covenant on Economic, Social and Cultural Rights follows, as an example.

International Covenant on Economic, Social and Cultural Rights 1966 Art 27

1. The present Covenant shall enter into force three months after the date of the deposit with the Secretary-General of the United Nations of the thirty-fifth instrument of ratification or instrument of accession.

2. For each State ratifying the present Covenant or acceding to it after the deposit of the thirty-fifth instrument of ratification or instrument of accession, the present Covenant shall enter into force three months after the date of deposit of its own instrument of ratification or instrument of accession.

Note

Given the growth in the international community in recent years (the United Nations now has 191 Member States, having been created by 51 States in 1945), the issue of new States is important. Many of the older international human rights treaties have experienced a dramatic expansion in the numbers of Contracting States. This has in itself produced many problems with respect to implementing the treaties, as is discussed in Chapter 3. Many treaties enter into force with a small number of States then experience an increase in membership as the years, or even decades go by. The International Covenant on Economic, Social and Cultural Rights took around 10 years to achieve the necessary number of ratifications to enter into force. It was opened for signature in 1966, yet only achieved the necessary ratifications to enter into force in 1976.

Question

What reasons are there for such a delay between opening for signature and entry into force? Can delays ever be a positive or essential element in creating a binding web of obligations for the protection of human rights?

States which sign up to a treaty can be referred to as High Contracting Parties, States Party, Parties, Signatories or even Member States. The terminology of choice depends on the instrument and the host organisation. It is important to ascertain whether a particular State is bound by a particular instrument. The internet is a valuable resource in this respect. For example, a list of States which are party to the major United Nations human rights treaties is located at www.ohchr.org.

Question

Which major human rights treaties concluded under the auspices of the United Nations has the United States of America ratified?

Once a treaty has entered into force, all contracting parties are required to act in accordance with its binding terms and to discharge any obligations in good faith. This is known as the doctrine of *pacta sund servanda* (see Vienna Convention on the Law of Treaties Art 26). Unless otherwise agreed or specified, treaties are binding throughout the territory of the contracting State (Vienna Convention on the Law of Treaties Art 29). For human rights treaties, this means that all individuals under the jurisdiction of the State can benefit from the terms of the instrument. Furthermore, States may not invoke principles of their national (internal) law as justification for failing to comply with treaty obligations (Vienna Convention on the Law of Treaties Art 27). This is again relevant in the context of human rights as the rights of individuals are frequently prescribed by national constitutions and it is clear that such national instruments may not supersede the terms of a binding international human rights instrument. The relationship between national and international law is considered in Chapter 7.

1.1.4 What happens if a treaty is concluded in a foreign language?

Treaties are often concluded in one or more authentic language(s), that is, the language(s) in which the treaty text is confirmed as being legally binding. For most international human rights instruments, the official languages of the organisation which has organised the drafting of the treaty will be deemed authentic. Consider the following examples.

Convention on the Elimination of All Forms of Discrimination against Women 1979 (United Nations) Art 30

The present Convention, the Arabic, Chinese, English, French, Russian and Spanish texts of which are equally authentic, shall be deposited with the Secretary-General of the United Nations.

International Labour Organisation Convention No 182 on the Worst Forms of Child Labour 1999 Art 16

The English and French versions of the text of this Convention are equally authoritative.

Organisation of African Unity Convention Governing the Specific Aspects of the Refugee Problems in Africa 1969 Art X(2)

The original instrument, done if possible in African languages, and in English and French, all texts being equally authentic, shall be deposited with the Administrative Secretary-General of the Organisation of African Unity.

Council of Europe's European Convention for the Protection of Human Rights and Fundamental Freedoms 1950 concluding clause

Done at Rome this 4th day of November 1950, in English and French, both texts being equally authentic, in a single copy which shall remain deposited in the archives of the Council of Europe.

Question

What problems can having multiple authentic versions of a treaty cause in terms of enforcement?

The Vienna Convention gives guidance on reconciling conflicting authentic texts:

Vienna Convention on the Law of Treaties 1969 Art 33

1. When a treaty has been authenticated in two or more languages, the text is equally authoritative in each language, unless the treaty provides or the parties agree that, in case of divergence, a particular text shall prevail.

2. A version of the treaty in a language other than one of those in which the text was authenticated shall be considered an authentic text only if the treaty so provides or the parties so agree.

3. The terms of the treaty are presumed to have the same meaning in each authentic text.

4. Except where a particular text prevails in accordance with paragraph 1, when a comparison of the authentic texts discloses a difference of meaning which the application of articles 31 and 32 does not remove, the meaning which best reconciles the texts, having regard to the object and purpose of the treaty, shall be adopted.

1.1.5 Subsequent amendments and additions to treaties

Treaties may subsequently be amended, often by a device called a protocol. Protocols are simply international instruments added on to a treaty. They are usually optional, so a State may be party to the main treaty but avoid obligations under any associated protocols. In the field of human rights, protocols frequently provide additional rights and freedoms. Examples include the two protocols to the United Nations Convention on the Rights of the Child on the involvement of children in armed conflicts and on the sale of children, child prostitution and child pornography. Both were adopted in 2000. Other protocols may provide an optional enforcement mechanism. For political reasons, the enforcement mechanism may have been omitted from the main treaty. The First Optional Protocol to the International Covenant on Civil and Political Rights is such an example. It enshrines a system of individual petitions which many States have elected not to sign up to. Within the African regional system, the protocol on establishing an African Court on Human Rights was added to the African Charter on Human and Peoples' Rights several years after the original treaty. This happened because the system and political will had developed to the extent that it was feasible to establish a human rights court.

1.1.6 Principal international human rights treaties

The following list contains the most common international human rights instruments, the 'core texts' of the United Nations. The full text of each instrument can be obtained from the website of the Office of the UN High Commissioner for Human Rights (www.ohchr.org):

The International Covenant on Civil and Political Rights 1966
The International Covenant on Economic, Social and Cultural Rights 1966
The International Convention on the Elimination of all Forms of Racial Discrimination 1965
The Convention on the Elimination of Discrimination against Women 1979
The Convention against Torture and other Cruel Inhuman or Degrading Treatment or Punishment 1984
The UN Convention on the Rights of the Child 1989
The Convention on the Rights of Migrant Workers and their Families 1990

These are the seven core United Nations treaties, though many other important instruments are adopted under the auspices of the United Nations and its main organs, institutions and associated organisations which pertain to human rights. The International Labour Organisation, for example, has adopted more than 100 treaties on workers' rights. From those, the governing body has identified eight Conventions as 'fundamental to the rights of human beings at work, irrespective of levels of developments of . . . States'. There are two conventions in each of four principal categories.

Forced labour

Convention No. 29 on forced labour 1930
Convention No. 105 on the abolition of forced labour 1957

Child labour

Convention No. 138 on minimum age 1973
Convention No. 182 on worst forms of child labour 1999

Freedom of association

Convention No. 87 on freedom of association and protection of the right to organise 1948
Convention No. 98 on the right to organise and collective bargaining 1949

Equality

Convention No. 111 on discrimination (employment and occupation) 1958
Convention No. 100 on equal remuneration 1951

These are discussed in more detail in Chapter 8.

Regional organisations have also contributed towards the development of international human rights, creating tabulations of fundamental rights and enforcement mechanisms for ensuring their protection.

Council of Europe

European Convention for the Protection of Human Rights and Fundamental Freedoms 1950

Organisation of American States

American Convention on Human Rights 1969

African Union

African Charter on Human and Peoples' Rights 1981

Regional organisations and the protection of human rights under regional law are discussed more in Chapter 4.

1.1.7 The issue of overlapping treaty obligations

Often the rights contained within the various human rights instruments overlap. The prohibition on torture is thus found in the UN and European treaties on torture, the European, American, African, Arab and CIS conventions on human rights, the International Covenant on Civil and Political Rights and the instruments on discrimination against women, race discrimination, children and migrant workers, to give a few examples. The following list illustrates the overlap in the main international and regional human rights instruments. The table reflects which rights from the Universal Declaration on Human Rights (which is used here as the core standard) appear in which subsequent international and regional instruments. The two international covenants (which provide a binding tabulation of the Universal Declaration on Human Rights) and the Convention on the Rights of the Child (which has attracted almost universal ratification) represent the international system; the three major regional systems are deployed as examples of regional instruments. Note that the table provides only an approximation of the overlap in rights and freedoms.

Right/freedom (UDHR)	ICCPR	ICESCR	CRC	ECHR	AmCHR	AfCHPR
Art 2 Non-discrimination	Art 2, 3	Art 2, 3	Art 2	Art 14		Art 2
Art 3 Life and liberty	Art 6, 9, 10		Art 6	Art 2, 5	Art 4, 7	Art 4
Art 4 Slavery	Art 8			Art 4	Art 6	Art 5
Art 5 Torture	Art 7		Art 37	Art 3	Art 5	Art 5
Art 7 Equal before the law	Art 14, 26		Art 40	Art 6	Art 3, 24	Art 3
Art 8 Effective national remedy				Art 13	Art 25	Art 7

Art 9 Arbitrary arrest and detention	Art 11		Art 40	Art 5		
Art 10 Fair trial	Art 14		Art 40	Art 6	Art 8	Art 7
Art 11 Presumption of innocence non-retrospective crimes	Art 14		Art 40	Art 6, 7	Art 8, 9	Art 7
Art 12 Private and family life	Art 17		Art 9, 10, 16	Art 8	Art 11	
Art 13 Freedom of movement	Art 12		Art 10			
Art 14 Asylum			Art 22		Art 22	Art 12
Art 15 Nationality	Art 24		Art 7			
Art 16 Marriage and family	Art 23	Art 10		Art 12	Art 17	Art 18
Art 17 Property				Prot 1	Art 21	Art 14
Art 18 Thought, conscience and religion	Art 18		Art 14	Art 9	Art 12	Art 8
Art 19 Opinion and expression	Art 19		Art 13	Art 10	Art 13	Art 9
Art 20 Assembly and association	Art 21, 22	Art 8	Art 15	Art 11	Art 15, 16	Art 10, 11
Art 21 Political participation	Art 25		Art 12, if it affects them		Art 23	Art 13
Art 22 Social security ESCR		Art 9	Art 26			
Art 23 Work		Art 6, 7	Art 32 exploit			Art 15
Art 24 Rest and leisure		Art 7	Art 31			
Art 25 Adequate standard of living, health, food, etc.		Art 11, 12	Art 24, 27			Art 16

Art 26 Education		Art 13, 14	Art 28, 29	Prot 1		Art 17
Art 27 Cultural life	Art 27	Art 15	Art 30			Art 17
Art 28 Social and international order						Art 23

KEY
ICCPR: International Covenant on Civil and Political Rights
ICESCR: International Covenant on Economic, Social and Cultural Rights
CRC: United Nations Convention on the Rights of the Child
ECHR: European Convention on Human Rights
AmCHR: American Convention on Human Rights
AfCHPR: African Charter on Human and Peoples' Rights

The regional instruments in Africa and the Americas contain additional rights that are expressly mentioned in the Universal Declaration. These are therefore excluded from the table. Evidently, many rights are replicated in several instruments. Non-discrimination clauses are virtually uniform, although recent treaties contain more expansive grounds of discrimination. The Charter of Fundamental Rights of the European Union 2000 Art 21 has one of the most comprehensive non-discrimination clauses.

Question

What advantages may there be in the same right appearing in several instruments?

Question

Look at the ratification history of various States (available online)—why will some States ratify one instrument but not another which has the same or lesser rights?

1.2 CUSTOMARY INTERNATIONAL LAW

Not all international human rights are located in written treaties. Some rights may be found in customary international law. This has some advantages as not all States have signed up to and ratified the principal international human rights instruments yet they still remain bound by some of the provisions of human rights. Similarly, elements of customary international law predate the emergence of treaties enshrining generic norms of human rights. (See also Alston, P, 'The Sources of Human Rights Law: Custom, Jus Cogens, General Principles' (1992) Australian Yearbook of International Law 82).

Smith, R, 'Customary international law' in Smith and van den Anker (eds),
The Essentials of Human Rights pp. 79–80

Customary international law is binding on States and may have the force of law. In accordance with the Statute of the International Court of Justice, the laws which the Court applies to resolve disputes includes international custom, as evidence of a general practice accepted as law and the general principles of law recognised by civilised nations (Article 38). Customary international law differs from Treaties in that customary international law may not be written down. States do not 'sign up' to customary international law or ratify it in the conventional way. Rather, customary international law refers to a practice which States follow because they feel legally obligated to do so. Customary international law was a very early form of international law. To a large extent, particularly in human rights, it has been superseded by treaties—prescribed formal legal obligations in written form.

There are two criteria which must be met for customary international law:

(1) Actual behaviour/practice of states. The International Court of Justice demands that for behaviour to constitute customary international law, it must be 'constant and uniform'. Consistency is a key requirement—States must act in conformity with the rule. Not all states must act in the specified manner; particular emphasis is given to those states who are particularly affected by the law in question. For international human rights, it would be necessary that almost all States act in conformity with the measure. There is no prescribed length of time during which states should engage in the behaviour. As with so many norms of law, much depends on the circumstances of the law in question. With international human rights, the practice will usually have evolved over a long period of time. State practice can be evidenced in a number of different ways. Recourse can be had to actual practice, diplomatic statements, national law, treaties agreed to etc. With international human rights, treaties and national law are probably the easiest elements of state practice/behaviour to identify. National constitutions and legal systems can be surveyed to gather evidence of consistency. The number of states acquiescing to international and regional human rights instruments is another obvious indicator.

(2) Legal reason for such behaviour. There is a need for *opinio juris* to be demonstrated when establishing customary international law. In other words, it is necessary to demonstrate that states are acting in a consistent practice because they feel they are under a legal obligation to do so. The International Court of Justice has noted that it is essential that states feel they are acting in conformity with what amounts to a legal obligation. Mere social usage does not suffice, the obligatory quality of the practice must be demonstrated. Of course it is difficult to prove the reasons for the actions of any given state. Politics, economics and diplomacy may all influence state practice. With international human rights, the problem is compounded as human rights by nature involve the actions of a state towards its nationals and other residents. It is necessary to indicate that the state feels subservient to international law in its actions. In other words, the state does not have the option to treat its nationals in a different manner. This has broad repercussions for the notion of national/parliamentary supremacy as it requires a state to acknowledge that it does not exist in a vacuum but rather its actions, even within its own territory, are shaped by international obligations.

Both actual state practice and a legal obligation to comply with the 'law' must be demonstrated before a rule of customary international law can be found. In the event of an international dispute, it is the state arguing the existence of a rule of customary international law which must demonstrate the criteria are met and thus the other state should have acted in conformity with it.

Question

National laws can be used as evidence of opinio juris. *Written constitutions are an obvious example. South Africa is notable for its new human rights based constitution, while in other States, human rights may not be tabulated in a written constitution. What other national law sources could thus be used as evidence of intent?*

The voting practices of States in regional and international fora may be indicative of a given State's approach to particular issues. While it is clear that politics and diplomacy have an impact, voting may provide evidence of State practice and even *opinio juris.*

In this respect, soft law (discussed below) is also of relevance. Declarations, trade agreement terms etc. can all provide evidence of State practice. They can also reflect accepted norms.

1.2.1 Altering and rejecting emergent customs

Custom can and does change over time and, just as with treaties, States can elect not to be bound by the norm. However for custom, a State must be more overt than passive in negating the rule in question. A passive State may find itself bound by rules of custom through inactivity.

Smith, R, 'Customary international law' in Smith and van den Anker (eds), *The Essentials of Human Rights* p. 80

. . . any state refuting a customary rule must do so from the inception of the practice in question. If a state only becomes part of the international community after the rule of customary international law has been established, then that state is bound by the rule whether it likes it or not. Given the international community has increased almost fourfold in the last fifty years, the importance of pre-existing binding customary international law cannot be overlooked.

Note that for most States, this means that they are bound by customary provisions on international human rights. Few, if any States, have negated customary provisions. Indeed, it appears that for the international community, ever more rights, freedoms and associated principles are entering into the realm of customary international law thereby lessening the imperative for State ratifications of treaties.

Given the vagaries of establishing customary international law, the most common alteration to custom occurs not through altered State usage but through codification of the customary practice in a treaty.

1.2.2 Customary guarantees against torture and slavery

The prohibition on slavery and on torture are two obvious examples of human rights' provisions which transcend the fundamental treaties and now can be regarded as customary international law. Consequently, States are bound to refrain from engaging in slavery or torture irrespective of whether or not they have ratified any international human rights instruments.

Slavery Convention 1926 Art 2

The High Contracting Parties undertake, each in respect of the territories placed under its sovereignty, jurisdiction, protection, suzerainty or tutelage, so far as they have not already taken the necessary steps:

(a) To prevent and suppress the slave trade

(b) To bring about, progressively and as soon as possible, the complete abolition of slavery in all its forms.

As the prohibition on slavery has roots traceable some 200 years back, few States have had the opportunity (and none have availed themselves of it) to steadfastly indicate an intention not to be bound by this norm. The United Nations itself is predicated on respect for the dignity and worth of the human person (Preamble, Charter of the United Nations 1945), a respect which clearly presupposes the abolition of slavery.

More recent condemnations of slavery and the slave trade, such as those issued at the World Conference against Racism and Racial Discrimination, Xenophobia and Related Intolerance 2001, add further universal support for the customary nature of the prohibition. The number and identity of treaties which the State in question has ratified is irrelevant as the State is bound purely because the prohibition on slavery is so well established that States feel legally bound by it and act in accordance with it.

Universal Declaration of Human Rights Art 5

No one shall be subjected to torture or to cruel, inhuman or degrading treatment or punishment.

For torture (as opposed to degrading or cruel treatment), the same is arguably true. Most States have ratified at least one article prohibiting torture. Difficulties remain due to problems of definition. Only the most abhorrent treatments fall within the prohibition on torture. It would be more difficult to extend the remit of custom to other infringing treatment which falls short of torture.

International and universal revulsion over practices of genocide make it another candidate for customary law, indeed *jus cogens*. Indeed, the international community roundly condemned genocide and pledged to take steps to prevent further occurrences in April 2004 on the tenth anniversary of the Rwandan Genocide. Genocide now gives rise to individual liability not only under the universal jurisdiction doctrine (whereby any State may prosecute an individual responsible for genocide irrespective of where the acts in point occurred) but also in terms of the Rome Statute of the International Criminal Court (see Chapters 5 and 15).

1.2.3   Case study: extracting custom from the United Nations Convention on the Rights of the Child

The United Nations Convention on the Rights of the Child has been ratified by all but two member States of the United Nations. Both the United States of America and Somalia have failed to ratify it, although Somalia has indicated its willingness to endorse the provisions and proceed to ratification as and when the turbulent political situation permits. Leaving aside for the moment the question of why States will ratify an expansive list of children's rights and yet avoid ratifying much shorter lists of basic human rights, the mere fact that most of the world has accepted the rights of the child produces the potential for customary law. However, it is not possible to infer that all the articles of the Convention form customary international law. Obviously, not all States comply with all the norms and some are, in essence, more aspirational than others, as the concluding observations of the Committee on the Rights of the Child demonstrate. Nevertheless, several principles underpin the UN Convention, including the best interest of the child, a concept central to decision-making processes.

UN Convention on the Rights of the Child Art 3(1)

In all actions concerning children whether undertaken by public or private social welfare institutions, courts of law, administrative authorities or legislative bodies, the best interests of the child shall be a primary consideration.

Similar provisions appear throughout the Convention. It is alluded to in Art 40 on juvenile offenders and Art 18 acknowledges the best interests of the child as the 'basic concern' of parents and legal guardians. Arguably, the 'best interests of the child' principle now transcends the treaty and is rightly considered part of customary international law. This is the view of some prominent international commentators including Geraldine Van Beuren.

Question

While rendering the best interests of the child part of customary international law may have little impact in the USA, which has been resilient to diplomatic efforts in favour of securing ratification, an emergent customary norm may have significant impact in the national laws of many contracting states. Why?

While some treaties can crystallise into customary international law, other treaties may from the outset reflect norms of customary law. Such treaties codify the custom. They do not override it, other than in respect of the States which sign up to the instrument.

1.2.4 *Jus cogens*

Related to customary international law is the concept of *jus cogens*: those norms of law which are effectively entrenched in the international regime and are non-negotiable.

Vienna Convention on the Law of Treaties Art 53
Treaties conflicting with a peremptory norm of general international law (*jus cogens*)

A treaty is void if, at the time of its conclusion, it conflicts with a peremptory norm of general international law. For the purposes of the present Convention, a peremptory norm of general international law is a norm accepted and recognized by the international community of States as a whole as a norm from which no derogation is permitted and which can be modified only by a subsequent norm of general international law having the same character.

Such peremptory norms, or *jus cogens*, are binding on all States irrespective of their treaty obligations and irrespective of their evidenced State practice. No State can legally act against these principles. In terms of international human rights, the prohibitions on slavery and genocide, the prohibition on racial discrimination (as discussed at the World Conference against Racism, Racial Discrimination, Xenophobia and Related Intolerance, Durban, South Africa 2001) and the right of all peoples to self-determination (in the sense of decolonisation) are obvious examples.

In *jus cogens*, one effectively finds the immutable public policy provisions, or entrenched concepts of the international community. Some elements of international human rights law apply *erga omnes*—that is all states are bound by the provision. (See for example *Barcelona Traction Light and Power Company* case *(Belgium v Spain)* [1970] ICJ Reps 32, para 33 re genocide, protection from slavery and racial discrimination; *Case concerning East Timor (Portugal v Australia)* [1995] ICJ Reps 102.)

Further examples can be drawn from judgments of the International Court with respect to international humanitarian and criminal law. See for example, the *Advisory Opinion on the Legality of the Threat or Use of Nuclear Weapons* [1996] ICJ Reps 257 referring to fundamentals of international humanitarian law as 'intrangressible principles of international customary law'.

1.3 OTHER INTERNATIONAL AND REGIONAL INSTRUMENTS

In addition to legally binding law enshrined in treaties or reflecting customary practice, international law also has a large body of material known as 'soft law'. 'Soft law' includes an array of different measures which can considerably influence and shape State practice. In essence, they can be regarded as statements of intent on the part of States. Moreover, they can be important indicators of State practice, thereby contributing towards the evolution of customary law.

Key instruments include declarations of international and regional organisations. These can prove to be of extreme importance. The Universal Declaration of Human Rights is a declaration of the General Assembly of the United Nations. As such, it is not strictly legally enforceable, although obviously it is of strong moral force and represents the agreed viewpoint of the international community. Moreover, as is mentioned above, some elements of the Universal Declaration are now so widely accepted as to be deemed customary international law.

Consider the impact of decolonisation. It swept the world in the era of the adoption of the following declaration and thereafter.

General Assembly Resolution 1514 (XV) Declaration on the Granting of Independence to Colonial Countries and Peoples 1960

1. The subjection of peoples to alien subjugation, domination and exploitation constitutes a denial of fundamental human rights, is contrary to the Charter of the United Nations and is an impediment to the promotion of world peace and co-operation.

2. All peoples have the right to self-determination; by virtue of that right they freely determine their political status and freely pursue their economic, social and cultural development.

3. Inadequacy of political, economic, social or educational preparedness should never serve as a pretext for delaying independence.

4. All armed action or repressive measures of all kinds directed against dependent peoples shall cease in order to enable them to exercise peacefully and freely their right to complete independence, and the integrity of their national territory shall be respected.

5. Immediate steps shall be taken, in Trust and Non-Self-Governing Territories or all other territories which have not yet attained independence, to transfer all powers to the peoples of those territories, without any conditions or reservations, in accordance with their freely expressed will and desire, without any distinction as to race, creed or colour, in order to enable them to enjoy complete independence and freedom.

6. Any attempt aimed at the partial or total disruption of the national unity and the territorial integrity of a country is incompatible with the purposes and principles of the Charter of the United Nations.

7. All States shall observe faithfully and strictly the provisions of the Charter of the United Nations, the Universal Declaration of Human Rights and the present Declaration on the basis of equality, non-interference in the internal affairs of all States, and respect for the sovereign rights of all peoples and their territorial integrity.

As is discussed in Chapter 8, the General Assembly's Declaration on the Rights and Responsibility of Individuals, Groups and Organs of Society to Promote and Protect Universally Recognised Human Rights and Fundamental Freedoms (GA Resn 53/144 (1999)) has also had considerable impact on human rights. This instrument seeks to lay some responsibility for human rights at the door of individuals and other non-State entities.

From the perspective of the international human rights lawyer, many declarations of the General Assembly are also indicative of consensual political will among States and many are important precursors to more legally enforceable international human rights. Frequently, major declarations are followed by international treaties.

Children's Rights

Declaration on the Rights of the Child 1959—United Nations Convention on the Rights of the Child 1989

Racial Discrimination

Declaration on the Elimination of all forms of Racial Discrimination 1963—International Convention on the Elimination of All Forms of Racial Discrimination 1965

Discrimination against Women

Declaration on the Elimination of Discrimination against Women 1967—Convention on the Elimination of All Forms of Discrimination against Women 1979

Question

Compare and contrast the rights in the declaration and the subsequent convention—some of the texts are reproduced below; are there many differences?

Other declarations are evidence of international concern although their content is yet to be consolidated in an international treaty.

Declaration on the Elimination of All Forms of Intolerance and of Discrimination based on Religion or Belief 1981
Declaration on the Right to Development 1986
Declaration on the Rights of Persons belonging to National or Ethnic, Religious and Linguistic Minorities 1992

Question

Why might international consensus on the terms of a binding treaty on these issues be difficult to achieve?

1.3.1 Jurisprudence

Considerable jurisprudence has emerged over the last half century, elaborating on a wide range of international human rights provisions. Some of this jurisprudence emanates from the international and regional treaty monitoring bodies, other elements from national courts. A major feature of international human rights law is the use of jurisprudence from other jurisdictions to shape judgments. Advocates and judges frequently employ cases from other regional and national systems to help extrapolate principles of law and determine the scope and nature of particular human rights. Accordingly, it is not possible to definitively state which laws will be applied to a particular case. First, international and regional systems do not operate within a system of binding precedents and thus decide cases based on the facts before them along with contemporary opinions and practices. Secondly, as human rights are constantly evolving, tribunals and courts may have recourse to the dicta of bodies in other organisations and States in order to ascertain current thought on a particular issue. Reference to other sources may be covert or overt, depending on the body involved. There is thus a degree of consistency in the jurisprudence. Similarly, it is important to bear in mind that restricting study to a single treaty will not afford the reader a complete understanding of the subject. Human rights are indivisible, interdependent and universal, thus justifying treating the various instruments as elements of an organic whole.

1.3.2   Case study: corporal punishment of children

The issue of corporal punishment of children has evoked considerable discussion around the world in recent years. Much of the jurisprudence is based on the prohibition on torture and other cruel, inhuman and degrading treatment or punishment, a provision common to most instruments and subject to more detailed tabulation in the UN and European conventions on torture.

1.3.2.1   The salient treaty provisions

Most instruments contain a prohibition on torture, cruel, inhuman and degrading treatment or punishment—these provisions are also used to assess whether corporal punishment is acceptable. For example, the European Court of Human Rights considered that judicial corporal punishment was contrary to Art 3 of the European Convention on Human Rights (see e.g. *Tyrer v United Kingdom*, Series A, vol. 26 European Court of Human Rights). Note also that corporal punishment of convicted prisoners had been condemned in South Africa (*S v Staggie* (1990) 1 SA Criminal Law Reports 669 and *S v Daniels* (1991) 2 SA Criminal Law Reports 403).

UN Convention on the Rights of the Child 1989 Art 19

1. States Parties shall take all appropriate legislative, administrative, social and educational measures to protect the child from all forms of physical or mental violence, injury or abuse, neglect or negligent treatment, maltreatment or exploitation, including sexual abuse, while in the care of parent(s), legal guardian(s) or any other person who has the care of the child.

2. Such protective measures should, as appropriate, include effective procedures for the establishment of social programmes to provide necessary support for the child and for those who have the care of the child, as well as for other forms of prevention and for identification, reporting, referral, investigation, treatment and follow-up of instances of child maltreatment described heretofore, and, as appropriate, for judicial involvement.

Concluding Observations of the Committee on the Rights of the Child: United Kingdom of Great Britain and Northern Ireland, UN Doc. CRC/C/15/Add.188, 4 October 2002, at para 35 et seq.

Corporal punishment

35. The Committee welcomes the abolition of corporal punishment in all schools in England, Wales and Scotland following its 1995 recommendations (ibid., para. 32), but is concerned that this abolition has not yet been extended to cover all private schools in Northern Ireland. It welcomes the adoption by the National Assembly for Wales of regulations prohibiting corporal punishment in all forms of day care, including childminding, but is very concerned that legislation prohibiting all corporal punishment in this context is not yet in place in England, Scotland or Northern Ireland.

36. In light of its previous recommendation (ibid., para. 31), the Committee deeply regrets that the State party persists in retaining the defence of 'reasonable chastisement' and has taken no significant action towards prohibiting all corporal punishment of children in the family.

37. The Committee is of the opinion that the Government's proposals to limit rather than to remove the 'reasonable chastisement' defence do not comply with the principles and provisions of the Convention and the aforementioned recommendations, particularly since they constitute a serious violation of the dignity of the child (see similar observations of the Committee on Economic, Social and Cultural Rights, E/C.12/1/Add.79, para. 36). Moreover, they suggest that some forms of corporal punishment are acceptable, thereby undermining educational measures to promote positive and non-violent discipline.

38. The Committee recommends that the State party:

(a) With urgency adopt legislation throughout the State party to remove the 'reasonable chastisement' defence and prohibit all corporal punishment in the family and in any other contexts not covered by existing legislation;

(b) Promote positive, participatory and non-violent forms of discipline and respect for children's equal right to human dignity and physical integrity, involving children and parents and all those who work with and for them, and carry out public education programmes on the negative consequences of corporal punishment.

Consider also the European Social Charter.

European Social Charter (Revised) Art 17
The right of children and young persons to social, legal and economic protection

With a view to ensuring the effective exercise of the right of children and young persons to grow up in an environment which encourages the full development of their personality and of their physical and mental capacities, the Parties undertake, either directly or in co-operation with public and private organisations, to take all appropriate and necessary measures designed:

1. . . .

(b) to protect children and young persons against negligence, violence or exploitation;

2. to provide to children and young persons a free primary and secondary education as well as to encourage regular attendance at schools.

The European Committee of Social Rights supervises the implementation of the European Social Charter and has expounded its view of Article 17:

Council of Europe European Committee of Social Rights, Conclusions XV-2, Vol. 1 (2001)

Article 17 requires a prohibition in legislation against any form of violence against children, whether at school, in other institutions, in their home or elsewhere.

1.3.2.2 The jurisprudence

The following cases demonstrate how national and regional law has approached the issue of corporal punishment. These cases also illustrate how jurisprudence can evolve—international human rights are constantly advancing to provide an ever greater standard of care for individuals.

European Court of Human Rights

A v United Kingdom (1998) Vol. 1998-VI, No. 90

The stepfather of A (a nine-year-old boy) was charged with assault. The boy had sustained severe bruising and markings (which lasted several days) from beatings with a cane. At trial in England, the jury accepted the stepfather's defence of reasonable chastisement. As a result, the stepfather was acquitted and freed. Representatives of the boy raised a case before the European Court of Human Rights claiming that the United Kingdom Government had allowed the boy's right to freedom from inhuman and degrading treatment or punishment to be infringed. In essence, the argument which prevailed was that the State owed a positive obligation to protect the right of the child. This could only be discharged through the application of criminal law.

1. The Court recalls that the applicant, who was then nine years old, was found by the consultant paediatrician who examined him to have been beaten with a garden cane which had been applied with considerable force on more than one occasion (see paragraph 9 above).

The Court considers that treatment of this kind reaches the level of severity prohibited by Article 3.

2. It remains to be determined whether the State should be held responsible, under Article 3, for the beating of the applicant by his stepfather.

The Court considers that the obligation on the High Contracting Parties under Article 1 of the Convention to secure to everyone within their jurisdiction the rights and freedoms defined in the Convention, taken together with Article 3, requires States to take measures designed to ensure that individuals within their jurisdiction are not subjected to torture or inhuman or degrading treatment or punishment, including such ill-treatment administered by private individuals (see, *mutatis mutandis*, the H.L.R. v. France judgment of 29 April 1997, *Reports* 1997-III, p. 758, § 40). Children and other vulnerable individuals, in particular, are entitled to State protection, in the form of effective deterrence, against such serious breaches of personal integrity (see, *mutatis mutandis*, the X and Y v. the Netherlands judgment of 26 March 1985, Series A no. 91, pp. 11–13, §§ 21–27; the Stubbings and Others v. the United Kingdom judgment of 22 October 1996, *Reports* 1996-IV, p. 1505, §§ 62–64; and also the United Nations Convention on the Rights of the Child, Articles 19 and 37).

3. The Court recalls that under English law it is a defence to a charge of assault on a child that the treatment in question amounted to 'reasonable chastisement' (see paragraph 14 above). The burden of proof is on the prosecution to establish beyond reasonable doubt that the assault went beyond the limits of lawful punishment. In the present case, despite the fact that the applicant had been subjected to treatment of sufficient severity to fall within the scope of Article 3, the jury acquitted his stepfather, who had administered the treatment (see paragraphs 10–11 above).

4. In the Court's view, the law did not provide adequate protection to the applicant against treatment or punishment contrary to Article 3. Indeed, the Government have accepted that this law currently fails to provide adequate protection to children and should be amended.

In the circumstances of the present case, the failure to provide adequate protection constitutes a violation of Article 3 of the Convention.

(Note that this notion of a positive obligation to protect rights will be considered in Chapter 2. It is also of relevance when discussing violence against women in the home, Chapter 14.)

Perhaps unsurprisingly, a ban on physical chastisement of children was not deemed an interference with the rights to family life which are protected under the European Convention for the Protection of Human Rights and Fundamental Freedoms.

Similar issues have been raised and the approach of the European Court and United Nations Committee on the Rights of the Child is discussed in the South African Constitutional Court (*S v Williams et al.* (1995) 3 SA 362 (Constitutional Court)) and the English House of Lords (*R v Secretary of State for Education and Employment and others ex p Williamson* [2005] UKHL 15).

Note the approach of the Canadian Supreme Court.

Canadian Foundation for Children, Youth and the Law v Canada [2004] 1 SCR 76

The Supreme Court of Canada was asked to consider the constitutionality of s 43 of the Criminal Code which provides 'Every schoolteacher, parent or person standing in the place of a parent is justified in using force by way of correction toward a pupil or child, as the case may be, who is under his care, if the force does not exceed what is reasonable under the circumstances'. The Canadian Foundation for Children, Youth and the Law contended that this provision was contrary to three provisions of the Canadian Charter of Rights and Freedoms: s 7 as the exception doesn't further the interests of the child, s 12 as it condones cruel and unusual punishment or treatment and s 15 by denying children the protection against assault to which adults are entitled. The Court dismissed the appeal although Justices Deschamps and Arbour (now the UN High Commissioner for Human Rights) dissented, deeming the provision contrary to human rights.

32. Canada is a party to the United Nations *Convention on the Rights of the Child*. Article 5 of the Convention requires state parties to

> respect the responsibilities, rights and duties of parents or . . . other persons legally responsible for the child, to provide, in a manner consistent with the evolving capacities of the child, appropriate direction and guidance in the exercise by the child of the rights recognized in the present Convention.

Article 19(1) requires the state party to

> protect the child from all forms of physical or mental violence, injury or abuse, neglect or negligent treatment, maltreatment or exploitation, including sexual abuse, while in the care of parent(s), legal guardian(s) or any other person who has the care of the child [emphasis added].

Finally, Article 37(*a*) requires state parties to ensure that '[n]o child shall be subjected to torture or other cruel, inhuman or degrading treatment or punishment' [emphasis added]. This language is also found in the *International Covenant on Civil and Political Rights*, Can. T.S. 1976 No. 47, to which Canada is a party. Article 7 of the Covenant states that '[n]o one shall be subjected to torture or to cruel, inhuman or degrading treatment or punishment.' The preamble to the *International Covenant on Civil and Political Rights* makes it clear that its provisions apply to 'all members of the human family'. From these international obligations, it follows that what is 'reasonable under the circumstances' will seek to avoid harm to the child and will never include cruel, inhuman or degrading treatment.

33. Neither the *Convention on the Rights of the Child* nor the *International Covenant on Civil and Political Rights* explicitly require state parties to ban all corporal punishment of children. In the process of monitoring compliance with the *International Covenant on Civil and Political Rights*, however, the Human Rights Committee of the United Nations has expressed the view that corporal punishment of children in schools engages Article 7's prohibition of degrading treatment or punishment: see for example, *Report of the Human Rights Committee*, vol. I, UN GAOR, Fiftieth Session, Supp. No. 40 (A/50/40) (1995), at paras. 426 and 434; *Report of the Human Rights Committee*, vol. I, UN GAOR, Fifty-fourth Session, Supp. No. 40 (A/54/40) (1999), at para. 358; *Report of the Human Rights Committee*, vol. I, UN GAOR, Fifty-fifth Session, Supp. No. 40 (A/55/40) (2000), at paras. 306 and 429. The Committee has not expressed a similar opinion regarding parental use of mild corporal punishment.

34. Section 43's ambit is further defined by the direction to consider the circumstances under which corrective force is used. National and international precedents have set out factors to be considered. Article 3 of the *European Convention on Human Rights*, 213 U.N.T.S. 221, forbids inhuman and degrading treatment. The European Court of Human Rights, in determining whether parental treatment of a child was severe enough to fall within the scope of Article 3, held that assessment must take account of 'all the circumstances of the case, such as the nature and context of the treatment, its duration, its physical and mental effects and, in some instances, the sex, age and state of health of the victim': Eur. Court H.R., *A. v. United Kingdom*, judgment of 23 September 1998, *Reports of Judgments and Decisions* 1998-VI, p. 2699. These factors properly focus on the prospective effect of the corrective force upon the child, as required by s. 43.

Note however, that a limitation on corporal punishment, in the form of prohibiting it in schools and other forms of organised day care, has been upheld even where no similar ban is imposed on parents.

1.3.2.3   Comment

Although in no international or regional instrument is the corporal punishment of children explicitly proscribed, it is clear that the issue is being monitored and States are being encouraged to dramatically limit the use of the defence of reasonable chastisement, if not abolish it altogether. The cross-referencing of the various bodies is also apparent. Momentum is building in support of the abolition of corporal punishment of children. This also indicates the evolving nature of human rights—after all, it took many years last century before domestic violence legislation evolved to prevent physical punishment intra-spouses.

1.4   A PRACTICAL GUIDE TO SOURCES

For the student of international human rights law, there are three main sources to which one will most likely have recourse: treaties, jurisprudence and academic commentaries. In this section, each will be considered in turn, evaluating the importance of each and guiding the reader to appropriate (and accessible) locations.

1.4.1   Treaties

Just as with public international law itself, treaties are the primary source of international human rights law. There are hundreds of instruments, all legally binding, which contribute towards the creation of law in the area. The full text of selections of the main international and regional instruments can be found on the internet. Each organisation publishes its primary texts on its own website. The following are the principal portal websites for the named organisations. Clearly marked links go to the main documents and instruments associated with each organisation:

United Nations: www.un.org
United Nations Office of the High Commissioner for Human Rights: www.ohchr.org
International Labour Organisation: www.ilo.org
Council of Europe: www.coe.int
Organisation of Security and Cooperation in Europe: www.osce.org
European Union: europa.eu
Organisation of American States: www.oas.org
African Union: www.african-union.org
League of Arab States: www.leagueofarabstates.org.

It is useful for students to familiarise themselves with the portal sites of the main organisations which they will be studying. Create a list or bookmark the individual document homepages to provide easy access to your own online library of source materials.

Each host organisation holds the authentic texts of its treaties in its archives and each contracting State holds copies of the treaties to which it is party in its archives. This means that it is sometimes possible to trace the text of a treaty through the archives (physical or electronic) of any State. Obviously the principal limitation is that

States only hold the texts of the treaties to which they are party. The advantage is that some States place all the relevant texts online, thereby facilitating access by all.

In addition, there are a number of compilations of documents which have been published as edited volumes. These contain a selection of treaties, selected and sometimes edited down by the editors. The following are examples:

Brownlie, I and Goodwin-Gill, G (eds), *Basic Documents on Human Rights*, 5th edn, 2006, Oxford: OUP

Ghandhi, P, *Blackstone's International Human Rights Documents*, 5th edn, 2006, Oxford: OUP

Wallace, R, *International Human Rights, text and materials*, 2nd edn, 2001, London: Sweet and Maxwell

Martin, JP, *25+ Human Rights Documents*, 3rd edn, 2001, New York: Center for the Study of Human Rights, Columbia University

Irrespective of the source used, with treaties, there are several important questions which must be considered when researching treaties as a source of human rights:

(1) **What rights and obligations does it contain?** This information is easily ascertainable from the text of the treaty. Further elaboration may be available in an explanatory memorandum published alongside the treaty which contains the rationale behind the adoption of the instrument and an explanation of the intended effect of its provisions.

(2) **Is it in force?** Most treaties require a minimum number of States to ratify/accede before the instrument enters into force. The principal websites usually indicate whether or not a particular treaty is in force, failing which it is possible to ascertain the relevant criteria (usually found in the General Provisions near the end of a treaty) and then determine the exact number of Contracting States. The treaty will enter into force the stated number of days/months following receipt of the required number of ratifications/instruments of accession.

(3) **Who has ratified it?** Lists of High Contracting Parties are available from the websites of the principal organisations. Check the date of ratification as there may be a delay between ratification and entry into force of the treaty for a given State. The period of any such delay will be specified in the treaty.

(4) **What impact has it had on national law?** This is particularly important if a State is required under national law to adopt specific legal measures implementing a treaty. Regard must be had to the Constitution of the State, national laws and decisions of national courts. Such information is obviously country-specific.

1.4.2 Jurisprudence

Alongside the primary texts, recourse will be had to the evolving jurisprudence, in its widest context, which supports the treaties. This jurisprudence may be classified as interpretative and guiding comments, reports from States and treaty monitoring bodies, caselaw and reports from NGOs and other interested parties. As with treaties, most of this information can now be found online. This greatly facilitates research as it is sometimes difficult to find the originals in the archives of individual States. The material relevant to each State is normally located in the archives of the Foreign Affairs Ministry (in the UK, the Foreign and Commonwealth Office: www.fco.gov.uk).

1.4.2.1   Interpretative and guiding comments

In order to better understand the scope and nature of the various instruments, it is necessary to examine what the drafters intended and what the monitoring bodies consider important. The *travaux préparatoires* of the treaty can provide evidence of the drafters' intention but may not always be easily accessible. They are often kept in the archives of the regional or international organisation under whose auspices the instrument was drafted (or the drafting conference was convened). Many such archives are now being transferred into web-friendly formats and are thus available online. Others require visits to specialised libraries and/or the relevant archives.

Explanatory memoranda may accompany the treaty which, although not legally binding, may also prove informative. Bodies such as the Council of Europe regularly publish explanatory memorandum to accompany new treaties. These are usually available online. United Nations Treaty Monitoring Bodies issue statements on the scope and nature of the obligations incumbent on States. These General Comments are discussed further in Chapter 6.

1.4.2.2   State and Treaty Monitoring Bodies Reports

All seven major United Nations international human rights treaties have treaty monitoring bodies established to oversee their operation. Compliance by States is monitored primarily through a system of regular self-evaluative reports (see Chapter 6). Regional treaties such as the European Social Charter are also implemented through reports from States to a regional committee. Reading State reports and the observations of the salient committee thereon indicates the extent to which a State is complying with the treaty and the views of the committee as to examples of good practice, issues requiring further attention, areas of concern etc. As the extract from the Concluding observations of the United Nations Committee on the Rights of the Child (above) demonstrates, the concluding observations on State reports may also be valuable in extending the scope of the rights and freedoms. They may also provide an explanation of the practical nature of the rights.

Question

Look up concluding observations of the Committee on Economic Social and Cultural Rights—most of the rights and freedoms in the associated treaty are to be achieved 'progressively'. Follow through some State reports and observations to see whether progressive realisation of rights is in fact achieved.

In locating the observations of the treaty monitoring bodies, reference should be had to the websites of the body in question. The website of the Office of the High Commissioner for Human Rights, for example, provides full copies of most State reports and concluding observations. These can be searched by country, by treaty, or by symbol (UN Document number); the latter is useful for searching the Treaty Bodies Database.

The following is an example of the information available online. The reports are available in various languages: in the United Nations, E-English, F-French, S-Spanish, R-Russian (Cyrillic), C-Chinese (Mandarin), A-Arabic.

State	Date of meeting	State report	List of issues	Reply	Delegate comments	Concluding observations of committee	Reply from State (if applicable)
	Session	E/F/R	E	E	E	E/F/R/S	E/F

Note that not every committee examines all aspects of the treaty and the State's compliance therewith at each session. Further, note that recourse to the views concerning other States can be useful as they may be indicative of the view of the Committee and the direction in which the right is evolving.

1.4.2.3 Caselaw

Although there are not as many cases on international human rights as national law, the African, American and European Courts and Commissions on Human Rights have made valuable contributions to the breadth and depth of understanding of human rights. Their cases and comments evidence the nature and scope of human rights and may sometimes be transferable. The extracts on corporal punishment (above) provide an example. Similarly, the opinions of the United Nations Treaty Monitoring Bodies on individual communications enrich our understanding of the rights and obligations in the various treaties as well as reinforcing the indivisibility and universality of human rights. (Note that not all United Nations human rights treaties permit individual communications—see Chapter 6.)

The following websites provide access to the caselaw and individual communications.

www.unhchr.ch/tbs/doc.nsf—United Nations Treaty Bodies database
www.ohchr.org/english/bodies/hrc/index.htm—United Nations Human Rights Committee
www.ohchr.org/english/bodies/cerd/index.htm—Committee on the Elimination of Racial Discrimination
www.ohchr.org/english/bodies/cat/index.htm—Committee against Torture
www.un.org/womenwatch/daw/cedaw/—Committee on the Elimination of Discrimination against Women
www.echr.coe.int—website of the European Court of Human Rights. The HUDOC search engine allows for searches on articles, parties or topics.
www.achpr.org—website of the African Commission on Human and Peoples' Rights with a section on decisions (under construction as of November 2006).
www.corteidh.or.cr—website of the Inter-American Court of Human Rights with access to its caselaw.

Consulting these sources will provide an excellent overview of the contemporary nature of any given treaty or, indeed, of any particular right or freedom.

A few websites consolidate the primary materials, providing ready access to the texts of the instruments, the reports of States and monitoring bodies and caselaw. These can be an excellent resource as they are effectively virtual libraries with the added benefit of clear categorisation of the materials and/or search engines.

1.4.2.4   Virtual library websites

Although the Office of the High Commissioner for Human Rights and the principal regional bodies have a comprehensive range of materials available online, additional external sites may also prove useful.

www.sim.law.uu.nl—the SIM document centre of the University of Utrecht. Searches can be made for individual treaty articles and jurisprudence thereon as well as the texts of the relevant materials. A schematic system classifies all the material and facilitates navigation.

www1.umn.edu.humarts—the University of Minnesota virtual human rights library. This also provides links to selected jurisprudence of the regional bodies.

www.bayefsky.com—Professor Ann Bayefsky established this site with access to the main UN materials. There is also a useful search facility which enables the user to identity all materials (treaty articles, monitoring bodies' reports and jurisprudence) which impact on a particular subject or theme. Searches can also be made for materials related to individual countries.

1.4.2.5   Reports of NGOs and other bodies

In addition, NGO sites frequently contain the relevant treaty texts and extracts from relevant State reports. The quality of NGO sites can vary and, of course, some may specifically select material in order to provide a polemical view on a topic. However, as recourse can easily be had to the primary materials through the official organisation sites, the relevance of NGO sites can easily be ascertained. Without doubt they have great value in concentrating all the materials on a given topic, often providing practical and theoretical analysis thereof. It is impossible to list all the NGOs which have useful websites as there are so many; thus only a few examples are given.

www.ngos.net/—United Nations NGO Network
www.amnesty.org/—Amnesty International
www.hrw.org/—Human Rights Watch
www.savethechildren.org—Save the Children
www.antislavery.org/—Slavery International
www.survival-international.org/—Survival International
www.right-to-education.org/—Right to Education
www.childrenareunbeatable.org.uk/—Corporal punishment
www.article19.org/—Global Campaign for Free Expression

In addition, many other bodies publish material of use in ascertaining the content and scope of the main human rights.

1.4.3   Academic Commentaries

Finally, academic commentaries can elaborate on the rights and freedoms which comprise international human rights law. It is not feasible to list all the relevant texts here. Many books address sections of human rights law or the impact of human rights provisions within particular States or sections of the community. Other books focus on a single right or freedom. Different theoretical considerations are also published. A perusal of any good bookshop, library catalogue, or the online catalogues of major law and international relations publishers provides a wealth of information.

Suggestions for further reading will be provided at the end of each chapter in this text. As far as possible, the texts mentioned will be those available in most law libraries and/or online.

FURTHER READING

For information on treaties and customary international law, recourse should be had to Public International Law texts.

Brownlie, I, *Principles of Public International Law*, 6th edn, 2003, Oxford: OUP

Evans, M, (ed) *International Law*, 2004, Oxford: OUP

Cassesse, A, *International Law*, 2004, Oxford: OUP

Shaw, M, *International Law*, 5th edn, 2003, Cambridge: CUP

Dixon, M, and McCorquodale, R, *Cases and Materials on International Law*, 4th edn, 2003, Oxford: OUP

Harris, D, *Cases and Materials on International Law*, 6th edn, 2004, London: Sweet and Maxwell

Sinclair, I, *The Vienna Convention on the Law of Treaties*, 1984, Manchester: MUP

Tams, C, *Enforcing Obligations Erga Omnes in International Law*, 2005, Cambridge: CUP

For general texts on international human rights, the following may prove to be of use:

Alfredsson, G, and Eide, A (eds), *The Universal Declaration of Human Rights—A Common Standard of Achievement*, 1999, The Hague: Martinus Nijhof

Buergenthal, T, Shelton, D, and Stewart, D, *International Human Rights in a Nutshell*, 3rd edn, 2002, St Paul, Minn.: West Group

Nowak, M, *Introduction to the International Human Rights Regime: No. 14 (Raoul Wallenberg Institute Series of Intergovernmental Human Rights Documentation)*, 2004, Leiden: Brill

O'Byrne, D, *Human Rights: an Introduction*, 2003, Harlow: Longman

Rehman, J, *International Human Rights Law, a practical approach*, 2003, Harlow: Pearson Education

Smith, R, *Textbook on International Human Rights*, 3rd edn, 2007, Oxford: OUP

Smith, R and van den Anker, C (eds), *The Essentials of Human Rights*, 2005, London: Hodder Arnold

Steiner, H, and Alston, P, *International Human Rights in Context—Law Politics Morals*, 2000, Oxford: OUP. 3rd edition due 2006

Tomuschat, C, *Human Rights—between idealism and realism*, 2003, Oxford: OUP

KEY CONCEPTS: UNIVERSALITY, INTERDEPENDENCE AND CATEGORIES OF RIGHTS

There are clearly many recognised examples of international human rights and fundamental freedoms. These are derived from many different sources as Chapter 1 indicated. As with so many legal systems, there are certain principles which undermine those rights and govern their operation. For human rights, most importantly, they are deemed to be universal. Thus absolutely everyone is entitled to human rights and fundamental freedoms.

2.1 UNIVERSALITY

Universal Declaration of Human Rights 1948 Art 1

All human beings are born free and equal in dignity and rights. They are endowed with reason and conscience and should act towards one another in a spirit of brotherhood.

The text of the Universal Declaration is an unequivocal endorsement of the universality of the rights contained therein. Similar statements appear in subsequent instruments which couch the beneficiaries of rights in terms such as 'everyone' and 'all persons'. Nevertheless, an issue which has long plagued academics and practitioners alike is whether human rights are truly universal. Obviously, the idea of human rights as externally verified and intrinsically applicable to all human beings suggests that rights are universal. However, only 56 States were members of the United Nations and thus party to the creation of the Universal Declaration. Membership of the United Nations has since more than trebled to some 191 States today. Africa and Asia (in a pre-decolonisation era) were particularly under-represented in strict geographical terms. Despite this, there is evidence of universal acceptance of universal rights. When the two International Covenants were adopted, the membership of the United Nations had more than doubled, while in comparison to the Universal Declaration an additional 133 States (Switzerland and Timor L'est (East Timor) only joined in 2002) were party to the UN Millennium Declaration which emphasised universal respect for the Universal Declaration.

General Assembly Millennium Declaration, Resolution A/Res/55/2
V. Human rights, democracy and good governance

24. We will spare no effort to promote democracy and strengthen the rule of law, as well as respect for all internationally recognized human rights and fundamental freedoms, including the right to development.

25. We resolve therefore:

• To respect fully and uphold the Universal Declaration of Human Rights.

• To strive for the full protection and promotion in all our countries of civil, political, economic, social and cultural rights for all.

• To strengthen the capacity of all our countries to implement the principles and practices of democracy and respect for human rights, including minority rights.

• To combat all forms of violence against women and to implement the Convention on the Elimination of All Forms of Discrimination against Women.

• To take measures to ensure respect for and protection of the human rights of migrants, migrant workers and their families, to eliminate the increasing acts of racism and xenophobia in many societies and to promote greater harmony and tolerance in all societies.

- To work collectively for more inclusive political processes, allowing genuine participation by all citizens in all our countries.

- To ensure the freedom of the media to perform their essential role and the right of the public to have access to information.

Perhaps more significantly, every Member State of the United Nations is party to additional enforceable human rights treaties which, almost without exception, pay homage to the influencing role of the Universal Declaration. Consider the following preambular statements:

International Covenant on Civil and Political Rights 1966

Recognising that, in accordance with the Universal Declaration of Human Rights, the ideal of free human beings enjoying civil and political freedom and freedom from fear and want can be achieved only if conditions are created whereby everyone may enjoy his civil and political rights, as well as his economic, social and cultural rights.

International Covenant on Economic, Social and Cultural Rights 1966

Recognising that, in accordance with the Universal Declaration of Human Rights, the ideal of free human beings enjoying civil and political freedom and freedom from fear and want can be achieved only if conditions are created whereby everyone may enjoy his economic, social and cultural rights, as well as his civil and political rights.

Perhaps this is to be expected in the twin Covenants which, after all, were drafted specifically to give legal effect to the terms of the Universal Declaration on Human Rights. Similar sentiments are also to be found expressed in other instruments, regional instruments and even in some national constitutions.

Convention against Torture and Other Cruel Inhuman or Degrading Treatment of Punishment 1984

. . . *Having* regard to article 5 of the Universal Declaration of Human Rights and article 7 of the International Covenant on Civil and Political Rights, both of which provide that no one shall be subject to torture or to cruel, inhuman or degrading treatment or punishment.

European Convention for the Protection of Human Rights and Fundamental Freedoms 1950

Considering the Universal Declaration of Human Rights proclaimed by the General Assembly of the United Nations on 10th December 1948 . . .

American Convention on Human Rights 1969

. . . *Reiterating* that, in accordance with the Universal Declaration of Human Rights, the ideal of free men enjoying freedom from fear and want can be achieved only if conditions are created whereby everyone may enjoy his economic, social and cultural rights, as well as his civil and political rights.

African Charter on Human and Peoples' Rights 1981

. . . *Reaffirming* the pledge they made . . . to co-ordinate and intensify their co-operation and efforts to achieve a better life for the peoples of Africa and to promote international co-operation, having regard to the Charter of the United Nations and the Universal Declaration of Human Rights.

Arab Charter on Human Rights 1994

. . . *Reaffirming* the principles of the Charter of the United Nations and the Universal Declaration of Human Rights, as well as provisions of the United Nations International Covenants on Civil and Political Rights and Economic, Social and Cultural Rights and the Cairo Declaration on Human Rights in Islam.

Today it would appear that, for whatever reason, universal acknowledgement of the importance of the Universal Declaration of Human Rights is a reality. This remains true despite sometimes vigorous disputes over the factual content of the Declaration and the legal enforceability of its provisions.

Indeed, many newly independent States incorporate swathes of the Universal Declaration in their Constitutions:

Constitution of the Republic of South Africa 1996

Rights

7. (1) This Bill of Rights is a cornerstone of democracy in South Africa. It enshrines the rights of all people in our country and affirms the democratic values of human dignity, equality and freedom.

(2) The state must respect, protect, promote and fulfil the rights in the Bill of Rights.

(3) The rights in the Bill of Rights are subject to the limitations contained or referred to in section 36, or elsewhere in the Bill.

Application

8. (1) The Bill of Rights applies to all law, and binds the legislature, the executive, the judiciary and all organs of state.

(2) A provision of the Bill of Rights binds a natural or a juristic person if, and to the extent that, it is applicable, taking into account the nature of the right and the nature of any duty imposed by the right.

(3) When applying a provision of the Bill of Rights to a natural or juristic person in terms of subsection (2), a court

a. in order to give effect to a right in the Bill, must apply, or if necessary develop, the common law to the extent that legislation does not give effect to that right; and

b. may develop rules of the common law to limit the right, provided that the limitation is in accordance with section 36(1).

(4) A juristic person is entitled to the rights in the Bill of Rights to the extent required by the nature of the rights and the nature of that juristic person.

The subsequent sections address the following rights, enforcement and protection guarantees.

9. Equality

10. Human Dignity

11. Life

12. Freedom and Security of the Person

13. Slavery, Servitude and Forced Labour

14. Privacy

15. Freedom of Religion, Belief and Opinion

16. Freedom of Expression

17. Assembly, Demonstration, Picket and Petition

18. Freedom of Association

19. Political Rights

20. Citizenship

21. Freedom of Movement and Residence

22. Freedom of Trade, Occupation and Profession

23. Labour Relations

24. Environment

25. Property

26. Housing

27. Health Care, Food, Water and Social Security

28. Children

29. Education

30. Language and Culture

31. Cultural, Religious and Linguistic Communities

32. Access to Information

33. Just Administrative Action

34. Access to Courts

35. Arrested, Detained and Accused Persons

Such incorporation of human rights arguably negates the exclusion of these States from the initial drafting process of international human rights. Of course, it can equally be argued that this reflects the desire of newly independent States to be recognised as actors on the international stage and to be deemed worthy of international trade, aid and co-operation. Compliance with international human rights standards is frequently a prerequisite to major international trade and aid agreements.

No State wishes to be regarded as infringing human rights in the current political and diplomatic climate, thus all States, at least overtly (albeit superficially), adhere to the notion of universal rights.

However, the concept of universality is not without problems as the recent report of the Secretary-General notes.

Kofi Annan, In larger freedom, towards development, security and human rights for all, UN Doc. A/59/2005

para 136 Support for the rule of law must be strengthened by universal participation in multilateral conventions. At present, many States remain outside the multilateral convention framework, in some cases preventing important conventions from entering into force. Five years ago, I provided special facilities for State to sign or ratify treaties of which I am the Depositary. This proves a major success and treaty events have been held annually ever since. This year's events will focus on 31 multilateral treaties to helps us respond to global challenges, with emphasis on human rights, refugees, . . . **I urge leaders especially to ratify and implement all treaties relating to the protection of civilians**.

2.1.1   Non-discrimination in the application of human rights

No one is excluded from the ambit of human rights instruments. Human rights extend equally to children and adults, prisoners, terrorists, all racial groupings, men and women, educated and non-educated, etc. Some rights are, however, restricted in the sense that not everyone can exercise them. Rights to marry, for example, do not apply to young children. As this is uniform, there is no discrimination. The non-discrimination clauses common to most instruments make the principle of non-discrimination abundantly clear.

Universal Declaration of Human Rights 1948 Art 2

Everyone is entitled to all rights and freedoms set forth in this Declaration, without distinction of any kind, such as race, colour, sex, language, religion, political or other opinion, national or social origin, property, birth or other status.

Furthermore, no distinction shall be made on the basis of the political, jurisdictional or international status of the country or territory to which a person belongs, whether it be independent, trust, non-self-governing or under any other limitation of sovereignty.

Charter of Fundamental Rights of the European Union 2000 Art 21(1)

Any discrimination based on any ground such as sex, race, colour, ethnic or social origin, genetic features, language, religion or belief, political or any other opinion, membership of a national minority, property, birth, disability, age or sexual orientation shall be prohibited.

Question

What reasons are there for the expansion of grounds between 1948 (the Universal Declaration) and 2000 (the European Charter)?

2.1.2   Minority protection

Clearly everyone is entitled to enjoy the basic human rights and fundamental freedoms enshrined in the various instruments. Traditionally international law was the exclusive preserve of States. Human rights violations were only actioned by States when there was an international dimension. For example, if State R has a majority population of religion L and its neighbour, State S, has a minority population of religion L, then State R may elect to act in defence of the minority religion L group in State S. Many wars were prompted by such a situation. More recently, the minority guarantee system operated by the League of Nations demonstrates this principle. One of the consequential results of the new world order is that the obligations of States have extended—it is no longer accepted that States have exclusive competence over individuals within their jurisdiction. There is an increasing emphasis on international supervision of international human rights. Obviously, this is the main focus of the current text. However, further refining of the concept of international human rights by international and regional bodies has resulted in an extension of the obligations undertaken by States. Today, States must not only ensure that they act in conformity with their international obligations but also ensure that there are legal provisions which ensure that others (States, individuals) also act in conformity with these obligations.

Initial instruments impinging on human rights sought to provide protection for identified vulnerable groups. Thus, the peace treaties concluding the First World War included 'minority guarantee clauses'.

2.1.3   The League of Nations and minority rights

Minority guarantee clauses were monitored by a special unit of the League of Nations (the predecessor to the United Nations). The following extract illustrates the provisions which such guarantees contained.

Treaty of Lausanne

Article 37

Turkey undertakes that the stipulations contained in Articles 38 to 44 shall be recognized as fundamental laws, and that no law, no regulation, nor official action shall conflict or interfere with these stipulations, nor shall any law, regulation, nor official action prevail over them.

Article 38

The Turkish Government undertakes to assure full and complete protection of life and liberty to all inhabitants of Turkey without distinction of birth, nationality, language, race or religion.

All inhabitants of Turkey shall be entitled to free exercise, whether in public or private, of any creed, religion or belief, the observance of which shall not be incompatible with public order and good morals.

Non-Moslem minorities will enjoy full freedom of movement and of emigration. Subject to the measures applied, on the whole or on part of the territory, to all Turkish nationals, and which may be taken by the Turkish Government for national defence, or for the maintenance of public order.

Article 39

Turkish nationals belonging to non-Moslem minorities will enjoy the same civil political rights as Moslems.

All the inhabitants of Turkey, without distinction of religion, shall be equal before the law.

Differences of religion, creed or confession shall not prejudice any Turkish national in matters relating to the enjoyment of civil or political rights, as, for instance, admission to public employments, functions and honours, or the exercise of professions and industries.

No restrictions shall be imposed on the free use by any Turkish national of any language in private intercourse, in commerce, religion, in the press, or in publications of any kind or at public meetings.

Notwithstanding the existence of the official language, adequate facilities shall be given to Turkish nationals of non-Turkish speech for the oral of their own language before the Courts.

Article 40

Turkish nationals belonging to non-Moslem minorities shall enjoy the same treatment and security in law and in fact as other Turkish nationals. In particular, they shall have an equal right to establish, manage and control at their own expense, any charitable, religious and social institutions, any schools and other establishments for instruction and education, with the right to use their own language and to exercise their own religion freely therein.

Article 41

As regards public instruction, the Turkish Government will grant in those towns and districts, where a considerable proportion of non-Moslem nationals are resident, adequate facilities for ensuring that in the primary schools the instruction shall be given to the children of such Turkish nationals through the medium of their own language. This provision will not prevent the Turkish Government from making the teaching of the Turkish language obligatory in the said schools.

In towns and districts where there is a considerable proportion of Turkish nationals belonging to non-Moslem minorities, these minorities shall be assured an equitable share in the enjoyment and application of the sums which may be provided out of public junks under the State, municipal or other budgets for educational, religious, or charitable purposes.

The sums in question shall be paid to the qualified representatives of the establishments and institutions concerned.

Article 42

The Turkish Government undertakes to take, as regards non-Moslem minorities, in so far as concerns their family law or personal status, measures permitting the settlement of these questions in accordance with the customs of those minorities.

These measures will be elaborated by special Commissions composed of representatives of the Turkish Government and of representatives of each of the minorities concerned in equal number. In case of divergence, the Turkish Government and the Council of the League of Nations will appoint in agreement an umpire chosen from amongst European lawyers.

The Turkish Government undertakes to grant full protection to the churches, synagogues, cemeteries, and other religious establishments of the above-mentioned minorities. All facilities and authorization will be granted to the pious foundations, and to the religious and charitable institutions of the said minorities at present existing in Turkey, and the Turkish Government will not refuse, for the formation of new religious and charitable institutions, any of the necessary facilities which are granted to other private institutions of that nature.

Article 43

Turkish nationals belonging to non-Moslem minorities shall not be compelled to perform any act which constitutes a violation of their faith or religious observances, and shall not be placed under any disability by reason of their regal to attend Courts of Law or to perform any legal business on their weekly day of rest.

This provision, however, shall not exempt such Turkish nationals from such obligations as shall be imposed upon all other Turkish nationals for the preservation of public order.

Article 44

Turkey agrees that, in so far as the preceding Articles of this Section affect non-Moslem nationals of Turkey, these provisions constitute obligations of international concern and shall be placed under the guarantee of the League of Nations. They shall not be modified without the assent of the majority of the Council of the League of Nations. The British Empire, France, Italy and Japan hereby agree not to withhold their assent to any modification in these Articles which is in due form assented to by a majority of the Council of the League of Nations.

Turkey agrees that any Member of the Council of the League of Nations shall have the right to bring to the attention of the Council any infraction or danger of infraction of any of these obligations, and that the Council thereupon take such action and give such directions as it may deem proper and effective in the circumstances.

Turkey further agrees that any difference of opinion as to questions of law or of fact arising out of these Articles between the Turkish Government and any one of the other Signatory Powers or any other Power, a member of the Council of the League of Nations, shall be held to be a dispute of an international character under Article 14 of the Government of the League of Nations. The Turkish Government hereby consents that any such dispute shall, if the other party thereto demands, be referred to the Permanent Court of International Justice. The decision of the Permanent Court shall be final and shall have the same force and effect as an award under Article 19 of the Covenant.

Article 45

The rights conferred by the provisions of the present Section on the non-Moslem minorities of Turkey will be similarly conferred by Greece on the Moslem minority in her territory.

The use of minority guarantee clauses allowed the targeting of groups likely to be subjected to discrimination.

Question

To what extent were the clauses successfully implemented? Consider cases such as Minority School in Albania and the exchange of Greek and Turkish populations.

It is interesting to note that in the twenty-first century, complaints of discrimination against Turkey have concerned Muslim people: *Sahin v Turkey*, a case dismissed by the Grand Chamber of the European Court of Human Rights in November 2005 arose through the imposition of secularity in Turkey and a ban on Muslim women wearing head coverings in universities!

The fate of minorities was mixed under the League of Nations. Ultimately, however, the League of Nations proved impotent in the face of systematic challenges to its authority and the Second World War broke out in Europe and spread further.

2.1.4   A change in emphasis: universal rights

The United Nations, since inception, elected to focus on universal human rights founded on respect for the innate human dignity. Focussing on universal rights, as designated in the Universal Declaration of Human Rights, minority rights were effectively deemed outmoded. As Professor Ian Brownlie notes, the 'assumption lying behind the classical formulation of standards of human rights . . . has been that group rights would be taken care of automatically as the result of the protection of the rights of individuals' (Brownlie, 'The Rights of Peoples in Modern International Law' in Crawford (ed), *The Rights of Peoples*, 1988, Oxford: Clarendon Press, 1 at 2). The new international regime thus sought to obviate the need for minority guarantees by guaranteeing the same rights and freedoms to all, irrespective of status. The concept of universalism is considered above.

Question

What are the political and legal problems with securing international universal norms of human rights?

2.1.5 A return to minority rights?

The theory and reality did not, however, meet. Today, there is evidence of a return to minority protection with many instruments creating regimes of protection for distinctive minority groups.

The following list contains European instruments aimed at protecting specific minority groups:

European Charter for Regional or Minority Languages 1992 (Council of Europe)
Framework Convention for the Protection of National Minorities 1995 (Council of Europe)
Hague Recommendations Regarding the Education Rights of National Minorities 1996 (OSCE)
Lund Recommendations on the Effective Participation of National Minorities in Public Life 1999 (OSCE)
Oslo Recommendations on the Linguistic Rights of National Minorities 1998 (OSCE)

Question

These instruments are primarily European which reflects international practice. The United Nations has but a Declaration on the rights of minorities. What reasons are there for Europe being the focal point of contemporary minority protection guarantees?

2.1.6   Developing sectoral and group rights

Other sectoral approaches to human rights have characterised the work of the international community in recent years. The reason is simple: universal rights have not been as effective as anticipated. The sectoral approach can reinforce existing universal rights or even highlight the plight of particular groups. However, it is arguable that their existence does not detract from the universality of rights. As is apparent from reading the texts, there are few innovative additions to the pre-existing tabulations of rights. The principal exception is possibly the UN Convention on the Rights of the Child, which enshrines the most comprehensive tabulation of rights and arguably extends the scope of the pre-existing instruments. Despite this, the Convention on the Rights of the Child has achieved the highest number of ratifications of any major international human rights instrument.

The preambles to the instruments indicate the rationale behind their adoption.

International Convention on the Elimination of All Forms of Racial Discrimination 1965

Considering that the Universal Declaration of Human Rights proclaims that all human beings are born free and equal in dignity and rights and that everyone is entitled to all the rights and freedoms set out therein, without distinction of any kind, in particular as to race, colour or national origin,

Considering that all human beings are equal before the law and are entitled to equal protection of the law against any discrimination and against any incitement to discrimination, . . .

Alarmed by manifestations of racial discrimination still in evidence in some areas of the world and by governmental policies based on racial superiority or hatred, such as policies of apartheid, segregation or separation,

Resolved to adopt all necessary measures for speedily eliminating racial discrimination in all its forms and manifestations, and to prevent and combat racist doctrines and practices in order to promote understanding between races and to build an international community free from all forms of racial segregation and racial discrimination.

Convention on the Elimination of All Forms of Discrimination against Women 1979

Concerned that in situations of poverty women have the least access to food, health, education, training and opportunities for employment and other needs,

Convinced that the establishment of the new international economic order based on equity and justice will contribute significantly towards the promotion of equality between men and women, . . .

Convinced that the full and complete development of a country, the welfare of the world and the cause of peace require the maximum participation of women on equal terms with men in all fields,

Bearing in mind the great contribution of women to the welfare of the family and to the development of society, so far not fully recognized, the social significance of maternity and the role of both parents in the family and in the upbringing of children, and aware that the role of women in procreation should not be a basis for discrimination but that the upbringing of children requires a sharing of responsibility between men and women and society as a whole,

Aware that a change in the traditional role of men as well as the role of women in society and in the family is needed to achieve full equality between men and women.

United Nations Convention on the Rights of the Child 1989

Recalling that, in the Universal Declaration of Human Rights, the United Nations has proclaimed that childhood is entitled to special care and assistance,

Convinced that the family, as the fundamental group of society and the natural environment for the growth and well-being of all its members and particularly children, should be afforded the necessary protection and assistance so that it can fully assume its responsibilities within the community,

Recognizing that the child, for the full and harmonious development of his or her personality, should grow up in a family environment, in an atmosphere of happiness, love and understanding,

Considering that the child should be fully prepared to live an individual life in society, and brought up in the spirit of the ideals proclaimed in the Charter of the United Nations, and in particular in the spirit of peace, dignity, tolerance, freedom, equality and solidarity, . . .

Bearing in mind that, as indicated in the Declaration of the Rights of the Child, 'the child, by reason of his physical and mental immaturity, needs special safeguards and care, including appropriate legal protection, before as well as after birth'.

International Convention on the Protection of the Rights of All Migrant Workers and Members of Their Families

Recognizing the importance of the work done in connection with migrant workers and members of their families in various organs of the United Nations, in particular in the Commission on Human Rights and the Commission for Social Development, and in the Food and Agriculture Organization of the United Nations, the United Nations Educational, Scientific and Cultural Organization and the World Health Organization, as well as in other international organizations,

Recognizing also the progress made by certain States on a regional or bilateral basis towards the protection of the rights of migrant workers and members of their families, as well as the importance and usefulness of bilateral and multilateral agreements in this field,

Realizing the importance and extent of the migration phenomenon, which involves millions of people and affects a large number of States in the international community,

Aware of the impact of the flows of migrant workers on States and people concerned, and desiring to establish norms which may contribute to the harmonization of the attitudes of States through the acceptance of basic principles concerning the treatment of migrant workers and members of their families,

Considering the situation of vulnerability in which migrant workers and members of their families frequently find themselves owing, among other things, to their absence from their State of origin and to the difficulties they may encounter arising from their presence in the State of employment,

Convinced that the rights of migrant workers and members of their families have not been sufficiently recognized everywhere and therefore require appropriate international protection,

Taking into account the fact that migration is often the cause of serious problems for the members of the families of migrant workers as well as for the workers themselves, in particular because of the scattering of the family,

Bearing in mind that the human problems involved in migration are even more serious in the case of irregular migration and convinced therefore that appropriate action should be encouraged in order to prevent and eliminate clandestine movements and trafficking in migrant workers, while at the same time assuring the protection of their fundamental human rights,

Considering that workers who are non-documented or in an irregular situation are frequently employed under less favourable conditions of work than other workers and that certain employers find this an inducement to seek such labour in order to reap the benefits of unfair competition,

Considering also that recourse to the employment of migrant workers who are in an irregular situation will be discouraged if the fundamental human rights of all migrant workers are more widely recognized and, moreover, that granting certain additional rights to migrant workers and members of their families in a regular situation will encourage all migrants and employers to respect and comply with the laws and procedures established by the States concerned.

Question

Are the foregoing categories representative of vulnerable groups? Are such instruments compatible with a concept of universal rights?

In addition, occasional instruments have focussed on specific rights or freedoms. The most obvious example is torture. Torture is deemed so abhorrent as to justify its own instrument under the auspices of the United Nations, the Council of Europe and the Organisation of American States.

Different regions have identified other areas of particular concern and adopted specific instruments protecting groups which are minorities or otherwise deemed particularly vulnerable. For example, the Organisation of African Unity (predecessor to the African Union) adopted a convention governing the specific aspects of refugee problems in Africa in 1969. The African Union has also passed treaties aimed at protecting children's rights and women's rights (the latter has yet to enter into force). Meanwhile, in the Americas, a convention on forced disappearance of persons and another on the prevention, punishment and eradication of violence against women have been adopted.

Question

To what extent do the regional additions reflect political and historical events within the region? Are such instruments thus reactive?

In addition, a number of declarations under the auspices of the United Nations, while not legally binding, provide further evidence of the moves towards sectoralising international human rights. Hence, there is a Declaration on the Rights of Persons belonging to National or Ethnic, Religious and Linguistic Minorities, a Declaration on the Rights of Indigenous Peoples (see Chapter 12) and a Convention on the Rights of Persons with Disabilities under discussion at present. In addition, international attention is currently focussed on the rights of those with AIDS and HIV, in light of the present pandemic and the significant impact it is having on demographics in large swathes of the globe.

These developments are accompanied by some controversy. Some commentators argued against the adoption of optional protocols to the Convention on the Rights of the Child, for example, considering that additional protocols undermined and detracted from the principal rights and freedoms enunciated in the treaty.

2.2 CULTURAL SENSITIVITY

One of the main challenges to the universality of contemporary human rights lies with cultural pluralism. Can anything but a very broad generalisation of rights ever be truly and equally applicable to all peoples, cultures, religions and languages? Obviously, in different countries, different rights will be prioritised by the State and by its residents. The unassailable expectation, however, is that all peoples are entitled to the same rights and freedoms irrespective of national origin and status. Note the view of the international community, as expressed in the Vienna Declaration adopted by the World Conference on Human Rights in 1993. This was the most significant global discussion of human rights to date with unprecedented numbers of States and non-governmental organisations meeting together to prioritise human rights protection, assess progress to date and agree a plan of action for securing the goal of universal respect and promotion of human rights and fundamental freedoms.

Vienna Declaration and Programme of Action 1993, para 5

While the significance of national and regional particularities and various historical, cultural and religious backgrounds must be borne in mind, it is the duty of States, regardless of their political, economic and cultural systems, to promote and protect all human rights and fundamental freedoms.

It appears therefore, that the universal system is considered to embody the fundamental rights and freedoms which should apply to all irrespective of their different 'particularities'. As many commentators note, there is an unfortunate reality/rhetoric deficit in this respect. A pervasive view remains that the tabulated universal rights are drawn from a western European Christian-influenced school of thought, which reached its zenith in the post-enlightenment era.

2.2.1 Celebrating cultural diversity

However, the current global climate is conducive to celebrating cultural diversity. Indeed, plurality of language, religion and culture is a *sine qua non* of globalisation and modern politics. The following extracts are preambular paragraphs and articles from the Universal Declaration on Cultural Diversity.

Universal Declaration on Cultural Diversity Adopted by the General Conference of the United Nations Educational, Scientific and Cultural Organization at its thirty-first session on 2 November 2001

Recalling that the Preamble to the Constitution of UNESCO affirms 'that the wide diffusion of culture, and the education of humanity for justice and liberty and peace are indispensable to the dignity of man and constitute a sacred duty which all the nations must fulfil in a spirit of mutual assistance and concern',

Reaffirming that culture should be regarded as the set of distinctive spiritual, material, intellectual and emotional features of society or a social group, and that it encompasses, in addition to art and literature, lifestyles, ways of living together, value systems, traditions and beliefs,

Noting that culture is at the heart of contemporary debates about identity, social cohesion, and the development of a knowledge-based economy,

Affirming that respect for the diversity of cultures, tolerance, dialogue and cooperation, in a climate of mutual trust and understanding are among the best guarantees of international peace and security,

Aspiring to greater solidarity on the basis of recognition of cultural diversity, of awareness of the unity of humankind, and of the development of intercultural exchanges,

Considering that the process of globalization, facilitated by the rapid development of new information and communication technologies, though representing a challenge for cultural diversity, creates the conditions for renewed dialogue among cultures and civilizations.

Article 1—Cultural diversity: the common heritage of humanity

Culture takes diverse forms across time and space. This diversity is embodied in the uniqueness and plurality of the identities of the groups and societies making up humankind. As a source of exchange, innovation and creativity, cultural diversity is as necessary for humankind as bio-diversity is for nature. In this sense, it is the common heritage of humanity and should be recognized and affirmed for the benefit of present and future generations.

Article 2—From cultural diversity to cultural pluralism

In our increasingly diverse societies, it is essential to ensure harmonious interaction among people and groups with plural, varied and dynamic cultural identities as well as their willingness to live together. Policies for the inclusion and participation of all citizens are guarantees of social cohesion, the vitality of civil society and peace. Thus defined, cultural pluralism gives policy expression to the reality of cultural diversity. Indissociable from a democratic framework, cultural pluralism is conducive to cultural exchange and to the flourishing of creative capacities that sustain public life.

Article 3—Cultural diversity as a factor in development

Cultural diversity widens the range of options open to everyone; it is one of the roots of development, understood not simply in terms of economic growth, but also as a means to achieve a more satisfactory intellectual, emotional, moral and spiritual existence.

Cultural diversity and human rights

Article 4—Human rights as guarantees of cultural diversity

The defence of cultural diversity is an ethical imperative, inseparable from respect for human dignity. It implies a commitment to human rights and fundamental freedoms, in particular the rights of persons belonging to minorities and those of indigenous peoples. No one may invoke cultural diversity to infringe upon human rights guaranteed by international law, nor to limit their scope.

2.2.2   Reconciling traditional culture with human rights

Some treaties exhibit evidence of cultural sensitivity. The Convention on the Rights of the Child, for example, includes a provision on child care which includes reference to different cultural practices.

UN Convention on the Rights of the Child Art 20

1. A child temporarily or permanently deprived of his or her family environment, or in whose own best interests cannot be allowed to remain in that environment, shall be entitled to special protection and assistance provided by the State.

2. States Parties shall in accordance with their national laws ensure alternative care for such a child.

3. Such care could include, *inter alia*, foster placement, kafalah of Islamic law, adoption or if necessary placement in suitable institutions for the care of children. When considering solutions, due regard shall be paid to the desirability of continuity in a child's upbringing and to the child's ethnic, religious, cultural and linguistic background.

Such provisions demonstrate recognition of cultural diversity and, as such, are to be commended. However, on the other hand, that particular provision may be attributed to difficulties in translation and communication, resulting in a provision which takes into account the various traditions of child care.

However, some cultural practices are effectively proscribed. No cultural argument is accepted as justification for female circumcision and female genital mutilation.

2.2.2.1 Female genital mutilation

Female circumcision is widely practised in areas of Africa and elsewhere. The practice has no identified health benefits but appears rather to be undertaken in accordance with cultural tradition. Some young women agree to be circumcised, arguably due to peer pressure and the need to secure a husband, others have little choice. The international community has repeatedly condemned the practice and called for its eradication.

Committee on the Elimination of Discrimination against Women, General Recommendation 14 (1990)

Recommends that States parties:

(a) Take appropriate and effective measures with a view to eradicating the practice of female circumcision. Such measures could include:

  (i) The collection and dissemination by universities, medical or nursing associations, national women's organizations or other bodies of basic data about such traditional practices;

  (ii) The support of women's organizations at the national and local levels working for the elimination of female circumcision and other practices harmful to women;

  (iii) The encouragement of politicians, professionals, religious and community leaders at all levels, including the media and the arts, to co-operate in influencing attitudes towards the eradication of female circumcision;

  (iv) The introduction of appropriate educational and training programmes and seminars based on research findings about the problems arising from female circumcision;

(b) Include in their national health policies appropriate strategies aimed at eradicating female circumcision in public health care. Such strategies could include the special responsibility of health personnel, including traditional birth attendants, to explain the harmful effects of female circumcision;

(c) Invite assistance, information and advice from the appropriate organizations of the United Nations system to support and assist efforts being deployed to eliminate harmful traditional practices;

(d) Include in their reports to the Committee under articles 10 and 12 of the Convention on the Elimination of All Forms of Discrimination against Women information about measures taken to eliminate female circumcision.

Consider also Fact Sheet No. 241 (2000) of the World Health Organisation. This explains the work being undertaken by that organisation to eradicate female genital mutilation (FGM), working towards the education of those condoning the practice. The eradication of FGM practices is an inter-organisational project also involving UNICEF. Challenging the culture of the countries and peoples concerned is a major objective and the most important step towards stamping out the practice. Once a cultural shift is achieved, legal measures will be more successful in perpetuating its abolition. Should the culture be changed, proscription will result merely in the practice going 'underground' with potentially devastating consequences for the health of women. The World Health Organisation estimates that up to two million young women a year are at risk of undergoing FGM and related practices.

Question

Can the international community effectively proscribe a cultural practice while maintaining respect for cultural diversity? Is female circumcision a special case?

2.2.3   The role of regional organisations

There is a clear role for regional and sectoral organisations in creating human rights instruments that are more tailored towards cultural requirements. Although there are exceptions, generally speaking, most regions of the world exhibit some heterogeneity and some common historical or cultural traits. Part of the rationale behind the creation of regional systems of human rights was to capitalise on this and establish systems which were more enforceable. Politics and diplomacy obviously had an impact on this too. Several regions have adopted instruments, some containing generic rights, others deemed to be adapted for the region concerned.

Question

Look at the regional instruments and the Universal Declaration. Are any of the rights in the Universal Declaration not applicable to people in a particular country region? Do the regional instruments miss them out?

2.2.3.1   Europe

The European system, although boasting a comparatively sophisticated enforcement machinery, contains one of the most basic catalogues of rights in its flagship instrument: the European Convention on Human Rights and Fundamental Freedoms 1950. The rights and freedoms in the Convention relate to the following:

Article 2—the right to life
Article 3—prohibition on torture and other inhuman or degrading treatment or punishment
Article 4—prohibition on slavery and forced labour
Article 5—the right to liberty and security of person
Article 6—the right to a fair trial
Article 7—prohibition on retrospective penal legislation
Article 8—the right to private and family life, home and correspondence
Article 9—freedom of thought, conscience and religion
Article 10—freedom of expression and opinion
Article 11—freedom of assembly and association
Article 12—right to marry and found a family

Question

Can the limited scope of the European Convention be justified in cultural terms? What reasons are there for this?

Admittedly, the European Convention has since been supplemented by a range of additional protocols, many of which add further rights and freedoms. Furthermore, the range of subjects covered by European human rights has been augmented by the European Social Charter of 1961, its protocols and the revised 1996 version, as well as by the minority instruments mentioned above and a convention on human rights and fundamental freedoms in the sphere of biomedicine, cloning and transplantations. These latter instruments are the only human rights instruments to specifically address such contemporary matters. While many of the developments in science and technology are focussed in Europe, it is by no means the sole geographical centre of innovation.

Question

What reasons may there be for the Council of Europe being the first major organisation to adopt a treaty on bioscience technology?

2.2.3.2 State's Margin of Appreciation

Within the European system, the European Court of Human Rights has developed the concept of the margin of appreciation which facilitates national determination of certain 'cultural' issues such as moral standards. This concept has evolved through the jurisprudence of the Court and is best illustrated by its classic exposition in *Handyside v United Kingdom*. The case concerned primarily Art 10 of the European Convention.

European Convention on Human Rights Art 10

1. Everyone has the right to freedom of expression. This right shall include freedom to hold opinions and to receive and impart information and ideas without interference by public authority and regardless of frontiers. This Article shall not prevent States from requiring the licensing of broadcasting, television or cinema enterprises.

2. The exercise of these freedoms, since it carries with it duties and responsibilities, may be subject to such formalities, conditions, restrictions or penalties as are prescribed by law and are necessary in a democratic society, in the interests of national security, territorial integrity or public safety, for the protection of disorder or crime, for the protection of health or morals, for the protection of the reputation or rights of others, for preventing the disclosure of information received in confidence, or for maintaining the authority and impartiality of the judiciary.

Freedom of expression is a qualified right under the European Convention. In other words, it is not absolute. In certain situations, States may curtail the right or even remove it completely. The important aspects to note are that the limitation must be :

(1) prescribed by law;

(2) necessary in a democratic society;

(3) in furtherance of a legitimate aim.

It is for the Court, as final arbiter, to determine whether or not any given limitation on a right is permissible. In determining this, the Court may accord States a margin of appreciation—permit a degree of discretion.

Handyside v United Kingdom (1979–80) I EHRR 737

Handyside published *The Little Red Schoolbook*, a book intended for young people. The book was first published in Denmark in 1969 and was subsequently available or published in Austria, Belgium, Finland, France, the Federal Republic of Germany, Greece, Iceland, Italy, Luxembourg, the Netherlands, Norway, Sweden and Switzerland and beyond. The applicant was the publisher of the book and prosecuted under the Obscene Publications legislation in England. The State argued that the book was contrary to the relevant law as it satisfied the corrupt and deprave test, not least given that it was being aimed at children.

48. The Court points out that the machinery of protection established by the Convention is subsidiary to the national systems safeguarding human rights (judgment of 23 July 1968 on the merits of the 'Belgian Linguistic' case, Series A no. 6, p. 35, para. 10 in fine). The Convention leaves to each Contracting State, in the first place, the task of securing the rights and liberties it enshrines. The institutions created by it make their own contribution to this task but they become involved only through contentious proceedings and once all domestic remedies have been exhausted (Article 26) (art. 26).

These observations apply, notably, to Article 10 para. 2 (art. 10–2). In particular, it is not possible to find in the domestic law of the various Contracting States a uniform European conception of morals. The view taken by their respective laws of the requirements of morals varies from time to time and from place to place, especially in our era which is characterised by a rapid and far-reaching evolution of opinions on the subject. By reason of their direct and continuous contact with the vital forces of their countries, State authorities are in principle in a better position than the international judge to give an opinion on the exact content of these requirements as well as on the 'necessity' of a 'restriction' or 'penalty' intended to meet them. The Court notes at this juncture that, whilst the adjective 'necessary', within the meaning of Article 10 para. 2 (art. 10–2), is not synonymous with 'indispensable' (cf., in Articles 2 para. 2 (art. 2–2) and 6 para. 1 (art. 6–1), the words 'absolutely necessary' and 'strictly necessary' and, in Article 15 para. 1 (art. 15–1), the phrase 'to the extent strictly required by the exigencies of the situation'), neither has it the flexibility of such expressions as 'admissible', 'ordinary' (cf. Article 4 para. 3) (art. 4–3), 'useful' (cf. the French text of the first paragraph of Article 1 of Protocol No. 1) (P1–1), 'reasonable' (cf. Articles 5 para. 3 and 6 para. 1) (art. 5–3, art. 6–1) or 'desirable'. Nevertheless, it is for the national authorities to make the initial assessment of the reality of the pressing social need implied by the notion of 'necessity' in this context.

Consequently, Article 10 para. 2 (art. 10–2) leaves to the Contracting States a margin of appreciation. This margin is given both to the domestic legislator ('prescribed by law') and to the bodies, judicial amongst others, that are called upon to interpret and apply the laws in force (Engel and others judgment of 8 June 1976, Series A no. 22, pp. 41–42, para. 100; cf., for Article 8 para. 2 (art. 8–2), De Wilde, Ooms and Versyp judgment of 18 June 1971, Series A no. 12, pp. 45–46, para. 93, and the Golder judgment of 21 February 1975, Series A no. 18, pp. 21–22, para. 45).

49. Nevertheless, Article 10 para. 2 (art. 10–2) does not give the Contracting States an unlimited power of appreciation. The Court, which, with the Commission, is responsible for ensuring the observance of those States' engagements (Article 19) (art. 19), is empowered to give the final ruling on whether a 'restriction' or 'penalty' is reconcilable with freedom of expression as protected by Article 10 (art. 10). The domestic margin of appreciation thus goes hand in hand with a European supervision. Such supervision concerns both the aim of the measure challenged and its 'necessity'; it covers not only the basic legislation but also the decision applying it, even one given by an independent court. In this respect, the Court refers to Article 50 (art. 50) of the Convention ('decision or . . . measure taken by a legal authority or any other authority') as well as to its own case-law (Engel and others judgment of 8 June 1976, Series A no. 22, pp. 41–42, para. 100).

The Court's supervisory functions oblige it to pay the utmost attention to the principles characterising a 'democratic society'. Freedom of expression constitutes one of the essential foundations of such a society, one of the basic conditions for its progress and for the development of every man. Subject to paragraph 2 of Article 10 (art. 10–2), it is applicable not only to 'information' or 'ideas' that are favourably received or regarded as inoffensive or as a matter of indifference, but also to those that offend, shock or disturb the State or any sector of the population. Such are the demands of that pluralism, tolerance and broadmindedness without which there is no 'democratic society'. This means, amongst other things, that every 'formality', 'condition', 'restriction' or 'penalty' imposed in this sphere must be proportionate to the legitimate aim pursued.

From another standpoint, whoever exercises his freedom of expression undertakes 'duties and responsibilities' the scope of which depends on his situation and the technical means he uses. The Court cannot overlook such a person's 'duties' and 'responsibilities' when it enquires, as in this case, whether 'restrictions' or 'penalties' were conducive to the 'protection of morals' which made them 'necessary' in a 'democratic society'.

50. It follows from this that it is in no way the Court's task to take the place of the competent national courts but rather to review under Article 10 (art. 10) the decisions they delivered in the exercise of their power of appreciation.

However, the Court's supervision would generally prove illusory if it did no more than examine these decisions in isolation; it must view them in the light of the case as a whole, including the publication in question and the arguments and evidence adduced by the applicant in the domestic legal system and then at the international level. The Court must decide, on the basis of the different data available to it, whether the reasons given by the national authorities to justify the actual measures of 'interference' they take are relevant and sufficient under Article 10 para. 2 (art. 10–2) (cf., for Article 5 para. 3 (art. 5–3), the Wemhoff judgment of 27 June 1968, Series A no. 7, pp. 24–25, para. 12, the Neumeister judgment of 27 June 1968, Series A no. 8, p. 37, para. 5, the Stogmuller judgment of 10 November 1969, Series A no. 9, p. 39, para. 3, the Matznetter judgment of 10 November 1969, Series A no. 10, p. 31, para. 3, and the Ringeisen judgment of 16 July 1971, Series A no. 13, p. 42, para. 104).

52 ...

Basically the book contained purely factual information that was generally correct and often useful, as the Quarter Sessions recognised. However, it also included, above all in the section on sex and in the passage headed 'Be yourself' in the chapter on pupils (paragraph 32 above), sentences or paragraphs that young people at a critical stage of their development could have interpreted as an encouragement to indulge in precocious activities harmful for them or even to commit certain criminal offences. In these circumstances, despite the variety and the constant evolution in the United Kingdom of views on ethics and education, the competent English judges were entitled, in the exercise of their discretion, to think at the relevant time that the Schoolbook would have pernicious effects on the morals of many of the children and adolescents who would read it.

The Court concluded that there was no breach of the European provisions on freedom of expression, the State being entitled to exercise discretion as to what constituted the moral standard within the State.

Recourse to the concluding observations of the treaty monitoring bodies of the United Nations reveals similar approaches to certain international human rights. Particularly in respect to economic, social and cultural 'progressive' rights, the committees appear to strive to advance the rights from periodic report to periodic report. Cultural (and indeed economic and political) reasons restricting the fulfilment of the full range of treaty obligations are taken into consideration.

Question

Enforcing human rights is essentially a matter for States. The international and regional systems can but monitor and supervise national efforts. Is the margin of appreciation device simply a consequence of this? Does it reflect appropriate discretion to be accorded to States or is it indicative of a weakening of the concept of universal rights?

2.2.3.3 Africa

From the outset, the African Union (or to be precise, the Organisation of African Unity) strove to encapsulate a uniquely African approach to human rights in its signature treaty, the African Charter on Human and Peoples' Rights.

African Charter on Human and Peoples' Rights Preamble

... *Taking into consideration* the virtues of their historical tradition and the values of African civilization which should inspire and characterise their reflection on the concept of human and peoples' rights.

Certainly the African Charter is innovative in that it strives towards including peoples' rights. Some of the rights are unusual and reflect particular problems endemic in Africa and particular injustices which require redress. For example, the emphasis on decolonisation and slavery. However, most of the basic human rights in the African Charter reflect clearly the terms of the Universal Declaration on Human Rights and the International Covenants. Of particular note, the African Charter is one of the only treaties to integrate the full range of rights covered in the Universal Declaration: civil, cultural, economic, political and social. The UN Convention on the Rights of the Child comes closest to matching the range of rights enshrined in the African Charter.

Question

What reasons are there to justify the advanced range of human rights contained in the African Charter as compared to the other principal regional (and indeed international) instruments?

Consider the scope of the peoples' rights in the African Charter:

African Charter on Human and Peoples' Rights

Article 19

All peoples shall be equal; they shall enjoy the same respect and shall have the same rights. Nothing shall justify the domination of a people by another.

Article 20

1. All peoples shall have the right to existence. They shall have the unquestionable and inalienable right to self-determination. They shall freely determine their political status and shall pursue their economic and social development according to the policy they have freely chosen.

2. Colonized or oppressed peoples shall have the right to free themselves from the bonds of domination by resorting to any means recognized by the international community.

3. All peoples shall have the right to the assistance of the States parties to the present Charter in their liberation struggle against foreign domination, be it political, economic or cultural.

Article 21

1. All peoples shall freely dispose of their wealth and natural resources. This right shall be exercised in the exclusive interest of the people. In no case shall a people be deprived of it.

2. In case of spoliation the dispossessed people shall have the right to the lawful recovery of its property as well as to an adequate compensation.

3. The free disposal of wealth and natural resources shall be exercised without prejudice to the obligation of promoting international economic cooperation based on mutual respect, equitable exchange and the principles of international law.

4. States parties to the present Charter shall individually and collectively exercise the right to

free disposal of their wealth and natural resources with a view to strengthening African unity and solidarity.

5. States parties to the present Charter shall undertake to eliminate all forms of foreign economic exploitation particularly that practiced by international monopolies so as to enable their peoples to fully benefit from the advantages derived from their national resources.

Article 22

1. All peoples shall have the right to their economic, social and cultural development with due regard to their freedom and identity and in the equal enjoyment of the common heritage of mankind.

2. States shall have the duty, individually or collectively, to ensure the exercise of the right to development.

Article 23

1. All peoples shall have the right to national and international peace and security. The principles of solidarity and friendly relations implicitly affirmed by the Charter of the United Nations and reaffirmed by that of the Organization of African Unity shall govern relations between States.

2. For the purpose of strengthening peace, solidarity and friendly relations, States parties to the present Charter shall ensure that: (a) any individual enjoying the right of asylum under 12 of the present Charter shall not engage in subversive activities against his country of origin or any other State party to the present Charter; (b) their territories shall not be used as bases for subversive or terrorist activities against the people of any other State party to the present Charter.

Question

Is the concept of peoples' rights indicative of African cultural values? What reasons are there for these rights?

The African Charter is also the most prominent instrument which makes reference to duties.

African Charter on Human and Peoples' Rights
Chapter II—Duties

Article 27

1. Every individual shall have duties towards his family and society, the State and other legally recognized communities and the international community.

2. The rights and freedoms of each individual shall be exercised with due regard to the rights of others, collective security, morality and common interest.

Article 28

Every individual shall have the duty to respect and consider his fellow beings without discrimination, and to maintain relations aimed at promoting, safeguarding and reinforcing mutual respect and tolerance.

Article 29

The individual shall also have the duty:

1. To preserve the harmonious development of the family and to work for the cohesion and respect of the family; to respect his parents at all times, to maintain them in case of need;

2. To serve his national community by placing his physical and intellectual abilities at its service;

3. Not to compromise the security of the State whose national or resident he is;

4. To preserve and strengthen social and national solidarity, particularly when the latter is threatened;

5. To preserve and strengthen the national independence and the territorial integrity of his country and to contribute to its defence in accordance with the law;

6. To work to the best of his abilities and competence, and to pay taxes imposed by law in the interest of the society;

7. To preserve and strengthen positive African cultural values in his relations with other members of the society, in the spirit of tolerance, dialogue and consultation and, in general, to contribute to the promotion of the moral well being of society;

8. To contribute to the best of his abilities, at all times and at all levels, to the promotion and achievement of African unity.

Question

Does the tabulation of duties specifically reflect African values?

2.2.3.4 Americas

The rights in the American system are essentially civil and political but expand considerably those encapsulated in the European Convention. The rights are as follows:

Art 3—right to juridical personality
Art 4—right to life
Art 5—right to humane treatment
Art 6—freedom from slavery
Art 7—right to liberty
Art 8—right to a fair trial
Art 9—freedom from ex post facto laws
Art 10—right to compensation
Art 11—right to privacy
Art 12—freedom of conscience and religion
Art 13—freedom of thought and expression
Art 14—right to reply
Art 15—right to assembly
Art 16—freedom of association
Art 17—family rights
Art 18—right to a name
Art 19—right of the child
Art 20—right to nationality
Art 21—right to property
Art 22—freedom of movement and residence
Art 23—right to participate in government
Art 24—equality before the law
Art 25—right to judicial protection

Question

To what extent does this tabulation of rights reflect the views of the American States of human rights? Does it adequately respond to historical and political issues characterising the region?

Note the term of Art 4 of the American Convention on Human Rights.

American Convention on Human Rights Art 4

1. Every person has the right to have his life respected. This right shall be protected by law and, in general, from the moment of conception. No one shall be arbitrarily deprived of his life.

2. In countries that have not abolished the death penalty, it may be imposed only for the most serious crimes and pursuant to a final judgment rendered by a competent court and in accordance with a law establishing such punishment, enacted prior to the commission of the crime. The application of such punishment shall not be extended to crimes to which it does not presently apply.

3. The death penalty shall not be reestablished in states that have abolished it.

4. In no case shall capital punishment be inflicted for political offenses or related common crimes.

5. Capital punishment shall not be imposed upon persons who, at the time the crime was committed, were under 18 years of age or over 70 years of age; nor shall it be applied to pregnant women.

6. Every person condemned to death shall have the right to apply for amnesty, pardon, or commutation of sentence, which may be granted in all cases. Capital punishment shall not be imposed while such a petition is pending decision by the competent authority.

Question

Consider Art 4(1) of the American Convention on Human Rights. In what way does it differ from other instruments articulating the right to life and what cultural reasons may there be for this?

2.2.4   Reservations and declarations: a practical solution?

Reservations and declarations are discussed in Chapter 3. For the present purposes it is enough to note that they are of importance in permitting States wide practical discretion on applying rights and freedoms, ostensibly to take account of cultural issues.

2.2.4.1   Case study: CEDAW and Islamic States

The Convention on the Elimination of All Forms of Discrimination against Women 1979 (CEDAW) seeks in essence to ensure the equal enjoyment of all civil, cultural, economic, political and social rights by men and women. This reflects the importance placed on gender equality in the Charter of the United Nations and the Universal Declaration of Human Rights.

Preamble, Convention on the Elimination of All Forms of Discrimination against Women 1979

Recalling that discrimination against women violates the principles of equality of rights and respect for human dignity, is an obstacle to the participation of women, on equal terms with men, in the political, social, economic and cultural life of their countries, hampers the growth of the prosperity of society and the family and makes more difficult the full development of the potentialities of women in the service of their countries and of humanity.

The perceived international importance of advocating gender equality prompted many States to sign and ratify this instrument, irrespective of the potential practical difficulties which realising its terms would encounter. Expansive reservations were treated as an essential tool, permitting ratification while retaining national laws which undermine the effectiveness of the Convention.

Saudi Arabia is frequently reported as pursuing and endorsing many practices prejudicial to women and contrary to gender equality.

However, the Kingdom of Saudi Arabia duly ratified the Convention on the Elimination of All Forms of Discrimination against Women in 2000 but added a declaration in the following terms:

> 1. In case of contradiction between any term of the Convention and the norms of islamic law, the Kingdom is not under obligation to observe the contradictory terms of the Convention.

This has been objected to by a number of States. Similar reservations/declarations have been lodged by other Islamic States. Note that reservations and their effect are discussed in Chapter 3.

Question

Is the submission of such reservations an appropriate payoff for the inclusion of these States in the international regime and their participation in the public international monitoring systems?

2.3 POSITIVE OBLIGATIONS ON STATES TO CONFORM TO HUMAN RIGHTS

A further characteristic of international human rights law is that the obligations imposed on States are not necessarily negative, requiring a passive response. Such an approach characterises liberty-based systems—the State should not limit the freedoms of its population unless there are good reasons for such interference. With right-based systems, individuals acquire positive rights which are enforceable against their State. The State may thus be required to actively ensure that the rights for which they proclaim respect are actively enforceable in the State.

A major development has been the extension of the territorial application of international human rights law. This phenomenon is based on the obligations of States and so can be distinguished from International Criminal Law (discussed in Chapter 15) which is grounded in universal jurisdiction. States are under a positive obligation to ensure that the rights and freedoms they accept under the relevant human rights treaties are extended to all within their jurisdiction. This can mean that States must have regard to the consequences of any decisions they take. In respect of extradition and deportation, the positive obligation can give rise to far-reaching consequences. Once again, the European Court's jurisprudence illustrates the point.

Soering v UK (1989) II EHRR 439

Soering, a German national, was detained in the United Kingdom pursuant to an extradition request from the United States of America for murder. Soering and his American girlfriend had allegedly admitted the murders of her parents in Virginia, United States of America. The girlfriend was extradited and convicted, sentenced to serve 90 years in prison. Germany also requested the extradition of Soering (to Germany). The following element of the judgment concerns whether extradition from the United Kingdom to a country likely to impose a capital sentence would violate the United Kingdom's obligations under the European Convention on Human Rights to respect freedom from torture and other inhuman or degrading treatment or punishment. Such a violation would arise through the so-called 'death row phenomena'—a prolonged period of waiting for execution with numerous appeals and raised hopes and expectations.

85. As results from Article 5 § 1 (f) (art. 5–1-f), which permits 'the lawful . . . detention of a person against whom action is being taken with a view to . . . extradition', no right not to be extradited is as such protected by the Convention. Nevertheless, in so far as a measure of extradition has consequences adversely affecting the enjoyment of a Convention right, it may, assuming that the consequences are not too remote, attract the obligations of a Contracting State under the relevant Convention guarantee (see, *mutatis mutandis*, the Abdulaziz, Cabales and Balkandali judgmentof 25 May 1985, Series A no. 94, pp. 31–32, §§ 59–60—in relation to rights in the field of immigration). What is at issue in the present case is whether Article 3 (art. 3) can be applicable when the adverse consequences of extradition are, or may be, suffered outside the jurisdiction of the extraditing State as a result of treatment or punishment administered in the receiving State.

86. Article 1 (art. 1) of the Convention, which provides that 'the High Contracting Parties shall secure to everyone within their jurisdiction the rights and freedoms defined in Section I', sets a limit, notably territorial, on the reach of the Convention. In particular, the engagement undertaken by a Contracting State is confined to 'securing' ('reconnaître' in the French text) the listed rights and freedoms to persons within its own 'jurisdiction'. Further, the Convention does not govern the actions of States not Parties to it, nor does it purport to be a means of requiring the Contracting States to impose Convention standards on other States. Article 1 (art. 1) cannot be read as justifying a general principle to the effect that, notwithstanding its extradition obligations, a Contracting State may not surrender an individual unless satisfied that the conditions awaiting him in the country of destination are in full accord with each of the safeguards of the Convention. Indeed, as the United Kingdom Government stressed, the beneficial purpose of extradition in preventing fugitive offenders from evading justice cannot be ignored in determining the scope of application of the Convention and of Article 3 (art. 3) in particular. In the instant case it is common ground that the United Kingdom has no power over the practices and arrangements of the Virginia authorities which are the subject of the applicant's complaints. It is also true that in other international instruments cited by the United Kingdom Government—for example the 1951 United Nations Convention relating to the Status of Refugees (Article 33), the 1957 European Convention on Extradition (Article 11) and the 1984 United Nations Convention against Torture and Other Cruel, Inhuman and Degrading Treatment or Punishment (Article 3)—the problems of removing a person to another jurisdiction where unwanted consequences may follow are addressed expressly and specifically. These considerations cannot, however, absolve the Contracting Parties from responsibility under Article 3 (art. 3) for all and any foreseeable consequences of extradition suffered outside their jurisdiction.

87. In interpreting the Convention regard must be had to its special character as a treaty for the collective enforcement of human rights and fundamental freedoms (see the Ireland v. the United Kingdom judgment of 18 January 1978, Series A no. 25, p. 90, § 239). Thus, the object and purpose of the Convention as an instrument for the protection of individual human beings require that its provisions be interpreted and applied so as to make its safeguards practical and effective (see, *inter alia*, the Artico judgment of 13 May 1980, Series A no. 37, p. 16, § 33). In addition, any interpretation of the rights and freedoms guaranteed has to be consistent with 'the general spirit of the Convention, an instrument designed to maintain and promote the ideals and values of a democratic society' (see the Kjeldsen, Busk Madsen and Pedersen judgment of 7 December 1976, Series A no. 23, p. 27, § 53).

88. Article 3 (art. 3) makes no provision for exceptions and no derogation from it is permissible under Article 15 (art. 15) in time of war or other national emergency. This absolute prohibition of torture and of inhuman or degrading treatment or punishment under the terms of the Convention shows that Article 3 (art. 3) enshrines one of the fundamental values of the democratic societies making up the Council of Europe. It is also to be found in similar terms in other international instruments such as the 1966 International Covenant on Civil and Political Rights

and the 1969 American Convention on Human Rights and is generally recognised as an internationally accepted standard. The question remains whether the extradition of a fugitive to another State where he would be subjected or be likely to be subjected to torture or to inhuman or degrading treatment or punishment would itself engage the responsibility of a Contracting State under Article 3 (art. 3). That the abhorrence of torture has such implications is recognised in Article 3 of the United Nations Convention Against Torture and Other Cruel, Inhuman or Degrading Treatment or Punishment, which provides that 'no State Party shall ... extradite a person where there are substantial grounds for believing that he would be in danger of being subjected to torture'. The fact that a specialised treaty should spell out in detail a specific obligation attaching to the prohibition of torture does not mean that an essentially similar obligation is not already inherent in the general terms of Article 3 (art. 3) of the European Convention. It would hardly be compatible with the underlying values of the Convention, that 'common heritage of political traditions, ideals, freedom and the rule of law' to which the Preamble refers, were a Contracting State knowingly to surrender a fugitive to another State where there were substantial grounds for believing that he would be in danger of being subjected to torture, however heinous the crime allegedly committed. Extradition in such circumstances, while not explicitly referred to in the brief and general wording of Article 3 (art. 3), would plainly be contrary to the spirit and intendment of the Article, and in the Court's view this inherent obligation not to extradite also extends to cases in which the fugitive would be faced in the receiving State by a real risk of exposure to inhuman or degrading treatment or punishment proscribed by that Article (art. 3).

89. What amounts to 'inhuman or degrading treatment or punishment' depends on all the circumstances of the case (see paragraph 100 below). Furthermore, inherent in the whole of the Convention is a search for a fair balance between the demands of the general interest of the community and the requirements of the protection of the individual's fundamental rights. As movement about the world becomes easier and crime takes on a larger international dimension, it is increasingly in the interest of all nations that suspected offenders who flee abroad should be brought to justice. Conversely, the establishment of safe havens for fugitives would not only result in danger for the State obliged to harbour the protected person but also tend to undermine the foundations of extradition. These considerations must also be included among the factors to be taken into account in the interpretation and application of the notions of inhuman and degrading treatment or punishment in extradition cases.

90. It is not normally for the Convention institutions to pronounce on the existence or otherwise of potential violations of the Convention. However, where an applicant claims that a decision to extradite him would, if implemented, be contrary to Article 3 (art. 3) by reason of its foreseeable consequences in the requesting country, a departure from this principle is necessary, in view of the serious and irreparable nature of the alleged suffering risked, in order to ensure the effectiveness of the safeguard provided by that Article (art. 3) (see paragraph 87 above).

91. In sum, the decision by a Contracting State to extradite a fugitive may give rise to an issue under Article 3 (art. 3), and hence engage the responsibility of that State under the Convention, where substantial grounds have been shown for believing that the person concerned, if extradited, faces a real risk of being subjected to torture or to inhuman or degrading treatment or punishment in the requesting country. The establishment of such responsibility inevitably involves an assessment of conditions in the requesting country against the standards of Article 3 (art. 3) of the Convention. Nonetheless, there is no question of adjudicating on or establishing the responsibility of the receiving country, whether under general international law, under the Convention or otherwise. In so far as any liability under the Convention is or may be incurred, it is liability incurred by the extraditing Contracting State by reason of its having taken action which has as a direct consequence the exposure of an individual to proscribed ill-treatment.

The Court unanimously found that, in the event of the Secretary of State's decision to extradite the applicant to the United States of America being implemented, there would be a violation of Art 3 of the Convention.

Note that the European Court of Human Rights would obviously have no jurisdiction over the USA had Soering been extradited. The actual violation of the Convention would thus occur in a non-member State. Indeed, no international body would have jurisdiction over the US in this situation. However, the possibility of the UK infringing the treaty through foreseeable third State actions has been corroborated by subsequent jurisprudence. *D v United Kingdom* Application 146/1996/767/964 (1997) concerned the deportation of a convicted (in the UK) drug offender who had been released from prison but was diagnosed with HIV/AIDS. The European Court held there would be a violation of Art 3 of the European Convention if he was deported back to St Kitts and Nevis due to the lack of medical care for AIDS patients there.

The principle espoused in *Soering v United Kingdom* has thus been refined in the case of *D v United Kingdom*. Today, States must be acutely aware of the foreseeable consequence of any actions they may take. Clearly the legal responsibility of States for human rights can extend beyond the geographical limit of the State, presupposing that the State is directly involved in the process of subjecting an individual to the potential violation.

Question

Do you agree with the reasoning of the European Court in these cases? To what extent does the dicta of the Court alter the accepted limits of State responsibility in International Law? Does the logical implication of D v United Kingdom *extend the notion of responsibility for human rights too far or does it merely reflect the universality of human rights?*

Note also the opinion of the United Nations' Committee Against Torture in *Mutombo v Switzerland*, UN Doc.CAT/C/12/D/13/1993. Compare this with *X v the Netherlands*, UN Doc. CAT/C/16/D/36/1995.

Responsibility of States for international human rights also impacts on the use made by States of their criminal law. States must ensure that individuals within their territory are punished for violating norms of human rights. Examples of this can be drawn from existing caselaw.

The first case illustrates the argument supporting this impact of human rights:

A v United Kingdom (1998) Vol. 1998-VI, No. 90

The facts of this case are discussed above, in Chapter 1. A child was beaten by his stepfather. At trial, the stepfather was acquitted following submission of the defence that the punishment of the child was 'reasonable chastisement' and thus permissible.

22. It remains to be determined whether the State should be held responsible, under Article 3, for the beating of the applicant by his stepfather.

The Court considers that the obligation on the High Contracting Parties under Article 1 of the Convention to secure to everyone within their jurisdiction the rights and freedoms defined in the Convention, taken together with Article 3, requires States to take measures designed to ensure that individuals within their jurisdiction are not subjected to torture or inhuman or degrading treatment or punishment, including such ill-treatment administered by private individuals (see, *mutatis mutandis*, the H.L.R. v. France judgment of 29 April 1997, *Reports* 1997-III, p. 758, § 40). Children and other vulnerable individuals, in particular, are entitled to State protection, in the form of effective deterrence, against such serious breaches of personal integrity (see, *mutatis mutandis*, the X and Y v. the Netherlands judgment of 26 March 1985, Series A no. 91, pp. 11–13, §§ 21–27; the Stubbings and Others v. the United Kingdom judgment of 22 October 1996, *Reports* 1996-IV, p. 1505, §§ 62–64; and also the United Nations Convention on the Rights of the Child, Articles 19 and 37).

23. The Court recalls that under English law it is a defence to a charge of assault on a child that the treatment in question amounted to 'reasonable chastisement' (see paragraph 14 above). The burden of proof is on the prosecution to establish beyond reasonable doubt that the assault went beyond the limits of lawful punishment. In the present case, despite the fact that the applicant had been subjected to treatment of sufficient severity to fall within the scope of Article 3, the jury acquitted his stepfather, who had administered the treatment (see paragraphs 10–11 above).

24. In the Court's view, the law did not provide adequate protection to the applicant against treatment or punishment contrary to Article 3. Indeed, the Government have accepted that this law currently fails to provide adequate protection to children and should be amended.

In the circumstances of the present case, the failure to provide adequate protection constitutes a violation of Article 3 of the Convention.

Such developments are not confined to Europe, as the *Velásquez Rodrigues* decision of the Inter-American Court of Human Rights (discussed below in Chapter 11) illustrates.

2.4   INDIVISIBILITY AND INTERDEPENDENCE OR A HIERARCHY OF RIGHTS?

The major international instruments clearly prescribe a wide range of human rights. Assuming they are all universally applicable, are they all equally applicable, or is there an overt or covert hierarchy? Are some rights more important than others? Perhaps most obviously, the right to life has to be accorded some degree of paramountcy, even if only as a matter of practicality. Quite clearly life is a precursor to enjoyment of any human rights, albeit some discussion remains as to the point at which life begins: birth or conception? Thereafter, the importance ascribed to rights is a matter of individual preference. People suffering in the aftermath of a catastrophic natural emergency will most likely prioritise clean water and food over the right to vote in democratic elections. Political prisoners may value freedom of expression over liberty. Indeed, some people value freedom of religion above the right to life. Can such conflicting views be reconciled with universality of rights?

Vienna Declaration and Programme of Action 1993, para 5

All human rights are universal, indivisible and interdependent and interrelated. The international community must treat human rights globally in a fair and equal manner, on the same footing, and with the same emphasis.

The most significant categorisation of rights is that between civil and political rights and economic, social and cultural rights. A third major category of rights has emerged too—group rights (or collective rights). The distinction between civil and political rights and economic, social and cultural rights arguably has historical and political origins.

2.4.1   A cold war product?—two categories of rights

The welfare state as a concept, is predicated on the idea that the State owes assistance to categories of people in great need. Such social and economic rights require positive action on the part of the State, while arguably some civil and political rights may be met by passivity on the part of the State, i.e. a failure to interfere with the individual exercise of the right. However, it is a myth that all social and economic rights require financial outlay on the part of the State and all civil and political rights do not. Social and economic rights are usually rights to tangible items, as opposed to civil and political rights which are rights to intangible actions.

Theories such as communism and Marxism emphasised many elements of economic and social rights. The State assisted the population with their basic needs. Of course, such rights came at a cost and many people living in such countries were arguably denied civil and political rights such as freedom of expression and democratic rights.

In contrast, the other side of the proverbial 'Iron Curtain' emphasised civil and political rights, the concepts which underpinned democratic societies. Many of these rights may also be traced back to the Reformation and Enlightenment period in Europe. The French Declaration on the Rights of Man, the American Declaration of Independence and its amendments (the Bill of Rights) focus on individual freedoms of liberty, speech and equality. Such rights are primarily civil and political in essence.

When the United Nations was preparing the legal tabulation of the Universal Declaration of Human Rights, the onset of the Cold War forced the division of the Universal Declaration. Two International Covenants emerged: one on economic, social and cultural rights, the other on civil and political rights. Even today, there remains a slight difference in the numbers of States parties to each.

2.5   INTERDEPENDENCE AND INDIVISIBILITY

A further factor to consider is the overlap between rights and the interdependence of all rights: for example failure to secure the right to adequate healthcare (a social/ economic right) may result in a threat to life, the right to life being a primary civil and political right. Many more examples can be found: right to education and right to vote and political participation; right to adequate rest periods for workers and freedom from degrading and even life-threatening treatment.

2.5.1   Example of right to clean water and adequate sanitation

The diagram opposite illustrates the interdependence of rights, focussing on the right to clean water and adequate sanitation.

Access to clean water and sanitation clearly has a bearing on a number of other rights and freedoms. A standalone right to clean water and adequate sanitation would not, of course, be sufficient to ensure that all elements of the right to education or the right to health are satisfied. On the other hand, fully implementing the right to health would require the supply of clean water and adequate sanitation.

2.5.2   The right to life

Life, and thus the right to life, is clearly a fundamental prerequisite to the exercise of many of the other rights and freedoms. However, this does not mean that the right to life is totally sacrosanct. That would place unrealistic burdens on the State—to preserve all life! Rather, each instrument notes the instances in which life may be forfeited.

European Convention on Human Rights Art 2

1. Everyone's right to life shall be protected by law. No one shall be deprived of his life intentionally save in the execution of a sentence of a court following his conviction of a crime for which this penalty is provided by law.

2. Deprivation of life shall not be regarded as inflicted in contravention of this article when it results from the use of force which is no more than absolutely necessary:

(a) in defence of any person from unlawful violence;
(b) in order to effect a lawful arrest or to prevent the escape of a person lawfully detained;
(c) in action lawfully taken for the purpose of quelling a riot or insurrection.

Not all rights are necessarily equal at all times, despite the concept of universalism outlined above. Moreover, individual situations will affect which rights are prioritised at any given time. This will usually be a subjective decision. Someone under house arrest for a prolonged period of time on account of political activities may well prioritise civil and political rights. Indeed, such a person may be willing to die for freedom of expression and political freedoms. In contrast, a child caught up in HIV/AIDS with a terminally ill parent and three younger siblings to support is unlikely to be as interested in political participation, freedom of expression and equality before the law. These rights are all factors and may be important to the child. However, his or her focus is more likely to be on the rights needed for immediate survival.

Question

Consider the plight of those involved in recent natural disasters: the Indian Ocean Tsunami, December 2004; famine in Niger, Ethiopia and Mali, 2006; the Pakistan and Indonesian earthquakes, 2005 and 2006; Hurricane Katrina in southern USA, 2005; catastrophic mudslides in Guatemala, 2005. Tragically, the list could continue. Which rights would be a priority for those caught up in the trauma and why?

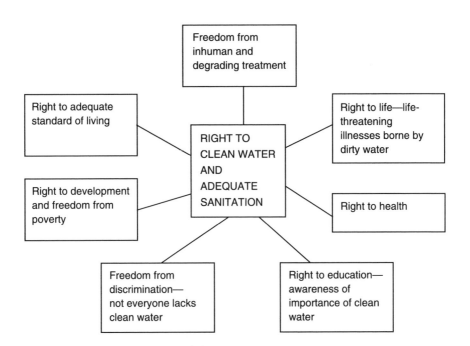

2.5.3   A family of rights

Having addressed the issue of a 'hierarchy' of rights, now consider the extent to which the following three rights and freedoms overlap. Is it possible to have full political participation without at least some freedom of expression? Can education and freedom of expression be mutually exclusive? Does an education (of whatever kind) assist with participation in the political process and the exercise of associated democratic rights?

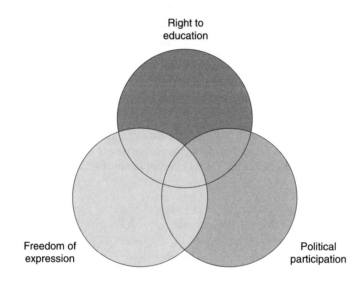

Rather than consider human rights in diverse categories, it is perhaps best to consider them as an organic whole, a family of rights, each category performing an important function; each contributing towards vibrant richness of rights and freedoms.

2.6   EVOLVING AND DEVELOPING RIGHTS

Finally, the rights enshrined in the various international and regional instruments are not static. Rather than remain frozen in time, the rights constantly evolve, responding to international events, reacting to social advancements and political change. The role of the courts and committees in achieving this change was discussed in Chapter 1, see also Chapter 6.

In conclusion, it appears true to say that international human rights are universal, indivisible, interdependent and inalienable.

FURTHER READING

An-Na'im, A (ed), *Human Rights in Cross-Cultural Perspectives: a quest for consensus*, 1992, Philadelphia: PUP

Ayton-Shenker, D, 'The Challenge of Human Rights and Cultural Diversity', United Nations Background Note. Available at www.un.org/rights/dpi1627e.htm

Baehr, P, *Universality in Practice*, 1999, New York: St. Martin's Press

Bell, L, Nathan, A and Peleg, I (eds), *Negotiating Culture and Human Rights*, 2001, New York: NYUP

Benvenisti, E, 'Margin of Appreciation, Consensus and Universal Standards' (1999) 31 International Law and Politics 843

Caney, S, 'Human Rights, Compatibility and Diverse Cultures' in Caney, S and Jones, P (eds), *Human Rights and Global Diversity*, 2001, London: Frank Cass

Eriksen, T, 'Between Universalism and Relativism: a critique of the UNESCO concepts of culture?' in Cowan, J, Dembour, M and Wilson, R (eds), *Culture and Rights: Anthropological Perspectives*, 2001, Cambridge: CUP

Evans, T, 'Universal Human Rights: as much round and round as ever onward?' (2003) 7.4 International Journal of Human Rights 155

Harris-Short, S, 'International Human Rights Law: Imperialist, Inept and Ineffective? Cultural Relativism and the UN Convention on the Rights of the Child' (2003) 25 Human Rights Quarterly 130

Hutchinson, M, 'The Margin of Appreciation Doctrine in the European Court of Human Rights' (1999) 48 International and Comparative Law Quarterly 638

Lavender, N, 'The Problem of the Margin of Appreciation' (1997) European Human Rights Law Review 380

McGoldrick, D, 'Multiculturalism and its Discontents' (2005) 5.1 Human Rights Law Review 27

Perry, M, 'Are Human Rights Universal? The Relativist Challenge and Related Matters' (1997) 19 Human Rights Quarterly 461

Renteln A, *International Human Rights: Universalism versus Relativism*, 1990, Newbury Park, CA: Sage

Wilkins, B, 'International Human Rights and National Discretion' (2002) 6.4 Journal of Ethics 373

CHAPTER 3

STATES AND TREATY OBLIGATIONS

The Millennium Declaration adopted by the General Assembly of the United Nations in 2000 emphasised the need for respect for the Universal Declaration of Human Rights (UN Doc. A/55/L.2, para 25) and for the Heads of State and Government to spare no effort promoting democracy and strengthening the rule of law, respecting all internationally recognised human rights and fundamental freedoms (para 24). For any system of international human rights to work, it is essential that as large a number of States as possible participate, embracing the rights and obligations enshrined in the salient instruments. In other words, their participation should be absolute.

> **Vienna Declaration and Programme of Action WORLD CONFERENCE ON HUMAN RIGHTS Vienna, 14–25 June 1993, UN Doc. A/CONF.157/23**
>
> 26. The World Conference on Human Rights welcomes the progress made in the codification of human rights instruments, which is a dynamic and evolving process, and urges the universal ratification of human rights treaties. All States are encouraged to accede to these international instruments; all States are encouraged to avoid, as far as possible, the resort to reservations.

By definition, international human rights are adopted in the understanding they will achieve international and, indeed, universal acceptance. To date, the only instrument to come close is the Convention on the Rights of the Child, with ratification by all but two member States of the UN (USA and Somalia). This chapter will encapsulate material relating to the obligations incumbent on States and the methods by which States may limit them. The next chapter will focus more on the systems of monitoring and enforcing human rights.

3.1   UNIVERSAL HUMAN RIGHTS AND RATIFICATION

An essential part of the new world order created through the United Nations is the concept of universal rights. Materials relating to the debate between universality and cultural pluralism have already been discussed in Chapter 2. In contrast, this section examines the practical problems encountered by the international community in trying to ensure the universal application of rights. Problems arise through the myriad of ways a State can legitimately limit its obligations under any given instrument. It is inevitable that universality was the goal of the United Nations: a truly global organisation derives continued legitimacy from international endorsement. However, even without the problems caused by cultural relativism, the goal of universality encounters hurdles with a lack of State ratifications.

Compare and contrast the following views of universal ratification.

A critical viewpoint

Professor Anne F. Bayefsky, York University, Canada. Committee on International Human Rights Law and Practice Report on the UN Human Rights Treaties: Facing the Implementation Crisis, International Law Association Helsinki Conference (1996)

The implementation crisis facing the principle UN human rights legal standards is now of danger-ous proportions. For a great many states ratification has become an end in itself, a means to easy accolades for empty gestures. The problem has arisen in part because of a deliberate emphasis on ratification.

The primary goal of the UN community has been to achieve universal ratification of the human rights treaties. The underlying belief is that once universal ratification is realized, the implementa-tion techniques can be strengthened. Once committed to participation, states will find it difficult to pull out and will find themselves ensnared in an ever-expanding network of international supervision and accountability.

In the meantime, ratification by human rights adversaries is purchased at a price, namely, dimin-ished obligations, lax supervision, and few adverse consequences from non-compliance. The cost of membership has been deliberately minimized. One significant example of this phenomenon is the acceptance into the treaty regime of states that ratify only with broad reservations. These reservations purport to limit the obligations assumed. For example, many Islamic and Asian states only ratify the treaties with the caveat that any obligation sustained must first be compatible with Islamic law or a similar broad reservation.

29 Such reservations are inconsistent with international law which requires reservations to conform to the object and purpose of the treaty, and in the case of human rights treaties means identifying and applying overriding, universal standards. Nevertheless, few states are prepared to challenge other states on the legitimacy of their reservations, and some important states like the United States and the United Kingdom currently are resisting attempts by the treaty bodies themselves to challenge reservations.

Question

Are Bayefsky's criticisms realistic and justified or unduly pessimistic?

Bayefsky's criticisms should be borne in mind when progressing through this chapter, not least as you re-evaluate whether or not they are justified.

A programme of practical solutions in the push towards universal ratification was suggested by Professor Philip Alston, the United Nations appointed Independent Expert who prepared a series of reports on rendering the United Nations process more efficient.

United Nations support of universalism

Professor Philip Alston, UN Independent Expert. Final report on enhancing the long-term effectiveness of the United Nations human rights treaty system, UN Doc. E/CN.4/1997/74

23. The emphasis upon promoting universal ratification is an essential one in order to strengthen and consolidate the universalist foundations of the United Nations human rights regime. Despite the fears of some critics, the quest for universal ratification need not have any negative con-sequences for the treaty regime as a whole. One such critic, Professor Bayefsky, has argued that the 'implementation crisis' which she perceives to exist is due in part to 'a deliberate emphasis on ratification' which for many States, has 'become an end in itself, a means to easy accolades for empty gestures'. In her view, ratification is often 'purchased at a price, namely, diminished obliga-tions, lax supervision, and few adverse consequences from non-compliance'. But such an analysis

would seem to confuse two processes which should remain, and for the most part have remained, separate. It is difficult to accept the proposition that the treaty bodies have been lax in their supervision in order to entice more States to accept the obligations in question. Indeed, the experience of the Convention on the Rights of the Child would seem clearly incompatible with such an analysis. The Committee on the Rights of the Child has, to date, been one of the most demanding and conscientious of the treaty bodies, but this has in no way impeded the dramatic movement towards the achievement of near-universal ratification of the Convention. In the view of the independent expert more, rather than less, should be done to explore ways in which to overcome the legitimate, as opposed to the inappropriate, concerns of certain identifiable groups of countries that have so far been reluctant to ratify.

24. Perhaps the most obvious such group consists of those States with a population of 1 million or less. Twenty-nine such States have not ratified either of the two International Covenants on Human Rights. As of 1996, 21 of those were estimated to have a Gross National Product per capita of below US$ 5,000 per annum, and with 11 of them being below the $2,000 per annum level.

. . .

25. This in turn raises the question of whether the international community should be providing resources to facilitate the ratification of treaties by such States and to assist them in meeting the subsequent reporting burden, at least initially. Curiously, it has yet to be acknowledged that such activities, which are essential to laying the foundations for a stable and peaceful world in which human rights are respected, should be funded adequately within the United Nations framework. It almost seems to be thought that efforts to promote the acceptance of human rights norms would somehow be tainted if progress were purchased at a price, in terms of the necessary technical assistance. In contrast, the principle was recognized long ago in the environmental area in which many of the arrangements made in relation to key treaties provide for financial and other forms of assistance to help States to undertake the necessary monitoring, to prepare reports and to implement some of the measures required in order to ensure compliance with treaty obligations.

To this end, Alston made a number of recommendations, including:

(1) examining the role of international agencies in encouraging ratifications;

(2) adopting systematic approach to overcoming identified obstacles to ratification;

(3) employing specific funding to support preparation of initial State reports;

(4) identifying appropriate ways of streamlining the reporting burden particularly for those States which have already ratified the Convention on the Rights of the Child and/or the Convention on the Elimination of All Forms of Racial Discrimination/ Discrimination against Women (the most commonly ratified instruments by States within this category) thereby encouraging the State to ratify more extensively.

Question
To what extent could such an approach prove successful? What are the advantages and disadvantages of this proposed approach? Should such an approach adequately address the problems identified by Alston and Bayefsky?

3.1.1 The unusual position of the Convention on the Rights of the Child

Following Alston's analysis, the paradox inherent in the ratification levels of the UN Convention on the Rights of the Child is remarkable. The Committee on the Rights of the Child is very progressive in its approach to the Convention. Accordingly, States are already being held to account for virtually all the rights in the International

Covenants and other principal instruments. A perusal of State reports indicates that many States do not have specific enforceable national instruments on children's rights—the rights enshrined in the Convention must then be supported by the same laws and regulations that protect the rights of adults. While few question the need for protection of children, it appears that most States already afford the same rights to adults and children, with little discrimination. Why then do they not exalt their positive universalist approach by ratifying the other instruments? Should the law fully support the range of children's rights in the Convention, few, if any, changes in national law would be required for implementing the two international covenants and, indeed, the other major instruments.

This issue is addressed by Philip Alston in his seminal report.

Philip Alston, final report, UN Doc. E/CN.4/1997/74, 27 March, paras 19–21

19. There are some important lessons to be learned from the successes achieved in relation to the [.] conventions which have attracted so many new ratifications in recent years. The first concerns the importance of political will, whether expressed through the holding of international conferences which place appropriate emphasis upon the convention in question or through consistent efforts by international organizations. In contrast, the lead-up to international conferences focusing on social development (Copenhagen) and human settlements (Istanbul) saw no attention at all to efforts to promote ratification of the relevant human rights treaties. The second lesson concerns the importance of mobilizing domestic constituencies (in this case, women's and children's non-governmental organizations) in support of the goals and mechanisms reflected in the treaty, thus making it easier for Governments to undertake ratification.

20. The third lesson, and in the case of the Convention on the Rights of the Child the most important, concerns the provision of assistance and advice by an international agency, which in this instance was the United Nations Children's Fund. Such agencies can, whenever requested, assist Governments and the principal social partners in various ways, including: by explaining the significance of the treaty as a whole and of its specific provisions; by promoting an awareness of the treaty which facilitates domestic consultations and discussions; by shedding light upon the requirements of the treaty in the event of ratification; by providing assistance to enable any necessary pre-ratification measures to be identified and implemented; by assisting in relation to the preparation of reports, both indirectly through the agency's own situation analyses, and directly through the provision of expert assistance where appropriate; and by reassuring developing countries in particular that ratification should bring with it enhanced access to at least some of the expert or financial resources needed to implement key provisions of the treaty.

21. In this respect the success of the effort to promote ratification of the Convention on the Rights of the Child indicates that there is no (or at least no longer) deep-rooted resistance to the principle of participation in human rights supervisory arrangements. Given the relative comprehensiveness of the Convention, along with the integral links between respect for children's rights and those of the rest of the community, it might be thought that the reasons which had previously led various States not to ratify all six of the core human rights treaties are no longer compelling and that there will be a new openness to increased participation in the overall treaty regime. Indeed, there is something odd about a situation in which all States but four have become parties to such a far-reaching Convention while almost one State in every three has not become a party to either of the two International Covenants.

Question

What reasons are there for reticent States to ratify the Convention on the Rights of the Child yet not even sign other instruments? What lessons can be learnt from the success of this instrument?

The Convention on the Rights of the Child is not alone in attracting multiple State ratifications, though certainly it is a unique beacon of hope for those advocating universal ratification of all major instruments. Notable advances in ratification have followed some other major conferences. The Fourth World Conference on Women (Beijing 1995) attracted significant public attention as the largest ever gathering of government and NGO representatives. It prompted anew a global commitment to the advancement of women through empowerment and provided a focus for increasing ratification of the UN Convention on the Elimination of All Forms of Discrimination against Women and the erosion of reservations thereto. Similarly, the Convention on the Elimination of All Forms of Racial Discrimination and the Migrant Workers Convention experienced a revival in interest in the wake of the Third World Conference against Racism, Racial Discrimination, Xenophobia and Related Intolerance (Durban 2001). Indeed, the Migrant Workers Convention finally entered into force in July 2003, following Guatemala's ratification. As a consequence, all the designated principal international human rights instruments are now in force, albeit the goal of universal ratification remains some way off.

3.2 LIMITATIONS ON STATE COMPLIANCE: RESERVATIONS, DECLARATIONS, DEROGATIONS AND DENUNCIATIONS

Ratification is not the sole problem encountered by proponents of a universal human rights regime. A State which ratifies any or all of the major instruments may still avoid the necessity of giving effect to the provisions of the instrument concerned. There are a number of ways that a State which has signed up to a human rights instrument can limit the range of obligations it assumes: reservations, declarations, derogations and denunciations. Each of these will be considered in turn.

3.3 RESERVATIONS

A reservation is the means by which a State can be party to a Treaty while excluding or modifying one or more provisions. The Vienna Convention on the Law of Treaties attempted to codify customary international law on the matter, though in some aspects represented progressive development of the pre-existing customary law.

3.3.1 Nature and scope of reservations

Vienna Convention on the Law of Treaties 1969
Article 2(1)(d)

For the purpose of the present Convention, 'reservation' means a unilateral statement, however phrased or named, made by a State, when signing, ratifying, accepting, approving or acceding to a treaty, whereby it purports to exclude or to modify the legal effect of certain provisions of the treaty in their application to that State.

Article 19
Formulation of reservations

A State may, when signing, ratifying, accepting, approving or acceding to a treaty, formulate a reservation unless:

(a) the reservation is prohibited by the treaty;

(b) the treaty provides that only specified reservations, which do not include the reservation in question, may be made; or

(c) in cases not falling under sub-paragraphs (a) and (b), the reservation is incompatible with the object and purpose of the treaty.

Not all reservations are termed such and thus the definition of a reservation is of crucial importance. As is seen in the following extract from a General Comment of the Human Rights Committee, it is the substance, not the title, of the measure which is determinative. The approach outlined by the Human Rights Committee probably pervades other international instruments and thus is of general relevance.

Human Rights Committee, General Comment 24 (1994)
Issues relating to reservations made upon ratification or accession to the Covenant or the Optional Protocols thereto, or in relation to declarations under article 41 of the Covenant

3. It is not always easy to distinguish a reservation from a declaration as to a State's understanding of the interpretation of a provision, or from a statement of policy. Regard will be had to the intention of the State, rather than the form of the instrument. If a statement, irrespective of its name or title, purports to exclude or modify the legal effect of a treaty in its application to the State, it constitutes a reservation. Conversely, if a so-called reservation merely offers a State's understanding of a provision but does not exclude or modify that provision in its application to that State, it is, in reality, not a reservation.

Traditionally, a reservation to a bilateral treaty would result in renegotiation to achieve consensus between parties. On the other hand, States ratifying or acceding to a multilateral treaty (most international human rights instruments) could only enter a reservation if said reservation was accepted by all other contracting parties. Should one or more State object to the reservation, then the State seeking to join the Convention would have to withdraw its reservation or leave the Convention. Clearly, in a system of international multilateral human rights instruments, such an approach could prove problematic, significantly limiting the number of States brought within the ambit of the international human rights system. Universalism would become impossibly idealistic. The need for a balance between universal participation in human rights instruments and the political expediency of reservations was addressed by the International Court of Justice.

3.3.2   The ICJ's approach developing reservations

Reservations to the Convention on the Prevention and Punishment of the Crime of Genocide, Advisory Opinion of 28 May 1951 (1951 ICJ 15)

The General Assembly of the United Nations referred questions to the International Court of Justice for an advisory opinion (G.A. resolution of 16 November 1950). The Court was asked whether a State ratifying or acceding to the Convention with a reservation can be regarded as being a party to the Convention, if the reservation is objected to by one or more of the parties to the Convention though not by all. Additional questions related to the effect of such a reservation *inter partes*:

It may, however, be asked whether the General Assembly of the United Nations, in approving the Genocide Convention, had in mind the practice according to which the Secretary-General, in exercising his functions as a depositary, did not regard a reservation as definitively accepted until it had been established that none of the other contracting States objected to it. If this were the case, it might be argued that the implied intention of the contracting parties was to make the effectiveness of any reservation to the Genocide Convention conditional on the assent of all the parties.

The Court does not consider that this view corresponds to reality. It must be pointed out, first of all, that the existence of an administrative practice does not in itself constitute a decisive factor in ascertaining what views the contracting States to the Genocide Convention may have had concerning the rights and duties resulting therefrom. It must also be pointed out that there existed among the American States members both of the United Nations and of the Organization of American States, a different practice which goes so far as to permit a reserving State to become a party irrespective of the nature of the reservations or of the objections raised by other contracting States. The preparatory work of the Convention contains nothing to justify the statement that the contracting States implicitly had any definite practice in mind. Nor is there any such indication in the subsequent attitude of the contracting States: neither the reservations made by certain States nor the position adopted by other States towards those reservations permit the conclusion that assent to one or the other of these practices had been given. Finally, it is not without interest to note, in view of the preference generally said to attach to an established practice, that the debate on reservations to multilateral treaties which took place in the Sixth Committee at the fifth session of the General Assembly reveals a profound divergence of views, some delegations being attached to the idea of the absolute integrity of the Convention, others favouring a more flexible practice which would bring about the participation of as many States as possible.

The Court concluded by seven votes to five that a State entering a reservation to the Genocide Convention which is objected to by one or more, though not all, parties to the Convention may be regarded as a party to the Convention as long as the reservation is compatible with the object and purpose of the Convention.

Comment

As far as the International Court is concerned, the special nature of the Genocide Convention rendered it an exceptional circumstance. In order to further universal ratification of this major humanitarian instrument, it was acceptable that States could enter reservations yet become a party. For those States objecting to the reservation, there would be no *inter partes* agreement, though each would independently remain party to the Convention.

3.3.3 The effect of reservations

Vienna Convention on the Law of Treaties 1969

Article 21

Legal effects of reservations and of objections to reservations

1. A reservation established with regard to another party in accordance with articles 19, 20 and 23:

(a) modifies for the reserving State in its relations with that other party the provisions of the treaty to which the reservation relates to the extent of the reservation; and

(b) modifies those provisions to the same extent for that other party in its relations with the reserving State.

2. The reservation does not modify the provisions of the treaty for the other parties to the treaty *inter se*.

3. When a State objecting to a reservation has not opposed the entry into force of the treaty between itself and the reserving State, the provisions to which the reservation relates do not apply as between the two States to the extent of the reservation.

It is clear that a valid reservation removes the provision concerned from the legal obligations of a State. A State is neither bound by the reserved provision, nor, in the interest of reciprocity, can it hold another State to account for infringing said provision. Clearly, the use of reservations can seriously undermine universality. The various international human rights monitoring bodies have had cause to discuss issues arising from the use of reservations. As the following extract demonstrates, problems arise not only through the existence of reservations but also through their creation, use and effect.

The Human Rights Committee's view

Human Rights Committee, General Comment 24 (1994)

Issues relating to reservations made upon ratification or accession to the Covenant or the Optional Protocols thereto, or in relation to declarations under article 41 of the Covenant

4. The possibility of entering reservations may encourage States which consider that they have difficulties in guaranteeing all the rights in the Covenant none the less to accept the generality of obligations in that instrument. Reservations may serve a useful function to enable States to adapt specific elements in their laws to the inherent rights of each person as articulated in the Covenant. However, it is desirable in principle that States accept the full range of obligations, because the human rights norms are the legal expression of the essential rights that every person is entitled to as a human being.

. . .

7. In an instrument which articulates very many civil and political rights, each of the many articles, and indeed their interplay, secures the objectives of the Covenant. The object and purpose of the Covenant is to create legally binding standards for human rights by defining certain civil and political rights and placing them in a framework of obligations which are legally binding for those States which ratify; and to provide an efficacious supervisory machinery for the obligations undertaken.

The Committee proceeded to expand on this with more detailed examples of reservations and their view thereon. The Committee was obviously focused on existing reservations and proposed reservations to the International Covenant on Civil and Political Rights.

The Committee identified certain reservations which would not be compatible with the Covenant:

Human Rights Committee, General Comment 24 (1994)

Issues relating to reservations made upon ratification or accession to the Covenant or the Optional Protocols thereto, or in relation to declarations under article 41 of the Covenant

8. Reservations that offend peremptory norms would not be compatible with the object and purpose of the Covenant. Although treaties that are mere exchanges of obligations between States allow them to reserve *inter se* application of rules of general international law, it is otherwise in human rights treaties, which are for the benefit of persons within their jurisdiction. Accordingly, provisions in the Covenant that represent customary international law (and *a fortiori* when they have the character of peremptory norms) may not be the subject of reservations. Accordingly, a State may not reserve the right to engage in slavery, to torture, to subject persons to cruel, inhuman or degrading treatment or punishment, to arbitrarily deprive persons of their lives, to arbitrarily arrest and detain persons, to deny freedom of thought, conscience and religion, to presume a person guilty unless he proves his innocence, to execute pregnant women or children, to permit the advocacy of national, racial or religious hatred, to deny to persons of marriageable age the right to marry, or to deny to minorities the right to enjoy their own culture,

profess their own religion, or use their own language. And while reservations to particular clauses of article 14 may be acceptable, a general reservation to the right to a fair trial would not be.

. . .

12. The intention of the Covenant is that the rights contained therein should be ensured to all those under a State party's jurisdiction. . . . Domestic laws may need to be altered properly to reflect the requirements of the Covenant; and mechanisms at the domestic level will be needed to allow the Covenant rights to be enforceable at the local level. Reservations often reveal a tendency of States not to want to change a particular law. And sometimes that tendency is elevated to a general policy. Of particular concern are widely formulated reservations which essentially render ineffective all Covenant rights which would require any change in national law to ensure compliance with Covenant obligations. No real international rights or obligations have thus been accepted. And when there is an absence of provisions to ensure that Covenant rights may be sued on in domestic courts, and, further, a failure to allow individual complaints to be brought to the Committee under the first Optional Protocol, all the essential elements of the Covenant guarantees have been removed.

. . .

19. . . . Reservations may [.] not be general, but must refer to a particular provision of the Covenant and indicate in precise terms its scope in relation thereto. When considering the compatibility of possible reservations with the object and purpose of the Covenant, States should also take into consideration the overall effect of a group of reservations, as well as the effect of each reservation on the integrity of the Covenant, which remains an essential consideration. States should not enter so many reservations that they are in effect accepting a limited number of human rights obligations, and not the Covenant as such. So that reservations do not lead to a perpetual non-attainment of international human rights standards, reservations should not systematically reduce the obligations undertaken only to those presently existing in less demanding standards of domestic law. Nor should interpretative declarations or reservations seek to remove an autonomous meaning to Covenant obligations, by pronouncing them to be identical, or to be accepted only in so far as they are identical, with existing provisions of domestic law. States should not seek through reservations or interpretative declarations to determine that the meaning of a provision of the Covenant is the same as that given by an organ of any other international treaty body.

Question

Why would States wish to ratify an instrument yet avoid full responsibility through reservations? Does the need for reservations, as outlined in the HRC General Comment, on balance override the problems caused, in other words are reservations a necessary evil in any international system? (Consider again the criticisms levied by Bayefsky, above.)

Reservations are a creature of international law. While they are undoubtedly widely used, questions arise over whether they are appropriate in a scheme of allegedly universal rights.

Reservations and human rights

Can reservations be made to international human rights treaties? This has been the subject of some debate and a major advisory opinion from the International Court of Justice. A test has evolved concerning the nature of any reservation and its purported compatibility with the object and purpose of the instrument concerned.

Reservations to the Convention on the Prevention and Punishment of the Crime of Genocide, Advisory Opinion of 28 May 1951 (1951 ICJ 15)

The solution of these problems must be found in the special characteristics of the Genocide Convention. The origins and character of that Convention, the objects pursued by the General

Assembly and the contracting parties, the relations which exist between the provisions of the Convention, *inter se*, and between those provisions and these objects, furnish elements of interpretation of the will of the General Assembly and the parties. The origins of the Convention show that it was the intention of the United Nations to condemn and punish genocide as 'a crime under international law' involving a denial of the right of existence of entire human groups, a denial which shocks the conscience of mankind and results in great losses to humanity, and which is contrary to moral law and to the spirit and aims of the United Nations (Resolution 96 (I) of the General Assembly, December 11th 1946). The first consequence arising from this conception is that the principles underlying the Convention are principles which are recognized by civilized nations as binding on States, even without any conventional obligation. A second consequence is the universal character both of the condemnation of genocide and of the cooperation required 'in order to liberate mankind from such an odious scourge' (Preamble to the Convention). The Genocide Convention was therefore intended by the General Assembly and by the contracting parties to be definitely universal in scope. It was in fact approved on December 9th, 1948, by a resolution which was unanimously adopted by fifty-six States.

The objects of such a convention must also be considered. The Convention was manifestly adopted for a purely humanitarian and civilizing purpose. It is indeed difficult to imagine a convention that might have this dual character to a greater degree, since its object on the one hand is to safeguard the very existence of certain human groups and on the other to confirm and endorse the most elementary principles of morality. In such a convention the contracting States do not have any interests of their own; they merely have, one and all, a common interest, namely, the accomplishment of those high purposes which are the raison d'être of the convention. Consequently, in a convention of this type one cannot speak of individual advantages or disadvantages to States, or of the maintenance of a perfect contractual balance between rights and duties. The high ideals which inspired the Convention provide, by virtue of the common will of the parties, the foundation and measure of all its provisions.

The foregoing considerations, when applied to the question of reservations, and more particularly to the effects of objections to reservations, lead to the following conclusions.

The object and purpose of the Genocide Convention imply that it was the intention of the General Assembly and of the States which adopted it that as many States as possible should participate. The complete exclusion from the Convention of one or more States would not only restrict the scope of its application, but would detract from the authority of the moral and humanitarian principles which are its basis. It is inconceivable that the contracting parties readily contemplated that an objection to a minor reservation should produce such a result. But even less could the contracting parties have intended to sacrifice the very object of the Convention in favour of a vain desire to secure as many participants as possible. The object and purpose of the Convention thus limit both the freedom of making reservations and that of objecting to them. It follows that it is the compatibility of a reservation with the object and purpose of the Convention that must furnish the criterion for the attitude of a State in making the reservation on accession as well as for the appraisal by a State in objecting to the reservation. Such is the rule of conduct which must guide every State in the appraisal which it must make, individually and from its own standpoint, of the admissibility of any reservation.

Any other view would lead either to the acceptance of reservations which frustrate the purposes which the General Assembly and the contracting parties had in mind, or to recognition that the parties to the Convention have the power of excluding from it the author of a reservation, even a minor one, which may be quite compatible with those purposes.

However, this opinion was not unanimous with several judges annexing dissenting opinions thereto. Consider the opinion of Judges Guerrero, McNair, Read and Hsu Mo as to whether distinctions between reservations are possible and indeed desirable.

It is clear that the 'classification' advocated by the majority of the court did not attract unanimous support.

Question

Do you think the same circumstances should pervade other basic international human rights treaties, thereby limiting the right to reservations? To what extent are other instruments derived from customary international law?

In accordance with the Vienna Convention, some instruments explicitly preclude the possibility of reservations. More commonly, however, only reservations incompatible with the object and purpose of the instrument are prohibited. This reflects the opinion of the International Court of Justice on the Genocide Convention and also the opinion of the Human Rights Committee which has elaborated on this in respect of the International Covenant on Civil and Political Rights.

Question

Should the Genocide Convention be treated as a unique case or should the same approach pervade the other multilateral instruments?

3.3.4 The International Covenant on Civil and Political Rights and Reservations

Human Rights Committee, General Comment 24 (1994)
Issues relating to reservations made upon ratification or accession to the Covenant or the Optional Protocols thereto, in relation to declarations under article 41 of the Covenant

14. The Committee considers that reservations relating to the required procedures under the first Optional Protocol would not be compatible with its object and purpose. The Committee must control its own procedures as specified by the Optional Protocol and its rules of procedure. Reservations have, however, purported to limit the competence of the Committee to acts and events occurring after entry into force for the State concerned of the first Optional Protocol. In the view of the Committee this is not a reservation but, most usually, a statement consistent with its normal competence *ratione temporis*. At the same time, the Committee has insisted upon its competence, even in the face of such statements or observations, when events or acts occurring before the date of entry into force of the first Optional Protocol have continued to have an effect on the rights of a victim subsequent to that date. Reservations have been entered which effectively add an additional ground of inadmissibility under article 5, paragraph 2, by precluding examination of a communication when the same matter has already been examined by another comparable procedure. In so far as the most basic obligation has been to secure independent third party review of the human rights of individuals, the Committee has, where the legal right and the subject-matter are identical under the Covenant and under another international instrument, viewed such a reservation as not violating the object and purpose of the first Optional Protocol.

15. The primary purpose of the Second Optional Protocol is to extend the scope of the substantive obligations undertaken under the Covenant, as they relate to the right to life, by prohibiting execution and abolishing the death penalty. It has its own provision concerning reservations, which is determinative of what is permitted. Article 2, paragraph 1, provides that only one category of reservation is permitted, namely one that reserves the right to apply the death penalty in time of war pursuant to a conviction for a most serious crime of a military nature committed during wartime. Two procedural obligations are incumbent upon States parties wishing to avail themselves of such a reservation. Article 2, paragraph 1, obliges such a State to inform the Secretary-General, at the time of ratification or accession, of the relevant provisions of its national legislation during warfare. This is clearly directed towards the objectives of specificity and transparency and in the view of the Committee a purported reservation unaccompanied by such information is without legal effect. Article 2, paragraph 3, requires a State making such a reservation to notify the Secretary-General of the beginning or ending of a state of war applicable

to its territory. In the view of the Committee, no State may seek to avail itself of its reservation (that is, have execution in time of war regarded as lawful) unless it has complied with the procedural requirement of article 2, paragraph 3.

. . .

20. States should institute procedures to ensure that each and every proposed reservation is compatible with the object and purpose of the Covenant. It is desirable for a State entering a reservation to indicate in precise terms the domestic legislation or practices which it believes to be incompatible with the Covenant obligation reserved; and to explain the time period it requires to render its own laws and practices compatible with the Covenant, or why it is unable to render its own laws and practices compatible with the Covenant. States should also ensure that the necessity for maintaining reservations is periodically reviewed, taking into account any observations and recommendations made by the Committee during examination of their reports. Reservations should be withdrawn at the earliest possible moment. Reports to the Committee should contain information on what action has been taken to review, reconsider or withdraw reservations.

Not all instruments permit reservations. As noted in the Genocide Convention case, it is desirable that the drafters stipulate whether reservations are permitted or not to clarify the matter. Art 17 of the Optional Protocol to the Convention on the Elimination of All Forms of Discrimination against Women, for example, stipulates that no reservations are permitted.

Question

Why are reservations to the Optional Protocol to CEDAW excluded and why were similar clauses not be inserted into other instruments?

3.3.5 Case study: the Convention on the Elimination of All Forms of Discrimination against Women and Reservations

The Beijing World Conference on Women noted with concern the impact of reservations on the enjoyment of human rights by women.

Beijing Fourth World Conference on Women Platform for Action

218. In order to protect the human rights of women, it is necessary to avoid, as far as possible, resorting to reservations and to ensure that no reservation is incompatible with the object and purpose of the Convention or is otherwise incompatible with international treaty law. Unless the human rights of women, as defined by international human rights instruments, are fully recognized and effectively protected, applied, implemented and enforced in national law as well as in national practice in family, civil, penal, labour and commercial codes and administrative rules and regulations, they will exist in name only.

219. In those countries that have not yet become parties to the Convention on the Elimination of All Forms of Discrimination against Women and other international human rights instruments, or where reservations that are incompatible with the object or purpose of the Convention have been entered, or where national laws have not yet been revised to implement international norms and standards, women's *de jure* equality is not yet secured. Women's full enjoyment of equal rights is undermined by the discrepancies between some national legislation and international law and international instruments on human rights. Overly complex administrative procedures, lack of awareness within the judicial process and inadequate monitoring of the violation of the human rights of all women, coupled with the under representation of women in justice systems, insufficient information on existing rights and persistent attitudes and practices perpetuate women's *de facto* inequality. De facto inequality is also perpetuated by the lack of enforcement

of, *inter alia*, family, civil, penal, labour and commercial laws or codes, or administrative rules and regulations intended to ensure women's full enjoyment of human rights and fundamental freedoms.

Note the following fundamental provisions of the Convention on the Elimination of All Forms of Discrimination against Women

Convention on the Elimination of All Forms of Discrimination against Women

Article 1

For the purposes of the present Convention, the term 'discrimination against women' shall mean any distinction, exclusion or restriction made on the basis of sex which has the effect or purpose of impairing or nullifying the recognition, enjoyment or exercise by women, irrespective of their marital status, on a basis of equality of men and women, of human rights and fundamental freedoms in the political, economic, social, cultural, civil or any other field.

Article 2

States Parties condemn discrimination against women in all its forms, agree to pursue by all appropriate means and without delay a policy of eliminating discrimination against women and, to this end, undertake:

(a) To embody the principle of the equality of men and women in their national constitutions or other appropriate legislation if not yet incorporated therein and to ensure, through law and other appropriate means, the practical realization of this principle;

(b) To adopt appropriate legislative and other measures, including sanctions where appropriate, prohibiting all discrimination against women;

(c) To establish legal protection of the rights of women on an equal basis with men and to ensure through competent national tribunals and other public institutions the effective protection of women against any act of discrimination;

(d) To refrain from engaging in any act or practice of discrimination against women and to ensure that public authorities and institutions shall act in conformity with this obligation;

(e) To take all appropriate measures to eliminate discrimination against women by any person, organization or enterprise;

(f) To take all appropriate measures, including legislation, to modify or abolish existing laws, regulations, customs and practices which constitute discrimination against women;

(g) To repeal all national penal provisions which constitute discrimination against women.

Article 3

States Parties shall take in all fields, in particular in the political, social, economic and cultural fields, all appropriate measures, including legislation, to ensure the full development and advancement of women, for the purpose of guaranteeing them the exercise and enjoyment of human rights and fundamental freedoms on a basis of equality with men.

Article 4

1. Adoption by States Parties of temporary special measures aimed at accelerating *de facto* equality between men and women shall not be considered discrimination as defined in the present Convention, but shall in no way entail as a consequence the maintenance of unequal or separate standards; these measures shall be discontinued when the objectives of equality of opportunity and treatment have been achieved.

2. Adoption by States Parties of special measures, including those measures contained in the present Convention, aimed at protecting maternity shall not be considered discriminatory.

Article 5

States Parties shall take all appropriate measures:

(a) To modify the social and cultural patterns of conduct of men and women, with a view to achieving the elimination of prejudices and customary and all other practices which are based on the idea of the inferiority or the superiority of either of the sexes or on stereotyped roles for men and women;

(b) To ensure that family education includes a proper understanding of maternity as a social function and the recognition of the common responsibility of men and women in the upbringing and development of their children, it being understood that the interest of the children is the primordial consideration in all cases.

Question

Look at Articles 1–5 of the Convention on the Elimination of All Forms of Discrimination against Women. A number of States have entered reservations to it yet become/remain State parties. Consider to what extent a reservation to these articles go to the merits of the convention itself.

For example, look at this extract from Egypt's reservation.

Convention on the Elimination of All Forms of Discrimination against Women Reservation made by Egypt

General reservation on article 2

The Arab Republic of Egypt is willing to comply with the content of this article, provided that such compliance does not run counter to the Islamic Shari'a.

Question

Is this compatible with the object and purpose of Art 2?

Note the views of Christine Chinkin when commenting on the many general reservations entered in respect of the first articles of the Convention with reference to Shari'a law:

'Reservations and Objections to the convention on the Elimination of All Forms of Discrimination against Women' in Chinkin et al., *Human Rights as General Norms and a State's Right to Opt Out*, 1997, London: BCIL, pp 64–84 at 66

Many criticisms can be made of these reservations: their indeterminacy, imprecision and openendedness are contrary to the certainty required for the acceptance of a clear legal obligation. These reservations have not been accompanied by explanations of their intended legal or practical scope, which itself is subject to doubt in that there are disagreements among Islamic scholars as to the requirements of Shari'a law.

Question

Does the element of uncertainty over the precise scope and application of Shari'a law demonstrate a failure to comply with the object and purpose test?

Reservations and Objections thereto—Case Study on Djibouti and The Convention on The Rights of the Child

A number of States have made reservations to the Convention on the Rights of the Child. The following example indicates a reservation which other States consider detrimental to the object and purpose of the Convention. The reservation made by Djibouti concerns Arts 1–54 of the Convention.

Reservation made by Djibouti

[the Government of the Republic of Djibouti] shall not consider itself bound by any provisions or articles that are incompatible with its religion and its traditional values.

Four objections were lodged in the following terms:

Objection lodged by Ireland

The Government of Ireland consider that such reservations, which seek to limit the responsibilities of the reserving State under the Convention, by invoking general principles of national law, may create doubts as to the commitment of those States to the object and purpose of the Convention.

This objection shall not constitute an obstacle to the entry into force of the Convention between Ireland and the aforementioned States.

Objection lodged by Norway

A reservation by which a State party limits its responsibilities under the Convention by invoking general principles of national law may create doubts about the commitments of the reserving state to the object and purpose of the Convention and, moreover, contribute to undermining the basis of international treaty law. It is in the common interest of states that treaties to which they have chosen to become parties also are respected, as to object and purpose, by all parties. The Government of Norway, therefore, objects to this reservation.

This objection shall not constitute an obstacle to the entry into force of the Convention between Norway and the Republic of Djibouti.

The Netherlands and Portugal lodged similarly framed objections.

Question

Does the reservation undermine the object and purpose of the Convention and thus are the objections justified?

3.3.6 United Nations' pressure to remove reservations

Removal of reservations is a key point highlighted by the UN treaty monitoring bodies when examining State periodic reports. In furtherance of the Vienna Declaration and Programme of Action and in pursuance of the universality of rights, the treaty monitoring bodies carefully examine all reservations in periodic reports, questioning the continuation thereof, prompting the State to carefully examine the necessity for the reservation. Obviously, such an approach fits comfortably with the progressive nature of economic social and cultural rights. However, given the number of reservations entered in respect of other instruments, it is a grave matter for concern.

The following are some examples:

Yemen, CERD, A/57/18 (2002) 74

462. While noting that the State party has provided information under article 5 of the Convention despite the reservations lodged, the Committee invites the State party to continue to provide specific information on how this article is implemented and to consider formally withdrawing those reservations.

463. Given recent political developments, the Committee also invites the State party to consider formally withdrawing its reservations to articles 17, 18 and 20 of the Convention.

France, ICESCR, E/2002/22 (2001) 121

874. The Committee suggests that the State party review its position with regard to minorities, ensuring that minority groups have the right to exist and to be protected as such in the State party. The Committee recommends that the State party withdraw its reservation with regard to article 27 of the International Covenant on Civil and Political Rights and that it ratify the Framework Convention on the Protection of National Minorities, as well as the European Charter for Regional and Minority Languages, signed by State members of the Council of Europe in 1995 and 1992, respectively

United Kingdom of Great Britain and Northern Ireland, CRC, CRC/C/121 (2002) 23

98. While welcoming the State party's withdrawal of its reservations made to articles 37 (d) and 32, the Committee remains concerned that the State party does not intend to withdraw its wide-ranging reservation on immigration and citizenship, which is against the object and purpose of the Convention. In addition, the Committee is concerned that the State party is not in a position to withdraw its reservation to article 37 (c) owing to the fact that children are still detained with adults in the State party. In that regard, the Committee is concerned that, while the State party has made efforts to reduce the number of children detained with adults, it appears that only resource considerations now prevent the withdrawal of the reservation.

99. The Committee, in line with its previous recommendation (CRC/C/15/Add.34, paras. 22 and 29), and in light of the Vienna Declaration and Programme of Action, recommends that the State party take all necessary measures to end the detention of children in the same facilities as adults and to withdraw its reservation to article 37 (c). The Committee also recommends that the State party reconsider its reservation to article 22 with a view to withdrawing it given the State party's observation that this reservation is formally unnecessary because the State party's law is in accordance with article 22 of the Convention.

3.3.7   Comment on reservations and human rights treaties

The Convention on the Elimination of All Forms of Discrimination against Women is among the most heavily reserved instruments in international human rights. Many commentators consider that the effectiveness of this instrument is so undermined as to render it little more than declaratory in stature. The push towards ratification following the Beijing conference and Platform for Action is one of the reasons for the increase in contracting States. The problem occurs when the new (and indeed existing) ratifications are so numerous and prevalent. The reality is that many States have very few obligations under the Convention. Consulting the website of the OHCHR Treaty Monitoring Bodies gives an indication of the range of reservations entered by States to this instrument. From a practical point of view, reservations are usually notified to the Secretary-General of the United Nations (treaty depository). In the absence of a relevant reservation clause, States may be deemed to accept any reservation unless they explicitly lodge an objection.

In summation, the current system of reservations has resulted in a flexible system by which States may, to an extent and subject to the aforementioned tests, limit their obligations under international human rights instruments.

3.4   DECLARATIONS

Declarations differ from reservations primarily in that they have more limited legal effect on the application of the instrument in the jurisdiction of the States concerned.

A Declaration which purports to add, limit or modify the terms of a convention will be treated as a reservation (hence the Vienna Convention defines a reservation with reference to its purpose 'however named or phrased'). Common declarations may relate to ratification not indicating legal recognition of a named State Party—this is used most commonly for reiterations of non-recognition of Israel and Taiwan. A purely political matter, the impact on the instrument is negligible. However, other declarations have greater consequences, for example declaring that the instrument will not be applied in a manner incompatible with national law or that the meaning of a particular article will be as specified. These will frequently be treated as reservations, in accordance with the Vienna Convention and customary law.

Note also para 3 of the Human Rights Committee, General Comment 24, see above. The important element to note is the intention of the State and the purpose of the declaration, not the actual title.

3.4.1 Declarations as reservations

Consider the following two 'declarations'.

Declaration by Jordan upon ratification of the Convention on the Elimination of All Forms of Discrimination against Women

Jordan does not consider itself bound by the following provisions:

1. Article 9, paragraph 2;

2. Article 15, paragraph 4 (a wife's residence is with her husband);

3. Article 16, paragraph (1) (c), relating to the rights arising upon the dissolution of marriage with regard to maintenance and compensation;

4. Article 16, paragraph (1) (d) and (g).

Declaration by the People's Republic of China in respect of the UN Convention on the Rights of the Child

The Government of the People's Republic of China, on behalf of the Hong Kong Special Administrative Region, interprets the Convention as applicable only following a live birth.

Question

Are the foregoing reservations or declarations in nature? Are they compatible with the object and purpose of the Treaty at issue?

3.4.2 Case study on reservations/declarations

To demonstrate the effect of reservations/declarations, consider the following situation arising from a reservation/declaration entered by France in respect of Art 27 of the International Covenant on Civil and Political Rights. Art 27 of the Covenant enshrines the so-called 'minorities' provision.

Treaty provision

International Covenant on Civil and Political Rights 1966 Art 27

In those States in which ethnic, religious or linguistic minorities exist, persons belonging to such minorities shall not be denied the right, in community with the other members of their group, to enjoy their own culture, to profess and practice their own religion, or to use their own language.

Human Rights Committee view thereon

According to the Human Rights Committee, it appears that the rights enshrined in this article are of fundamental importance and thus the right of a State to derogate or use reservations to avoid responsibility is limited. Authority for this can be drawn from the terms of its General Comment on the subject of reservations

General Comment No. 24 (1994), Human Rights Committee at para 10

10. While there is no hierarchy of importance of rights under the Covenant, the operation of certain rights may not be suspended, even in times of national emergency. This underlines the great importance of non-derogable rights. But not all rights of profound importance, such as articles 9 and 27 of the Covenant, have in fact been made non-derogable. . . . While there is no automatic correlation between reservations to non-derogable provisions, and reservations which offend against the object and purpose of the Covenant, a State has a heavy onus to justify such a reservation.

French declaration and reservation

However, in spite of this, it appears that States can and have entered qualifications to the article.

International Covenant on Civil and Political Rights, Declaration and Reservation made by France

(8) In the light of article 2 of the Constitution of the French Republic, the French Government declares that article 27 is not applicable so far as the Republic is concerned.

The relevant provisions of the French constitution are as follows:

The 1958 Constitution of the French Republic and its amendments

(Note that this English translation was prepared under the joint responsibility of the Press, Information and Communication Directorate of the Ministry of Foreign Affairs and the European Affairs Department of the National Assembly. The French original is the sole authentic text.)

Article 2

The language of the Republic shall be French.

The national emblem shall be the blue, white and red tricolour flag.

The national anthem shall be La Marseillaise.

The motto of the Republic shall be 'Liberty, Equality, Fraternity'.

Its principle shall be: government of the people, by the people and for the people.

National sovereignty shall belong to the people, who shall exercise it through their representatives and by means of referendum.

No section of the people nor any individual may arrogate to itself, or to himself, the exercise thereof.

Suffrage may be direct or indirect as provided by the Constitution. It shall always be universal, equal and secret.

All French citizens of either sex who have reached their majority and are in possession of their civil and political rights may vote as provided by statute.

The effect of the reservation/declaration emerges when examining relevant jurisprudence.

Case arising therefrom

Guedson v France, Communication No. 219/1986: France, 23/08/90, CCPR/C/39/D/219/1986

The author of the communication, a Breton whose mother tongue is Breton, appeared before the Tribunal Correctionnel of Rennes on charges of having damaged public property by defacing road signs in French. He never admitted his participation in the offences he was charged with. On the day of the hearing, he requested that his witnesses and himself gave testimony in Breton, which was the language used daily by most of them and in which they could most easily express themselves for the purposes of his defence. The request was refused by the court, as was an appeal on that ground. The French court was of the opinion that Guedson was capable of defending himself without interpretation before the trial court. Guedson claimed infringement of a number of rights under the International Covenant on Civil and Political Rights, most pertinently here, Art 27.

> 5.6 Finally, with respect to the alleged violation of article 27, the State party recalls that upon ratification of the Covenant, the French Government entered [the aforequoted reservation]. Thus, the State party argues that 'the idea of membership of an "ethnic, religious or linguistic minority" which the applicant invokes is irrelevant in the case in point, and cannot be held against the French Government which does not recognize the existence of "minorities" in the Republic, defined, in article 2 of the Constitution as "indivisible, secular, democratic and social".'

The minority language issue raised by Guedson could not be examined by the Committee due to the invocation of France's reservation. This graphically demonstrates the potential problems associated with reservations. Obviously, individuals (or States) wishing to bring complaints should clarify the status of any given article in advance to ensure the claim is admissible.

Question

There are a number of similar examples—balance the necessity for such reservations (in terms of public international law) with the potential for their misuse by States. Are reservations an 'evil necessity' of the universal system?

3.5 DEROGATIONS

It is inevitable that rights and freedoms can not be couched in absolute terms. A degree of flexibility may always be a political expediency. Most notably in times of civil strife and extreme situations, a State may wish to limit rights and freedoms. For example, requisitioning of property, detention of 'enemies', monitoring of communications, limiting of rights to demonstrate and free speech. Such extreme circumstances are taken into account by the various international and regional instruments through rights of derogation. Generally, derogations are only permitted in specified situations—usually those threatening the State. States must notify a central body, and by consequence, the States Party, as to the extent and duration of the derogation. Derogations should only be to the extent strictly required by the exigencies of the situation and only for the time the emergency situation remains. Indeterminate derogations are not viewed favourably. Perceived terrorist threats, extreme famine, major geographical catastrophes and armed conflict are all potential reasons for derogating from convention obligations.

3.5.1   A typical derogation clause—the ICCPR

The International Covenant on Civil and Political Rights contains the following derogation clause:

International Covenant on Civil and Political Rights Art 4

1. In time of public emergency which threatens the life of the nation and the existence of which is officially proclaimed, the States Parties to the present Covenant may take measures derogating from their obligations under the present Covenant to the extent strictly required by the exigencies of the situation, provided that such measures are not inconsistent with their other obligations under international law and do not involve discrimination solely on the ground of race, colour, sex, language, religion or social origin.

2. No derogation from articles 6, 7, 8 (paragraphs 1 and 2), 11, 15, 16 and 18 may be made under this provision.

3. Any State Party to the present Covenant availing itself of the right of derogation shall immediately inform the other States Parties to the present Covenant, through the intermediary of the Secretary-General of the United Nations, of the provisions from which it has derogated and of the reasons by which it was actuated. A further communication shall be made, through the same intermediary, on the date on which it terminates such derogation.

3.5.2   The approach of the Human Rights Committee

The Human Rights Committee expanded upon the nature of circumstances justifying the invocation of Art 4 in a General Comment. General Comment 29 replaces General Comment 5 in this regard. General Comments 13 and 20 also contain relevant material. It is clear that the use of derogation clauses should be restricted to extreme situations.

Human Rights Committee, General Comment 29 (2001)

1. Article 4 of the Covenant is of paramount importance for the system of protection for human rights under the Covenant. On the one hand, it allows for a State party unilaterally to derogate temporarily from a part of its obligations under the Covenant. On the other hand, article 4 subjects both this very measure of derogation, as well as its material consequences, to a specific regime of safeguards. The restoration of a state of normalcy where full respect for the Covenant can again be secured must be the predominant objective of a State party derogating from the Covenant. In this general comment, replacing its General Comment No 5, adopted at the thirteenth session (1981), the Committee seeks to assist States parties to meet the requirements of article 4.

2. Measures derogating from the provisions of the Covenant must be of an exceptional and temporary nature. Before a State moves to invoke article 4, two fundamental conditions must be met: the situation must amount to a public emergency which threatens the life of the nation, and the State party must have officially proclaimed a state of emergency. The latter requirement is essential for the maintenance of the principles of legality and rule of law at times when they are most needed. When proclaiming a state of emergency with consequences that could entail derogation from any provision of the Covenant, States must act within their constitutional and other provisions of law that govern such proclamation and the exercise of emergency powers; it is the task of the Committee to monitor the laws in question with respect to whether they enable and secure compliance with article 4. In order that the Committee can perform its task, States parties to the Covenant should include in their reports submitted under article 40 sufficient and precise information about their law and practice in the field of emergency powers. . . .

4. A fundamental requirement for any measures derogating from the Covenant, as set forth in

article 4, paragraph 1, is that such measures are limited to the extent strictly required by the exigencies of the situation. This requirement relates to the duration, geographical coverage and material scope of the state of emergency and any measures of derogation resorted to because of the emergency. Derogation from some Covenant obligations in emergency situations is clearly distinct from restrictions or limitations allowed even in normal times under several provisions of the Covenant. Nevertheless, the obligation to limit any derogations to those strictly required by the exigencies of the situation reflects the principle of proportionality which is common to derogation and limitation powers. Moreover, the mere fact that a permissible derogation from a specific provision may, of itself, be justified by the exigencies of the situation does not obviate the requirement that specific measures taken pursuant to the derogation must also be shown to be required by the exigencies of the situation. In practice, this will ensure that no provision of the Covenant, however validly derogated from will be entirely inapplicable to the behaviour of a State party. When considering States parties' reports the Committee has expressed its concern over insufficient attention being paid to the principle of proportionality.

3.5.3 Regional examples of derogation clauses

Derogation clauses also appear in regional instruments although, most conspicuously, there is no such clause in the African Charter on Human and Peoples' Rights.

European Convention on Human Rights Art 15

1. In time of war or other public emergency threatening the life of the nation any High Contracting Party may take measures derogating from its obligations under this Convention to the extent strictly required by the exigencies of the situation, provided that such measures are not inconsistent with its other obligations under international law.

2. No derogation from Article 2, except in respect of deaths resulting from lawful acts of war, or from Articles 3, 4 (paragraph 1) and 7 shall be made under this provision.

3. Any High Contracting Party availing itself of this right of derogation shall keep the Secretary-General of the Council of Europe fully informed of the measures which it has taken and the reasons therefor. It shall also inform the Secretary-General of the Council of Europe when such measures have ceased to operate and the provisions of the Convention are again being fully executed.

Inter-American Convention on Human Rights Art 27

1. In time of war, public danger, or other emergency that threatens the independence or security of a State Party, it may take measures derogating from its obligations under the present Convention to the extent and for the period of time strictly required by the exigencies of the situation, provided that such measures are not inconsistent with its other obligations under international law and do not involve discrimination on the ground of race, color, sex, language, religion, or social origin.

2. The foregoing provision does not authorize any suspension of the following articles: Article 3 (Right to Juridical Personality), Article 4 (Right to Life), Article 5 (Right to Humane Treatment), Article 6 (Freedom from Slavery), Article 9 (Freedom from Ex Post Facto Laws), Article 12 (Freedom of Conscience and Religion), Article 17 (Rights of the Family), Article 18 (Right to a Name), Article 19 (Rights of the Child), Article 20 (Right to Nationality), and Article 23 (Right to Participate in Government), or of the judicial guarantees essential for the protection of such rights.

3. Any State Party availing itself of the right of suspension shall immediately inform the other States Parties, through the Secretary-General of the Organization of American States, of the provisions the application of which it has suspended, the reasons that gave rise to the suspension, and the date set for the termination of such suspension.

Although derogations are meant to be of limited duration, there are a number of examples of derogations remaining in force for many years.

3.5.4 Case study: United Kingdom

Consider the position of the United Kingdom which entered a derogation to the European Convention on Human Rights in respect of the emergency situation in Northern Ireland. The derogation was maintained for many years and its withdrawal in 1984 prompted the case of *Brogan and others v United Kingdom* (1988) Series A, No 145-B, 11 EHRR 117 in which the European Court found infringements of Art 5 of the Convention. The UK reinstated its derogation, the legitimacy of which was upheld in *Brannigan and McBride v United Kingdom* (1993) Series A, No 258-B, 17 EHRR 539.

Brannigan and McBride v United Kingdom (1993) Series A, No 258-B, 17 EHRR 539

The applicants were arrested in Northern Ireland and detained for prolonged periods of time in accordance with the relevant anti-terrorist legislation. Brannigan was detained for six days, fourteen and one-half hours, interrogated on 43 occasions and denied access to books, newspapers and writing materials as well as radio and television. McBride was detained for four days, six hours and 25 minutes, interrogated on 22 occasions and subjected to the same regime as Brannigan. The European Court was asked to comment on the invocation by the United Kingdom of an Art 15 derogation to justify non-compliance with Art 5 of the European Convention—protection of liberty and guarantees for detainees.

41. The applicants argued that it would be inconsistent with Article 15 para 2 (art. 15–2) if, in derogating from safeguards recognised as essential for the protection of non-derogable rights such as Articles 2 and 3 (art. 2, art. 3), the national authorities were to be afforded a wide margin of appreciation. This was especially so where the emergency was of a quasi-permanent nature such as that existing in Northern Ireland. To do so would also be inconsistent with the Brogan and Others judgment where the Court had regarded judicial control as one of the fundamental principles of a democratic society and had already—they claimed—extended to the Government a margin of appreciation by taking into account in paragraph 58 (p. 32) the context of terrorism in Northern Ireland (loc. cit.).

42. In their written submissions, Amnesty International maintained that strict scrutiny was required by the Court when examining derogation from fundamental procedural guarantees which were essential for the protection of detainees at all times, but particularly in times of emergency. Liberty, Interights and the Committee on the Administration of Justice ('Liberty and Others') submitted for their part that, if States are to be allowed a margin of appreciation at all, it should be narrower the more permanent the emergency becomes.

43. The Court recalls that it falls to each Contracting State, with its responsibility for 'the life of [its] nation', to determine whether that life is threatened by a 'public emergency' and, if so, how far it is necessary to go in attempting to overcome the emergency. By reason of their direct and continuous contact with the pressing needs of the moment, the national authorities are in principle in a better position than the international judge to decide both on the presence of such an emergency and on the nature and scope of derogations necessary to avert it. Accordingly, in this matter a wide margin of appreciation should be left to the national authorities (see the Ireland v. the United Kingdom judgment of 18 January 1978, Series A no. 25, pp. 78–79, para. 207).

Nevertheless, Contracting Parties do not enjoy an unlimited power of appreciation. It is for the Court to rule on whether *inter alia* the States have gone beyond the 'extent strictly required by the exigencies' of the crisis. The domestic margin of appreciation is thus accompanied by a European supervision (ibid.). At the same time, in exercising its supervision the Court must give appropriate weight to such relevant factors as the nature of the rights affected by the derogation, the circumstances leading to, and the duration of, the emergency situation.

Following the ceasefire in Northern Ireland, the derogation was again withdrawn. This would indicate compliance with Art 15, as the perceived emergency situation had ceased to be a threat to the State. However, following the terrorist attacks on the United States of America in 2001, the United Kingdom elected to enter a new, and arguably broader, derogation.

Statutory Instrument 2001 No. 3644, The Human Rights Act 1998 (Designated Derogation) Order 2001, Sched

There exists a terrorist threat to the United Kingdom from persons suspected of involvement in international terrorism. In particular, there are foreign nationals present in the United Kingdom who are suspected of being concerned in the commission, preparation or instigation of acts of international terrorism, of being members of organisations or groups which are so concerned or of having links with members of such organisations or groups, and who are a threat to the national security of the United Kingdom.

. . .

Derogation under Art 15 of the Convention

The Government has considered whether the exercise of the extended power to detain contained in the Anti-terrorism, Crime and Security [Act 2001] may be inconsistent with the obligations under Article 5(1) of the Convention. As indicated above, there may be cases where, notwithstanding a continuing intention to remove or deport a person who is being detained, it is not possible to say that 'action is being taken with a view to deportation' within the meaning of Article 5(1)(f) as interpreted by the Court in the Chahal case. To the extent, therefore, that the exercise of the extended power may be inconsistent with the United Kingdom's obligations under Article 5(1), the Government has decided to avail itself of the right of derogation conferred by Article 15(1) of the Convention and will continue to do so until further notice.

Note that pursuant to the entry into force of the Terrorism Act 2005, which changes the detention provisions in English law, this derogation has been withdrawn. The explanatory note to the relevant statutory instrument explains the position.

Statutory Instrument 2005 No. 1071, The Human Rights Act 1998 (Amendment) Order 2005

EXPLANATORY NOTE *(This note is not part of the Order)*

This Order amends Schedule 3 to the Human Rights Act 1998 to reflect the withdrawal by the United Kingdom of the derogation designated by the Human Rights Act 1998 (Designated Derogation) Order 2001 (S.I. 2001/3644) ('the derogation'). The derogation was from Article 5(1) of the Convention for the Protection of Human Rights and Fundamental Freedoms, agreed by the Council of Europe at Rome on 4th November 1950 ('the Convention'). The derogation concerned detention provisions in the Anti-terrorism, Crime and Security Act 2001 (c. 24). Those detention provisions were repealed with effect from 14th March 2005 by section 16(2)(a) of the Prevention of Terrorism Act 2005 (c. 2). On 16th March 2005, the United Kingdom Government informed the Secretary-General of the Council of Europe, pursuant to Article 15(3) of the Convention, of the withdrawal of the derogation.

While arguably a relevant emergency situation pertained throughout the period covered by the various UK Prevention of Terrorism (Temporary Provisions) Acts, due to the problems in Northern Ireland, the duration of the various derogations may give rise to justifiable concern. Naturally, any abuse of the derogation powers may undermine the universality of rights, as derogation clauses represent a legitimate method of limiting rights. In respect of the case study, greater problems arguably arise with the most recent derogation entered by the United Kingdom. The terrorism threat is not as clearly defined, as was the case previously in Northern Ireland. Thus, the derogation may potentially apply to a greater range of situations. While the United Nations Security Council deemed the September 2001 events a threat to international peace and security, there are a number of obvious issues arising if States are entitled to enter derogations on the basis of perceived international terrorist threats, particularly derogations of indeterminate duration. During the original derogations, a series of bombing attacks in England and civil unrest in Northern Ireland evidenced the imminence of the terrorist threat, thereby justifying a protracted derogation.

Question

On the basis of your understanding of the current international terrorist threat, can the United Kingdom, or indeed any other country, be entitled to enter derogations to appropriate instruments?

3.5.5 Non-derogable provisions

As is apparent from the foregoing clauses, derogation is not an absolute right. Rather it is of practical necessity in extreme situations. States cannot absolve themselves from responsibility under many articles of each instrument, irrespective of the circumstances. For example, no instrument permits derogations from provisions on slavery or torture. Other instruments, including the African Charter, as noted above, prohibit any derogation.

Convention against Torture and other Cruel, Inhuman or Degrading Treatment or Punishment Arts 2(2) and 2(3)

2. No exceptional circumstances whatsoever, whether a state of war or a threat of war, internal political in stability or any other public emergency, may be invoked as a justification of torture.

3. An order from a superior officer or a public authority may not be invoked as a justification of torture.

Question

Why is torture always excluded from the ambit of derogation clauses? What other rights and freedoms are always beyond the reach of derogation clauses and why?

Question

Provision for derogation is predominantly a characteristic of instruments tabulating civil and political rights rather than those on non-discrimination or on economic and social rights. What are the reasons for this?

The classification of some rights as non-derogable is taken by many commentators to imply a hierarchy of rights and freedoms, through implying that some rights and freedoms are more fundamental than others. Clearly, this can present challenges to the universality and indivisibility of human rights. However, it can be argued that derogations are essential to allow States the flexibility to deal appropriately with emergency situations, in order to expedite a return to 'normality' and full respect for all rights and freedoms.

Question

Can derogations be more easily reconciled with universal ratification than reservations?

Despite the prevalence of derogation clauses in human rights treaties, there is growing evidence of the restrictive approach taken to restrictions on recognised rights by the international community. Thus, it appears that a State's right to derogate is not unfettered. Consider the view of the Human Rights Committee in General Comment 29. This refers to the derogation clause in the International Covenant on Civil and Political Rights which is excerpted above.

Human Rights Committee General Comment 29

3. Not every disturbance or catastrophe qualifies as a public emergency which threatens the life of the nation, as required by article 4, paragraph 1. During armed conflict, whether international or non-international, rules of international humanitarian law become applicable and help, in addition to the provisions in article 4 and article 5, paragraph 1, of the Covenant, to prevent the abuse of a State's emergency powers. The Covenant requires that even during an armed conflict measures derogating from the Covenant are allowed only if and to the extent that the situation constitutes a threat to the life of the nation. If States parties consider invoking article 4 in other situations than an armed conflict, they should carefully consider the justification and why such a measure is necessary and legitimate in the circumstances. On a number of occasions the Committee has expressed its concern over States parties that appear to have derogated from rights protected by the Covenant, or whose domestic law appears to allow such derogation in situations not covered by article 4.

. . .

5. The issues of when rights can be derogated from, and to what extent, cannot be separated from the provision in article 4, paragraph 1, of the Covenant according to which any measures derogating from a State party's obligations under the Covenant must be limited 'to the extent strictly required by the exigencies of the situation'. This condition requires that States parties provide careful justification not only for their decision to proclaim a state of emergency but also for any specific measures based on such a proclamation. If States purport to invoke the right to derogate from the Covenant during, for instance, a natural catastrophe, a mass demonstration including instances of violence, or a major industrial accident, they must be able to justify not only that such a situation constitutes a threat to the life of the nation, but also that all their measures derogating from the Covenant are strictly required by the exigencies of the situation. In the opinion of the Committee, the possibility of restricting certain Covenant rights under the terms of, for instance, freedom of movement (article 12) or freedom of assembly (article 21) is generally sufficient during such situations and no derogation from the provisions in question would be justified by the exigencies of the situation.

6. The fact that some of the provisions of the Covenant have been listed in article 4 (paragraph 2), as not being subject to derogation does not mean that other articles in the Covenant may be subjected to derogations at will, even where a threat to the life of the nation exists. The legal obligation to narrow down all derogations to those strictly required by the exigencies of the situation establishes both for States parties and for the Committee a duty to conduct a careful analysis under each article of the Covenant based on an objective assessment of the actual situation.

7. Article 4, paragraph 2, of the Covenant explicitly prescribes that no derogation from the following articles may be made: article 6 (right to life), article 7 (prohibition of torture or cruel, inhuman or degrading punishment, or of medical or scientific experimentation without consent), article 8, paragraphs 1 and 2 (prohibition of slavery, slave-trade and servitude), article 11 (prohibition of imprisonment because of inability to fulfil a contractual obligation), article 15 (the principle of legality in the field of criminal law, i.e. the requirement of both criminal liability and

punishment being limited to clear and precise provisions in the law that was in place and applicable at the time the act or omission took place, except in cases where a later law imposes a lighter
penalty), article 16 (the recognition of everyone as a person before the law), and article 18
(freedom of thought, conscience and religion). The rights enshrined in these provisions are non-
derogable by the very fact that they are listed in article 4, paragraph 2. The same applies, in relation
to States that are parties to the Second Optional Protocol to the Covenant, aiming at the
abolition of the death penalty, as prescribed in article 6 of that Protocol. Conceptually, the
qualification of a Covenant provision as a non-derogable one does not mean that no limitations or
restrictions would ever be justified. The reference in article 4, paragraph 2, to article 18, a
provision that includes a specific clause on restrictions in its paragraph 3, demonstrates that the
permissibility of restrictions is independent of the issue of derogability. Even in times of most
serious public emergencies, States that interfere with the freedom to manifest one's religion or
belief must justify their actions by referring to the requirements specified in article 18, paragraph
3. On several occasions the Committee has expressed its concern about rights that are non-
derogable according to article 4, paragraph 2, being either derogated from or under a risk of
derogation owing to inadequacies in the legal regime of the State party.

8. According to article 4, paragraph 1, one of the conditions for the justifiability of any derogation
from the Covenant is that the measures taken do not involve discrimination solely on the ground
of race, colour, sex, language, religion or social origin. Even though article 26 or the other Covenant provisions related to non-discrimination (articles 2, 3, 14, paragraph 1, 23, paragraph 4, 24,
paragraph 1, and 25) have not been listed among the non-derogable provisions in article 4,
paragraph 2, there are elements or dimensions of the right to non-discrimination that cannot be
derogated from in any circumstances. In particular, this provision of article 4, paragraph 1, must be
complied with if any distinctions between persons are made when resorting to measures that
derogate from the Covenant.

9. Furthermore, article 4, paragraph 1, requires that no measure derogating from the provisions
of the Covenant may be inconsistent with the State party's other obligations under international
law, particularly the rules of international humanitarian law. Article 4 of the Covenant cannot be
read as justification for derogation from the Covenant if such derogation would entail a breach of
the State's other international obligations, whether based on treaty or general international law.
This is reflected also in article 5, paragraph 2, of the Covenant according to which there shall be
no restriction upon or derogation from any fundamental rights recognized in other instruments
on the pretext that the Covenant does not recognize such rights or that it recognizes them to a
lesser extent.

10. Although it is not the function of the Human Rights Committee to review the conduct of a
State party under other treaties, in exercising its functions under the Covenant the Committee
has the competence to take a State party's other international obligations into account when it
considers whether the Covenant allows the State party to derogate from specific provisions of
the Covenant. Therefore, when invoking article 4, paragraph 1, or when reporting under article 40
on the legal framework related to emergencies, States parties should present information on
their other international obligations relevant for the protection of the rights in question, in
particular those obligations that are applicable in times of emergency. In this respect, States
parties should duly take into account the developments within international law as to human
rights standards applicable in emergency situations.

3.5.6   The approach of the European Court of Human Rights

At a regional level, derogations entered by the United Kingdom have been discussed
above. However, it is also instructive to consider the dicta of the European Court of
Human Rights as regards derogations.

Aksoy v Turkey, Application 21987/93, 18/12/1996

Aksoy was suspected of being involved in the PKK and had been detained by Turkish security forces. He alleged ill-treatment during detention and received medical treatment upon his eventual release from captivity. Following alleged threats over his application to the European Commission on Human Rights regarding his detention and ill-treatment, he was shot and killed in south-east Turkey. The applicant's relatives continued the application on his behalf but many of the facts were disputed by the Turkish Government. Moreover, the Government maintained that the security situation justified the detention.

68. The Court recalls that it falls to each Contracting State, with its responsibility for 'the life of [its] nation', to determine whether that life is threatened by a 'public emergency' and, if so, how far it is necessary to go in attempting to overcome the emergency. By reason of their direct and continuous contact with the pressing needs of the moment, the national authorities are in principle better placed than the international judge to decide both on the presence of such an emergency and on the nature and scope of the derogations necessary to avert it. Accordingly, in this matter a wide margin of appreciation should be left to the national authorities. Nonetheless, Contracting Parties do not enjoy an unlimited discretion. It is for the Court to rule whether, *inter alia*, the States have gone beyond the 'extent strictly required by the exigencies' of the crisis. The domestic margin of appreciation is thus accompanied by a European supervision. In exercising this supervision, the Court must give appropriate weight to such relevant factors as the nature of the rights affected by the derogation and the circumstances leading to, and the duration of, the emergency situation (see the Brannigan and McBride v. the United Kingdom judgment of 26 May 1993, Series A no. 258-B, pp. 49–50, para. 43). 2. Existence of a public emergency threatening the life of the nation . . .

70. The Court considers, in the light of all the material before it, that the particular extent and impact of PKK terrorist activity in South-East Turkey has undoubtedly created, in the region concerned, a 'public emergency threatening the life of the nation' (see, *mutatis mutandis*, the Lawless v. Ireland judgment of 1 July 1961, Series A no. 3, p. 56, para. 28, the above-mentioned Ireland v. the United Kingdom judgment, p. 78, para. 205, and the above-mentioned Brannigan and McBride judgment, p. 50, para. 47). . . .

76. The Court would stress the importance of Article 5 (art. 5) in the Convention system: it enshrines a fundamental human right, namely the protection of the individual against arbitrary interference by the State with his or her right to liberty. Judicial control of interferences by the executive with the individual's right to liberty is an essential feature of the guarantee embodied in Article 5 para. 3 (art. 5–3), which is intended to minimise the risk of arbitrariness and to ensure the rule of law (see the above-mentioned Brogan and Others judgment, p. 32, para. 58). Furthermore, prompt judicial intervention may lead to the detection and prevention of serious ill-treatment, which, as stated above (paragraph 62), is prohibited by the Convention in absolute and non-derogable terms.

77. In the Brannigan and McBride judgment (cited at paragraph 68 above), the Court held that the United Kingdom Government had not exceeded their margin of appreciation by derogating from their obligations under Article 5 of the Convention (art. 5) to the extent that individuals suspected of terrorist offences were allowed to be held for up to seven days without judicial control. In the instant case, the applicant was detained for at least fourteen days without being brought before a judge or other officer. The Government have sought to justify this measure by reference to the particular demands of police investigations in a geographically vast area faced with a terrorist organisation receiving outside support (see paragraph 72 above).

78. Although the Court is of the view—which it has expressed on several occasions in the past (see, for example, the above-mentioned Brogan and Others judgment)—that the investigation of terrorist offences undoubtedly presents the authorities with special problems, it cannot accept that it is necessary to hold a suspect for fourteen days without judicial intervention. This period is

exceptionally long, and left the applicant vulnerable not only to arbitrary interference with his right to liberty but also to torture (see paragraph 64 above). Moreover, the Government have not adduced any detailed reasons before the Court as to why the fight against terrorism in South-East Turkey rendered judicial intervention impracticable. . .?

79. The Government emphasised that both the derogation and the national legal system provided sufficient safeguards to protect human rights. Thus, the derogation itself was limited to the strict minimum required for the fight against terrorism; the permissible length of detention was prescribed by law and the consent of a public prosecutor was necessary if the police wished to remand a suspect in custody beyond these periods. Torture was prohibited by Article 243 of the Criminal Code (see paragraph 24 above) and Article 135 (a) stipulated that any statement made in consequence of the administration of torture or any other form of ill-treatment would have no evidential weight. . . .

83. . . . the Court considers that in this case insufficient safeguards were available to the applicant, who was detained over a long period of time. In particular, the denial of access to a lawyer, doctor, relative or friend and the absence of any realistic possibility of being brought before a court to test the legality of the detention meant that he was left completely at the mercy of those holding him.

84. The Court has taken account of the unquestionably serious problem of terrorism in South-East Turkey and the difficulties faced by the State in taking effective measures against it. However, it is not persuaded that the exigencies of the situation necessitated the holding of the applicant on suspicion of involvement in terrorist offences for fourteen days or more in incommunicado detention without access to a judge or other judicial officer. . . .

87. In conclusion, the Court finds that there has been a violation of Article 5 para. 3 of the Convention (art. 5–3).

Ultimately, humanitarian law is human rights for extreme situations, a body of law from which no derogation is possible prescribing the parameters within which hostilities are conducted. Its relevance is recognised by the Human Rights Committee in its General Comment 29 on Derogations.

For more information on humanitarian law, see Chapter 15.

Question

Humanitarian law may apply in extreme situations but consider the status of detainees in Camp X-Ray at Guantanamo Bay, Cuba. US officials have consistently maintained that the detainees are not prisoners of war in terms of the Geneva Conventions. Rather they are 'unlawful combatants' and thus fall outwith the Geneva regime. However, the State and Defense departments have reiterated that the detainees are treated in accordance with Geneva principles. On 29 June 2006 in Handan v Rumsfeld, *the US Supreme Court ruled against military tribunals for the detainees, prompting further debate on the status of the detainees. The US had not ratified the major international human rights instruments. Should States be able to sidestep humanitarian law by terminological changes? In what ways can the international community regulate such actions?*

3.6 DENUNCIATIONS

As with contracts in national law, there are rules and regulations governing the circumstances in which treaties are frustrated, terminated and revoked. Joining many human rights treaties is a one-way process—once ratified, a State cannot simply remove itself from the ambit of the provisions, thereby thwarting progress towards universal ratification! Others permit unilateral denunciation. Some conventions terminate at a specified time on following securement of their objectives: the operation of the 1973 International Convention on the Suppression and Punishment of the Crime of Apartheid, for example, has now been suspended. The general position for denunciation is covered by the Vienna Convention on the Law of Treaties.

3.6.1   Terminating treaty obligations

Vienna Convention on the Law of Treaties 1969

Article 43
Obligations imposed by international law independently of a treaty

The invalidity, termination or denunciation of a treaty, the withdrawal of a party from it, or the suspension of its operation, as a result of the application of the present Convention or of the provisions of the treaty, shall not in any way impair the duty of any State to fulfil any obligation embodied in the treaty to which it would be subject under international law independently of the treaty.

Article 54
Termination of or withdrawal from a treaty under its provisions or by consent of the parties

The termination of a treaty or the withdrawal of a party may take place:

(a) in conformity with the provisions of the treaty; or

(b) at any time by consent of all the parties after consultation with the other contracting States.

Article 56
Denunciation of or withdrawal from a treaty containing no provision regarding termination, denunciation or withdrawal

1. A treaty which contains no provision regarding its termination and which does not provide for denunciation or withdrawal is not subject to denunciation or withdrawal unless:

(a) it is established that the parties intended to admit the possibility of denunciation or withdrawal; or

(b) a right of denunciation or withdrawal may be implied by the nature of the treaty.

2. A party shall give not less than twelve months' notice of its intention to denounce or withdraw from a treaty under paragraph 1.

With respect to international human rights instruments, clearly a number of factors are relevant. First, the instrument must be examined for any clause permitting denunciation. Not all instruments contain such an article. Failure to find a relevant article clearly prompts recourse to the *travaux préparatoires* to elucidate the intention of the drafters and initial parties. If a right to denunciation can be found, or inferred, then consent of all other States Parties is required. This can be a time-consuming and problematic business in contemporary multilateral instruments—agreement of more than 100 States will frequently be required. It should be noted, that even should a State be successful in denouncing a particular instrument, it remains bound by customary international law. Given that some aspects of international human rights instruments codify customary international law, the actual effect of such denunciation may simply be to remove the State from the reporting mechanism. States may still be subject to investigation under the 1503 procedure before the Human Rights Council (see Chapter 5).

3.6.2   Denunciation and United Nations Human Rights Treaties

Some instruments explicitly provide for denunciation—e.g. Art 21 of Convention on the Elimination of all Forms of Racial Discrimination—others do not, and so customary law and the Vienna Convention apply. Given the importance attached to human rights instruments and the goal of universal ratification, allowing denunciation when not explicitly provided for in the treaty could be viewed as a backward step. When Korea attempted to withdraw from the ICCPR in 1997, the Human Rights Committee issued a General Comment on the matter

General Comment 26 (1997): Issues Relating to the Continuity of Obligations to the International Covenant on Civil and Political Rights, A/53/40 vol. I (1998) 102

1. The International Covenant on Civil and Political Rights does not contain any provision regarding its termination and does not provide for denunciation or withdrawal. Consequently, the possibility of termination, denunciation or withdrawal must be considered in the light of applicable rules of customary international law which are reflected in the Vienna Convention on the Law of Treaties. On this basis, the Covenant is not subject to denunciation or withdrawal unless it is established that the parties intended to admit the possibility of denunciation or withdrawal or a right to do so is implied from the nature of the treaty.

2. That the parties to the Covenant did not admit the possibility of denunciation and that it was not a mere oversight on their part to omit reference to denunciation is demonstrated by the fact that article 41 (2) of the Covenant does permit a State party to withdraw its acceptance of the competence of the Committee to examine inter-State communications by filing an appropriate notice to that effect while there is no such provision for denunciation of or withdrawal from the Covenant itself. Moreover, the Optional Protocol to the Covenant, negotiated and adopted contemporaneously with it, permits States parties to denounce it. Additionally, by way of comparison, the International Convention on the Elimination of All Forms of Racial Discrimination, which was adopted one year prior to the Covenant, expressly permits denunciation. It can therefore be concluded that the drafters of the Covenant deliberately intended to exclude the possibility of denunciation. The same conclusion applies to the Second Optional Protocol in the drafting of which a denunciation clause was deliberately omitted.

3. Furthermore, it is clear that the Covenant is not the type of treaty which, by its nature, implies a right of denunciation. Together with the simultaneously prepared and adopted International Covenant on Economic, Social and Cultural Rights, the Covenant codifies in treaty form the universal human rights enshrined in the Universal Declaration of Human Rights, the three instruments together often being referred to as the 'International Bill of Human Rights'. As such, the Covenant does not have a temporary character typical of treaties where a right of denunciation is deemed to be admitted, notwithstanding the absence of a specific provision to that effect.

4. The rights enshrined in the Covenant belong to the people living in the territory of the State party. The Human Rights Committee has consistently taken the view, as evidenced by its longstanding practice, that once the people are accorded the protection of the rights under the Covenant, such protection devolves with territory and continues to belong to them, notwithstanding change in government of the State party, including dismemberment in more than one State or State succession or any subsequent action of the State party designed to divest them of the rights guaranteed by the Covenant.

5. The Committee is therefore firmly of the view that international law does not permit a State which has ratified or acceded or succeeded to the Covenant to denounce it or withdraw from it.

Question

While this approach clearly aims at advancing international human rights, is it advisable? Can it be reconciled with the more flexible approach towards reservations and derogations?

3.6.3 Regional human rights instruments and denunciations

The regional instruments too can be the subject of denunciations, where so specified. For example, Greece denounced the European Convention in 1969 following a *coup d'état*. It later withdrew from the Council of Europe, rejoining at a later date and re-acceding to the Convention in 1974. Clearly, a State can only be bound by an instrument if it so consents. Denunciations therefore are an essential aspect of the international human rights system, though obviously it is regrettable if denunciations occur, not least for the negative effect on universality. In any event, denunciations are not particularly common in international human rights, a fact attributable in part to the lack of sanctions attributable to non-compliance.

3.6.4 Individual petitions and denunciations

Under international human rights law, some treaties permit individual communications to the associated treaty monitoring body for consideration. These systems are usually optional (see Chapter 6). Of the regional systems, the European Convention on Human Rights rendered individual complaints to the Court compulsory after its reform in the 1990s.

Of growing concern to the international community have been denunciations of the provisions on the right of individual petitions. The realisation of International Human Rights is traditionally the preserve of States, international and regional bodies primarily producing observations on periodic reports voluntarily submitted by States. However, in many instruments inter-State complaints and individual communications are optional processes. Accordingly, States can elect whether to submit themselves to these processes and in doing so renounce the potential for complaints against them. Such action, while counter-productive to the protection and promotion of human rights, is legitimate. The most notable example is the States subject to many individual petitions who have sought to withdraw from the optional protocol to the ICCPR. These States are drawn primarily from the Caribbean region.

3.6.5 Case study of denunciation: International Covenant on Civil and Political Rights, First Optional Protocol

The denunciation clause

> #### International Covenant on Civil and Political Rights, Optional Protocol Art 12
>
> 1. Any State Party may denounce the present Protocol at any time by written notification addressed to the Secretary-General of the United Nations. Denunciation shall take effect three months after the date of receipt of the notification by the Secretary-General.
>
> 2. Denunciation shall be without prejudice to the continued application of the provisions of the present Protocol to any communication submitted under article 2 before the effective date of denunciation.

Three States indicated their intention to denounce the Optional Protocol: Jamaica; Guyana; and Trinidad and Tobago. Jamaica had 177 individual communications lodged against it (the highest number against any State Party), Trinidad and Tobago 48 and Guyana 11. Only Jamaica proceeded with denouncement (as of 23 January

1998), the others re-acceded with reservations. However, following numerous objections to its reservations, Trinidad and Tobago denounced the protocol for a second time (as of 27 June 2000). Individual communications under consideration before the effective dates of denunciation are dealt with in accordance with the optional protocol provisions.

Guyana's denunciation

Guyana proceeded to denounce, then re-accede on the same day (5 April 1999), the re-accession being accompanied by the following reservation:

'[. . .] Guyana re-accedes to the Optional Protocol to the International Covenant on Civil and Political Rights with a Reservation to article 6 thereof with the result that the Human Rights Committee shall not be competent to receive and consider communications from any persons who is under sentence of death for the offences of murder and treason in respect of any matter relating to his prosecution, detention, trial, conviction, sentence or execution of the death sentence and any matter connected therewith.

Accepting the principle that States cannot generally use the Optional Protocol as a vehicle to enter reservations to the International Covenant on Civil and Political Rights itself, the Government of Guyana stresses that its Reservation to the Optional Protocol in no way detracts from its obligations and engagements under the Covenant, including its undertaking to respect and ensure to all individuals within the territory of Guyana and subject to its jurisdiction the rights recognised in the Covenant (in so far as not already reserved against) as set out in article 2 thereof, as well as its undertaking to report to the Human Rights Committee under the monitoring mechanism established by article 40 thereof.'

International response—the Netherlands

Response of States to this move was critical. Consider the following statements:

2. The Government of the Kingdom of the Netherlands is of the view that this reservation, which seeks to limit the obligations of the reserving State towards individuals under sentence of death, raises doubts as to the object and purpose of the Optional Protocol.

3. The Government of the Netherlands considers that the purpose of the Optional Protocol [to the International Covenant on Civil and Political Rights] is to strengthen the position of the individual under the Covenant. Denying the benefits of the Optional Protocol in relation to the Covenant to a group of individuals under the most severe sentence is fundamentally in conflict with the object and purpose of the Optional Protocol.

4. Also the Government of the Kingdom of the Netherlands considers the procedure followed by Guyana, of denouncing the Optional Protocol followed by a re-accession with reservations, as contrary to the rules of the law of treaties that prohibit the formulation of reservations after ratification. The procedure followed by Guyana circumvents such well-established rules.

5. The Government of the Kingdom of the Netherlands therefore objects to the aforementioned reservation made by the Government of Guyana to the Optional Protocol to the International Covenant on Civil and Political Rights.

Question

Do you agree with the criticism levied by the Netherlands? To what extent does the Guyanan approach conform to international law and to what extent does it corroborate Bayefsky's critical view of the international system?

FURTHER READING

Lijnzaad, L, *Reservations to UN Human Rights Treaties, Ratify and Ruin?*, 1995, The Hague: Martinus Nijhof

Clark, B, 'The Vienna Convention Reservations Regime and the Convention on Discrimination against Women' (1991) 85 AJIL 281

Conforti, B, and Francioni, F, *Enforcing International Human Rights in Domestic Courts*, 1997, Leiden: Brill

Chinkin, C et al., *Human Rights as General Norms and a State's right to opt out*, 1997, London: BIICL

Higgins, R, *Problems and Process: International Law and How we Use it*, 1995, Clarendon: Oxford

Helfer, L, 'Exiting Treaties' (2005) 91 Virginia Law Review 1579

Ziemele, I (ed), *Reservations to Human Rights Treaties and the Vienna Convention regime: Conflict, Harmony or Reconciliation*, 2004, Leiden: Brill

CHAPTER 4

HUMAN RIGHTS ORGANISATIONS AND KEY INSTITUTIONS

Human rights do not exist in a vacuum. Inevitably, they are formulated by individuals and States and they are implemented by States themselves. However, a number of national, regional and international bodies exercise responsibility for overseeing the monitoring of human rights and ensuring that States comply with the obligations. This chapter will focus on the principal international and regional systems. National human rights institutions are considered in Chapter 7 on implementing international human rights. This chapter concerns itself with the key international organisations and institutions which operate regimes of human rights protection.

4.1 INTERNATIONAL ORGANISATIONS

International human rights are, by definition, global in character. They apply to all individuals and transcend national law and regulation. As such they were developed under the auspices of the international community although they apply nationally. To assist in this, a number of international organisations created norms of human rights and structures for monitoring their realisation. Predominant among them is the United Nations.

4.2 THE UNITED NATIONS

The United Nations is the primary international organisation enjoying responsibility for international human rights protection. However, human rights protection was not the driving force behind the creation of the Organisation in 1945.

4.2.1 Purpose of the United Nations

The preamble indicates the rationale underpinning the Organisation while Art 1 explains its agreed purposes.

United Nations Charter 1945

Preamble

WE THE PEOPLES OF THE UNITED NATIONS DETERMINED

to save succeeding generations from the scourge of war, which twice in our lifetime has brought untold sorrow to mankind, and

to reaffirm faith in fundamental human rights, in the dignity and worth of the human person, in the equal rights of men and women and of nations large and small, and

to establish conditions under which justice and respect for the obligations arising from treaties and other sources of international law can be maintained, and

to promote social progress and better standards of life in larger freedom,

Article 1
Purposes of the United Nations

The Purposes of the United Nations are:

1. To maintain international peace and security, and to that end: to take effective collective measures for the prevention and removal of threats to the peace, and for the suppression of acts of aggression or other breaches of the peace, and to bring about by peaceful means, and in conformity with the principles of justice and international law, adjustment or settlement of international disputes or situations which might lead to a breach of the peace;

2. To develop friendly relations among nations based on respect for the principle of equal rights and self-determination of peoples, and to take other appropriate measures to strengthen universal peace;

3. To achieve international co-operation in solving international problems of an economic, social, cultural, or humanitarian character, and in promoting and encouraging respect for human rights and for fundamental freedoms for all without distinction as to race, sex, language, or religion; and

4. To be a centre for harmonizing the actions of nations in the attainment of these common ends.

As is apparent, the maintenance of international peace and security is the primary function of the United Nations. However, in furtherance thereof, respect for human rights is identified of being of importance. Grounded in the work of the League of Nations, the then international community was of the opinion that securing respect for equal rights would inevitably lead to a more peaceful world. The emphasis on economic cooperation resonated with post-war contemporary politics—large swathes of the European population were displaced, the European economy was in disarray.

Steiner, H and Alston, P (eds), *International Human Rights in Context—Law Politics Morals*, 2nd edn, 2000, Oxford: OUP at p 138

The Charter's references to human rights are scattered, terse, even cryptic. The term 'human rights' appears infrequently, although in vital contexts . . . Several striking characteristics of these provisions [which mention human rights] emerge. Many have a promotional or programmatic character, for they refer principally to the purposes or goals of the UN or to the competencies of different UN organs: 'encouraging respect for human rights', 'assisting in the realization of human rights', 'promote . . . universal respect for, and observance of, human rights'. Not even a provision such as Article 56, which refers to obligations of the Member States rather than of the UN, contains the language of obligation.

Steiner and Alston note that only the right to equal protection is mentioned directly in the Charter, no other human right is accorded such status.

Perhaps an explanation for this can be extracted from a potential problem with the development of international human rights law which appears in the text of the principles governing the Organisation and its members:

United Nations Charter, Art 2, Principle 7

Nothing contained in the present Charter shall authorize the United Nations to intervene in matters which are essentially within the domestic jurisdiction of any state or shall require the Members to submit such matters to settlement under the present Charter; but this principle shall not prejudice the application of enforcement measures under Chapter VII.

While this would appear to preclude international human rights, it must be remembered that international human rights are of concern to the international community as dignity and worth of each person is recognised by the international community and transcends national law. The individual is no longer deemed the property of the State or to be treated as such. However, this was perhaps rather a novel concept in 1945.

4.2.2   Structure of the United Nations

In accordance with the Charter of the United Nations, Art 7, the principal organs of the Organisation are a General Assembly, a Security Council, an Economic and Social Council, a Trusteeship Council, an International Court of Justice and a secretariat. Of these, the Trusteeship Council is obsolete, with the successful transition to independence of the non-self-governing territories (see Arts 73–85, UN Charter). Not all the remaining organs significantly impact on international human rights. Moreover, the original framework has been supplemented by a range of ancillary and auxiliary bodies, many of whom have direct responsibilities for international human rights. What must be borne in mind is that most of these bodies derive their powers from the member States, that is, they only enjoy such powers as the States agree to give them, either explicitly through a specific treaty, or implicitly through a declaration and evolving practice.

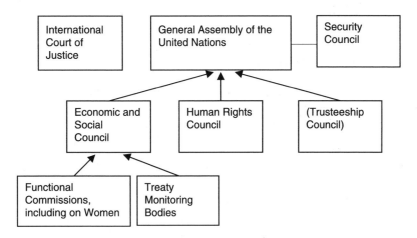

Although human rights permeate through many operational areas within the United Nations, the above diagram focuses on those institutions most involved with international human rights. In effect, this is a human rights driven structure of the United Nations. For more information of the structure and organs of the United Nations itself, recourse should be had to the website of the United Nations (www.un.org) and/or to any of the principal textbooks on Public International Law. The following text is limited to the main organs and institutions having responsibility for/impacting on international human rights and their report structure.

4.2.3   General Assembly

The General Assembly is the principal forum for the congregation of the United Nations member States. It consists of all the members of the United Nations (UN Charter Art 9), each member having one vote (Art 18). In accordance with the Charter, the General Assembly meets annually (Art 20) though can meet in extraordinary special sessions as and when required. The General Assembly has wide-ranging powers.

UN Charter

Article 10

The General Assembly may discuss any questions or any matters within the scope of the present Charter or relating to the powers and functions of any organs provided for in the present Charter, and, except as provided in Article 12, may make recommendations to the Members of the United Nations or to the Security Council or to both on any such questions or matters.

Article 13

1. The General Assembly shall initiate studies and make recommendations for the purpose of:

a. promoting international co-operation in the political field and encouraging the progressive development of international law and its codification;

b. promoting international co-operation in the economic, social, cultural, educational, and health fields, and assisting in the realization of human rights and fundamental freedoms for all without distinction as to race, sex, language, or religion.

2. The further responsibilities, functions and powers of the General Assembly with respect to matters mentioned in paragraph 1 (b) above are set forth in Chapters IX and X.

Examples of the impact of the General Assembly on Human Rights

The General Assembly has adopted many resolutions which impact significantly on the work of the United Nations in human rights. Indeed, much of the responsibility for human rights ultimately relates back to or is initiated by the General Assembly. All human rights bodies ultimately report to the General Assembly. Even the Security Council must submit annual reports to the Assembly. Whatever the practical (particularly time) limitations, the central focus in the Charter on the General Assembly substantiates the emphasis on the States having responsibility for the operation of the organisation, rather than any individual body.

As far as the generation of 'soft' law, several resolutions of the General Assembly have had significant impact. Some have been declaratory of international law, others have initiated studies which have had dramatic impact on human rights.

Resolution 1514 (XV) (1960) on the Granting of Independence to Colonial Countries and Peoples

Resolution 36/55 (1981), Declaration on the Elimination of All Forms of Intolerance and of Discrimination Based on Religion or Belief

Resolution 40/144 (1985), Declaration on the Human Rights of Individuals who are not Nationals of the Country in which they Live

Resolution 41/128 (1986), Declaration on the Right to Development

Resolution 43/115 (1988) on the establishment of an independent expert to review the treaty monitoring bodies

Resolution 43/173 (1988), Principles for the Protection of All Persons Under Any Form of Detention or Imprisonment

Resolution 45/111 (1990), Basic Principles for the Treatment of Prisoners

Resolution 45/113 (1990), United Nations Rules for the Protection of Juveniles Deprived of their Liberty

Resolution 47/135 (1992), Declaration on the Rights of Persons Belonging to National or Ethnic, Religions and Linguistic Minorities

Resolution 48/104 (1993), Declaration on the Elimination of Violence against Women

Resolution 56/115 (2001) on a world programme of action concerning disabled peoples

As the above list indicates, many elements of freedom of liberty and right to a fair trial are governed by General Assembly guidelines. The importance of these guidelines are that they apply to all States. While some codify existing international practice, others contain rules which are agreed by the member States and thus form new and emergent rules of international practice. General Assembly declarations and principles can be, and are referred to in national courts when determining the scope and nature of particular human rights provisions.

In addition, most of the major United Nations treaties on human rights were preceded by a declaration of the General Assembly. The following are the main examples.

Resolution 217(III) (1948), Universal Declaration of Human Rights

— **International Covenants on Civil and Political Rights and on Economic, Social and Cultural Rights 1966**

Resolution 1386 (XIV) (1959), Declaration on the Rights of the Child

— **UN Convention on the Rights of the Child 1989**

Resolution 1904 (XVIII) (1963), Declaration on the Elimination of All Forms of Racial Discrimination

— **International Convention on the Elimination of All Forms of Racial Discrimination 1965**

Resolution 2263 (XXII) (1967), Declaration on the Elimination of Discrimination against Women

— **Convention on the Elimination of All Forms of Discrimination against Women 1979**

Resolution 3452 (XXX) (1975), Declaration on the Protection of All Persons from Being Subjected to Torture and Other Cruel, Inhuman or Degrading Treatment or Punishment

— **Convention against Torture and Other Cruel, Inhuman or Degrading Treatment or Punishment 1984**

While the main international treaties stem from General Assembly Declarations, there is often a considerable time lapse between declaration and treaty: some 18 years between the Universal Declaration and the International Covenants, 30 years for the rights of the child, yet only two years for racial discrimination.

Question

Although several declarations adopted in resolutions have resulted in treaties, many have not. What reasons may there be for the wealth of human rights declarations and principles adopted by the General Assembly? Why are such instruments not adopted by the international community in a legally binding form?

4.2.4 Economic and Social Council

Art 61 of the Charter of the United Nations provides that the Economic and Social Council (ECOSOC) shall comprise 54 members of the United Nations (this represents the culmination of a series of increases from the original 18 agreed in 1945), each serving three year terms of office. A wide mandate is extended to the Council, thereby facilitating its evolution into a key player in contemporary international human rights law.

Charter of the United Nations

Article 62

1. The Economic and Social Council may make or initiate studies and reports with respect to international economic, social, cultural, educational, health, and related matters and may make recommendations with respect to any such matters to the General Assembly to the Members of the United Nations, and to the specialized agencies concerned.

2. It may make recommendations for the purpose of promoting respect for, and observance of, human rights and fundamental freedoms for all.

3. It may prepare draft conventions for submission to the General Assembly, with respect to matters falling within its competence.

4. It may call, in accordance with the rules prescribed by the United Nations, international conferences on matters falling within its competence.

Article 64

1. The Economic and Social Council may take appropriate steps to obtain regular reports from the specialized agencies. It may make arrangements with the Members of the United Nations and with the specialized agencies to obtain reports on the steps taken to give effect to its own recommendations and to recommendations on matters falling within its competence made by the General Assembly.

2. It may communicate its observations on these reports to the General Assembly.

ECOSOC receives all the reports of the main international human rights bodies, including the treaty monitoring bodies (see Chapter 6). Moreover, it coordinates various UN programmes which aim at improving human rights standards. The United Nations Development Programme is a prime example.

4.2.4.1   Reform?

Significant reform proposals currently tabled before the General Assembly (see Chapter 9) include plans for the strengthening of ECOSOC. While noting the work of the Council, the Secretary-General considers five areas which require consideration: integrating, reviewing and implementing the development agenda; reviewing trends in international development cooperation; addressing economic and social challenges; monitoring and addressing economic and social dimensions of conflicts and asserting its leadership in driving a global development agenda (Kofi Annan, *In larger Freedom, towards development, security and human rights for all*, UN Doc. A/59/2005 paras 175–179).

Kofi Annan, In larger freedom: towards development, security and human rights for all, UN Doc. A/59/2005

171. The Charter of the United Nations gives the Economic and Social Council a range of important functions that involve coordination, policy review and policy dialogue. Most of these seem more critical than ever in this age of globalization, in which a comprehensive United Nations development agenda has emerged from the summits and conferences of the 1990s. More than ever, the United Nations needs to be able to develop and implement policies in this area in a coherent manner. The functions of the Council are generally thought to be uniquely relevant to these challenges, but it has not as yet done justice to them.

. . .

172. In 1945, the framers of the Charter did not give the Economic and Social Council enforce-ment powers. Having agreed at Bretton Woods in the previous year to create powerful

international financial institutions and expecting that these would be complemented by a world trade organization in addition to the various specialized agencies, they clearly intended that international economic decision-making would be decentralized. But this only makes the Council's potential role as coordinator, convener, forum for policy dialogue and forger of consensus the more important. It is the only organ of the United Nations explicitly mandated by the Charter to coordinate the activities of the specialized agencies and to consult with non-governmental organizations. And it has a network of functional and regional commissions operating under its aegis which are increasingly focused on the implementation of development goals.

173. The Economic and Social Council has put these assets to good use in the recent years, building bridges through an annual special high-level meeting with the trade and financial institutions, for instance . . .

180. Implementing all these recommendations would require the Economic and Social Council to function with a new and more flexible structure, not necessarily restricted by the current annual calendar of 'segments' and 'substantive session'. In addition, the Council needs an effective, efficient and representative intergovernmental mechanism for engaging its counterparts in the institutions dealing with finance and trade. This could either be achieved by expanding its Bureau or by establishing an Executive Committee with a regionally balanced composition.

Question

To what extent are such reforms likely to be viewed favourably by member States? What opposition may such reforms encounter?

4.2.4.2   ECOSOC's Functional Commissions

Delegation is pivotal to the completion of the work of ECOSOC and it has created a number of Commissions and specialist committees and appointed various expert bodies to assist it in the discharge of its broad range of functions. At present ECOSOC has 10 functional commissions, many of which impact on human rights.

Functional Commissions of ECOSOC (2006)

Statistical Commission
Commission on Population and Development
Commission for Social Development
Commission on Human Rights—last session 27 March 2006
Commission on the Status of Women
Commission on Narcotic Drugs
Commission on Crime Prevention and Criminal Justice
Commission on Science and Technology for Development
Commission on Sustainable Development
United Nations Forum on Forests

All the Commissions are subject to the same rules of procedures (extracts appear below on the Commission on Human Rights).

Question

What are the obvious practical and political limitations on the powers and functioning of the Council?

Two of these Commissions play significant roles in the protection and promotion of human rights: the Commission on Human Rights and the Commission on the Status of Women. Note the Commission on Human Rights has formally ceased operations now.

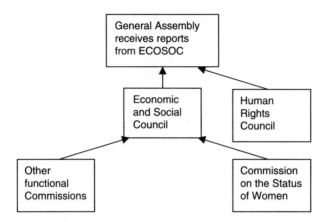

4.2.5   Human Rights Council

Not to be confused with the Human Rights Committee, a body established to monitor the International Covenant on Civil and Political Rights, the Human Rights Council is the newest human rights body in the United Nations system. It was created in 2006 to replace the Commission on Human Rights. The Commission was a functional Commission of the Economic and Social Council, established in 1947. It was originally tasked with drafting the Universal Declaration on Human Rights. This it did, under the leadership of Eleanor Roosevelt within its first year of operation. Perhaps this will remain the most significant achievement of the Commission. Plans for reforming the United Nations human rights machinery focussed on the Commission. In December 2004, the Secretary-General presented to the General Assembly of the United Nations the report of the High-level Panel on Threats, Challenges and Changes. Although only nine of some 300 pages in the report address human rights, the comments of the panel attracted considerable interest. The Secretary-General then issued his own report on United Nations reform, 'In larger freedom: towards development, security and human rights for all'. This report proposed replacing the Commission with a smaller standing Human Rights Council which could be accorded status as a principal organ of the United Nations or could be a subsidiary of the United Nations General Assembly. Note the criticisms levied at the Commission.

Kofi Annan, *In larger freedom: towards development, security and human rights for all*, available from www.un.org/largerfreedom, UN Doc. A/59/2005

181. The Commission on Human Rights has given the international community a universal human rights framework, comprising the Universal Declaration on Human Rights, the two International Covenants[21] and other core human rights treaties. During its annual session, the Commission draws public attention to human rights issues and debates, provides a forum for the development of United Nations human rights policy and establishes a unique system of independent and expert special procedures to observe and analyse human rights compliance by theme and by country. The Commission's close engagement with hundreds of civil society organizations provides an opportunity for working with civil society that does not exist elsewhere.

182. Yet the Commission's capacity to perform its tasks has been increasingly undermined by its declining credibility and professionalism. In particular, States have sought membership of the Commission not to strengthen human rights but to protect themselves against criticism or to

criticize others. As a result, a credibility deficit has developed, which casts a shadow on the reputation of the United Nations system as a whole.

The Commission on Human Rights met in March 2006 and considered the report of the Secretary-General and the High-level Panel. This was its final meeting.

Question

The Commission was the original body for enforcing, monitoring and developing international human rights. Much of its work has perhaps now been subsumed by the treaty monitoring bodies (see Chapter 6) established with specific competency for each of the main international human rights treaties. Consider the benefits in retaining an independent (of the human rights treaties) council and how such a resource could best be maximised.

4.2.5.1   Creating the new Council

In accordance with General Assembly Resolution 60/251 (2006), the peoples of the United Nations decided to establish the Human Rights Council in Geneva to replace the Commission on Human Rights (at para 1). The Council is established as a subsidiary body of the General Assembly but the Assembly will review its status in five years (2011) at which time it may be elevated to a full organ of the United Nations. Even as a subsidiary body, the Council enjoys a higher status than the Commission. This reinforces the importance of human rights within the United Nations today.

The Council is tasked to meet throughout the year, a change from the annual meetings of the former Commission. It operates under the normal rules of procedure for committees of the General Assembly and can draw on the skills and knowledge of a wide range of bodies, including NGOs, in accordance with the pre-existing arrangements observed by the Commission under ECOSOC Resolution 1996/31 (1996) (GA Resn 60/251 at paras 10–11).

General Assembly Resolution 60/251 (2006) para 12

12. . . . the methods of work of the Council shall be transparent, fair and impartial and shall enable genuine dialogue, be results-oriented, allow for subsequent follow-up discussions to recommendations and their implementation and also allow for substantive interaction with special procedures and mechanisms;

4.2.5.2   Membership of the Council

Little time was given to the General Assembly to create the Council. Elections were scheduled for 9 May with the first meeting of the Council on 19 June. Detailed procedures were provided in the enabling resolution:

General Assembly Resolution 60/251 (2006) paras 7–9

7. . . . the Council shall consist of forty-seven Member States, which shall be elected directly and individually by secret ballot by the majority of the members of the General Assembly; the membership shall be based on equitable geographical distribution, and seats shall be distributed as follows among regional groups: Group of African States, thirteen; Group of Asian States, thirteen; Group of Eastern European States, six; Group of Latin American and Caribbean States, eight; and Group of Western European and other States, seven; the members of the Council shall serve for a period of three years and shall not be eligible for immediate re-election after two consecutive terms;

8. ... the membership in the Council shall be open to all States Members of the United Nations; when electing members of the Council, Member States shall take into account the contribution of candidates to the promotion and protection of human rights and their voluntary pledges and commitments made thereto; the General Assembly, by a two-thirds majority of the members present and voting, may suspend the rights of membership in the Council of a member of the Council that commits gross and systematic violations of human rights;

9. ... members elected to the Council shall uphold the highest standards in the promotion and protection of human rights, shall fully cooperate with the Council and be reviewed under the universal periodic review mechanism during their term of membership.

Forty-seven members represent only a small reduction on the membership of the former Commission – fifty-three. It remains to be seen whether such a reduction renders the Council less unwieldy than its predecessor as regards decision-making. Note particularly the power of the General Assembly to suspend the membership of States committing gross and serious violations of human rights. Obviously no State has a perfect Human Rights record. However there is a clear underlying intention in the resolution to make States in the Council accountable for their human rights record. The following States were elected to serve on the inaugural Council:

Argentina	Mali
Azerbaijan	Mauritius
Bahrain	Mexico
Bangladesh	Morocco
Brazil	Netherlands
Cameroon	Nigeria
Canada	Pakistan
China	Peru
Cuba	Philippines
Czech Republic	Poland
Djibouti	Republic of Korea
Ecuador	Romania
Finland	Russian Federation
France	Saudi Arabia
Gabon	Senegal
Germany	South Africa
Ghana	Sri Lanka
Guatemala	Switzerland
India	Tunisia
Indonesia	Ukraine
Japan	United Kingdom
Jordan	Uruguay
Malaysia	Zambia

Many applicant countries submitted pledged on their human rights agenda in advance of the elections.

Question

Do these States satisfy the criteria in Resolution 60/251?

4.2.5.3 Powers of the Council

Resolution 60/251 specifies the powers of the new body.

General Assembly Resolution 60/251 (2006) paras 2–5

2. . . . the Council shall be responsible for promoting universal respect for the protection of all human rights and fundamental freedoms for all, without distinction of any kind and in a fair and equal manner;

3. . . . the Council should address situations of violations of human rights, including gross and systematic violations, and make recommendations thereon. It should also promote the effective coordination and the mainstreaming of human rights within the United Nations system;

4. . . . the work of the Council shall be guided by the principles of universality, impartiality, objectivity and non-selectivity, constructive international dialogue and cooperation, with a view to enhancing the promotion and protection of all human rights, civil, political, economic, social and cultural rights, including the right to development;

5. . . . the Council shall, inter alia:

(a) Promote human rights education and learning as well as advisory services, technical assistance and capacity-building, to be provided in consultation with and with the consent of Member States concerned;

(b) Serve as a forum for dialogue on thematic issues on all human rights;

(c) Make recommendations to the General Assembly for the further development of international law in the field of human rights;

(d) Promote the full implementation of human rights obligations undertaken by States and follow-up to the goals and commitments related to the promotion and protection of human rights emanating from United Nations conferences and summits;

(e) Undertake a universal periodic review, based on objective and reliable information, of the fulfilment by each State of its human rights obligation and commitments in a manner which ensures universality of coverage and equal treatment with respect to all States; the review shall be a cooperative mechanism, based on an interactive dialogue, with the full involvement of the country concerned and with consideration given to its capacity-building needs; such a mechanism shall complement and not duplicate the work of treaty bodies; the Council shall develop the modalities and necessary time allocation for the universal periodic review mechanism within one year after the holding of its first session;

(f) Contribute, through dialogue and cooperation, towards the prevention of human rights violations and respond promptly to human rights emergencies;

(g) Assume the role and responsibilites of the Commission on Human Rights relating to the work of the Office of the United Nations High Commissioner for Human Rights, as decided by the General Assembly in its resolution 48/141 of 20 December 1993;

(h) Work in close cooperation in the field of human rights with Governments, regional organizations, national human rights institutions and civil society;

(i) Make recommendations with regard to the promotion and protection of human rights;

(j) Submit an annual report to the General Assembly.

Ultimately the Council has been established as the focal point for human rights endeavours in the United Nations. It should help member States meet their human rights obligations.

4.2.6 Sub-Commission on the Protection and Promotion of Human Rights

In 1946, a Sub-Commission on the Prevention of Discrimination and the Protection of Minorities was created under the Commission on Human Rights and ECOSOC. Originally a partial successor to the problem of minority rights, the Sub-Commission underwent a name change in 1999 to the Sub-Commission on the Protection and Promotion of Human Rights. While this perhaps better reflects the breadth of its advisory role, it simultaneously removes the last vestige of specific minority rights mechanisms from the United Nations.

At present, 26 independent experts in the field of human rights sit on the Sub-Commission. Each serves in an individual capacity for the promotion of international human rights. They are elected by the Human Rights Council and, in accordance with normal United Nations practice, the membership reflects an equitable geographical distribution. A rolling system of re-election ensures continuity of the work in progress.

The following list is the 2006 membership. The geographical distribution is obvious. Some of the members are career diplomats, others are pre-eminent academics, all experts in international human rights.

Membership of the Sub-Commission 2006 (updates available from www.ohchr.org/english/bodies/subcom/membership.htm

Mr Miguel Alfonso Martínez (Cuba)
Mr Gudmundur Alfredsson (Iceland)
Mr José Bengoa (Chile)
Mr Gáspár Bíró (Hungary)
Mr Marc Bossuyt (Belgium)
Mr Shiqiu Chen (China)
Mr Mohammed Habib Cherif (Tunisia)
Ms Chin Sung Chung (Republic of Korea)
Mr Emmanuel Decaux (France)
Mr Rui Baltazar Dos Santos Alves (Mozambique)
Mr El-Hadji Guissé (Senegal)
Ms Françoise Jane Hampson (United Kingdom)
Mr Vladimir A. Kartashkin (Russian Federation)
Ms Kalliopi Koufa (Greece)
Ms Iulia-Antoanella Motoc (Romania)
Ms Florizelle O'Connor (Jamaica)
Mr Paulo Sérgio Pinheiro (Brazil)
Ms Lalaina Rakotoarisoa (Madagascar)
Mr David Rivkin (United States of America)
Mr Ibrahim Salama (Egypt)
Mr Abdul Sattar (Pakistan)
Mr Soli Jehangir Sorabjee (India)
Mr Janio Iván Tuñón Veilles (Panama)
Ms N.U.O Wadibia-Anyanwu (Nigeria)
Ms Halima Embarek Warzazi (Morocco)
Mr Yozo Yokota (Japan)

The Sub-Commission can undertake studies and make recommendations on any aspect of discrimination and perform any other function entrusted to it by the Human Rights Council or the Economic and Social Council.

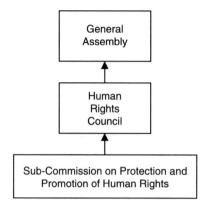

4.2.7 Commission on the Status of Women (CSW)

ECOSOC Resolution 11(11) (1946) established the Commission on the Status of Women. Membership has increased to 45, with a clear balance in favour of women members! Unlike most of the international human rights machinery, the Commission on the Status of Women has its own secretariat, partially provided by the Division for the Advancement of Women (DAW). The functions of the Commission are governed by the powers granted to it in the enabling resolution (Economic and Social Council Resolution 11(II) of 21 June 1946). This was expanded in Resolution 1987/22.

The most significant body of work before the Commission at present is the ongoing review of progress towards the goals agreed in Beijing by the Fourth World Conference on Women in 1995.

ECOSOC Resolution 1996/6
FRAMEWORK FOR THE FUNCTIONING OF THE COMMISSION

Recalling that the General Assembly, in resolution 50/203, decided that the Assembly, the Economic and Social Council and the Commission on the Status of Women, in accordance with their respective mandates and in accordance with Assembly resolution 48/162 of 20 December 1993 and other relevant resolutions, should constitute a three-tiered intergovernmental mechanism that would play the primary role in the overall policy-making and follow-up, and in coordinating the implementation and monitoring of the Platform for Action, reaffirming the need for a coordinated follow-up to and implementation of the results of major international conferences in the economic, social and related fields,

Convinced that the follow-up to the Fourth World Conference on Women should be undertaken on the basis of an integrated approach to the advancement of women within the framework of a coordinated follow-up to and implementation of the results of major international conferences in the economic, social and related fields, as well as the overall responsibilities of the General Assembly and the Economic and Social Council,

1. Decides that the Commission on the Status of Women shall have a catalytic role in mainstreaming a gender perspective in policies and programmes;

2. Decides that the inter-agency committee on the follow-up to the Fourth World Conference on Women, established by the Administrative Committee on Coordination, shall inform the Commission and the Economic and Social Council of the progress of its work, for the purpose of system-wide coordination, and that a gender perspective shall also be fully integrated in the work of all thematic task forces established by the Administrative Committee on Coordination;

3. Decides that the Platform for Action should be implemented through the work of all the bodies and organizations of the United Nations system during the period 1995–2000, and notes that the institutions of the United Nations especially devoted to the advancement of women, including the International Research and Training Institute for the Advancement of Women and the United Nations Development Fund for Women, are in the process of reviewing their programmes of work in the light of the Platform for Action and its implementation;

4. Decides, in view of the traditional importance of non-governmental organizations in the advancement of women, that such organizations should be encouraged to participate in the work of the Commission and in the monitoring and implementation process related to the Conference to the maximum extent possible, and requests the Secretary-General to make appropriate arrangements to ensure full utilization of existing channels of communication with non-governmental organizations in order to facilitate broad-based participation and dissemination of information;

5. Decides, in recognition of the valuable contribution of non-governmental organizations to the Fourth World Conference on Women, that the Council and its Committee on Non-Governmental Organizations will review the applications of those non-governmental organizations under Council resolution 1296 (XLIV) of 23 May 1968 as expeditiously as possible, and also decides that, prior to the forty-first session of the Commission on the Status of Women, the Council will take a decision on the participation of the non-governmental organizations that were accredited to the Conference and that have applied for consultative status, in Conference follow-up and in the work of the Commission on the Status of Women, without prejudice to the work of the Open-ended Working Group on the Review of Arrangements for Consultation with Non-Governmental Organizations;

6. Requests the Secretary-General urgently to draw the attention of non-governmental organizations accredited to the Fourth World Conference on Women to the provisions of the present resolution and to the process established under Council resolution 1296 (XLIV).

II
TERMS OF REFERENCE

1. Confirms the existing mandate of the Commission on the Status of Women as set out in Council resolutions 11 (II), 48 (IV) and 1987/22, bearing in mind that the Platform for Action builds upon the Nairobi Forward-looking Strategies for the Advancement of Women;

2. Decides that the Commission shall:

(a) Assist the Economic and Social Council in monitoring, reviewing and appraising progress achieved and problems encountered in the implementation of the Beijing Declaration and Platform for Action at all levels, and shall advise the Council thereon;

(b) Continue to ensure support for mainstreaming a gender perspective in United Nations activities and develop further its catalytic role in this regard in other areas;

(c) Identify issues where United Nations system-wide coordination needs to be improved in order to assist the Council in its coordination function;

(d) Identify emerging issues, trends and new approaches to issues affecting the situation of women or equality between women and men that require urgent consideration, and make substantive recommendations thereon;

(e) Maintain and enhance public awareness and support for the implementation of the Platform for Action.

Question

Much of the work of the functional Commissions is based on compilation of reports, investigations and discussions. To what extent do such activities promote and protect human rights?

4.3   INTERNATIONAL COURTS

There are two 'international' courts, neither of which actually has cause to consider international human rights on a regular basis. The International Court of Justice is part of the United Nations and is established in accordance with the Charter of the United Nations itself. Standing alone, independent of the United Nations machinery, yet accepted by many member States, the International Criminal Court is a peculiar hybrid body. Although operating within the ambit of international law, it serves solely to prosecute individuals for violations of selected, very serious elements of international humanitarian and criminal law.

4.3.1   International Court of Justice

The International Court of Justice was established by Art 92 of the UN Charter as the principal judicial organ of the United Nations. It sits in the Hague, the Netherlands and succeeds the Permanent Court of International Court. In some texts, it is referred to as the World Court. All member States of the United Nations are *ipso facto* parties to the Statute of the International Court of Justice, which is annexed to the UN Charter (Art 93). This Statute contains all relevant information on the creation, membership, competencies and procedure of the Court. The Court comprises 15 judges, no two of whom can be nationals of the same State. Judges serve for terms of nine years though the system of appointments is staggered to ensure continuity with a third of the judges retiring every three years. Judges may be re-elected in accordance with the procedure laid down in the Statute.

Statute of the International Court of Justice Art 2

The Court shall be composed of a body of independent judges, elected regardless of their nationality from among persons of high moral character, who possess the qualifications required in their respective countries for appointment to the highest judicial offices, or are jurisconsults of recognized competence in international law.

Only States may be parties in cases before the Court (Art 34(1), Statute of the International Court of Justice), thus seemingly precluding consideration of international human rights law. However, the International Court enjoys consensual jurisdiction whereby States may accept its jurisdiction either in respect of all or any specific cases (Art 36).

Statute of the International Court of Justice Art 36(2)

1. The jurisdiction of the Court comprises all cases which the parties refer to it and all matters specially provided for in the Charter of the United Nations or in treaties and conventions in force.

2. The states parties to the present Statute may at any time declare that they recognize as compulsory *ipso facto* and without special agreement, in relation to any other state accepting the same obligation, the jurisdiction of the Court in all legal disputes concerning:

a. the interpretation of a treaty;

b. any question of international law;

c. the existence of any fact which, if established, would constitute a breach of an international obligation;

d. the nature or extent of the reparation to be made for the breach of an international obligation.

3. The declarations referred to above may be made unconditionally or on condition of reciprocity on the part of several or certain states, or for a certain time.

4. Such declarations shall be deposited with the Secretary-General of the United Nations, who shall transmit copies thereof to the parties to the Statute and to the Registrar of the Court.

5. Declarations made under Article 36 of the Statute of the Permanent Court of International Justice and which are still in force shall be deemed, as between the parties to the present Statute, to be acceptances of the compulsory jurisdiction of the International Court of Justice for the period which they still have to run and in accordance with their terms.

6. In the event of a dispute as to whether the Court has jurisdiction, the matter shall be settled by the decision of the Court.

Question

States are reluctant to bring complaints before the International Court of Justice. Considering examples of disputes which have been brought, what reasons are there for national recalcitrance to use the Court for human rights issues?

As final arbiter of treaty law, there is clear potential for cases to enter the docket of the Court which concern international human rights agreements. However, the Court has been accorded little opportunity to examine human rights. Nevertheless, some decisions and opinions of the Court have impacted on international human rights law.

While the Court can and does adjudicate on inter-State complaints, it also has jurisdiction to give advisory opinions on any legal questions at the request of any authorised body (Art 65, Statute of the International Court of Justice). Opinions have ranged over a number of areas from the legal personality of the United Nations, to the status of nuclear weapons and whether they constitute a threat to humanity.

A range of laws may be applied by the International Court to assist it in determining a case. Obviously, it is not open to the Court to determine that a matter is non-juridical on account of no relevant law being available.

Statute of the International Court of Justice Art 38

1. The Court, whose function is to decide in accordance with international law such disputes as are submitted to it, shall apply:

a. international conventions, whether general or particular, establishing rules expressly recognized by the contesting states;

b. international custom, as evidence of a general practice accepted as law;

c. the general principles of law recognized by civilized nations;

d. subject to the provisions of Article 59, judicial decisions and the teachings of the most highly qualified publicists of the various nations, as subsidiary means for the determination of rules of law.

2. This provision shall not prejudice the power of the Court to decide a case *ex aequo et bono*, if the parties agree thereto.

A number of cases have actual or tangential impact on aspects of human rights. Given the seriousness of instituting international proceedings in this venue, the relevant cases concern primarily the most serious aspects of international human rights, usually crimes against humanity and genocide. Some cases have general impact on the nature and substance of international human rights, others, such as the one currently following due judicial process on the application of the Genocide Convention in the Balkans, concern the actual application of human rights treaties. See also the *Armed Activities on the Territory of the Congo (Democratic Republic of the Congo v Uganda)* case under deliberation at present in which the parties were urged to refrain from further activities infringing the various instruments (including human rights).

4.3.2   International Criminal Court

The International Criminal Court is somewhat a hybrid body. It is not part of the United Nations organisational structure but was created at the behest of the international community and enjoys support from a wide variety of member States of the United Nations. In terms of the preamble to its constituent document, the Rome Statute of the International Criminal Court 1998, the States Parties were 'determined . . . for the sake of present and future generations, to establish an independent permanent International Criminal Court established in relationship with the United Nations system, with jurisdiction over the most serious crimes of concern to the international community as a whole' (Chapter 15 discusses International Criminal Law). An Assembly of States Parties oversees the functioning of the Court (Art 112) and its operation. The Court is co-financed by assessed contributions from States Parties and funds from the United Nations (Art 115).

Statute of the International Criminal Court Art 1

An International Criminal Court ('the Court') is hereby established. It shall be a permanent institution and shall have the power to exercise its jurisdiction over persons for the most serious crimes of international concern, as referred to in this Statute, and shall be complementary to national criminal jurisdictions. The jurisdiction and functioning of the Court shall be governed by the provisions of this Statute.

Like the International Court of Justice, the International Criminal Court is situated in the Hague, although it retains the power to sit elsewhere, thus conceivably it could go 'on circuit' to locations with a density of alleged perpetrators. Unlike the Court of Justice, the International Criminal Court comprises a Presidency, an Appeals Division, a Trial Division and a Pre-trial Division, the Office of Prosecutor and the Registry. A total of 18 judges were appointed initially, though this number may be increased if deemed necessary. Judges are subject to staggered election systems, with elections every three years and they generally cannot be re-elected.

Statute of the International Criminal Court Art 5
Crimes within the jurisdiction of the Court

1. The jurisdiction of the Court shall be limited to the most serious crimes of concern to the international community as a whole. The Court has jurisdiction in accordance with this Statute with respect to the following crimes:

(a) The crime of genocide;

(b) Crimes against humanity;

(c) War crimes;

(d) The crime of aggression.

2. The Court shall exercise jurisdiction over the crime of aggression once a provision is adopted in accordance with articles 121 and 123 defining the crime and setting out the conditions under which the Court shall exercise jurisdiction with respect to this crime. Such a provision shall be consistent with the relevant provisions of the Charter of the United Nations.

Given the nature of the jurisdictional competence of the International Criminal Court, a separate independent Office of Prosecutor is necessary to instigate investigations, authorise detention and extradition/surrender and bring relevant cases to trial. In this respect, the International Criminal Court shares some similarities with the national criminal law systems of many States.

Question

What problems may be anticipated in securing the necessary evidence to institute proceedings and to bring an alleged perpetrator to trial?

A wide range of legal materials may be employed in determining cases brought before the International Criminal Court. Of particular note, in the current context, all proceedings must be in accordance with norms of international human rights.

Statute of the International Criminal Court Art 21

Applicable law

1. The Court shall apply:

   (a) In the first place, this Statute, Elements of Crimes and its Rules of Procedure and Evidence;

   (b) In the second place, where appropriate, applicable treaties and the principles and rules of international law, including the established principles of the international law of armed conflict;

   (c) Failing that, general principles of law derived by the Court from national laws of legal systems of the world including, as appropriate, the national laws of States that would normally exercise jurisdiction over the crime, provided that those principles are not inconsistent with this Statute and with international law and internationally recognized norms and standards.

2. The Court may apply principles and rules of law as interpreted in its previous decisions.

3. The application and interpretation of law pursuant to this article must be consistent with internationally recognized human rights, and be without any adverse distinction founded on grounds such as gender as defined in article 7, paragraph 3, age, race, colour, language, religion or belief, political or other opinion, national, ethnic or social origin, wealth, birth or other status.

The Statute of the Court makes detailed provision for the collection of evidence, the rights of the accused, the conduct of all stages of the case, the applicable law, the appeal process and even sanctions. Those found guilty can be sentenced to imprisonment and will be imprisoned in whichever State the Court decides (from a list of nominees). On completion of sentence, the convictee will be returned to his/her home State or a State which agrees to accept him or her. Convictees may also be subject to fines and forfeiture measures (Art 77). The Statute itself makes clear the procedures to be followed at every stage of proceedings. Relevant international human rights standards prevail at all times. Cognisance is also given to various sets of principles and standards governing criminal trials and detention, as declared by the General Assembly of the United Nations.

The International Criminal Court has concurrent jurisdiction with national courts. This State may elect to prosecute alleged perpetrators under national law rather than facilitate an international investigation.

Statute of the International Criminal Court Art 19(2(b))

2. Challenges to the admissibility of a case on the grounds referred to in article 17 or challenges to the jurisdiction of the Court may be made by: . . .

(b) A State which has jurisdiction over a case, on the ground that it is investigating or prosecuting the case or has investigated or prosecuted.

Question

Why may States prove reluctant to permit international investigations, preferring to use national criminal law? Consider recent examples of crimes which fall within the Statute— which States could prosecute?

No case has yet been heard by the International Criminal Court, though summons have been issued. In time, the jurisprudence of the Court has the potential to contribute significantly to international criminal and humanitarian law. In the short term, much can be learned from the practice of the Office of Prosecutor and the Court as to the practical exercise of the highest standards of international rights on a fair trial, detention and the rights of the accused.

4.4   THE INTERNATIONAL LABOUR ORGANISATION

The International Labour Organisation was established in 1919 after the conclusion of the First World War. Indeed, its constitution is annexed to the Treaty of Versailles. Its original remit was to address issues of social justice, leaving political and military issues to the League of Nations. The two organisations were initially viewed as being complementary.

International Labour Organisation Constitution, Preamble

Whereas universal and lasting peace can be established only if it is based upon social justice;

And whereas conditions of labour exist involving such injustice hardship and privation to large numbers of people as to produce unrest so great that the peace and harmony of the world are imperilled; and an improvement of those conditions is urgently required; as, for example, by the regulation of the hours of work including the establishment of a maximum working day and week, the regulation of the labour supply, the prevention of unemployment, the provision of an adequate living wage, the protection of the worker against sickness, disease and injury arising out of his employment the protection of children, young persons and women, provision for old age and injury, protection of the interests of workers when employed in countries other than their own, recognition of the principle of equal remuneration for work of equal value, recognition of the principle of freedom of association, the organization of vocational and technical education and other measures;

Whereas also the failure of any nation to adopt humane conditions of labour is an obstacle in the way of other nations which desire to improve the conditions in their own countries;

The International Labour Organisation (ILO) remained, despite the collapse of the League of Nations. Today it is officially a specialised agency of the United Nations. In furtherance of its remit, the ILO has adopted a range of conventions and recommendations aimed at standard-setting international labour law and policy.

Swepston, L, 'The ILO's System of Human Rights Protection' in Symonides, J (ed), *Human Rights: International Protection, Monitoring, Enforcement*, 2003, Aldershot: Ashgate/UNESCO, pp 91–109

The ILO was founded before the term 'human rights' became current in the international world. Neither the ILO Constitution nor the other fundamental documents of the Organization use the term, and the constitution speaks instead of 'social justice' as the basis for the ILO's work . . . The concept of 'social justice' is wider [than 'human rights' as used by the United Nations] . . . In addition the ILO's instruments do not suppose that important human relations exist only between the state and individuals.

Question

What impact does standard-setting of labour relations have for States? What obligations can be imposed on States by the international labour codes evinced by the ILO? What effect do such instruments have on individuals?

Constitution of the International Labour Organisation Arts 22, 24, 26

Article 22

Each of the Members agrees to make an annual report to the International Labour Office on the measures which it has taken to give effect to the provisions of Conventions to which it is a party. These reports shall be made in such form and shall contain such particulars as the Governing Body may request.

Article 24

In the event of any representation being made to the International Labour Office by an industrial association of employers or of workers that any of the Members has failed to secure in any respect the effective observance within its jurisdiction of any Convention to which it is a party, the Governing Body may communicate this representation to the government against which it is made, and may invite that government to make such statement on the subject as it may think fit.

Article 26

1. Any of the Members shall have the right to file a complaint with the International Labour Office if it is not satisfied that any other Member is securing the effective observance of any Convention which both have ratified in accordance with the foregoing articles.

2. The Governing Body may, if it thinks fit, before referring such a complaint to a Commission of Inquiry, as hereinafter provided for, communicate with the government in question in the manner described in article 24.

3. If the Governing Body does not think it necessary to communicate the complaint to the government in question, or if, when it has made such communication, no statement in reply has been received within a reasonable time which the Governing Body considers to be satisfactory, the Governing Body may appoint a Commission of Inquiry to consider the complaint and to report thereon.

4. The Governing Body may adopt the same procedure either of its own motion or on receipt of a complaint from a delegate to the Conference.

5. When any matter arising out of article 25 or 26 is being considered by the Governing Body, the government in question shall if not already represented thereon, be entitled to send a representative to take part in the proceedings of the Governing Body while the matter is under consideration. Adequate notice of the date on which the matter will be considered shall be given to the government in question.

One notable feature of the ILO is the composition of its key organs. All have three elements: State governments; employers' representatives; employee representatives. States have either one third or one half the voting power in the institution (the exact division depends on the organ). This means that the ILO is unique in that workers and employers are involved at all levels. It took more than half a century for the benefits of extending participation in standard-setting to be recognised by the wider international community—see above re the Commission on Human Rights of the United Nations and Chapter 8 for the role of non-governmental organisations in advancing international human rights.

In accordance with Art 2 of the Constitution, there are three main organs:

(a) a General Conference of representatives of the Members;

(b) a Governing Body composed as described in Art 7; and

(c) an International Labour Office controlled by the Governing Body.

Note the composition arrangements in the following extracts.

Constitution of the ILO Art 3

1. The meetings of the General Conference of representatives of the Members shall be held from time to time as occasion may require, and at least once in every year. It shall be composed of four representatives of each of the Members, of whom two shall be Government delegates and the two others shall be delegates representing respectively the employers and the workpeople of each of the Members.

In terms of Art 4(1), each delegate has one vote; thus States have half the voting power.

ILO Constitution (the Governing Body) Art 7

1. The Governing Body shall consist of fifty-six persons

- Twenty-eight representing governments,

- Fourteen representing the employers, and

- Fourteen representing the workers.

2. Of the twenty-eight persons representing governments, ten shall be appointed by the Members of chief industrial importance, and eighteen shall be appointed by the Members selected for that purpose by the Government delegates to the Conference, excluding the delegates of the ten Members mentioned above.

3. The Governing Body shall as occasion requires determine which are the Members of the Organization of chief industrial importance and shall make rules to ensure that all questions relating to the selection of the Members of chief industrial importance are considered by an impartial committee before being decided by the Governing Body. Any appeal made by a Member from the declaration of the Governing Body as to which are the Members of chief industrial importance shall be decided by the Conference, but an appeal to the Conference shall not suspend the application of the declaration until such time as the Conference decides the appeal.

4. The persons representing the employers and the persons representing the workers shall be elected respectively by the Employers' delegates and the Workers' delegates to the Conference.

5. The period of office of the Governing Body shall be three years. If for any reason the Governing Body elections do not take place on the expiry of this period, the Governing Body shall remain in office until such elections are held. . . .

7. The Governing Body shall, from time to time, elect from its number a chairman and two vice-chairmen, of whom one shall be a person representing a government, one a person representing the employers, and one a person representing the workers.

Question

Evaluate the merits of the innovative work of the ILO, not least in light of the fact it achieves little external publicity and is often discounted in preference to the principal United Nations human rights mechanisms. Account for the low profile of the ILO.

Note that another specialised agency of the United Nations, UNESCO is considered in Chapter 5 as the organisation has established a mechanism for individual complaints.

4.5   REGIONAL ORGANISATIONS

The evolution of regional organisations with responsibility for monitoring human rights compliance is a comparatively new phenomenon, even by the youthful standards of international human rights law.

The first regional system to develop was in Europe. Its landmark international human rights instrument, the European Convention on Human Rights 1950 professed a basis in the Universal Declaration of Human Rights.

European Convention on Human Rights 1950, Preamble

Considering the Universal Declaration of Human Rights proclaimed by the General Assembly of the United Nations on 10th December 1948;

Considering that this Declaration aims at securing the universal and effective recognition and observance of the Rights therein declared;

Considering that the aim of the Council of Europe is the achievement of greater unity between its members and that one of the methods by which that aim is to be pursued is the maintenance and further realisation of human rights and fundamental freedoms;

Reaffirming their profound belief in those fundamental freedoms which are the foundation of justice and peace in the world and are best maintained on the one hand by an effective political democracy and on the other by a common understanding and observance of the human rights upon which they depend;

Being resolved, as the governments of European countries which are like-minded and have a common heritage of political traditions, ideals, freedom and the rule of law, to take the first steps for the collective enforcement of certain of the rights stated in the Universal Declaration,

Indeed, almost all subsequent regional human rights instruments, irrespective of their origin, make similar statements. While this would seem to indicate solidarity among international and regional bodies pursuing the goal of protection of international human rights instruments, initially the concept of regional human rights attracted considerable criticism as it was deemed to be in competition with the embryonic international system.

Question

Is there any merit in the early concerns of the United Nations—have these concerns proven justified?

Inevitably, as the European and American systems developed and achieved considerable measurable successes, the United Nations stance perceptibly altered.

Indeed the United Nations has been proactive in advocating regional international human rights systems. Success was found in Africa, with the creation of the Organisation of African Unity and its Charter on Human and Peoples' Rights. Calls continue to be made for the development of a regional system in Asia. Note the comments of Kofi Annan with respect to regional organisations and their relationship to the United Nations.

In larger freedom, towards development, security and human rights for all, UN Doc. A/59/2005

213. A considerable number of regional and subregional organizations are now active around the world, making important contributions to the stability and prosperity of their members, as well as of the broader international system. The United Nations and regional organizations should play complementary roles in facing the challenges to international peace and security. In this connection, donor countries should pay particular attention to the need for a 10-year plan for capacity-building with the African Union. To improve coordination between the United Nations and regional organizations, within the framework of the Charter of the United Nations, I intend to introduce memoranda of understanding between the United Nations and individual organizations, governing the sharing of information, expertise and resources, as appropriate in each case. For regional organizations that have a conflict prevention or peacekeeping capacity, these memoranda of understanding could place those capacities within the framework of the United Nations Standby Arrangements System.

214. I also intend to invite regional organizations to participate in meetings of United Nations system coordinating bodies, when issues in which they have a particular interest are discussed.

Three major regional systems operate today, each with an established machinery for monitoring State compliance with regionally agreed tabulations of international human rights and fundamental freedoms: Europe; the Americas and Africa. Today, the regional systems are an integral part of the global effort to secure the protection and promotion of international human rights and fundamental freedoms. International opinion now appears to support frequent expansion in the number of bodies and organisations imbued with responsibility for protecting and enforcing human rights. The Global Compact extends responsibility to multinational corporations while national institutions (discussed in Chapter 7) are encouraged to create appropriate channels for ensuring the realisation of human rights within States.

4.6   EUROPE

Europe was the centre of two world wars within 30 years. The political climate was conducive to the development of a regime aimed at protecting citizens. Much of the minority protection regime of the League of Nations was aimed at protecting groups in Europe, mainly in the newly delineated States after the conclusion of the First World War. Following the Second World War, the leaders in Europe looked at developing various regional organisations with different functions. A Congress of Europe was convened in 1948. This resulted in various new organisations in Europe—the relevant developments are discussed below.

4.6.1   Council of Europe

The Council of Europe is one of the premier organisations with an established system for not only monitoring international human rights but also ensuring the implementation of human rights. Human rights have long been at the forefront of the organisation.

Statute of the Council of Europe: Aims, Art 1

a   The aim of the Council of Europe is to achieve a greater unity between its members for the purpose of safeguarding and realising the ideals and principles which are their common heritage and facilitating their economic and social progress.

b   This aim shall be pursued through the organs of the Council by discussion of questions of common concern and by agreements and common action in economic, social, cultural, scientific, legal and administrative matters and in the maintenance and further realisation of human rights and fundamental freedoms.

c   Participation in the Council of Europe shall not affect the collaboration of its members in the work of the United Nations and of other international organisations or unions to which they are parties.

Note that protection of human rights is a fundamental requirement made by the Council of all Member States. Those States wishing to join must evidence their compliance with the rule of law and respect for human rights. Given that the Statute was adopted in May 1949, such a statement was fairly radical and, arguably, goes further than the comparable requirement of the United Nations.

Statute of the Council of Europe Art 3

Every member of the Council of Europe must accept the principles of the rule of law and of the enjoyment by all persons within its jurisdiction of human rights and fundamental freedoms, and collaborate sincerely and effectively in the realisation of the aim of the Council as specified in Chapter I.

The following bodies are most involved with human rights: the European Commissioner on Human Rights, the Committee of Ministers which has responsibility for the implementation of the judgments of the European Court and, established by the European Convention on Human Rights, the European Court of Human Rights and its Grand Chamber.

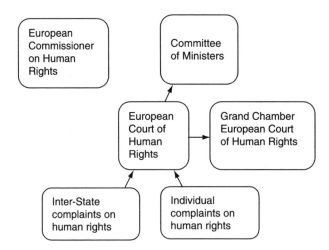

The European Court of Human Rights, as it is established in terms of the European Convention on Human Rights, is discussed in more detail in Chapter 6. The Court is thus treated as a conventional mechanism, being established in terms of, and limited in its powers by, the relevant treaty.

4.6.1.1   Committee of Ministers

Statute of the Council of Europe

Article 13

The Committee of Ministers is the organ which acts on behalf of the Council of Europe in accordance with Articles 15 and 16.

Article 14

Each member shall be entitled to one representative on the Committee of Ministers, and each representative shall be entitled to one vote. Representatives on the Committee shall be the Ministers for Foreign Affairs. When a Minister for Foreign Affairs is unable to be present or in other circumstances where it may be desirable, an alternate may be nominated to act for him, who shall, whenever possible, be a member of his government.

Article 15

a   On the recommendation of the Consultative Assembly or on its own initiative, the Committee of Ministers shall consider the action required to further the aim of the Council of Europe, including the conclusion of conventions or agreements and the adoption by governments of a common policy with regard to particular matters. Its conclusions shall be communicated to members by the Secretary-General.

b   In appropriate cases, the conclusions of the Committee may take the form of recommendations to the governments of members, and the Committee may request the governments of members to inform it of the action taken by them with regard to such recommendations. . . .

Article 17

The Committee of Ministers may set up advisory and technical committees or commissions for such specific purposes as it may deem desirable. . . .

Article 21

a   Unless the Committee decides otherwise, meetings of the Committee of Ministers shall be held:

i   in private, and

ii   at the seat of the Council.

b   The Committee shall determine what information shall be published regarding the conclusions and discussions of a meeting held in private.

c   The Committee shall meet before and during the beginning of every session of the Consultative Assembly and at such other times as it may decide.

In terms of human rights, the Committee of Ministers has primary responsibility for ensuring that the States comply with the judgments of the European Court of Human Rights.

European Convention on Human Rights Art 46

1   The High Contracting Parties undertake to abide by the final judgment of the Court in any case to which they are parties.

2   The final judgment of the Court shall be transmitted to the Committee of Ministers, which shall supervise its execution.

Moreover, the Committee has the right to ask the Court for an advisory opinion on any legal question concerning the Convention.

European Convention on Human Rights Art 47

1 The Court may, at the request of the Committee of Ministers, give advisory opinions on legal questions concerning the interpretation of the Convention and the protocols thereto.

2 Such opinions shall not deal with any question relating to the content or scope of the rights or freedoms defined in Section 1 of the Convention and the protocols thereto, or with any other question which the Court or the Committee of Ministers might have to consider in consequence of any such proceedings as could be instituted in accordance with the Convention.

4.6.1.2   European Commissioner on Human Rights

Note the mandate of the European Commissioner, as specified by the initiating resolution of the committee of Ministers.

Council of Europe Committee of Ministers Resolution 99/50 (1999)

Article 1

1. The Commissioner shall be a non-judicial institution to promote education in, awareness of and respect for human rights, as embodied in the human rights instruments of the Council of Europe.

2. The Commissioner shall respect the competence of, and perform functions other than those fulfilled by, the supervisory bodies set up under the European Convention of Human Rights or under other human rights instruments of the Council of Europe. The Commissioner shall not take up individual complaints.

Article 2

The Commissioner shall function independently and impartially.

Article 3

The Commissioner shall:

a.   promote education in and awareness of human rights in the member States;

b.   contribute to the promotion of the effective observance and full enjoyment of human rights in the member States;

c.   provide advice and information on the protection of human rights and prevention of human rights violations. When dealing with the public, the Commissioner shall, wherever possible, make use of and co-operate with human rights structures in the member States. Where such structures do not exist, the Commissioner will encourage their establishment;

d.   facilitate the activities of national ombudsmen or similar institutions in the field of human rights;

e.   identify possible shortcomings in the law and practice of member States concerning the compliance with human rights as embodied in the instruments of the Council of Europe, promote the effective implementation of these standards by member States and assist them, with their agreement, in their efforts to remedy such shortcomings;

f.   address, whenever the Commissioner deems it appropriate, a report concerning a specific matter to the Committee of Ministers or to the Parliamentary Assembly and the Committee of Ministers;

g.   respond, in the manner the Commissioner deems appropriate, to requests made by the Committee of Ministers or the Parliamentary Assembly, in the context of their task of ensuring compliance with the human rights standards of the Council of Europe;

h.   submit an annual report to the Committee of Ministers and the Parliamentary Assembly;

   i.   co-operate with other international institutions for the promotion and protection of human rights while avoiding unnecessary duplication of activities.

Article 4

The Commissioner shall take into account views expressed by the Committee of Ministers and the Parliamentary Assembly of the Council of Europe concerning the Commissioner's activities.

Article 5

1. The Commissioner may act on any information relevant to the Commissioner's functions. This will notably include information addressed to the Commissioner by governments, national parliaments, national ombudsmen or similar institutions in the field of human rights, individuals and organisations.

2. The gathering of information relevant to the Commissioner's functions shall not give rise to any general reporting system for member States.

Article 6

1. Member States shall facilitate the independent and effective performance by the Commissioner of his or her functions. In particular, they shall facilitate the Commissioner's contacts, including travel, in the context of the mission of the Commissioner and provide in good time information requested by the Commissioner.

2. The Commissioner shall be entitled, during the exercise of his or her functions, to the privileges and immunities provided for in Article 40 of the Statute of the Council of Europe and in the agreements made thereunder.

Article 7

The Commissioner may directly contact governments of member States of the Council of Europe.

Article 8

1. The Commissioner may issue recommendations, opinions and reports.

2. The Committee of Ministers may authorise the publication of any recommendation, opinion or report addressed to it.

Alvaro Gil-Robles is the first (and present) Commissioner; he was elected in 1999.

Note that certain changes are proposed in terms of Protocol Fourteen to the European Convention on Human Rights (not yet in force – ratification awaited). Art 13 of the new protocol seeks to amend the existing Art 36 of the Convention to the effect that the Commissioner may submit written comments or intervene in any case before a Chamber or Grand Chamber. The reality may prove that little changes as the Commissioner enjoys audience by invitation at present.

4.6.1.3 European Social Committee

Mention must also be made of the European Committee of Social Rights which oversees the implementation of the European Social Charter by a system of reports. The following extract details the bodies involved in reviewing State reports. Note that the text of the Charter has been subject to additional protocols and was completely revised and reopened for signature in 1996.

European Social Charter 1961

Article 25—Committee of Experts

1 The Committee of Experts shall consist of not more than seven members appointed by the Committee of Ministers from a list of independent experts of the highest integrity and of recognised competence in international social questions, nominated by the Contracting Parties.

2 The members of the committee shall be appointed for a period of six years. They may be reappointed. However, of the members first appointed, the terms of office of two members shall expire at the end of four years.

3 The members whose terms of office are to expire at the end of the initial period of four years shall be chosen by lot by the Committee of Ministers immediately after the first appointment has been made.

4 A member of the Committee of Experts appointed to replace a member whose term of office has not expired shall hold office for the remainder of his predecessor's term.

Article 26—Participation of the International Labour Organisation

The International Labour Organisation shall be invited to nominate a representative to participate in a consultative capacity in the deliberations of the Committee of Experts.

Article 27—Sub-committee of the Governmental Social Committee

1 The reports of the Contracting Parties and the conclusions of the Committee of Experts shall be submitted for examination to a sub-committee of the Governmental Social Committee of the Council of Europe.

2 The sub-committee shall be composed of one representative of each of the Contracting Parties. It shall invite no more than two international organisations of employers and no more than two international trade union organisations as it may designate to be represented as observers in a consultative capacity at its meetings. Moreover, it may consult no more than two representatives of international non-governmental organisations having consultative status with the Council of Europe, in respect of questions with which the organisations are particularly qualified to deal, such as social welfare, and the economic and social protection of the family.

3 The sub-committee shall present to the Committee of Ministers a report containing its conclusions and append the report of the Committee of Experts.

Article 28—Consultative Assembly

The Secretary-General of the Council of Europe shall transmit to the Consultative Assembly the conclusions of the Committee of Experts. The Consultative Assembly shall communicate its views on these conclusions to the Committee of Ministers.

Article 29—Committee of Ministers

By a majority of two-thirds of the members entitled to sit on the Committee, the Committee of Ministers may, on the basis of the report of the sub-committee, and after consultation with the Consultative Assembly, make to each Contracting Party any necessary recommendations.

An additional protocol on collective complaints was adopted in 1995. Provision is made in the revised Social Charter for its continuance, pursuant to States' approval.

Additional Protocol to the European Social Charter Providing for a System on Collective Complaints ETS 158, 1998

Article 1

The Contracting Parties to this Protocol recognise the right of the following organisations to submit complaints alleging unsatisfactory application of the Charter:

a   international organisations of employers and trade unions referred to in paragraph 2 of Article 27 of the Charter;

b   other international non-governmental organisations which have consultative status with the Council of Europe and have been put on a list established for this purpose by the Governmental Committee;

c   representative national organisations of employers and trade unions within the jurisdiction of the Contracting Party against which they have lodged a complaint.

Article 2

1   Any Contracting State may also, when it expresses its consent to be bound by this Protocol, in accordance with the provisions of Article 13, or at any moment thereafter, declare that it recognises the right of any other representative national non-governmental organisation within its jurisdiction which has particular competence in the matters governed by the Charter, to lodge complaints against it.

2   Such declarations may be made for a specific period.

3   The declarations shall be deposited with the Secretary-General of the Council of Europe who shall transmit copies thereof to the Contracting Parties and publish them.

Article 3

The international non-governmental organisations and the national non-governmental organisations referred to in Article 1.b and Article 2 respectively may submit complaints in accordance with the procedure prescribed by the aforesaid provisions only in respect of those matters regarding which they have been recognised as having particular competence. . . .

Article 10

The Contracting Party concerned shall provide information on the measures it has taken to give effect to the Committee of Ministers' recommendation, in the next report which it submits to the Secretary-General under Article 21 of the Charter.

4.6.2   Organisation of Security and Cooperation in Europe

The Organisation of Security and Cooperation in Europe is one of the major political achievements of the Cold War. Not only did States from both sides of the 'Iron Curtain' sit down together to discuss common aims, but human rights was high on the agenda from the outset. Admittedly, many areas of crucial importance reflecting a partial détente were also included—prior notification of military manoeuvres, for example.

Final Recommendations of the Helsinki Consultations 1973, Para 19

The reaffirmation, with such clarifications and additions as may be deemed desirable, and the precise statement, in conformity with the purposes and principles of the United Nations, of the following principles of primary significance guiding the mutual relations of the participating States, are deemed to be of particular importance:

- sovereign equality, respect for the rights inherent in sovereignty;

- refraining from the threat or use of force;

- inviolability of frontiers;

- territorial integrity of States;

- peaceful settlement of disputes;

- non-intervention in internal affairs;

- respect for human rights and fundamental freedoms, including the freedom of thought, conscience, religion or belief;
- equal rights and self-determination of peoples;
- co-operation among States;
- fulfilment in good faith of obligations under international law.

Final Act of the Helsinki Conference on Security and Cooperation in Europe 1979

VII. Respect for human rights and fundamental freedoms, including the freedom of thought, conscience, religion or belief

The participating States will respect human rights and fundamental freedoms, including the freedom of thought, conscience, religion or belief, for all without distinction as to race, sex, language or religion.

They will promote and encourage the effective exercise of civil, political, economic, social, cultural and other rights and freedoms all of which derive from the inherent dignity of the human person and are essential for his free and full development.

Within this framework the participating States will recognize and respect the freedom of the individual to profess and practice, alone or in community with others, religion or belief acting in accordance with the dictates of his own conscience.

The participating States on whose territory national minorities exist will respect the right of persons belonging to such minorities to equality before the law, will afford them the full opportunity for the actual enjoyment of human rights and fundamental freedoms and will, in this manner, protect their legitimate interests in this sphere.

The participating States recognize the universal significance of human rights and fundamental freedoms, respect for which is an essential factor for the peace, justice and well-being necessary to ensure the development of friendly relations and co-operation among themselves as among all States.

They will constantly respect these rights and freedoms in their mutual relations and will endeavour jointly and separately, including in co-operation with the United Nations, to promote universal and effective respect for them.

They confirm the right of the individual to know and act upon his rights and duties in this field.

In the field of human rights and fundamental freedoms, the participating States will act in conformity with the purposes and principles of the Charter of the United Nations and with the Universal Declaration of Human Rights. They will also fulfil their obligations as set forth in the international declarations and agreements in this field, including *inter alia* the International Covenants on Human Rights, by which they may be bound.

VIII. Equal rights and self-determination of peoples

The participating States will respect the equal rights of peoples and their right to self-determination, acting at all times in conformity with the purposes and principles of the Charter of the United Nations and with the relevant norms of international law, including those relating to territorial integrity of States.

By virtue of the principle of equal rights and self-determination of peoples, all peoples always have the right, in full freedom, to determine, when and as they wish, their internal and external political status, without external interference, and to pursue as they wish their political, economic, social and cultural development.

The participating States reaffirm the universal significance of respect for and effective exercise of equal rights and self-determination of peoples for the development of friendly relations among themselves as among all States; they also recall the importance of the elimination of any form of violation of this principle.

Further elaboration of the 'human dimension' appears in the text of the Copenhagen meeting a decade later. Note the emphasis on human rights.

Question

Is the year (1990) instructive in explaining why such a reinforcement of human rights was possible?

Document on the Copenhagen Meeting of the Conference on Human Dimension of the CSCE 1990, paras 1–5

(1) The participating States express their conviction that the protection and promotion of human rights and fundamental freedoms is one of the basic purposes of government, and reaffirm that the recognition of these rights and freedoms constitutes the foundation of freedom, justice and peace.

(2) They are determined to support and advance those principles of justice which form the basis of the rule of law. They consider that the rule of law does not mean merely a formal legality which assures regularity and consistency in the achievement and enforcement of democratic order, but justice based on the recognition and full acceptance of the supreme value of the human personality and guaranteed by institutions providing a framework for its fullest expression.

(3) They reaffirm that democracy is an inherent element of the rule of law. They recognize the importance of pluralism with regard to political organizations.

(4) They confirm that they will respect each other's right freely to choose and develop, in accordance with international human rights standards, their political, social, economic and cultural systems. In exercising this right, they will ensure that their laws, regulations, practices and policies conform with their obligations under international law and are brought into harmony with the provisions of the Declaration on Principles and other CSCE commitments.

(5) They solemnly declare that among those elements of justice which are essential to the full expression of the inherent dignity and of the equal and inalienable rights of all human beings are the following:

(5.1) —free elections that will be held at reasonable intervals by secret ballot or by equivalent free voting procedure, under conditions which ensure in practice the free expression of the opinion of the electors in the choice of their representatives;

(5.2) —a form of government that is representative in character, in which the executive is accountable to the elected legislature or the electorate;

(5.3) —the duty of the government and public authorities to comply with the constitution and to act in a manner consistent with law;

(5.4) —a clear separation between the State and political parties; in particular, political parties will not be merged with the State;

(5.5) —the activity of the government and the administration as well as that of the judiciary will be exercised in accordance with the system established by law. Respect for that system must be ensured;

(5.6) —military forces and the police will be under the control of, and accountable to, the civil authorities;

(5.7) —human rights and fundamental freedoms will be guaranteed by law and in accordance with their obligations under international law;

(5.8) —legislation, adopted at the end of a public procedure, and regulations will be published, that being the condition for their applicability. Those texts will be accessible to everyone;

(5.9) —all persons are equal before the law and are entitled without any discrimination to the equal protection of the law. In this respect, the law will prohibit any discrimination and guarantee to all persons equal and effective protection against discrimination on any ground;

(5.10) —everyone will have an effective means of redress against administrative decisions, so as to guarantee respect for fundamental rights and ensure legal integrity;

(5.11) —administrative decisions against a person must be fully justifiable and must as a rule indicate the usual remedies available;

(5.12) —the independence of judges and the impartial operation of the public judicial service will be ensured;

(5.13) —the independence of legal practitioners will be recognized and protected, in particular as regards conditions for recruitment and practice;

(5.14) —the rules relating to criminal procedure will contain a clear definition of powers in relation to prosecution and the measures preceding and accompanying prosecution;

(5.15) —any person arrested or detained on a criminal charge will have the right, so that the lawfulness of his arrest or detention can be decided, to be brought promptly before a judge or other officer authorized by law to exercise this function;

(5.16) —in the determination of any criminal charge against him, or of his rights and obligations in a suit at law, everyone will be entitled to a fair and public hearing by a competent, independent and impartial tribunal established by law;

(5.17) —any person prosecuted will have the right to defend himself in person or through prompt legal assistance of his own choosing or, if he does not have sufficient means to pay for legal assistance, to be given it free when the interests of justice so require;

(5.18) —no one will be charged with, tried for or convicted of any criminal offence unless the offence is provided for by a law which defines the elements of the offence with clarity and precision;

(5.19) —everyone will be presumed innocent until proved guilty according to law;

(5.20) —considering the important contribution of international instruments in the field of human rights to the rule of law at a national level, the participating States reaffirm that they will consider acceding to the International Covenant on Civil and Political Rights, the International Covenant on Economic, Social and Cultural Rights and other relevant international instruments, if they have not yet done so;

(5.21) —in order to supplement domestic remedies and better to ensure that the participating States respect the international obligations they have undertaken, the participating States will consider acceding to a regional or global international convention concerning the protection of human rights, such as the European Convention on Human Rights or the Optional Protocol to the International Covenant on Civil and Political Rights, which provide for procedures of individual recourse to international bodies.

Charter of Paris for A New Europe 1990
Human Rights, Democracy and Rule of Law

We undertake to build, consolidate and strengthen democracy as the only system of government of our nations. In this endeavour, we will abide by the following:

Human rights and fundamental freedoms are the birthright of all human beings, are inalienable and are guaranteed by law. Their protection and promotion is the first responsibility of government.

Respect for them is an essential safeguard against an over-mighty State. Their observance and full exercise are the foundation of freedom, justice and peace.

Democratic government is based on the will of the people, expressed regularly through free and fair elections. Democracy has as its foundation respect for the human person and the rule of law. Democracy is the best safeguard of freedom of expression, tolerance of all groups of society, and equality of opportunity for each person.

Democracy, with its representative and pluralist character, entails accountability to the electorate, the obligation of public authorities to comply with the law and justice administered impartially. No one will be above the law.

We affirm that, without discrimination,

every individual has the right to freedom of thought, conscience and religion or belief,

freedom of expression,

freedom of association and peaceful assembly,

freedom of movement;

no one will be:

subject to arbitrary arrest or detention,

subject to torture or other cruel, inhuman or degrading treatment or punishment;

everyone also has the right:

to know and act upon his rights,

to participate in free and fair elections,

to fair and public trial if charged with an offence,

to own property alone or in association and to exercise individual enterprise,

to enjoy his economic, social and cultural rights.

We affirm that the ethnic, cultural, linguistic and religious identity of national minorities will be protected and that persons belonging to national minorities have the right freely to express, preserve and develop that identity without any discrimination and in full equality before the law.

We will ensure that everyone will enjoy recourse to effective remedies, national or international, against any violation of his rights.

Full respect for these precepts is the bedrock on which we will seek to construct the new Europe.

Our States will co-operate and support each other with the aim of making democratic gains irreversible.

The Human Dimension of the OSCE, however, has burgeoned into an active system for promoting human rights and advancing democracy and minority rights in Europe. The following diagram schematically represents the main bodies involved with human rights.

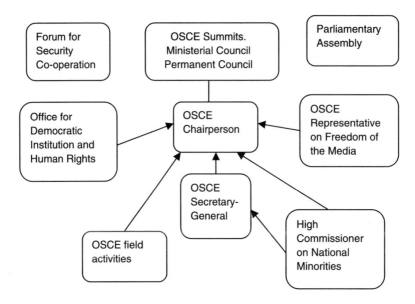

4.6.2.1   Office for Democratic Institutions and Human Rights

The office for Democratic Institutions and Human Rights is a specialised institution of the OSCE dealing with various issues of concern to human rights. It oversees the democratisation of states, assisting in electoral reform and monitoring electoral processes. It assists States in developing appropriate mechanisms for implementing human rights and anti-terrorism obligations and all elements of the human dimension of the OSCE (see above). Concerning specific groups of concern to the OSCE, the Office also acts as the main focal point of integrationist activities for the Sinti and Roma peoples.

4.6.2.2   Representative on Freedom of the Media

Elements of human rights are also addressed by the Representative on Freedom of the Media.

Permanent Council decision No. 193, paras 2 and 3

2. Based on OSCE principles and commitments, the OSCE Representative on Freedom of the Media will observe relevant media developments in all participating States and will, on this basis, and in close co-ordination with the Chairman-in-Office, advocate and promote full compliance with OSCE principles and commitments regarding freedom of expression and free media. In this respect he or she will assume an early-warning function. He or she will address serious problems caused by, *inter alia*, obstruction of media activities and unfavourable working conditions for journalists. He or she will closely co-operate with the participating States, the Permanent Council, the Office for Democratic Institutions and Human Rights (ODIHR), the High Commissioner on National Minorities and, where appropriate, other OSCE bodies, as well as with national and international media associations.

3. The OSCE Representative on Freedom of the Media will concentrate, as outlined in this paragraph, on rapid response to serious non-compliance with OSCE principles and commitments by participating States in respect of freedom of expression and free media. In the case of an allegation of serious non-compliance therewith, the OSCE Representative on Freedom of the

Media will seek direct contacts, in an appropriate manner, with the participating State and with other parties concerned, assess the facts, assist the participating State, and contribute to the resolution of the issue. He or she will keep the Chairman-in-Office informed about his or her activities and report to the Permanent Council on their results, and on his or her observations and recommendations.

4.6.2.3   High Commissioner for National Minorities

The High Commissioner's role is to provide early warning and take appropriate early action to diffuse national tensions and assist preventing the escalating of tension. His mandate is drawn from the Helsinki Document of 1992. Extracts as below.

CSCE Helsinki Document 1992, The Challenges of Change
CSCE HIGH COMMISSIONER ON NATIONAL MINORITIES

(1) The participating States decide to establish a High Commissioner on National Minorities.

Mandate

(2) The High Commissioner will act under the aegis of the CSO and will thus be an instrument of conflict prevention at the earliest possible stage.

(3) The High Commissioner will provide 'early warning' and, as appropriate, 'early action' at the earliest possible stage in regard to tensions involving national minority issues which have not yet developed beyond an early warning stage, but, in the judgement of the High Commissioner, have the potential to develop into a conflict within the CSCE area, affecting peace, stability or relations between participating States, requiring the attention of and action by the Council or the CSO.

(4) Within the mandate, based on CSCE principles and commitments, the High Commissioner will work in confidence and will act independently of all parties directly involved in the tensions.

(5a) The High Commissioner will consider national minority issues occurring in the State of which the High Commissioner is a national or a resident, or involving a national minority to which the High Commissioner belongs, only if all parties directly involved agree, including the State concerned.

(5b) The High Commissioner will not consider national minority issues in situations involving organized acts of terrorism.

(5c) Nor will the High Commissioner consider violations of CSCE commitments with regard to an individual person belonging to a national minority.

(6) In considering a situation, the High Commissioner will take fully into account the availability of democratic means and international instruments to respond to it, and their utilization by the parties involved.

(7) When a particular national minority issue has been brought to the attention of the CSO, the involvement of the High Commissioner will require a request and a specific mandate from the CSO.

Profile, appointment, support

(8) The High Commissioner will be an eminent international personality with long-standing relevant experience from whom an impartial performance of the function may be expected.

(9) The High Commissioner will be appointed by the Council by consensus upon the recommendation of the CSO for a period of three years, which may be extended for one further term of three years only.

(10)   The High Commissioner will draw upon the facilities of the ODIHR in Warsaw, and in particular upon the information relevant to all aspects of national minority questions available at the ODIHR.

Early warning

(11)   The High Commissioner will:

(11a) collect and receive information regarding national minority issues from sources described below (see Supplement paragraphs (23)–(25));

(11b) assess at the earliest possible stage the role of the parties directly concerned, the nature of the tensions and recent developments therein and, where possible, the potential consequences for peace and stability within the CSCE area;

(11c) to this end, be able to pay a visit, in accordance with paragraph (17) and Supplement paragraphs (27)–(30), to any participating State and communicate in person, subject to the provisions of paragraph (25), with parties directly concerned to obtain first-hand information about the situation of national minorities.

(12)   The High Commissioner may during a visit to a participating State, while obtaining first-hand information from all parties directly involved, discuss the questions with the parties, and where appropriate promote dialogue, confidence and co-operation between them.

Provision of early warning

(13)   If, on the basis of exchanges of communications and contacts with relevant parties, the High Commissioner concludes that there is a *prima facie* risk of potential conflict (as set out in paragraph (3)) he/she may issue an early warning, which will be communicated promptly by the Chairman-in-Office to the CSO.

(14)   The Chairman-in-Office will include this early warning in the agenda for the next meeting of the CSO. If a State believes that such an early warning merits prompt consultation, it may initiate the procedure set out in Annex 2 of the Summary of Conclusions of the Berlin Meeting of the Council ('Emergency Mechanism').

(15)   The High Commissioner will explain to the CSO the reasons for issuing the early warning.

Early action

(16)   The High Commissioner may recommend that he/she be authorized to enter into further contact and closer consultations with the parties concerned with a view to possible solutions, according to a mandate to be decided by the CSO. The CSO may decide accordingly.

Accountability

(17)   The High Commissioner will consult the Chairman-in-Office prior to a departure for a participating State to address a tension involving national minorities. The Chairman-in-Office will consult, in confidence, the participating State(s) concerned and may consult more widely.

(18)   After a visit to a participating State, the High Commissioner will provide strictly confidential reports to the Chairman-in-Office on the findings and progress of the High Commissioner's involvement in a particular question.

(19)   After termination of the involvement of the High Commissioner in a particular issue, the High Commissioner will report to the Chairman-in-Office on the findings, results and conclusions. Within a period of one month, the Chairman-in-Office will consult, in confidence, on the findings, results and conclusions the participating State(s) concerned and may consult more widely. Thereafter the report, together with possible comments, will be transmitted to the CSO.

Question

How effective is the system likely to be? What are its advantages?

4.6.2.4 Field activities

The OSCE undertakes a wide variety of field activities in furtherance of its key objectives. It runs many field offices throughout eastern and central Europe.

4.6.3 European Union

While the initial objective of the European Union was to rebuild the decimated economies of the region (European Coal and Steel Community, European Economic
Community, European Atomic Energy Community), as the communities developed
ever more areas encroached upon their competencies. Today, the new European
Union enjoys a wide range of responsibilities and competencies. Alongside this has
developed recognition of the importance of human rights. Indeed the European
Union now has agreed a Charter of Fundamental Rights which reaffirms the organisation's commitment to universal human rights.

The European Union has five main institutions, four of which (see diagram) are
involved with elements of human rights (the Court of Auditors is omitted). Decision-
making in the European Union is undertaken by the Council, Commission and Parliament. The Court has the power to consider actions against all three institutions in
certain circumstances. The Court also has competency to hear certain actions brought
by the Commission against States failing to correctly implement Community law and
can hear certain individual actions (usually staff cases). In addition, the Court has an
advisory jurisdiction (preliminary rulings) and can assist national courts in interpreting and applying Community law. For further information, regard should be had to
the Consolidated Version of the Treaty Establishing the European Community. It
should be noted that the composition of the aforementioned bodies and certain

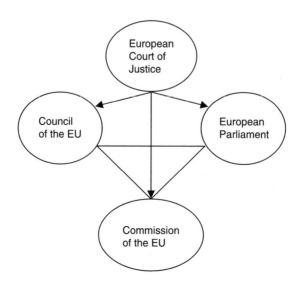

elements of procedures will be affected by the provisions of the Constitution. The Constitution is currently tabled before States. However, it has already been rejected by some member States and thus the process of internal reform has effectively stalled.

With a primarily economic remit, most of the 'human rights' impact of the Union is in the area of discrimination, particularly in employment. However, the Union has contributed considerably to the concept of sex discrimination, discrimination on national origin and associated rights. In this respect, there may occasionally be an overlap (reinforcement) of the work of the International Labour Organisation.

Note Protocol 14 to the European Convention on Human Rights.

Protocol 14 to the European Convention on Human Rights Art 17

Article 59 of the Convention shall be amended as follows:

1 A new paragraph 2 shall be inserted which shall read as follows:

'2 The European Union may accede to this Convention.'

2 Paragraphs 2, 3 and 4 shall become paragraphs 3, 4 and 5 respectively.

This clarifies a long-running academic debate on whether or not accession is possible.

Irrespective of the status of the Council of Europe's European Convention under the jurisdiction of the European Court of Justice and the European Union, considerable advancements have been made towards securing human rights within the Union. The Fundamental Charter on Rights was adopted at the Nice Summit and will form part of the overall Constitution of the European Union (should the Constitution be adopted—at the time of writing the process of ratification seems stalled following 'no' referenda in various States early in 2005). With a proclaimed goal of guiding the institutions of the Union, the impact of the Charter will nevertheless be felt.

4.7   THE AMERICAS

4.7.1   Organisation of American States

Much of the human rights work of the Organisation of American States is undertaken by institutions established to oversee the Inter-American Convention on Human Rights. These are thus discussed in Chapter 6. However, other bodies have roles which impact, at times significantly, on human rights. Most notable is the Inter-American Commission on Human Rights.

Inter-American Commission on Human Rights

The Inter-American Commission operates independently of the American Convention on Human Rights. However the Commission also has responsibilities under the Convention. This gives rise to dual jurisdiction, almost overlapping, albeit complementary, functions. However, it also extends the protection of human rights beyond those States which have accepted the American Convention and, indeed, the distinct category within that of those States which have accepted the compulsory jurisdiction of the Court. The potential for individual petitions through to the Court, as a treaty-based mechanism, is discussed in Chapter 6.

The United States of America has not accepted the jurisdiction of the Inter-American Court to hear complaints of violations of human rights. However, as the country is a member of the Organisation, the Commission has jurisdiction to investigate abuses of human rights, albeit it primarily in accordance with the general American Declaration on the Rights and Duties of Man. See, for example, *Mary and Carrie Dann v United States of America*, Report No 75/02 (2002) whereby the petitioners claimed that various rights under the American Declaration on the Rights and Duties of Man had been infringed.

The following diagram outlines the procedure for bringing a complaint before the Inter-American Commission (see also Chapter 5).

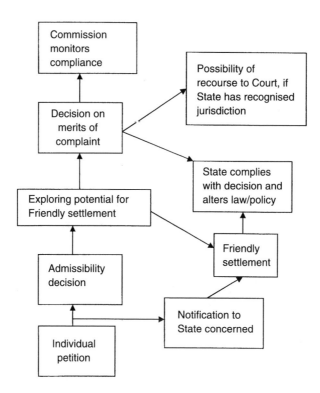

4.8   AFRICA

4.8.1   African Union

The African Union was launched by the 2002 Durban Summit, of the then Organisation of African Unity. Interim arrangements remain in place at present to assist in the transition from Organisation to Union.

The African Union now comprises various organs: the Assembly; the Executive Council; the Pan-African Parliament; the African Court of Justice; the Commission; the Permanent Representatives Committee; the Specialized Technical Committee; the Economic Social and Cultural Council; the Peace and Security Council and various financial institutions. Most of these institutions are in the early stages of operation at present. Their impact on human rights remains to be seen.

4.9 OTHERS

No other region has achieved comprehensive human rights guarantees and enforcement/monitoring mechanisms.

4.9.1 Commonwealth of Independent States

The Commonwealth of Independent States did not wait long before adopting a Convention on Human Rights and Fundamental Freedoms. The Convention envisaged a Court to monitor compliance. However, as some commentators note, a major goal of the system was to assist with the democratisation of member States and to help them establish sufficient democratic credibility for membership applications to the Council of Europe.

Question

Note the terms of the Commonwealth's Convention on Human Rights—to what extent do the rights and freedoms vary from those enshrined in the European Convention on Human Rights to which members of the Commonwealth of Independent States are now party?

4.9.2 Arab League

Although the Arab League has succeeded in drafting a regional instrument on international human rights, achieving support for the instrument and any enforcement or monitoring machinery has been more problematic. At present, the Arab system is undergoing reform.

Within the Arab League system, many issues of cultural relativism of rights and freedoms could be addressed. As is discussed elsewhere in this text, many States which adhere to Islamic teaching and laws enter a number of reservations to international human rights treaties containing, *inter alia*, family rights and equal rights for women in marriage. Creating a specific Arab-based system has clear potential.

4.9.3 Asia

To date, no specific organisation or mechanism for guaranteeing the protection of human rights has emerged in Asia.

FURTHER READING

Badawi-el-Sheikh, I, 'The African Commission on Human and Peoples' Rights: Prospects and Problems' (1989) 7.3 Netherlands Quarterly of Human Rights 272

Benedek, W, 'The African Charter and Commission on Human and Peoples' Rights' (1993) 11 Netherlands Quarterly of Human Rights 25

Buergenthal, T, Norris, R, and Shelton, D, *Protecting Human Rights in the Americas*, 3rd edn, 1990, Arlington: Engel

Cerna, C, 'The Inter-American Commission of Human Rights' in Smith, R, and Van den Anker, C (eds), *The Essentials of Human Rights*, 2005, London: Hodder Arnold, pp 180–185

Davidson, S, *The Inter-American Human Rights System*, 1997, Dartmouth: Aldershot

Hanski, R, and Suksi, M (eds), *An Introduction to the International Protection of Human Rights*, 2nd edn, 1999, Turku/Abo: Abo Akademi

Harris, D, and Livingstone, S, *The Inter-American System of Human Rights*, 1998, Oxford: OUP

Lempinen, M, *Challenges facing the system of special procedures of the United Nations Commission on Human Rights*, 2001, Turku/Abo: Abo Akademi

Shelton, D, *Remedies in International Human Rights Law*, 1999, Oxford: OUP

Swepston, L, 'The International Labour Organization's System of Human Rights Protection' in Symonides, J (ed), *Human Rights: International Protection, Monitoring, Enforcement*, 2003, Aldershot/Burlington, VT: Ashgate/UNESCO, pp 91–109

Symonides, J (ed), *Human Rights: International Protection, Monitoring, Enforcement*, 2003, Aldershot/Burlington, VT: Ashgate/UNESCO.

Tomasevski, K, 'Sanctions and Human Rights', in Symonides, J (ed), *Human Rights: International Protection, Monitoring, Enforcement*, 2003, Aldershot/Burlington, VT: Ashgate/UNESCO, pp 303–323

Websites

www.un.org—United Nations

www.ohchr.int—Office of the High Commissioner for Human Rights

www.icj-cij.org—International Court of Justice

www.ict-cpi.int—International Criminal Court

www.coe.int—Council of Europe

www.europa.eu—European Union

www.osce.org—Organisation for Security and Cooperation in Europe

www.osce.org/odihr/—OSCE Office for Democratic Institutions and Human Rights

www.osce.org/fom/—OSCE Representative on Freedom of the Media

www.osce.org/hcnm/—OSCE High Commissioner on National Minorities

www.oas.org—Organisation of American States

www.cidh.org/—Inter-American Commission on Human Rights

www.africa-union.org—African Union

www.arableagueonline.org—League of Arab States

CHAPTER 5

IMPLEMENTING INTERNATIONAL HUMAN RIGHTS LAW

Creating tabulations of international human rights law remains a significant achievement of both regional and international systems. However, the success of such treaties and other instruments can best be gauged by the extent to which States modify their behaviour and conform to the standards set. In other words, it is the extent to which individuals enjoy respect for their fundamental rights and freedoms in an environment which promotes and protects international human rights. There are two principal systems for implementing international human rights norms: the procedures available generally under the international and regional bodies and the procedures which are only available as a result of ratification of one or more of the major international or regional human rights instruments. This chapter will focus on those systems operating outwith the principal specific international human rights instruments, that is, those systems which are generally available to everyone within the relevant territories. The next chapter looks at the systems established by the various international human rights treaties.

What are the general systems for monitoring human rights? The Human Rights Council and UNESCO both have systems for reviewing complaints against States, irrespective of their international human rights obligations. Naturally, the Security Council of the United Nations, with its primary obligation to maintain peace and order, may also take action when peace is threatened by flagrant violations of human rights. These powers of the Security Council transcend the international human rights instruments and can be applied to all member States of the United Nations. Moving to regional arrangements, some regional systems, particularly in the Americas, have investigative systems for violations of human rights, irrespective of ratification of the principal regional conventions. Finally, a brief look at International Criminal Law completes this chapter. In terms of international criminal law, perpetrators of designated war crimes and crimes against humanity, naturally involving violations of human rights, can be held to account.

5.1 HUMAN RIGHTS COUNCIL

The Human Rights Council was created in 2006. It assumes the competencies of the former Commission on Human Rights which held its last meeting in March 2006. It enjoys a general mandate to address human rights issues. However, its predecessor, the Commission on Human Rights, primarily focused on standard-setting, drafting international human rights instruments and forging agreements on the parameters of human rights obligations. From the Universal Declaration on Human Rights to the Draft Convention on Indigenous Peoples' Rights, the Commission frequently spearheaded advancements on standard-setting. Arguably, some of the instruments drafted by the Commission, in themselves, represent a response to violations on human rights.

Question

Look at a list of international human rights instruments. Consider the relevant political climate in which they were drafted. Has the Commission been proactive or reactive?

In 1947, the Commission opined that it had no power to take action in regard to any human rights complaints. This was agreed by Economic and Social Council. Considerable progress has been made since then.

Economic and Social Council Resolution 728 F (XXVIII) 1959

The Economic and Social Council,

Having considered chapter V of the report of the Commission on Human Rights on its first session, concerning communications, and chapter IX of the report of the Commission on its fifteenth session,

1. *Approves* the statement that the Commission on Human Rights recognizes that it has no power to take any action in regard to any complaints concerning human rights.

In 1959, the Economic and Social Council approved a Commission statement that it had no power to take any action in regard to complaints concerning human rights (Resolution 728 F (XXVIII)). It then requested the Secretary-General to assume responsibility for disseminating communications concerning violations of human rights and fundamental freedoms.

Economic and Social Council Resolution 728 F (XXVIII) 1959, Communications concerning human rights

The Economic and Social Council, . . .

2. *Requests* the Secretary-General:

(a) To compile and distribute to members of the Commission on Human Rights before each session a non-confidential list containing a brief indication of the substance of each communication, however addressed, which deals with the principles involved in the promotion of universal respect for, and observance of, human rights and to divulge the identity of the authors of such communications unless they indicate that they wish their names to remain confidential;

(b) To compile before each session of the Commission a confidential list containing a brief indication of the substance of other communications concerning human rights, however addressed, and to furnish this list to members of the Commission, in private meeting, without divulging the identity of the authors of communications except in cases where the authors state that they have already divulged or intend to divulge their names or that they have no objection to their names being divulged;

(c) To enable members of the Commission, upon request, to consult the originals of communications dealing with the principles involved in the promotion of universal respect for, and observance of, human rights;

(d) To inform the writers of all communications concerning human rights, however addressed, that their communications will be handled in accordance with this resolution, indicating that the Commission has no power to take any action in regard to any complaint concerning human rights;

(e) To furnish each Member State concerned with a copy of any communication concerning human rights which refers explicitly to that State or to territories under its jurisdiction, without divulging the identity of the author, except as provided for in sub-paragraph (b) above;

(f) To ask Governments sending replies to communications brought to their attention in accordance with sub-paragraph (e) whether they wish their replies to be presented to the Commission in summary form or in full.

The same provisions extend to the Sub-Commission on Prevention of Discrimination and Protection of Minorities should the communication relate to areas within its competence. An *ad hoc* committee of the Commission may elect to review communications in advance of its session, in order to determine which communications will apply (para 2(c) (extracted above)).

This however, was not the end of the matter. More substantial powers were given to the Commission in light of information evidencing gross and systematic violations of rights in certain African territories. This emerged into a confidential system for examining complaints, which exists in terms of Resolution 1503, with further elucidation and streamlining in Resolution 2000/3. Additionally, Thematic or Special Rapporteurs may be appointed to examine specific violations. General Assembly Resolution 60/251 confirms that the Human Rights Council continues the work of the Commission in examining complaints and appointing rapporteurs.

5.1.1   Gross and systematic violations: 1235 and 103 procedures

Since 1967 the Commission has had certain powers, indeed responsibilities, to investigate serious violations of human rights. However, the procedure is not akin to a judicial investigation. Rather, it is a facility for achieving an overview of a deteriorating and serious human rights situation in a particular State. The system was first devised as a response to prominent violations of human rights in certain areas.

Economic and Social Council Resolution 1235 (XLII) 1967, Question of the violation of human rights and fundamental freedoms, including policies of racial discrimination and segregation and of apartheid, in all countries, with particular reference to colonial and other dependent countries and territories

The Economic and Social Council, noting resolutions 8(XXIII) and 9(XXIII) of the Commission on Human Rights,

1. Welcomes the decision of the Commission on Human Rights to give annual consideration to the item entitled 'Question of the violation of human rights and fundamental freedoms, including policies of racial discrimination and segregation and of apartheid, in all countries, with particular reference to colonial and other dependent countries and territories', without prejudice to the functions and powers of organs already in existence or which may be established within the framework of measures of implementation included in international covenants and conventions on the protection of human rights and fundamental freedoms, and concurs with the requests for assistance addressed to the Sub-Commission on Prevention of Discrimination and Protection of Minorities and to the Secretary-General;

2. Authorises the Commission on Human Rights and the Sub-Commission on Prevention of Discrimination and Protection of Minorities, in conformity with the provisions of paragraph 1 of the Commission's resolution 8(XXIII), to examine information relevant to gross violations of human rights and fundamental freedoms, as exemplified by the policy of apartheid as practised in the Republic of South Africa and the Territory of South West Africa under the direct responsibility of the United Nations and now illegally occupied by the Government of South Africa, and to racial discrimination as practised notably in Southern Rhodesia, contained in the communications listed by the Secretary-General pursuant to Economic and Social Council Resolution 728 F (XXVIII) of 30 July 1959;

3. Decides that the Commission on Human Rights may, in appropriate cases, and after careful consideration of the information this made available to it, in conformity with the provisions of paragraph 1 above, make a thorough study of situations which reveal a consistent pattern of violations of human rights, as exemplified by the policy of apartheid as practised in the Republic of South Africa and the Territory of South West Africa under the direct responsibility of the United

Nations and now illegally occupied by the Government of South Africa, and to racial discrimination as practised notably in Southern Rhodesia, and report, with recommendations thereon, to the Economic and Social Council;

4. Decides to review the provisions of paragraphs 2 and 3 of the present resolution after the entry into force of the International Covenants on Human Rights;

5. Takes note of the fact that the Commission on Human Rights, in its resolution 6 (XXIII), has instructed an *ad hoc* study group to study in all its aspects the question of the ways and means by which the Commission might be enabled or assisted to discharge functions in relation to violations of human rights and fundamental freedoms, whilst maintaining and fulfilling its other functions.

6. Requests the Commission on Human Rights to report to it on the result of this study after having given consideration to the conclusions of the *ad hoc* study group referred to in paragraph 5 above.

It would appear that the initial emphasis was on empowering the Commission to monitor the human rights situation in South Africa, Southern Rhodesia (now Zimbabwe) and South West Africa (now Namibia), three territories giving rise to increasing concern in the 1960s. Commission powers were viewed as complementary to those of the treaty monitoring bodies and indeed, the other organs of the United Nations organisation: the General Assembly or, more likely, the Security Council. In many ways, this system is part of the tools by which the Commission discharged its primary functions in terms of its mandate.

Economic and Social Council Resolution 1503 (XLVIII), Procedure for dealing with communications relating to violations of human rights and fundamental freedoms

The Economic and Social Council, noting resolutions 7 (XXVI) and 17 (XXV) of the Commission on Human Rights and resolution 2 (XXI) of the Sub-Commission on Prevention of Discrimination and Protection of Minorities,

1. *Authorizes* the Sub-Commission on Prevention of Discrimination and Protection of Minorities to appoint a working group consisting of not more than twenty-five members, with due regard to geographical distribution, to meet once a year in private meetings for a period not exceeding ten days immediately before the sessions of the Sub-Commission to consider all communications, including replies of Governments thereon, received by the Secretary-General under Council resolution 728 F (XXVIII) of 30 July 1959 with a view to bringing to the attention of the Sub-Commission those communications, together with replies of Governments, if any, which appear to reveal a consistent pattern of gross and reliably attested violations of human rights and fundamental freedoms within the terms of reference of the Sub-Commission;

2. *Decides* that the Sub-Commission on Prevention of Discrimination and Protection of Minorities should, as the first step in the implementation of the present resolution, devise at its twenty-third session appropriate procedures for dealing with the question of admissibility of communications received by the Secretary-General under Council resolution 728 F (XXVIII) and in accordance with Council resolution 1235 (XLII) of 6 June 1967;

3. *Requests* the Secretary-General to prepare a document on the question of admissibility of communications for the Sub-Commission's consideration at its twenty-third session;

4. *Further requests* the Secretary-General:

    (a) To furnish to the members of the Sub-Commission every month a list of communications prepared by him in accordance with Council resolution 728 F (XXVIII) and a brief description of them together with the text of any replies received from Governments;

(b) To make available to the members of the working group at their meetings the originals of such communications listed as they may request, having due regard to the provisions of paragraph 2(b) of Council resolution 728 F (XXVIII) concerning the divulging of the identity of the authors of communications;

(c) To circulate to the members of the Sub-Commission, in the working languages, the originals of such communications as are referred to the Sub-Commission by the working group;

5. Requests the Sub-Commission on Prevention of Discrimination and Protection of Minorities to consider in private meetings, in accordance with paragraph 1 above, the communications brought before it in accordance with the decision of a majority of the members of the working group and any replies of Governments relating thereto and other relevant information, with a view to determining whether to refer to the Commission on Human Rights particular situations which appear to reveal a consistent pattern of gross and reliably attested violations of human rights requiring consideration by the Commission;

6. Requests the Commission on Human Rights after it has examined any situation referred to it by the Sub-Commission to determine:

(a) Whether it requires a thorough study by the Commission and a report and recommendations thereon to the Council in accordance with paragraph 3 of Council resolution 1235 (XLII);

(b) Whether it may be a subject of an investigation by an *ad hoc* committee to be appointed by the Commission which shall be undertaken only with the express consent of the State concerned and shall be conducted in constant co-operation with that State and under conditions determined by agreement with it. In any event, the investigation may be undertaken only if:

   (i) All available means at the national level have been resorted to and exhausted;

   (ii) The situation does not relate to a matter which is being dealt with under other procedures prescribed in the constituent instruments of, or conventions adopted by, the United Nations and the specialized agencies, or in regional conventions, or which the State concerned wishes to submit to other procedures in accordance with general or special international agreements to which it is a party;

7. Decides that if the Commission on Human Rights appoints an *ad hoc* committee to carry on an investigation with the consent of the State concerned:

(a) The composition of the committee shall be determined by the Commission. The members of the committee shall be independent persons whose competence and impartiality is beyond question. Their appointment shall be subject to the consent of the Government concerned;

(b) The committee shall establish its own rules of procedure. It shall be subject to the quorum rule. It shall have authority to receive communications and hear witnesses, as necessary. The investigation shall be conducted in co-operation with the Government concerned;

(c) The committee's procedure shall be confidential, its proceedings shall be conducted in private meetings and its communications shall not be publicized in any way;

(d) The committee shall strive for friendly solutions before, during and even after the investigation;

(e) The committee shall report to the Commission on Human Rights with such observations and suggestions as it may deem appropriate;

8. Decides that all actions envisaged in the implementation of the present resolution by the Sub-Commission on Prevention of Discrimination and Protection of Minorities or the

Commission on Human Rights shall remain confidential until such time as the Commission may decide to make recommendations to the Economic and Social Council;

9. Decides to authorize the Secretary-General to provide all facilities which may be required to carry out the present resolution, making use of the existing staff of the Division of Human Rights of the United Nations Secretariat;

10. *Decides* that the procedure set out in the present resolution for dealing with communications relating to violations of human rights and fundamental freedoms should be reviewed if any new organ entitled to deal with such communications should be established within the United Nations or by international agreement.

Question

Some commentators argue that the confidentiality element allows violations of human rights to be 'swept under the carpet'. Does it? Contrast this with the more transparent process before the treaty monitoring bodies, a system also open to frequent criticism despite being more 'public'.

The Sub-Commission on Prevention of Discrimination and Protection of Minorities adopted guidelines on the admissibility criteria to be deployed in the 1503 procedure.

Sub-Commission on Prevention of Discrimination and Protection of Minorities, Resolution I (XXIV), UN Doc. E/CN.4/1070 (1971)

The Sub-Commission on Prevention of Discrimination and Protection of Minorities

Considering that the Economic and Social Council, by its resolution 1503 (XLVIII), decided that the Sub-Commission should devise appropriate procedures for dealing with the question of admissibility of communications received by the Secretary-General under Council resolution 728 F (XXVIII) of 30 July 1959 and in accordance with Council resolution 1235 (XLII) of 6 June 1967,

Adopts the following provisional procedures for dealing with the question of admissibility of communications referred to above:

(1) *Standards and criteria*

(a) The object of the communication must not be inconsistent with the relevant principles of the Charter, of the Universal Declaration of Human Rights and of the other applicable instruments in the field of human rights.

(b) Communications shall be admissible only if, after consideration thereof, together with the replies of any of the Governments concerned, there are reasonable grounds to believe that they may reveal a consistent pattern of gross and reliably attested violations of human rights and fundamental freedoms, including policies of racial discrimination and segregation and of *apartheid* in any country, including colonial and other dependent countries and peoples.

(2) *Source of communications*

(a) Admissible communications may originate from a person or group of persons, who, it can be reasonably presumed, are victims of the violations referred to in subparagraph (1) (b) above, any person or group of persons who have direct and reliable knowledge of those violations, or non-governmental organizations acting in good faith in accordance with recognized principles of human rights, not resorting to politically motivated stands contrary to the provisions of the Charter of the United Nations and having direct and reliable knowledge of such violations.

(b) Anonymous communications shall be inadmissible; subject to the requirements of subparagraph (2) (b) of resolution 728 F (XXVIII) of the Economic and Social Council, the author of a communication, whether an individual, a group of individuals or an organization, must be clearly identified.

    (c) Communications shall not be inadmissible solely because the knowledge of the individual authors is second-hand, provided that they are accompanied by clear evidence.

(3) *Contents of communications and nature of allegations*

    (a) The communication must contain a description of the facts and must indicate the purpose of the petition and the rights that have been violated.

    (b) Communications shall be inadmissible if their language is essentially abusive and in particular if they contain insulting reference to the State against which the complaint is directed. Such communications may be considered if they meet the other criteria for admissibility after deletion of the abusive language.

    (c) A communication shall be inadmissible if it has manifestly political motivations and its subject is contrary to the provisions of the Charter of the United Nations.

    (d) A communication shall be inadmissible if it appears that it is based exclusively on report disseminated by mass media.

(4) *Existence of other remedies*

    (a) Communications shall be inadmissible if their admission would prejudice the functions of the specialized agencies of the United Nations system.

    (b) Communications shall be inadmissible if domestic remedies have not been exhausted, unless it appears that such remedies would be ineffective or unreasonably prolonged. Any failure to exhaust remedies should be satisfactorily established.

    (c) Communications relating to cases which have been settled by the State concerned in accordance with the principles set forth in the Universal Declaration of Human Rights and other applicable documents in the field of human right will not be considered.

(5) *Timeliness*

A communication shall be inadmissible if it is not submitted to the United Nations within a reasonable time after the exhaustion of the domestic remedies as provided above.

Question

To what extent are these criteria consonant with those used by the Treaty Monitoring Bodies of the United Nations and the regional courts (see Chapter 6)?

The system was refined and partially reformed in 2000. The following resolution provides details of the system as it operates today. Note, however, that in accordance with Decision 2006/102 of 30 June 2006, the Human Rights Council extended the operation of the 1503 procedure for a year, subject to review.

ECOSOC Resolution 2000/3, 2000 Procedure for dealing with communications concerning human rights

The Economic and Social Council,

Recalling its resolution 728 F (XXVIII) of 30 July 1959 concerning the handling of communications concerning human rights and its decision 79 (LVIII) of 6 May 1975 relating thereto,

Recalling also its resolution 1235 (XLII) of 6 June 1967 authorizing the Commission on Human Rights to examine information relevant to gross violations of human rights and fundamental freedoms, its resolution 1503 (XLVIII) of 27 May 1970 establishing a procedure for dealing with communications relating to violations of human rights and fundamental freedoms and its resolution 1990/41 of 25 May 1990 concerning the establishment, composition and designation of the members of the Working Group on Situations,

Recalling further resolution 1 (XXIV) of the Subcommission on Prevention of Discrimination and Protection of Minorities (now the Subcommission for the Promotion and Protection of Human Rights) of 13 August 1971 concerning criteria for the admissibility of communications, (1) as well as Subcommission resolution 2 (XXIV) of 16 August 1971 concerning the establishment, composition and designation of the members of the Working Group on Communications, (2) *Recalling* Commission on Human Rights decisions 3 (XXX) of 6 March 1974, (3) 5 (XXXIV) of 3 March 1978 (4) and 9 (XXXVI) of 7 March 1980, (5) all aimed at facilitating government participation and cooperation under the procedure, and decision 3 (XXXIV) of 3 March 1978 (6) inviting the Chairman-Rapporteur of the Working Group on Communications to be present during the deliberations of the Commission on that item,

Noting decision 2000/109 of 26 April 2000 of the Commission on Human Rights, (7) *inter alia*, approving the recommendations of its inter-sessional open-ended Working Group on Enhancing the Effectiveness of the Mechanisms of the Commission on Human Rights concerning the review of the procedure governed by Economic and Social Council resolution 1503 (XLVIII) and related resolutions and decisions, (8)

1. *Endorses* Commission decision 2000/109 of 26 April 2000, 12 insofar as it concerns the review of the procedure governed by Economic and Social Council resolution 1503 (XLVIII) and related resolutions and decisions;

2. *Decides*, accordingly, that the Working Group on Communications designated in conformity with paragraph 37 of the report of the inter-sessional open-ended Working Group on Enhancing the Effectiveness of the Mechanisms of the Commission on Human Rights (9) shall henceforth meet annually for two weeks, immediately following the annual session of the Subcommission on the Promotion and Protection of Human Rights, to examine the communications received under Council resolution 728 F (XXVIII) that have been transmitted to the Governments concerned not later than 12 weeks prior to the meeting of the Working Group, and any government replies relating thereto, in conformity with the criteria for the admissibility of communications contained in resolution 1 (XXIV) of the Subcommission, (6) with a view to bringing to the attention of the Working Group on Situations any particular situations which appear to reveal a consistent pattern of gross and reliably attested violations of human rights and fundamental freedoms;

3. *Requests* the Secretary-General, with the approval of the Chairman-Rapporteur of the Working Group on Communications, to screen out manifestly ill-founded communications in the preparation of the monthly confidential summaries of communications (confidential lists of communications) communicated to the members of the Working Group, it being understood that communications screened out would not be transmitted to the Governments concerned for reply;

4. *Calls upon* the Secretary-General to inform the countries concerned, immediately after the conclusion of the meeting of the Working Group on Communications, of the actions taken in regard to them;

5. *Entrusts* to the Working Group on Situations designated in conformity with paragraph 40 of the report of the inter-sessional open-ended Working Group on Enhancing the Effectiveness of the Mechanisms of the Commission on Human Rights, (14) which shall meet annually for one week not less than one month prior to the annual session of the Commission, the role of examining the confidential report and recommendations of the Working Group on Communications and determining whether or not to refer a particular situation thus brought before it to the Commission on Human Rights, as well as of examining the particular situations kept under review by the Commission under the procedure, and, accordingly, to place before the Commission a confidential report identifying the main issues of concern, normally together with a draft resolution or draft decision recommending the action to be taken by the Commission in respect of the situations referred to it;

6. *Requests* the Secretary-General to make the confidential files available, at least one week in advance of the first closed meeting, to all members of the Commission on Human Rights;

7. *Authorizes* the Commission on Human Rights, as it deems appropriate, to consider the par-

ticular situations placed before it by the Working Group on Situations, as well as the situations kept under review, in two separate closed meetings, employing the following modalities:

(a) At the first closed meeting, each country concerned would be invited to make opening presentations; a discussion would then follow between members of the Commission and the Government concerned, based on the contents of confidential files and the report of the Working Group on Situations;

(b) In the interim between the first and second closed meetings, any member or members of the Commission could submit an alternative or an amendment to any texts forwarded by the Working Group on Situations; any such draft texts would be circulated confidentially by the secretariat, in accordance with the rules of procedure of the functional commissions of the Economic and Social Council, in advance of the second closed meeting;

(c) At the second closed meeting, members of the Commission would discuss and take action on the draft resolutions or decisions; a representative or representatives of the Governments concerned would have the right to be present during the adoption of the final decision/resolution taken in regard to the human rights situation in that country; as has been the established practice, the Chairperson of the Commission would subsequently announce in a public meeting which countries had been examined under the 1503 procedure, as well as the names of countries no longer being dealt with under the procedure; the 1503 dossiers would remain confidential, except where the Government concerned has indicated the wish that they become public;

(d) In accordance with the established practice, the action taken in respect of a particular situation should be one of the following options:

(i) To discontinue consideration of the matter when further consideration or action is not warranted;

(ii) To keep the situation under review in the light of any further information received from the Government concerned and any further information which may reach the Commission under the 1503 procedure;

(iii) To keep the situation under review and to appoint an independent expert;

(iv) To discontinue consideration of the matter under the confidential procedure governed by Council resolution 1503 (XLVIII) in order to take up consideration of the same matter under the public procedure governed by Council resolution 1235 (XLII);

8. *Decides* that the provisions of Council resolution 1503 (XLVIII) and related resolutions and decisions not affected by the present reorganization of work shall remain in force, including:

(a) Provisions relating to the duties and responsibilities of the Secretary-General, it being understood that in respect of the handling of communications and government replies relating thereto the duties and responsibilities are as follows:

(i) The compilation, as before, of monthly confidential summaries of incoming communications concerning alleged violations of human rights; the identity of authors may be deleted upon request;

(ii) The transmittal of a copy of each summarized communication, in the language received, to the Government concerned for reply, without divulging the identity of the author if he or she so requests;

(iii) Acknowledging the receipt of communications to their authors;

(iv) The reproduction and circulation to the members of the Commission, as before, of the replies received from Governments;

(b) Provisions aimed at facilitating government cooperation and participation in the procedure, including the provisions of Commission decision 3 (XXX) of 6 March 1974, now to be applied following the meetings of the Working Group on Communications;

9. *Decides* that all actions envisaged in the implementation of the present resolution by the Working Group on Communications, the Working Group on Situations and the Commission on Human Rights shall remain confidential until such time as the Commission may decide to make recommendations to the Economic and Social Council;

10. *Decides* that the procedure as amended may continue to be referred to as the 1503 procedure.

Question

To what extent do the reforms in Resolution 2000/3 achieve the goal of maximising human rights protection?

The only evidence of consideration under the communication procedure is the release of names of States. Given the nature of the system, no information is released on the subject matter of the complaints or whether the matter was satisfactorily resolved.

While this may be viewed as unsatisfactory, all States being the subject of communications are treated in an identical fashion, thus few deductions can be made as to the human rights situation based solely on the list of States.

Around 85 States have been considered under this process to date, in other words, almost half the members of the United Nations itself. Permanent members of the Security Council such as the United Kingdom and the United States of America have also been considered. Many of the States are brought to the attention of the Commission during periods of political upheaval, e.g. the dissolution of the former Soviet socialist eastern bloc countries and their transitions to democracy. The following lists the States which have been considered since 2000, the years indicate every session during which they have been examined, including the most recent.

States considered under the 1503 procedure from 2000–2006

Bolivia 1977–1981, 2004
Chad 1991–1999, 2002–2003
Chile 1975–1976, 1978–1979, 1981, 2000
Democratic Republic of the Congo (ex. Zaire) 2000, 2001
Djibouti 2003, 2004
Honduras 1988–1989, 2004–2005
Kenya 1993, 2000
Latvia 1995, 1997, 2000
Liberia 2002–2003
Maldives 2001
Nigeria 2002
Republic of the Congo 2000, 2001
Togo 2001–2002
Uganda 1975–1981, 1995, 2000–2001
United Arab Emirates 2000
Uzbekistan 1996–1997, 2003–2005
Vietnam 1994, 2000
Yemen 1998–1999, 2000
Zambia 2002
Zimbabwe 2000

Question

Look at the list of countries being considered recently under the 1253/1503 procedure. Compare it to the countries ratifying the main human rights treaties and complying with the reporting requirements thereunder. To what extent does this procedure permit States currently outwith the treaty monitoring system to be scrutinised?

5.1.2   Thematic and country rapporteurs

In addition, the Commission enjoyed considerable powers in respect of other special procedures, principally the creation of a system of mandates in furtherance of monitoring either specific human rights (thematic rapporteurs) or specific countries or areas (country rapporteurs). Over time, the role of rapporteurs has evolved into a complex web, designed to further the promotion of international standards of human rights. These mechanisms are also continued by the Human Rights Council.

Strengthening Special Procedures: The way forward from www.ohchr.org/english/bodies/chr/special/complaints.htm

Although the mandates given to special procedure mechanisms vary, they are usually to examine, monitor, advise and publicly report on human rights situations in specific countries or territories (country mandates), or on major phenomena of human rights violations worldwide (thematic mandates). Various activities can be undertaken by special procedures, including:

Receiving and analysing information on the situation of human rights from various sources on an ongoing basis;

Networking and information sharing with partners, both Governmental and non-governmental, within and outside the UN, in a spirit of complementarity of roles and responsibilities;

Seeking—often on an urgent basis—clarification from Governments, and where required requesting them to implement protection measures to guarantee or restore the enjoyment of human rights;

Raising awareness about specific human rights, situations and phenomena attesting threats to and violations of human rights;

When specific circumstances so warrant, raising public concerns through media and other public statements;

Undertaking country visits to assess the human rights situation pertaining to their respective mandates and making recommendations to the Governments concerned with a view to improving the situation;

Reporting and making recommendations to the CHR, and when specified in their mandates to the GA (in some cases to the SC) on the regular activities under the mandate, on field visits as well as specific thematic trends and phenomena;

Participating in the global partnership to consolidate national protection systems through the follow-up to their recommendations.

To fulfil these tasks, the mandates are entrusted to individuals who serve as a special rapporteur, representative, independent expert or member of a working group. They are usually appointed by the Chairperson of the Commission on Human Rights (with a few being appointed by the Secretary-General as his [Special] Representatives. The experts entrusted with these mandates come from all parts of the world. They are independent prominent human rights personalities from various backgrounds and include academics, lawyers, economists and eminent representatives of the civil society. They serve in a personal capacity for a maximum of 6 years and do not receive salaries or financial compensation for their work. . . .

Management of mandates

Mandates have grown in an *ad hoc* fashion, with each mandate-holder developing specific methods of work. At the same time a number of basic rules and common methodological tools have been developed which are of interest and use to all, and become particularly useful for new mandate-holders, whose number is increasing not only with the creation of new mandates but also as a result of the rules on turnover of mandate-holders developed and applied by the CHR so as to encourage renewal.

A compilation of current methods of work of special procedures mandate-holders is being prepared by OHCHR as a first step to a comparative study of such methods and the possible further rationalization of working methods, the development of standard criteria for certain activities (such as fact-finding, consideration of individual cases, evaluation of responses on individual cases, follow-up action by mandate-holders etc.) and identification of best practices.

Database, information sharing and information support system

As part of its efforts to ensure a coordinated approach of communications to Governments in a systematized way, OHCHR created in June 2001 a Quick Response Desk through which all communications with governments concerning allegations of violations of human rights, including Urgent Appeals are channelled. It is expected that such increased coordination will assist in establishing criteria for follow-up on communications by interested mandates.

The Quick Response Desk extended coverage of the urgent action database to all thematic and geographic mandates. The number of communications sent to governments and the number of communications sent jointly by two or more mandate-holders increased over the previous year. In 2003, over 650 urgent appeals were communicated, some 60 per cent of which were joint appeals. During the same period, more than 100 letters of allegations were processed through the urgent action database. The increase in the number of communications on individual cases sent to governments benefits victims of human rights violations: more cases are brought to the attention of governments and of the international community, and efforts are being made in order to more systematically follow-up on these cases. . . .

Cooperation with the Commission on Human Rights

. . . The essential foundation on which the effectiveness of the CHR and its mechanisms rests is the responsibility of all Governments to cooperate fully with those mechanisms. Since 1999, 49 countries have extended standing invitations to the thematic special procedures of the Commission on Human Rights to visit their countries, including 9 since the beginning of 2003. Country visits provide an essential opportunity for gathering first-hand information and establishing direct contact with relevant authorities and representatives of the civil society, as well as members of the UNCT present in the field. In 2003, mandate-holders undertook over 80 fact-finding missions and the information contained in the respective reports proved to be useful and relevant in supporting the work of UN country teams activities or/and in the development of technical cooperation projects. . . .

Follow-up and prevention

As already mentioned, the Special Procedures Branch is developing criteria and strengthening methodologies for the selection, operations and reporting functions of special procedures; it is also engaged in facilitating increased interaction between the special procedures and their various partners within the international human rights system, i.e. States members of the CHR and the General Assembly, treaty bodies, national institutions and non-governmental organizations, as well as partner organizations and bodies within the UN system-wide, so as to encourage better follow-up to their activities at the national level. Efforts are also being made to better disseminate knowledge and awareness of the special procedures. This in turn may provide better opportunities to use the expertise and wealth of information developed by the special procedures in order to devise early warning mechanisms, alert relevant UN instances, including the Security Council, to emerging crisis situations and provide suggestions for an adequate response.

As the above extract demonstrates, the United Nations is aware of the need to strengthen the follow-up to any report under the special procedures mechanisms. Failure to do so will obviously undermine the effectiveness of the process.

There are a number of special procedures mechanisms currently in operation. Most are thematic with a trans-national dimension but others are concerned exclusively with one State. Mandates are generally for a fixed period of time though can be renewed. If and when renewed, sometimes a different individual is appointed. Indeed, sometimes rapporteurs change half way through a mandate. Inevitably, a rapporteur's impact partially depends on their identity and lasting enthusiasm (sometimes in the face of adversity) as well as finance.

There are a number of special procedure mechanisms currently in operation. Most are thematic with trans-national dimensions, but a number are concerned exclusively with one State. The mandates are generally for a fixed period of time. If (or when) renewed, sometimes a different individual will be appointed. Individual rapporteurs can have a significant impact on the role—their personal enthusiasm, available time and finance, can shape how proactive they are in advancing their remit. Some mandates offer questionnaires for individuals wishing to lodge complaints: torture, enforced disappearances, arbitrary detention and violence against women are some examples (see www.ohchr.org/english/bodies/chr/special/questionnaires.htm).

A sample mandate for a rapporteur is as follows:

Commission on Human Rights Resolution 2000/61

The Commission on Human Rights,

Recalling General Assembly resolution 53/144 of 9 December 1998 by which the Assembly adopted by consensus the Declaration on the Right and Responsibility of Individuals, Groups and Organs of Society to Promote and Protect Universally Recognized Human Rights and Fundamental Freedoms,

Reiterating the importance of this Declaration and its promotion and implementation,

Emphasizing the important role that individuals, non-governmental organizations and groups play in the promotion and protection of all human rights and fundamental freedoms,

Noting with deep concern that, in many countries, persons and organizations engaged in promoting and defending human rights and fundamental freedoms are often subjected to threats, harassment, insecurity, arbitrary detention and extrajudicial executions,

1. *Welcomes* the report of the Secretary-General (E/CN.4/2000/95) on ways for effective promotion and implementation of the Declaration on the Right and Responsibility of Individuals, Groups and Organs of Society to Promote and Protect Universally Recognized Human Rights and Fundamental Freedoms, submitted pursuant to Commission resolution 1999/66 of 28 April 1999;

2. *Calls upon* all States to promote and give effect to the Declaration;

3. *Requests* the Secretary-General to appoint, for a period of three years, a special representative who shall report on the situation of human rights defenders in all parts of the world and on possible means to enhance their protection in full compliance with the Declaration; the main activities of the special representative shall be:

(a) To seek, receive, examine and respond to information on the situation and the rights of anyone, acting individually or in association with others, to promote and protect human rights and fundamental freedoms;

(b) To establish cooperation and conduct dialogue with Governments and other interested actors on the promotion and effective implementation of the Declaration;

(c) To recommend effective strategies better to protect human rights defenders and follow up on these recommendations;

4. *Urges* all Governments to cooperate with and assist the Special Representative of the Secretary-General in the performance of his or her tasks and to furnish all information in the fulfilment of his or her mandate upon request;

5. *Requests* the Secretary-General to provide the Special Representative with all necessary assistance, in particular the staff and resources deemed necessary to fulfil his or her mandate;

6. *Requests* the Special Representative to submit annual reports on his/her activities to the Commission and to the General Assembly and to make any suggestions and recommendations enabling him or her better to carry out his or her tasks and activities.

In 2005, the Rapporteur lodged a report summarising all individual cases raised by the Special Representative of the Secretary-General with Governments, including Government responses (UN Doc. E/CN.4/2005/101/Add.1) as well as an annual report (UN Doc. E/CN.4/2005/101).

Question

Evaluate the work undertaken by the Rapporteur and the scope of the mandate.

The following table lists the current rapporteurs (effective 2006)

Special Procedures of the Human Rights Council: Country Mandates

Afghanistan
Belarus
Burundi
Cambodia
Cuba
Democratic People's Republic of Korea
Democratic Republic of the Congo (ex-Zaire)
Haiti
Liberia
Myanmar
Palestinian Territories Occupied since 1967
Somalia
Sudan
Uzbekistan

Special Procedures of the Human Rights Council: Thematic Mandates

Special Rapporteur on adequate housing as a component of the right to an adequate standard of living
Working Group on people of African descent
Working Group on Arbitrary Detention
Special Rapporteur on the sale of children, child prostitution and child pornography
Special Rapporteur on the right to education
Working Group in Enforced or Involuntary Disappearances
Special Rapporteur on extrajudicial, summary or arbitrary executions
Independent Expert on the question of human rights and extreme poverty
Special Rapporteur on the right to food
Special Rapporteur on the promotion and protection of the right to freedom of expression
Special Rapporteur on freedom of religion or belief
Special Rapporteur on the right of everyone to the enjoyment of the highest attainable Standard of physical and mental health

Special Representative of the Secretary-General on the situation of human rights defenders

Special Rapporteur on the independence of judges and lawyers

Special Rapporteur on the situation of indigenous peoples

Representative of the Secretary-General on internally displaced persons

Working Group on the use of mercenaries as a means of impeding the exercise of the right of peoples to self-determination

Special Rapporteur on the human rights of migrants

Special Rapporteur on contemporary forms of racism, racial discrimination, xenophobia and related intolerance

Independent Expert on the effects of structural adjustment policies and foreign debt

Special Rapporteur on torture and other cruel, inhuman or degrading treatment or punishment

Special Rapporteur on the adverse effects of the illicit movement and dumping of toxic and dangerous products and wastes on the enjoyment of human rights

Special Rapporteur on trafficking in persons, especially in women and children

Special Rapporteur on violence against women, its causes and consequences

Special Representative of the Secretary-General on human rights and transnational corporations and other business enterprises

Independent Expert on minority issues

Independent Expert on human rights and international solidarity

Special Rapporteur on the promotion and protection of human rights while countering terrorism

Rapporteurs are drawn from international academics, legal and political experts and others with recognised special competence and interest in the subject concerned. They are appointed from across a range of countries. Funding can be problematic as the United Nations has sparse resources. Thus, sometimes rapporteurs are effectively self-funded and undertake visits partially subsidised by other agencies. This does not necessarily affect their independence.

Question

Consider aspects of one or more rapporteurs (available at www.ohchr.org). How effective are rapporteurs/working groups in redressing violations of human rights? Does the publicity element work/serve a valuable purpose?

Annual sessions of the Commission can receive more than a hundred different reports under the various special procedures operated by the Commission. The principal problem is the lack of follow-up mechanisms. Time and money prevents the rapporteurs themselves from undertaking further work on individual State reports and especially on allegations of human rights violations.

The Human Rights Council is in the process of reviewing all former Commission mechanisms to assess their effectiveness and ascertain the most successful systems for progressing human rights. The Office of the High Commissioner for Human Rights has begun issuing Special Procedures Bulletins. The first was published online, covering January–April 2006. Bulletins will be published thrice yearly and provide details of visits, communications and contacting using the Special Procedures.

5.2   THE UNITED NATIONS EDUCATIONAL, SCIENTIFIC AND CULTURAL ORGANISATION (UNESCO)

The United Nations Educational, Scientific and Cultural Organisation also operates a non-contentious individual communications procedure for violations of education, culture and science rights.

Given the process operates under the auspices of UNESCO, it naturally applies to a limited range of rights, essentially those falling within the competence of UNESCO. In terms of the Universal Declaration of Human Rights, these rights include the right to information—including freedom of opinion and expression, right to education, the right to participate freely in cultural life and the right to share in scientific advancement (Arts 19, 26 and 27 of the Universal Declaration of Human Rights). UNESCO notes that these rights may imply the exercise of other rights, such as freedom of thought, conscience and religion, the right to receive and impart information and ideas through any media and regardless of frontiers, moral rights resulting from scientific, literary or artistic production and freedom of assembly and association for activities related to education, science and culture.

The process was established by a decision adopted by the Executive Board of UNESCO in furtherance of the duties incumbent upon the organisation in terms of its constitutive document. The text of the decision follows.

Decision 104 Ex/3.3, 1978 Study of the procedures which should be followed in the examination of cases and questions which might be submitted to UNESCO concerning the exercise of human rights in the spheres of its competence, in order to make its action more effective: Report of the Working Party of the Executive Board

The Executive Board,

1. Mindful that the competence and role of UNESCO in the field of human rights derive primarily from Article I.1 of the Constitution of UNESCO, which states: 'The purpose of the Organization is to contribute to peace and security by promoting collaboration among the nations through education, science and culture in order to further universal respect for justice, for the rule of law and for the human rights and fundamental freedoms which are affirmed for the peoples of the world, without distinction of race, sex, language or religion, by the Charter of the United Nations', and from the Charter of the United Nations, . . .

6. Mindful of Article I.3 of the Constitution of UNESCO, which states: 'With a view to preserving the independence, integrity and fruitful diversity of the cultures and educational systems of the States members of the Organization, the Organization is prohibited from intervening in matters which are essentially within their domestic jurisdiction',

7. Considering that, in matters concerning human rights within its fields of competence, UNESCO, basing its efforts on moral considerations and its specific competence, should act in a spirit of international co-operation, conciliation and mutual understanding, and recalling that UNESCO should not play the role of an international judicial body,

8. Recognizing the important role of the Director-General, in:

(a) seeking continually to strengthen the action of UNESCO in the promotion of human rights, both through the settlement of cases and the elimination of massive, systematic or flagrant violations of human rights and fundamental freedoms, and

(b) initiating consultations, in conditions of mutual respect, confidence and confidentiality, to help reach solutions to particular problems concerning human rights,

9. Invites the Director-General to pursue this role;

10. Considering that, in the exercise of its competence in the field of human rights, UNESCO is called upon to examine:

(a) cases concerning violations of human rights which are individual and specific,

(b) questions of massive, systematic or flagrant violations of human rights which result either from a policy contrary to human rights applied *de jure* or *de facto* by a State or from an accumulation of individual cases forming a consistent pattern,

11. Considering the terms of reference of the Committee on Conventions and Recommendations in Education,

12. Taking into account the tasks already entrusted to the Committee concerning human rights matters within the Organization's fields of competence,

13. Decides that the Committee will henceforth be designated 'the Committee on Conventions and Recommendations';

14. Decides that the Committee will continue to carry out its functions with respect to conventions and recommendations and will consider communications received by the Organization concerning cases and questions of violations of human rights within UNESCO's fields of competence in accordance with the following conditions and procedures.

The admissibility criteria are also specified in the decision. In many respects they reflect the criteria commonly applied to applications to other international and human rights regional bodies. Of particular interest is the fact that the process is not limited solely to individuals/groups and the time limit criterion, which are perhaps more flexible than other instruments. Admissibility is not a contentious issue; rather the lack of knowledge of the system and therefore a lack of applications reflects the comparatively 'low' impact of this procedure.

Decision 104 Ex/3.3 continued

Conditions:

(a) Communications shall be deemed admissible if they meet the following conditions:

   (i)   the communication must not be anonymous;

   (ii)   the communication must originate from a person or a group of persons who, it can be reasonably presumed, are victims of an alleged violation of any of the human rights referred to in paragraph (iii) below. It may also originate from any person, group of persons or organization having reliable knowledge of those violations;

   (iii) the communication must concern violations of human rights falling within UNESCO's competence in the fields of education, science, culture and information and must not be motivated exclusively by other considerations;

   (iv)   the communication must be compatible with the principles of the Organization, the Charter of the United Nations, the Universal Declaration of Human Rights, the international covenants on human rights and other international instruments in the field of human rights;

   (v)   the communication must not be manifestly ill-founded and must appear to contain relevant evidence;

   (vi)   the communication must be neither offensive nor an abuse of the right to submit communications. However, such a communication may be considered if it meets all other criteria or admissibility, after the exclusion of the offensive or abusive parts;

   (vii) the communication must not be based exclusively on information disseminated through the mass media;

    (viii) the communication must be submitted within a reasonable time-limit following the facts which constitute its subject-matter or within a reasonable time-limit after the facts have become known;

    (ix) the communication must indicate whether an attempt has been made to exhaust available domestic remedies with regard to the facts which constitute the subject-matter of the communication and the result of such an attempt, if any;

    (x) communications relating to matters already settled by the States concerned in accordance with the human rights principles set forth in the Universal Declaration of Human Rights and the international covenants on human rights shall not be considered;

Decision 104 Ex/3.3 finally details the procedures to be followed by the Director-General and Committee in considering communications. Note that this provides an element of transparency of process, despite the confidentiality of the procedure. Those submitting complaints are at least aware of the stages their complaint will encounter before any result occurs.

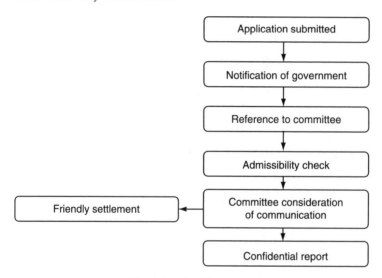

Decision 104 Ex/3.3 continued

Procedures:

(b) The Director-General shall:

    (i) acknowledge receipt of communications and inform the authors thereof of the above-mentioned conditions governing admissibility;

    (ii) ascertain that the author of the communication has no objection to his communication, after having been communicated to the government concerned, being brought to the notice of the Committee and to his name being divulged;

    (iii) upon receipt of an affirmative answer from the author of the communication, transmit the communication to the government concerned, informing it that the communication will be brought to the notice of the Committee, together with any reply the government may wish to make;

    (iv) transmit the communication to the Committee, together with the reply, if any, of the government concerned and additional relevant information from the author, taking into account the need to proceed without undue delay;

(c) the Committee shall examine in private session the communications transmitted to it by the Director-General;

(d) the Committee shall decide on the admissibility of communications in accordance with the above-mentioned conditions;

(e) representatives of the governments concerned may attend meetings of the Committee in order to provide additional information or to answer questions from members of the Committee on either admissibility or the merits of the communication;

(f) the Committee may avail itself of the relevant information at the disposal of the Director-General;

(g) in consideration of a communication, the Committee may, in exceptional circumstances, request the Executive Board to authorize it under Rule 29 of the Rules of Procedure to take appropriate action;

(h) the Committee may keep a communication submitted to it on its agenda while seeking additional information it may consider necessary for the disposition of the matter;

(i) the Director-General shall notify the author of the communication and the government concerned of the Committee's decision on the admissibility of the communication;

(j) the Committee shall dismiss any communication which, having been found admissible, does not, upon examination of the merits, appear to warrant further action. The author of the communication and the government concerned shall be notified accordingly;

(k) communications which warrant further consideration shall be acted upon by the Committee with a view to helping to bring about a friendly solution designed to advance the promotion of the human rights falling within UNESCO's fields of competence;

15. Decides further that the Committee shall submit confidential reports to the Executive Board at each session on the carrying out of its mandate under the present decision. These reports shall contain appropriate information arising from its examination of the communications which the Committee considers it useful to bring to the notice of the Executive Board. The reports shall also contain recommendations which the Committee may wish to make either generally or regarding the disposition of a communication under consideration;

16. Decides to consider confidential reports of the Committee in private session and to take further action as necessary in accordance with Rule 28 of the Rules of Procedure;

17. Decides also that communications transmitted to it by the Committee which testify to the existence of a question shall be dealt with in accordance with paragraph 18 below;

18. Considers that questions of massive, systematic or flagrant violations of human rights and fundamental freedoms—including, for example, those perpetrated as a result of policies of aggression, interference in the internal affairs of States, occupation of foreign territory and implementation of a policy of colonialism, genocide, apartheid, racialism, or national and social oppression— falling within UNESCO's fields of competence should be considered by the Executive Board and the General Conference in public meetings.

Question

Compare this approach to that of the United Nations Human Rights Council (1503 procedure). Are there any advantages in the UNESCO system over and above that of the Council?

Note the emphasis on securing a friendly solution. This appears to be the primary purpose of the procedure and obviously reinforces the statement at the beginning of the Decision, that the process is not intended to be judicial in nature. The UNESCO procedure is, in general, confidential although as the decision notes, massive, systematic or flagrant violations of human rights are to be considered in public meetings. While arguably creating a system which is attractive to States, this also demonstrates respect for the State's powers and responsibilities. Establishing a confidential dialogue with a State should permit a full exploration of the facts and any contentious issues.

Question

Is the UNESCO system unduly limited? Are there any lessons to be learned for the other international systems?

The UNESCO system has been reasonably successful—according to statistics published by UNESCO, from 1978–2005, 529 communications were considered by the Committee on Conventions and Recommendations. Of this, some 330 were settled. Given the confidential nature of the procedure, it is difficult to obtain information thereon. However, according to UNESCO, the following results were achieved for the alleged victims:

Summary of results of application of 104 Ex/3.3 procedure (from http:// portal.unesco.org, autumn 2006)

Released/acquitted—194
Released after completion of sentence—11
Authorised to leave the State in question—20
Authorised to return to the State in question—35
Able to resume their employment or activity—29
Able to resume a banned publication or broadcast programme—14
Able to resume normal life following a cessation of threats—3
Able to benefit from changes in certain education laws which were discriminatory towards ethnic or religious minorities—10
Able to obtain passports and/or grants, or receive diplomas—12
Able to resume studies—2

With reference to the list of rights which may be considered by the Committee (above), tentative conclusions can thus be drawn on the subject matter of issues raised before the Committee, although, of course, no assumptions can be made as to the identity of the States involved.

The Committee on Conventions and Recommendations, which receives and considers individual and group communications, has a renewable mandate to examine considerations under the procedure outlined above and to consider various matters relating to the human rights instruments adopted by UNESCO (see, more recently, Executive Board Decision 168 Ex/6.2, 2003). The current Committee has 30 members and a chairperson.

5.3   UNITED NATIONS SECURITY COUNCIL AND SANCTIONS

The Security Council, primary organ of the United Nations, has an array of powers to ensure States comply with international law. While these powers can be extended to include international human rights, the most significant hurdle to be overcome with respect to international human rights law lies in a premise underpinning the Charter of the United Nations itself.

Charter of the United Nations Art 2(7)

Nothing contained in the present Charter shall authorise the United Nations to intervene in matters which are essentially within the domestic jurisdiction of any State or shall require the Members to submit such matters to settlement under the present Charter; but this principle shall not prejudice the application of enforcement measures under Chapter VII.

The most startling example of the Security Council, indeed the entire United Nations system failing to address a major abuse of international human rights because it was deemed to be an internal affair of the State, is the genocide in Rwanda in 1994.

United Nations Secretary-General's address on the tenth anniversary of the genocide in Rwanda, April 2004, available from www.un.org/events/rwanda/sgmessage.html

The genocide in Rwanda should never have happened. But it did. Neither the UN Secretariat, nor the Security Council, nor Member States in general, nor the international media, paid enough attention to the gathering signs of disaster. Eight hundred thousand men, women and children were abandoned to the most brutal of deaths, as neighbour killed neighbour and sanctuaries such as churches and hospitals were turned into slaughterhouses. The international community failed Rwanda, and that must leave us always with a sense of bitter regret and abiding sorrow.

Given the very nature of international human rights, monitoring requires interference in areas within the normal internal competence of the State, the situation in Rwanda is perhaps all the more tragic. Obviously there are a number of reasons contributing towards the neglect evidenced by the international community in this extreme situation. It can be contrasted with the situation a year or so earlier in the then Yugoslavia. International intervention was forthcoming through NATO and allied troops.

Question

What reasons are there for the difference in treatment experienced by Rwanda and Yugoslavia?

More significantly, the Security Council enjoys a range of powers in terms of the Charter to intervene in matters threatening international peace or security, including violations of international human rights. The powers are primarily peaceful (Chapter VI) but extend to authorisation of the use of force (Chapter VII). One characteristic of contemporary international human rights is the increased willingness of the Security Council, indeed the United Nations, to intervene in quasi-internal matters. There are a number of examples, what follows are but a few:

Resolution 1641 (2005) on Burundi, following on from Resolution 1545 (2004)

Resolution 1368 (2001) on threats to international peace and security caused by terrorist acts

Resolution 1333 (2000) on Afghanistan, reiterating deep concern over violations of human rights.

Resolution 569 (1985) on South Africa, condemning a number of human rights infringements

Resolution 4 (1946) on the Spanish question demonstrating the relationship between internal politics and international peace and security.

Question

Ascertain the veracity of the allegation that politics and not respect for human dignity dictate the actions of the Security Council. Especially have regard to the potential for veto by the permanent members of the Security Council (i.e. France, People's Republic of China, Russia, United Kingdom and United States of America).

In accordance with the provisions of the United Nations Charter, the Security Council has primary responsibility for peace and security matters. Accordingly, it may act when violations of human rights constitute a threat to international peace and security. Among the powers available to the Security Council in fulfilment of its mandate are the use of force (as a last resort) and a variety of mechanisms for ensuring the peaceful resolution of disputes. One peaceful option open to the Security Council is the imposition of sanctions on a State. The most substantive raft of sanctions ever imposed were against Iraq in 1991.

Security Council Resolution 661 (1990)

Acting under Chapter VII of the Charter,

1. *Determines* that Iraq so far has failed to comply with paragraph 2 of resolution 660 (1990) and has usurped the authority of the legitimate Government of Kuwait;

2. *Decides*, as a consequence, to take the following measures to secure compliance of Iraq with paragraph 2 of resolution 660 (1990) and to restore the authority of the legitimate Government of Kuwait;

3. *Decides* that all States shall prevent:

(a) The import into their territories of all commodities and products originating in Iraq or Kuwait exported therefrom after the date of the present resolution;

(b) Any activities by their nationals or in their territories which would promote or are calculated to promote the export or trans-shipment of any commodities or products from Iraq or Kuwait; and any dealings by their nationals or their flag vessels or in their territories in any commodities or products originating in Iraq or Kuwait and exported therefrom after the date of the present resolution, including in particular any transfer of funds to Iraq or Kuwait for the purposes of such activities or dealings;

(c) The sale or supply by their nationals or from their territories or using their flag vessels of any commodities or products, including weapons or any other military equipment, whether or not originating in their territories but not including supplies intended strictly for medical purposes, and, in humanitarian circumstances, foodstuffs, to any person or body in Iraq or Kuwait or to any person or body for the purposes of any business carried on in or operated from Iraq or Kuwait, and any activities by their nationals or in their territories which promote or are calculated to promote such sale or supply of such commodities or products;

4. *Decides* that all States shall not make available to the Government of Iraq, or to any commercial, industrial or public utility undertaking in Iraq or Kuwait, any funds or any other financial or economic resources and shall prevent their nationals and any persons within their territories from removing from their territories or otherwise making available to that Government or to any such undertaking any such funds or resources and from remitting any other funds to persons or bodies within Iraq or Kuwait, except payments exclusively for strictly medical or humanitarian purposes and, in humanitarian circumstances, foodstuffs;

5. *Calls upon* all States, including States non-members of the United Nations, to act strictly in accordance with the provisions of the present resolution notwithstanding any contract entered into or licence granted before the date of the present resolution;

6. *Decides* to establish, in accordance with rule 28 of the provisional rules of procedure, a Committee of the Security Council consisting of all the members of the Council, to undertake the following tasks and to report on its work to the Council with its observations and recommendations:

(a) To examine the reports on the progress of the implementation of the present resolution which will be submitted by the Secretary-General;

(b) To seek from all States further information regarding the action taken by them concerning the effective implementation of the provisions laid down in the present resolution;

7. *Calls upon* all States to co-operate fully with the Committee in the fulfilment of its tasks, including supplying such information as may be sought by the Committee in pursuance of the present resolution.

Perhaps it could have been anticipated but the impact of these sanctions was most dramatic on Iraqi civilians. Consequently, the United Nations implemented its now somewhat discredited oil-for-food programme. Investigations are ongoing into the programme and its effect. There is little doubt that the United Nations will be more reticent over the issue of sanctions in the future. Note the provisions of Security Council Resolution 1718 (2006) following the Democratic Peoples' Republic of Korea's nuclear test in October 2006. Humanitarian actions are clearly protected. The following resolution heralded the easing of sanctions against Iraq for humanitarian reasons.

Security Council Resolution 986 (1995)

The Security Council

Recalling its previous relevant resolutions,

Concerned by the serious nutritional and health situation of the Iraqi population, and by the risk of a further deterioration in this situation,

Convinced of the need as a temporary measure to provide for the humanitarian needs of the Iraqi people until the fulfilment by Iraq of the relevant Security Council resolutions, including notably resolution 687 (1991) of 3 April 1991, allows the Council to take further action with regard to the prohibitions referred to in resolution 661 (1990) of 6 August 1990, in accordance with the provisions of those resolutions,

Convinced also of the need for equitable distribution of humanitarian relief to all segments of the Iraqi population throughout the country,

Reaffirming the commitment of all Member States to the sovereignty and territorial integrity of Iraq,

Acting under Chapter VII of the Charter of the United Nations,

1. *Authorizes* States, notwithstanding the provisions of paragraphs 3 (a), 3 (b) and 4 of resolution 661 (1990) and subsequent relevant resolutions, to permit the import of petroleum and petroleum products originating in Iraq, including financial and other essential transactions directly relating thereto, sufficient to produce a sum not exceeding a total of one billion United States dollars every 90 days for the purposes set out in this resolution and subject to the following conditions:

(a) Approval by the Committee established by resolution 661 (1990), in order to ensure the transparency of each transaction and its conformity with the other provisions of this resolution, after submission of an application by the State concerned, endorsed by the Government of Iraq, for each proposed purchase of Iraqi petroleum and petroleum products, including details of the purchase price at fair market value, the export route, the opening of a letter of credit payable to the escrow account to be established by the Secretary-General for the purposes of this resolution, and of any other directly related financial or other essential transaction;

(b) Payment of the full amount of each purchase of Iraqi petroleum and petroleum products directly by the purchaser in the State concerned into the escrow account to be established by the Secretary-General for the purposes of this resolution;

Question

Why are the United Nations, and indeed regional organisations, reluctant to use the 'ultimate sanction' of expulsion against a State which does not comply with norms of international and regional law?

5.4 INTERNATIONAL CRIMINAL COURTS, TRIBUNALS AND PROCESSES

While technically not international human rights, but rather international criminal law, the International Criminal Court continues to appear in many syllabi of international human rights law, not least, driven by student interest. International

Criminal Law has, as it has evolved, made it clear that individuals may be prosecuted for very serious infringements of international human rights. International criminal law builds on the work of the Nuremberg and Tokyo tribunals after the Second World War and, more recently, the work of the two International Criminal Tribunals (for Rwanda and the Former Yugoslavia).

5.4.1   *Ad hoc* International Criminal Tribunals

Ad hoc International Criminal Tribunals were established under the auspices of the United Nations to oversee the prosecution of those involved in the atrocities in Rwanda and the former Yugoslavia. Both these bodies were established by the Security Council and operate as international bodies.

Resolution 955(1994) on the establishment of an international tribunal for Rwanda

1. *Decides* hereby, having received the request of the Government of Rwanda (S/1994/1115), to establish an international tribunal for the sole purpose of prosecuting persons responsible for genocide and other serious violations of international humanitarian law committed in the territory of Rwanda and Rwandan citizens responsible for genocide and other such violations committed in the territory of neighbouring States, between 1 January 1994 and 31 December 1994 and to this end to adopt the Statute of the International Criminal Tribunal for Rwanda annexed hereto;

2. *Decides* that all States shall cooperate fully with the International Tribunal and its organs in accordance with the present resolution and the Statute of the International Tribunal and that consequently all States shall take any measures necessary under their domestic law to implement the provisions of the present resolution and the Statute, including the obligation of States to comply with requests for assistance or orders issued by a Trial Chamber under Article 28 of the Statute, and *requests* States to keep the Secretary-General informed of such measures;

3. *Considers* that the Government of Rwanda should be notified prior to the taking of decisions under articles 26 and 27 of the Statute;

4. *Urges* States and intergovernmental and non-governmental organizations to contribute funds, equipment and services to the International Tribunal, including the offer of expert personnel;

5. *Requests* the Secretary-General to implement this resolution urgently and in particular to make practical arrangements for the effective functioning of the International Tribunal, including recommendations to the Council as to possible locations for the seat of the International Tribunal at the earliest time and to report periodically to the Council;

6. *Decides* that the seat of the International Tribunal shall be determined by the Council having regard to considerations of justice and fairness as well as administrative efficiency, including access to witnesses, and economy, and subject to the conclusion of appropriate arrangements between the United Nations and the State of the seat, acceptable to the Council, having regard to the fact that the International Tribunal may meet away from its seat when it considers it necessary for the efficient exercise of its functions; and *decides* that an office will be established and proceedings will be conducted in Rwanda, where feasible and appropriate, subject to the conclusion of similar appropriate arrangements;

7. *Decides* to consider increasing the number of judges and Trial Chambers of the International Tribunal if it becomes necessary.

Resolution 827 (1993) on a tribunal for Yugoslavia

2. *Decides* hereby to establish an international tribunal for the sole purpose of prosecuting persons responsible for serious violations of international humanitarian law committed in the

territory of the former Yugoslavia between 1 January 1991 and a date to be determined by the Security Council upon the restoration of peace and to this end to adopt the Statute of the International Tribunal annexed to the above-mentioned report;

3. *Requests* the Secretary-General to submit to the judges of the International Tribunal, upon their election, any suggestions received from States for the rules of procedure and evidence called for in Article 15 of the Statute of the International Tribunal;

4. *Decides* that all States shall cooperate fully with the International Tribunal and its organs in accordance with the present resolution and the Statute of the International Tribunal and that consequently all States shall take any measures necessary under their domestic law to implement the provisions of the present resolution and the Statute, including the obligation of States to comply with requests for assistance or orders issued by a Trial Chamber under Article 29 of the Statute;

5. *Urges* States and intergovernmental and non-governmental organizations to contribute funds, equipment and services to the International Tribunal, including the offer of expert personnel;

6. *Decides* that the determination of the seat of the International Tribunal is subject to the conclusion of appropriate arrangements between the United Nations and the Netherlands acceptable to the Council, and that the International Tribunal may sit elsewhere when it considers it necessary for the efficient exercise of its functions;

7. *Decides* also that the work of the International Tribunal shall be carried out without prejudice to the right of the victims to seek, through appropriate means, compensation for damages incurred as a result of violations of international humanitarian law;

8. *Requests* the Secretary-General to implement urgently the present resolution and in particular to make practical arrangements for the effective functioning of the International Tribunal at the earliest time and to report periodically to the Council;

9. *Decides* to remain actively seized of the matter.

Some of the jurisprudence of these tribunals is considered in Chapter 15.

5.4.2   Mixed Courts and Tribunals

Mixed courts are primarily established under domestic law with the purpose of examining atrocities committed within the State. They usually apply national and elements of international criminal law. While not necessarily part of the international system, they merit brief consideration as their increasing number was perhaps a factor contributing towards the development of the permanent International Criminal Court. Indeed, the substantial cost of funding *ad hoc* tribunals was of concern to the United Nations and as such procedures became viewed as a necessary part of post-conflict nation-building/re-building, the potential for increased costs was dramatic. To many commentators, the mixed courts were thus a cost-saving initiative. Note however, that the jurisdiction of the International Criminal Court is concurrent with national courts, thus the potential for further mixed courts and tribunals remains.

5.4.2.1   Sierra Leone Special Court

The Sierra Leone Special Court is part of the normal Sierra Leonean judicial system. It was established on the basis of a treaty concluded between Sierra Leone and the United Nations. Civil war has raged in Sierra Leone for many years with only short respites in the immediate aftermath of sporadic peace agreements.

Report of the Secretary-General on the Establishment of a Special Court for Sierra Leone, UN Doc. S/2000/915 (2000)

25. It is generally accepted that the decade-long civil war in Sierra Leone dates back to 1991, when on 23 March of that year forces of the Revolutionary United Front (RUF) entered Sierra Leone from Liberia and launched a rebellion to overthrow the one-party military rule of the All People's Congress (APC). In determining a beginning date of the temporal jurisdiction of the Special Court within the period since 23 March 1991, the Secretary-General has been guided by the following considerations: (a) the temporal jurisdiction should be reasonably limited in time so that the Prosecutor is not overburdened and the Court overloaded; (b) the beginning date should correspond to an event or a new phase in the conflict without necessarily having any political connotations; and (c) it should encompass the most serious crimes committed by persons of all political and military groups and in all geographical areas of the country. A temporal jurisdiction limited in any of these respects would rightly be perceived as a selective or discriminatory justice.

Following the most recent peace agreement, the Secretary-General of the United Nations, in concert with the Government of Sierra Leone, negotiated the terms for the establishment of an independent court and concluded its Statute (UN Doc. S/2000/915, 4/10/00). Being based in a treaty means the court has a different authority than the *ad hoc* tribunals which were established by a resolution of the Security Council. However, although it is established in Sierra Leonean law, the court retains evidence of its international authority.

Statute of the Special Court for Sierra Leone Arts 12–14

Article 12
Composition of the Chambers

1. The Chambers shall be composed of eleven independent judges, who shall serve as follows:

(a) Three judges shall serve in each of the Trial Chambers, of whom one shall be a judge appointed by the Government of Sierra Leone, and two judges appointed by the Secretary-General of the United Nations (hereinafter 'the Secretary-General');

(b) Five judges shall serve in the Appeals Chamber, of whom two shall be judges appointed by the Government of Sierra Leone, and three judges appointed by the Secretary-General.

2. Each judge shall serve only in the Chamber to which he or she has been appointed.

3. The judges of the Appeals Chamber and the judges of the Trial Chambers, respectively, shall elect a presiding judge who shall conduct the proceedings in the Chamber to which he or she was elected. The presiding judge of the Appeals Chamber shall be the President of the Special Court.

4. In addition to the judges sitting in the Chambers and present at every stage of the proceedings, the presiding judge of a Trial Chamber or the Appeals Chamber shall designate an alternate judge appointed by either the Government of Sierra Leone or the Secretary-General, to be present at each stage of the trial, and to replace a judge, if that judge is unable to continue sitting.

Article 13
Qualification and appointment of judges

1. The judges shall be persons of high moral character, impartiality and integrity who possess the qualifications required in their respective countries for appointment to the highest judicial offices. They shall be independent in the performance of their functions, and shall not accept or seek instructions from any Government or any other source.

2. In the overall composition of the Chambers, due account shall be taken of the experience of the judges in international law, including international humanitarian law and human rights law, criminal law and juvenile justice.

3. The judges shall be appointed for a four-year period and shall be eligible for reappointment.

Article 14
Rules of Procedure and Evidence

1. The Rules of Procedure and Evidence of the International Criminal Tribunal for Rwanda obtaining at the time of the establishment of the Special Court shall be applicable *mutatis mutandis* to the conduct of the legal proceedings before the Special Court.

2. The judges of the Special Court as a whole may amend the Rules of Procedure and Evidence or adopt additional rules where the applicable Rules do not, or do not adequately, provide for a specific situation. In so doing, they may be guided, as appropriate, by the Criminal Procedure Act, 1965, of Sierra Leone.

Statute of the Special Court for Sierra Leone Arts 1–5
Article 1
Competence of the Special Court

The Special Court shall have the power to prosecute persons most responsible for serious violations of international humanitarian law and Sierra Leonean law committed in the territory of Sierra Leone since 30 November 1996.

Article 2
Crimes against humanity

The Special Court shall have the power to prosecute persons who committed the following crimes as part of a widespread or systematic attack against any civilian population:

(a) Murder;

(b) Extermination;

(c) Enslavement;

(d) Deportation;

(e) Imprisonment;

(f) Torture;

(g) Rape, sexual slavery, enforced prostitution, forced pregnancy and any other form of sexual violence;

(h) Persecution on political, racial, ethnic or religious grounds;

(i) Other inhumane acts.

Article 3
Violations of article 3 common to the Geneva Conventions and of Additional Protocol II

The Special Court shall have the power to prosecute persons who committed or ordered the commission of serious violations of article 3 common to the Geneva Conventions of 12 August 1949 for the Protection of War Victims, and of Additional Protocol II thereto of 8 June 1977. These violations shall include:

(a) Violence to life, health and physical or mental well-being of persons, in particular murder as well as cruel treatment such as torture, mutilation or any form of corporal punishment;

(b) Collective punishments;

(c) Taking of hostages;

(d) Acts of terrorism;

(e) Outrages upon personal dignity, in particular humiliating and degrading treatment, rape, enforced prostitution and any form of indecent assault;

(f) Pillage;

(g) The passing of sentences and the carrying out of executions without previous judgement pronounced by a regularly constituted court, affording all the judicial guarantees which are recognized as indispensable by civilized peoples;

(h) Threats to commit any of the foregoing acts.

Article 4
Other serious violations of international humanitarian law

The Special Court shall have the power to prosecute persons who committed the following serious violations of international humanitarian law:

(a) Intentionally directing attacks against the civilian population as such or against individual civilians not taking direct part in hostilities;

(b) Intentionally directing attacks against personnel, installations, material, units or vehicles involved in a humanitarian assistance or peacekeeping mission in accordance with the Charter of the United Nations, as long as they are entitled to the protection given to civilians or civilian objects under the international law of armed conflict;

(c) Abduction and forced recruitment of children under the age of 15 years into armed forces or groups for the purpose of using them to participate actively in hostilities.

Article 5
Crimes under Sierra Leonean law

The Special Court shall have the power to prosecute persons who have committed the following crimes under Sierra Leonean law:

(a) Offences relating to the abuse of girls under the Prevention of Cruelty to Children Act, 1926 (Cap. 31):

  (i) Abusing a girl under 13 years of age, contrary to section 6;

  (ii) Abusing a girl between 13 and 14 years of age, contrary to section 7;

  (iii) Abduction of a girl for immoral purposes, contrary to section 12.

(b) Offences relating to the wanton destruction of property under the Malicious Damage Act, 1861:

  (i) Setting fire to dwelling-houses, any person being therein to section 2;

  (ii) Setting fire to public buildings, contrary to sections 5 and 6;

  (iii) Setting fire to other buildings, contrary to section 6.

Note that the jurisdiction is concurrent with other Sierra Leonean courts. Jurisdiction is over international crimes and national crimes. There are some differences with the wordings of the Statute and that of the *ad hoc* tribunals and the Statute of Rome.

The conflict in Sierra Leone was noted for the involvement of children. Indeed, the role of children in the conflict and their need for special rehabilitation measures has been a feature of the Truth and Reconciliation Process which is ongoing in the country. It is perhaps interesting to note that the Sierra Leonean court has jurisdiction over those aged 15 and over, albeit in accordance with international guidelines and the Truth and Reconciliation Process.

As to why the United Nations elected to establish a mixed court for Sierra Leone, perhaps a hint can be found in the provisions on funding the court. Funding is initially through voluntary contributions from the international community.

5.4.2.2   East Timor Special Panels

Conflict in East Timor accompanied its moves towards independence. Originally a Portuguese colony, it became a self-governing territory in 1960 (UN General Assembly Resolution 1542 (XV) 1960) under Portuguese administration but was occupied in 1975 by Indonesian forces and deemed part of Indonesia. Following negotiations between Indonesia, Portugal and Timorese representatives, a referendum on self-determination was held in August 1999. Over three-quarters of the population voted for independence, despite increased violence and reports of intimidation. The Security Council authorised the intervention of an international force to restore peace and order (Security Council Resolution 1264, 1999) and proceeded to establish the United Nations Transitional Administration in East Timor (Resolution 1272, 1999) as part of the nation-building process. Securing independence and full self-determination was a slow process but successful and East Timor became the 191st member State of the United Nations in 2002.

Part of the Transitional Administration's mandate was to create a judicial system though the issue of prosecuting those implicated in the violence and atrocities during Indonesian rule was problematic. A United Nations Commission of Inquiry was established and supported the creation of international tribunal with Timorese and Indonesian representatives (UN Doc. A/54/726, 2000). However, the United Nations eventually supported the national prosecution of offenders. Special Panels were established to prosecute international and serious criminal law offences. Similarly, Indonesian law was invoked to ensure the prosecution of those resident within Indonesia. However, the operation of the Timorese justice system and the Indonesian prosecutorial system has fallen short of the normal standard of international law. A United Nations independent Commission of Experts reviewed the prosecution of serious violations of human rights in Timor-L'este (East Timor) in 1999 (UN Doc. S/2005/458) and, while recognising the positive impact of the judicial process, raised a number of concerns. Partially in light of this, Indonesia has agreed to review its proceedings and has been accorded time by the international community to do so. Failing which, international intervention is likely.

5.4.2.3   Others

Cambodia: The reign of Pol Pot and the Khmer Rouge in Cambodia and the subsequent civil conflict resulted in significant violence and genocide. Within Cambodia, the UN-Cambodia peace agreement was not signed until 1991 (Cold War politics arguably slowed the process). The United Nations created an interim administration to oversee the transfer of authority to the new Cambodian authorities. Thereafter, Cambodia requested UN assistance in the prosecution of Khmer Rouge members. An expert panel was appointed to consider the options (GA Resolution 52/135 (1997)) and recommended an *ad hoc* tribunal. This was rejected by Cambodia and agreement was eventually reached on the establishment of a mixed tribunal. Extraordinary Chambers located within the Cambodian legal system have jurisdiction over international crimes and include international judges. The Chambers are only just entering their operational phase. In July 2006, one of the most senior accused persons died in custody, thereby avoiding trial. The length of time between the genocide and trials renders this scenario likely to be repeated with negative implications for justice.

Kosovo: Kosovo was enmeshed in the growing conflict in the Balkans in 1989–1999.

Although previously an autonomous region of the Socialist Federal Republic of Yugoslavia, the revocation of that autonomy by then President Slobodan Milosevic signalled the start of mounting ethnic tension and escalating violence. Following bombings by NATO in 1999, Yugoslavia agreed to retreat from Kosovo (SC Resolution 1244 (1999)). As also happened in Timor, the Secretary-General established an interim administrative authority in a region. Creating a functional judicial system was one of the administration's roles and despite some dispute over whether Kosovan, Yugoslavian or international law should apply, a number of prosecutions have been actioned. Obviously, some aspects of the work of the *ad hoc* International Criminal Tribunal for the Former Yugoslavia overlaps with this.

Iraq: Note the trial of Saddam Hussein and his co-accused, though for crimes against humanity, are being held in Iraqi courts in accordance with Iraqi law.

5.4.3 International Criminal Court

The present law relevant to international criminal law can be found in the Statute of Rome creating the International Criminal Court. Note that this treaty is not signed by all Member States of the international community and, for those falling outwith its jurisdiction, customary international law alone applies. The International Criminal Court operates alongside but outwith the United Nations system. It is thus independent.

Rome Statute of the International Criminal Court Art 5

The jurisdiction of the Court shall be limited to the most serious crimes of concern to the international community as a whole. The Court has jurisdiction in accordance with this Statute with respect to the following crimes:

(a) The crime of genocide;

(b) Crimes against humanity;

(c) War crimes;

(d) The crime of aggression.

Articles 6–8 define the crimes identified in (a)–(c) above, the crime of aggression is defined separately. The definitions of the crimes are relatively detailed as is appropriate for an instrument which will serve as the basis of legal prosecutions.

Question

Look up the definitions of the above-mentioned crimes (see also Chapter 15 of this text). Do they possess the necessary legal quality to identify appropriate prosecutions?

Question

Compare the definition of genocide with that enshrined in the Genocide Convention. Has the definition altered? It is also interesting to read the jurisprudence of the two International Criminal Tribunals which have considerably developed the scope of genocide.

Statute of the International Criminal Court Art 13

The Court may exercise its jurisdiction with respect to a crime referred to in Article 5 in accordance with the provisions of this Statute if:

(a) A situation in which one or more of such crimes appears to have been committed is referred to the Prosecutor by a State Party in accordance with article 14;

(b) A situation in which one or more of such crimes appears to have been committed is referred to the Prosecutor by the Security Council acting under Chapter VII of the Charter of the united nations; or

(c) The Prosecutor has initiated an investigation in respect of such a crime in accordance with article 15.

There are a couple of important limitations in respect of jurisdiction. In accordance with Art 11 of the Statute, the Court only has jurisdiction in respect of crimes committed after the entry into force of the Statute and after the entry into force of the Statute for the State concerned (unless the State has agreed to backdate jurisdiction to the entry into force of the Statute). Perhaps more important are the admissibility criteria which are found in Art 17 of the Statute.

However, unlike other areas of International Human Rights, International Criminal Law can be enforced against individuals.

Rome Statute of the International Criminal Court Art 25

(1) The Court shall have jurisdiction over natural persons pursuant to this Statute.

(2) A person who commits a crime within the jurisdiction of the Court shall be individually responsible and liable for punishment in accordance with this Statute.

The scope of individual liability is considerable. Read Arts 25(3)–33 which detail provisions regarding the establishment and avoidance of individual liability.

Question

To what extent can individuals avoid liability for their actions? Do these provisions undermine the effectiveness of international criminal law?

Individual liability for violations of human rights, albeit violations of a limited range of very serious abuses of human rights, in many respects challenges traditional views of international law, in so far that States no longer suffer sole responsibility for implementing human rights. In extreme situations, individuals too must recognise and respect the dignity and worth of their fellow human beings and act accordingly.

Question

Is the extension of liability for violations of rights to individuals implicated in international crimes acceptable under international law?

5.4.3.1   Comment

Consider the recent example of the United States of America led action in Iraq. While the United States has not ratified the Rome Statute, the United Kingdom has. Consequently, should any action of the United Kingdom's forces infringe the provisions of the Statute, there is the possibility of reference to the international Prosecutor. However, as the nature of international criminal law encourages concurrent jurisdiction, the UK has elected to invoke national law, through the courts martial system, to investigate and prosecute those allegedly involved in breaching international criminal and humanitarian law. For the record, the United States of America has also instituted national proceedings against several of its troops allegedly involved in war crimes and other inappropriate behaviour in Iraq.

5.4.4   Case study: first International Criminal Court warrants

In October 2005, the first five arrest warrants were unsealed by the Office of the Prosecutor of the International Criminal Court. These were issued in accordance with the procedure prescribed by the Statute of Rome and followed referral of the conflict in northern Uganda to the Court by the Government of Uganda in December 2003. Following discussions the Prosecutor, Luis Moreno-Ocampo, decided to open a formal investigation. This culminated in the application for arrest warrants, made to the Pre-Trial Chamber II in May 2005. Warrants were issued in July 2005 but remained sealed until the Pre-Trial Chamber was satisfied that all necessary measures had been taken to protect victims and potential witnesses.

All five accused are senior members of the Lord's Resistance Army, an armed rebel group claiming to fight on behalf of the Acholi peoples of northern Uganda but in fact frequently attacking the Acholi people themselves. The conflict has been ongoing for 19 years and, according to the Prosecutor, almost half the civilian population of northern Uganda have lost their freedom and now live in camps for internally displaced persons. During the period under investigation, July 2002 until July 2004, the Prosecutor's office amassed evidence of thousands of killings and abductions. Murder and enslavement were of particular concern.

The suspects were all involved in the conflict in Northern Uganda. Joseph Kony, the leader of the Lord's Resistance Army, is connected with 12 counts of crimes against humanity and 21 counts of war crimes. These include rape, murder, sexual enslavement, forced enlisting of children and enslavement. Vincent Otti, the second in command of the Lord's Resistance Army, is named for 11 counts of crimes against humanity and 21 counts of war crimes. Other high ranked members of the Lord's Resistance Army's command who are under warrant are Raska Lukwiya, Okot Odhiambo and Dominic Ongwen (although the Prosecutor notes that he has reputedly been killed in combat). In accordance with the terms of the Statute of Rome, the alleged crimes have all been committed after July 2002 when the jurisdiction of the Court commenced. The first arrest was made in March 2006. The trial should begin late 2006/early 2007.

At the news conference launching the search for the suspects, the Prosecutor took care to highlight the importance attached to adequate victim and witness protection measures.

The Prosecutor is continuing to investigate situations in Uganda, the Democratic Republic of the Congo and Darfur, Sudan. The latter was referred to the Court by the Security Council under Chapter VII of the UN Charter.

Question

Read the report on the Indonesian prosecutions for crimes in Timor L'este (referenced above). Note the problems with witness protection in Indonesia during the conduct of the international criminal trials. Can this be avoided?

Following systematic and gross violations of human rights, the United Nations initially favoured the establishment of *ad hoc* mechanisms. Hence the establishment of the two *ad hoc* International Criminal Tribunals, one for Rwanda, located in Arusha, Tanzania, the other for the Former Yugoslavia and situated in the Hague, the Netherlands. Increasingly desperate situations worldwide, including the tragic transition to independence of East Timor, prompted a rethink. States were encouraged to take responsibility for the prosecution of individuals responsible for human rights violations. Indeed, in Rwanda and the former Yugoslavia, some domestic prosecutions have taken place. An increased range of *ad hoc* tribunals was proving costly and cumbersome. Hence local solutions were sought in Sierra Leone, Indonesia etc.

5.5   ORGANISATION OF AMERICAN STATES INTER-AMERICAN COMMISSION ON HUMAN RIGHTS

In general, the regional human rights systems are limited by the powers granted to the salient monitoring body in terms of the principal human rights instrument. The European Court of Human Rights operates under the European Convention for the Protection of Human Rights and Fundamental Freedoms and the African Commission on Human and Peoples' Rights operates in accordance with the African Charter on Human and Peoples' Rights. The African Court of Human Rights, while formed under the protocol to the Charter also may assume some potential for human rights implementation in terms of the new Treaty on African Union, as well the African Court of Justice. The less judicial mechanisms created under the auspices of the Organisation for Security and Cooperation in Europe (see Chapter 4) have a broad jurisdiction over States, albeit with the consent of States.

Uniquely among regional organisations, the OAS incorporates a system for monitoring compliance with human rights norms which exists outwith the confines of the formal treaty mechanism. The Inter-American Commission enjoys a pervasive jurisdiction to monitor human rights generally within the Organisation of American States. As previously noted (Chapter 4), this means it has jurisdiction over all member States rather than just those States ratifying the Convention and accepting its jurisdiction thereunder. For those States who have not accepted the Convention, the Commission is limited to its residual consultative powers under the OAS Charter.

Charter of the Organisation of American States, as amended
Chapter XV
THE INTER-AMERICAN COMMISSION ON HUMAN RIGHTS
Article 106

There shall be an Inter-American Commission on Human Rights, whose principal function shall be to promote the observance and protection of human rights and to serve as a consultative organ of the Organization in these matters.

An inter-American convention on human rights shall determine the structure, competence, and procedure of this Commission, as well as those of other organs responsible for these matters. . . .

Article 145

Until the inter-American convention on human rights, referred to in Chapter XV, enters into force, the present Inter-American Commission on Human Rights shall keep vigilance over the observance of human rights.

The composition and procedures are addressed in detail in the American Convention on Human Rights and associated documentation (see Arts 34–51).

American Convention on Human Rights 1969
Article 35

The Commission shall represent all the member countries of the Organization of American States. . . .

Article 41

The main function of the Commission shall be to promote respect for and defense of human rights. In the exercise of its mandate, it shall have the following functions and powers:

a.   to develop an awareness of human rights among the peoples of America;

b. to make recommendations to the governments of the member states, when it considers such action advisable, for the adoption of progressive measures in favor of human rights within the framework of their domestic law and constitutional provisions as well as appropriate measures to further the observance of those rights;

c. to prepare such studies or reports as it considers advisable in the performance of its duties;

d. to request the governments of the member states to supply it with information on the measures adopted by them in matters of human rights;

e. to respond, through the General Secretariat of the Organization of American States, to inquiries made by the member states on matters related to human rights and, within the limits of its possibilities, to provide those states with the advisory services they request;

f. to take action on petitions and other communications pursuant to its authority under the provisions of Articles 44 through 51 of this Convention; and

g. to submit an annual report to the General Assembly of the Organization of American States.

Article 42

The States Parties shall transmit to the Commission a copy of each of the reports and studies that they submit annually to the Executive Committees of the Inter-American Economic and Social Council and the Inter-American Council for Education, Science, and Culture, in their respective fields, so that the Commission may watch over the promotion of the rights implicit in the economic, social, educational, scientific, and cultural standards set forth in the Charter of the Organization of American States as amended by the Protocol of Buenos Aires.

The Statute of the Commission provides details of its operational procedures, as does its rules of procedures.

Statute of the Inter-American Commission on Human Rights Approved by Resolution No 447 taken by the General Assembly of the OAS 9th session, 1979

Article 1

1. The Inter-American Commission on Human Rights is an organ of the Organization of the American States, created to promote the observance and defence of human rights and to serve as consultative organ of the Organization in this matter.

2. For the purposes of the present Statute, human rights are understood to be:

a. The rights set forth in the American Convention on Human Rights, in relation to the States Parties thereto;

b. The rights set forth in the American Declaration of the Rights and Duties of Man, in relation to the other member states. . . .

Article 18

The Commission shall have the following powers with respect to the member states of the Organization of American States:

a. to develop an awareness of human rights among the peoples of the Americas;

b. to make recommendations to the governments of the states on the adoption of progressive measures in favour of human rights in the framework of their legislation, constitutional provisions and international commitments, as well as appropriate measures to further observance of those rights;

c. to prepare such studies or reports as it considers advisable for the performance of its duties;

d. to request that the governments of the states provide it with reports on measures they adopt in matters of human rights;

e. to respond to inquiries made by any member state through the General Secretariat of the Organization on matters related to human rights in the state and, within its possibilities, to provide those states with the advisory services they request;

f. to submit an annual report to the General Assembly of the Organization, in which due account shall be taken of the legal regime applicable to those States Parties to the American Convention on Human Rights and of that system applicable to those that are not Parties;

g. to conduct on-site observations in a state, with the consent or at the invitation of the government in question; and

h. to submit the program-budget of the Commission to the Secretary-General, so that he may present it to the General Assembly. . . .

Article 20

In relation to those member states of the Organization that are not parties to the American Convention on Human Rights, the Commission shall have the following powers, in addition to those designated in Article 18:

a. to pay particular attention to the observance of the human rights referred to in Articles I, II, III, IV, XVIII, XXV, and XXVI of the American Declaration of the Rights and Duties of Man;

b. to examine communications submitted to it and any other available information, to address the government of any member state not a Party to the Convention for information deemed pertinent by this Commission, and to make recommendations to it, when it finds this appropriate, in order to bring about more effective observance of fundamental human rights; and,

c. to verify, as a prior condition to the exercise of the powers granted under subparagraph b. above, whether the domestic legal procedures and remedies of each member state not a Party to the Convention have been duly applied and exhausted.

The United States of America has not accepted the American Convention on Human Rights and thus complaints against it cannot be brought before the Inter-American Court of Human Rights. However, it has more general responsibilities to adhere to than the American Declaration on the Rights and Duties of Man. This has prompted a number of complaints to the Inter-American Commission and a number of findings of violations of the American Declaration of the Rights and Duties of Man: *Mary and Carrie Dann v United States of America*, Report No. 75/02 (2002) is one major example concerning indigenous people's rights. Many of the other complaints relate to criminal and appeal procedures for those convicted of capital offences and held on death row (for example: Report No. 1/05 Case 12.430 *Roberto Moreno Ramos v United States* (2005) or Report No. 100/03, Case 12.240 *Douglas Thomas v United States* (2003)).

FURTHER READING

General Public International Law textbooks provide information on the basic United Nations organs—see Chapter 1 for some suggestions.

Buergenthal, T, Shelton, D, and Stewart, D, *International Human Rights in a Nutshell*, 3rd edn, 2002, St Paul, Minn.: West Group

Cassesse, A, *International Criminal Law*, 2003, Oxford: Oxford University Press

Fitzpatrick, J, *Human Rights in Crisis. The International System for Protecting Rights during States of Emergency*, 1994, Philadelphia: University of Pennsylvania Press

Frulli, M, 'The Special Court for Sierra Leone: Some Preliminary Comments' (2000) 19 European Journal of International Law 857

Kelsall, T, 'Truth, Lies, Ritual: Preliminary Reflections on the Truth and Reconciliation Commission in Sierra Leone' (2005) 27 Human Rights Quarterly 361

Nowak, M, 'Introduction to the International Human Rights Regime: No. 14 (Raoul Wallenberg Institute Series of Intergovernmental Human Rights' Documentation), 2004, Leiden: Brill

OHCHR, Fact Sheet No. 3 Advisory Services and technical Cooperation in the Field of Human Rights, Geneva: OHCHR

OHCHR, Fact Sheet No. 27 Seventeen Frequently Asked Questions about United Nations Special Rapporteurs, 2001, Geneva: OHCHR

Ratner, R, 'The Cambodian Settlement Accords' (1993) 87 American Journal of International Law 1.

Ratner, M and Abrams, J, Accountability for Human Rights Atrocities in International Law, 2001, Oxford: OUP.

Websites

www.un.org—United Nations
www.un.org/ga—General Assembly of the United Nations
www.un.org/Docs/sc/—Security Council of the United Nations
www.un.org/docs/ecosoc/—Economic and Social Council
www.un.org/womenwatch/daw/csw—Commission on the Status of Women
www.ohchr.org/english/bodies/hrcouncil—Human Rights Council
www.unesco.org—UNESCO
www.ilo.org—International Labour Organisation

CHAPTER 6

IMPLEMENTING HUMAN RIGHTS: COMMITTEES AND COURTS

A number of conventional mechanisms have evolved to oversee the implementation of human rights. Most of these are created and operate under the terms agreed by the relevant High Contracting Parties. The seven treaty monitoring bodies established to monitor compliance with the principal UN international human rights treaties are the prime example of this. However, there are also a number of other committees under regional arrangements or separate international arrangements which operate in a similar way.

Regional organisations have been successful in developing the concept further, evolving courts with jurisdiction to consider infringements of international human rights by States, publicly holding the States to account.

This chapter will focus on these mechanisms, leading on to Chapter 7 which discusses national institutions.

6.1 UNITED NATIONS TREATY MONITORING BODIES: CONVENTIONAL MECHANISMS

Compliance of States with the primary international human rights instruments is monitored by committees created explicitly for this purpose. With the exception of the Committee on Economic, Social and Cultural Rights, each of the treaty monitoring bodies is established by the treaty in question. Accordingly, all power is derived from the provisions of the relevant treaty. Given the similarity between the seven committees, generic examples will be utilised in this section, selected from the various committees. Obviously, the text will be augmented by illustrations of the main variations from the general procedures.

The United Nations system supports seven treaty monitoring bodies.

United Nations Conventional Mechanisms: Committees and their constitutive Treaties

The Human Rights Committee (HRC) oversees the International Covenant on Civil and Political Rights;

The Committee on Economic, Social and Cultural Rights (CESCR) for the International Covenant on Economic, Social and Cultural Rights;

The Committee on the Elimination of Racial Discrimination (CERD) for the International Convention on the Elimination of All Forms of Racial Discrimination;

The Committee on the Elimination of Discrimination against Women (CEDAW) in respect of the Convention on the Elimination of All Forms of Discrimination against Women;

The Committee on the Rights of the Child (CRC) for the Convention on the Rights of the Child; and

The Committee on Migrant Workers (CMW) for the International Convention on Protection of the Rights of all Migrant Workers and Members of their Families.

6.1.1   Creation of Committees

Most Committees are created in terms of their parent instrument and derive powers based thereon. The Human Rights Committee was one of the first Committees to be established and as Steiner states, 'has transformed what was a novel and in some ways radical mandate into one that now appears conventional' (Steiner, H, 'Individual complaints in a world of massive violations: what role for the Human Rights Committee?' in Alston, P, and Crawford, J (eds), *The Future of UN Human Rights Treaty Monitoring*, 2000, Cambridge: Cambridge University Press). In some respects the Human Rights Committee continues to be the benchmark by which other international committees are measured. Indeed, it has evolved dynamically into an active and reasonably effective (given the constraints under which it operates) mechanism for monitoring the implementation of a range of human rights globally.

Most of the international human rights treaty monitoring committees operate under similar conditions. These committees are usually established in accordance with the terms of the relevant treaty which prescribes how many members each committee has, the requisite terms of appointment, the function and role of the committee, how often and where it meets etc. The following extract provides the relevant information for the Human Rights Committee, the appropriate section of the other instruments should be consulted for specific details applicable to any of the other committees.

International Covenant on Civil and Political Rights 1966

Article 28

1. There shall be established a Human Rights Committee (hereafter referred to in the present Covenant as the Committee). It shall consist of eighteen members and shall carry out the functions hereinafter provided.

2. The Committee shall be composed of nationals of the States Parties to the present Covenant who shall be persons of high moral character and recognized competence in the field of human rights, consideration being given to the usefulness of the participation of some persons having legal experience.

3. The members of the Committee shall be elected and shall serve in their personal capacity.

Article 29

1. The members of the Committee shall be elected by secret ballot from a list of persons possessing the qualifications prescribed in article 28 and nominated for the purpose by the States Parties to the present Covenant.

2. Each State Party to the present Covenant may nominate not more than two persons. These persons shall be nationals of the nominating State.

3. A person shall be eligible for renomination.

Article 30

1. The initial election shall be held no later than six months after the date of the entry into force of the present Covenant.

2. At least four months before the date of each election to the Committee, other than an election to fill a vacancy declared in accordance with article 34, the Secretary-General of the United Nations shall address a written invitation to the States Parties to the present Covenant to submit their nominations for membership of the Committee within three months.

3. The Secretary-General of the United Nations shall prepare a list in alphabetical order of all the

persons thus nominated, with an indication of the States Parties which have nominated them, and shall submit it to the States Parties to the present Covenant no later than one month before the date of each election.

4. Elections of the members of the Committee shall be held at a meeting of the States Parties to the present Covenant convened by the Secretary-General of the United Nations at the Head-quarters of the United Nations. At that meeting, for which two thirds of the States Parties to the present Covenant shall constitute a quorum, the persons elected to the Committee shall be those nominees who obtain the largest number of votes and an absolute majority of the votes of the representatives of States Parties present and voting.

Article 31

1. The Committee may not include more than one national of the same State.

2. In the election of the Committee, consideration shall be given to equitable geographical distribution of membership and to the representation of the different forms of civilization and of the principal legal systems.

Article 32

1. The members of the Committee shall be elected for a term of four years. They shall be eligible for re-election if renominated. However, the terms of nine of the members elected at the first election shall expire at the end of two years; immediately after the first election, the names of these nine members shall be chosen by lot by the Chairman of the meeting referred to in article 30, paragraph 4.

2. Elections at the expiry of office shall be held in accordance with the preceding articles of this part of the present Covenant.

Article 33

1. If, in the unanimous opinion of the other members, a member of the Committee has ceased to carry out his functions for any cause other than absence of a temporary character, the Chairman of the Committee shall notify the Secretary-General of the United Nations, who shall then declare the seat of that member to be vacant.

2. In the event of the death or the resignation of a member of the Committee, the Chairman shall immediately notify the Secretary-General of the United Nations, who shall declare the seat vacant from the date of death or the date on which the resignation takes effect.

Article 34

1. When a vacancy is declared in accordance with article 33 and if the term of office of the member to be replaced does not expire within six months of the declaration of the vacancy, the Secretary-General of the United Nations shall notify each of the States Parties to the present Covenant, which may within two months submit nominations in accordance with article 29 for the purpose of filling the vacancy.

2. The Secretary-General of the United Nations shall prepare a list in alphabetical order of the persons thus nominated and shall submit it to the States Parties to the present Covenant. The election to fill the vacancy shall then take place in accordance with the relevant provisions of this part of the present Covenant.

3. A member of the Committee elected to fill a vacancy declared in accordance with article 33 shall hold office for the remainder of the term of the member who vacated the seat on the Committee under the provisions of that article.

Article 35

The members of the Committee shall, with the approval of the General Assembly of the United Nations, receive emoluments from United Nations resources on such terms and conditions as the General Assembly may decide, having regard to the importance of the Committee's responsibilities.

Article 36

The Secretary-General of the United Nations shall provide the necessary staff and facilities for the effective performance of the functions of the Committee under the present Covenant.

Article 37

1. The Secretary-General of the United Nations shall convene the initial meeting of the Committee at the Headquarters of the United Nations.

2. After its initial meeting, the Committee shall meet at such times as shall be provided in its rules of procedure.

3. The Committee shall normally meet at the Headquarters of the United Nations or at the United Nations Office at Geneva.

Article 38

Every member of the Committee shall, before taking up his duties, make a solemn declaration in open committee that he will perform his functions impartially and conscientiously.

Article 39

1. The Committee shall elect its officers for a term of two years. They may be re-elected.

2. The Committee shall establish its own rules of procedure, but these rules shall provide, *inter alia*, that:

(a) Twelve members shall constitute a quorum;

(b) Decisions of the Committee shall be made by a majority vote of the members present.

Article 40

1. The States Parties to the present Covenant undertake to submit reports on the measures they have adopted which give effect to the rights recognized herein and on the progress made in the enjoyment of those rights:

(a) Within one year of the entry into force of the present Covenant for the States Parties concerned;

(b) Thereafter whenever the Committee so requests.

2. All reports shall be submitted to the Secretary-General of the United Nations, who shall transmit them to the Committee for consideration. Reports shall indicate the factors and difficulties, if any, affecting the implementation of the present Covenant.

3. The Secretary-General of the United Nations may, after consultation with the Committee, transmit to the specialized agencies concerned copies of such parts of the reports as may fall within their field of competence.

4. The Committee shall study the reports submitted by the States Parties to the present Covenant. It shall transmit its reports, and such general comments as it may consider appropriate, to the States Parties. The Committee may also transmit to the Economic and Social Council these comments along with the copies of the reports it has received from States Parties to the present Covenant.

5. The States Parties to the present Covenant may submit to the Committee observations on any comments that may be made in accordance with paragraph 4 of this article.

Note that the membership of the Committee is re-elected in a staggered system, thus ensuring some continuity throughout. Note the basic (limited) powers of the Committee. Remember that the States had to negotiate the terms of the treaty in the first place, thus the Committee only has the powers which the international community was willing to bestow on it.

Question

Consider how many high contracting parties there are now to the International Covenant on Civil and Political Rights. What problems therefore arise from the fact that there are currently three annual three-week sessions of the part-time Committee?

6.1.1.1 Exception: Committee on Economic, Social and Cultural Rights

The Committee on Economic, Social and Cultural Rights is an exception to the general rule in that it was not created by its parent treaty, the International Covenant on Economic, Social and Cultural Rights 1966. Rather it was created by the Economic and Social Council to assist it with monitoring the Covenant.

ECOSOC Resolution 1985/17, 28 May 1985

Review of the composition, organization and administrative arrangements of the Sessional Working Group of Governmental Experts on the Implementation of the International Covenant on Economic, Social and Cultural Rights

(*a*) The Working Group established by Economic and Social Council decision 1978/10 and modified by Council decision 1981/158 and resolution 1982/33 shall be renamed 'Committee on Economic, Social and Cultural Rights' (hereinafter referred to as 'the Committee'):

(*b*) The Committee shall have eighteen members who shall be experts with recognized competence in the field of human rights, serving in their personal capacity, due consideration being given to equitable geographical distribution and to the representation of different forms of social and legal systems; to this end, fifteen seats will be equally distributed among the regional groups, while the additional three seats will be allocated in accordance with the increase in the total number of States parties per regional group;

(*c*) The members of the Committee shall be elected by the Council by secret ballot from a list of persons nominated by States parties to the International Covenant on Economic, Social and Cultural Rights under the following conditions:

(i) The members of the Committee shall be elected for a term of four years and shall be eligible for re-election at the end of their term, if renominated;

(ii) One half of the membership of the Committee shall be renewed every second year, bearing in mind the need to maintain the equitable geographical distribution mentioned in subparagraph (*b*) above;

(iii) The first elections shall take place during the Council's first regular session of 1986; immediately after the first elections, the President of the Council shall choose by lot the names of nine members whose term shall expire at the end of two years;

(iv) The terms of office of members elected to the Committee shall begin on 1 January following their election and expire on 31 December following the election of members that are to succeed them as members of the Committee;

(v) Subsequent elections shall take place every second year during the first regular session of the Council;

(vi) At least four months before the date of each election to the Committee the Secretary-General shall address a written invitation to the States parties to the Covenant to submit their nominations for membership of the Committee within three months; the Secretary-General shall prepare a list of the persons thus nominated, with an indication of the States parties which have nominated them, and shall submit it to the Council no later than one month before the date of each election;

(*d*) The Committee shall meet annually for a period of up to three weeks, taking into account the number of reports to be examined by the Committee, with the venue alternating between Geneva and New York;

(e) The members of the Committee shall receive travel and subsistence expenses from United Nations resources;

(f) The Committee shall submit to the Council a report on its activities, including a summary of its consideration of the reports submitted by States parties to the Covenant, and shall make suggestions and recommendations of a general nature on the basis of its consideration of those reports and of the reports submitted by the specialized agencies, in order to assist the Council to fulfil, in particular, its responsibilities under articles 21 and 22 of the Covenant;

(g) The Secretary-General shall provide the Committee with summary records of its proceedings, which shall be made available to the Council at the same time as the report of the Committee; the Secretary-General shall further provide the Committee with the necessary staff and facilities for the effective performance of its functions, bearing in mind the need to give adequate publicity to its work;

(h) The procedures and methods of work established by Council resolution 1979/43 and the other resolutions and decisions referred to in the preamble lo the present resolution shall remain in force in so far as they are not superseded or modified by the present resolution;

(i) The Council shall review the composition, organization and administrative arrangements of the Committee at its first regular session of 1990, and subsequently every five years, taking into account the principle of equitable geographical distribution of its membership.

Question

Look at the Covenant and the rights and obligations assumed by States thereunder. What reasons are there for failing to create a conventional review mechanism to oversee the Covenant on Economic, Social and Cultural Rights when the Covenant was drafted?

6.1.2   Administrative, secretarial and research support

Given the increased workload of the Committees through the burgeoning number of States submitting reports, inevitably the functioning of the Committees is reliant on the support provided by the international secretariat. Most of the Committees are supported by the Office of the High Commissioner for Human Rights (OHCHR). The following extract is taken from the OHCHR's mission statement available online:

OHCHR aims to ensure the practical implementation of universally recognized human rights norms. It is committed to strengthening the United Nations human rights programme and providing the United Nations treaty monitoring bodies and special mechanisms established by the Commission on Human Rights with the highest quality support.

The High Commissioner for Human Rights is the official with principal responsibility for United Nations human rights activities. OHCHR is committed to working with other parts of the United Nations to integrate human rights standards throughout the work of the Organization.

The role of the High Commissioner for Human Rights, www.ohchr.org/ english/about/hc/index.htm
Supporting international human rights bodies

The High Commissioner seeks to offer the highest quality research, expertise, advice and administrative services to the main UN human rights bodies. OHCHR provides support for the meetings of the United Nations Commission on Human Rights and its Sub-Commission and follow-up to their deliberations. Its staff assist the numerous experts appointed by these bodies in investigating and reporting on human rights issues. It also prepares the work of the UN committees that monitor how States fulfil their human rights obligations. OHCHR ensures a communication flow between these international bodies to maximize the impact of their efforts.

The Office of the High Commissioner for Human Rights normally provides secretarial assistance to the committees and appropriate accommodation for staff and meetings. The Committee members are thus better able to maximise the (comparatively) short time they have in Geneva to focus on monitoring the implementation of the relevant treaty by contracting states. One of the criticisms levelled at the current system is that the increase in the number of treaties and the proliferation in accessions thereto (due to the increase in membership of the United Nations) have not been matched in an increase in resources to the committees to facilitate implementation. This is discussed in more detail in Chapter 9 on reforming the international system.

6.1.2.1   Exception: Committee on the Elimination of Discrimination against Women

Unlike the other committees, CEDAW is supported by the Division for the Advancement of Women (DAW). The protection of women has early origins in the United Nations: a Sub-Commission on the Status of Women was established by ECOSOC Resolution E/20, 1946 with a nucleus of nine members. The Commission on the Status of Women (CSW) was established as a functional commission of the Economic and Social Council by Council Resolution 11(II) of 21 June 1946 to prepare recommendations and reports to the Council on promoting women's rights in political, economic, civil, social and educational fields. It now has 45 members.

Mission Statement of Division for Advancement of Women, www.un.org/ womenwatch/daw/daw/

Grounded in the vision of equality of the United Nations Charter, the Division for the Advancement of Women (DAW) advocates the improvement of the status of women of the world and the achievement of their equality with men. Aiming to ensure the participation of women as equal partners with men in all aspects of human endeavour, the Division promotes women as equal participants and beneficiaries of sustainable development, peace and security, governance and human rights. As part of its mandate, it strives to stimulate the mainstreaming of gender perspectives both within and outside the United Nations system.

The Division:

- is a catalyst for advancing the global agenda on women's issues and gender equality, and works closely with Governments, its partners in the United Nations system and civil society

- conducts research and develops policy options, fosters interaction between Governments and civil society

- aims to strengthen communication between the international and national policy-making processes by the promotion of global standards and norms, awareness-raising, and the sharing of best practices

- supports the implementation of the Beijing Platform for Action (1995), the outcome of the 23rd special session of the General Assembly (2000), relevant recommendations of other global conferences and their reviews, and relevant decisions taken by the General Assembly, Economic and Social Council, the Commission on the Status of Women, and other functional commissions of the ECOSOC

- provides substantive servicing to the Commission on the Status of Women with the mandate to elaborate global policies and norms

- provides substantive and technical servicing to the Committee on the Elimination of

Discrimination against Women (CEDAW)—the expert treaty body which monitors the implementation of the Convention on the Elimination of all Forms of Discrimination against Women and its Optional Protocol

- promotes and supports the mainstreaming of gender perspectives into the work of inter-governmental bodies, the policies and programmes of departments and offices of the United Nations, as well as at national, regional and international levels

- provides advisory services and technical cooperation programmes to developing countries in connection with its work on policy formulation and implementation related to the Beijing Declaration and Platform for Action, the outcome of the 23rd special session of the General Assembly; as well as its work related to the Convention on the Elimination of All Forms of Discrimination against Women and its Optional Protocol.

6.1.3   Powers of Committees

The power of each Committee is derived from the relevant instrument. It follows that each Committee only enjoys such power as the High Contracting States agree. The terminology employed in the treaties is prosaic, indicating little actual power: committees consider reports and communications then forward their views thereon to the appropriate parties following discussion in closed meetings. It is clear that States did not envisage the role of Committees as being judicial, quasi-judicial or even particularly pro-active in monitoring the implementation of international human rights norms. However, within the terms of their remit, the committees have succeeded in developing their powers. The impact of the Committees have been quite far reaching—of perhaps particular note, both the Human Rights Committee and the Committee on the Rights of the Child have considerably developed the rights and freedoms enshrined in their parent document.

Committees each have the same principal function of monitoring the compliance with the terms of the relevant treaty by States Parties. Receiving, considering and opining on reports is the principal function, inter-State and individual complaints sit alongside this in most systems. Additionally, most of the Committees take the opportunity to shape the law through issuing general comments on specific issues and some have the opportunity of conducting visits to States Parties to investigate their compliance record.

6.1.4   Initial and periodic reports by states to treaty monitoring bodies

The primary mechanism for monitoring the implementation of human rights is reports. States compile reports on the actions they have taken to realise the obligations undertaken in terms of the relevant human rights instrument.

The Committees generally draw up reporting guidelines for the use of States when compiling reports. The compilation of multiple reports is one of the consequential burdens on States as a result of the flourishing human rights treaty system. As a consequence, attempts are being made to standardise some aspects of the information. This is discussed further in the chapter on reform (Chapter 9). Technical assistance with the compilation of initial periodic reports can be provided by the Office of the High Commissioner for Human Rights to contracting States. The following diagram indicates the process.

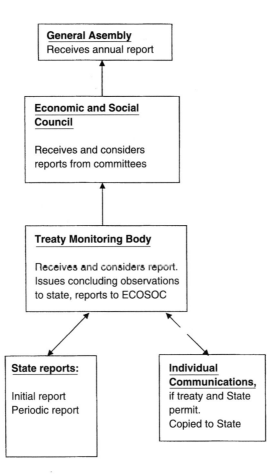

The following extract is of rights in the International Covenant on Economic, Social and Cultural Rights.

International Covenant on Economic, Social and Cultural Rights
Arts 1,2 and 11

Article 1

1. All peoples have the right of self-determination. By virtue of that right they freely determine their political status and freely pursue their economic, social and cultural development.

2. All peoples may, for their own ends, freely dispose of their natural wealth and resources without prejudice to any obligations arising out of international economic co-operation, based upon the principle of mutual benefit, and international law. In no case may a people be deprived of its own means of subsistence.

3. The States Parties to the present Covenant, including those having responsibility for the administration of Non-Self-Governing and Trust Territories, shall promote the realization of the right of self-determination, and shall respect that right, in conformity with the provisions of the Charter of the United Nations.

Article 2

1. Each State Party to the present Covenant undertakes to take steps, individually and through international assistance and co-operation, especially economic and technical, to the maximum of

its available resources, with a view to achieving progressively the full realization of the rights recognized in the present Covenant by all appropriate means, including particularly the adoption of legislative measures.

2. The States Parties to the present Covenant undertake to guarantee that the rights enunciated in the present Covenant will be exercised without discrimination of any kind as to race, colour, sex, language, religion, political or other opinion, national or social origin, property, birth or other status.

3. Developing countries, with due regard to human rights and their national economy, may determine to what extent they would guarantee the economic rights recognized in the present Covenant to non-nationals.

Article 11

1. The States Parties to the present Covenant recognize the right of everyone to an adequate standard of living for himself and his family, including adequate food, clothing and housing, and to the continuous improvement of living conditions. The States Parties will take appropriate steps to ensure the realization of this right, recognizing to this effect the essential importance of international co-operation based on free consent.

2. The States Parties to the present Covenant, recognizing the fundamental right of everyone to be free from hunger, shall take, individually and through international co-operation, the measures, including specific programmes, which are needed:

(a) To improve methods of production, conservation and distribution of food by making full use of technical and scientific knowledge, by disseminating knowledge of the principles of nutrition and by developing or reforming agrarian systems in such a way as to achieve the most efficient development and utilization of natural resources;

(b) Taking into account the problems of both food-importing and food-exporting countries, to ensure an equitable distribution of world food supplies in relation to need.

Question

Consider the difficulty for a State seeking to compile relevant reports to submit to the Committee.

Extracts from Revised general guidelines regarding the form and contents of reports to be submitted by states parties under articles 16 and 17 of the International Covenant on Economic, Social and Cultural Rights, 17/06/91, UN Doc. E/C.12/1991/1

A. Part of the report relating to general provisions of the Covenant
Article 1 of the Covenant

In what manner has the right to self-determination been implemented?

Article 2 of the Covenant

1. To what extent and in what manner are non-nationals not guaranteed the rights recognized in the Covenant? What justification is there for any difference?

2. Which of the rights are specifically subject to non-discrimination provisions in national law? Attach the text of such provisions.

3. If your State participates in development cooperation, is any effort made to ensure that it is used, on a priority basis, to promote the realization of economic, social and cultural rights?

B. Part of the report relating to specific rights

. . .

Article 11 of the Covenant

1. (a) Please supply information on the current standard of living of your population, in respect of both the aggregate and different socio-economic, cultural, and other groups within the society. How has the standard of living changed over time (e.g., compared with 10 years ago and 5 years ago) with regard to these different groups? Has there been a continuous improvement of living conditions for the entire population or for what groups?

(b) In case your Government has recently submitted reports relevant to the situation with respect to all or some of the rights contained in article 11 to the United Nations or a specialized agency, you may wish to refer to the relevant parts of those reports rather than repeat the information here.

(c) Please indicate the per capita GNP for the poorest 40 per cent of your population. Is there a 'poverty line' in existence in your country and, if so, what is the basis for this line?

(d) Please indicate your country's Physical Quality of Life Index.

2. The right to adequate food

(a) Please provide a general overview of the extent to which the right to adequate food has been realized in your country. Describe the sources of information that exist in this regard, including nutritional surveys and other monitoring arrangements.

(b) Please provide detailed information (including statistical data broken down in terms of different geographical areas) on the extent to which hunger and/or malnutrition exists in your country. This information should deal in particular with the following issues:

(i) The situation of especially vulnerable or disadvantaged groups, including:

Landless peasants

Marginalized peasants

Rural workers

Rural unemployed

Urban unemployed

Urban poor

Migrant workers

Indigenous peoples

Children

Elderly people

Other especially affected groups;

(ii) Any significant differences in the situation of men and women within each of the above groups;

(iii) The changes that have taken place over the past five years with respect to the situation of each of the above groups.

(c) During the reporting period, have there been any changes in national policies, laws and practices negatively affecting the access to adequate food by these groups or sectors or within the worse-off regions? If so, please describe these changes and evaluate their impact.

(d) Please indicate what measures are considered necessary by your Government to guarantee access to adequate food for each of the vulnerable or disadvantaged groups mentioned above and for the worse-off areas, and for the full implementation of the right to food for both men and women. Indicate the measures taken and specify time-related goals and nutritional bench-marks for measuring achievements in this regard.

(e) Please indicate in what ways measures taken to improve methods of production, conservation and distribution of food by making full use of technical and scientific knowledge have contributed towards, or have impeded the realization of the right to adequate food. Please describe the impact of these measures in terms of ecological sustainability and the protection and conservation of food producing resources.

(f) Please indicate what measures are taken to disseminate knowledge of the principles of nutrition and specify whether any significant groups or sectors within society seem to lack such knowledge.

(g) Please describe any measures of agrarian reform taken by your Government to ensure that the agrarian system is efficiently utilized in order to promote food security at household level without negatively affecting human dignity both in the rural and urban settings taking into account articles 6 to 8 of the Covenant. Describe the measures taken:

(i) To legislate to this effect;

(ii) To enforce existing law to this effect;

(iii) To facilitate monitoring through governmental and non-governmental organizations.

(h) Please describe and evaluate the measures taken by your Government in order to ensure an equitable distribution, in terms of both production and trade, of world food supplies in relation to need, taking into account the problems of both food-importing and food-exporting countries.

3. The right to adequate housing

(a) Please furnish detailed statistical information about the housing situation in your country.

(b) Please provide detailed information about those groups within your society that are vulnerable and disadvantaged with regard to housing. Indicate, in particular:

(i) The number of homeless individuals and families;

(ii) The number of individuals and families currently inadequately housed and without ready access to basic amenities such as water, heating (if necessary), waste disposal, sanitation facilities, electricity, postal services, etc. (in so far as you consider these amenities relevant in your country). Include the number of people living in over-crowded, damp, structurally unsafe housing or other conditions which affect health;

(iii) The number of persons currently classified as living in 'illegal' settlements or housing;

(iv) The number of persons evicted within the last five years and the number of persons currently lacking legal protection against arbitrary eviction or any other kind of eviction;

(v) The number of persons whose housing expenses are above any government-set limit of affordability, based upon ability to pay or as a ratio of income;

(vi) The number of persons on waiting lists for obtaining accommodation, the average length of waiting time and measures taken to decrease such lists as well as to assist those on such lists in finding temporary housing;

(vii) The number of persons in different types of housing tenure by: social or public housing; private rental sector; owner-occupiers; 'illegal' sector; and other.

(c) Please provide information on the existence of any laws affecting the realization of the right to housing, including:

(i) Legislation which gives substance to the right to housing in terms of defining the content of this right;

(ii) Legislation such as housing acts, homeless person acts, municipal corporation acts, etc;

(iii) Legislation relevant to land use, land distribution; land allocation, land zoning, land ceilings, expropriations including provisions for compensation; land planning, including procedures for community participation;

(iv)   Legislation concerning the rights of tenants to security of tenure, to protection from eviction; to housing finance and rental control (or subsidy), housing affordability, etc;

(v)   Legislation concerning building codes, building regulations and standards and the provision of infrastructure;

(vi)   Legislation prohibiting any and all forms of discrimination in the housing sector, including groups not traditionally protected;

(vii) Legislation prohibiting any form of eviction;

(viii) Any legislative repeal or reform of existing laws which detracts from the fulfilment of the right to housing;

(ix)   Legislation restricting speculation on housing or property, particularly when such speculation has a negative impact on the fulfilment of housing rights for all sectors of society;

(x)   Legislative measures conferring legal title to those living in the 'illegal' sector;

(xi)   Legislation concerning environmental planning and health in housing and human settlements.

(d) Please provide information on all other measures taken to fulfil the right to housing, including:

(i)   Measures taken to encourage 'enabling strategies' whereby local community-based organizations and the 'informal sector' can build housing and related services. Are such organizations free to operate? Do they receive Government funding?

(ii)   Measures taken by the State to build housing units and to increase other construction of affordable, rental housing;

(iii) Measures taken to release unutilized, under-utilized or mis-utilized land;

(iv)   Financial measures taken by the State including details of the budget of the Ministry of Housing or other relevant Ministry as a percentage of the national budget;

(v)   Measures taken to ensure that international assistance for housing and human settlements is used to fulfil the needs of the most disadvantaged groups;

(vi)   Measures taken to encourage the development of small and intermediate urban centres, especially at the rural level;

(vii) Measures taken during, *inter alia*, urban renewal programmes, redevelopment projects, site upgrading, preparation for international events (Olympics, expositions, conferences, etc.), 'beautiful city campaigns', etc., which guarantee protection from eviction or guaranteed rehousing based on mutual agreement, by any persons living on or near to affected sites.

(e) During the reporting period, have there been any changes in national policies, laws and practices negatively affecting the right to adequate housing? If so, please describe the changes and evaluate their impact.

4. Please give details on any difficulties or shortcomings encountered in the fulfilment of the rights enshrined in article 11 and on the measures taken to remedy these situations (if not already described in the present report).

5. Please indicate the role of international assistance in the full realization of the rights enshrined in article 11.

As with this example, the reporting guidelines can be quite specific. The Office of the High Commissioner of Human Rights and various NGOs and regional government funded bodies are willing to provide any necessary training for State officials tasked with compiling and submitting reports.

Consider the following extracts of the report from Denmark and the Russian Federation to the Economic, Social and Cultural Rights Committee. Each extract relates only to the right to self-determination (Art 1 of the Covenant).

Fourth Periodic Report submitted by Denmark, considered 2004
E/C.12/4/Add.12

Article 1. The right to self-determination
Greenland
Introduction

1. Greenland is a geographically separate and well-defined part of the Danish Realm covering an area of 2,175,600 square kilometres. The population of Greenland is almost exclusively made up of an indigenous people (ethnic Greenlanders/Kalaallit or Inuit) with a language and culture distinct from the Danish. As of 1 January 2002, the total population of Greenland amounted to 49,814 persons, the vast majority of whom are ethnic Greenlanders. Additionally, 6,728 ethnic Greenlanders live in various other parts of the Realm.

2. Denmark regards the right of peoples to self-determination as also being applicable to indigenous peoples. How the observance of this right has been achieved in the case of the indigenous people of Greenland, the only indigenous people living within the Kingdom of Denmark, is described below.

3. The Danish Constitution applies to all parts of the Danish Realm. Since 1953, Greenland has been represented by two permanent members in the Danish Parliament.

4. The Home Rule Act of 1978 permitted Greenland to take over responsibility for almost all policy areas pertaining exclusively to its own affairs (the Greenland Home Rule Act is enclosed as Annex I). Reference is made to reports submitted by the Government of Denmark under article 40 of the International Covenant on Civil and Political Rights concerning the introduction of Home Rule in Greenland, contained in documents CCPR/G/Add.19, CCPR/C/37/Add.5 and CCPR/64/Add.11.

5. Denmark has ratified ILO Convention No. 169 concerning Indigenous and Tribal Peoples in Independent Countries. This Convention applies to the indigenous people of Greenland. The Home Rule authorities encouraged Denmark to ratify the Convention and thereby declare that the Home Rule Act for Greenland fulfils the obligations of the Convention.

Home Rule in Greenland

6. In 1972, the Provincial Council of Greenland recommended to the Danish Government that the issue of granting the Provincial Council increased influence on and joint responsibility for the development of Greenland be studied. The Danish Government established a Commission on Home Rule in Greenland composed of Greenlandic and Danish politicians. On the basis of the recommendations and proposals of the Commission, the Danish Parliament passed the Greenland Home Rule Act in November 1978. By a referendum held in Greenland, on 17 January 1979, a large majority of the population of Greenland approved the coming into force of the Act. Seventy per cent of the votes cast favoured the introduction of Home Rule in Greenland, which became effective as of 1 May 1979.

Home Rule powers

7. Greenland Home Rule is an extensive type of self-government. By the Greenland Home Rule Act the Danish Parliament has delegated legislative and executive powers to the Home Rule Authority, consisting of a popularly elected legislative assembly: the Greenland Home Rule Parliament (Landsting) and the Greenland Home Rule Government (Landsstyre). The powers transferred by statute are in principle identical to the powers exercised by the central authorities of the Realm in other parts of Denmark. Consequently, the Danish Parliament and the Danish Government refrain from enacting legislation and exercising administrative powers in the fields where these powers have been transferred to the Home Rule authorities. . . .

Procedures for the transfer of powers to Home Rule

10. Greenland Home Rule rests on the basic principle that legislative power and 'the power of the purse' should not be divided. Consequently, the Home Rule Act provides that when the Danish Parliament transfers a field to the Home Rule, the Home Rule Authority must take on the associated expenditures. Conversely, the Home Rule Authority is the sole beneficiary of taxes and revenue generated in fields transferred to Home Rule. Since Greenland is not yet able to fully self-finance a number of capital-intensive fields, an instrument has been created under the Home Rule Act to facilitate transfer of powers to Home Rule in fields requiring Danish subsidies.

Unity of the Realm and constitutional limits to Home Rule

13. The Home Rule Act has not altered Greenland's constitutional status as a part of the Danish Realm. The principle of the unity of the Realm, derived from the Danish Constitution and expressed in the Home Rule Act, sets certain limits to the scope of Greenland Home Rule: sovereignty continues to rest with the central authorities of the Realm; Greenland remains a part of the Danish Realm; only policy areas pertaining exclusively to Greenland may be transferred to the Home Rule Authority; the delegation of powers cannot be unlimited and must be precisely defined by statute; certain fields such as the so-called affairs of State may not be transferred to Home Rule. These exclusive affairs of State include external relations, defence and monetary policy.

Joint decision on mineral resources

15. The Home Rule Act states that the resident population of Greenland has fundamental rights to the natural resources of Greenland. In respect of mineral resources, the Home Rule Act contains a special provision vesting joint decision-making power in the national authorities and the Home Rule authorities, making it possible for either party to oppose, and ultimately to veto, a development policy or specific resolutions considered by the party in question as being undesirable. The Commission on Home Rule applied the principle that, in the wording of the legislation on mineral resources as well as of the Home Rule Act, due respect must be paid to the unity of the Realm and thus also to the interests of the Realm as a whole.

'Greenlandization'

16. With the introduction of Home Rule an intensive process of 'Greenlandization' commenced. The autonomy of Greenland was symbolized by the bringing into existence of an official flag and coat of arms of Greenland. The Home Rule Authority has made great efforts to preserve the culture and heritage of Greenland. The language is of vital importance and the Home Rule Act proclaims Greenlandic to be the principal language in Greenland.

17. After having had Home Rule for more than 20 years the Government of Greenland decided, in 2000, to establish a commission on the expansion of Home Rule. The Commission is to make a report on the current extent of Home Rule and to identify and describe new arrangements that will satisfy the self-government aspirations of Greenland within the Danish Realm. Some of the areas which the Commission is exploring are presently within the jurisdiction of the Danish Government, such as the judicial system, foreign affairs and security policy. Furthermore, the Commission will put forward proposals for moving Greenland further in the direction of economic self-sufficiency. See paragraph 30 below.

Recent developments in Greenland

25. In January 2000, a Commission on Self-Government, established by the Greenland Home Rule Government, commenced its work. The Commission, which is made up of representatives of the political parties as well as experts appointed in their personal capacities, has the following terms of reference:

> The Commission's task is to prepare a report on the possibilities for expanding Greenland's autonomy within the unity of the Realm, based on the principle of conformity between rights and responsibilities.

The Commission shall describe the Home Rule's current position with respect to consti-tutional law—including questions of jurisdiction and delegation between the central and Home Rule governments—and identify and describe alternative arrangements that will better satisfy self-government aspirations within the unity of the Realm.

The Commission shall explore the possibilities for expanding Greenland's authority, role and ability to act in the foreign and security policy areas. To this end, it shall:

— consider Greenland's role in security policy from the standpoint of its geographical situation, and how Greenland's interests can most appropriately be safeguarded from this point of view; and

— consider the need and potential for independent Greenlandic representation in inter-national forums at which Greenlandic representatives currently form part of Danish government delegations.

The Commission shall describe the areas in which the Home Rule has taken over jurisdiction, the areas in which the central Government has retained jurisdiction, and those areas in which jurisdiction is shared in various ways between the Home Rule and the central Government. In this connection the Commission shall consider possibilities for the transfer to Greenland in whole or part of the judicial system in Greenland, now or in the long term, in view of the report to be tabled by the Greenlandic Commission on the Administration of Justice.

The Commission shall put forward proposals for moving Greenland further in the direction of economic self-sufficiency, including the conditions for the block transfer. It shall describe and discuss changes to the Greenland Treasury's various subsidy schemes.

The Commission shall consider the need and feasibility of transferring other areas of responsibility to the Home Rule, and explore the advantages and disadvantages.

The Commission is asked to explore and assess possibilities for Greenlandic participation in assertion of sovereignty and fisheries inspection.

The Commission may put forward proposals for amending the Home Rule Act and existing enabling legislation, and amendments to administrative and framework agreements between the central Government and the Home Rule in the above-mentioned areas of concern.

The report goes on to address the Faroe Islands.

Fourth periodic report of the Russian federation, UN Doc. E/C.12/4/Add.10, considered 2001

The right to self-determination (article 1)

1. Article 5, paragraph 3 of the Russian Federation's Constitution states: 'The federated structure of the Russian Federation shall be based on its state integrity, a uniform system of state power, delimitation of scopes of authority and powers between the bodies of state power of the Russian Federation and the bodies of state power of the Russian Federation's constituent members, equality and self-determination of the peoples in the Russian Federation'.

2. Over 140 nationalities and ethnic groups live in the Russian Federation. The Russian Feder-ation is made up of 21 republics, 6 territories (krai), 49 regions (oblast), 1 autonomous region and 10 autonomous areas (okrug), each with its own constitution or charter and its own legislation.

3. To extend its constitutional provisions concerning the self-determination of peoples, the Rus-sian Federation adopted the Act 'National cultural autonomy' in 1996, and the Act 'Guarantees of the rights of indigenous peoples whose numbers are small' in 1999. National cultural autonomy is a form of national cultural self-determination in which citizens belonging to specific nationalities come together into one community, on a freely organized basis, in order to resolve independently matters relating to the preservation of their independence, language, education and culture. By 2000, eleven ethnic groups in the Russian Federation had availed themselves of the law on establishing national cultural autonomy: Ukrainians, Kurds, Germans, Roma, Azerbaijanis, Lezgins, Belorussians, Tatars, Koreans, Serbs and Jews.

4. Further information concerning this article is contained in paragraphs 1–14 of the Russian Federation's third periodic report submitted in 1994.

Question

To what extent do either or both of the reports extracted above comply with the guidelines issues by the Committee? Moreover, to what extent does the report reflect the reality of the region concerned?

6.1.4.1   Comment on reports

Although primarily a mechanism for complying with the treaty obligations, the reports form part of a constructive dialogue between the treaty monitoring body and the State. Reports may also be employed as a self-evaluation exercise, allowing the State to identify problems and areas in which the international community may help. Given the beneficial aspects of reports, States are actively encouraged to submit reports, as per the treaty obligations. The frequency of reports varies from instrument to instrument, as the table below indicates.

Treaty	Frequency of periodic reports
International Convention on the Elimination of all Forms of Racial Discrimination	Every 2 years
International Covenant on Economic, Social and Cultural Rights	Not specified
International Covenant on Civil and Political Rights	Not specified Generally every 5 years
Convention on the Elimination of Discrimination against Women	Every 4 years
Convention against Torture	Every 4 years
UN Convention on the Rights of the Child	Every 5 years
International Convention on the Protection of the Rights of all Migrant Workers and Members of Their Families	Every 5 years

If each new State ratifies each instrument, it will have seven reports to submit within a year and thereafter regular periodic reports. This can be unduly onerous on some States and thus is one of the issues currently under review—see Chapter 9.

6.1.4.2   Non-submission of reports/incomplete reports

Should a State fail to submit a report on time, reminders may be sent. Thereafter, the matter will be drawn to the attention of the relevant bodies in accordance with the hierarchy. Similarly, States can be asked to provide further information to supplement their report. Such requests may be based on information the Committee received from NGOs, other United Nations entities and organisations, or even from general news coverage. Even if a report is complete and submitted on time, before the scheduled meeting, Committees may elect to refer a list of issues to a State for response.

Question

This system allows the Committee to focus on particular issues and set the agenda for the discussion. What other advantages does it afford a system which is currently stretched in terms of time?

Note the following guidelines from the Committee on the Elimination of Racial Discrimination which apply to the submission of reports.

Rules of Procedure adopted for CERD: 01/01/89.
UN Doc. CERD/C/35/Rev.3.

PART TWO. RULES RELATING TO THE FUNCTIONS OF THE COMMITTEE
XV. REPORTS AND INFORMATION FROM STATES PARTIES UNDER ARTICLE 9 OF THE CONVENTION
Form and contents of reports
Rule 63

The Committee may, through the Secretary-General, inform the States parties of its Wishes regarding the form and contents of the periodic reports required to be submitted under article 9 of the Convention.

Attendance by States parties at examination of reports
Rule 64

The Committee shall, through the Secretary-General, notify the States parties (as early as possible) of the opening date, duration and place of the session at which their respective reports will be examined. Representatives of the States parties may be present at the meetings of the Committee when their reports are examined. The Committee may also inform a State party from which it decides to seek further information that it may authorize its representative to be present at a specified meeting. Such a representative should be able to answer questions which may be put to him by the Committee and make statements on reports already submitted by his State, and may also submit additional information from his State.

Request for additional information
Rule 65

If the Committee decides to request an additional report or further information from a State party under the provisions of article 9, paragraph 1, of the Convention, it may indicate the manner as well as the time within which such additional report or further information shall be supplied and shall transmit its decision to the Secretary-General for communication, within two weeks, to the State party concerned.

Non-receipt of reports
Rule 66

1. At each session, the Secretary-General shall notify the Committee of all cases of non-receipt of reports or additional information, as the case may be, provided for under article 9 of the Convention. The Committee, in such cases, may transmit to the State party concerned, through the Secretary-General, a reminder concerning the submission of the report or additional information.

2. If even after the reminder, referred to in paragraph 1 of this rule, the State party does not submit the report or additional information required under article 9 of the Convention, the Committee shall include a reference to this effect in its annual report to the General Assembly.

Suggestions and general recommendations
Rule 67

1. When considering a report submitted by a State party under article 9, the Committee shall first determine whether the report provides the information referred to in the relevant communications of the Committee.

2. If a report of the State party to the Convention, in the opinion of the Committee, does not contain sufficient information, the Committee may request that State to furnish additional information.

3. If, on the basis of its examination of the reports and information supplied by the State party, the Committee determines that some of the obligations of that State under the Convention have not been discharged, it may make suggestions and general recommendations in accordance with article 9, paragraph 2, of the Convention.

Transmission of suggestions and general recommendations
Rule 68

1. Suggestions and general recommendations made by the Committee based on the examination of the reports and information received from States parties under article 9, paragraph 2, of the Convention shall be communicated by the Committee through the Secretary-General to the States parties for their comments.

2. The Committee may, where necessary, indicate a time-limit within which comments from States parties are to be received.

3. Suggestions and general recommendations of the Committee, referred to in paragraph 1, shall be reported to the General Assembly, together with comments, if any, from States parties.

Should States fail to submit reports, certain Committees, such as CERD, reserve the right to consider the status of human rights in the State on the basis of other information available to them. Such a situation would only follow repeated requests to the State to engage in dialogue with the Committee. In the first instance, following repeated failure to submit reports, the State is usually sent a list of questions for written responses. (See for example, the letter and list of issues in connection with the 5th to 14th overdue periodic reports due from 1989 to 2005 of the Republic of the Seychelles, 19 August 2005, from the website of the Office of the High Commissioner of Human Rights.)

Question

What advantages are offered by delivering a list of issues/questions when a series of reports have failed to be forthcoming?

Note that letters and requests for information are often accompanied by an offer of technical assistance should it be required by the State. Should no information be forthcoming, the Committee will issue concluding observations.

Committee on the Elimination of Racial Discrimination, CERD/C/64/Dec.1 Guyana, 2004

Decision (1) 64 on Guyana

1. The Committee on the Elimination of Racial Discrimination recalls its Decision 2 (62) adopted on 21 March 2003, and regrets that the State party has been unable to fulfill its commitment to submit its initial to fourteenth periodic reports combined in one document, in time for consideration at the 64th session of the Committee. However, it takes note of the submission by Guyana of its report to the Committee on the Elimination of Discrimination against Women and of its report to the Committee on the Rights of the Child.

2. The Committee notes that, following repeated requests from the State party for technical assistance from the Office of the High Commissioner for Human Rights, a decision was recently taken to appoint a consultant to assist the State party in the preparation of the report. In this connection, the Committee also takes note of the State party's assurances that it remains committed to the preparation and submission to the Committee of its initial to fourteenth periodic reports, combined in one document.

3. The Committee recognises the difficult economic and social conditions facing Guyana and remains deeply concerned about the extensive political and ethnic conflicts which have aggravated the situation in the country and led to serious divisions in society, and that this has affected the ability of the State party to conform to the requirements of the Convention.

4. The Committee agrees with intergovernmental and non-governmental organisations and United Nations agencies that a vicious circle of political and ethnic tensions has adversely affected human rights, weakened civil society, increased racial violence and poverty and exclusion among indigenous population groups, and hampered the administration of justice and the application of human rights standards in Guyana.

5. The Committee reiterates that the purpose of the system whereby States parties submit reports is to establish and maintain a dialogue with the Committee on actions taken, progress made and difficulties encountered in complying with obligations arising under the Convention. It further reiterates that any State party's failure to honour its reporting obligations under article 9 of the Convention is a serious impediment to the operation of the monitoring system established under the Convention.

6. The Committee is particularly encouraged by the indication made to the Committee by the United Nations Special Rapporteur on Contemporary Forms of Racism, Racial Discrimination, Xenophobia and Related Intolerance, that the process of political dialogue currently underway will make a fundamental contribution to the long-term resolution to the problem of ethnic polarisation in the country (see also E/CN.4/2004/18/Add.1).

7. The Committee recommends that the initial to fourteenth reports of Guyana, combined in one document, be submitted before 30 September 2004, so that they can be processed and scheduled for examination in 2005. In the event of the non-receipt of the report by the above date, the Committee will re-schedule the examination of the situation in Guyana under the review procedure at its sixty-sixth session, to be held in March 2005.

Question

Compare and contrast these observations with those issued in response to a State report. What benefit does the issuing of reports regardless of State submissions have?

6.1.4.3   Exception: Early warning measures and urgent action procedures

The Committee on the Elimination of Racial Discrimination may also take action to prevent racial discrimination under its early warning and urgent action provisions. This reflects the importance attached to maintaining the prohibition on racial discrimination, not least as a contribution to international peace and security.

CERD Prevention of Racial Discrimination including early warning measures and urgent action procedures, Decision 1(67), UN Doc. CERD/C/DEC/SUR/2 (2005)

Decision 1(67) on Suriname

1. The Committee recalls that in Decision 3 (66) of 9 March 2005, it expressed concern about the fact that a revised version of the draft Mining Act, which was approved by Suriname's Council

of Ministers at the end of 2004, may not be in conformity with the Committee's recommendations adopted in March 2004 following the consideration of the first to tenth periodic reports of Suriname (A/59/18, paras. 180–210).

2. The Committee deeply regrets that it has not received any comment under the follow-up procedure from the State party on the above assessment of the draft law, as requested in Decision 3 (66).

3. The Committee expresses deep concern about information alleging that Suriname is actively disregarding the Committee's recommendations by authorizing additional resource exploitation and associated infrastructure projects that pose substantial threats of irreparable harm to indigenous and tribal peoples, without any formal notification to the affected communities and without seeking their prior agreement or informed consent.

4. Drawing once again the attention of the State party to its General Recommendation 23 (1997) on the rights of indigenous peoples, the Committee urges the State party to ensure the compliance of the revised draft Mining Act with the International Convention on the Elimination of All Forms of Racial Discrimination, as well as with the Committee's 2004 recommendations. In particular, the Committee urges the State party to:

— Ensure legal acknowledgement of the rights of indigenous and tribal peoples to possess, develop, control and use their communal lands and to participate in the exploitation, management and conservation of the associated natural resources;

— Strive to reach agreements with the peoples concerned, as far as possible, before awarding any concessions;

— Ensure that indigenous and tribal peoples are granted the right of appeal to the courts, or any independent body specially created for that purpose, in order to uphold their traditional rights and their right to be consulted before concessions are granted and to be fairly compensated for any damage.

5. The Committee recommends once again that a framework law on the rights of indigenous and tribal peoples be elaborated and that the State Party take advantage of the technical assistance available under the advisory services and technical assistance Programme of the Office of the United Nations High Commissioner for Human Rights for that purpose.

7. The Committee urges the Secretary-General of the United Nations to draw the attention of the competent United Nations bodies to the particularly alarming situation in relation to the rights of indigenous peoples in Suriname, and to request them to take all appropriate measures in this regard.

Question

What advantages are there for the Committee to adopt such decisions in the face of State non-action?

Similarly, the Committee against Torture has the power to initiate investigations into information on systematic torture in the territory of any of the High Contracting States:

Convention against Torture Art 20

1. If the Committee receives reliable information which appears to it to contain well-founded indications that torture is being systematically practised in the territory of a State Party, the Committee shall invite that State Party to co-operate in the examination of the information and to this end to submit observations with regard to the information concerned.

2. Taking into account any observations which may have been submitted by the State Party concerned, as well as any other relevant information available to it, the Committee may, if it decides that this is warranted, designate one or more of its members to make a confidential inquiry and to report to the Committee urgently.

3. If an inquiry is made in accordance with paragraph 2 of this article, the Committee shall seek the co-operation of the State Party concerned. In agreement with that State Party, such an inquiry may include a visit to its territory.

4. After examining the findings of its member or members submitted in accordance with paragraph 2 of this article, the Commission shall transmit these findings to the State Party concerned together with any comments or suggestions which seem appropriate in view of the situation.

5. All the proceedings of the Committee referred to in paragraphs 1 to 4 of this article shall be confidential, and at all stages of the proceedings the co-operation of the State Party shall be sought. After such proceedings have been completed with regard to an inquiry made in accordance with paragraph 2, the Committee may, after consultations with the State Party concerned, decide to include a summary account of the results of the proceedings in its annual report made in accordance with article 24.

Question

Why are CERD and CAT most likely to require these additional powers?

6.1.5   Inter-State complaints

Given the early systems evolved under traditional concepts of human rights, it is not surprising that inter-State complaints were viewed as being the primary mechanism for enforcing human rights, as would be the case for any other element of international law. International law being primarily concerned with the law of nations, it follows that States are both the subjects and enforcers.

Both the Convention against Torture (Art 21) and the Migrant Workers' Convention (Art 74) offer the option of inter-State complaints. Note that States must overtly agree in advance to this, that is, a State declaration recognising the necessary competence of the Committee is a necessary precursor to the filing of a State complaint. A more complex system, though still commencing with an appropriate declaration recognising the competence of the Committee, is provided for under the International Covenant on Civil and Political Rights Arts 41–43. In contrast, the procedure under the International Convention on the Elimination of All Forms of Racial Discrimination is not optional. It applies to all State parties to the Convention upon ratification.

International Convention on the Elimination of All Forms of Racial Discrimination 1965

Article 11

1. If a State Party considers that another State Party is not giving effect to the provisions of this Convention, it may bring the matter to the attention of the Committee. The Committee shall then transmit the communication to the State Party concerned. Within three months, the receiving State shall submit to the Committee written explanations or statements clarifying the matter and the remedy, if any, that may have been taken by that State.

2. If the matter is not adjusted to the satisfaction of both parties, either by bilateral negotiations or by any other procedure open to them, within six months after the receipt by the receiving State of the initial communication, either State shall have the right to refer the matter again to the Committee by notifying the Committee and also the other State.

3. The Committee shall deal with a matter referred to it in accordance with paragraph 2 of this article after it has ascertained that all available domestic remedies have been invoked and exhausted in the case, in conformity with the generally recognized principles of international law. This shall not be the rule where the application of the remedies is unreasonably prolonged.

4. In any matter referred to it, the Committee may call upon the States Parties concerned to supply any other relevant information.

5. When any matter arising out of this article is being considered by the Committee, the States Parties concerned shall be entitled to send a representative to take part in the proceedings of the Committee, without voting rights, while the matter is under consideration.

Article 12

1. (a) After the Committee has obtained and collated all the information it deems necessary, the Chairman shall appoint an *ad hoc* Conciliation Commission (hereinafter referred to as the Commission) comprising five persons who may or may not be members of the Committee. The members of the Commission shall be appointed with the unanimous consent of the parties to the dispute, and its good offices shall be made available to the States concerned with a view to an amicable solution of the matter on the basis of respect for this Convention;

   (b) If the States parties to the dispute fail to reach agreement within three months on all or part of the composition of the Commission, the members of the Commission not agreed upon by the States parties to the dispute shall be elected by secret ballot by a two-thirds majority vote of the Committee from among its own members

2. The members of the Commission shall serve in their personal capacity. They shall not be nationals of the States parties to the dispute or of a State not Party to this Convention.

3. The Commission shall elect its own Chairman and adopt its own rules of procedure.

4. The meetings of the Commission shall normally be held at United Nations Headquarters or at any other convenient place as determined by the Commission.

5. The secretariat provided in accordance with article 10, paragraph 3, of this Convention shall also service the Commission whenever a dispute among States Parties brings the Commission into being.

6. The States parties to the dispute shall share equally all the expenses of the members of the Commission in accordance with estimates to be provided by the Secretary-General of the United Nations.

7. The Secretary-General shall be empowered to pay the expenses of the members of the Commission, if necessary, before reimbursement by the States parties to the dispute in accordance with paragraph 6 of this article.

8. The information obtained and collated by the Committee shall be made available to the Commission, and the Commission may call upon the States concerned to supply any other relevant information.

Article 13

1. When the Commission has fully considered the matter, it shall prepare and submit to the Chairman of the Committee a report embodying its findings on all questions of fact relevant to the issue between the parties and containing such recommendations as it may think proper for the amicable solution of the dispute.

2. The Chairman of the Committee shall communicate the report of the Commission to each of the States parties to the dispute. These States shall, within three months, inform the Chairman of the Committee whether or not they accept the recommendations contained in the report of the Commission.

3. After the period provided for in paragraph 2 of this article, the Chairman of the Committee shall communicate the report of the Commission and the declarations of the States Parties concerned to the other States Parties to this Convention.

Note also that States may refer matters concerning the interpretation, application and effect of certain instruments to the International Court of Justice in accordance with provisions of the conventions itself (e.g. Art 29, Convention of the Elimination of All Forms of Discrimination against Women) or indeed in accordance with normal international law procedure for disputes between States. The relevant conventions prescribe a preliminary procedure in order to effect a peaceful and non-contentious resolution of any dispute arising between State Parties.

Convention on the Elimination of All Forms of Discrimination against Women 1979 Art 29

1. Any dispute between two or more States Parties concerning the interpretation or application of the present Convention which is not settled by negotiation shall, at the request of one of them, be submitted to arbitration. If within six months from the date of the request for arbitration the parties are unable to agree on the organization of the arbitration, any one of those parties may refer the dispute to the International Court of Justice by request in conformity with the Statute of the Court.

2. Each State Party may at the time of signature or ratification of the present Convention or accession thereto declare that it does not consider itself bound by paragraph 1 of this article. The other States Parties shall not be bound by that paragraph with respect to any State Party which has made such a reservation.

3. Any State Party which has made a reservation in accordance with paragraph 2 of this article may at any time withdraw that reservation by notification to the Secretary-General of the United Nations.

Question

States Parties have proven reluctant to institute inter-State proceedings. What reasons are there for this? Irrespective of your reasons, why does it remain astute to include inter-State complaints in most international human rights instruments?

The only other option for inter-State complaints is recourse to the International Court of Justice. Obviously this comes with its own limitations. Indeed, the 1948 Convention on the Prevention and Punishment of Genocide is the main international human rights related instrument which has been raised in contentious cases before the International Court of Justice.

Question

Look at the two cases arising from the Balkans conflict in the early 1990s which are in the docket of the International Court of Justice (www.icj-cij.org). Explain why these cases were brought. Why would recourse to the ICJ be unlikely to benefit international human rights law enforcement?

As inter-State complaints have not proven to be a useful tool in enforcing international human rights norms, recourse must be had to other available mechanisms.

6.1.6   Individual communications

Individual communications, thought not compulsory under any international system, have emerged as an important element in protecting and preserving international human rights. States must explicitly declare their acceptance of the individual petition system of the salient treaty or, alternatively, ratify a separate protocol (where appropriate) which details the individual system. Only in Europe are individual communication procedures compulsory for all States ratifying the European Convention for the Protection of Human Rights and Fundamental Freedoms. This was not always the case, initially the system was optional. For other regional systems, they remain optional.

The following table shows which of the fundamental international human rights instruments create a system of individual petitions.

Treaty	Possibility of individual petition?
International Convention for the Elimination of all forms of Racial Discrimination	Yes, Art 14
International Covenant on Economic, Social and Cultural Rights	No, though draft optional protocol under discussion
International Covenant on Civil and Political Rights	Yes, first optional protocol
Convention on the Elimination of Discrimination against Women	Yes, optional protocol
Convention against Torture	Yes, Art 22
UN Convention on the Rights of the Child	No
International Convention on the Protection of the Rights of all Migrant Workers and Members of Their Families	Yes, Art 77 but not yet in force

6.1.6.1   Comment

It should be remembered that due to the overlap in rights, it may be possible for individual communications against a State which either does not recognise the right to individual petition or in respect of a treaty with no right of individual petition to be raised in a different forum. For example, elements of the Convention on the Rights of the Child could be raised before the Human Rights Committee as there is an overlap in the rights contained in these instruments. This is one of the advantages of overlapping treaty obligations. This also reflects the general guidance that to determine the scope of a State's obligations, you must examine all of its treaty obligations, regional and international.

Question

Note the terminology employed—generally communications, not cases or complaints. Why is such 'neutral', 'non-contentious' terminology more likely to be acceptable to States?

Compare and contrast the terminology with that employed in the European Convention on Human Rights and the Inter-American Convention on Human Rights. Both regional systems have a designated Human Rights Court, as opposed to Committee (though note the concurrent and complementary role of the Inter-American Commission). Unsurprisingly both Courts can render judgments although they also have competence to issue advisory opinions (a jurisdiction more commonly invoked by the Inter-American Court).

Question

How can the distinct differences between the international and regional systems be explained?

6.1.6.2   Admissibility criteria and communications process

In all instances, individual communications must satisfy certain criteria to be deemed admissible and be in an appropriate format. Relevant specifications may be found in the instrument in point.

Consider Article 77 of the Migrant Workers' Convention, noting particularly the conditions specified in 77(2)+(3).

International Convention on the Protection of the Rights of All Migrant Workers and Members of Their Families Art 77

1. A State Party to the present Convention may at any time declare under the present article that it recognizes the competence of the Committee to receive and consider communications from or on behalf of individuals subject to its jurisdiction who claim that their individual rights as established by the present Convention have been violated by that State Party. No communication shall be received by the Committee if it concerns a State Party that has not made such a declaration.

2. The Committee shall consider inadmissible any communication under the present article which is anonymous or which it considers to be an abuse of the right of submission of such communications or to be incompatible with the provisions of the present Convention.

3. The Committee shall not consider any communication from an individual under the present article unless it has ascertained that:

(a) The same matter has not been, and is not being, examined under another procedure of international investigation or settlement;

(b) The individual has exhausted all available domestic remedies; this shall not be the rule where, in the view of the Committee, the application of the remedies is unreasonably prolonged or is unlikely to bring effective relief to that individual.

4. Subject to the provisions of paragraph 2 of the present article, the Committee shall bring any communications submitted to it under this article to the attention of the State Party to the present Convention that has made a declaration under paragraph 1 and is alleged to be violating any provisions of the Convention. Within six months, the receiving State shall submit to the Committee written explanations or statements clarifying the matter and the remedy, if any, that may have been taken by that State.

5. The Committee shall consider communications received under the present article in the light of all information made available to it by or on behalf of the individual and by the State Party concerned.

6. The Committee shall hold closed meetings when examining communications under the present article.

7. The Committee shall forward its views to the State Party concerned and to the individual.

8. The provisions of the present article shall come into force when ten States Parties to the present Convention have made declarations under paragraph 1 of the present article. Such declarations shall be deposited by the States Parties with the Secretary-General of the United Nations, who shall transmit copies thereof to the other States Parties. A declaration may be withdrawn at any time by notification to the Secretary-General. Such a withdrawal shall not prejudice the consideration of any matter that is the subject of a communication already transmitted under the present article; no further communication by or on behalf of an individual shall

be received under the present article after the notification of withdrawal of the declaration has been received by the Secretary-General, unless the State Party has made a new declaration.

The relevant treaty provision provides for the appropriate procedures to be followed by the Committee. More information is contained in the relevant optional protocols where such a mechanism contains the relevant provisions. Complaints are normally brought by the alleged victim but can also be brought by a third party with the consent of the alleged victim or on his/her behalf where he/she is unable to bring the complaint.

Compare such provisions with the admissibility criteria for the compulsory procedure under the European Convention on Human Rights.

European Convention on Human Rights 1950

Article 34—Individual applications

The Court may receive applications from any person, non-governmental organisation or group of individuals claiming to be the victim of a violation by one of the High Contracting Parties of the rights set forth in the Convention or the protocols thereto. The High Contracting Parties undertake not to hinder in any way the effective exercise of this right.

Article 35—Admissibility criteria

1 The Court may only deal with the matter after all domestic remedies have been exhausted, according to the generally recognised rules of international law, and within a period of six months from the date on which the final decision was taken.

2 The Court shall not deal with any application submitted under Article 34 that

a   is anonymous; or

b   is substantially the same as a matter that has already been examined by the Court or has already been submitted to another procedure of international investigation or settlement and contains no relevant new information.

3 The Court shall declare inadmissible any individual application submitted under Article 34 which it considers incompatible with the provisions of the Convention or the protocols thereto, manifestly ill-founded, or an abuse of the right of application.

4 The Court shall reject any application which it considers inadmissible under this Article. It may do so at any stage of the proceedings.

As to the procedure to be followed in the event of the receipt of a communication, although this varies between the Committees, there are certain similarities. Consider the optional protocol to the Covenant on Civil and Political Rights, the body with the greatest number of individual communications received to date.

Optional Protocol to the International Covenant on Civil and Political Rights

Article 1

A State Party to the Covenant that becomes a Party to the present Protocol recognizes the competence of the Committee to receive and consider communications from individuals subject to its jurisdiction who claim to be victims of a violation by that State Party of any of the rights set forth in the Covenant. No communication shall be received by the Committee if it concerns a State Party to the Covenant which is not a Party to the present Protocol.

Article 2

Subject to the provisions of article 1, individuals who claim that any of their rights enumerated in the Covenant have been violated and who have exhausted all available domestic remedies may submit a written communication to the Committee for consideration.

Article 3

The Committee shall consider inadmissible any communication under the present Protocol which is anonymous, or which it considers to be an abuse of the right of submission of such communications or to be incompatible with the provisions of the Covenant.

Article 4

1. Subject to the provisions of article 3, the Committee shall bring any communications submitted to it under the present Protocol to the attention of the State Party to the present Protocol alleged to be violating any provision of the Covenant.

2. Within six months, the receiving State shall submit to the Committee written explanations or statements clarifying the matter and the remedy, if any, that may have been taken by that State.

Article 5

1. The Committee shall consider communications received under the present Protocol in the light of all written information made available to it by the individual and by the State Party concerned.

2. The Committee shall not consider any communication from an individual unless it has ascertained that:

(a) The same matter is not being examined under another procedure of international investigation or settlement;

(b) The individual has exhausted all available domestic remedies. This shall not be the rule where the application of the remedies is unreasonably prolonged.

3. The Committee shall hold closed meetings when examining communications under the present Protocol.

4. The Committee shall forward its views to the State Party concerned and to the individual.

Article 6

The Committee shall include in its annual report under article 45 of the Covenant a summary of its activities under the present Protocol. . . .

Article 10

The provisions of the present Protocol shall extend to all parts of federal States without any limitations or exceptions. . . .

Article 12

1. Any State Party may denounce the present Protocol at any time by written notification addressed to the Secretary-General of the United Nations. Denunciation shall take effect three months after the date of receipt of the notification by the Secretary-General.

2. Denunciation shall be without prejudice to the continued application of the provisions of the present Protocol to any communication submitted under article 2 before the effective date of denunciation.

Question

Compare and contrast the admissibility criteria with those of regional bodies such as those overseeing the European, African and American systems. Is it more difficult to bring a complaint before the international bodies?

Question

Does the lengthy procedure outlined in the examples above reflect traditional international practice or indicate a move towards recognition of the importance of the individual?

6.1.6.3   Remedies available to the individual

As is apparent, complaints to the treaty monitoring bodies are not *per se* cases. There is no system of public 'hearings' and no 'judgments'. In many respects this emphasises the role of the treaty monitoring bodies in overseeing the implementation of rights within States rather than enforcing them, this is in accordance with general principles of international law. For individuals, communications may thus seem a 'weak' remedy.

Question

What remedies are available to individuals against a State?

Note the regional provisions on remedies.

European Convention on Human Rights Art 41

If the Court finds that there has been a violation of the Convention or the protocols thereto, and if the internal law of the High Contracting Party concerned allows only partial reparation to be made, the Court shall, if necessary, afford just satisfaction to the injured party.

American Convention on Human Rights Art 63

1. If the Court finds that there has been a violation of a right or freedom protected by this Convention, the Court shall rule that the injured party be ensured the enjoyment of his right or freedom that was violated. It shall also rule, if appropriate, that the consequences of the measure or situation that constituted the breach of such right or freedom be remedied and that fair compensation be paid to the injured party.

2. In cases of extreme gravity and urgency, and when necessary to avoid irreparable damage to persons, the Court shall adopt such provisional measures as it deems pertinent in matters it has under consideration. With respect to a case not yet submitted to the Court, it may act at the request of the Commission.

6.1.7   Independent Enquiries by Committees

Certain of the treaties permit investigation by the Committees. The Committee against Torture and the Committee on the Elimination of All Forms of Discrimination against Women may take the initiative and investigate human rights situations in any given State. The right is not unfettered but subject to procedures agreed by states at the time of drafting, adopting and ratifying the relevant instrument. As with inter-State complaints, States may opt out of the relevant provisions and thus no independent investigation can commence.

Optional Protocol to the Convention on the Elimination of Discrimination against Women 1999

Article 8

1. If the Committee receives reliable information indicating grave or systematic violations by a State Party of rights set forth in the Convention, the Committee shall invite that State Party to cooperate in the examination of the information and to this end to submit observations with regard to the information concerned.

2. Taking into account any observations that may have been submitted by the State Party concerned as well as any other reliable information available to it, the Committee may designate one or more of its members to conduct an inquiry and to report urgently to the Committee. Where warranted and with the consent of the State Party, the inquiry may include a visit to its territory.

3. After examining the findings of such an inquiry, the Committee shall transmit these findings to the State Party concerned together with any comments and recommendations.

4. The State Party concerned shall, within six months of receiving the findings, comments and recommendations transmitted by the Committee, submit its observations to the Committee.

5. Such an inquiry shall be conducted confidentially and the cooperation of the State Party shall be sought at all stages of the proceedings.

Article 9

1. The Committee may invite the State Party concerned to include in its report under article 18 of the Convention details of any measures taken in response to an inquiry conducted under article 8 of the present Protocol.

2. The Committee may, if necessary, after the end of the period of six months referred to in article 8.4, invite the State Party concerned to inform it of the measures taken in response to such an inquiry.

Article 10

1. Each State Party may, at the time of signature or ratification of the present Protocol or accession thereto, declare that it does not recognize the competence of the Committee provided for in articles 8 and 9.

2. Any State Party having made a declaration in accordance with paragraph 1 of the present article may, at any time, withdraw this declaration by notification to the Secretary-General.

Note particularly that the procedure is strictly confidential and that the State concerned must agree to the investigation taking place.

Question

What purpose may be served by such a 'closed' investigation?

Note also the power of the African Commission on Human and Peoples' Rights which has a broad mandate and a broad range of investigative powers.

African Charter on Human and Peoples' Rights Arts 45(1)(a) and 46

The functions of the Commission shall be:

1. To promote Human and Peoples' Rights and in particular:

(a) to collect documents, undertake studies and researches on African problems in the field of human and peoples' rights, organize seminars, symposia and conferences, disseminate information, encourage national and local institutions concerned with human and peoples' rights, and should the case arise, give its views or make recommendations to Governments. . . .

Article 46

The Commission may resort to any appropriate method of investigation; it may hear from the Secretary-General of the Organization of African Unity or any other person capable of enlightening it.

6.1.8 General Comments

General Comments are issued by most of the UN treaty monitoring bodies.

General Comments adopted by the Human Rights Committee (number of comment, subject and year of adoption)

1 Reporting obligation 1981

2 Reporting guidelines 1981

3 Article 2 (Implementation at the national level) 1981

4   Article 3 (Equal enjoyment of civil and political rights by men and women) 1981

5   Article 4 (Derogations) 1981

6   Article 6 (Right to life) 1982

7   Article 7 (Prohibition of torture or cruel, inhuman or degrading treatment or punishment) 1982

8   Article 9 (Right to liberty and security of persons) 1982

9   Article 10 (Humane treatment of persons deprived of their liberty) 1982

10   Article 19 (Freedom of opinion) 1983

11   Article 20 1983

12   Article 1 (Right to self-determination) 1984

13   Article 14 (Administration of justice) 1984

14   Article 6 (Right to life) 1984

15   The position of aliens under the Covenant 1986

16   Article 17 (Right to privacy) 1988

17   Article 24 (Rights of the child) 1989

18   Non-discrimination 1989

19   Article 23 (The family) 1990

20   Article 7 (Prohibition of torture or cruel, inhuman or degrading treatment or punishment) 1992

21   Article 10 (Humane treatment of persons deprived of their liberty) 1992

22   Article 18 (Freedom of thought, conscience or religion) 1993

23   Article 27 (Rights of minorities) 1994

24   Reservations to the Covenant or Optional Protocols or declarations under article 41 of the Covenant 1994

25   Article 25 (Participation in public affairs and the right to vote) 1996

26   Continuity of obligations 1997

27   Article 12 (Freedom of movement) 1999

28   Article 3 (The equality of rights between men and women) 2000

29   Article 4 (Derogations during a state of emergency) 2001

30   Reporting obligations of States parties under article 40 2002

31   The nature of the general legal obligation imposed on States parties 2004.

The full text of General Comments of all the treaty monitoring bodies can be found either online or in UN Doc. HRI/GEN/1/Rev.7. General comments provide further elaboration of the rights and freedoms contained in a treaty. They may provide guidance for States seeking to establish the scope and nature of their obligations under the treaty. Moreover, they indicate the views of the Committee as to the scope of treaty rights, thereby forewarning States as to the likely approach to be followed by the Committee in its concluding observations to periodic reports. As the above list demonstrates, some reports concern the reporting obligations under the treaty, offering advice to States in that regard.

Note, as an example, the General Comment on the nature of minority rights—Art 27, International Covenant on Civil and Political Rights.

General Comment 23 (1994) Human Rights Committee

1. Article 27 of the Covenant provides that, in those States in which ethnic, religious or linguistic minorities exist, persons belonging to these minorities shall not be denied the right, in community with the other members of their group, to enjoy their own culture, to profess and practise their own religion, or to use their own language. The Committee observes that this article establishes and recognizes a right which is conferred on individuals belonging to minority groups and which is distinct from, and additional to, all the other rights which, as individuals in common with everyone else, they are already entitled to enjoy under the Covenant.

2. In some communications submitted to the Committee under the Optional Protocol, the right protected under article 27 has been confused with the right of peoples to self-determination proclaimed in article 1 of the Covenant. Further, in reports submitted by States parties under article 40 of the Covenant, the obligations placed upon States parties under article 27 have sometimes been confused with their duty under article 2.1 to ensure the enjoyment of the rights guaranteed under the Covenant without discrimination and also with equality before the law and equal protection of the law under article 26.

3.1. The Covenant draws a distinction between the right to self-determination and the rights protected under article 27. The former is expressed to be a right belonging to peoples and is dealt with in a separate part (Part I) of the Covenant. Self-determination is not a right cognizable under the Optional Protocol. Article 27, on the other hand, relates to rights conferred on individuals as such and is included, like the articles relating to other personal rights conferred on individuals, in Part III of the Covenant and is cognizable under the Optional Protocol.

3.2. The enjoyment of the rights to which article 27 relates does not prejudice the sovereignty and territorial integrity of a State party. At the same time, one or other aspect of the rights of individuals protected under that article—for example, to enjoy a particular culture—may consist in a way of life which is closely associated with territory and use of its resources. This may particularly be true of members of indigenous communities constituting a minority. . . .

5.1. The terms used in article 27 indicate that the persons designed to be protected are those who belong to a group and who share in common a culture, a religion and/or a language. Those terms also indicate that the individuals designed to be protected need not be citizens of the State party. In this regard, the obligations deriving from article 2.1 are also relevant, since a State party is required under that article to ensure that the rights protected under the Covenant are available to all individuals within its territory and subject to its jurisdiction, except rights which are expressly made to apply to citizens, for example, political rights under article 25. A State party may not, therefore, restrict the rights under article 27 to its citizens alone.

5.2. Article 27 confers rights on persons belonging to minorities which 'exist' in a State party. Given the nature and scope of the rights envisaged under that article, it is not relevant to determine the degree of permanence that the term 'exist' connotes. Those rights simply are that individuals belonging to those minorities should not be denied the right, in community with members of their group, to enjoy their own culture, to practise their religion and speak their language. Just as they need not be nationals or citizens, they need not be permanent residents. Thus, migrant workers or even visitors in a State party constituting such minorities are entitled not to be denied the exercise of those rights. As any other individual in the territory of the State party, they would, also for this purpose, have the general rights, for example, to freedom of association, of assembly, and of expression. The existence of an ethnic, religious or linguistic minority in a given State party does not depend upon a decision by that State party but requires to be established by objective criteria.

5.3. The right of individuals belonging to a linguistic minority to use their language among them-selves, in private or in public, is distinct from other language rights protected under the Covenant. In particular, it should be distinguished from the general right to freedom of expression protected under article 19. The latter right is available to all persons, irrespective of whether they belong to minorities or not. Further, the right protected under article 27 should be distinguished from the particular right which article 14.3 (f) of the Covenant confers on accused persons to interpretation where they cannot understand or speak the language used in the courts. Article 14.3 (f) does not, in any other circumstances, confer on accused persons the right to use or speak the language of their choice in court proceedings.

6.1. Although article 27 is expressed in negative terms, that article, nevertheless, does recognize the existence of a 'right' and requires that it shall not be denied. Consequently, a State party is under an obligation to ensure that the existence and the exercise of this right are protected against their denial or violation. Positive measures of protection are, therefore, required not only against the acts of the State party itself, whether through its legislative, judicial or administrative authorities, but also against the acts of other persons within the State party.

6.2. Although the rights protected under article 27 are individual rights, they depend in turn on the ability of the minority group to maintain its culture, language or religion. Accordingly, positive measures by States may also be necessary to protect the identity of a minority and the rights of its members to enjoy and develop their culture and language and to practise their religion, in community with the other members of the group. In this connection, it has to be observed that such positive measures must respect the provisions of articles 2.1 and 26 of the Covenant both as regards the treatment between different minorities and the treatment between the persons belonging to them and the remaining part of the population. However, as long as those measures are aimed at correcting conditions which prevent or impair the enjoyment of the rights guaranteed under article 27, they may constitute a legitimate differentiation under the Covenant, provided that they are based on reasonable and objective criteria.

7. With regard to the exercise of the cultural rights protected under article 27, the Committee observes that culture manifests itself in many forms, including a particular way of life associated with the use of land resources, especially in the case of indigenous peoples. That right may include such traditional activities as fishing or hunting and the right to live in reserves protected by law. The enjoyment of those rights may require positive legal measures of protection and measures to ensure the effective participation of members of minority communities in decisions which affect them.

8. The Committee observes that none of the rights protected under article 27 of the Covenant may be legitimately exercised in a manner or to an extent inconsistent with the other provisions of the Covenant.

9. The Committee concludes that article 27 relates to rights whose protection imposes specific obligations on States parties. The protection of these rights is directed towards ensuring the survival and continued development of the cultural, religious and social identity of the minorities concerned, thus enriching the fabric of society as a whole. Accordingly, the Committee observes that these rights must be protected as such and should not be confused with other personal rights conferred on one and all under the Covenant. States parties, therefore, have an obligation to ensure that the exercise of these rights is fully protected and they should indicate in their reports the measures they have adopted to this end.

Question

Does this provide adequate and appropriate guidance to States as to minority rights?

6.1.9   On-site visits

While the foregoing methods permit 'remote' monitoring of the human rights situation in the various states, inevitably such a system does not produce a truly accurate reflection of human rights. Consequently, additional sources may be consulted to 'round out' the reports of the State. But there remains no viable alternative to *in situ* investigations. Some treaty monitoring bodies have been given powers permitting this. As their powers are granted by the high contracting States, it is inevitable that the

States themselves have limited the powers of the committees in this respect. Most notably, there is no power of 'surprise' visits, all visits must be at the invitation of the States and agreed in advance. Essentially, State visits are currently only undertaken in the UN by rapporteurs; the UN treaty monitoring bodies, unlike their regional counterparts, do not enjoy these powers.

At the international level, the Committee against Torture now has this power as its optional protocol is in force with more than twenty parties.

Optional Protocol to the Convention against Torture and other Cruel, Inhuman or Degrading Treatment or Punishment 2002

Article 1

The objective of the present Protocol is to establish a system of regular visits undertaken by independent international and national bodies to places where people are deprived of their liberty, in order to prevent torture and other cruel, inhuman or degrading treatment or punishment.

Article 2

1. A Subcommittee on Prevention of Torture and Other Cruel, Inhuman or Degrading Treatment or Punishment of the Committee against Torture (hereinafter referred to as the Subcommittee on Prevention) shall be established and shall carry out the functions laid down in the present Protocol.

2. The Subcommittee on Prevention shall carry out its work within the framework of the Charter of the United Nations and shall be guided by the purposes and principles thereof, as well as the norms of the United Nations concerning the treatment of people deprived of their liberty.

3. Equally, the Subcommittee on Prevention shall be guided by the principles of confidentiality, impartiality, non-selectivity, universality and objectivity.

4. The Subcommittee on Prevention and the States Parties shall cooperate in the implementation of the present Protocol.

Article 3

Each State Party shall set up, designate or maintain at the domestic level one or several visiting bodies for the prevention of torture and other cruel, inhuman or degrading treatment or punishment (hereinafter referred to as the national preventive mechanism).

Article 4

1. Each State Party shall allow visits, in accordance with the present Protocol, by the mechanisms referred to in articles 2 and 3 to any place under its jurisdiction and control where persons are or may be deprived of their liberty, either by virtue of an order given by a public authority or at its instigation or with its consent or acquiescence (hereinafter referred to as places of detention). These visits shall be undertaken with a view to strengthening, if necessary, the protection of these persons against torture and other cruel, inhuman or degrading treatment or punishment.

2. For the purposes of the present Protocol, deprivation of liberty means any form of detention or imprisonment or the placement of a person in a public or private custodial setting which that person is not permitted to leave at will by order of any judicial, administrative or other authority. . . .

Article 11

1. The Subcommittee on Prevention shall:

(a) Visit the places referred to in article 4 and make recommendations to States Parties concerning the protection of persons deprived of their liberty against torture and other cruel, inhuman or degrading treatment or punishment;

(b) In regard to the national preventive mechanisms:

    (i) Advise and assist States Parties, when necessary, in their establishment;

    (ii) Maintain direct, and if necessary confidential, contact with the national preventive mechanisms and offer them training and technical assistance with a view to strengthening their capacities;

    (iii) Advise and assist them in the evaluation of the needs and the means necessary to strengthen the protection of persons deprived of their liberty against torture and other cruel, inhuman or degrading treatment or punishment;

    (iv) Make recommendations and observations to the States Parties with a view to strengthening the capacity and the mandate of the national preventive mechanisms for the prevention of torture and other cruel, inhuman or degrading treatment or punishment;

(c) Cooperate, for the prevention of torture in general, with the relevant United Nations organs and mechanisms as well as with the international, regional and national institutions or organizations working towards the strengthening of the protection of all persons against torture and other cruel, inhuman or degrading treatment or punishment.

Article 12

In order to enable the Subcommittee on Prevention to comply with its mandate as laid down in article 11, the States Parties undertake:

(a) To receive the Subcommittee on Prevention in their territory and grant it access to the places of detention as defined in article 4 of the present Protocol;

(b) To provide all relevant information the Subcommittee on Prevention may request to evaluate the needs and measures that should be adopted to strengthen the protection of persons deprived of their liberty against torture and other cruel, inhuman or degrading treatment or punishment;

(c) To encourage and facilitate contacts between the Subcommittee on Prevention and the national preventive mechanisms;

(d) To examine the recommendations of the Subcommittee on Prevention and enter into dialogue with it on possible implementation measures.

Article 13

1. The Subcommittee on Prevention shall establish, at first by lot, a programme of regular visits to the States Parties in order to fulfil its mandate as established in article 11.

2. After consultations, the Subcommittee on Prevention shall notify the States Parties of its programme in order that they may, without delay, make the necessary practical arrangements for the visits to be conducted.

3. The visits shall be conducted by at least two members of the Subcommittee on Prevention. These members may be accompanied, if needed, by experts of demonstrated professional experience and knowledge in the fields covered by the present Protocol who shall be selected from a roster of experts prepared on the basis of proposals made by the States Parties, the Office of the United Nations High Commissioner for Human Rights and the United Nations Centre for International Crime Prevention. In preparing the roster, the States Parties concerned shall propose no

more than five national experts. The State Party concerned may oppose the inclusion of a specific expert in the visit, whereupon the Subcommittee on Prevention shall propose another expert.

4. If the Subcommittee on Prevention considers it appropriate, it may propose a short follow-up visit after a regular visit.

Article 14

1. In order to enable the Subcommittee on Prevention to fulfil its mandate, the States Parties to the present Protocol undertake to grant it:

(a) Unrestricted access to all information concerning the number of persons deprived of their liberty in places of detention as defined in article 4, as well as the number of places and their location;

(b) Unrestricted access to all information referring to the treatment of those persons as well as their conditions of detention;

(c) Subject to paragraph 2 below, unrestricted access to all places of detention and their installations and facilities;

(d) The opportunity to have private interviews with the persons deprived of their liberty without witnesses, either personally or with a translator if deemed necessary, as well as with any other person who the Subcommittee on Prevention believes may supply relevant information;

(e) The liberty to choose the places it wants to visit and the persons it wants to interview.

2. Objection to a visit to a particular place of detention may be made only on urgent and compelling grounds of national defence, public safety, natural disaster or serious disorder in the place to be visited that temporarily prevent the carrying out of such a visit. The existence of a declared state of emergency as such shall not be invoked by a State Party as a reason to object to a visit.

Article 15

No authority or official shall order, apply, permit or tolerate any sanction against any person or organization for having communicated to the Subcommittee on Prevention or to its delegates any information, whether true or false, and no such person or organization shall be otherwise prejudiced in any way.

Article 16

1. The Subcommittee on Prevention shall communicate its recommendations and observations confidentially to the State Party and, if relevant, to the national preventive mechanism.

2. The Subcommittee on Prevention shall publish its report, together with any comments of the State Party concerned, whenever requested to do so by that State Party. If the State Party makes part of the report public, the Subcommittee on Prevention may publish the report in whole or in part. However, no personal data shall be published without the express consent of the person concerned.

3. The Subcommittee on Prevention shall present a public annual report on its activities to the Committee against Torture.

4. If the State Party refuses to cooperate with the Subcommittee on Prevention according to articles 12 and 14, or to take steps to improve the situation in the light of the recommendations of the Subcommittee on Prevention, the Committee against Torture may, at the request of the Subcommittee on Prevention, decide, by a majority of its members, after the State Party has had an opportunity to make its views known, to make a public statement on the matter or to publish the report of the Subcommittee on Prevention.

Such a system of visits is already operational at a regional level. Indeed establishing the European Torture Committee was the primary *raison d'être* of the European

Convention for the Prevention of Torture and Inhuman or Degrading Treatment or Punishment 1987.

European Convention for the Prevention of Torture and Inhuman or Degrading Treatment or Punishment 1989

Article 1

There shall be established a European Committee for the Prevention of Torture and Inhuman or Degrading Treatment or Punishment (hereinafter referred to as the 'Committee'). The Committee shall, by means of visits, examine the treatment of persons deprived of their liberty with a view to strengthening, if necessary, the protection of such persons from torture and from inhuman or degrading treatment or punishment.

Article 2

Each party shall permit visits, in accordance with this Convention, to any place within its jurisdiction where persons are deprived of their liberty by a public authority.

Article 3

In the application of this Convention, the Committee and the competent national authorities of the party concerned shall co-operate with each other. . . .

Article 7

1. The Committee shall organise visits to places referred to in Article 2. Apart from periodic visits, the Committee may organise such other visits as appear to it to be required in the circumstances.

2. As a general rule, the visits shall be carried out by at least two members of the Committee. The Committee may, if it considers it necessary, be assisted by experts and interpreters.

Article 8

1. The Committee shall notify the Government of the Party concerned of its intention to carry out a visit. After such notification, it may at any time visit any place referred to in Article 2.

2. A Party shall provide the Committee with the following facilities to carry out its task:

a. access to its territory and the right to travel without restriction;

b. full information on the place where persons deprived of their liberty are being held;

c. unlimited access to any place where persons are deprived of their liberty, including the right to move inside such places without restriction;

d. other information available to the Party which is necessary for the Committee to carry out its task. In seeking such information, the Committee shall have regard to applicable rules of national law and professional ethics.

3. The Committee may interview in private persons deprived of their liberty.

4. The Committee may communicate freely with any person whom it believes can supply relevant information.

5. If necessary, the Committee may immediately communicate observations to the competent authorities of the Party concerned.

Article 9

1. In exceptional circumstances, the competent authorities of the Party concerned may make representations to the Committee against a visit at the time or to the particular place proposed by the Committee. Such representations may only be made on grounds of national defence, public safety, serious disorder in places where persons are deprived of their liberty, the medical condition of a person or that an urgent interrogation relating to a serious crime is in progress.

2. Following such representations, the Committee and the Party shall immediately enter into consultations in order to clarify the situation and seek agreement on arrangements to enable the Committee to exercise its functions expeditiously. Such arrangements may include the transfer to another place of any person whom the Committee proposed to visit. Until the visit takes place, the Party shall provide information to the Committee about any person concerned.

Article 10

1. After each visit, the Committee shall draw a report on the facts found during the visit, taking account of any observations which may have been submitted by the Party concerned. It shall transmit to the latter its report containing any recommendations it considers necessary. The Committee may consult with the Party with a view to suggesting, if necessary, improvements in the protection of persons deprived of their liberty.

2. If the Party fails to co-operate or refuses to improve the situation in the light of the Committee's recommendations, the Committee may decide, after the Party has had an opportunity to make known its views, by a majority of two-thirds of its members to make a public statement on the matter.

Question

Consider the balance that must be struck by the Committee—while undertaking relevant visits, they must also respect the rights of States, their territorial integrity and their political sovereignty. To what extent are States likely to permit full access to treaty-monitoring committees?

The European Committee intends visiting the following countries during 2006: Armenia, Azerbaijan, Bulgaria, Czech Republic, France, Ireland, Monaco, Romania, Slovenia, 'the former Yugoslav Republic of Macedonia'. The following extract relates to a visit made by the Committee to the United Kingdom. The official response of the Government is contained in CPT/Inf (2005) 10. These documents were released in June 2005 and are published with the consent of the government concerned. In July 2005, a follow-up visit included a return to Belmarsh (CPT/Inf(2006)26).

Report to the Government of the United Kingdom on the visit to the United Kingdom carried out by the European Committee for the Prevention of Torture and Inhuman or Degrading Treatment or Punishment (CPT) from 14 to 19 March 2004 CPT/Inf (2005) 10

D. Immediate observation pursuant to Article 8, paragraph 5, of the Convention in relation to three persons detained under the Anti-Terrorism, Crime and Security Act 2001

7. At the meeting with the authorities which took place at the end of the visit, the CPT's delegation made an immediate observation, pursuant to Article 8, paragraph 5, of the Convention, concerning three persons detained under the ATCSA.

The first person, who had been transferred from Belmarsh Prison to Broadmoor Special Hospital, was suffering from a most severe post-traumatic stress disorder, a condition which requires a safe and calm environment as a basis for treatment. In Broadmoor, this person has endured frequent episodes of verbal abuse by members of staff (a fact acknowledged by other staff members) as well as assaults from other patients. The delegation itself witnessed such an unprovoked attack, which might have led to injury had its members not been able to intervene. His mental state also appeared to have deteriorated seriously, risking permanent damage. The delegation stressed that it was clinically inappropriate to place this person in an establishment that was mainly tasked with the care of dangerous and violent patients. It asked for him to be transferred as a matter of urgency to a different type of treatment facility.

The second person ('G'), imprisoned in Belmarsh Prison, suffered from major physical disabilities. Moreover, the depression provoked by his detention had led to significant weight loss and a further loss of function, which necessitated the use of a wheelchair or crutches. The delegation stressed that if this person remained in these conditions in Belmarsh, which did not offer the appropriate treatment facilities, his state of health was likely to deteriorate further. It asked for immediate steps to be taken to ensure that he received the care and treatment warranted by his condition.

The third person ('P'), who was also imprisoned in Belmarsh, suffered from a disability (amputation of both forearms) that prevented him from urinating or defecating unaided. However, he did not always receive the necessary assistance. Moreover, his mental state had deteriorated seriously as a result of his detention, leading to both severe depression and post-traumatic stress disorder. The delegation asked for urgent consideration to be given to his transfer to an establishment with proper facilities to deal with his physical disability and to treat his mental disorder, in a humane environment. It also stressed that psychiatric treatment for this detainee—which must not be delayed any longer—was both an acute, life-saving measure and an essential prerequisite for any rehabilitative effort.

The delegation asked the authorities to report, within two months, on measures taken in the light of its immediate observation. By letter of 11 June 2004, the United Kingdom authorities responded to the immediate observation made by the delegation. This response will be assessed later in this report. . . .

B. Response to the immediate observation pursuant to Article 8, paragraph 5, of the Convention in relation to three persons detained under the Anti-Terrorism, Crime and Security Act 2001

11. In the case of the patient placed in Broadmoor Special Hospital, the authorities state in their response that the Home Office considers that, in view of his clinical needs and also the risks he presents to the public, this is the most appropriate setting for him. The Committee is not convinced by this reply. It conflicts with the conclusions of a number of medical experts, including those—and this is acknowledged by the authorities—of the Broadmoor Special Hospital medical team. Moreover, the medical doctor responsible for this patient has requested authority to transfer him to local psychiatric services, but has apparently never received a reply.

Even if, following the CPT's visit, the patient was transferred to another hospital ward offering a 'more stable' environment and steps were taken to deal with his psychological needs, the wisdom of keeping him in a setting intended for the care and treatment of violent and dangerous patients with a quite different clinical profile is highly debatable. Such a decision, which appears to give little weight to therapeutic considerations—and thus to the patient's well-being—is not, in the opinion of the Committee, acceptable.

In the light of the delegation's request and of the conclusions and proposals of the Broadmoor Special Hospital medical team and other expert reports, **the CPT recommends that the United Kingdom authorities take the necessary steps to ensure that this patient, whose mental health has deteriorated seriously whilst in detention, benefits without further delay from the whole range of treatment required by his condition in care facilities that correspond to his clinical profile.**

The CPT would also like to receive precise information on the individualised treatment plan for this patient drawn up since the delegation's visit.

12. The CPT notes in connection with the allegations of verbal abuse by staff that disciplinary proceedings have been launched against one staff member while in two other cases the allegations were found after investigation to be unsubstantiated. **It would like to receive in due course the results of the disciplinary proceedings in the first mentioned case, as well as further details concerning the grounds for the conclusions reached in the two other**

cases. It would also like to be informed of the response of the National Health Service to the other complaints submitted by the patient.

13. Finally, for so long as this patient is held in Broadmoor, **the CPT trusts that all possible steps will be taken to ensure that he can practise his religion and receives food which is in keeping with his dietary habits**.

14. In the case of detainee 'G', the Special Immigration Appeals Commission (SIAC) ruled on 20 January 2004 that he should be given bail because of the effects of his detention on his mental health. The SIAC considered that 'detention [had] created a mental illness' and that 'the open-ended nature of the detention was such as to ensure that the condition did not improve'. The release on bail, on very strict terms, took place in April 2004. The Committee welcomes this decision.

15. In the case of detainee 'P', the authorities state that the mental health team at Belmarsh do not agree with the delegation's request that he should be transferred, without further delay, to a suitable facility for physical rehabilitation and for treatment of his mental disorder. In their opinion, if 'P' were prepared to accept the treatments and assistance currently being offered to him they would be sufficient to ameliorate any deterioration in his physical and mental states. They add that Belmarsh Prison is able to provide the support required for both physical rehabilitation and the treatment of his mental disorder, under the conditions of security required by his detention. Should the mental health team consider at any time that he required in-patient treatment for his mental disorder, the team would take the necessary steps under the provisions of the Mental Health Act 1983.

In the CPT's opinion, this approach indicates a profound lack of awareness of the state of this person, who suffers from severe depression and post-traumatic stress disorder, bordering on psychosis. Efforts to help him accept his new prosthesis were inevitably doomed to failure because of the recurrent symptoms of extreme traumatisation (consequences of the torture inflicted in his country of origin, the explosion that cost him both forearms and damaged his lower legs, his current conditions of detention and the experience of police confiscation and non-restitution of his prosthesis), which were not adequately identified or taken into account, and because of the anti-therapeutic and punitive methods used in Belmarsh Prison to force him to use the prostheses, including threats and the temporary withdrawal of nursing assistance necessary for him to perform his everyday functions. It is therefore unreasonable to expect such a person to exhibit the confidence in and cooperation with the current prison environment necessary for treatment. It is widely recognised that severe depressive symptoms can prevent full cooperation with assistance offered.

The CPT considers that maintaining this person in his current conditions of detention while waiting for him to accept the treatment offered by the Belmarsh Prison health facility creates an imminent risk of a serious deterioration in his mental and physical condition. For so long as this person is deprived of his liberty, **the CPT calls on the United Kingdom authorities to take the necessary steps, without delay, to address the risk of permanent damage, in accordance with the request made by its delegation at the end of the visit**.

Question

To what extent is the guidance of the Committee valuable for the State? Ascertain the extent to which the Committee was permitted to examine the 'real' situation within the State.

6.2 REGIONAL SYSTEMS AND CREATING JUDICIAL MECHANISMS

For general human rights, court systems only occur at the regional level. Some have argued for the creation of a World Human Rights Court (see, for example,

Thomas Buergenthal, 'A Court and Two Consolidated Treaty Bodies' in Bayefsky, A (ed), *The UN Human Rights Treaty System in the 21ˢᵗ Century*, 2000, The Hague: Kluwer) but no progress has been made to date. The International Criminal Court clearly has the potential to give effect to certain human rights though obviously this is by prosecuting the individuals responsible for war crimes, crimes against humanity etc. rather than holding the State to account for infringements of human rights.

Question

What benefits could courts have over committees?

There is provision in terms of each of the principal regional instruments for a court to be established to oversee the implementation of regional human rights. The CIS Convention makes similar provision for a Court to be established in Minsk. Given that the courts are established in accordance with treaty and protocol provisions, they too are conventional mechanisms, and restricted in their power to that permitted by the founding States.

6.2.1   European Court of Human Rights

The European Court of Human Rights is probably the most effective court yet established to monitor and implement human rights. Its impact extends beyond Europe as various national courts in other regions of the world have recourse to the jurisprudence of the European Court of Human Rights when determining the nature and scope of certain contentious rights.

Of particular note, all contracting States must permit complaints to be brought before the European Court of Human Rights.

European Convention on Human Rights 1950

Article 19—Establishment of the Court

To ensure the observance of the engagements undertaken by the High Contracting Parties in the Convention and the Protocols thereto, there shall be set up a European Court of Human Rights, hereinafter referred to as 'the Court'. It shall function on a permanent basis. . . .

Article 32—Jurisdiction of the Court

1 The jurisdiction of the Court shall extend to all matters concerning the interpretation and application of the Convention and the protocols thereto which are referred to it as provided in Articles 33, 34 and 47.

2 In the event of dispute as to whether the Court has jurisdiction, the Court shall decide.

Article 33—Inter-State cases

Any High Contracting Party may refer to the Court any alleged breach of the provisions of the Convention and the protocols thereto by another High Contracting Party.

Article 34—Individual applications

The Court may receive applications from any person, non-governmental organisation or group of individuals claiming to be the victim of a violation by one of the High Contracting Parties of the rights set forth in the Convention or the protocols thereto. The High Contracting Parties undertake not to hinder in any way the effective exercise of this right. . . .

Article 47—Advisory opinions

1 The Court may, at the request of the Committee of Ministers, give advisory opinions on legal questions concerning the interpretation of the Convention and the protocols thereto.

2 Such opinions shall not deal with any question relating to the content or scope of the rights or freedoms defined in Section 1 of the Convention and the protocols thereto, or with any other question which the Court or the Committee of Ministers might have to consider in consequence of any such proceedings as could be instituted in accordance with the Convention.

3 Decisions of the Committee of Ministers to request an advisory opinion of the Court shall require a majority vote of the representatives entitled to sit on the Committee.

Note that no reporting system operates for the European Convention on Human Rights although reports are the principal mechanism deployed for ensuring compliance with the European Social Charter.

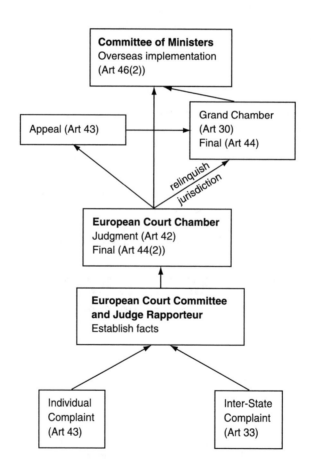

Despite the terminology, the European Court of Human Rights continues to regard its function as supervisory—that is, it seeks to guide States in their application of the Convention. There is copious evidence of this—the Court rarely awards punitive damages as just satisfaction (Art 41 of the Convention); the Court will determine a violation and rarely proceeds to elaborate on subsequent articles of the Convention which may also have been infringed.

Examples of the impact of the Court's judgments can be found online at www.coe.int/T/E/Human_rights/execution/01_Introduction/01_Introduction.asp #TopOfPage

6.2.2 Inter-American Court and Commission of Human Rights

The Inter-American system, as discussed in Chapter 4 operates with both a Commission and a Court. As was the case initially with the European Court of Human Rights, individuals have no *locus standi* before the Inter-American Court of Human Rights. However, complaints can still reach the Court by individuals referring the matter first to the Commission.

American Convention on Human Rights

Article 44

Any person or group of persons, or any nongovernmental entity legally recognized in one or more member states of the Organization, may lodge petitions with the Commission containing denunciations or complaints of violation of this Convention by a State Party.

Article 45

1. Any State Party may, when it deposits its instrument of ratification of or adherence to this Convention, or at any later time, declare that it recognizes the competence of the Commission to receive and examine communications in which a State Party alleges that another State Party has committed a violation of a human right set forth in this Convention.

2. Communications presented by virtue of this article may be admitted and examined only if they are presented by a State Party that has made a declaration recognizing the aforementioned competence of the Commission. The Commission shall not admit any communication against a State Party that has not made such a declaration.

3. A declaration concerning recognition of competence may be made to be valid for an indefinite time, for a specified period, or for a specific case.

Subsequent articles explain in detail the procedure employed in processing complaints, including the admissibility criteria and the need to seek a friendly settlement if possible. The extra-conventional competence of the Commission is addressed in Chapter 5. As was noted, the Commission was established pursuant to the Convention but alterations to the OAS Charter provided more substantive competence for the body.

American Convention on Human Rights

Article 57

The Commission shall appear in all cases before the Court. . . .

Article 61

1. Only the States Parties and the Commission shall have the right to submit a case to the Court.

2. In order for the Court to hear a case, it is necessary that the procedures set forth in Articles 48 and 50 shall have been completed.

Article 62

1. A State Party may, upon depositing its instrument of ratification or adherence to this Convention, or at any subsequent time, declare that it recognizes as binding, ipso facto, and not requiring special agreement, the jurisdiction of the Court on all matters relating to the interpretation or application of this Convention.

2. Such declaration may be made unconditionally, on the condition of reciprocity, for a specified period, or for specific cases. It shall be presented to the Secretary-General of the Organization, who shall transmit copies thereof to the other member states of the Organization and to the Secretary of the Court.

3. The jurisdiction of the Court shall comprise all cases concerning the interpretation and application of the provisions of this Convention that are submitted to it, provided that the States Parties to the case recognize or have recognized such jurisdiction, whether by special declaration pursuant to the preceding paragraphs, or by a special agreement.

Article 63

1. If the Court finds that there has been a violation of a right or freedom protected by this Convention, the Court shall rule that the injured party be ensured the enjoyment of his right or freedom that was violated. It shall also rule, if appropriate, that the consequences of the measure or situation that constituted the breach of such right or freedom be remedied and that fair compensation be paid to the injured party.

2. In cases of extreme gravity and urgency, and when necessary to avoid irreparable damage to persons, the Court shall adopt such provisional measures as it deems pertinent in matters it has under consideration. With respect to a case not yet submitted to the Court, it may act at the request of the Commission.

Article 64

1. The member states of the Organization may consult the Court regarding the interpretation of this Convention or of other treaties concerning the protection of human rights in the American states. Within their spheres of competence, the organs listed in Chapter X of the Charter of the Organization of American States, as amended by the Protocol of Buenos Aires, may in like manner consult the Court.

2. The Court, at the request of a member state of the Organization, may provide that state with opinions regarding the compatibility of any of its domestic laws with the aforesaid international instruments. . . .

Article 67

The judgment of the Court shall be final and not subject to appeal. In case of disagreement as to the meaning or scope of the judgment, the Court shall interpret it at the request of any of the parties, provided the request is made within ninety days from the date of notification of the judgment.

Article 68

1. The States Parties to the Convention undertake to comply with the judgment of the Court in any case to which they are parties.

2. That part of a judgment that stipulates compensatory damages may be executed in the country concerned in accordance with domestic procedure governing the execution of judgments against the state.

The following diagram indicates the various stages of a complaint being brought to the Court.

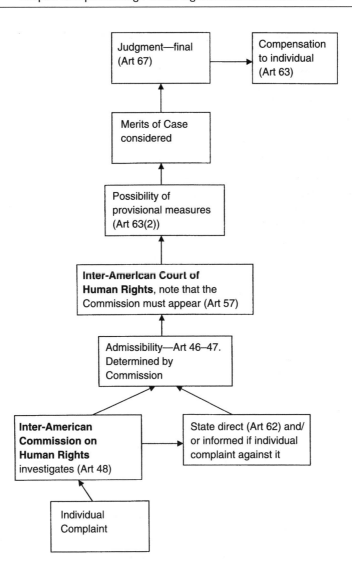

With respect to provisional measures, it is noteworthy that the Commission retains power to request these, even if the Court is not seized of the matter.

Note that more substantive remedies are often awarded by the Inter-American Court. The compensation can be for pecuniary and non-pecuniary damages. The Court can, and has, also made specific orders—e.g. for a State to release a prisoner (*Loayza Tamayo* (Ser.C, No. 33 (1997)) or change domestic law (*Barrios Altos* (Ser.C, No. 75 (2001)). (Note that both these examples involve Peru but other States have received similar judgments from the Inter-American Court).

6.2.3   African Commission and Court of Human and Peoples' Rights

Under the African system, a Commission and Court oversee the application of the African Charter on Human and Peoples' Rights.

African Charter on Human and Peoples' Rights 1981

Article 30

An African Commission on Human and Peoples' Rights, hereinafter called 'the Commission', shall be established within the Organization of African Unity to promote human and peoples' rights and ensure their protection in Africa. . . .

Article 45

The functions of the Commission shall be:

1. To promote Human and Peoples' Rights and in particular:

(a) to collect documents, undertake studies and researches on African problems in the field of human and peoples' rights, organize seminars, symposia and conferences, disseminate information, encourage national and local institutions concerned with human and peoples' rights, and should the case arise, give its views or make recommendations to Governments;

(b) to formulate and lay down, principles and rules aimed at solving legal problems relating to human and peoples' rights and fundamental freedoms upon which African Governments may base their legislations;

(c) co-operate with other African and international institutions concerned with the promotion and protection of human and peoples' rights.

2. Ensure the protection of human and peoples' rights under conditions laid down by the present Charter.

3. Interpret all the provisions of the present Charter at the request of a State party, an institution of the OAU or an African Organization recognized by the OAU.

4. Perform any other tasks which may be entrusted to it by the Assembly of Heads of State and Government.

Article 46

The Commission may resort to any appropriate method of investigation; it may hear from the Secretary-General of the Organization of African Unity or any other person capable of enlightening it.

Article 47

If a State party to the present Charter has good reasons to believe that another State party to this Charter has violated the provisions of the Charter, it may draw, by written communication, the attention of that State to the matter. This communication shall also be addressed to the Secretary-General of the OAU and to the Chairman of the Commission. Within three months of the receipt of the communication, the State to which the communication is addressed shall give the enquiring State, written explanation or statement elucidating the matter. This should include as much as possible relevant information relating to the laws and rules of procedure applied and applicable, and the redress already given or course of action available . . .

Article 55

1. Before each Session, the Secretary of the Commission shall make a list of the communications other than those of States parties to the present Charter and transmit them to the members of the Commission, who shall indicate which communications should be considered by the Commission.

2. A communication shall be considered by the Commission if a simple majority of its members so decide.

Article 56

Communications relating to human and peoples' rights referred to in 55 received by the Commission, shall be considered if they:

1. Indicate their authors even if the latter request anonymity,

2. Are compatible with the Charter of the Organization of African Unity or with the present Charter,

3. Are not written in disparaging or insulting language directed against the State concerned and its institutions or to the Organization of African Unity,

4. Are not based exclusively on news discriminated through the mass media,

5. Are sent after exhausting local remedies, if any, unless it is obvious that this procedure is unduly prolonged,

6. Are submitted within a reasonable period from the time local remedies are exhausted or from the date the Commission is seized of the matter, and

7. Do not deal with cases which have been settled by these States involved in accordance with the principles of the Charter of the United Nations, or the Charter of the Organization of African Unity or the provisions of the present Charter.

Article 57

Prior to any substantive consideration, all communications shall be brought to the knowledge of the State concerned by the Chairman of the Commission.

Article 58

1. When it appears after deliberations of the Commission that one or more communications apparently relate to special cases which reveal the existence of a series of serious or massive violations of human and peoples' rights, the Commission shall draw the attention of the Assembly of Heads of State and Government to these special cases.

2. The Assembly of Heads of State and Government may then request the Commission to undertake an in-depth study of these cases and make a factual report, accompanied by its findings and recommendations.

3. A case of emergency duly noticed by the Commission shall be submitted by the latter to the Chairman of the Assembly of Heads of State and Government who may request an in-depth study.

No Court was provided for in the original African Charter. This appeared to be a deliberate decision. Although dissimilar from the other regional systems (Europe and the Americas), it reflects the prevailing international (United Nations) practice of non-judicial mechanisms for addressing violations of human rights.

Van der Mei, A, 'The new African Court on Human and Peoples' Rights: towards an effective human rights protection mechanism for Africa?' (2005) 18.1 Leiden Journal of International Law 113 at 115

According to commentators, the choice to establish a commission and not a court was motivated by African norms and values. These would favour negotiation, conciliation, and other amicable forms as the appropriate methods for dispute settlement, and would oppose the confrontational judicial settlement in the West.

The African Court is established by virtue of an optional protocol to the Charter. Details concerning the Court, its jurisdiction and function can be found in that instrument.

6.3 REMEDIES FOR INDIVIDUALS

For individuals, one of the main problems with the foregoing procedures is the perceived lack of remedies. Obviously, the treaties make frequent reference to the need for adequate remedies (at a national level) for infringements of human rights.

Convention on the Elimination of All Forms of Racial Discrimination Art 6

States Parties shall assure to everyone within their jurisdiction effective protection and remedies, through the competent national tribunals and other State institutions, against any acts of racial discrimination which violate his human rights and fundamental freedoms contrary to this Convention, as well as the right to seek from such tribunals just and adequate reparation or satisfaction for any damage suffered as a result of such discrimination.

The view of the Committee on this was clarified in a General Comment in 2000.

CERD General Recommendation 26 (2000)

1. The Committee on the Elimination of Racial Discrimination believes that the degree to which acts of racial discrimination and racial insults damage the injured party's perception of his/her own worth and reputation is often underestimated.

2. The Committee notifies States parties that, in its opinion, the right to seek just and adequate reparation or satisfaction for any damage suffered as a result of such discrimination, which is embodied in article 6 of the Convention, is not necessarily secured solely by the punishment of the perpetrator of the discrimination; at the same time, the courts and other competent authorities should consider awarding financial compensation for damage, material or moral, suffered by a victim, whenever appropriate.

See also the following articles from selected treaties:

International Covenant on Civil and Political rights

Article 9(5)

Anyone who has been the victim of unlawful arrest or detention shall have an enforceable right to compensation.

Article 14(6)

When a person has by a final decision been convicted of a criminal offence and when subsequently his conviction has been reversed or he has been pardoned on the ground that a new or newly discovered fact shows conclusively that there has been a miscarriage of justice, the person who has suffered punishment as a result of such conviction shall be compensated according to law, unless it is proved that the non-disclosure of the unknown fact in time is wholly or partly attributable to him.

Convention against Torture

Article 14

1. Each State Party shall ensure in its legal system that the victim of an act of torture obtains redress and has an enforceable right to fair and adequate compensation, including the means for as full rehabilitation as possible. In the event of the death of the victim as a result of an act of torture, his dependants shall be entitled to compensation.

2. Nothing in this article shall affect any right of the victim or other persons to compensation which may exist under national law.

Note also the view of the Committee on Economic, Social and Cultural Rights as regards the exercise of the right to the highest attainable standard of health.

Committee on Economic, Social and Cultural Rights General Comment 14 (2000): Article 12: The Right to the Highest Attainable Standard of Health
Remedies and accountability

59. Any person or group victim of a violation of the right to health should have access to effective judicial or other appropriate remedies at both national and international levels. All victims of such violations should be entitled to adequate reparation, which may take the form of restitution,

compensation, satisfaction or guarantees of non-repetition. National ombudsmen, human rights commissions, consumer forums, patients' rights associations or similar institutions should address violations of the right to health.

60. The incorporation in the domestic legal order of international instruments recognizing the right to health can significantly enhance the scope and effectiveness of remedial measures and should be encouraged in all cases. Incorporation enables courts to adjudicate violations of the right to health, or at least its core obligations, by direct reference to the Covenant.

61. Judges and members of the legal profession should be encouraged by States parties to pay greater attention to violations of the right to health in the exercise of their functions.

62. States parties should respect, protect, facilitate and promote the work of human rights advocates and other members of civil society with a view to assisting vulnerable or marginalized groups in the realization of their right to health.

For a practical example, consider the opinion of the Human Rights Committee

Burgos v Uruguay, Communication 52/1979, UN Doc. CCPR/C/13/D/52/1979

The author is a political refugee of Uruguayan nationality, living in Austria. She submitted a communication on behalf of her husband, who was in Uruguay. He was allegedly kidnapped in Buenos Aires by members of the 'Uruguayan security and intelligence forces', detained in Buenos Aires for about two weeks and clandestinely transported to Uruguay, where he was detained incommunicado by the special security forces at a secret prison for three months. During the entire period of detention, allegedly the man suffered from physical and mental torture and other cruel, inhuman or degrading treatment. He sustained a broken jaw and perforated eardrums. Burgos was then transferred to a military hospital. Over a year later, he was charged and brought to trial before a military court. He was not entitled to his own counsel and the final verdict was still pending at the time of the communication.

13. The Human Rights Committee, acting under article 5 (4) of the Optional Protocol to the International Covenant on Civil and Political Rights is of the view that the communication discloses violations of the Covenant, in particular of:

- Article 7, because of the treatment (including torture) suffered by Lopez Burgos at the hands of Uruguayan military officers in the period from July to October 1976 both in Argentina and Uruguay;

- Article 9 (1), because the act of abduction into Uruguayan territory constituted an arbitrary arrest and detention;

- Article 9 (3), because Lopez Burgos was not brought to trial within a reasonable time;

- Article 14 (3) (d), because Lopez Burgos was forced to accept Colonel Mario Rodriguez as his legal counsel;

- Article 14 (3) (g), because Lopez Burgos was compelled to sign a statement incriminating himself;

- Article 22 (1) in conjunction with article 19 (1) and (2), because Lopez Burgos has suffered persecution for his trade union activities.

14. The Committee, accordingly, is of the view that the State party is under an obligation, pursuant to article 2 (3) of the Covenant, to provide effective remedies to Lopez Burgos, including immediate release, permission to leave Uruguay and compensation for the violations which he has suffered, and to take steps to ensure that similar violations do not occur in the future.

Note the very specific references to compensation. Not all Committees (indeed not all communications) offer the same comments.

The Inter-American system probably offers the highest financial compensation. However, from its jurisprudence, it is possible to discern the process of evaluating compensation.

Case of Velásquez-Rodríguez v Honduras Compensatory damages (Art 63(1) American Convention on Human Rights), Series C, No. 7, Judgment of July 21 1989

The facts of this case are discussed in Chapter 11. In some respects they are similar to that of *Burgos*. Essentially the applicant had disappeared and the Inter-American court of Human Rights had found infringements of many rights and freedoms contained in the American Convention. The applicant could be presumed dead. The judgment on the merits of the case is reported in Series C, No. 4 (1988). The issue of compensation was reserved for the court.

25. It is a principle of international law, which jurisprudence has considered 'even a general concept of law,' that every violation of an international obligation which results in harm creates a duty to make adequate reparation. Compensation, on the other hand, is the most usual way of doing so . . .

26. Reparation of harm brought about by the violation of an international obligation consists in full restitution (*restitutio in integrum*), which includes the restoration of the prior situation, the reparation of the consequences of the violation, and indemnification for patrimonial and non-patrimonial damages, including emotional harm.

27. As to emotional harm, the Court holds that indemnity may be awarded under international law and, in particular, in the case of human rights violations. Indemnification must be based upon the principles of equity.

. . . .

34. However, in its judgment on the merits . . ., the Court has already pointed out the Government's continuing duty to investigate so long as the fate of a disappeared person is unknown . . . . The duty to investigate is in addition to the duties to prevent involuntary disappearances and to punish those directly responsible . . . .

35. Although these obligations were not expressly incorporated into the resolutory part of the judgment on the merits, it is a principle of procedural law that the bases of a judicial decision are a part of the same. Consequently, the Court declares that those obligations on the part of Honduras continue until they are fully carried out.

36. Otherwise, the Court understands that the judgment on the merits of July 29, 1988, is in itself a type of reparation and moral satisfaction of significance and importance for the families of the victims. . . .

38. The expression 'fair compensation,' used in Article 63 (1) of the Convention to refer to a part of the reparation and to the 'injured party,' is compensatory and not punitive. Although some domestic courts, particularly the Anglo-American, award damages in amounts meant to deter or to serve as an example, this principle is not applicable in international law at this time.

39. Because of the foregoing, the Court believes, then, that the fair compensation, described as 'compensatory' in the judgment on the merits of July 29, 1988, includes reparation to the family of the victim of the material and moral damages they suffered because of the involuntary disappearance of Manfredo Velásquez. . . .

46. The Court notes that the disappearance of Manfredo Velásquez cannot be considered an accidental death for the purposes of compensation, given that it is the result of serious acts imputable to Honduras. The amount of compensation cannot, therefore, be based upon guidelines

such as life insurance, but must be calculated as a loss of earnings based upon the income the victim would have received up to the time of his possible natural death. In that sense, one can take as a point of departure the salary that, according to the certification of the Honduran Vice-Minister of Planning on October 19, 1988, Manfredo Velásquez was receiving at the time of his disappearance (1,030 lempiras per month) and calculate the amount he would have received at the time of his obligatory retirement at the age of sixty, as provided by Article 69 of the Law of the National Institute of Social Security for Teachers and which the Government itself considers the most favorable. At retirement, he would have been entitled to a pension until his death.

47. However, the calculation of the loss of earnings must consider two distinct situations. When the beneficiary of the indemnity is a victim who is totally and permanently disabled, the compensation should include all he failed to receive, together with appropriate adjustments based upon his probable life expectancy. In that circumstance, the only income for the victim is what he would have received, but will not receive, as earnings.

48. If the beneficiaries of the compensation are the family members, the situation is different. In principle, the family members have an actual or future possibility of working or receiving income on their own. The children, who should be guaranteed the possibility of an education which might extend to the age of twenty-five, could, for example, begin to work at that time. It is not correct, then, in these cases, to adhere to rigid criteria, more appropriate to the situation described in the above paragraph, but rather to arrive at a prudent estimate of the damages, given the circumstances of each case.

49. Based upon a prudent estimate of the possible income of the victim for the rest of his probable life and on the fact that, in this case, the compensation is for the exclusive benefit of the family of Manfredo Velásquez identified at trial, the Court sets the loss of earnings in the amount of five hundred thousand lempiras to be paid to the wife and to the children of Manfredo Velásquez as set out below.

50. The Court must now consider the question of the indemnification of the moral damages . . ., which is primarily the result of the psychological impact suffered by the family of Manfredo Velásquez because of the violation of the rights and freedoms guaranteed by the American Convention, especially by the dramatic characteristics of the involuntary disappearance of persons.

51. The moral damages are demonstrated by expert documentary evidence and the testimony of Dr. Federico Allodi . . ., psychiatrist and Professor of Psychology at the University of Toronto, Canada. According to his testimony, the above doctor examined the wife of Manfredo Velásquez, Mrs. Emma Guzmán Urbina de Velásquez and his children, Héctor Ricardo, Herling Lizzett and Nadia Waleska Velásquez. According to those examinations, they had symptoms of fright, anguish, depression and withdrawal, all because of the disappearance of the head of the family. The Government could not disprove the existence of psychological problems that affect the family of the victim. The Court finds that the disappearance of Manfredo Velásquez produced harmful psychological impacts among his immediate family which should be indemnified as moral damages.

52. The Court believes the Government should pay compensation for moral damages in the amount of two hundred and fifty thousand lempiras, to be paid to the wife and children of Manfredo Velásquez as specified below. . . .

56. The Court now determines how the Government is to pay compensation to the family of Manfredo Velásquez.

57. Payment of the seven hundred and fifty thousand lempiras awarded by the Court must be carried out within ninety days from the date of notification of the judgment, free from any tax that might eventually be considered applicable. Nevertheless, the Government may pay in six equal monthly installments, the first being payable within ninety days and the remainder in successive months. In this case, the balance shall be incremented by the appropriate interest, which shall be at the interest rates current at the moment in Honduras.

58. One-fourth of the indemnity is awarded to the wife who shall receive that sum directly. The remaining three-fourths shall be distributed among the children. With the funds from the award to the children, a trust fund shall be set up in the Central Bank of Honduras under the most favorable conditions permitted by Honduran banking practice. The children shall receive monthly payments from this trust fund, and at the age of twenty-five shall receive their proportionate part.

59. The Court shall supervise the implementation of the compensatory damages at all of its stages. The case shall be closed when the Government has fully complied with the instant judgment.

The European system, in contrast, retains an altruistic approach and often regards a pending change in national law remedy enough, thus restricting the award to the financial outlay for bringing the case.

Question

Given the nature of international human rights law (living instrument etc.), what rationale may there be for the approach of the European Court to remedies?

However, in some circumstances, it does award compensation

Selmouni v France, Application no. 25803/94, judgment 1999

Mr Selmouni was arrested following a series of drug related arrests, he denied involvement. He was held in custody for three days and questioned by police from the Criminal Investigation Department. His detention was extended and he was repeatedly examined by a medical officer who noted various injuries. Selmouni alleged police brutality (including sexual assault) and accordingly an infringement to his freedom from torture, inhuman and degrading treatment (Art 3, European Convention). The Court found a violation of Art 3 of the Convention, corroborating the claims of assault.

120. The applicant claimed 750,000 French francs (FRF) for personal injury. That amount comprised general compensation for the injuries occasioned by the violence he had endured during police custody and special compensation for the effects on his visual acuity, the condition of his eye not yet having stabilised. He claimed FRF 1,500,000 for non-pecuniary damage resulting from his treatment in police custody, the length of the proceedings and the impossibility of obtaining a transfer to the Netherlands to serve his sentence there.

121. The French Government submitted, having regard both to the lack of any distinction between the damage sustained as a result of violations of Article 3 and Article 6 and to the fact that proceedings were in progress before the domestic courts, that the question of the application of Article 41 was not ready for decision. . . .

123. The Court first reiterates its finding that the applicant has neither proved that he was raped nor established a causal link between the violence suffered and the loss of visual acuity relied on (see paragraph 90 above). Nevertheless, it finds, having regard, *inter alia*, to the five days' ITTP (see paragraph 31 above) and, in part, to his pain and suffering, that the applicant sustained personal injury in addition to non-pecuniary damage. Accordingly, having regard to the extreme seriousness of the violations of the Convention of which Mr **Selmouni** was a victim, the Court considers that he suffered personal injury and non-pecuniary damage for which the findings of violations in this judgment do not afford sufficient satisfaction. It considers, having regard to its previous conclusions, that the question of the application of Article 41 is ready for decision and, making its assessment on an equitable basis as required by that Article, it awards him FRF 500,000.

Question

Can human rights violations ever satisfactorily be compensated from the perspective of the individual? Consider the purpose of human rights monitoring and thus the purpose of the committees and courts. To what extent does the award of compensation act as a deterrent to States?

FURTHER READING

Alston, P and Crawford, J, *The Future of UN Human Rights Treaty Monitoring*, 2000, Cambridge: CUP

Bayefsky, A, *How to Complain to the UN Human Rights Treaty System*, 2002: Ardsley, NY: Transnational Press

Cancado Trinidade, A, 'The Development of International Human Rights Law by the Operation and the caselaw of the European and Inter-American Courts of Human Rights' (2004) 25 Human Rights Law Journal 157

Cerna, C, 'The Inter-American Court of Human Rights', in Smith, R, and van den Anker, C (eds), *The Essentials of Human Rights*, 2005, London: Hodder, pp 180–185

McGoldrick, D, *The Human Rights Committee, its role in the development of the International Covenant on Civil and Political Rights*, 1994, Oxford. Clarendon Press

Moir, L, 'Law and the Inter-American Human Rights System' (2003) 25 Human Rights Quarterly 182

Murray, R, *African Commission on Human and Peoples' Rights and International Law*, 2000, Hart Publishing

Murray, R, and Wheatly, S, 'Groups and the African Charter on Human and Peoples' right' (2003) 25 Human Rights Quarterly 213

Pasqualucci, J, 'The Inter-American Court of Human Rights', in Smith, R and van den Anker, C (eds), *The Essentials of Human Rights*, 2005, London: Hodder, pp 185–187

Shelton, D, *Remedies in International Human Rights Law*, 2nd edn, 2005, Oxford: OUP

Van Dijk and van Hoof, *Theory and Practice of the European Convention on Human Rights*, 1998, The Hague: Kluwer

United Nations Office of the High Commissioner for Human Rights, *Complaint Procedures*, Fact Sheet No. 7 (Rev.1), Geneva: OHCHR

United Nations Office of the High Commissioner for Human Rights, *The Committee on the Elimination of Racial Discrimination*, Fact Sheet No. 12, Geneva: OHCHR

United Nations Office of the High Commissioner for Human Rights, *Civil and Political rights: The Human Rights Committee*, Fact Sheet No. 15 (Rev.1), 2005, Geneva: OHCHR

United Nations Office of the High Commissioner for Human Rights, *The Committee on Economic, Social and Cultural Rights*, Fact Sheet No. 16 (Rev.1) 1991, Geneva: OHCHR

United Nations Office of the High Commissioner for Human Rights, *The Committee against Torture*, Fact Sheet No. 17, Geneva: OHCHR

United Nations Office of the High Commissioner for Human Rights, *The United Nations Human Rights treaty System, an introduction to the core human rights treaties and the treaty bodies* (2005) Fact Sheet No. 30, Geneva: OHCHR (also available online from www.ohchr.org)

Websites

www.ohchr.org/english/bodies/cerd/index.htm—Committee on the Elimination of Racial Discrimination www.ohchr.org/english/bodies/hrc/index.htm—Human Rights Committee

www.ohchr.org/english/bodies/cescr/index.htm—Committee on Economic, Social and Cultural Rights

www.un.org/womenwatch/daw/cedaw/—Committee on the Elimination of Discrimination against Women

www.ohchr.org/english/bodies/cat/index.htm—Committee against Torture

www.ohchr.org/english/bodies/crc/index.htm—Committee on the Rights of the Child

www.ohchr.org/english/bodies/cmw/index.htm—Committee on Migrant Workers

www.echr.coe.int—European Court of Human Rights

http://www.cpt.coe.int—European Committee against Torture

CHAPTER 7

NATIONAL INSTITUTIONS FOR PROTECTING AND PROMOTING HUMAN RIGHTS

'We the peoples of the united nations' (United Nations Charter). 'The States Parties to the present Covenant . . . considering the obligation of States under the Charter of the United Nations to promote universal respect for, and observance of, human rights and freedoms . . . agree' in the words of the preamble to the International Covenant on Economic, Social and Cultural Rights and that on Civil and Political Rights. Clearly, the obligation to protect human rights is imposed on States themselves and not on the international community or any given international organisation. It follows that responsibility for realising international human rights is a matter primarily within the competence of States. While the last 60 years have witnessed an enormous expansion of international human rights, issues relating to implementation and enforcement remain unresolved. As the chapter on monitoring and enforcing international human rights demonstrated, by definition the international legal system is consensual in nature, dependent on the will of States. With the passing years, attention has focused on additional ways to give effect to norms of human rights. It is perhaps logical that attention has thus turned to the primary obligees under international human rights instruments (the States themselves) and mechanisms by which national institutions can protect and promote human rights. After all, consider the view of the General Assembly on the nature of human rights responsibility.

Declaration on the Right and Responsibility of Individuals, Groups and Organs of Society to Promote and Protect Universally Recognized Human Rights and Fundamental Freedoms, General Assembly Resolution 53/144 of 9 December 1998

Article 2

1. Each State has a prime responsibility and duty to protect, promote and implement all human rights and fundamental freedoms, *inter alia*, by adopting such steps as may be necessary to create all conditions necessary in the social, economic, political and other fields, as well as the legal guarantees required to ensure that all persons under its jurisdiction, individually and in association with others, are able to enjoy all those rights and freedoms in practice.

2. Each State shall adopt such legislative, administrative and other steps as may be necessary to ensure that the rights and freedoms referred to in the present Declaration are effectively guaranteed.

Article 3

Domestic law consistent with the Charter of the United Nations and other international obligations of the State in the field of human rights and fundamental freedoms is the juridical framework within which human rights and fundamental freedoms should be implemented and enjoyed and within which all activities referred to in the present Declaration for the promotion, protection and effective realization of those rights and freedoms should be conducted.

7.1 STATES AND INTERNATIONAL (HUMAN RIGHTS) LAW

States can be monistic or dualistic in their approach to international law (including international human rights law). The approach they take shapes their view of international human rights and affects their relationship with international treaty monitoring bodies and courts.

7.1.1 Monistic State

Put simply, in those States advocating a monistic view to international law, international, regional and national law all form part of the same single legal system. International law usually enjoys primacy over national law. Law is viewed as a unitary concept with an inbuilt hierarchy favouring the transnational systems.

National institutions in those systems in the monistic tradition will usually employ international human rights as the standard against which to measure national law. They will uphold principles of international human rights law in the face of conflicting national law. (The same will usually be true of national courts in monistic States.) National institutions in such States will often be involved in compiling reports for the treaty monitoring bodies and play an active role in publicising and promoting the rights protected under the international and regional systems.

Question

How would courts in a monistic State generally resolve the following:

1. *a conflict between national and international law?*

2. *a subsequent national measure which conflicts with international law?*

3. *a subsequent alteration to international law?*

With respect to enforcing international human rights in the national courts, monistic systems have a clear advantage over dualistic systems.

7.1.2 Dualistic State

In contrast, dualistic States maintain a distinction between international (usually including regional law) and national law. As the two systems are deemed to serve different functions (inter-State relations and State-civilian/intra-civilian relations) they are mutually exclusive. This poses problems for international human rights as obviously international human rights law impacts on the rights of civilians *vis-à-vis* the State, and indeed the rights of the population among themselves. However, provision is made in dualistic theory for a transfer from international to national law. This is dependent on the explicit consent of the national legislature.

The format of the enabling measure is dependent upon the provisions of the constitution of the State concerned. For some States it will be a simple legislative measure, for

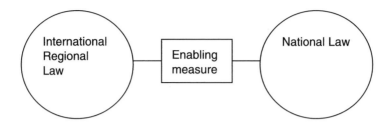

others, consent of the national legislature. Once the enabling measure is in place, it acts as a bridge, a gate, permitting the international and regional laws to enter the realm of national law. Thereafter, it will usually enjoy the same status before the national courts as other national law. Sometimes the enabling measure is a specific act of the legislature which gives effect to provisions of the treaty, in whole or in part. Whichever, the effect of international law is limiting to the extent permitted by the enabling act. International law is thus not prioritised unless the enabling act (or the Constitution of the State) explicitly provides that this is so.

7.1.3   Case study: the United Kingdom, dualism and the Human Rights Act

The United Kingdom has a dualistic approach to treaty law (though a monistic approach to customary international law). Consequently, its international human rights obligations do not in general form an actionable part of national law. Treaty-making is an exercise of royal prerogative powers by the executive. Approval by the legislature (the democratically elected representatives of British citizens) is required to authorise national courts to enforce a particular treaty. Until 1998, no enabling act of Parliament was passed to cause national courts to have regard to international human rights treaties. There is a presumption against Parliament violating international human rights. However, Parliament enjoys supreme legislative autonomy in terms of the United Kingdom's (unwritten) constitution.

Mortensen v Peters (1906) 8 F(J) 93 (Scotland)

Under a Scottish byelaw, it was an offence to engage in certain fishing practices within the Moray Firth (an expanse of water in the northeast of Scotland, east of Inverness). Mortensen was Danish but master of a Norwegian ship. He was convicted in Scotland for this offence. He had been fishing in the Moray Firth as defined in the byelaw, but at a point beyond the then prevailing international standard of territorial waters—a three mile limit offshore. In terms of international law, fishing on the High Seas (beyond the three mile limit) was permitted. His appeal was rejected by the High Court of Justiciary, the most senior criminal court in Scotland.

> **Lord Dunedin** at p 100: For us an Act of Parliament duly passed by Lords and Commons and assented to by the King, is supreme, and we are bound to give effect to its terms.

> **Lord Kyllachy** at p 103: it may probably be conceded that there is always a certain presumption against the Legislature of a country asserting or assuming the existence of a territorial jurisdiction going clearly beyond limits established by the common consent of nations—that is to say, by international law . . . But then it is only a presumption, and as such it must always give way to the language used if it is clear, and also to all counter presumptions which may legitimately be had in view in determining, on ordinary principles, the true meaning and intent of the legislation. Express words will of course be conclusive, and so also will plain implication.

International law could only be used to resolve ambiguities and fill in gaps in common and statute law. Individuals cannot rely on treaties before the national courts 'unless and until' they are incorporated into national law—see *Maclaine Watson v Department of Trade* [1990] 2 AC 418 at 500 per Lord Oliver in the House of Lords.

International human rights did not form part of the national law of the United Kingdom although the State ratified the key international and regional (European) instruments on human rights. Arguably, many rights were already provided for under national law. However, as the burgeoning caselaw of the European Court of Human Rights indicated, the United Kingdom had a far from perfect record of compliance with regional human rights. Perusing the periodic reports submitted to the various international treaty monitoring bodies reveals the same.

In 1998, the Labour government enacted the Human Rights Act 1998. This Act entered into force in 2001. Consider its long title:

Human Rights Act 1998, chapter 42, Long title

An Act to give further effect to rights and freedoms guaranteed under the European Convention on Human Rights; to make provision with respect to holders of certain judicial offices who become judges of the European Court of Human Rights; and for connected purposes.

The Human Rights Act thus gives further effect to elements of the European Convention on Human Rights. It does not incorporate the convention into national law thereby making it directly enforceable in national courts. Rather, it enables national courts to use the Convention in various ways:

Human Rights Act 1998, ss 2–4

Interpretation of Convention rights

2.—(1) A court or tribunal determining a question which has arisen in connection with a Convention right must take into account any—

(a) judgment, decision, declaration or advisory opinion of the European Court of Human Rights,

(b) opinion of the Commission given in a report adopted under Article 31 of the Convention,

(c) decision of the Commission in connection with Article 26 or 27(2) of the Convention, or

(d) decision of the Committee of Ministers taken under Article 46 of the Convention,

whenever made or given, so far as, in the opinion of the court or tribunal, it is relevant to the proceedings in which that question has arisen.

(2) Evidence of any judgment, decision, declaration or opinion of which account may have to be taken under this section is to be given in proceedings before any court or tribunal in such manner as may be provided by rules.

(3) In this section 'rules' means rules of court or, in the case of proceedings before a tribunal, rules made for the purposes of this section—

(a) by the Lord Chancellor or the Secretary of State, in relation to any proceedings outside Scotland;

(b) by the Secretary of State, in relation to proceedings in Scotland; or

(c) by a Northern Ireland department, in relation to proceedings before a tribunal in Northern Ireland—

    (i) which deals with transferred matters; and

    (ii) for which no rules made under paragraph (a) are in force.

Interpretation of legislation

3.—(1) So far as it is possible to do so, primary legislation and subordinate legislation must be read and given effect in a way which is compatible with the Convention rights.

(2) This section—

(a) applies to primary legislation and subordinate legislation whenever enacted;

(b) does not affect the validity, continuing operation or enforcement of any incompatible primary legislation; and

(c) does not affect the validity, continuing operation or enforcement of any incompatible subordinate legislation if (disregarding any possibility of revocation) primary legislation prevents removal of the incompatibility.

Declaration of incompatibility

4.—(1) Subsection (2) applies in any proceedings in which a court determines whether a provision of primary legislation is compatible with a Convention right.

(2) If the court is satisfied that the provision is incompatible with a Convention right, it may make a declaration of that incompatibility.

(3) Subsection (4) applies in any proceedings in which a court determines whether a provision of subordinate legislation, made in the exercise of a power conferred by primary legislation, is compatible with a Convention right.

(4) If the court is satisfied—

(a) that the provision is incompatible with a Convention right, and

(b) that (disregarding any possibility of revocation) the primary legislation concerned prevents removal of the incompatibility,

it may make a declaration of that incompatibility.

(5) In this section 'court' means—

(a) the House of Lords;

(b) the Judicial Committee of the Privy Council;

(c) the Courts-Martial Appeal Court;

(d) in Scotland, the High Court of Justiciary sitting otherwise than as a trial court or the Court of Session;

(e) in England and Wales or Northern Ireland, the High Court or the Court of Appeal.

(6) A declaration under this section ('a declaration of incompatibility')—

(a) does not affect the validity, continuing operation or enforcement of the provision in respect of which it is given; and

(b) is not binding on the parties to the proceedings in which it is made.

Note that even should the national courts determine that national law is incompatible with the Convention (s 4), national law remains legally in force. This reflects the dualistic heritage of the country: international law is not viewed as superior and thus not automatically able to take priority over national law. Within the United Kingdom, the view of the domestic legislature dominates in accordance with the entrenched principle of parliamentary supremacy which characterises the British constitution.

Compare and contrast the two following extracts from judgments before and after the entry into force of the Human Rights Act in the United Kingdom.

R v Secretary of State for the Home Department ex parte Brind **[1991] AC 696**
(House of Lords)

The case concerned journalists who sought judicial review of a decision by the Home Secretary requiring the BBC and IBA to refrain from broadcasting on television or radio actual spoken words of persons involved in organisations proscribed under the then Prevention of Terrorism (Temporary Provisions) Act 1984 and the Northern Ireland (Emergency Provisions) Act 1978. Their arguments on appeal were partially based on Article 10 of the European Convention on Human Rights but dismissed unanimously.

> **Lord Bridge** (pp 747–748): It is accepted, . . . that, like any other treaty obligations which have not been embodied in the law by statute, the Convention is not part of the domestic law, that the courts accordingly have no power to enforce Convention rights directly and that, if domestic legislation conflicts with the Convention, the courts must nevertheless enforce it. But it is already well settled that, in construing any provision in domestic legislation which is ambiguous in the sense that it is capable of a meaning which either conforms to or conflicts with the Convention, the courts will presume that Parliament intended to legislate in conformity with the Convention, not in conflict with it. . . .
>
> When Parliament has been content for so long to leave those who complain that their Convention rights have been infringed to seek their remedy in Strasbourg, it would be surprising suddenly to find that the judiciary has, without Parliament's aid, the means to incorporate the Convention into such an important area of domestic law and I cannot escape the conclusion that this would be a judicial usurpation of the legislative function.

Obviously the Human Rights Act altered this view. Section 3 of the Human Rights Act is examined in the following case.

R v A **[2002] AC 45**

The respondent had been tried for rape. His defence was that the complainant consented, or that he had honestly believed she had consented. Defence counsel thus wished to lead evidence about the complainant's prior (consensual) sexual relations with the accused and his friend. In accordance with the relevant statute (s 41, Youth Justice and Criminal Evidence Act 1999), the judge ruled that only questions concerning consensual sex with the friend could be put to the complainant in cross-examination, not any questions concerning prior relations with the defendant. Leave to appeal was granted, the House of Lords being asked 'May a sexual relationship between a defendant and complainant be relevant to the issue of consent so as to render its exclusion . . . a contravention of the defendant's rights to a fair trial [as protected under Article 6 of the European Convention and given further effect under the Human Rights Act 1998]?'

> **Lord Steyn** (para 44) . . . the interpretative obligation under section 3 is a strong one. It applies even if there is no ambiguity in the language in the sense of the language being capable of two different meanings . . . The White Paper made clear that the obligation goes far beyond the rule which enabled the courts to take the Convention into account in resolving any ambiguity in a legislative provision. . . . Section 3 places a duty on the court to strive to find a possible interpretation compatible with Convention rights. Under ordinary methods of interpretation a court may depart from the language of the statute to avoid absurd consequences: section 3 goes much further. Undoubtedly, a court must always look for a contextual and purposive interpretation: section 3 is more radical in its effect. It is a general principle of the interpretation of legal instruments that the text is the primary source of interpretation: other sources are subordinate to it: compare, for example, Article 31 to 33 of the Vienna Convention on the Law of Treaties

(1980)(Cmnd 7964). Section 3 qualifies this general principle because it requires a court to find an interpretation compatible with Convention rights if it is possible to do so . . . In accordance with the will of parliament as reflected in section 3, it will sometimes be necessary to adopt an interpretation which linguistically may appear strained. The techniques to be used will not only involve the reading down of express language in a statute but also the implication of provisions. A declaration of incompatibility is a measure of last resort. It must be avoided unless it is plainly impossible to do so. If a *clear* limitation on Convention rights is stated *in terms*, such an impossibility will arise . . .

Lord Hope of Craighead (para 51): It is plain a balance must be struck between the right of the defendant to a fair trial and the right of the complainant not to be subjected to unnecessary humiliation and distress when giving evidence. The right of the defendant to a fair trial has now been reinforced by the incorporation into our law of Article 6 of the European Convention for the Protection of Human Rights and Fundamental freedoms by the Human Rights Act 1998.

Lord Hope of Craighead (para 108): The rule of construction which section 3 lays down is quite unlike any previous rule of statutory interpretation. There is no need to identify an ambiguity or absurdity. Compatibility with Convention rights is the sole guiding principle. That is the paramount object which the rule seeks to achieve. But the rule is only a rule of interpretation. It does not entitle judges to act as legislators.

Question

To what extent are the judges in R v A *securing a balance between respecting human rights and respecting parliamentary sovereignty? Should judges be given such a scope to change the meaning of statutes to give effect to human rights?*

7.1.4   Different rules for different rights?

Some commentators suggest that not all human rights can be realised under national law. Tomuschat suggests that first generation rights (primarily civil and political rights) are the simplest to enact as the rights directly relate to interference of the State with individual rights and liberties (Christian Tomuschat, *Human Rights—between idealism and realism*, 2003, Oxford: OUP, p 93). The extent of the obligations incumbent on States under the International Covenant on Civil and Political Rights has been discussed by the Human Rights Committee.

Human Rights Committee General Comment No. 3: Implementation at the national level (Art 2) (1981)

1. The Committee notes that article 2 of the Covenant generally leaves it to the States parties concerned to choose their method of implementation in their territories within the framework set out in that article. It recognizes, in particular, that the implementation does not depend solely on constitutional or legislative enactments, which in themselves are often not *per se* sufficient. The Committee considers it necessary to draw the attention of States parties to the fact that the obligation under the Covenant is not confined to the respect of human rights, but that States parties have also undertaken to ensure the enjoyment of these rights to all individuals under their jurisdiction. This aspect calls for specific activities by the States parties to enable individuals to enjoy their rights. This is obvious in a number of articles (e.g. art. 3 which is dealt with in General Comment 4 below), but in principle this undertaking relates to all rights set forth in the Covenant.

2. In this connection, it is very important that individuals should know what their rights under the Covenant (and the Optional Protocol, as the case may be) are and also that all administrative and judicial authorities should be aware of the obligations which the State party has assumed under the Covenant. To this end, the Covenant should be publicized in all official languages of the State and steps should be taken to familiarize the authorities concerned with its contents as part of

their training. It is desirable also to give publicity to the State party's cooperation with the Committee.

In contrast, Tomuschat points out that some second generation rights (economic, social and cultural rights) lack the necessary specificity for national level enforcement (p 92). This is corroborated by the terms of the International Covenant on Civil and Political Rights and General Comment 9 (1998) of the Committee on Economic, Social and Cultural Rights.

General Comment No. 9 (1998) Committee on Economic, Social and Cultural Rights, UN Doc. E/C.12/1998/24

1. In its General Comment No. 3 (1990) on the nature of States parties' obligations (art. 2, para. 1, of the Covenant) the Committee addressed issues relating to the nature and scope of States parties' obligations. The present general comment seeks to elaborate further certain elements of the earlier statement. The central obligation in relation to the Covenant is for States parties to give effect to the rights recognized therein. By requiring Governments to do so 'by all appropriate means', the Covenant adopts a broad and flexible approach which enables the particularities of the legal and administrative systems of each State, as well as other relevant considerations, to be taken into account.

2. But this flexibility coexists with the obligation upon each State party to use all the means at its disposal to give effect to the rights recognized in the Covenant. In this respect, the fundamental requirements of international human rights law must be borne in mind. Thus the Covenant norms must be recognized in appropriate ways within the domestic legal order, appropriate means of redress, or remedies, must be available to any aggrieved individual or group, and appropriate means of ensuring governmental accountability must be put in place . . .

4. In general, legally binding international human rights standards should operate directly and immediately within the domestic legal system of each State party, thereby enabling individuals to seek enforcement of their rights before national courts and tribunals. The rule requiring the exhaustion of domestic remedies reinforces the primacy of national remedies in this respect. The existence and further development of international procedures for the pursuit of individual claims is important, but such procedures are ultimately only supplementary to effective national remedies.

5. The Covenant does not stipulate the specific means by which it is to be implemented in the national legal order. And there is no provision obligating its comprehensive incorporation or requiring it to be accorded any specific type of status in national law. Although the precise method by which Covenant rights are given effect in national law is a matter for each State party to decide, the means used should be appropriate in the sense of producing results which are consistent with the full discharge of its obligations by the State party. The means chosen are also subject to review as part of the Committee's examination of the State party's compliance with its obligations under the Covenant.

Tomuschat suggests that many of the rights in the Covenant 'boil down to nothing more than an objective of social policy' (p 92), just as third generation rights are essentially political objectives. 'No third generation right possesses the accuracy which would be necessary to legitimate adjudication by judicial bodies' (Tomuschat ibid.).

For States, the issue is particularly pressing with human rights. When the early instruments were drafted in the middle of last century, it was almost inconceivable that international (and indeed regional) organisations could directly affect the national law of Member States, and most certainly not conceivable with respect to the rights of citizens against their State. Creating a culture of respect for human rights has been an incremental process.

Stages of creating a culture of human rights in a State

States recognise and ratify international human rights instruments

States adjust national law as necessary to conform to standards

States comply with international and regional monitoring arrangements

Generation of national awareness of standards of international rights

Promotion of standards within State

National enforcement and monitoring of all rights and freedoms

The stages are not necessarily discreet and are not inevitably adhered to in a particular order. However, the foregoing indicates some of the problems of ensuring compliance with international human rights standards within States. As the previous chapters have indicated, States are often enjoined to accede to instruments for political and diplomatic reasons. Some do not progress past the stage of ratification to amending national law.

Question

Note the requirements in Art 2 of the International Covenant on Civil and Political Rights, Art 2 of the International Covenant on Economic, Social and Cultural Rights and Art 2 of the Convention against Torture and Other Cruel, Inhuman or Degrading Treatment or Punishment. To what extent does each instrument require States to change their national laws/ implement specific measures to give effect to the treaty obligations?

7.2   THE INTERNATIONAL APPROACH TO NATIONAL INSTITUTIONS

National human rights institutions are viewed favourably by the United Nations. This has been apparent from the outset and was reiterated by the world community during the World Conference on Human Rights in 1993.

Vienna Declaration, para 36

The World Conference on Human Rights reaffirms the important and constructive role played by national institutions for the promotion and protection of human rights, in particular in their advisory capacity to the competent authorities, their role in remedying human rights violations, in the dissemination of human rights information, and education in human rights.

The World Conference on Human Rights encourages the establishment and strengthening of national institutions, having regard to the 'Principles relating to the status of national institutions' and recognising that it is the right of each State to choose the framework which is best suited to its particular needs at the national level.

Note the discretion accorded to each State to adjudge the most appropriate mechanism for pursuing human rights in its own jurisdiction.

Question

Why are the scope and form of national institutions left to each State to determine?

Shortly after the establishment of the organisation in 1946, the Economic and Social Council expressed support for local (national) human rights bodies to support the work of the Commission on Human Rights. A resolution in 1960 called for the formation (and continuation) of national human rights bodies.

Further developments occurred in a number of United Nations workshops and meetings over the next three decades. During this period, guidelines as to the functioning of human rights institutions were drafted and a number of national bodies were established. Developments culminated in a 1991 workshop held in Paris which aimed at discussing mechanisms for increasing the effectiveness of national human rights bodies. Many national institutions participated in the sessions. The result, the Paris Principles relating to the status and functioning of national institutions for protection and promotion of human rights, remain the blueprint today (approved by the General Assembly, UN Doc. A/RES/48/134, 20 December 1993). The General Assembly approves and supports the creation of national institutions.

General Assembly Resolution 48/134, UN Doc. A/RES/48/134, 20 December 1993

2. *Reaffirms* the importance of developing, in accordance with national legislation, effective national institutions for the promotion and protection of human rights and of ensuring the pluralism of their membership and their independence;

3. *Encourages* Member States to establish or, where they already exist, to strengthen national institutions for the promotion and protection of human rights and to incorporate those elements in national development plans;

4. *Encourages* national institutions for the promotion and protection of human rights established by Member States to prevent and combat all violations of human rights as enumerated in the Vienna Declaration and Programme of Action and relevant international instruments;

Approval has also been expressed by several of the treaty monitoring bodies.

Committee on the Elimination of Racial Discrimination, General Recommendation No. 17: Establishment of national institutions to facilitate implementation of the Convention

1. *Recommends* that States parties establish national commissions or other appropriate bodies, taking into account, *mutatis mutandis*, the principles relating to the status of national institutions annexed to Commission on Human Rights resolution 1992/54 of 3 March 1992, to serve, *inter alia*, the following purposes:

(a) To promote respect for the enjoyment of human rights without any discrimination, as expressly set out in article 5 of the International Convention on the Elimination of All Forms of Racial Discrimination;

(b) To review government policy towards protection against racial discrimination;

(c) To monitor legislative compliance with the provisions of the Convention;

(d) To educate the public about the obligations of States parties under the Convention;

(e) To assist the Government in the preparation of reports submitted to the Committee on the Elimination of Racial Discrimination.

2. *Also recommends* that, where such commissions have been established, they should be associated with the preparation of reports and possibly included in government delegations in order to intensify the dialogue between the Committee and the State party concerned.

See also, General Comment No. 10 of the Committee on Economic, Social and Cultural Rights UN Doc. E/C.12/1998/25—The role of national human rights institutions in the protection of economic, social and cultural rights—and General Comment No. 2 of the Committee on the Rights of the Child.

The Principles are divided into four sections addressing the competence and responsibilities of national human rights institutions, their composition, their operation and their status.

7.2.1   Powers of national institutions: the Paris Principles

The Paris Principles themselves begin by examining the powers a national institution requires. Clearly, the focus is on developing the competence to promote and develop national awareness of, and compliance with international human rights.

Paris Principles relating to the status and functioning of national institutions for protection and promotion of human rights

A. Competence and responsibilities

1. A national institution shall be vested with competence to protect and promote human rights.

2. A national institution shall be given as broad a mandate as possible, which shall be clearly set forth in a constitutional or legislative text, specifying its composition and its sphere of competence.

3. A national institution shall, *inter alia*, have the following responsibilities:

(a) To submit to the government, parliament and any other competent body, on an advisory basis either at the request of the authorities concerned or through the exercise of its power to hear a matter without higher referral, opinions, recommendations, proposals and reports on any matters concerning the protection and promotion of human rights. The national institution may decide to publicize them. These opinions, recommendations, proposals and reports, as well as any prerogative of the national institution, shall relate to the following areas:

   (i) Any legislative or administrative provisions, as well as provisions relating to judicial organization, intended to preserve and extend the protection of human rights. In that connection, the national institution shall examine the legislation and administrative provisions in force, as well as bills and proposals, and shall make such recommendations as it deems appropriate in order to ensure that these provisions conform to the fundamental principles of human rights. It shall, if necessary, recommend the adoption of new legislation, the amendment of legislation in force and the adoption or amendment of administrative measures;

   (ii) Any situation of violation of human rights which it decides to take up;

   (iii) The preparation of reports on the national situation with regard to human rights in general, and on more specific matters;

   (iv) Drawing the attention of the government to situations in any part of the country where human rights are violated and making proposals to it for initiatives to put an end to such situations and, where necessary, expressing an opinion on the positions and reactions of the government;

(b) To promote and ensure the harmonization of national legislation, regulations and practices with the international human rights instruments to which the State is a party, and their effective implementation;

(c) To encourage ratification of the above-mentioned instruments or accession to those instruments, and to ensure their implementation;

(d) To contribute to the reports which States are required to submit to United Nations bodies and committees, and to regional institutions, pursuant to their treaty obligations, and, where necessary, to express an opinion on the subject, with due respect for their independence;

(e) To cooperate with the United Nations and any other agency in the United Nations system, the regional institutions and the national institutions of other countries which are competent in the areas of the protection and promotion of human rights;

(f) To assist in the formulation of programmes for the teaching of, and research into, human rights and to take part in their execution in schools, universities and professional circles;

(g) To publicize human rights and efforts to combat all forms of discrimination, in particular racial discrimination, by increasing public awareness, especially through information and education and by making use of all press organs.

In many respects, national institutions appear to be a potential panacea for many ills of the international system: encouraging State ratification of key instruments; contributing to periodic reports; investigating and reporting on human rights situations within the State; and generally spearheading a raising of awareness of human rights thereby promulgating the promotion and protection of human rights within the State. Clearly the State must give consideration to the mandate of any national institution and seek to ensure the necessary breadth for carrying out the required duties.

Question

Where do national institutions fit in the stages of implementing international human rights instruments (above)?

Note that a national institution should be vested with competence to protect and promote human rights and be given as broad a mandate as possible embedded in law. This should guarantee the operation of the institution and contributes towards the independence thereof. The Paris Principles explore this further, advocating the methods of operation for national institutions (part C below) and exploring the potential for receiving and administrating complaints against the State and State bodies (part D below).

The role of national human rights institutions in the protection of economic, social and cultural rights : General Comment No. 10 Committee on Economic, Social and Cultural Rights, UN Doc. E/C.12/1998/25

3. The Committee notes that national institutions have a potentially crucial role to play in promoting and ensuring the indivisibility and interdependence of all human rights. Unfortunately, this role has too often either not been accorded to the institution or has been neglected or given a low priority by it. It is therefore essential that full attention be given to economic, social and cultural rights in all of the relevant activities of these institutions. The following list is indicative of the types of activities that can be, and in some instances already have been, undertaken by national institutions in relation to these rights:

(a) The promotion of educational and information programmes designed to enhance awareness and understanding of economic, social and cultural rights, both within the population at large and among particular groups such as the public service, the judiciary, the private sector and the labour movement;

(b) The scrutinizing of existing laws and administrative acts, as well as draft bills and other proposals, to ensure that they are consistent with the requirements of the International Covenant on Economic, Social and Cultural Rights;

(c) Providing technical advice, or undertaking surveys in relation to economic, social and cultural rights, including at the request of the public authorities or other appropriate agencies;

(d) The identification of national-level benchmarks against which the realization of Covenant obligations can be measured;

(e) Conducting research and inquiries designed to ascertain the extent to which particular economic, social and cultural rights are being realized, either within the State as a whole or in areas or in relation to communities of particular vulnerability;

(f) Monitoring compliance with specific rights recognized under the Covenant and providing reports thereon to the public authorities and civil society; and

(g) Examining complaints alleging infringements of applicable economic, social and cultural rights standards within the State.

Note the similarities with the guidelines suggested by the Committee on the Elimination of All Forms of Discrimination against Women.

Committee on the Elimination of Discrimination against Women, General recommendation No. 6 (1988), Effective national machinery and publicity

The Committee on the Elimination of Discrimination against Women,

Having considered the reports of States parties to the Convention on the Elimination of All Forms of Discrimination against Women,

Noting United Nations General Assembly resolution 42/60 of 30 November 1987,

Recommends that States parties:

1. Establish and/or strengthen effective national machinery, institutions and procedures, at a high level of Government, and with adequate resources, commitment and authority to:

(a) Advise on the impact on women of all government policies;

(b) Monitor the situation of women comprehensively;

(c) Help formulate new policies and effectively carry out strategies and measures to eliminate discrimination.

7.2.2   Operational guidelines for national institutions

The problem with simply establishing national human rights institutions is ensuring they have the competence to undertake the tasks required of them. Careful consideration thus should precede the creation of any given State's national institution. What is the body required to do? What is it empowered to do? Finally what powers and functions does it require to fulfil its mandate?

Paris Principles relating to the status and functioning of national institutions for protection and promotion of human rights

C. Methods of operation

Within the framework of its operation, the national institution shall:

1. Freely consider any questions falling within its competence, whether they are submitted by the government or taken up by it without referral to a higher authority, on the proposal of its members or of any petitioner,

2. Hear any person and obtain any information and any documents necessary for assessing situations falling within its competence;

3. Address public opinion directly or through any press organ, particularly in order to publicize its opinions and recommendations;

4. Meet on a regular basis and whenever necessary in the presence of all its members after they have been duly consulted;

5. Establish working groups from among its members as necessary, and set up local or regional sections to assist it in discharging its functions;

6. Maintain consultation with the other bodies, whether jurisdictional or otherwise, responsible for the protection and promotion of human rights (in particular, ombudsmen, mediators and similar institutions);

7. In view of the fundamental role played by the non-governmental organizations in expanding the work of the national institutions, develop relations with the non-governmental organizations devoted to protecting and promoting human rights, to economic and social development, to combating racism, to protecting particularly vulnerable groups (especially children, migrant workers, refugees, physically and mentally disabled persons) or to specialized areas.

Special consideration must be given to the mandate of those institutions required to undertake judicial functions, or even quasi-judicial functions. Regard must be had to the functions of a body empowered to adjudicate on national compliance with human rights standards. There must be appropriate legal safeguards to ensure due process of law is followed, guarantees any decision has appropriate validity and a reasonable follow-up mechanism to ensure enforcement of decisions.

Paris Principles relating to the status and functioning of national institutions for protection and promotion of human rights
D. Additional principles concerning the status of commissions with quasi-jurisdictional competence

A national institution may be authorized to hear and consider complaints and petitions concerning individual situations. Cases may be brought before it by individuals, their representatives, third parties, non-governmental organizations, associations of trade unions or any other representative organizations. In such circumstances, and without prejudice to the principles stated above concerning the other powers of the commissions, the functions entrusted to them may be based on the following principles:

1. Seeking an amicable settlement through conciliation or, within the limits prescribed by the law, through binding decisions or, where necessary, on the basis of confidentiality;

2. Informing the party who filed the petition of his rights, in particular the remedies available to him, and promoting his access to them;

3. Hearing any complaints or petitions or transmitting them to any other competent authority within the limits prescribed by the law;

4. Making recommendations to the competent authorities, especially by proposing amendments or reforms of the laws, regulations or administrative practices, especially if they have created the difficulties encountered by the persons filing the petitions in order to assert their rights.

The complaints system has potentially far-reaching consequences, as it may be interpreted by some States as quasi-judicial in nature. Given the resistance often encountered against establishing transnational human rights courts, this may prove problematic.

Note also the recommendations of the Committee on the Rights of the Child concerning the status of national human rights institutions.

Committee on the Rights of the Child, General Comment No. 2 (2002) the role of independent national human rights institutions in the promotion and protection of the rights of the child, para 8

[National Human Rights Institutions] should, if possible, be constitutionally entrenched and must at least be legislatively mandated. It is the view of the Committee that their mandate should include as broad a scope as possible for promoting and protecting human rights.

Question

Consider various examples of national human rights institutions. What is their role in administrative law? Do they perform a judicial function or are they primarily a reviewer of administrative process (a traditional ombudsperson)?

7.2.3   A separation of powers?—independence from the State

Having considered the role of national institutions, it is apparent that a degree of independence from the executive of a State is essential to facilitate satisfactory discharge of functions. However, the institution must also be sanctioned by the State, and to an extent actively supported by it, to permit full exercise of the prescribed functions. This can often cause problems as State support and State control must clearly be distinguished to guarantee independence and genuine effectiveness. The Paris Principles make provision for the composition and independence of national institutions.

Paris Principles relating to the status and functioning of national institutions for protection and promotion of human rights

B. Composition and guarantees of independence and pluralism

1. The composition of the national institution and the appointment of its members, whether by means of an election or otherwise, shall be established in accordance with a procedure which affords all necessary guarantees to ensure the pluralist representation of the social forces (of civilian society) involved in the protection and promotion of human rights, particularly by powers which will enable effective cooperation to be established with, or through the presence of, representatives of:

> Non-governmental organizations responsible for human rights and efforts to combat racial discrimination, trade unions, concerned social and professional organizations, for example, associations of lawyers, doctors, journalists and eminent scientists;
>
> Trends in philosophical or religious thought;
>
> Universities and qualified experts;
>
> Parliament;
>
> Government departments (if they are included, these representatives should participate in the deliberations only in an advisory capacity).

2. The national institution shall have an infrastructure which is suited to the smooth conduct of its activities, in particular adequate funding. The purpose of this funding should be to enable it to have its own staff and premises, in order to be independent of the government and not be subject to financial control which might affect this independence.

3. In order to ensure a stable mandate for the members of the institution, without which there can be no real independence, their appointment shall be effected by an official act which shall establish the specific duration of the mandate. This mandate may be renewable, provided that the pluralism of the institution's membership is ensured.

Question

Do the Paris Principles enshrine sufficient workable guarantees for both the independence of national institutions and the effectiveness of the discharge of their duties?

While the creation of effective national human rights institutions will clearly be of advantage in reinforcing human rights at the national level, increasingly a new role is emerging: that of primary enforcer and guarantor of human rights. As has been noted elsewhere, there are many problems with the existing international system. For a multitude of reasons, many beyond the reasonable control of the international and regional organisations, the system lacks the necessary powers to enforce protection of human rights. National institutions that are free from such constraints thus represent a potential vehicle for progressing the active enforcement and realisation of human rights at the national level. Could national institutions be the salvation of the human rights movement?

7.2.4 Funding

While the issue of funding clearly relates to the independence of national institutions, support is available from other avenues for States wishing to create and establish national institutions. Consider the following extract from the Economic and Social Council.

National institutions for the promotion and protection of human rights, Economic and Social Council Decision 1998/258

At its 46th plenary meeting, on 30 July 1998, the Economic and Social Council, taking note of Commission on Human Rights resolution 1998/55 of 17 April 1998, approved the Commission's requests to the Secretary-General:

(a) To continue to provide, from within existing resources, the necessary assistance for holding meetings of the Coordinating Committee created by national institutions for the promotion and protection of human rights during the sessions of the Commission on Human Rights, under the auspices of and in cooperation with the Office of the United Nations High Commissioner for Human Rights;

(b) To continue to provide, from within existing resources and the United Nations Voluntary Fund for Technical Cooperation in the Field of Human Rights, the necessary assistance for regional meetings of national institutions

7.2.5 A lifeline for the international human rights system?

In 2002, the Secretary-General, Kofi Annan, emphasised the need for the United Nations to assist and support states wishing to create national human rights institutions; this was, he opined 'what in the long run will ensure that human rights are protected and advanced in a sustained manner' (UN Doc. A/57/387).

Strengthening of the United Nations: An agenda for change, UN Doc. A/57/387

50. In paragraphs 25 and 26 of the Millennium Declaration, Member States resolved to strengthen their capacity at the country level to implement the principles and practices of human rights, including minority rights, the rights of women, the rights of children and the rights of migrants. Building strong human rights institutions at the country level is what in the long run will ensure that human rights are protected and advanced in a sustained manner. The emplacement or

enhancement of a national protection system in each country, reflecting international human rights norms, should therefore be a principal objective of the Organization. These activities are especially important in countries emerging from conflict.

51. In order to achieve these goals, the Office of the United Nations High Commissioner for Human Rights has begun to work through the resident coordinator system to ensure that human rights are incorporated into country level analysis, planning and programme implementation. United Nations country teams—including United Nations funds and programmes, the specialized agencies and the World Bank—need access to information, analysis and examples of how to include human rights in country programmes. The Office of the High Commissioner must have the capacity to train country teams, assess and disseminate best practice, and develop monitoring mechanisms for measuring the impact of its human rights programming. To avoid duplication and ensure the best use of resources, the High Commissioner will need to draw upon the support of partner institutions to the maximum extent possible while maintaining a capacity to deploy the Office's own staff when necessary.

The Chief Commissioner of the United Kingdom's first established Commission (in Northern Ireland) is of the opinion that human rights commissions can add value to the work of the international treaty monitoring bodies and agencies as '[t]hey can acquire a special status for human rights' (Dickson, B, 'The Contribution of Human Rights Commissions to the Protection of Human Rights' (2003) Public Law 272 at 284). Few can argue with the fact that human rights are most successfully enforced at a national/local level. There the power exists to change laws and policies. Real power to effect human rights standards remains with the States. Dickson goes further, concluding 'as we move forward into the complexities and challenges of the twenty-first century a human rights commission is a *sine qua non* of a democratic society' (p 285).

Question

What practical reasons are there for seeking to enforce human rights at a national level? Why should enforcement prove more successful at a national level?

The Office of the High Commissioner for Human Rights supports the sharing of good practice among states in furtherance of the development of national human rights institutions. It also promotes the development of regional networks for the same purpose. A National Institutions Unit is located within the Capacity Building and Field Operations Branch of the OHCHR in Geneva. Elsewhere at the international level, national institutions may be accredited for participation in the sessions of the Human Rights Council and the National Human Rights Institutions Forum.

National institutions for the promotion and protection of human rights Report of the Secretary-General submitted in accordance with Commission on Human Rights Resolution 1997/40, UN Doc. E/CN.4/1998/47

5. In the last few years, the number of national institutions has increased significantly and in a number of cases their functions in promoting and protecting human rights at the national level have evolved. While national institutions are usually either constitutionally entrenched or established by national legislation and depend upon financial resources provided by Government, an effective national institution will be one which is capable of acting independently of Government, party politics and other external influences. National institutions are playing an increasing role in the work of the United Nations and are in a position to implement, at the national level, action to ensure the promotion and protection of internationally recognized human rights.

6. The participation of national institutions in human rights forums is not a new idea. They have, in the past, been granted status in several international meetings. At the World Conference on Human Rights in Vienna in 1993, national institutions were granted the right to participate *de jure*

in the debates. Since the World Conference, national institutions have participated as independent entities in a number of international and regional seminars and workshops organized in conjunction with the United Nations and some have addressed the Commission on Human Rights (as separate entities, but generally speaking from the seats of their official government delegations). At the fifty-second session of the Commission, the Chairman of the Commission decided to allocate separate speaking time for national institutions during consideration of the sub-item of the agenda on national institutions. A similar arrangement was adopted at subsequent meetings.

7.3   THE REGIONAL POSITION ON NATIONAL INSTITUTIONS

At a regional level too, there is growing support for national institutions. While many of these support the existing regional systems: e.g. Europe and Africa, others are in regions without such mechanisms.

The Council of Europe has hosted a number of roundtable meetings of national human rights institutions and ombudspersons while in Asia, for example, the Asia Pacific Forum of National Human Rights Institutions represents significant progress towards the creation of national institutions within the region and the awareness, more generally, of human rights.

7.4   NATURE OF NATIONAL INSTITUTIONS

There are many examples of national human rights institutions ranging from government advisory committees to quasi-judicial and fully independent bodies constantly reviewing state practice. Titles and functions vary from State to State. Some are independent while others are linked to the government in power or the primary legislative body (although the Paris Principles specify that their composition should be pluralistic, any government participation should be advisory only and funding mechanisms should ensure independence from government—principle B1). For example, within Europe, many States have created a human rights national entity to ensure compliance with the European Convention standards. Similarly, many emerging democracies hail the establishment of a national human rights institution as evidence of democracy and respect for the rule of law. This is especially evident in countries with a chequered history of human rights and those striving to emerge from the shadow of human rights abuses. Within the Organisation for Security and Cooperation in Europe, national human rights institutions are recognised as having a role to play in furthering democracy and the rule of law throughout the region.

Additionally, the creation of a national human rights body may contribute to the truth and reconciliation process as the experience of South Africa demonstrates.

The Paris Principles specify that a national institution shall be vested with competence to protect and promote human rights and shall be given as broad a mandate as possible (embedded in law) (Principles A1 and 2). Among the responsibilities of national institutions are 'to submit to the government, parliament and any other competent body, on an advisory basis . . . opinions, recommendation, proposals and reports on any matters concerning the protection and promotion of human rights' (Principle A3(a)). The areas covered by this include violations of human rights, legislative and administrative provisions and even foreign policy. National institutions also have the responsibility for promoting human rights standards and ensuring national legislation is harmonised therewith, encouraging ratification of the international human rights instruments, contributing towards State reports to treaty monitoring bodies, cooperating with UN and regional human rights agencies, formulating programmes for teaching human rights in schools and universities and publicising human rights and the need to combat all forms of discrimination (Principle A3). Not all national human rights institutions have jurisdiction to receive complaints. Irrespective of that, their establishment should raise awareness of human rights and promote the protection of human rights.

7.5   EXAMPLES OF NATIONAL INSTITUTIONS

There follows some examples of different bodies which meet some or all of the criteria for National Institutions as specified in the Paris Principles. The Norwegian children's commissioner is discussed below. This section will focus on other regional institutions.

7.5.1   Brazil

In Brazil, regional attorneys/public prosecutors are appointed to oversee the rights of certain groups. For example, litigation on behalf of the rights of indigenous peoples is often instigated by publicly funded prosecutors. These people are partly funded by the State but obviously must remain independent thereof when instituting actions against the State of State-affiliated organisations.

Question

List the advantages and disadvantages of State funded human rights defenders—is this an appropriate model for other States to emulate?

7.5.2   Northern Ireland

In Northern Ireland, the role of Human Rights Commissioner was created in the wake of the establishment of a Northern Irish Assembly with quasi-legislative functions. Its constitutive document is the devolution agreement, the Northern Ireland Act of 1998.

Northern Ireland Act 1998, c47

68.—(1) There shall be a body corporate to be known as the Northern Ireland Human Rights Commission.

(2) The Commission shall consist of a Chief Commissioner and other Commissioners appointed by the Secretary of State.

(3) In making appointments under this section, the Secretary of State shall as far as practicable secure that the Commissioners, as a group, are representative of the community in Northern Ireland.

69.—(1) The Commission shall keep under review the adequacy and effectiveness in Northern Ireland of law and practice relating to the protection of human rights.

(2) The Commission shall, before the end of the period of two years beginning with the commencement of this section, make to the Secretary of State such recommendations as it thinks fit for improving—

(a) its effectiveness;

(b) the adequacy and effectiveness of the functions conferred on it by this Part; and

(c) the adequacy and effectiveness of the provisions of this Part relating to it.

(3) The Commission shall advise the Secretary of State and the Executive Committee of the Assembly of legislative and other measures which ought to be taken to protect human rights—

(a) as soon as reasonably practicable after receipt of a general or specific request for advice; and

(b) on such other occasions as the Commission thinks appropriate.

(4) The Commission shall advise the Assembly whether a Bill is compatible with human rights—

(a) as soon as reasonably practicable after receipt of a request for advice; and

(b) on such other occasions as the Commission thinks appropriate.

(5) The Commission may—

(a) give assistance to individuals in accordance with section 70; and

(b) bring proceedings involving law or practice relating to the protection of human rights.

(6) The Commission shall promote understanding and awareness of the importance of human rights in Northern Ireland; and for this purpose it may undertake, commission or provide financial or other assistance for—

(a) research; and

(b) educational activities.

(7) The Secretary of State shall request the Commission to provide advice of the kind referred to in paragraph 4 of the Human Rights section of the Belfast Agreement.

(8) For the purpose of exercising its functions under this section the Commission may conduct such investigations as it considers necessary or expedient.

(9) The Commission may decide to publish its advice and the outcome of its research and investigations.

(10) The Commission shall do all that it can to ensure the establishment of the committee referred to in paragraph 10 of that section of that Agreement.

(11) In this section

(a) a reference to the Assembly includes a reference to a committee of the Assembly;

(b) 'human rights' includes the Convention rights.

The devolution agreements enabled the establishment of regional commissioners yet left the State as an entity, the United Kingdom took longer to create one. A Joint House of Lords and House of Commons Parliamentary Select Committee does consider human rights issues and has sought to influence government policy and publicise relevant issues. However, this body comprises members of the legislature.

7.5.3   United States of America

In the United States of America the Supreme Court is guardian of the Bill of Rights. As a corollary to its appellate functions, it acts as a barometer on conformity with the national human rights standards. The principal problem with such a model is that international human rights standards are not considered. The United States Commission on Civil Rights reports to Congress and the President on issues of Civil Rights in accordance with its statutory powers (Civil Rights Act 1957).

Mission Statement of the Commission on Civil Rights

To investigate complaints alleging that citizens are being deprived of their right to vote by reason of their race, color, religion, sex, age, disability, or national origin, or by reason of fraudulent practices.

To study and collect information relating to discrimination or a denial of equal protection of the laws under the Constitution because of race, color, religion, sex, age, disability, or national origin, or in the administration of justice.

To appraise federal laws and policies with respect to discrimination or denial of equal protection of the laws because of race, color, religion, sex, age, disability, or national origin, or in the administration of justice.

To serve as a national clearinghouse for information in respect to discrimination or denial of equal protection of the laws because of race, color, religion, sex, age, disability, or national origin.

To submit reports, findings, and recommendations to the President and Congress.

To issue public service announcements to discourage discrimination or denial of equal protection of the laws.

7.5.4   Australia

In Australia, a Human Rights and Equal Opportunity Commission assumes the role as a national human rights institution.

Human Rights and Equal Opportunity Commission Act 1986
SECTION 7
Human Rights and Equal Opportunity Commission

(1) There is established by this Act a Commission by the name of the Human Rights and Equal Opportunity Commission.

(2) The Commission:

(a) is a body corporate, with perpetual succession;

(b) shall have a common seal;

(c) may acquire, hold and dispose of real and personal property; and

(d) may sue and be sued in its corporate name.

(3) All courts, judges and persons acting judicially shall take judicial notice of the imprint of the common seal of the Commission appearing on a document and shall presume that the document was duly sealed.

SECTION 8B
The Human Rights Commissioner

(1) The Human Rights Commissioner is to be appointed by the Governor-General as a full-time member.

(2) A person is not qualified to be appointed as the Human Rights Commissioner unless the Governor-General is satisfied that the person has appropriate qualifications, knowledge or experience.

SECTION 10A
Duties of Commission

(1) It is the duty of the Commission to ensure that the functions of the Commission under this or any other Act are performed:

(a) with regard for:

    (i) the indivisibility and universality of human rights; and

    (ii) the principle that every person is free and equal in dignity and rights; and

(b) efficiently and with the greatest possible benefit to the people of Australia.

(2) Nothing in this section imposes a duty on the Commission that is enforceable by proceedings in a court.

SECTION 11
Functions of Commission

(1) The functions of the Commission are:

(a) such functions as are conferred on the Commission by the *Age Discrimination Act 2004*, the *Racial Discrimination Act 1975*, the *Sex Discrimination Act 1984* or any other enactment;

(aa) to inquire into, and attempt to conciliate, complaints of unlawful discrimination;

(ab) to deal with complaints lodged under Part IIC;

(b) such functions as are to be performed by the Commission pursuant to an arrangement in force under section 16;

(c) such functions as are expressed to be conferred on the Commission by any State enactment, being functions in relation to which the Minister has made a declaration under section 18;

(d) the functions conferred on the Commission by section 31;

(e) to examine enactments, and (when requested to do so by the Minister) proposed enactments, for the purpose of ascertaining whether the enactments or proposed enactments, as the case may be, are, or would be, inconsistent with or contrary to any human right, and to report to the Minister the results of any such examination;

(f) to inquire into any act or practice that may be inconsistent with or contrary to any human right, and:

    (i) where the Commission considers it appropriate to do so—to endeavour, by conciliation, to effect a settlement of the matters that gave rise to the inquiry; and

    (ii) where the Commission is of the opinion that the act or practice is inconsistent with or contrary to any human right, and the Commission has not considered it appropriate to endeavour to effect a settlement of the matters that gave rise to the inquiry or has endeavoured without success to effect such a settlement—to report to the Minister in relation to the inquiry;

(g) to promote an understanding and acceptance, and the public discussion, of human rights in Australia;

(h) to undertake research and educational programs and other programs, on behalf of the Commonwealth, for the purpose of promoting human rights, and to co-ordinate any such programs undertaken by any other persons or authorities on behalf of the Commonwealth;

(j) on its own initiative or when requested by the Minister, to report to the Minister as to the laws that should be made by the Parliament, or action that should be taken by the Commonwealth, on matters relating to human rights;

(k) on its own initiative or when requested by the Minister, to report to the Minister as to the action (if any) that, in the opinion of the Commission, needs to be taken by Australia in order to comply with the provisions of the Covenant, of the Declarations or of any relevant international instrument;

(m) on its own initiative or when requested by the Minister, to examine any relevant international instrument for the purpose of ascertaining whether there are any inconsistencies between that instrument and the Covenant, the Declarations or any other relevant international instrument, and to report to the Minister the results of any such examination;

(n) to prepare, and to publish in such manner as the Commission considers appropriate, guidelines for the avoidance of acts or practices of a kind in respect of which the Commission has a function under paragraph (f);

(o) where the Commission considers it appropriate to do so, with the leave of the court hearing the proceedings and subject to any conditions imposed by the court, to intervene in proceedings that involve human rights issues; and

(p) to do anything incidental or conducive to the performance of any of the preceding functions.

(2) The Commission shall not:

(a) regard an enactment or proposed enactment as being inconsistent with or contrary to any human right for the purposes of paragraph (1)(e) by reason of a provision of the enactment or proposed enactment that is included solely for the purpose of securing adequate advancement of particular persons or groups of persons in order to enable them to enjoy or exercise human rights equally with other persons; or

(b) regard an act or practice as being inconsistent with or contrary to any human right for the purposes of paragraph (1)(f) where the act or practice is done or engaged in solely for the purpose referred to in paragraph (a) of this subsection.

7.5.5   Canada

Canada has provincial and federal institutions with responsibility for human rights. Ontario established the first Human Rights Commission at a local level. This was followed more than 30 years later by the Canadian Commission, which operates at the federal level. Initially, the provincial bodies were concerned with promoting anti-discrimination laws though their remit is now significantly broader.

Canadian Human Rights Act (R.S. 1985, c. H-6)

26. (1) A commission is hereby established to be known as the Canadian Human Rights Commission, in this Part and Part III referred to as the 'Commission', consisting of a Chief Commissioner, a Deputy Chief Commissioner and not less than three or more than six other members, to be appointed by the Governor in Council.

(2) The Chief Commissioner and Deputy Chief Commissioner are full-time members of the Commission and the other members may be appointed as full-time or part-time members of the Commission.

(3) Each full-time member of the Commission may be appointed for a term not exceeding seven years and each part-time member may be appointed for a term not exceeding three years.

(4) Each member of the Commission holds office during good behaviour but may be removed by the Governor in Council on address of the Senate and House of Commons.

27. (1) In addition to its duties under Part III with respect to complaints regarding discriminatory practices, the Commission is generally responsible for the administration of this Part and Parts I and III and

(a) shall develop and conduct information programs to foster public understanding of this Act and of the role and activities of the Commission thereunder and to foster public recognition of the principle described in section 2;

(b) shall undertake or sponsor research programs relating to its duties and functions under this Act and respecting the principle described in section 2;

(c) shall maintain close liaison with similar bodies or authorities in the provinces in order to foster common policies and practices and to avoid conflicts respecting the handling of complaints in cases of overlapping jurisdiction;

(d) shall perform duties and functions to be performed by it pursuant to any agreement entered into under subsection 28(2);

(e) may consider such recommendations, suggestions and requests concerning human rights and freedoms as it receives from any source and, where deemed by the Commission to be appropriate, include in a report referred to in section 61 reference to and comment on any such recommendation, suggestion or request;

(f) shall carry out or cause to be carried out such studies concerning human rights and freedoms as may be referred to it by the Minister of Justice and include in a report referred to in section 61 a report setting out the results of each such study together with such recommendations in relation thereto as it considers appropriate;

(g) may review any regulations, rules, orders, by-laws and other instruments made pursuant to an Act of Parliament and, where deemed by the Commission to be appropriate, include in a report referred to in section 61 reference to and comment on any provision thereof that in its opinion is inconsistent with the principle described in section 2; and

(h) shall, so far as is practical and consistent with the application of Part III, try by persuasion, publicity or any other means that it considers appropriate to discourage and reduce discriminatory practices referred to in sections 5 to 14.1.

(2) The Commission may, on application or on its own initiative, by order, issue a guideline setting out the extent to which and the manner in which, in the opinion of the Commission, any provision of this Act applies in a class of cases described in the guideline.

(3) A guideline issued under subsection (2) is, until it is revoked or modified, binding on the Commission and any member or panel assigned under subsection 49(2) with respect to the resolution of a complaint under Part III regarding a case falling within the description contained in the guideline.

Question

Ascertain the efficacy of the above bodies from the information provided or additional information. Do they comply with the guidelines of the United Nations?

7.6 CONCLUSIONS

An ideal national human rights institution would have the power to monitor national legislation, prompting changes as necessary to comply with emerging international and regional norms. Moreover, there should be a mechanism by which individuals and groups could complain about violations of human rights. Ultimately, for as long as international law remains in its current consensual form, full realisation of international human rights standards is dependent on the actions of States. It is the States themselves who created the current regime of international human rights, as an act of good faith they should surely take all necessary steps to conform to their obligations thereunder. Establishing effective national institutions, as many have done, is clearly a positive development. Expanding the network of national institutions across the globe should ensure that the political rhetoric of international human rights becomes a tangible reality for the intended beneficiaries: you and me.

7.7 CHILDREN'S COMMISSIONERS—A SPECIAL CASE?

As Chapter 10 discusses, children are perhaps particularly vulnerable given their youth and, at least in early years, their dependence on adult (older) carers. To many, this means that national institutions have a significant role to play in advocating and representing the rights of children. Children's ombudspersons developed in the Nordic countries and are now common in many jurisdictions.

The implementation requirements of the Convention on the Rights of the Child do not differ dramatically from those of the other instruments.

United Nations Convention on the Rights of the Child Art 4

States Parties shall undertake all appropriate legislative, administrative, and other measures for the implementation of the rights recognized in the present Convention. With regard to economic, social and cultural rights, States Parties shall undertake such measures to the maximum extent of their available resources and, where needed, within the framework of international cooperation.

Two General Comments of the Committee on the Rights of the Child add further detail to this provision: General Comment No. 2(2002) (UN Doc. CRC/GC/2002/2) on the role of independent national human rights institutions in the promotion and protection of the rights of the child and General Comment No. 5(2003) on General measures of implementation of the Convention on the Rights of the Child (Arts 4, 42 and 44, para 6) (UN Doc. CRC/GC/2003/5).

Committee on the Rights of the Child General Comment No. 2 (2002), paras 5 and 7

While adults and children alike need independent NHRIs to protect their human rights, additional justifications exist for ensuring that children's human rights are given special attention. These include the facts that children's developmental state makes them particularly vulnerable to human rights violations; their opinions are still rarely taken into account; most children have no vote and cannot play a meaningful role in the political process that determines Governments' response to human rights; children encounter significant problems in using the judicial system to protect their rights or to seek remedies for violations of their rights; and children's access to organizations that may protect their rights is generally limited. . . .

It is the view of the Committee that every State needs an independent human rights institution with responsibility for promoting and protecting children's rights. The Committee's principal concern is that the institution, whatever its form, should be able, independently and effectively, to monitor, promote and protect children's rights. It is essential that promotion and protection of children's rights is 'mainstreamed' and that all human rights institutions existing in a country work closely together to this end.

Question

Do you agree that national human rights institutions may be insufficient to ensure that the rights of the child are properly protected within the State?

That children's rights are viewed distinctly and have produced an increase in the number of national institutions is apparent from the work of the Committee on the Rights of the Child.

Committee on the Rights of the Child General Comment No. 5 (2003), para 9

The general measures of implementation identified by the Committee and described in the present general comment are intended to promote the full enjoyment of all rights in the

Convention by all children, through legislation, the establishment of coordinating and monitoring bodies—governmental and independent—comprehensive data collection, awareness-raising and training and the development and implementation of appropriate policies, services and pro-grammes. One of the satisfying results of the adoption and almost universal ratification of the Convention has been the development at the national level of a wide variety of new child-focused and child-sensitive bodies, structures and activities—children's rights units at the heart of Government, ministers for children, inter-ministerial committees on children, parliamentary committees, child impact analysis, children's budgets and 'state of children's rights' reports, NGO coalitions on children's rights, children's ombudspersons and children's rights commissioners and so on.

There is clearly a role for national institutions in ensuring that children's voices are heard at all levels of decision-making and that their needs are considered by the power-makers of a State.

The Committee on the Rights of the Child advocates that children either have separate institutions or that a distinct division within the regular national human rights institution deals specifically with children's issues. Obviously part of the emphasis has to be on accessibility for children to the body concerned.

From the international perspective, children's commissioners fulfil many pur-poses. In essence they are a voice for children; an advocate for children's' rights; an investigator of complaints; and a governmental advisor.

Smith, R et al., 'The English Children's Commissioner: a Knight in Shining Armour?', Paper, Fourth World Congress on Children and Family Rights

Voice: Provide a mouthpiece for children, receiving and processing their views thereby giving effect to Article 12 of the Convention on the Rights of the Child. Van Beuren suggests that '[i]f the hallmark of a democratic society is a plurality of expressed opinion and contributions by those living within it then participation of children ought to be valued' (Van Beuren, G. (1994) *The International Law on the Rights of the Child*, Dordrecht: Martinus Nijhoff, 1994 at 131). This links to Hammarberg's argument (Hammarberg, T. (1990) 'The U.N. Convention on the Rights of the Child—and How to Make it Work' *Human Rights Quarterly* 12:97) for participation as once heard, children's opinions can be channelled in appropriate directions to facilitate participation in decision-making. The Norwegian ombudsman model, established in 1981, is a good example of this.

Advocate: Provide a platform from which to campaign for children's rights. Indeed the UN Committee recommends that children's organisations are involved in establishing salient com-missions (UN Committee on the Rights of the Child *Concluding Observations* UN Doc. CRC/C/15/Add.188a: para 17(d)). Even at the international level, a number of non-governmental organisa-tions contribute to the promotion of children's rights. Given the aforementioned vulnerability of children, the need for active advocacy cannot be underestimated. The importance is exacerbated when the child is too young or otherwise impeded from a more active role in decision-making. Moreover, advocacy can assist in changing the culture to a more child responsive one conducive to children's rights' realisation and possibly even proactive in their preemptive protection.

Investigator: Act as investigator and mediator for considering individual or groups complaints. While children can use existing international and regional individual complaint mechanisms (none exist under UNCRC), these are not necessarily child-friendly or accessible, the efficacy of each depending on a number of factors not least the age of the child. Commissioners should thus be 'easily accessible to children, able to determine their own agenda, empowered to investigate violations of children's rights in a child-sensitive manner and ensure that children have an effective remedy for violations of their rights.' (UN Committee on the Rights of the Child *Concluding Observations* UN Doc. CRC/C/15/Add.188a: para 17(a)). A number of factors must be considered including the language employed at each stage. Children must be made aware of their rights before any complaint process becomes effective. Securing human rights education is of key importance in this respect.

Governmental Advisor: Advise governments and legislatures on measures affecting children. The Committee recommended to the UK that it should '[e]nsure that all the human rights institutions have formal advisory functions with the respective legislative bodies and that they establish formal links, including of cooperation, with each other' (UN Committee on the Rights of the Child *Concluding Observations* UN Doc. CRC/C/15/Add.188a: para 17(b)). This links back to commissioners as a voice for children and the advocacy function. Participation projects in southern African States have demonstrated the potential positive impact children can have on the legislative process. Within Europe, youth parliaments perform a similar, albeit less official, function, channelling the views of young people towards the decision-makers in an informal manner.

The Council of Europe makes simple suggestions regarding the powers of national institutions for children:

European Convention on the Exercise of children's Rights 1996, ETS 160
Article 12

1   Parties shall encourage, through bodies which perform, *inter alia*, the functions set out in paragraph 2, the promotion and the exercise of children's rights.

2   The functions are as follows:

   a   to make proposals to strengthen the law relating to the exercise of children's rights;

   b   to give opinions concerning draft legislation relating to the exercise of children's rights;

   c   to provide general information concerning the exercise of children's rights to the media, the public and persons and bodies dealing with questions relating to children;

   d   to seek the views of children and provide them with relevant information.

Within Europe, the European Network of Ombudsmen for Children (ENOC) was established in 1997. It links independent offices for children from twelve countries in Europe with the aim of encouraging implementation of the Convention on the Rights of the Child, supporting collective lobbying for children's rights, to sharing information, approaches and strategies, and promoting the development of effective independent offices for children (see, generally www.ombudsnet.org/).

7.7.1   Case study: Norway

Norway created the world's first ever *ombud* (Commissioner) for children in 1981. Reidar Hjermann, the present incumbent appointed in 2004, is Norway's fourth Ombudsman for Children. The first was Målfrid Grude Flekkøy (1981–1989), followed by Trond Viggo Torgersen (1989–1995) and Trond Waage (1996–2004).

Three concepts are identified as underpinning the work of the ombudsman in Norway.

Objectives of ombudsman for Children in Norway (taken in English translation from www.barneombudet.no)

Safety measures: all efforts and initiatives the government and society have established, in order for vulnerable children to be intercepted by, for instance, child welfare authorities.

Participation: the society's ability to listen and act on behalf of children, their experience and expertise as well as letting children and youth be a part of the ever changing society.

Conditions for growth: an extensive concept to cover the basic ideas such as education, health and culture.

Note how different in expression these are from the goals expressed by the Committee on the Rights for the Child. Note also the scope which they encompass.

Constitutive Act, taken in English translation from www.barneombudet.no
ACT NO. 5 OF MARCH 6, 1981 RELATING TO THE OMBUDSMAN FOR CHILDREN (With changes from July 17 1998)

§1 Purpose

The purpose of this Act is to contribute to promoting the interests of children in society.

§2 Ombudsman for Children

The King shall appoint an Ombudsman for Children for a period of four years.

§3 Duties of the Ombudsman

The duties of the Ombudsman are to promote the interests of children vis-à-vis public and private authorities and to follow up the development of conditions under which children grow up.

In particular the Ombudsman shall:

(a) On own initiative or as a hearing instance protect the interests of children in connection with planning and study-reports in all fields,

(b) Ensure that legislation relating to the protection of children's interests is observed, including if Norwegian law and administrative routines are in accordance with Norway's obligations according to the UN convention on the Rights of the Child,

(c) Propose measures that can strengthen children's safety under the law,

(d) Put forward proposals for measures that can solve or prevent conflicts between children and society,

(e) Ensure that sufficient information is given to the public and private sectors concerning children's rights and measures required for children.

The Ombudsman may act on own initiative or at the request of other people. The Ombudsman for Children himself decides whether an application offers sufficient grounds for action.

§4 Access to institutions and duty to provide information, etc.

The Ombudsman shall have free access to all public and private institutions for children.

Government authorities and public and private institutions for children shall, notwithstanding the pledge of secrecy, give the Ombudsman the information needed to carry out the duties of the Ombudsman pursuant to this Act. Information that is needed for the accomplishment of the Ombudsman's tasks pursuant to §3, second paragraph, litra b, may also, notwithstanding the pledge of secrecy, be demanded from others. When information can be demanded pursuant to this item, it may also be required that records and other documents be produced.

The rules laid down in subsection 1, 204 and §§205–209 of the Civil Disputes Act are correspondingly applicable to the Ombudsman's right to demand information. Disputes as to the application of these rules may be brought before the District and City Courts, which decide the question by a court ruling.

§5 Statements from the Ombudsman

The Ombudsman has the right to make statements concerning conditions included in his working sphere, according to this Act and the Instructions for the Ombudsman. The Ombudsman himself decides to whom these statements shall be directed.

§6 Instructions for the Ombudsman

The King lays down general instructions for the organisation and procedures of the Ombudsman. Beyond this the Ombudsman carries out his functions independently.

A subsequent decree elaborates on the power of the Ombudsman to investigate cases.

INSTRUCTIONS FOR THE OMBUDSMAN FOR CHILDREN

Laid down by Royal Decree of September 11, 1981 with changes last by Royal Decree of July 17. 1998, taken in English translation from www.barneombudet.no

§2 How cases are taken up

The Ombudsman takes up cases on his own initiative or at the request of other people.

Anyone may apply to the Ombudsman. The Ombudsman shall ensure that verbal applications are put into writing.

A person applying to the Ombudsman should, in so far as possible, explain the grounds for the application and submit whatever information and documents are available in this case.

If an application concerns a specific child and the application does not come from the child itself, the Ombudsman shall not deal with the case without the permission of the relevant child. When the child's age so indicates, the permission of the guardian shall also be obtained. If general considerations so indicate, the Ombudsman may deal with the case even though permission as mentioned above has not been obtained.

§3 Rejection

The Ombudsman shall reject applications concerning specific, individual conflicts between a child and its guardians, between the guardians mutually concerning the exercise of parental responsibility and similar matters. The Ombudsman shall also reject applications that partly cover such conflicts, unless the Ombudsman, after a concrete assessment, finds that the interests of the child obviously will be neglected through this rejection.

The Ombudsman shall in such cases give the reason for the rejection and offer information about any existing instances established for the purpose of handling conflicts of this nature.

A rejection by the Ombudsman cannot be appealed.

§4 Referrals

Applications relating to conditions that in the main concern questions relating to the application of the law or the handling of the case are to be referred by the Ombudsman to the Storting's Ombudsman for Public Administration when this is relevant.

If an application concerns a situation that may be brought before an administrative agency, the person applying to the Ombudsman for Children shall be advised to take the matter up with the relevant body. The Ombudsman himself may also send the matter to this body.

If an application concerns a situation which can be referred to the Public Prosecution Authority or a special supervisory body, after a more detailed investigation of the circumstances of the case the Ombudsman may send the case to the relevant authority if the conditions pursuant to subsection 6 of §13 b of the Public Administration Act obtain.

§5 Shelving of cases

If the Ombudsman finds that application has been made for a situation that does not offer grounds for criticism or for any other follow-up procedure, the case may be shelved. The Ombudsman may also shelve a case if the situation that the application concerns has been remedied or has ceased to exist.

At any stage in the proceedings, the Ombudsman may also shelve a case for reasons connected with work. However, the Ombudsman should try to deal with a representative selection of cases.

Anyone who has applied to the Ombudsman shall be informed of the shelving of the case and the reason for this.

The shelving of the case by the Ombudsman cannot be appealed.

§6 Rules for dealing with cases

Chapters I–III of the Public Administration Act and the Freedom of Information Act are applicable to the activity of the Ombudsman.

Before making his statement the Ombudsman shall ensure that the case is clarified as far as possible. The Ombudsman determines what steps should be taken to clarify the circumstances in the case.

Also when this does not follow from other rules the Ombudsman shall preserve secrecy about the source of information he has used when the source has expressly requested this, or if the Ombudsman finds this appropriate on behalf of the child.

§7 The Ombudsman's statement on the case

The Ombudsman shall personally adopt a standpoint on all cases that have been taken up for discussion and have not been shelved pursuant to §5 of the Instruction. As a basic rule the opinion of the Ombudsman shall be formulated as a written statement, giving the grounds for this.

The Ombudsman himself decides to whom the statement shall be directed. The statement can also be directed to the press and the broadcasting corporation or others to the extent that the Ombudsman finds expedient.

The Ombudsman shall not express an opinion on the position in regard to the law when the Storting's Ombudsman for Public Administration has made a statement or when the situation has either been decided by the courts or has been brought before the courts for a decision.

Neither shall the Ombudsman express an opinion in cases that are under police investigation and where children might have been exposed to acts in violation with the law, insofar as somebody is under suspicion or indicted in the case. Even so, the Ombudsman may criticise the factual and legal situation that has been revealed by the Ombudsman for Public Administration's statement, by the police investigation or by the decision of the courts.

Question

Are the limitations in part three justified, given the nature of human rights, the benefactors and the duty incumbents?

FURTHER READING

Harland, C, 'The Status of the ICCPR in the Domestic Law of State Parties: an initial global survey through UN Human Rights Committee documents' (2000) 22 Human Rights Quarterly 187

Heyns, C, and Viljoen, F, 'The Impact of the United Nations Human Rights Treaties on the Domestic Level' (2000) 23 Human Rights Quarterly 483

Heyns, C, and Viljoen, F, *The Impact of UN Human Rights Treaties on the Domestic Level*, 2002, the Hague: Kluwer

Marie, Jean-Bernard, 'National Systems for the Protection of Human Rights' in Symonides, J, *Human Rights: International Protection, Monitoring, Enforcement*, 2003, Aldershot: Ashgate/UNESCO, pp 257–280

Shelton, D, *Remedies in International Human Rights Law*, 1999, Oxford: OUP

United Nations, Fact Sheet No. 19, *National Institutions for the Promotion and Protection of Human Rights*, 1993, Geneva, United Nations Office

Websites

www.nhri.org—United Nations Forum for National Human Rights Institutions

www.usccr.gov/—US Commission on Civil Rights

www.nihrc.org—Northern Ireland Human Rights Commission

www.hreoc.gov.au/—Australian Human Rights and Equal Opportunities Commission

www.chrc-ccdp.ca/—Canadian Human Rights Commission

CHAPTER 8

EXTENDING THE DUTIES TO PROTECT AND RESPECT HUMAN RIGHTS: NON-STATE ACTORS

International human rights are indivisible, inalienable and universal. Accordingly, everyone should contribute towards their development. Only Art 29 of the Universal Declaration alludes to duties of individuals. So far the role of international and regional institutions and treaty monitoring bodies have been discussed. Chapter 7 on National Human Rights Institutions reviews the nature of international human rights. In spite of these developments, still human rights are not enjoyed by everyone everywhere. This chapter therefore takes the discussion further, looking at the involvement of non-State actors in building a culture of respect and promotion of human rights.

Three categories will be considered in this chapter: Non-Governmental Organisations; Multinational Corporations (Business); and Educators. Of course, as the African regional instruments indicate, there is perhaps a corresponding duty upon individuals and those involved in human rights activities (lawyers for example) to familiarise themselves with human rights and to strive to secure their realisation. The 'power of the people' may produce a cumulative effect.

8.1 NON-GOVERNMENTAL ORGANISATIONS

Non-government organisations are evermore involved in the process of articulating and realising rights. They influenced the inclusion of references to human rights in the UN Charter during the drafting process at Dumbarton Oaks in San Francisco. Their involvement in the United Nations has increased since—today they engage with international human rights in a variety of ways. Inevitably therefore, the number of NGOs and the range of issues with which they work has also increased.

> **Richmond, O, 'The Role of Non-Governmental Organisation in Human Rights Protection', in Smith, RKM and Van Den Anker, C (eds), *The Essentials of Human Rights*, 2005, London: Hodder Arnold, pp 274–276 at 274**
>
> In 1914, there were 1083 non-governmental organisations (NGOs) and no firm conception of universal human rights affirmed by the international community, such as it was. Now the estimated number of NGOs stands at between 37,000 and 50,000 according to the UNDP Human Development Reports and the OECD Directory of NGOs . . . Many NGOs were formed in the 1990s as a response to the broad requirements of . . . peacebuilding, humanitarianism, human rights monitoring and advocacy. Most NGOs operate on specific issues or bridge several aspects of these areas.

8.1.1 What are NGOs?

Non-governmental organisations encompasses all bodies which are not part of the State or international organisations. Political pressure groups and grass-roots activists are covered, along with community initiatives and various bodies commonly accorded charitable status. Some NGOs are huge, with thousands of members and a broad geographical remit. They may have international membership and be active in international affairs. The December 2005 Montreal Summit on the Kyoto Protocol is an example of major international NGOs participating in a global conference. Large NGOs can exert considerable political influence within States and indeed at the regional or international level. Consider the impact of multiple NGO campaigns against the use of landmines/anti-personnel weapons which resulted, eventually, in the 1997 Convention on the Prohibition of the Use, Stockpiling, Production and Transfer of Anti-Personnel Mines and on their Destruction. Other NGOs operate at a community or State level. Their importance to furthering international human rights law remains, however. As Chapter 5 notes, groups have *locus standi* to initiate complaints against States under the African Charter on Human and Peoples' Rights.

8.1.1.1   List of Principal International Human Rights NGOs

Several hundred NGOs enjoy recognition by the United Nations and other international and regional bodies. Some represent a broad range of issues; others focus on a single issue/right/freedom. Some are peculiar to one country or region, others are international. It would be impossible to list all NGOs active in human rights, not least because the list would change hourly. New local organisations are continually being formed and single issue groups are inevitably created as a response to State and international policy.

Question

Consider the recent increase in groups and coalitions of NGOs against the United States and United Kingdom led military action in Iraq. What other recent events have produced significant NGO responses?

Examples of NGOs

Amnesty International
Oxfam
Save the Children International
Friends of the Earth
Human Rights Watch
Greenpeace
Survival International
Anti-Slavery International
Article 19

8.1.1.2   Case study: Amnesty International

The mission of Amnesty International can be extracted from its Statute, as amended in 2003.

Statute of Amnesty International, from web.amnesty.org/pages/aboutai-statute-eng

VISION AND MISSION

1. AMNESTY INTERNATIONAL's vision is of a world in which every person enjoys all of the human rights enshrined in the Universal Declaration of Human Rights and other international human rights standards.

In pursuit of this vision, AMNESTY INTERNATIONAL's mission is to undertake research and action focused on preventing and ending grave abuses of the rights to physical and mental integrity, freedom of conscience and expression, and freedom from discrimination, within the context of its work to promote all human rights.

CORE VALUES

2. AMNESTY INTERNATIONAL forms a global community of human rights defenders with the principles of international solidarity, effective action for the individual victim, global coverage, the universality and indivisibility of human rights, impartiality and independence, and democracy and mutual respect.

METHODS

3. AMNESTY INTERNATIONAL addresses governments, intergovernmental organizations, armed political groups, companies and other non-state actors.

AMNESTY INTERNATIONAL seeks to disclose human rights abuses accurately, quickly and persistently. It systematically and impartially researches the facts of individual cases and patterns of human rights abuses. These findings are publicized, and members, supporters and staff mobilize public pressure on governments and others to stop the abuses.

In addition to its work on specific abuses of human rights, AMNESTY INTERNATIONAL urges all governments to observe the rule of law, and to ratify and implement human rights standards; it carries out a wide range of human rights educational activities; and it encourages intergovernmental organizations, individuals, and all organs of society to support and respect human rights.

8.1.2 How do NGOs contribute to human rights?

There are many roles for NGOs and, at times, there seems a never-increasing range of innovative ways in which they can contribute towards the development of human rights: education; advocacy; training; fundraising; awareness-raising and participating in creating and developing international and regional norms of international human rights (standard-setting).

Economic and Social Council Resolution 1996/31, UN Doc. E/1996/96 (1996), Consultative relationship between the United Nations and non-governmental organizations

Part I

PRINCIPLES TO BE APPLIED IN THE ESTABLISHMENT OF CONSULTATIVE RELATIONS

The following principles shall be applied in establishing consultative relations with non-governmental organizations:

1. The organization shall be concerned with matters falling within the competence of the Economic and Social Council and its subsidiary bodies.

2. The aims and purposes of the organization shall be in conformity with the spirit, purposes and principles of the Charter of the United Nations.

3. The organization shall undertake to support the work of the United Nations and to promote knowledge of its principles and activities, in accordance with its own aims and purposes and the nature and scope of its competence and activities.

4. Except where expressly stated otherwise, the term 'organization' shall refer to non-governmental organizations at the national, subregional, regional or international levels.

5. Consultative relationships may be established with international, regional, subregional and national organizations, in conformity with the Charter of the United Nations and the principles and criteria established under the present resolution. The Committee, in considering applications for consultative status, should ensure, to the extent possible, participation of non-governmental organizations from all regions, and particularly from

developing countries, in order to help achieve a just, balanced, effective and genuine involvement of non-governmental organizations from all regions and areas of the world. The Committee shall also pay particular attention to non-governmental organizations that have special expertise or experience upon which the Council may wish to draw.

6. Greater participation of non-governmental organizations from developing countries in international conferences convened by the United Nations should be encouraged.

7. Greater involvement of non-governmental organizations from countries with economies in transition should be encouraged.

8. Regional, subregional and national organizations, including those affiliated to an international organization already in status, may be admitted provided that they can demonstrate that their programme of work is of direct relevance to the aims and purposes of the United Nations and, in the case of national organizations, after consultation with the Member State concerned. The views expressed by the Member State, if any, shall be communicated to the non-governmental organization concerned, which shall have the opportunity to respond to those views through the Committee on Non-Governmental Organizations.

9. The organization shall be of recognized standing within the particular field of its competence or of a representative character. Where there exist a number of organizations with similar objectives, interests and basic views in a given field, they may, for the purposes of consultation with the Council, form a joint committee or other body authorized to carry on such consultation for the group as a whole.

10. The organization shall have an established headquarters, with an executive officer. It shall have a democratically adopted constitution, a copy of which shall be deposited with the Secretary-General of the United Nations, and which shall provide for the determination of policy by a conference, congress or other representative body, and for an executive organ responsible to the policy-making body.

11. The organization shall have authority to speak for its members through its authorized representatives. Evidence of this authority shall be presented, if requested.

12. The organization shall have a representative structure and possess appropriate mechanisms of accountability to its members, who shall exercise effective control over its policies and actions through the exercise of voting rights or other appropriate democratic and transparent decision-making processes. Any such organization that is not established by a governmental entity or intergovernmental agreement shall be considered a non-governmental organization for the purpose of these arrangements, including organizations that accept members designated by governmental authorities, provided that such membership does not interfere with the free expression of views of the organization.

13. The basic resources of the organization shall be derived in the main part from contributions of the national affiliates or other components or from individual members. Where voluntary contributions have been received, their amounts and donors shall be faithfully revealed to the Council Committee on Non-Governmental Organizations. Where, however, the above criterion is not fulfilled and an organization is financed from other sources, it must explain to the satisfaction of the Committee its reasons for not meeting the requirements laid down in this paragraph. Any financial contribution or other support, direct or indirect, from a Government to the organization shall be openly declared to the Committee through the Secretary-General and fully recorded in the financial and other records of the organization and shall be devoted to purposes in accordance with the aims of the United Nations.

14. In considering the establishment of consultative relations with a non-governmental organization, the Council will take into account whether the field of activity of the organization is wholly or mainly within the field of a specialized agency, and whether or not it

could be admitted when it has, or may have, a consultative arrangement with a specialized agency.

15. The granting, suspension and withdrawal of consultative status, as well as the interpretation of norms and decisions relating to this matter, are the prerogative of Member States exercised through the Economic and Social Council and its Committee on Non-Governmental Organizations. A non-governmental organization applying for general or special consultative status or a listing on the Roster shall have the opportunity to respond to any objections being raised in the Committee before the Committee takes its decision.

16. The provisions of the present resolution shall apply to the United Nations regional commissions and their subsidiary bodies *mutatis mutandis*.

17. In recognizing the evolving relationship between the United Nations and non-governmental organizations, the Economic and Social Council, in consultation with the Committee on Non-Governmental Organizations, will consider reviewing the consultative arrangements as and when necessary to facilitate, in the most effective manner possible, the contributions of non-governmental organizations to the work of the United Nations. . . .

Part VII

PARTICIPATION OF NON-GOVERNMENTAL ORGANIZATIONS IN INTERNATIONAL CONFERENCES CONVENED BY THE UNITED NATIONS AND THEIR PREPARATORY PROCESS

41. Where non-governmental organizations have been invited to participate in an international conference convened by the United Nations, their accreditation is the prerogative of Member States, exercised through the respective preparatory committee. Such accreditation should be preceded by an appropriate process to determine their eligibility.

42. Non-governmental organizations in general consultative status, special consultative status and on the Roster, that express their wish to attend the relevant international conferences convened by the United Nations and the meetings of the preparatory bodies of the said conferences shall as a rule be accredited for participation. Other non-governmental organizations wishing to be accredited may apply to the secretariat of the conference for this purpose in accordance with the following requirements. . . .

49. A non-governmental organization that has been granted accreditation to attend a session of the preparatory committee, including related preparatory meetings of regional commissions, may attend all its future sessions, as well as the conference itself.

50. In recognition of the intergovernmental nature of the conference and its preparatory process, active participation of non-governmental organizations therein, while welcome, does not entail a negotiating role.

51. The non-governmental organizations accredited to the international conference may be given, in accordance with established United Nations practice and at the discretion of the chairperson and the consent of the body concerned, an opportunity to briefly address the preparatory committee and the conference in plenary meetings and their subsidiary bodies.

52. Non-governmental organizations accredited to the conference may make written presentations during the preparatory process in the official languages of the United Nations as they deem appropriate. Those written presentations shall not be issued as official documents except in accordance with United Nations rules of procedure.

53. Non-governmental organizations without consultative status that participate in international conferences and wish to obtain consultative status later on should apply through the normal procedures established under Council resolution 1296 (XLIV) as updated. Recognizing the

importance of the participation of non-governmental organizations that attend a conference in the follow-up process, the Committee on Non-Governmental Organizations, in considering their application, shall draw upon the documents already submitted by that organization for accreditation to the conference and any additional information submitted by the non-governmental organization supporting its interest, relevance and capacity to contribute to the implementation phase. The Committee shall review such applications as expeditiously as possible so as to allow participation of the respective organization in the implementation phase of the conference. In the interim, the Economic and Social Council shall decide on the participation of non-governmental organizations accredited to an international conference in the work of the relevant functional commission on the follow-up to and implementation of that conference.

54. The suspension and withdrawal of the accreditation of non-governmental organizations to United Nations international conferences at all stages shall be guided by the relevant provisions of the present resolution.

The United Nations has produced information for NGOs wishing to enter and use the United Nations system: *United Nations System: A Guide for NGOs*, 10th edn, 2003, New York: United Nations, also available online (www.un-ngls.org/ngo_guide.htm).

8.1.2.1   *Generating awareness of human rights*

One of the most significant impacts of NGOs lies in generating an awareness of human rights issues. Large and small NGOs campaign on a regular basis. Human rights awards have been given to several NGOs for their contribution to the raising of awareness of human rights issues. NGOs may collaborate across borders to provide a broader or stronger focus on any given issue. Examples include the global alliance of NGOs on corporal punishment. At the United Kingdom national level, NGOs formed an alliance: Children are Unbeatable (see www.childrenareunbeatable.co.uk) while at the international level, the Global Initiative with expansive NGO and organisation support is End Corporal Punishment (see www.endcorporalpunishment.org/).

Question

Consider the ways in which NGOs can raise the profile of human rights, both nationally and internationally.

8.1.2.2   *Contributing to international standard-setting*

The role of NGOs in drafting legislation should not be overlooked. At the international, regional and national levels, NGOs can play a significant role in creating and establishing human rights instruments. NGOs participate at a variety of world conferences. At the 2001 World Conference Against Racism, the NGO Forum conducted its own discussions and adopted its own declaration (see www.racism.org.za/index-2.html). The following is an extract from this lengthy document. It demonstrates the breadth of NGO activity.

WCAR NGO FORUM DECLARATION 2001

INDIGENOUS PEOPLES

140. Indigenous Peoples live in every region of the world, including the Arctic, Africa, Russia, the Americas, Europe, Asia, Australia and the Pacific amongst other areas, and everywhere they suffer gross discrimination and marginalization. The belief in the inferiority of Indigenous Peoples, in addition to the lack of consultation on matters that effect (*sic*) them, remains deeply embedded in

the legal, economic and social fabric of many States and has resulted in the dispossession and destruction of Indigenous territories and resources, political, religious and social systems.

141. Indigenous Peoples continue to suffer the loss of their territories and resources, the destruction of their cultures, and violence directed at their peoples. Indigenous women and children, in particular, endure multiple forms of discrimination. This dispossession, violence and discrimination constitute flagrant violations of our human rights in contravention of the Universal Declaration of Human Rights.

142. Indigenous Peoples are peoples within the full meaning of international law. Indigenous Peoples have the right to self-determination by virtue of which they freely determine their economic, social, political and cultural development and the inherent right to possession of all of their traditional and ancestral lands and territories. The knowledge and cultures of Indigenous Peoples cannot be separated from their unique spiritual and physical relationships with their lands, waters, resources and territories. The denial or qualification of the self-determination of Indigenous Peoples is racist and lies at the root of Indigenous suffering. Structural racism in past and current manifestations of colonialism, invasion, apartheid, ethnocide and genocide has denied, and continues to deny Indigenous Peoples their fundamental right to self-determination.

143. Racism against Indigenous Peoples manifests itself in discriminatory laws and policies that perpetuate and exacerbate racism against Indigenous Peoples. These laws and policies include the denial of the status of Indigenous Peoples with the right to self determination under international law, the militarization of indigenous lands and territories, doctrines that allow Indigenous territories to be taken without due process of law or adequate compensation, the unilateral extinguishment of indigenous land rights, the doctrine of plenary power, discrimination against Indigenous Peoples in the civil and criminal justice systems of States, failure to recognize the justice systems of Indigenous Peoples, the lack of equal participation of Indigenous Peoples in decision-making processes in matters that may affect their cultural, spiritual or physical integrity, the lack of respect for treaties, agreements and laws between Indigenous Peoples and States with no legal resource for Indigenous Peoples, the denial of protection of the religious freedom for Indigenous prisoners, the disproportionate incarceration of Indigenous Peoples, policies that deny, suppress or destroy Indigenous languages, and the presumption that Indigenous Peoples do not own subsoil resources under their lands.

144. Racism against Indigenous Peoples also manifests itself in many forms, including: forced and covert displacement; forced assimilation; forced removal of indigenous children from their communities; economic policies which exploit Indigenous resources without Indigenous consent and without returning any benefit to Indigenous communities; the use of sexual violence against Indigenous women as a weapon of war; misinformation and lack of reproductive information, imposition of dangerous contraceptives on Indigenous girls and women, and forced sterilization of Indigenous girls and women; the appropriation of Indigenous intellectual and cultural property, including genetic property, and the use of the images of Indigenous peoples and individuals without their consent.

145. Religious Intolerance towards Indigenous spiritual practices and the profaning of indigenous sacred sites and objects has been a fundamental instrument in the subjugation of Indigenous Peoples since the invasion and the beginning of colonialism, and is a persistent evil that States must take action to end.

146. Environmental racism—an historical form of racial discrimination—has led to and continues to lead to the ruination of indigenous lands, waters and environments by the implementation of unsustainable schemes, such as mining, biopiracy, deforestation, the dumping of contaminated waste, oil and gas drilling and other land use practices that do not respect indigenous ceremonies, spiritual beliefs, traditional medicines and life ways, the biodiversity of indigenous lands, indigenous economies and means of subsistence, and the right to health.

LABOUR

147. Racism, racial discrimination, xenophobia and related intolerance as experienced by most migrant, immigrant, indigenous as well as second generation descendent workers is manifested through multiple forms of discrimination practiced in the workplace and in the communities in which they live. These include restrictive and exclusionary immigration and labour laws and policies, the denial of trade union rights, exploitative working conditions, low wages and non payment of wages, denial or restriction of labour law protections based on types of job, lack of access to public services such as health, housing and social security. It also includes subtle and overt acts of hostility and violence based on colour, race, nationality, gender, age, caste, class and ethnicity. Full labour law protections must be afforded all workers with no discrimination based on occupation. This discrimination is structural in nature and contravenes international standards. Undocumented migrant workers are doubly at risk of racism and xenophobia. Their lack of legal status is too often used as an excuse to deny human rights, including access to the law and social services.

148. The negative effects of globalization has a specific impact on workers. In particular globalisation has a negative effect on women who are trafficked as as (sic) sex trade workers or employed as low wage and sweat shop workers.

149. Colonialism, slavery and other forms of servitude are primary sources of racism, race discrimination and xenophobia and despite international agreements to outlaw slavery, the trafficking of African children for slavery and forced labour is still ongoing whilst the enslavement and other forms of servitude of Africans and African descendants, Asian and Asian descendants and other marginalized groups have resulted in substantial and lasting economic, political and cultural damage to these peoples. This form of exploitation is particularly damaging to African and African descendant women, who are still victims of sexual trafficking and sexual exploitation, poverty and social exclusion.

150. The policies and programmes of the WTO and International Financial Institutions, in particular the IMF and World Bank, often aggravate racism and other discriminatory practices.

151. Recognizing the valuable role of trade unions, as democratic and representative organizations of working people and their unique functions of trade unions in fighting racism and discrimination in the labour market and in society generally, we recognize the central role of those affected by racism in developing, implementing and monitoring policies and programmes to eliminate racism.

Much of the text of the NGO forum reflects the principal document adopted by the World Conference itself.

Question

What limitations are there on the degree of participation of NGOs in various international and regional organisation events? Consider the voting procedures, access to material and the influencing of government.

8.1.2.3   Contributing towards work of treaty monitoring bodies

NGOs may enjoy considerable independence and thus democratic power within States and can impartially report on and investigate a given human rights' situation. This feature means that NGO reports can help to balance the reports submitted by States under the periodic reporting system to the Treaty Monitoring Bodies. Obviously, care must be taken to balance what can be two polemical viewpoints in a search for the truth.

In some instances, the United Nations Treaty Monitoring Bodies have even resorted to using NGO reports when a State has steadfastly failed to submit its periodic report.

8.1.2.4   Case study: CERD

With biennial reports in terms of Art 9(1) of the International Convention on the Elimination of Racial Discrimination, failures to submit reports quickly become problematic.

The following extract is based on Guyana failing to submit its initial to 14th periodic reports, even in a single document. It illustrates the latent power of NGOs and corroborates their importance given that treaty monitoring bodies clearly may have recourse to NGO reports.

Committee on the Elimination of Racial Discrimination, UN Doc. CERD/C/64/Dec.1, 1 May 2004

Decision (1) 64 on Guyana

1. The Committee on the Elimination of Racial Discrimination recalls its decision 2 (62) adopted on 21 March 2003 and regrets that the State party has been unable to fulfil its commitment to submit its initial to fourteenth periodic reports, combined in one document, in time for consideration at the sixty-fourth session of the Committee. However, it takes note of the submission by Guyana of its report to the Committee on the Elimination of Discrimination against Women and of its report to the Committee on the Rights of the Child.

2. The Committee notes that, following repeated requests from the State party for technical assistance from the Office of the High Commissioner for Human Rights, a decision was recently taken to appoint a consultant to assist the State party in the preparation of the report. In this connection, the Committee also takes note of the State party's assurances that it remains committed to the preparation and submission to the Committee of its initial to fourteenth periodic reports, combined in one document.

3. The Committee recognizes the difficult economic and social conditions facing Guyana and remains deeply concerned about the extensive political and ethnic conflicts which have aggravated the situation in the country and led to serious divisions in society, and that this has affected the ability of the State party to fulfil the requirements of the Convention.

4. The Committee agrees with intergovernmental and non-governmental organizations and United Nations agencies that a vicious circle of political and ethnic tensions has adversely affected human rights, weakened civil society, increased racial violence and poverty and exclusion among indigenous population groups, and hampered the administration of justice and the application of human rights standards in Guyana.

5. The Committee reiterates that the purpose of the system whereby States parties submit reports is to establish and maintain a dialogue with the Committee on actions taken, progress made and difficulties encountered in complying with obligations arising under the Convention. It further reiterates that any State party's failure to honour its reporting obligations under article 9 of the Convention is a serious impediment to the operation of the monitoring system established under the Convention.

6. The Committee is particularly encouraged by the indication made to the Committee by the United Nations Special Rapporteur on contemporary forms of racism, racial discrimination, xenophobia and related intolerance that the process of political dialogue currently under way will make a fundamental contribution to the long-term solution to the problem of ethnic polarization in the country (see also E/CN.4/2004/18/Add.1).

7. The Committee recommends that the initial to fourteenth reports of Guyana, combined in one document, be submitted before 30 September 2004, so that they can be processed and scheduled for examination in 2005. In the event of the non-receipt of the report by that date, the Committee will reschedule the examination of the situation in Guyana under the review procedure at its sixty-sixth session, to be held in March 2005.

8.1.2.5 Prompting the implementation of human rights

Naturally, NGOs have a prominent role to play in encouraging State compliance with human rights instruments and with the recommendations and observations of the various human rights treaty monitoring bodies (and regional courts).

8.2 BUSINESS AND MULTINATIONAL CORPORATIONS

The importance of global business lies in the economic, and even political, power wielded by some multinational corporations. This power often usurps that of government of the State being invested in with allegations of exploitation and corruption commonplace.

Undoubtedly globalisation brings prosperity for many and 'development' (whether positive or negative is a matter for debate) for others. The power of multinational corporations involved in the process has been noted by international organisations. It is in an attempt to ensure that the force of change is a force of good that the following international guidelines for business have emerged.

There is nothing novel in proclaiming guidelines to be followed by companies wishing to pursue ethical foreign transactions. A number of private initiatives have provided guidelines in the past, some deal with particular States: the Sullivan Principles governing US business in apartheid South Africa and the similar MacBride Principles for Northern Ireland, both aimed at limiting discriminatory employment and related work practices (see McCrudden, C, 'Human Rights Codes for Transnational Corporations: What can the Sullivan and MacBride Principles Tell Us?' (1999) 19 Oxford Journal of Legal Studies, pp 167–201); other particular issues, for example, the Valdez Principles on the environment. In addition, more specific sectoral codes have been adopted: for example the labour code of the International Confederation of Free Trade Unions, the European Community Codes on various trade-related developments and, more recently, a plethora of self-regulation codes from within companies anxious to be seen as promoting ethical trade. Many of these codes originated in the US. This is perhaps not surprising given that the US has a density of multinational corporations and a history of foreign investment and trade. Few of these codes are in any way binding—they are, in effect, political statements of intention and support for a policy objective.

8.2.1 International Labour Organisation (ILO)

The International Labour Organisation was established in 1919 in terms of the Treaty of Versailles. The governing body of the International Labour Organisation has identified eight Conventions as 'fundamental to the rights of human beings at work, irrespective of levels of developments of . . . States'. There are two conventions in each of four principal categories. The result is anticipated by the ILO to be 'a global consensus on social and labour issues, and serve as the major reference point in this sphere'.

ILO Declaration on Fundamental Principles and Rights at Work, 86th Session, Geneva, June 1998

The International Labour Conference

1. Recalls:

(a) that in freely joining the ILO, all Members have endorsed the principles and rights set out in its Constitution and in the Declaration of Philadelphia, and have undertaken to work towards attaining the overall objectives of the Organization to the best of their resources and fully in line with their specific circumstances;

(b) that these principles and rights have been expressed and developed in the form of specific rights and obligations in Conventions recognized as fundamental both inside and outside the Organization.

2. Declares that all Members, even if they have not ratified the Conventions in question, have an obligation arising from the very fact of membership in the Organization to respect, to promote and to realize, in good faith and in accordance with the Constitution, the principles concerning the fundamental rights which are the subject of those Conventions, namely:

(a) freedom of association and the effective recognition of the right to collective bargaining;

(b) the elimination of all forms of forced or compulsory labour;

(c) the effective abolition of child labour; and

(d) the elimination of discrimination in respect of employment and occupation.

3. Recognizes the obligation on the Organization to assist its Members, in response to their established and expressed needs, in order to attain these objectives by making full use of its constitutional, operational and budgetary resources, including, by the mobilization of external resources and support, as well as by encouraging other international organizations with which the ILO has established relations, pursuant to article 12 of its Constitution, to support these efforts:

(a) by offering technical cooperation and advisory services to promote the ratification and implementation of the fundamental Conventions;

(b) by assisting those Members not yet in a position to ratify some or all of these Conventions in their efforts to respect, to promote and to realize the principles concerning fundamental rights which are the subject of these Conventions; and

(c) by helping the Members in their efforts to create a climate for economic and social development.

4. Decides that, to give full effect to this Declaration, a promotional follow-up, which is meaningful and effective, shall be implemented in accordance with the measures specified in the annex hereto, which shall be considered as an integral part of this Declaration.

5. Stresses that labour standards should not be used for protectionist trade purposes, and that nothing in this Declaration and its follow-up shall be invoked or otherwise used for such purposes; in addition, the comparative advantage of any country should in no way be called into question by this Declaration and its follow-up.

Which conventions then are included in the identified categories? Each are examined in turn: forced labour, child labour, freedom of association and equality.

8.2.1.1   Forced Labour

The abolition of forced labour was one of the first areas to receive attention. Forced labour is prohibited (or severely restricted) by all major international and regional human rights' instruments. The 1930 Convention No. 29 on forced labour and the 1957 Convention No. 105 on the abolition of forced labour enshrine the salient rules. All States were encouraged to sign up to these conventions in May 1995, following the 75th anniversary of the International Labour Organisation. Forced labour is generally regarded by the international community as perilously close to slavery and analogous practices. Since 1930, it has been prohibited by the ILO's multilateral international instrument. A number of international and regional texts make similar provisions. See, for example Art 8(3) International Covenant on Civil and Political Rights 1966, Art 4, European Convention for the Protection of Human Rights and Fundamental Freedoms 1950.

ILO Convention No. 29 on forced labour (1930)

Article 1

1. Each Member of the International Labour Organisation which ratifies this Convention undertakes to suppress the use of forced or compulsory labour in all its forms within the shortest possible period.

2. With a view to this complete suppression, recourse to forced or compulsory labour may be had, during the transitional period, for public purposes only and as an exceptional measure, subject to the conditions and guarantees hereinafter provided.

3. At the expiration of a period of five years after the coming into force of this Convention, and when the Governing Body of the International Labour Office prepares the report provided for in Article 31 below, the said Governing Body shall consider the possibility of the suppression of forced or compulsory labour in all its forms without a further transitional period and the desirability of placing this question on the agenda of the Conference.

Article 2

1. For the purposes of this Convention the term *forced or compulsory labour* shall mean all work or service which is exacted from any person under the menace of any penalty and for which the said person has not offered himself voluntarily.

2. Nevertheless, for the purposes of this Convention, the term *forced or compulsory labour* shall not include—

(a) any work or service exacted in virtue of compulsory military service laws for work of a purely military character;

(b) any work or service which forms part of the normal civic obligations of the citizens of a fully self-governing country;

(c) any work or service exacted from any person as a consequence of a conviction in a court of law, provided that the said work or service is carried out under the supervision and control of a public authority and that the said person is not hired to or placed at the disposal of private individuals, companies or associations;

(d) any work or service exacted in cases of emergency, that is to say, in the event of war or of a calamity or threatened calamity, such as fire, flood, famine, earthquake, violent epidemic or epizootic diseases, invasion by animal, insect or vegetable pests, and in general any circumstance that would endanger the existence or the well-being of the whole or part of the population;

(e) minor communal services of a kind which, being performed by the members of the community in the direct interest of the said community, can therefore be considered as normal civic obligations incumbent upon the members of the community, provided that the members of the community or their direct representatives shall have the right to be consulted in regard to the need for such services. . . .

Article 11

1. Only adult able-bodied males who are of an apparent age of not less than 18 and not more than 45 years may be called upon for forced or compulsory labour. Except in respect of the kinds of labour provided for in Article 10 of this Convention, the following limitations and conditions shall apply:

(a) whenever possible prior determination by a medical officer appointed by the administration that the persons concerned are not suffering from any infectious or contagious disease and that they are physically fit for the work required and for the conditions under which it is to be carried out;

(b) exemption of school teachers and pupils and officials of the administration in general;

(c) the maintenance in each community of the number of adult able-bodied men indispensable for family and social life;

(d) respect for conjugal and family ties.

2. For the purposes of subparagraph (c) of the preceding paragraph, the regulations provided for in Article 23 of this Convention shall fix the proportion of the resident adult able-bodied males who may be taken at any one time for forced or compulsory labour, provided always that this proportion shall in no case exceed 25 per cent. In fixing this proportion the competent authority shall take account of the density of the population, of its social and physical development, of the seasons, and of the work which must be done by the persons concerned on their own behalf in their locality, and, generally, shall have regard to the economic and social necessities of the normal life of the community concerned.

Article 12

1. The maximum period for which any person may be taken for forced or compulsory labour of all kinds in any one period of twelve months shall not exceed sixty days, including the time spent in going to and from the place of work.

2. Every person from whom forced or compulsory labour is exacted shall be furnished with a certificate indicating the periods of such labour which he has completed.

Article 13

1. The normal working hours of any person from whom forced or compulsory labour is exacted shall be the same as those prevailing in the case of voluntary labour, and the hours worked in excess of the normal working hours shall be remunerated at the rates prevailing in the case of overtime for voluntary labour.

2. A weekly day of rest shall be granted to all persons from whom forced or compulsory labour of any kind is exacted and this day shall coincide as far as possible with the day fixed by tradition or custom in the territories or regions concerned.

Article 14

1. With the exception of the forced or compulsory labour provided for in Article 10 of this Convention, forced or compulsory labour of all kinds shall be remunerated in cash at rates not less than those prevailing for similar kinds of work either in the district in which the labour is employed or in the district from which the labour is recruited, whichever may be the higher.

2. In the case of labour to which recourse is had by chiefs in the exercise of their administrative functions, payment of wages in accordance with the provisions of the preceding paragraph shall be introduced as soon as possible.

3. The wages shall be paid to each worker individually and not to his tribal chief or to any other authority.

4. For the purpose of payment of wages the days spent in travelling to and from the place of work shall be counted as working days.

5. Nothing in this Article shall prevent ordinary rations being given as a part of wages, such rations to be at least equivalent in value to the money payment they are taken to represent, but deductions from wages shall not be made either for the payment of taxes or for special food, clothing or accommodation supplied to a worker for the purpose of maintaining him in a fit condition to carry on his work under the special conditions of any employment, or for the supply of tools. . . .

Article 25

The illegal exaction of forced or compulsory labour shall be punishable as a penal offence, and it shall be an obligation on any Member ratifying this Convention to ensure that the penalties imposed by law are really adequate and are strictly enforced.

Question

Note the potential sexist overtones—what justifications are there for this?

Subsequent development in society altered the perception of forced labour and, rather than regulate it, the International Labour Organisation is now seeking to proscribe it.

ILO Convention No. 105 on the abolition of forced labour (1957)
Article 1

Each Member of the International Labour Organisation which ratifies this Convention undertakes to suppress and not to make use of any form of forced or compulsory labour—

(a) as a means of political coercion or education or as a punishment for holding or expressing political views or views ideologically opposed to the established political, social or economic system;

(b) as a method of mobilising and using labour for purposes of economic development;

(c) as a means of labour discipline;

(d) as a punishment for having participated in strikes;

(e) as a means of racial, social, national or religious discrimination.

Article 2

Each Member of the International Labour Organisation which ratifies this Convention undertakes to take effective measures to secure the immediate and complete abolition of forced or compulsory labour as specified in Article 1 of this Convention.

8.2.1.2   Elimination of Child Labour

A further category of fundamental conventions is that of the elimination of child labour. The International Labour Organisation has been concerned with limiting working hours and restricting abusive working conditions for children since its inauguration. Two more recent instruments have been included in the ILO's eight fundamental instruments: Convention No. 138 (1973) on minimum age and the 1999 Convention No. 182 on worst forms of child labour. Children are viewed by the international community as the most precious resource. Inherently vulnerable, they can easily be exploited by adults. Their very size and physical underdevelopment renders them suitable for a variety of work unbecoming to adults. This was the original motivation at the start of the ILO's work in the area. Children continue to work to some extent in almost every country in the world. What is prohibited is the abusive exploitation of children. Health and safety concerns underpin many of the provisions of these concerns; of secondary importance are the international rights of children themselves (see for example, the United Nations' Convention on the Rights of the Child 1989 or the African Charter on the Rights and Welfare of the Child 1990, discussed in Chapter 10)—children are entitled to a childhood and, perhaps more importantly, to an education.

ILO Convention No. 138 minimum age 1973

Article 1

Each Member for which this Convention is in force undertakes to pursue a national policy designed to ensure the effective abolition of child labour and to raise progressively the minimum age for admission to employment or work to a level consistent with the fullest physical and mental development of young persons.

Article 2

1. Each Member which ratifies this Convention shall specify, in a declaration appended to its ratification, a minimum age for admission to employment or work within its territory and on means of transport registered in its territory; subject to Articles 4 to 8 of this Convention, no one under that age shall be admitted to employment or work in any occupation. . . .

3. The minimum age specified in pursuance of paragraph 1 of this Article shall not be less than the age of completion of compulsory schooling and, in any case, shall not be less than 15 years.

4. Notwithstanding the provisions of paragraph 3 of this Article, a Member whose economy and educational facilities are insufficiently developed may, after consultation with the organisations of employers and workers concerned, where such exist, initially specify a minimum age of 14 years. . . .

Article 3

1. The minimum age for admission to any type of employment or work which by its nature or the circumstances in which it is carried out is likely to jeopardise the health, safety or morals of young persons shall not be less than 18 years.

2. The types of employment or work to which paragraph 1 of this Article applies shall be determined by national laws or regulations or by the competent authority, after consultation with the organisations of employers and workers concerned, where such exist.

3. Notwithstanding the provisions of paragraph 1 of this Article, national laws or regulations or the competent authority may, after consultation with the organisations of employers and workers concerned, where such exist, authorise employment or work as from the age of 16 years on condition that the health, safety and morals of the young persons concerned are fully protected and that the young persons have received adequate specific instruction or vocational training in the relevant branch of activity. . . .

Article 6

This Convention does not apply to work done by children and young persons in schools for general, vocational or technical education or in other training institutions, or to work done by persons at least 14 years of age in undertakings, where such work is carried out in accordance with conditions prescribed by the competent authority, after consultation with the organisations of employers and workers concerned, where such exist, and is an integral part of—

(a) a course of education or training for which a school or training institution is primarily responsible;

(b) a programme of training mainly or entirely in an undertaking, which programme has been approved by the competent authority; or

(c) a programme of guidance or orientation designed to facilitate the choice of an occupation or of a line of training.

Article 7

1. National laws or regulations may permit the employment or work of persons 13 to 15 years of age on light work which is—

(a) not likely to be harmful to their health or development; and

(b) not such as to prejudice their attendance at school, their participation in vocational orientation or training programmes approved by the competent authority or their capacity to benefit from the instruction received.

2. National laws or regulations may also permit the employment or work of persons who are at least 15 years of age but have not yet completed their compulsory schooling on work which meets the requirements set forth in sub-paragraphs (a) and (b) of paragraph 1 of this Article.

3. The competent authority shall determine the activities in which employment or work may be permitted under paragraphs 1 and 2 of this Article and shall prescribe the number of hours during which and the conditions in which such employment or work may be undertaken.

4. Notwithstanding the provisions of paragraphs 1 and 2 of this Article, a Member which has availed itself of the provisions of paragraph 4 of Article 2 may, for as long as it continues to do so, substitute the ages 12 and 14 for the ages 13 and 15 in paragraph 1 and the age 14 for the age 15 in paragraph 2 of this Article.

See also Chapter 10 for the convention on the worst forms of child labour.

8.2.1.3   Freedom of Association

On freedom of association, Convention No. 87 (1948) on freedom of association and protection of the right to organise and Convention No. 98 (1949) on the right to organise and collective bargaining seek to ensure the right of all workers to associate and to negotiate terms and conditions of employment collectively. Collective rights of employees are viewed as fundamental to the control and improvement of working conditions and the prevention of exploitation of workers. Once again, this is a common theme in international and regional instruments on human rights and fundamental freedoms. See, for example, Art 23(4), Universal Declaration of Human Rights 1948, Art. 22, International Covenant on Civil and Political Rights 1966, Art 11, European Convention for the Protection of Human Rights and Fundamental Freedoms 1950.

ILO Convention No. 87 on freedom of association 1948

Article 2

Workers and employers, without distinction whatsoever, shall have the right to establish and, subject only to the rules of the organisation concerned, to join organisations of their own choosing without previous authorisation.

Article 3

1. Workers' and employers' organisations shall have the right to draw up their constitutions and rules, to elect their representatives in full freedom, to organise their administration and activities and to formulate their programmes.

2. The public authorities shall refrain from any interference which would restrict this right or impede the lawful exercise thereof.

Article 4

Workers' and employers' organisations shall not be liable to be dissolved or suspended by administrative authority.

Article 5

Workers' and employers' organisations shall have the right to establish and join federations and confederations and any such organisation, federation or confederation shall have the right to affiliate with international organisations of workers and employers.

Convention No. 98 on the right to organise and collective bargaining (1949)

Article 1

1. Workers shall enjoy adequate protection against acts of anti-union discrimination in respect of their employment.

2. Such protection shall apply more particularly in respect of acts calculated to—

(a) make the employment of a worker subject to the condition that he shall not join a union or shall relinquish trade union membership;

(b) cause the dismissal of or otherwise prejudice a worker by reason of union membership or because of participation in union activities outside working hours or, with the consent of the employer, within working hours.

Article 2

1. Workers' and employers' organisations shall enjoy adequate protection against any acts of interference by each other or each other's agents or members in their establishment, functioning or administration.

2. In particular, acts which are designed to promote the establishment of workers' organisations under the domination of employers or employers' organisations, or to support workers' organisations by financial or other means, with the object of placing such organisations under the control of employers or employers' organisations, shall be deemed to constitute acts of interference within the meaning of this Article.

Article 3

Machinery appropriate to national conditions shall be established, where necessary, for the purpose of ensuring respect for the right to organise as defined in the preceding Articles.

Article 4

Measures appropriate to national conditions shall be taken, where necessary, to encourage and promote the full development and utilisation of machinery for voluntary negotiation between employers or employers' organisations and workers' organisations, with a view to the regulation of terms and conditions of employment by means of collective agreements.

Article 5

1. The extent to which the guarantees provided for in this Convention shall apply to the armed forces and the police shall be determined by national laws or regulations.

2. In accordance with the principle set forth in paragraph 8 of Article 19 of the Constitution of the International Labour Organisation the ratification of this Convention by any Member shall not be deemed to affect any existing law, award, custom or agreement in virtue of which members of the armed forces or the police enjoy any right guaranteed by this Convention.

Article 6

This Convention does not deal with the position of public servants engaged in the administration of the State, nor shall it be construed as prejudicing their rights or status in any way.

Question

What reasons are there for the exceptions articulated in Article 6, why are such people excluded? What is the position in your State concerning trade unions and public servants?

8.2.1.4 Equality

The final category of deemed ILO fundamental conventions is a bedrock of international human rights, and underpins the entire United Nations' system—the commitment to the equality of men and women (see Preface, United Nations Charter 1945). A general prohibition on discrimination is also found in Convention No. 111 (1958) on discrimination (employment and occupation) while the second fundamental ILO conventions in this category: Convention No. 100 (1951), addresses the issue of equal remuneration.

ILO Convention No. 111 Discrimination (employment and occupation) 1958

Article 1

1. For the purpose of this Convention the term **discrimination** includes—

(a) any distinction, exclusion or preference made on the basis of race, colour, sex, religion, political opinion, national extraction or social origin, which has the effect of nullifying or impairing equality of opportunity or treatment in employment or occupation;

(b) such other distinction, exclusion or preference which has the effect of nullifying or impairing equality of opportunity or treatment in employment or occupation as may be determined by the Member concerned after consultation with representative employers' and workers' organisations, where such exist, and with other appropriate bodies.

2. Any distinction, exclusion or preference in respect of a particular job based on the inherent requirements thereof shall not be deemed to be discrimination.

3. For the purpose of this Convention the terms **employment** and **occupation** include access to vocational training, access to employment and to particular occupations, and terms and conditions of employment.

Article 2

Each Member for which this Convention is in force undertakes to declare and pursue a national policy designed to promote, by methods appropriate to national conditions and practice, equality of opportunity and treatment in respect of employment and occupation, with a view to eliminating any discrimination in respect thereof.

Article 3

Each Member for which this Convention is in force undertakes, by methods appropriate to national conditions and practice—

(a) to seek the co-operation of employers' and workers' organisations and other appropriate bodies in promoting the acceptance and observance of this policy;

(b) to enact such legislation and to promote such educational programmes as may be calculated to secure the acceptance and observance of the policy;

(c) to repeal any statutory provisions and modify any administrative instructions or practices which are inconsistent with the policy;

(d) to pursue the policy in respect of employment under the direct control of a national authority;

(e) to ensure observance of the policy in the activities of vocational guidance, vocational training and placement services under the direction of a national authority;

(f) to indicate in its annual reports on the application of the Convention the action taken in pursuance of the policy and the results secured by such action.

Article 4

Any measures affecting an individual who is justifiably suspected of, or engaged in, activities prejudicial to the security of the State shall not be deemed to be discrimination, provided that the individual concerned shall have the right to appeal to a competent body established in accordance with national practice.

Article 5

1. Special measures of protection or assistance provided for in other Conventions or Recommendations adopted by the International Labour Conference shall not be deemed to be discrimination.

2. Any Member may, after consultation with representative employers' and workers' organisations, where such exist, determine that other special measures designed to meet the particular requirements of persons who, for reasons such as sex, age, disablement, family responsibilities or social or cultural status, are generally recognised to require special protection or assistance, shall not be deemed to be discrimination.

Question

To what extent do the provisions of this Convention vary from the general discrimination provisions found in other conventions?

With respect to equality in employment, particularly between male and female employees, the most advanced body of laws is possibly that enacted under the auspices of the European Union. (The European Union is discussed briefly in Chapter 4.) The basic provision of the Consolidated Version of the Treaty Establishing the European Community is Art 141.

Treaty Establishing the European Community Art 141

1. Each Member State shall ensure that the principle of equal pay for male and female workers for equal work or work of equal value is applied.

2. For the purpose of this article, 'pay' means the ordinary basic or minimum wage or salary and any other consideration, whether in cash or in kind, which the worker receives directly or indirectly, in respect of his employment, from his employer.

Equal pay without discrimination based on sex means:

(a) that pay for the same work at piece rates shall be calculated on the basis of the same unit of measurement;

(b) that pay for work at time rates shall be the same for the same job.

3. The Council, acting in accordance with the procedure referred to in Article 251, and after consulting the Economic and Social Committee, shall adopt measures to ensure the application of the principle of equal opportunities and equal treatment of men and women in matters of employment and occupation, including the principle of equal pay for equal work or work of equal value.

4. With a view to ensuring full equality in practice between men and women in working life, the principle of equal treatment shall not prevent any Member State from maintaining or adopting measures providing for specific advantages in order to make it easier for the underrepresented sex to pursue a vocational activity or to prevent or compensate for disadvantages in professional careers.

This has been substantiated by various pieces of secondary legislation, most notably Council Directive No. 75/117/EEC (1975) on the approximation of the laws of the member States relating to the application of the principle of equal pay for men and women and Council Directive No. 76/207/EEC (1976) on the implementation of the principle of equal treatment for men and women as regards access to employment, vocational training and promotion, and working conditions. This latter directive has been amended by Council and Parliament Directive No. 2002/73 (2002). Additional directives address a range of gender equality issues in the sphere of social law and policy (a standard text on EU Law will provide an introduction). A significant body of jurisprudence from the European Court of Justice has shaped and informed the law in this area within the European Union, and indeed beyond. For those individuals living within the European Union, these provisions are particularly valuable because of the doctrine of direct effect: as a consequence of this, individuals may rely on the provisions of the Treaty and/or directive against the State in national courts.

The ILO Convention makes similar provision, but obviously has considerably wider geographical scope.

ILO Convention No. 100 equal remuneration 1951

Article 1

For the purpose of this Convention—

(a) the term **remuneration** includes the ordinary, basic or minimum wage or salary and any additional emoluments whatsoever payable directly or indirectly, whether in cash or in kind, by the employer to the worker and arising out of the worker's employment;

(b) the term **equal remuneration for men and women workers for work of equal value** refers to rates of remuneration established without discrimination based on sex.

Article 2

1. Each Member shall, by means appropriate to the methods in operation for determining rates of remuneration, promote and, in so far as is consistent with such methods, ensure the application to all workers of the principle of equal remuneration for men and women workers for work of equal value.

2. This principle may be applied by means of—

(a) national laws or regulations;

(b) legally established or recognised machinery for wage determination;

(c) collective agreements between employers and workers; or

(d) a combination of these various means.

8.2.1.5   Comment on ILO Contribution

The ILO has enjoyed some success in promoting these eight conventions within States. Therein lies the principal limitation of the conventions in the present context. The ILO is an international organisation, created by and operating in accordance with, international law. Consequently, its instruments are open to signature by States. Only if contracting States elect to enact implementing national legislation will non-State businesses be bound by the terms of these instruments. Corporate entities cannot, *per se*, ratify the instruments though, of course, it is open to any body to express support for the principles articulated therein. Moreover, the ILO operates primarily by consensual reports thus the means of implementing the conventions are limited. There is no incentive for corporations to conform to these standards as they are drafted in terms of State compliance. However, as States enact national laws to implement the conventions, then corporations will find themselves bound by the terms of national law and thus the conventions.

8.2.2 The Organisation of Economic Cooperation and Development

The Organisation of Economic Cooperation and Development has a more limited membership of some 30 States drawn primarily from the 'developed world', primarily Western Europe, North America and the Antipodes. Although considerably more limited in member States than the UN or the ILO, the importance in the OECD lies in the identity of its members—primarily those States which are home to the largest multinational enterprises. Increased foreign investment through globalisation highlighted the potential influence of such enterprises, thus in 1976 the OECD produced its first set of Guidelines for Multinational Enterprises. These guidelines have been periodically reviewed, the most recent set date to June 2000 (see, Tully, S, 'The 2000 Review of the OECD Guidelines for Multinational Enterprises' (2001) 50 International and Comparative Law Quarterly, pp 394–404).

Department of Trade and Industry, UK National Contact Point Information Booklet, HMSO, 2001, p. 7

The Guidelines provide a voluntary framework of 'principles of good conduct' for international companies conducting business. According to the Department of Trade and Industry (UK), the Guidelines 'aim to promote and develop a sustainable approach to business conduct, and build an atmosphere of confidence and predictability between business, labour, governments and society as a whole'.

For reasons of space, only the preface and the first two sections are reproduced here.

The OECD Guidelines for Multinational Enterprises

Preface

1. The *OECD Guidelines for Multinational Enterprises* (the *Guidelines*) are recommendations addressed by governments to multinational enterprises. They provide voluntary principles and standards for responsible business conduct consistent with applicable laws. The *Guidelines* aim to ensure that the operations of these enterprises are in harmony with government policies, to strengthen the basis of mutual confidence between enterprises and the societies in which they operate, to help improve the foreign investment climate and to enhance the contribution to sustainable development made by multinational enterprises. The *Guidelines* are part of the *OECD Declaration on International Investment and Multinational Enterprises* the other elements of which relate to national treatment, conflicting requirements on enterprises, and international investment incentives and disincentives.

2. International business has experienced far-reaching structural change and the *Guidelines* themselves have evolved to reflect these changes. With the rise of service and knowledge-intensive industries, service and technology enterprises have entered the international marketplace. Large enterprises still account for a major share of international investment, and there is a trend toward large-scale international mergers. At the same time, foreign investment by small- and medium-sized enterprises has also increased and these enterprises now play a significant role on the international scene. Multinational enterprises, like their domestic counterparts, have evolved to encompass a broader range of business arrangements and organisational forms. Strategic alliances and closer relations with suppliers and contractors tend to blur the boundaries of the enterprise.

3. The rapid evolution in the structure of multinational enterprises is also reflected in their operations in the developing world, where foreign direct investment has grown rapidly. In developing countries, multinational enterprises have diversified beyond primary production and extractive industries into manufacturing, assembly, domestic market development and services.

4. The activities of multinational enterprises, through international trade and investment, have strengthened and deepened the ties that join OECD economies to each other and to the rest of the world. These activities bring substantial benefits to home and host countries. These benefits accrue when multinational enterprises supply the products and services that consumers want to buy at competitive prices and when they provide fair returns to suppliers of capital. Their trade and investment activities contribute to the efficient use of capital, technology and human and natural resources. They facilitate the transfer of technology among the regions of the world and the development of technologies that reflect local conditions. Through both formal training and on-the-job learning enterprises also promote the development of human capital in host countries.

5. The nature, scope and speed of economic changes have presented new strategic challenges for enterprises and their stakeholders. Multinational enterprises have the opportunity to implement best practice policies for sustainable development that seek to ensure coherence between social, economic and environmental objectives. The ability of multinational enterprises to promote sustainable development is greatly enhanced when trade and investment are conducted in a context of open, competitive and appropriately regulated markets.

6. Many multinational enterprises have demonstrated that respect for high standards of business conduct can enhance growth. Today's competitive forces are intense and multinational enterprises face a variety of legal, social and regulatory settings. In this context, some enterprises may be tempted to neglect appropriate standards and principles of conduct in an attempt to gain undue competitive advantage. Such practices by the few may call into question the reputation of the many and may give rise to public concerns.

7. Many enterprises have responded to these public concerns by developing internal programmes, guidance and management systems that underpin their commitment to good corporate citizenship, good practices and good business and employee conduct. Some of them have called upon consulting, auditing and certification services, contributing to the accumulation of expertise in these areas. These efforts have also promoted social dialogue on what constitutes good business conduct. The *Guidelines* clarify the shared expectations for business conduct of the governments adhering to them and provide a point of reference for enterprises. Thus, the *Guidelines* both complement and reinforce private efforts to define and implement responsible business conduct.

8. Governments are co-operating with each other and with other actors to strengthen the international legal and policy framework in which business is conducted. The post-war period has seen the development of this framework, starting with the adoption in 1948 of the Universal Declaration of Human Rights. Recent instruments include the ILO Declaration on Fundamental Principles and Rights at Work, the Rio Declaration on Environment and Development and Agenda 21 and the Copenhagen Declaration for Social Development.

9. The OECD has also been contributing to the international policy framework. Recent developments include the adoption of the Convention on Combating Bribery of Foreign Public Officials in International Business Transactions and of the OECD Principles of Corporate Governance, the OECD Guidelines for Consumer Protection in the Context of Electronic Commerce, and ongoing work on the OECD Guidelines on Transfer Pricing for Multinational Enterprises and Tax Administrations.

10. The common aim of the governments adhering to the *Guidelines* is to encourage the positive contributions that multinational enterprises can make to economic, environmental and social progress and to minimise the difficulties to which their various operations may give rise. In working towards this goal, governments find themselves in partnership with the many businesses,

trade unions and other non-governmental organisations that are working in their own ways toward the same end. Governments can help by providing effective domestic policy frameworks that include stable macroeconomic policy, non-discriminatory treatment of firms, appropriate regulation and prudential supervision, an impartial system of courts and law enforcement and efficient and honest public administration. Governments can also help by maintaining and promoting appropriate standards and policies in support of sustainable development and by engaging in ongoing reforms to ensure that public sector activity is efficient and effective. Governments adhering to the *Guidelines* are committed to continual improvement of both domestic and international policies with a view to improving the welfare and living standards of all people.

I. Concepts and Principles

. . .

II. General Policies

Enterprises should take fully into account established policies in the countries in which they operate, and consider the views of other stakeholders. In this regard, enterprises should:

1. Contribute to economic, social and environmental progress with a view to achieving sustainable development.

2. Respect the human rights of those affected by their activities consistent with the host government's international obligations and commitments.

3. Encourage local capacity building through close co-operation with the local community, including business interests, as well as developing the enterprise's activities in domestic and foreign markets, consistent with the need for sound commercial practice.

4. Encourage human capital formation, in particular by creating employment opportunities and facilitating training opportunities for employees.

5. Refrain from seeking or accepting exemptions not contemplated in the statutory or regulatory framework related to environmental, health, safety, labour, taxation, financial incentives, or other issues.

6. Support and uphold good corporate governance principles and develop and apply good corporate governance practices.

7. Develop and apply effective self-regulatory practices and management systems that foster a relationship of confidence and mutual trust between enterprises and the societies in which they operate.

8. Promote employee awareness of, and compliance with, company policies through appropriate dissemination of these policies, including through training programmes.

9. Refrain from discriminatory or disciplinary action against employees who make *bona fide* reports to management or, as appropriate, to the competent public authorities, on practices that contravene the law, the *Guidelines* or the enterprise's policies.

10. Encourage, where practicable, business partners, including suppliers and sub-contractors, to apply principles of corporate conduct compatible with the *Guidelines*.

11. Abstain from any improper involvement in local political activities.

III. Disclosure

IV. Employment and Industrial Relations

V. Environment

VI. Combating Bribery

VII. Consumer Interests

VIII. Science and Technology

IX. Competition

X. Taxation

8.2.2.1   Comment on the OECD Guidelines

The OECD guidelines are drawn up by States, not companies. They are supported by many large enterprises but remain essentially a voluntary code of conduct. Governments are committed to the observance of the Guidelines, supporting multinational enterprises through the provision of National Contact Points to promote and ensure implementation of the Guidelines. National Contact Points report annually to the OECD thus some degree of monitoring is possible though, once again, there are no sanctions per se given the Guidelines are voluntary. National Contact Points may also arbitrate in the event of any dispute over the application of the Guidelines. Further limitations occur when the multinational enterprise is engaged in activities outwith the OECD member States (most likely). There will be no national contact point and thus there is limited assistance available to companies seeking advice. Similar problems may arise when it is difficult to elicit the national origin of the part of the company concerned, a growing problem in an increasingly globalised world.

The OECD Guidelines are irrefutably the most comprehensive set of guidelines available for companies to follow. A strict adherence to them would inevitably comply with all salient international standards. However, they are more limited in geographical scope than the less precise provisions of the United Nations Global Compact.

8.2.3   United Nations Global Compact

At the World Economic Forum in 1999, Kofi Annan, Secretary-General of the United Nations, challenged global business leaders to embrace human rights in their individual corporate practices. Observance of human rights is increasingly a key indicator of the social responsibility of a company. Many companies are anxious to avoid domestic litigation on account of their overseas practices. The terms of the Compact thus appeal as a political commitment to internationally accepted values. However, compliance with the Compact is voluntary, not least because the United Nations lacks the competence to enforce its will on corporate bodies. Sanctions against States are applied by virtue of national law, on the authority of the United Nations.

The Global Compact, at heart, is ten principles: two on general human rights; four on labour, three on the environment, and a late addition, one on anti-corruption. The environment is increasingly linked to emerging collective human rights on development and environment while clearly corruption is a major source of concern in some elements of international business. By 2006, the Global Compact boasts almost 3,000 participants worldwide covering some ninety states.

8.2.3.1   General human rights

United Nations Global Compact: General Human Rights

Principle 1: Businesses should support and respect the protection of internationally proclaimed human rights; and

Principle 2: make sure that they are not complicit in human rights abuses.

These principles seek to harness the economic power wielded by some corporations. Before entering new markets, human rights' assessments should be carried out to ensure companies are not implicit in abuse of human rights. Bribing official and tolerating corrupt systems of government render companies complicit in the abuse of rights. These principles thus have potentially far-reaching consequences for business. Continues investment in countries with poor human rights' records is problematic— the corporate policy and business acumen may in such circumstances be at odds.

8.2.3.2   Labour

United Nations Global Compact: Labour

Principle 3: Businesses should uphold the freedom of association and the effective recognition of the right to collective bargaining;

Principle 4: the elimination of all forms of forced and compulsory labour;

Principle 5: the effective abolition of child labour; and

Principle 6: the elimination of discrimination in respect of employment and occupation.

Many of these principles already form part of national law in States. In such situations, compliance is not elective for businesses. However, as recent press campaigns have shown, exploitative work practices are still common in many States and business explicitly condones this by investing in these States and taking advantage of cheap labour sources.

8.2.3.3   The environment

The next three principles concern the environment, an area of mounting concern since issues of toxic emissions, global warming and pollution were highlighted at the 1992 Rio Earth Summit.

United Nations Global Compact: The Environment

Principle 7: Businesses should support a precautionary approach to environmental challenges;

Principle 8: undertake initiatives to promote greater environmental responsibility; and

Principle 9: encourage the development and diffusion of environmentally friendly technologies.

Environmental impact assessments and built in safety margins should minimise the threat of serious damage to the environment (see Principle 15 of the Rio Declaration). Agenda 21 defines environmental responsibility, encouraging environmental management (see also the International Declaration on Cleaner Production) and supporting the use of environmentally sound technologies which protect the environment, use resources in a sustainable manner and limit waste products.

8.2.3.4   Anti-corruption

United Nations Global Compact: Anti-Corruption

Principle 10: Businesses should work against all forms of corruption, including extortion and bribery.

This, the newest principle, was added to the Global Compact in 2004. On 9 December 2004, in commemoration of the declared International Anti-Corruption Day, the

Global Compact launched a worldwide effort to raise awareness among its participants of the need to eliminate corruption. The Principle reflects evolving international concern and the United Nations Convention against Corruption which was adopted by General Assembly Resolution 58/4 of 31 October 2003.

8.2.3.5 Achieving the Compact

The Global Compact itself provides a system for the progressive realisation of the principles enshrined therein. A Nine Step Plan was produced under the auspices of the Office of the United Nations High Commissioner for Human Rights to assist corporations wishing to support the Global Compact:

United Nations High Commissioner for Human Rights: Nine Step Framework for Action, taken from www.unhchr.ch/business

The framework for action reflects the following broad set of steps that a company can take:

- **Identify Human Rights Issues:** The first step is to identify the issues that a company might face. These can vary significantly depending on the industrial sector and the countries in which a company has operations and business relationships. The past five years has demonstrated clearly that while most companies have the need to focus on labor standards, companies in the mineral extraction, apparel/footwear, and agricultural industries have distinct issues that require different approaches. Reviewing the potential human rights impact of a company's operations and relationships will help to focus policy setting and implementation.

- **Develop Policy Options:** As noted above, the Universal Declaration of Human Rights and the ILO's core labour standards are generally the foundation of a company's policies. These are expanded upon to address the unique issues facing a company. Several oil companies, for example, have developed policies and practices based on the UN Code of Conduct for Law Enforcement Officials to establish guidelines for security personnel working in or near their facilities.

- **Operationalizing Policy:** To ensure the policy has the desired impact, many companies have developed guidelines to aid implementation. This process of translating broad principle into practice is essential, and in some cases can be complicated. Yet without doing so, a company's ability to act, and to communicate internally, to business partners, and to the external world, is substantially limited. The development of policy will be enhanced both by seeking contributions from within the company and reaching out to NGOs and other relevant external stakeholders for their input.

- **Dialogue/Outreach/Collaboration:** For many companies, this is actually the first step. The efforts undertaken by Novo Nordisk, for example, involved outreach to academics, as well as stakeholders that expressed interest and concern about the company's approach to human rights issues, in advance of policy setting. Undertaken thoughtfully, advance consultation with human rights groups and social partners can enhance the basic structure a company puts in place to address human rights, and will help establish systems of public accountability.

- **Educating Key Staff/Training:** As with any aspect of business, it is critical to ensure that all personnel with the opportunity to 'make or break' the human rights policy are educated about what the policy means in practice as well as the philosophy behind the policy. This is a complicated task for a company with operations in numerous countries. Companies operating globally—whether large or small—also find that they have the need to communicate universal principles to staff coming from different cultures, and based in countries with widely varying practices and human rights records. This places a high premium on communicating a consistent message, while at the same time addressing cultural nuances that can make meaningful differences in implementation.

- **Developing Appropriate Internal Capacity:** Several companies in the past five years have found that managing human rights issues requires internal capacity and expertise. Just as environment, health and safety (EHS) functions have developed in most multinational companies, more and more such businesses are establishing human rights specialists. The value of doing so helps make sure that a company has: (1) proper expertise on this complex topic; (2) the ability to monitor a fast-changing environment; (3) sufficient knowledge and communication skills to engage in meaningful outreach with NGOs and the public sector; (4) the ability to manage instances when a human rights policy might be violated, and (5) the authority to ensure that company personnel are held accountable for implementation. Some companies have established freestanding human rights or labour standards units; some have attached them to broad corporate social responsibility groups or corporate affairs, and others have 'devolved' responsibility to country or regional managers.

- **Communication with Business Partners:** Just as internal capacity is critical, so too is ensuring that business partners understand and act upon a company's concern for human rights. Business partners take many forms: vendors, subcontractors, and governments, amongst others. This means that communication with business partners also takes many forms. Steps taken by companies include: training of vendors on codes of conduct and other human rights standards; including compliance with human rights and labor rights standards in contractual agreements, and appropriate dialogue with public officials about the need to ensure a climate in which human rights are respected.

- **Internal Accountability:** Few business policies are implemented effectively without systems of accountability, and human rights is no different. By establishing performance benchmarks and holding designated staff responsible for implementation, a company is more likely to be successful. This can happen in a range of ways: some companies have ultimate responsibility in senior management; some companies choose to take a country by country approach; some choose both. Internal accountability is taken one step further by companies that, through a variety of means, implement some form of independent verification or public, verified reporting.

- **Independent Verification and Public Reporting:** As noted throughout this report, several companies have begun to experiment with different forms of verification and reporting. Such practices are most highly developed on labor practice, and examples of recent initiatives are identified above. Recent events, including the WTO ministerial in Seattle, demonstrate the growing importance the consuming public places on increased transparency and independent systems of public accountability. Independent verification and reporting is one way that companies can contribute to, in the words of economist Paul Krugman, 'build[ing] a constituency that reaches beyond the sort of people who congregate at Davos.'

So in a nutshell, the recommended step-by-step guide is that corporations should

(1) Identify salient human rights issues,

(2) Develop an appropriate corporate policy,

(3) Enact the policy,

(4) Engage in dialogue to shape policy development and implementation,

(5) Educate key staff, providing human rights' training,

(6) Develop internal capacity for addressing human rights,

(7) Communicate regularly with business partners,

(8) Establish internal accountability, for example to stakeholders,

(9) Engage with the public reporting.

The United Nations offers itself as a partner in developing corporate policy in terms of the Compact. Companies signing up to the Compact are required to notify the UN Secretary-General of their decision, publicise their commitment to the Compact and submit annually to the Secretary-General an example of progress made or lessons learnt from implementing the principles. These Communications on Progress are posted on the Global Compact website as encouragement for other companies, part of an exchange of 'examples of 'good practice'. Through partnership with the United Nations, companies are encouraged to register their support for the Global Compact and share advice and experiences with other companies in a mutually supportive manner.

8.2.3.6 Involving NGOs

Through partnerships with NGOs, companies are encouraged to advance their observance of the principles. NGOs may assist in training officials, developing human rights' policies and formulating implementing strategies. Moreover, they can be an important source of knowledge on the human rights situation in various States. This is particularly useful with respect to States recalcitrant in submitting reports to the United Nations human rights treaty monitoring bodies, as information on human rights therein may not be otherwise accessible or reliable.

The Global Compact is effectively a virtual code; it appears primarily on the World Wide Web, rarely in paper print form. All information pertaining to the code is accessible remotely. Despite this, the importance of the Global Compact lies in its very existence. As companies increasingly discover, globalisation has resulted in greater global awareness of human rights and the ethical dimension of business. Customers become more environmentally and socially aware, human rights and environmental issues can shape customer decisions. The press given to Nike, Gap, Nestle etc. in the last few years testify to this. A growing number of companies now brand themselves as supporting fair trade and corporate responsibility. This is viewed in some quarters as key to capturing the youth and young adult market.

A new governance framework for the Global Compact was announced in September 2005 in New York. It aims to foster involvement in and ownership of the Compact by all participants at all levels.

Governance functions will be shared by the following entities with differentiated tasks:

- A triennial Leaders Summit (next one June 2007)
- A Board (meeting annually)
- Local Networks (self-governing)
- Annual Local Networks Forum
- The Global Compact Office and Inter-Agency Team (see also UN Doc A/RES/60/215)

8.2.4 Comment on business and human rights

Human rights policy in the United Nations has changed over the years since the adoption of the second part of the International Bill of Rights in 1966. As rights become more detailed and directed more at specific vulnerable groups in a sectoral approach, it could be argued that the zenith of international human rights in its present consensual form has been reached. To progress further, either a more comprehensive enforcement mechanism is needed (not possible under international law due to diverse opinions on sanctions) or more comprehensive implementation mechanisms (again not likely). The global reality is that business can be more influential than Governments, thus it is perhaps logical that the United Nations should direct its attention there. States retain a primary responsibility for the implementation of universal standards of rights within their jurisdictions. However, the might of global business is now being feted by the United Nations and productively employed to advocate rights, companies are now agreeing to act in accordance with these norms of rights and exert pressure on States where they do business to conform likewise. In a self-perpetuating circle, human rights are being reinforced and the United Nations role strengthened, thereby further advancing universal respect for universal rights.

Although routed in legal norms which currently bind States, the Global Compact remains essentially a political tool. It is an expression of support for international rights and freedoms on the part of those who sign up. Ultimately, adherence to the principles in articulating parameters for ethical trading might motivate States to address gross and systematic violations of rights and freedoms. In this respect, the Compact may in the long run assist in remedying the major deficiency of international human rights—in effect it may provide a sanction. Those States not complying with basic norms of human rights may no longer be viewed as attractive financial investments by multinational companies anxious to reduce costs. This may prompt States to re-evaluate their human rights' record. Globalisation may yet result in a subtle shift in opinion, an improvement in the overall global human rights' position. Undoubtedly this is the goal of the United Nations. Whether transnational corporations are willing to 'toe' the United Nations' line remains to be seen. The Global Compact may be viewed as a desperate measure by a United Nations without the power to enforce its will on recalcitrant States, or as tacit acknowledgement that the nation-State is no longer the sole powerful actor on the international stage. However, it is undeniable that, through globalisation, business is a powerful force in international economics and politics. Global corporate social responsibility is a major goal of the Global Compact. With its adoption and faithful adherence to its nine principles, globalisation could make an almost immeasurable contribution towards the realisation of international justice for all.

8.2.5 Case Study: *John Doe et al. v Unocal Corp.*, 1996–2005

In the United States of America, the Alien Tort Claims Act 1789 grants jurisdiction to the US Federal Court over torts committed overseas in violation of international law.

US Alien Tort Claims Act 1789
Section 1350. Alien's action for tort

> The district courts shall have original jurisdiction of any civil action by an alien for a tort only, committed in violation of the law of nations or a treaty of the United States.

The application of this provision to human rights became apparent after the litigation in *Filartiga v Pena-Irala* 1980 F. 2d 876 (2d cir) (US). The United States Circuit Court of Appeals considered the prohibition on torture part of customary international law and opened the way for human rights abuses overseas to be actioned within the United States. Suits have been filed against several State presidents and leaders in the intervening period, generally without success (for jurisdiction/territory issues—that is, securing attendance at court). However, the application of the law to multinational corporations has become apparent over the last decade.

John Doe et al. v Unocal Corp. 2002 WL 31063976 (9th Cir. (Cal.) September 18 2002

In 1996, people from the Tenasserim area of Myanmar (formerly Burma) assisted by two NGOs (EarthRights International and Center for Constitutional Rights) filed suit against Unocal alleging that the company directly or indirectly subjected the villagers to serial human rights abuses during the construction of a gas pipeline. (The plaintiffs filed as John, Jane and baby Doe to preserve anonymity with the consent of the court and in accordance with American legal practice.) The initially named co-defendants Total SA, a French oil firm of which Unocal has an interest, the Myanmar government and Myanmar Oil were dropped as Total had insufficient interest to be sued in the US and the other two had sovereign immunity. The action continued against Unocal on the basis of its interest in Total, the company involved in the pipeline. The gas pipeline was constructed under an agreement between Total SA and the two Myanmar defendants. The pipeline was built between 1992 and 1999. International human rights organisations reported evidence of human rights violations perpetrated by Myanmar authorities during the construction phase.

Unocal's Knowledge that the Myanmar Military was Providing Security and Other Services for the Project.

It is undisputed that the Myanmar Military provided security and other services for the Project, and that Unocal knew about this. The pipeline was to run through Myanmar's rural Tenasserim region. The Myanmar Military increased its presence in the pipeline region to provide security and other services for the Project. A Unocal memorandum documenting Unocal's meetings with Total on March 1 and 2, 1995 reflects Unocal's understanding that '[f]our battalions of 600 men each will protect the [pipeline] corridor' and '[f]ifty soldiers will be assigned to guard each survey team.' A former soldier in one of these battalions testified at his deposition that his battalion had been formed in 1996 specifically for this purpose. In addition, the Military built helipads and cleared roads along the proposed pipeline route for the benefit of the Project.

There is also evidence sufficient to raise a genuine issue of material fact whether the Project *hired* the Myanmar Military, through Myanmar Oil, to provide these services, and whether Unocal knew about this.

In March 2005, an unspecified out-of-court settlement was reached between Unocal and the villagers.

Unocal statement on settlement from www.unocal.com/myanmar/suit.htm

On March 21, 2005, Unocal announced that it had reached a final settlement with the parties to several lawsuits related to the company's investment through subsidiaries in the Yadana natural gas pipeline project in Myanmar (Burma). The lawsuits had alleged that Unocal was complicit in human rights violations committed by the Burmese military. Both state and federal courts will soon be acting to dismiss these claims.

Although terms of the settlement are confidential, we want to make the following very clear. Unocal has never condoned, encouraged or participated in human rights violations in any project. As indicated in the agreed joint press release that was published earlier, Unocal maintains, and has always maintained, that we did nothing wrong and have always respected human rights in Myanmar (Burma). Indeed, we received a ruling from the court that Unocal did nothing wrong with regard to the Yadana project.

It is absolutely against our principles, practices and Code of Conduct to tolerate the use of forced labour. Under the management of Total, the project operator, all workers on the Yadana project were paid and voluntary. All workers were paid directly, and these payments were carefully documented by Total. Further, no villages were relocated in connection with the Yadana project. Owners of land used for the project received fair compensation.

Unocal is not the only company to face litigation in the United States: a number of actions are in progress or have recently being concluded.

8.2.6   Case study: Shell in Nigeria and the Odoni peoples

The Social and Economic Rights Action Center and the Center for Economic and Social Rights v Nigeria, Comm. No. 155/96 (2001), African Commission for Human Rights

1. The Communication alleges that the military government of Nigeria has been directly involved in oil production through the State oil company, the Nigerian National Petroleum Company (NNPC), the majority shareholder in a consortium with Shell Petroleum Development Corporation (SPDC), and that these operations have caused environmental degradation and health problems resulting from the contamination of the environment among the Ogoni People.

2. The Communication alleges that the oil consortium has exploited oil reserves in Ogoniland with no regard for the health or environment of the local communities, disposing toxic wastes into the environment and local waterways in violation of applicable international environmental standards. The consortium also neglected and/or failed to maintain its facilities causing numerous avoidable spills in the proximity of villages. The resulting contamination of water, soil and air has had serious short and long-term health impacts, including skin infections, gastrointestinal and respiratory ailments, and increased risk of cancers, and neurological and reproductive problems.

3. The Communication alleges that the Nigerian Government has condoned and facilitated these violations by placing the legal and military powers of the State at the disposal of the oil companies. The Communication contains a memo from the Rivers State Internal Security Task Force, calling for 'ruthless military operations'. . . .

7. The Communication alleges that in the course of the last three years, Nigerian security forces have attacked, burned and destroyed several Ogoni villages and homes under the pretext of dislodging officials and supporters of the Movement of the Survival of Ogoni People (MOSOP). These attacks have come in response to MOSOP's non-violent campaign in opposition to the destruction of their environment by oil companies. Some of the attacks have involved uniformed combined forces of the police, the army, the air-force, and the navy, armed with armoured tanks and other sophisticated weapons. In other instances, the attacks have been conducted by unidentified gunmen, mostly at night. The military-type methods and the calibre of weapons used in such attacks strongly suggest the involvement of the Nigerian security forces. The complete failure of the Government of Nigeria to investigate these attacks, let alone punish the perpetrators, further implicates the Nigerian authorities. . . .

49. In accordance with Articles 60 and 61 of the African Charter, this communication is examined in the light of the provisions of the African Charter and the relevant international and regional human rights instruments and principles. The Commission thanks the two human rights NGOs who brought the matter under its purview: the Social and Economic Rights Action Center (Nigeria) and the Center for Economic and Social Rights (USA). Such is a demonstration of the usefulness to the Commission and individuals of *actio popularis*, which is wisely allowed under the African Charter. It is a matter of regret that the only written response from the government of Nigeria is an admission of the gravamen of the complaints which is contained in a note verbale and. . . . In the circumstances, the Commission is compelled to proceed with the examination of the matter on the basis of the uncontested allegations of the Complainants, which are consequently accepted by the Commission. . . .

53. Government compliance with the spirit of Articles 16 and 24 of the African Charter must also include ordering or at least permitting independent scientific monitoring of threatened environments, requiring and publicising environmental and social impact studies prior to any major industrial development, undertaking appropriate monitoring and providing information to those communities exposed to hazardous materials and activities and providing meaningful opportunities for individuals to be heard and to participate in the development decisions affecting their communities.

54. We now examine the conduct of the government of Nigeria in relation to Articles 16 and 24 of the African Charter. Undoubtedly and admittedly, the government of Nigeria, through NNPC has the right to produce oil, the income from which will be used to fulfil the economic and social rights of Nigerians. But the care that should have been taken as outlined in the preceding paragraph and which would have protected the rights of the victims of the violations complained of was not taken. To exacerbate the situation, the security forces of the government engaged in conduct in violation of the rights of the Ogonis by attacking, burning and destroying several Ogoni villages and homes. . . .

58. The Commission notes that in the present case, despite its obligation to protect persons against interferences in the enjoyment of their rights, the Government of Nigeria facilitated the destruction of the Ogoniland. Contrary to its Charter obligations and despite such internationally established principles, the Nigerian Government has given the green light to private actors, and the oil Companies in particular, to devastatingly affect the well-being of the Ogonis. By any measure of standards, its practice falls short of the minimum conduct expected of governments, and therefore, is in violation of Article 21 of the African Charter.

Additional rights were also found to have been violated with the Commission concluding that the Federal Republic of Nigeria was in violation of Arts 2, 4, 14, 16, 18(1), 21 and 24 of the African Charter on Human and Peoples' Rights.

Question

Note the comment of the Commission at the end of the opinion: Para 69 'The Commission does not wish to fault governments that are labouring under difficult circumstances to improve the lives of their people. The situation of the people of Ogoniland, however, requires, in the view of the Commission, a reconsideration of the Government's attitude to the allegations contained in the instant communication. The intervention of multinational corporations may be a potentially positive force for development if the State and the people concerned are ever mindful of the common good and the sacred rights of individuals and communities'. To what extent can regional and international law ensure that multinational corporations are a positive force in international development?

Note also that the action against Royal Dutch Petroleum/Shell was lodged in the US courts under the Alien Tort Claims Act concerning participation in crimes against humanity, torture, summary execution, arbitrary detention and other cruel, inhuman, and degrading treatment. The case was again relative to the Ogoni people with particular emphasis on the 1995 hangings of Ken Saro-Wiwa and John Kpuinen, two leaders of the Movement for the Survival of the Ogoni People, and reported torture. Various notions are still being processed for this class action.

8.3   EDUCATORS, LAWYERS AND INDIVIDUALS

The duty to promote and respect human rights arguably extends beyond the remit of States, NGOs and business to individuals themselves. While individuals are the primary beneficiary of human rights, those benefits bring with them duties.

Universal Declaration of Human Rights Art 29(1)

Everyone has duties to the community in which alone the free and full development of his personality is possible.

A general obligation to encourage human rights education may also be derived from the General Assembly's Declaration on the Rights and Responsibility of Individuals, Groups and Organs of Society to Promote and Protect Universally Recognised Human Rights and Fundamental Freedoms.

General Assembly's Declaration on the Rights and Responsibility of Individuals, Groups and Organs of Society to Promote and Protect Universally Recognised Human Rights and Fundamental Freedoms Resolution 53/144 (1999)

Article 16

Individuals, non-governmental organizations and relevant institutions have an important role to play in contributing to making the public more aware of questions relating to all human rights and fundamental freedoms through activities such as education, training and research in these areas to strengthen further, *inter alia*, understanding, tolerance, peace and friendly relations among nations and among all racial and religious groups, bearing in mind the various backgrounds of the societies and communities in which they carry out their activities.

Article 18

1. Everyone has duties towards and within the community, in which alone the free and full development of his or her personality is possible.

2. Individuals, groups, institutions and non-governmental organizations have an important role to play and a responsibility in safeguarding democracy, promoting human rights and fundamental freedoms and contributing to the promotion and advancement of democratic societies, institutions and processes.

3. Individuals, groups, institutions and non-governmental organizations also have an important role and a responsibility in contributing, as appropriate, to the promotion of the right of everyone to a social and international order in which the rights and freedoms set forth in the Universal Declaration of Human Rights and other human rights instruments can be fully realized.

This is obviously of particular importance to lawyers and law enforcement agents. Substantial guidelines and technical support is available from the United Nations to ensure that law enforcement personnel are familiar with the basics of international human rights and their practices and policies conform to the salient standards. For example, consider the United Nations guidelines for law enforcement officials.

Code of Conduct for Law Enforcement Officials, General Assembly Resolution 34/169 (1979)

Article 1

Law enforcement officials shall at all times fulfil the duty imposed upon them by law, by serving the community and by protecting all persons against illegal acts, consistent with the high degree of responsibility required by their profession.

Article 2

In the performance of their duty, law enforcement officials shall respect and protect human dignity and maintain and uphold the human rights of all persons.

Obviously, the human rights alluded to include provisions of the basic international (and indeed regional) instruments. Inevitably, it is necessary for all law enforcement officials to be aware of the provisions and accordingly their impact and effect on the scope of their work. Elements of human rights training thus have to be incorporated *inter alia* into police training. Some of the issues concerning the treatment of detainees are discussed in more detail in Chapter 11. Note that such a requirement has a precedent: the Geneva Conventions on the conduct of hostilities and protection of injured armed forces and the civilian population must be taught to all members of armed forces within each and every State (see Chapter 15).

For a State to discharge its positive obligation under international human rights law, all officials must be aware of the relevant international standards.

Question

Consider mechanisms by which States can discharge this positive obligation and ensure the practice of law enforcement officials conform to the international standard.

Similarly, lawyers require knowledge of human rights and the mechanisms for their enforcement. Through lawyers pushing the boundaries of international human rights, the parameters of protection will become clear. Consider the progress in the United Kingdom: England has a common law tradition with a strong civil liberties flavour, yet since the introduction of the Human Rights Act 1998 (cited above) lawyers have embraced human rights and fundamental freedoms with haste, resulting in a comprehensive jurisprudence in but a few years. More generally, if lawyers are unaware of the opportunities available at the international and regional levels to enforce and implement human rights, progress towards securing and realising rights will be slow.

8.3.1   Education

Education is a right recognised by international law.

Universal Declaration Art 26

Everyone has the right to education. Education shall be free, at least in the elementary and fundamental stages. Elementary education shall be compulsory. Technical and professional education shall be made generally available and higher education shall be equally accessible to all on the basis of merit.

United Nations Convention on the Rights of the Child

Article 28

1. States Parties recognize the right of the child to education, and with a view to achieving this right progressively and on the basis of equal opportunity, they shall, in particular:

(a) Make primary education compulsory and available free to all;

(b) Encourage the development of different forms of secondary education, including general and vocational education, make them available and accessible to every child, and take appropriate measures such as the introduction of free education and offering financial assistance in case of need;

(c) Make higher education accessible to all on the basis of capacity by every appropriate means;

(d) Make educational and vocational information and guidance available and accessible to all children;

(e) Take measures to encourage regular attendance at schools and the reduction of drop-out rates.

2. States Parties shall take all appropriate measures to ensure that school discipline is adminis-

tered in a manner consistent with the child's human dignity and in conformity with the present Convention.

3. States Parties shall promote and encourage international cooperation in matters relating to education, in particular with a view to contributing to the elimination of ignorance and illiteracy throughout the world and facilitating access to scientific and technical knowledge and modern teaching methods. In this regard, particular account shall be taken of the needs of developing countries.

Obviously these provisions impose obligations on the State. However, the right to education also imposes obligations as to the nature of the education provided. 'Education involves much more than the transmission of knowledge and skills', as the then Special Rapporteur commented in a report on her Mission to the United States of America (UN Doc. E/CN.4/2002/60/Add.1, para 76). Note therefore the international espoused purpose of education.

Universal Declaration Art 26(2)

Education shall be directed to the full development of the human personality and to the strengthening of respect for human rights and fundamental freedoms. It shall promote understanding, tolerance and friendship among all nations, racial or religious groups, and shall further the activities of the United Nations for the maintenance of peace.

Vienna Declaration of the World Conference on Human Rights 1993, para 33

The World Conference on Human Rights reaffirms that States are duty-bound, as stipulated in the Universal Declaration of Human Rights and the International Covenant on Economic, Social and Cultural Rights and in other international human rights instruments, to ensure that education is aimed at strengthening the respect of human rights and fundamental freedoms. The World Conference on Human Rights emphasizes the importance of incorporating the subject of human rights education programmes and calls upon States to do so. Education should promote understanding, tolerance, peace and friendly relations between the nations and all racial or religious groups and encourage the development of United Nations activities in pursuance of these objectives. Therefore, education on human rights and the dissemination of proper information, both theoretical and practical, play an important role in the promotion and respect of human rights with regard to all individuals without distinction of any kind such as race, sex, language or religion, and this should be integrated in the education policies at the national as well as international levels. The World Conference on Human Rights notes that resource constraints and institutional inadequacies may impede the immediate realization of these objectives.

Note in particular the link to international peace and security. Arguably, everyone has a duty to respect and preserve international peace and security. By making this link, the United Nations avoids complicated issues over jurisdictional competence (or at least attempts to). Comprehensive information on the obligation to provide education and on the nature of education permeate many international documents. Key provisions are found in the Convention on the Rights of the Child.

United Nations Convention on the Rights of the Child

Article 29

1. States Parties agree that the education of the child shall be directed to:

(a) The development of the child's personality, talents and mental and physical abilities to their fullest potential;

(b) The development of respect for human rights and fundamental freedoms, and for the principles enshrined in the Charter of the United Nations;

(c) The development of respect for the child's parents, his or her own cultural identity, language and values, for the national values of the country in which the child is living, the country from which he or she may originate, and for civilizations different from his or her own;

(d) The preparation of the child for responsible life in a free society, in the spirit of understanding, peace, tolerance, equality of sexes, and friendship among all peoples, ethnic, national and religious groups and persons of indigenous origin;

(e) The development of respect for the natural environment.

2. No part of the present article or article 28 shall be construed so as to interfere with the liberty of individuals and bodies to establish and direct educational institutions, subject always to the observance of the principle set forth in paragraph 1 of the present article and to the requirements that the education given in such institutions shall conform to such minimum standards as may be laid down by the State.

Question

To what extent do resource implications (Vienna Declaration) limit the nature of education as opposed to the basic provision of education?

Arguably education holds the key to the future of the human rights movement which has characterised international development in the last 50 years. Strong parallels can be drawn between the right to education and the development of respect for human dignity, the involvement of human rights in the equation strengthens this connection.

Having compared and contrasted the various provisions on education, Professor Manfred Nowak extracts four principal goals of education in accordance with international human rights.

Nowak, M, 'The Right to Education' in Eide, A, Krause, K, and Rosas, A (eds), *Economic, Social and Cultural Rights*, 2nd edn, 2001, Dordrecht: Martinus Nijhoff, pp 245–271 at p 251

Notwithstanding all the controversies about the universality of human right preceding the Vienna World Conference on Human Rights, one may conclude that there exists today at least a fairly broad universal consensus on the major aims and objectives of the right to education: a) to enable a human being freely to develop his or her personality and dignity; b) to enable a human being to actively participate in a free society in the spirit of mutual tolerance and respect for other civilisations, cultures and religions; c) to develop respect for one's parents, the national values of one's country and for the natural environment; and d) to develop respect for human rights, fundamental freedoms and the maintenance of peace.

Education is not just directed at children. Children obviously benefit from compulsory and free primary education and an evolving right to free education at subsequent levels. (Note the potential problem of university tuition fees.) Education extends to tertiary level (university) and beyond into community education and lifelong learning. As discussion enters the realm of adult learning (including universities in this), there is clearly an element of individual responsibility. It is not simply the State discharging an obligation, but rather an individual seeking educational provision. In this respect human rights education is most successful: teaching those who want to learn is easier than teaching those obliged to learn. However, this concept also places an onus on universities and further education centres to ensure that appropriate quality of education is provided.

UNESCO World Declaration on Higher Education for the Twenty-First Century 1998
Article 1—Mission to educate, to train and to undertake research

We affirm that the core missions and values of higher education, in particular the mission to contribute to the sustainable development and improvement of society as a whole, should be preserved, reinforced and further expanded, namely, to:

(a) educate highly qualified graduates and responsible citizens able to meet the needs of all sectors of human activity, by offering relevant qualifications, including professional training, which combine high-level knowledge and skills, using courses and content continually tailored to the present and future needs of society;

(b) provide opportunities (*espace ouvert*) **for higher learning and for learning throughout life,** giving to learners an optimal range of choice and a flexibility of entry and exit points within the system, as well as an opportunity for individual development and social mobility in order **to educate for citizenship and for active participation in society,** with a worldwide vision, for endogenous capacity-building, and for the consolidation of human rights, sustainable development, democracy and peace, in a context of justice;

(c) **advance, create and disseminate knowledge** through **research** and provide, as part of its service to the community, relevant expertise to assist societies in cultural, social and economic development, promoting and developing scientific and technological research as well as research in the social sciences, the humanities and the creative arts;

(d) help **understand, interpret, preserve, enhance, promote and disseminate national and regional, international and historic cultures,** in a context of cultural pluralism and diversity;

(e) help protect and enhance **societal values** by training young people in the values which form the basis of democratic citizenship and by providing critical and detached perspectives to assist in the discussion of strategic options and the reinforcement of humanistic perspectives;

(f) contribute to the development and improvement of education at all levels, including through the training of teachers.

Similarly, within Europe, the European Union and Council of Europe promulgate education grounded in cross-cultural democratic values. European bodies are particularly concerned with developing plurilingual skills and historical and cultural understanding. The work of the OSCE also impinges on this (as part of its Human Dimension). European integration and the harmonious coexistence of many small States is aided by developing appropriate education strategies underpinned by mutual tolerance and enhanced understanding of interrelated histories and cultural differences. Recommendation Rec (2000) 24 of the Committee of Ministers on the Development of European Studies for Democratic Citizenship.

The United Nations has recently concluded its Decade for Human Rights Education (ended December 2004) and now launched a World Programme for Human Rights Education. The rationale underpinning this initiative has partly the need to develop awareness of human rights. Generating an awareness of human rights clearly empowers individuals to call their State to account for violations and effects, over time, a cultural shift towards promotion and respect of norms of international human rights law.

Perhaps that is the final frontier for human rights—creating an environment in which all human beings can and do learn of their 'birthright' of human rights. With knowledge comes empowerment (as the Millennium Declaration and multiple United Nations declarations enforce). With empowerment comes the possibility of grass-roots activism and non-governmental organisations influencing State authorities. Thereafter, consumerism ethics can influence global business and corporations themselves may elect to acknowledge, at least in part, basic human rights standards. All of the foregoing should help to affect a cultural shift towards respect for human rights. There are many problems with individuals passively waiting for the State to conform to international and regional norms. There is a limit to the power of international and regional organisations as regards enforcement of international human rights (see Chapters 5, 6 and 9). Accordingly, it is perhaps reasonable to extend to non-State actors (individuals, non-governmental organisations and multi-national corporations) the opportunity to embrace, claim and develop international human rights. They can best exploit the opportunities presented by National Institutions (see Chapter 7), and can bring a State to account nationally and, if applicable (see Chapters 5 and 6) internationally. If the international and regional systems along with States cannot be relied on to secure human rights, alternative avenues of reinforcing the message of human rights must be employed.

FURTHER READING

Alfredsson, G, 'The Right to Human Rights Education' in Eide, A, Krause, K, and Rosas, A (eds), *Economic, Social and Cultural Rights*, 2001, 2nd edn, Dordrecht: Martinus Nijhoff, pp 273–288

Alston, P (ed), *Non-State Actors and Human Rights*, 2005, Oxford: OUP

Arajarvi, P, 'Article 26' in Alfredsson, G, and Eide, A (eds), *The Universal Declaration of Human Rights, a common standard of achievement*, 1999, the Hague: Kluwer, pp 551–574

Backer, L, 'Human Rights and Legal Education in the Western Hemisphere: Legal Parochialism and Hollow Universalism' (2002) 21 Penn State International Law Review 115

Baxi, U, 'Human Rights Education: the Promise of the Third Millennium' in Andreopoulos, G, and Claude, R (eds), *Human Rights Education for the Twenty-first Century*, 1997, Philadelphia: University of Pennsylvania Press

Baxi, U, 'Human Rights Education' in Smith, RKM, and Van Den Anker, C (eds), *The Essentials of Human Rights*, 2005, London: Hodder Arnold, pp 159–162

Breed, L, 'Regulating our 21st-Century Ambassadors: A New Approach to Liability for Human Rights Violations Abroad' (2002) 42 Virginia Journal of International Law 1005

Breen, C, 'The role of NGOs in the formulation of and compliance with the Optional Protocol to the Convention on the Rights of the Child on Involvement of Children in Armed Conflict' (2003) 25.2 Human Rights Quarterly 453

Carey, H, and Richmond, O, *Mitigating Conflict: the role of NGOs*, 2003, London: Frank Cass

Crick, B, et al. *Education for citizenship and the teaching of democracy in schools*, Final report of the Advisory Group on Citizenship, 1998, London: QCA

Joseph, S, 'Pharmaceutical Corporations and Access to drugs: the "Fourth Wave" of Corporate Human Rights Scrutiny' (2003) 25.2 Human Rights Quarterly 425

Josselin, D, and Wallace, W (eds), *Non-State Actors in World Politics*, 2001, London: Palgrave

Korey, W, *NGOs and the Universal Declaration of Human Rights*, New York: Palgrave

Kuper, A, *Global Responsibilities: Who Must Deliver on Human Rights*, 2005, London: Taylor and Francis

Lillich, R, 'The Teaching of International Human Rights Law in US Law Schools' (1983) 77 American Journal of International Law 855

Macleod, S, and Parkinson, J (eds), *Global Governance and the Quest for Justice: Corporations, Governance and Globalisation,* 2005, Oxford: Hart Publishing

Monshipouri, M, Welch, C, and Kennedy, E, 'Multinational Corporations and the Ethics of Global Responsibility: problems and possibilities' (2003) 25.4 Human Rights Quarterly 965

Muntarbhorn, V, 'Education for Human Rights' in Symonides, J (ed), *Human Rights: New Dimensions and Challenges*, 1998, Aldershot: Ashgate/ Dartmouth/ UNESCO, pp 281–301

Murray, R, and Wheatley, S, 'Groups and the African Charter on Human and Peoples' Rights' (2003) 25.1 Human Rights Quarterly 213

Nowak, M, 'The Right to Education' in Eide, A, Krause, K, and Rosas, A (eds), *Economic, Social and Cultural Rights,* 2001, 2nd edn, Dordrecht: Martinus Nijhoff, pp 245–271

Nowak, M, 'Prioritising Human Rights Education and Training' (2004) 3 European Human Rights Law Review 235

Pasternak, S, 'The International Legal Obligation to Teach Worldism in US Classrooms' (1999) 10 Indiana International and Comparative Law Review 51

Poullaos, I, 'The Nature of the Beast: Using the Alien Tort Claims Act to Combat International Human Rights Violations' (2002) 80 Washington University Law Quarterly 327

Steiner, H, 'The University's Critical Role in the Human Rights Movement' (2002) 15 Harvard Human Rights Journal 317

Stone, A, 'Human Rights Education and Public Policy in the United States: Mapping the Road Ahead' (2002) 24 Human Rights Quarterly 537

Tomasevski, K, *Human rights in education as prerequisite for human rights education*, 2001, Right to Education Primers 4, Lund: Raoul Wallenberg Institute

Tomasevski, K, *Report on the right to education by the Special Rapporteur* (2004) UN Doc. E/CN.4/2004/45

United Nations Office of the High Commissioner for Human Rights, *Human Rights Defenders: Protecting the Right to Defend Human Rights*, Fact Sheet No. 29, 2004, Geneva: OHCHR

United Nations, *Plan of Action for the United Nations Decade for Human Rights Education 1995–2004: Human rights education—lessons for life* (1996), UN. Doc. A/51/506/ Add.1, Appendix, 12 December 1996

UNESCO, *World Declaration on Higher Education for the Twenty-first Century 1998: Vision and Action*, 1998, Paris: UNESCO

Van Tujil, P, 'NGOs and human rights: sources of justice and democracy' (1999) 52(2) Journal of International Affairs 493

Weiss, T, and Gordenker, L (eds) *NGOs, the UN and Global Governance*, 1996 Boulder: Lynne Rienner

Websites

Information on Non-Governmental Organisations appears in Chapter 1.

www.unglobalcompact.org—The United Nations' Global Compact

www.unhchr.ch/business.htm—Office of the High Commissioner for Human Rights: Business and Human Rights: A Progress Report

www.ilo.org—The International Labour Organisation

www.oecd.org—The Organisation for Economic Cooperation and Development

amnesty.org.uk/business—Amnesty International UK Business Group

www.right-to-education.org—the website of the former United Nations Rapporteur on education, Katarina Tomasevski

www.unesco.org—UNESCO's portal with various instruments on education

www.europa.eu.int—The European Union's portal with links to its social policy and law provisions.

CHAPTER 9

REFORMING THE INTERNATIONAL AND REGIONAL HUMAN RIGHTS SYSTEMS

Many issues preventing the full realisation of human rights have been identified in the preceding chapters. Problems prevail at the regional as well as international levels. Inevitably, the very nature of international law exercises a restraint on developing a system of effectively implemented and protected human rights. Considerable advancements have been made over the last 50 years: the evolution of a permanent court within the structure of the Council of Europe has exerted a strong influence over the development of human rights not only in Europe, but also in the other regional systems; the expansion in ratified treaties under the United Nations system has led to increased human rights protection (at least on paper); and the continual rise in popular awareness of human rights has contributed towards the development of a human rights global culture. However, realising international human rights remains beset by problems as recognised by the Vienna World Conference.

Vienna Programme of Action 1993

17. The World Conference on Human Rights recognises the necessity for a continuing adaptation of the United Nations human rights machinery to the current and future needs in the promotion and protection of human rights, as reflected in the present Declaration and within the framework of a balanced and sustainable development for all people. In particular, the United Nations human rights organs should improve their coordination, efficiency and effectiveness.

More than a decade later, the need to improve the coordination, effectiveness and efficiency of the United Nations human rights organs remains an issue high on the international agenda. The importance of ensuring an effective functioning human rights system is self-evident.

Bayefsky, A, *The UN Human Rights Treaty System: Universality at the Crossroads*, 2001, Transnational: NY (pbk)/ Kluwer: the Hague (hbk), online from www.bayefsky.com/tree.php/id/9250

If rights are not followed by remedies, and standards have little to do with reality, then the rule of law is at risk. The extent of the shortfalls in the implementation of the treaties now threatens the integrity of the international legal regime. Ratification for a very large number of participants in the treaty system has become an end in itself. The large numbers of ratifications reflect the widely-held view by states parties that there are not serious consequences associated with ratification. The price of joining has generally been appearing relatively infrequently, before a small number of individuals, in comparatively remote sites in Geneva and New York, for a brief period of time taken up by frequent monologues by state representatives or committee members. Many states parties ratified precisely because the international scheme was evidently dysfunctional and the lack of democratic institutions at home made the likelihood of national consequences comfortably remote.

Considerable impetus has been given to calls for reform by the High-level Panel on Threats, Challenges and Changes whose report the Secretary-General transmitted to the General Assembly during its 59th session in December 2004. Kofi Annan opined that the report 'offers the United Nations a unique opportunity to refashion and renew our institutions'. Human rights issues formed but a tiny fraction of the report. However, it was followed by the Secretary-General's own report *In larger freedom, towards development, security and human rights for all*, UN Doc. A/59/2005. The report was directed towards the meeting of the heads of State in September 2005 which reviewed progress towards the Millennium Declaration. Many of the matters raised were on the agenda of the General Assembly for its December 2005 meeting.

This chapter will focus on two distinct processes: first, overall reform of the United Nations and its human rights monitoring system and second, the processes currently underway to improve the treaty monitoring bodies (conventional mechanisms) operating under the auspices of the United Nations. Progress towards the latter is ongoing, the former is more extensive and many of the reforms proposed will address the issues raised in the latter section. Finally, some additional comments will be made as to the current and pending regional reforms.

9.1   THE BIGGER PICTURE—HUMAN RIGHTS AND UNITED NATIONS REFORM

The present Secretary-General, Kofi Annan, has long been a proponent of change within the United Nations Organisation. (He will be succeeded by Ban Ki-Moon on 1 January 2007.) He has undertaken a number of initiatives aimed at reforming the organisation and increasing its efficiency.

United Nations Millennium Declaration

1. We, heads of State and Government, have gathered at United Nations Headquarters in New York from 6 to 8 September 2000, at the dawn of a new millennium, to reaffirm our faith in the Organization and its Charter as indispensable foundations of a more peaceful, prosperous and just world.

2. We recognize that, in addition to our separate responsibilities to our individual societies, we have a collective responsibility to uphold the principles of human dignity, equality and equity at the global level. As leaders we have a duty therefore to all the world's people, especially the most vulnerable and, in particular, the children of the world, to whom the future belongs.

3. We reaffirm our commitment to the purposes and principles of the Charter of the United Nations, which have proved timeless and universal. Indeed, their relevance and capacity to inspire have increased, as nations and peoples have become increasingly interconnected and interdependent.

4. We are determined to establish a just and lasting peace all over the world in accordance with the purposes and principles of the Charter. We rededicate ourselves to support all efforts to uphold the sovereign equality of all States, respect for their territorial integrity and political independence, resolution of disputes by peaceful means and in conformity with the principles of justice and international law, the right to self-determination of peoples which remain under colonial domination and foreign occupation, non-interference in the internal affairs of States, respect for human rights and fundamental freedoms, respect for the equal rights of all without distinction as to race, sex, language or religion and international cooperation in solving international problems of an economic, social, cultural or humanitarian character.

5. We believe that the central challenge we face today is to ensure that globalization becomes a positive force for all the world's people. For while globalization offers great opportunities, at present its benefits are very unevenly shared, while its costs are unevenly distributed. We recognize that developing countries and countries with economies in transition face special difficulties in responding to this central challenge. Thus, only through broad and sustained efforts to create a shared future, based upon our common humanity in all its diversity, can globalization be made fully inclusive and equitable. These efforts must include policies and measures, at the global level, which correspond to the needs of developing countries and economies in transition and are formulated and implemented with their effective participation.

The prevalence of conflict, the impact of the US 'War on Terror' in Iraq, Afghanistan and indeed the US itself, unprecedented (in recent times) natural disasters and a political climate which appears to recognise that the world is changing and an appropriate response is necessary. These combined to prompt the work of the Secretary-General in his report *In larger freedom, towards development, security and human rights for all*, UN Doc. A/59/2005.

In larger freedom, towards development, security and human rights for all, UN Doc. A/59/2005

154. Clearly our Organization, as an organization, was built for a different era. Equally clearly, not all our current practices are adapted to the needs of today. That is why Heads of State and Government, in the Millennium Declaration, recognized the need to strengthen the United Nations to make it a more effective instrument for pursuing their priorities.

155. Indeed, ever since I took office as Secretary-General in 1997, one of my main priorities has been to reform the internal structures and culture of the United Nations to make the Organization more useful to its Member States and to the world's peoples. And much has been achieved. Today, the Organization's structures are more streamlined, its working methods more effective and its various programmes better coordinated, and it has developed working partnerships in many areas with civil society and the private sector. In the economic and social spheres, the Millennium Development Goals now serve as a common policy framework for the entire United Nations system, and indeed for the broader international development community. United Nations peacekeeping missions today are much better designed than they used to be, and have a more integrated understanding of the many different tasks involved in preventing a recurrence of fighting and laying the foundations of lasting peace. And we have built strategic partnerships with a wide range of non-State actors who have an important contribution to make to global security, prosperity and freedom.

156. But many more changes are needed. As things stand now, different governance structures for the many parts of the system, overlapping mandates and mandates that reflect earlier rather than current priorities all combine to hobble our effectiveness. It is essential to give managers real authority so that they can fully align the system's activities with the goals endorsed by Member States—which I hope will be those outlined in the present report. We must also do more to professionalize the Secretariat and to hold its staff and management more rigorously accountable for their performance. And we need to ensure greater coherence, both among the various United Nations representatives and activities in each country and in the wider United Nations system, particularly in the economic and social fields.

157. But reform, if it is to be effective, cannot be confined to the executive branch. It is time to breathe new life also into the intergovernmental organs of the United Nations.

This report builds upon the Millennium Declaration, striving to create the blueprint for an organisation responsive to the needs of States in the twenty-first century and capable of realising the millennium goals. Kofi Annan also notes that the Charter of the United Nations has only been amended twice in the 60 years of the United Nations' operation: to enlarge membership of the Security Council and of the Economic and Social Council (*In larger freedom* at para 216).

Note the challenge presented in the final paragraph of the executive summary.

In larger freedom, towards development, security and human rights for all, UN Doc. A/59/2005, executive summary, second, third and last paragraphs

Events since the Millennium Declaration demand that consensus be revitalized on key challenges and priorities and converted into collective action. The guiding light in doing so must be the needs and hopes of people everywhere. The world must advance the causes of security, development and human rights together, otherwise none will succeed. Humanity will not enjoy security without development, it will not enjoy development without security, and it will not enjoy either without respect for human rights.

In a world of inter-connected threats and opportunities, it is in each country's self-interest that all of these challenges are addressed effectively. Hence, the cause of larger freedom can only be advanced by broad, deep and sustained global cooperation among States. The world needs strong and capable States, effective partnerships with civil society and the private sector, and agile and effective regional and global intergovernmental institutions to mobilize and coordinate collective action. The United Nations must be reshaped in ways not previously imagined, and with a boldness and speed not previously shown.

It is for the world community to decide whether this moment of uncertainty presages wider conflict, deepening inequality and the erosion of the rule of law, or is used to renew institutions for peace, prosperity and human rights. Now is the time to act. The annex to the report lists specific items for consideration by Heads of State and Government. Action on them is possible. It is within reach. From pragmatic beginnings could emerge a visionary change of direction for the world.

Bayefsky notes that '[w]hat began as an assertion of a few, is now a global proclamation of entitlements of the victims of human rights abuse' (Bayefsky, A, *The UN Human Rights System: Universality at the Crossroads*, 2001, available online from www.bayefsky.com).

As the Secretary-General notes, the world in the twenty-first century has a massive head start in realising respect for human dignity and the rule of law (see e.g. para 129). Moreover, human rights are of fundamental importance to the world today.

Kofi Annan, In larger freedom, towards development, security and human rights for all, UN Doc. A/59/2005

17. We will not enjoy development without security, we will not enjoy security without development, and we will not enjoy either without respect for human rights.

140. Human Rights are as fundamental to the poor as to the rich, and their protection is as important to the security and prosperity of the developed world as it is to that of the developing world. It would be a mistake to treat human rights as though they were a trade-off to be made between human rights and such goals as security or development. We only weaken our hand in fighting the horrors of extreme poverty or terrorism if, in our efforts to do so, we deny the very human rights that these scourges take away from citizens. Strategies based on the protection of human rights are vital for both our moral standing and the practical effectiveness of our actions.

141. Since its establishment, the United Nations has committed itself to striving for a world of peace and justice grounded in universal respect for human rights—a mission reaffirmed five years ago by the Millennium Declaration. But the system for protecting human rights at the international level is today under considerable strain. Change is needed if the United Nations is to sustain long-term, high-level engagement on human rights issues, across the range of the Organization's work.

9.1.1 Office of the High Commissioner for Human Rights

As noted in Chapter 4/5, the Office of the High Commissioner for Human Rights was established in 1993. Successive High Commissioners have made significant inroads into developing human rights although the Office of the High Commissioner receives only 1.8 per cent of the United Nations budget (A/59/2005/Annex, at page 3). More resources are thus a key concern.

The view of the Secretary-General is as follows:

Kofi Annan, In larger freedom, towards development, security and human rights for all, UN Doc. A/59/2005

144. The increasing frequency of the Security Council's invitations to the High Commissioner to brief it on specific situations shows that there is now a greater awareness of the need to take human rights into account in resolutions on peace and security. **The High Commissioner must play a more active role in the deliberations of the Security Council and of the proposed Peacebuilding Commission, with emphasis on the implementation of relevant provisions in Security Council resolutions.** Indeed, human rights must be incorporated into decision-making and discussion throughout the work of the Organization. The concept of 'mainstreaming' human rights has gained greater attention in recent years, but it has still not been adequately reflected in key policy and resource decisions.

145. These observations all point to the need to strengthen the Office of the High Commissioner for Human Rights. While the role of the High Commissioner has expanded in the areas of crisis response, national human rights capacity-building, support for the Millennium Development Goals and conflict prevention, her Office remains woefully ill-equipped to respond to the broad range of human rights challenges facing the international community. **Member States' proclaimed commitment to human rights must be matched by resources to strengthen the Office's ability to discharge its vital mandate. I have asked the High Commissioner to submit a plan of action within 60 days.**

146. The High Commissioner and her Office need to be involved in the whole spectrum of United Nations activities. But this can only work if the intergovernmental foundations of our human rights machinery are strong. In section V below, therefore, I shall make a proposal to transform the body which should be the central pillar of the United Nations human rights system—the Commission on Human Rights.

The High Commissioner herself (Louise Arbour) had the opportunity to respond to these comments in her plan of action submitted to the Secretary-General and General Assembly.

Plan of Action submitted by the United Nations High Commissioner for Human Rights, UN Doc. A/59/2005/Add.3, annex

70. Priority areas will be reviewed periodically to ensure that OHCHR is equipped to address emerging human rights challenges. The policy and planning unit being established, as described below, will assist us in priority-setting.

78. Despite repeated pledges as to the indivisibility of human rights and the need for the United Nations to pay due attention to all human rights, economic, social and cultural rights are still questioned by some, including regarding their justiciability—as seen in the discussions to create a procedure for hearing individual complaints of violations of the rights spelled out in the International Covenant on Economic, Social and Cultural Rights. These rights still enjoy a lesser status in law in most countries. Some believe that the principle of progressive realization of these rights creates special difficulties regarding accountability. The Committee on Economic, Social and Cultural Rights and many of the special procedures have addressed the legal issues involved and, over the past few years, have added much to our understanding of the scope and content of economic, social and cultural rights. Much work remains to be done, however, including in convincing often sceptical publics and Governments that human rights truly are interdependent and indivisible. . . .

81. Concerning conflict prevention, much of the existing United Nations human rights information could be used more extensively in United Nations preventive diplomacy. Information alone will be insufficient, however. The task is to ensure that it is analysed and brought to the

attention of those with a responsibility to act. One clear implication of greater OHCHR country engagement is that the Office will be much better equipped to anticipate looming human rights crises and to highlight the human rights implications of unfolding crises.

82. OHCHR needs to increase its capacity to contribute expert legal and policy input on human rights matters to conflict resolution efforts. Increasingly, OHCHR is called upon to assist countries emerging from conflict and periods of widespread abuse, including through procedures to uncover the truth about what happened, to investigate and verify massive human rights violations, to vet public officials and to reform and rehabilitate the justice system. To these ends, OHCHR will increase efforts with a host of partners, pursuing complementary action within peace missions, United Nations country teams and United Nations Headquarters-based policy and coordination bodies. Addressing impunity and the crimes of the past figure prominently, but there are many other human rights issues that need to be considered in order to build a sustainable peace. In addition, an expanded OHCHR field presence may itself help to create conflict resolution opportunities since engagements with belligerents on human rights issues create space for discussion of political issues.

83. In these areas, there is a clear need for OHCHR to expand its capacity, including especially in its New York Office, so as to ensure that it provides an effective input into both country and thematic issues.

In order to meet the challenges presented by a reformed United Nations, the Millennium Declaration and increased focus on making human rights protection a reality worldwide, the High Commissioner claims a need for significant strengthening of the management and planning capacity of the Office, supported naturally by an increase in resources.

Plan of Action submitted by the United Nations High Commissioner for Human Rights, UN Doc. A/59/2005/Add.3, annex

116. OHCHR is currently in the process of strengthening its management capacity, as elaborated in the budget proposals that I have recently made for the biennium 2006–2007. These will have to be further reviewed and strengthened if we are to deliver on the plans and commitments outlined in the present plan of action. We will need to improve our capacity to prioritize, plan and implement our work better in order to ensure effective delivery and greater accountability.

118. In order to enhance its capacity to support the human rights programme and to facilitate rapid deployment, OHCHR will require greater operational flexibility through a series of measures, including broader delegation of authority in financial and administrative matters. Its current authority, limited to initiating administrative actions, should gradually evolve towards an authority to approve and implement all such actions, applying the same procedures which have been successfully used by other United Nations departments and offices. As a first step, the following delegation of authority will be sought: establishment of an account to be accessed for emergency response purposes; acceptance of contributions; approval of allotments and temporary posts (against extrabudgetary contributions); authority for recruitment and administration of staff; emergency travel; and procurement. At the same time, new administrative policies will be developed to respond to the expanded operational needs of OHCHR, along the lines of those established by operational United Nations funds and programmes.

120. Achieving geographical balance in OHCHR will remain one of the priorities of the High Commissioner. While the primary consideration in the selection of staff is the need to secure the highest standards of competence, integrity and efficiency, OHCHR will also pay due regard to recruiting and selecting individuals on as wide a geographical basis as possible. In an effort to widen the pool of qualified human rights candidates, it will continue to work with the Office of Human Resources Management to organize specialized competitive human rights examinations, and successful candidates from underrepresented countries will be carefully considered.

122. Finally, numerous evaluations and studies have pointed to the need for OHCHR to ensure better linkages between its field presences and Headquarters, and in this regard a policy to encourage staff rotation has been under discussion for some time. Such a policy would increase the pool of specialized human rights staff willing and available for field deployment and raise the overall proportion of human rights staff with field experience. Enhancing field presence, as suggested in the present plan of action, should proceed with such a policy in place.

123. The location of OHCHR, away from Headquarters, presents certain obstacles to ensuring human rights issues are at the core of the Organization's work. Most core United Nations departments and agencies are headquartered in New York, and the Executive Committees and their sub-bodies convene in New York, as does the Security Council, the General Assembly and its committees and the Economic and Social Council. Further, most of the United Nations policy discussions on matters of peace, security and development take place in New York. The New York Office of OHCHR is actively engaged in these discussions, but its staffing has remained constant for some time while demands have continued to grow. The current round of reforms will again significantly expand the Office's New York-based work, bringing a heightened profile for human rights in the United Nations system, an expediting of the human rights mainstreaming imperative and, as seems likely, a Peacebuilding Commission and its support office. Meeting those demands will require that OHCHR in New York be equipped with a higher proportion of human and financial resources.

124. If the promotion and protection of human rights are to be at the core of the work of the United Nations, there must be a commitment to the providing of resources that are commensurate to the task. There is much that OHCHR can do in the immediate term to advance the objectives outlined in the present plan of action and it intends to take those steps, looking at how best it can utilize existing resources.

With respect to resources, the High Commissioner estimates a need to double finance in the next five to six years (at para 126). Significant consequences arise for the United Nations and member States from such a dramatic increase in funding.

Question

Consider the various issues arising with respect to funding, especially the implications for other areas of UN activity and assess the arguments for increasing human rights funding. Note that peacekeeping, development and nation building all represent growing and pressing demands on the scant resources of the United Nations.

Perhaps unsurprisingly, the High Commissioner considers engagement and dialogue with member States of key importance to ensuring the implementation of human rights. The following action points are identified in her response to the Secretary-General's *In larger freedom* report.

Plan of Action submitted by the United Nations High Commissioner for Human Rights, UN Doc. A/59/2005/Add.3, annex

127. Engagement and dialogue with countries will be the primary means through which OHCHR works to ensure the implementation of human rights. In particular:

- Geographic desks at headquarters will be strengthened through a substantial increase in staffing levels

- OHCHR will increasingly deploy staff in the field in country, regional and subregional offices, as required and on the basis of an analysis of deployment options now under way

- A rapid response capacity to deploy human rights officers at short notice will be developed, including identification, predeployment training, and rostering

- OHCHR will enhance its expertise to provide legal and technical advice and support for fact-finding missions and commissions of inquiry

- OHCHR is reviewing its support for human rights components in United Nations peace operations with a view to making it more effective and increasing its capacity to provide advice and training to their civilian police and military components.

128. The OHCHR technical cooperation programme will be strengthened and focused and implemented on the basis of a clear strategy agreed with the Government, OHCHR presence in the country and long-term engagement, and the participation of civil society.

129. All country engagement work will include dedicated attention to economic, social and cultural rights. OHCHR will increase work to protect these rights through law and we will consolidate an expert resource capacity on their legal aspects in OHCHR.

130. OHCHR will consolidate and further develop thematic human rights expertise, ensure its integration with OHCHR country work and periodically review priorities. On the basis of an inventory of all existing mandated studies and reports to United Nations bodies, we will make suggestions on rationalization to release research capacity.

131. The work of the treaty bodies and special procedures will be fully integrated into OHCHR dialogue and engagement with countries.

132. OHCHR will create a unit to lead on legal advocacy and advice on international human rights law, including on compliance and law reform at the national level.

133. OHCHR will allocate appropriate resources to meet the increasing demand for its rule-of-law work, including for support for system-wide rule-of-law and justice initiatives.

Question

Consider the obvious advantages for the treaty monitoring bodies in this plan. To what extent can the High Commissioner advance the work of the treaty monitoring bodies at the country level—what kind of activities could achieve this goal?

9.1.2   Human Rights Bodies

Kofi Annan, In larger freedom, towards development, security and human rights for all, UN Doc. A/59/2005

147. But the human rights treaty bodies, too, need to be much more effective and more responsive to violations of the rights that they are mandated to uphold. The treaty body system remains little known; is compromised by the failure of many States to report on time if at all, as well as the duplication of reporting requirements; and is weakened further by poor implementation of recommendations. **Harmonized guidelines on reporting to all treaty bodies should be finalized and implemented so that these bodies can function as a unified system.**

A number of measures reforming the treaty monitoring bodies are ongoing—these are discussed in more detail below.

As always, with any reform of the treaty monitoring bodies, finance is a key concern. The provision of additional resources for the Office of the High Commissioner for Human Rights has already been discussed; the need for further funding of the human rights treaty monitoring bodies is beyond question. This issue was also highlighted some time ago by the Independent Expert on enhancing the long-term effectiveness of the United Nations human rights system. He commented that his report was predicated on the following facts.

Report of the Independent Expert on Enhancing the Long-Term Effectiveness of the UN Human Rights Treaty System, Final Report E/CN.4/1997/74 (1997)

9. The present report is based upon several premises. The first is that the basic assumptions of the treaty supervisory system are sound and remain entirely valid. In other words, the principle of holding States accountable for non-compliance with their treaty obligations by means of an objective and constructive dialogue, on the basis of comprehensive information and inputs from all interested parties, has been vindicated in practice and has the potential to be an important and effective means by which to promote respect for human rights. The potential contribution that it can make has not in any way been superseded by other approaches or mechanisms that have been created. The second premise is that considerable achievements have been recorded by all of the treaty bodies in recent years, although there has been significant unevenness in that regard. The third is that progress, both in improving the quality and effectiveness of monitoring and in reforming the procedures and institutions, is inevitably a gradual process and there are no 'miracle cures' to be found.

10. The fourth premise is that the present system is unsustainable and that significant reforms will be required if the overall regime is to achieve its objectives. This is a function of several developments including the immense expansion of the human rights treaty system in a period of less than two decades, the expanding reach and increasing demands of regional human rights systems, the proliferation of reporting obligations in other contexts, especially in the environmental field, and the increasing pressures upon Governments and the United Nations system to reduce their budgetary outlays and streamline their programmes. The treaty bodies cannot, and nor should they seek to, remain immune to these pressures.

11. Indeed, predictions as to likely future levels of resource availability are critical to any assessment of what needs to be done in relation to the treaty system. While firm predictions are difficult at best, there is very little cause to think that there will be a dramatic increase in existing resource levels in the years ahead. In part this is a reflection of global budgetary pressures and their impact on the United Nations as a whole. But, more significantly, it reflects the perhaps inevitable, although nonetheless short-sighted and regrettable, reluctance of Governments to provide adequate resources for the development of mechanisms which might be able to monitor their human rights performance more effectively.

12. In many respects, this is the key issue both for those who are persuaded of the need to reform the system and for those who are not. In considering the future of the treaty supervisory system, much depends upon the assumptions that are made as to the future availability of resources. If it is assumed that, over time, even if not in the immediate future, considerably more resources will be made available, then the focus should be upon seeking to perfect, or at least improve, the system in the form in which it is currently developing. But if the assumption is that the existing level of funding is unlikely to be increased in the years ahead, then the current system is simply not sustainable and we will witness a steady diminution in the support available to each treaty body and in the ability of each to function in a meaningful way.

9.1.3   Proposing a Human Rights Council

From a human rights perspective, the most radical of the reform proposals related to the cessation of the Commission on Human Rights and the creation of a new Council, a Human Rights Council. Such a recommendation reflects the increased importance of human rights within the international community as there could be only three Councils within the UN framework: the Security Council, the Economic and Social Council and the Human Rights Council. Effectively it represents an increase in status for human rights as a Council would occupy a considerably higher place in the hierarchy than a Commission.

In larger freedom, towards development, security and human rights for all, UN Doc. A/59/2005

165. Its founders endowed the United Nations with three Councils, each having major responsibilities in its own area: the Security Council, the Economic and Social Council and the Trusteeship Council. Over time, the division of responsibilities between them has become less and less balanced: the Security Council has increasingly asserted its authority and, especially since the end of the cold war, has enjoyed greater unity of purpose among its permanent members but has seen that authority questioned on the grounds that its composition is anachronistic or insufficiently representative; the Economic and Social Council has been too often relegated to the margins of global economic and social governance; and the Trusteeship Council, having successfully carried out its functions, is now reduced to a purely formal existence.

166. I believe we need to restore the balance, with three Councils covering respectively, (a) international peace and security, (b) economic and social issues, and (c) human rights, the promotion of which has been one of the purposes of the Organization from its beginnings but now clearly requires more effective operational structures. These Councils together should have the task of driving forward the agenda that emerges from summit and other conferences of Member States, and should be the global forms in which the issues of security, development and justice can be properly addressed. The first two Councils, of course, already exist but need to be strengthened. The third requires a far-reaching overhaul and upgrading of our existing human rights machinery.

Creating a Human Rights Council strengthens the role of human rights within the United Nations, giving it credibility and recognition which was probably not conceivable at the establishment of the United Nations 60 years ago in an era before any universal declarations and conventions on a wide range of human rights existed.

In larger freedom, towards development, security and human rights for all, UN Doc. A/59/2005

183. If the United Nations is to meet the expectations of men and women everywhere—and indeed, if the Organization is to take the cause of human rights as seriously as those of security and development—then Member States should agree to replace the Commission on Human Rights with a smaller standing Human Rights Council. Member States would need to decide if they want the Human Rights Council to be a principal organ of the United Nations or a subsidiary body of the General Assembly, but in either case its members would be elected directly by the General Assembly by a two-thirds majority of members present and voting. The creation of the Council would accord human rights a more authoritative position, corresponding to the primacy of human rights in the Charter of the United Nations. Member States should determine the composition of the Council and the term of office of its members. Those elected to the Council should undertake to abide by the highest human rights standards.

Question

To what extent has the global community and its approach to human rights changed in the last 60 years? Are the changes sufficient to justify such an elevation of the position of human rights?

The work of the Commission had been criticised by the Secretary-General's High-level Panel on Threats, Challenges and Change: *A More Secure World: our shared responsibility* 2004.

'A more secure world: our shared responsibility' Report of the High-level Panel on Threats, Challenges and Change, UN Doc. A/59/565

282. One of the central missions of the United Nations is to protect human rights, a mission reaffirmed by the Millennium Declaration. The Commission on Human Rights is entrusted with promoting respect for human rights globally, fostering international cooperation in human rights,

responding to violations in specific countries and assisting countries in building their human rights capacity.

283. In recent years, the Commission's capacity to perform these tasks has been undermined by eroding credibility and professionalism. Standard-setting to reinforce human rights cannot be performed by States that lack a demonstrated commitment to their promotion and protection. We are concerned that in recent years States have sought membership of the Commission not to strengthen human rights but to protect themselves against criticism or to criticize others. The Commission cannot be credible if it is seen to be maintaining double standards in addressing human rights concerns.

284. Reform of this body is therefore necessary to make the human rights system perform effectively and ensure that it better fulfils its mandate and functions. We support the recent efforts of the Secretary-General and the United Nations High Commissioner for Human Rights to ensure that human rights are integrated throughout the work of the United Nations, and to support the development of strong domestic human rights institutions, especially in countries emerging from conflict and in the fight against terrorism. Member States should provide full support to the Secretary-General and the High Commissioner in these efforts.

285. In many ways, the most difficult and sensitive issue relating to the Commission on Human Rights is that of membership. In recent years, the issue of which States are elected to the Commission has become a source of heated international tension, with no positive impact on human rights and a negative impact on the work of the Commission. Proposals for membership criteria have little chance of changing these dynamics and indeed risk further politicizing the issue. Rather, **we recommend that the membership of the Commission on Human Rights be expanded to universal membership**. This would underscore that all members are committed by the Charter to the promotion of human rights, and might help to focus attention back on to substantive issues rather than who is debating and voting on them.

286. In the first half of its history, the Commission was composed of heads of delegation who were key players in the human rights arena and who had the professional qualifications and experience necessary for human rights work. Since then this practice has lapsed. We believe it should be restored, and we propose that **all members of the Commission on Human Rights designate prominent and experienced human rights figures as the heads of their delegations**.

An addendum to the report contains further details on the proposed Council.

In larger freedom, towards development, security and human rights for all, UN Doc. A/59/2005, Addendum 1, Human Rights Council, Explanatory note by the Secreatry-General

1. The establishment of a Human Rights Council would reflect in concrete terms the increasing importance being placed on human rights in our collective rhetoric. The upgrading of the Commission on Human Rights into a full-fledged Council would raise human rights to the priority accorded to it in the Charter of the United Nations. Such a structure would offer architectural and conceptual clarity, since the United Nations already has Councils that deal with two other main purposes—security and development.

2. The Commission on Human Rights in its current form has some notable strengths and a proud history, but its ability to perform its tasks has been overtaken by new needs and undermined by the politicization of its sessions and the selectivity of its work. A new Human Rights Council would help serve to overcome some growing problems—of perception and in substance—associated with the Commission, allowing for thorough reassessment of the effectiveness of United Nations intergovernmental machinery in addressing human rights concerns.

4. The Human Rights Council would be **a standing body**, able to meet regularly and at any time to deal with imminent crises and allow for timely and in-depth consideration of human rights issues. Moving human rights discussions beyond the politically charged six-week session would

also allow more time for substantive follow-up on the implementation of decisions and resolutions. Being **elected by the entire membership of the General Assembly** would make members more accountable and the body more representative. And being elected directly by the General Assembly—the principal United Nations legislative body—would also have greater authority than the Commission, which is a subsidiary body of the Economic and Social Council. Indeed, according to the Charter, responsibility for discharging the functions under the Economic and Social Council, including the promotion of human rights, is ultimately vested in the General Assembly. **A smaller membership** would allow the Human Rights Council to have more focused debate and discussions.

5. The Secretary-General believes that the Human Rights Council should be **located in Geneva**, allowing it to continue to work in close cooperation with the Office of the United Nations High Commissioner for Human Rights. The World Food Council (1974–1995) represents a precedent for a standing Council established by the General Assembly sitting outside New York. Similarly, the International Court of Justice at the Hague represents a principal Charter body located outside New York. While based in Geneva, as a standing body the Council would have the flexibility to 'enhance' its presence in New York. Options would include holding special sessions in New York or having specific subcomponents based in New York so as to better interface with the General Assembly, the Security Council and the Economic and Social Council.

6. The Secretary-General further elaborated on a proposed new key **peer review function** for the Human Rights Council in a speech to the Commission on Human Rights on 7 April 2005:

'It should have an explicitly defined function as a chamber of peer review. Its main task would be to evaluate the fulfilment by all States of all their human rights obligations. This would give concrete expression to the principle that human rights are universal and indivisible. Equal attention will have to be given to civil, political, economic, social and cultural rights, as well as the right to development. And it should be equipped to give technical assistance to States and policy advice to States and United Nations bodies alike. Under such a system, every Member State could come up for review on a periodic basis. Any such rotation should not, however, impede the Council from dealing with any massive and gross violations that might occur. Indeed, the Council will have to be able to bring urgent crises to the attention of the world community.'

7. The peer review mechanism would complement but would not replace reporting procedures under human rights treaties. The latter arise from legal commitments and involve close scrutiny of law, regulations and practice with regard to specific provisions of those treaties by independent expert panels. They result in specific and authoritative recommendations for action. Peer review would be a process whereby States voluntarily enter into discussion regarding human rights issues in their respective countries, and would be based on the obligations and responsibilities to promote and protect those rights arising under the Charter and as given expression in the Universal Declaration of Human Rights. Implementation of findings should be developed as a cooperative venture, with assistance given to States in developing their capacities.

8. Crucial to peer review is the notion of universal scrutiny, that is, that the performance of all Member States in regard to all human rights commitments should be subject to assessment by other States. The peer review would help avoid, to the extent possible, the politicization and selectivity that are hallmarks of the Commission's existing system. It should touch upon the entire spectrum of human rights, namely, civil, political, economic, social and cultural rights. The Human Rights Council will need to ensure that it develops a system of peer review that is fair, transparent and workable, whereby States are reviewed against the same criteria. A fair system will require agreement on the quality and quantity of information used as the reference point for the review. In that regard, the Office of the High Commissioner could play a central role in compiling such information and ensuring a comprehensive and balanced approach to all human rights. The findings of the peer reviews of the Human Rights Council would help the international community

better provide technical assistance and policy advice. Furthermore, it would help keep elected members accountable for their human rights commitments.

Question

Do these proposals adequately provide for a neutral, effective and proactive body capable of advancing and developing the human rights agenda in the new millennium?

The United Nations High Commissioner submitted a plan of action to the General Assembly addressing the issues raised in the Secretary-General's report. She is broadly supportive of the plan to upgrade the Commission to Human Rights Council and makes the following points:

Plan of Action submitted by the United Nations High Commissioner for Human Rights, UN Doc. A/59/2005/Add.3, annex

1. Commission on Human Rights

90. The Secretary-General has proposed the replacement of the Commission on Human Rights by an upgraded Human Rights Council. As this is under active discussion, the High Commissioner wishes to use this opportunity to set out a few points.

91. It is essential that a new body find effective means to carry out its supervisory responsibilities, which will necessarily entail some system for measuring States' human rights obligations against their actual practice. The present system for country scrutiny in the Commission is, all agree, unsatisfactory. At the same time, there must be some system in place for considering the actual human rights situation in countries.

92. For this reason, I strongly support the proposal that country scrutiny be exercised through a system of peer review, whether in a new Human Rights Council or a reformed Commission on Human Rights. This system should be built on the principle of universal scrutiny, whereby all States submit to a review of law and practice concerning their human rights obligations. For such a system to be credible and gain the confidence of all, it will be essential that a fair and transparent method be developed to compile information upon which to base the peer review. As the Secretary-General has emphasized, a new Human Rights Council should also continue the practice of the Commission regarding access for non-governmental organizations and preserve the independent role of the special procedures.

93. It is difficult for OHCHR to speculate in detail how the creation of a Human Rights Council would impact on our work since so many of the details concerning the scope, power and composition of the body are still under discussion. Certainly, a standing body that would be able to meet regularly throughout the year, although a welcome development, would also place new demands on OHCHR and we would need the capacity to respond. The precise details of the peer review will need to be worked out, and in particular it will be important to distinguish a system of peer review by other States from reporting to expert treaty bodies.

94. With respect to either a new Human Rights Council or the Commission on Human Rights, OHCHR intends to step up its efforts to play a more active role, in a spirit of partnership, in identifying means of strengthening efforts to protect human rights.

The exact relationship between the bodies was the subject of much debate. The General Assembly, the Security Council, the International Court of Justice and the Economic and Social Council will remain principal organs of the United Nations. The option for the Human Rights Council is either to be a separate principal organ as befits a Council of the United Nations or to be established as a subsidiary to the United Nations General Assembly.

9.1.4   The Human Rights Council

By General Assembly Resolution 60/251, the Human Rights Council was created. Its composition and powers are discussed in Chapter 4. As was noted earlier, the Council is a subsidiary body to the General Assembly, enjoying a higher status than its predecessor, a functional commission of the Economic and Social Council. The status of the Council is subject to review thus it may in time become a full principal organ of the United Nations.

The Human Rights Council reports directly to the General Assembly. It also assumes most powers of the Commission on Human Rights. The power of the Council to conduct universal human rights reviews is interesting and has potentially far-reaching consequences for States (Resolution 60/251 at para 5(e)). This system now operates alongside the review processes undertaken by the treaty monitoring bodies and the complaints procedure of the former Commission.

Perhaps the final words on the reform process should be those of Kofi Annan:

In larger freedom, towards development, security and human rights for all, UN Doc. A/59/2005

220. At no time in human history have the fates of every woman, man and child been so inter-twined across the globe. We are united both by moral imperatives and by objective interests. We can build a world in larger freedom—but to do it we must find common ground and sustain collective action. This task can seem daunting, and it is easy to descend into generalities or stray into areas of such deep disagreement that differences are reinforced not overcome.

221. Yet it is for us to decide whether this moment of uncertainty presages wider conflict, deepening inequality and the erosion of the rule of law, or is used to renew our common institutions for peace, prosperity and human rights. Now is the time to act. Enough words and good intentions: in the present report I have largely limited myself to the decisions that I believe are both needed and achievable in 2005 . . .

222. To make the right choice, leaders will need what United States President Franklin D. Roosevelt, whose vision was so central to the founding of the United Nations, called 'the courage to fulfil [their] responsibilities in an admittedly imperfect world'. They will also need the wisdom to transcend their differences. Given firm, clear-sighted leadership, both within States and among them, I am confident that they can. I am also certain that they must. What I have called for here is possible. It is within reach. From pragmatic beginnings could emerge a visionary change of direction in our world. That is our opportunity and our challenge.

9.2   ONGOING REFORM OF UNITED NATIONS TREATY MONITORING BODIES

Although the current proposals represent a dramatic overhauling of the fabric of the United Nations, other reform agendas have influenced the protection and advancement of human rights within the United Nations. Indeed, initiatives have been ongoing for a considerable time with the aim of streamlining and rendering more effective the treaty monitoring system.

As part of the Agenda for Change for the twenty-first century and part of the United Nations Secretary-General's process for rendering more effective human rights, attention has focused on ways in which certain key problems can be countered:

- Backlog of State reports
- Overlapping obligations/coexistence of monitoring systems

- Delays/non-submission of reports
- Follow-up mechanisms to ensure compliance.

The contemporary review perhaps can be dated to the appointment of Professor Philip Alston pursuant to General Assembly Resolution 43/115, 8 December 1988 and Commission on Human Rights Resolution 1989/47, 6 March 1989. This appointment followed a report of a meeting of the various chairs of the human rights treaty monitoring bodies.

Two interim reports were submitted—the first can be found in UN Doc. A/44/668 (1989), updated for submission to the World Conference on Human Rights in Vienna in 1993, UN Doc. A/CONF/157/PC/62/Add.11/Rev.1. The final report was submitted to the 53rd session of the Commission on Human Rights in 1997: UN Doc. E/CN.4/1997/74. The Commission asked the Secretary-General to solicit the views of States and other interested bodies on the study and report to the Commission on the enhancement of the human rights treaty system (see UN Doc. E/CN.4/1998/85 and UN Doc. E/CN.4/2000/98).

9.2.1   Evaluating the effectiveness of the United Nations' mechanisms approach evinced in the Alston report

The Independent Expert addresses the approach adopted in the report and the rationale behind it.

Report of Independent Expert, UN Doc. A/44/668

A. Mandate

1. The focus of the present study is on long-term approaches to enhancing the effective operation of existing and prospective bodies established under United Nations human rights instruments. Its preparation was entrusted by the Secretary-General to an independent expert in accordance with paragraph 15 (a) of General Assembly resolution 43/115 of 8 December 1988, which requested a study on possible long-term approaches to the supervision of new instruments on human rights, and paragraph 5 of Commission on Human Rights resolution 1989/47, which requested a study on possible long-term approaches to enhancing the effective operation of existing and prospective bodies established under United Nations human rights instruments. In accordance with those resolutions, the present study is being submitted to the General Assembly at its forty-fourth session and the Commission on Human Rights at its forty-sixth session.

2. The immediate impetus for the study was a recommendation made to the General Assembly by the meeting of persons chairing the human rights treaty bodies, which took place at Geneva from 10 to 14 October 1988 (A/44/98, para. 84). In preparing the study the expert was requested to take into account the conclusions and recommendations of that meeting. In addition account has been taken of recent discussions held under relevant agenda items in the General Assembly, the Economic and Social Council, the Commission on Human Rights and the Sub-Commission on Prevention of Discrimination and Protection of Minorities. Extensive reference has also been made to the reports of the various United Nations human rights treaty bodies and to a range of other relevant literature.

B. Approach adopted

3. It may reasonably be assumed that the present study has been entrusted to an independent expert in order to facilitate the task of addressing some of the more difficult and far-reaching issues raised by the problems currently facing the human rights treaty bodies as well as some of those which may reasonably be expected to arise over the next decade or so. Moreover, the quest

for enhanced effectiveness inevitably requires consideration of issues on which no consensus may immediately be discernible. An expert study is thus a useful means by which to shed further light on issues that require continuing reflection and debate. It may also be an appropriate mechanism for dealing with issues relating to the functioning of a diverse and somewhat disparate range of bodies that are not subject to the overall authority of any one body and that do not fit easily into any particular organizational structure or hierarchy.

4. The present study deals with a variety of issues raised in discussions within the relevant United Nations organs and in the deliberations of the treaty bodies themselves. It does not, however, purport to be comprehensive or to deal with each of the issues exhaustively.

5. In preparing the study, the author kept two rather different objectives in mind. The first was to place the issues in their wider context and to stimulate reflection on approaches that, in the short term, may seem impracticable or even unnecessary but, in the long term, may be unavoidable. Given the centrality of the treaty bodies within the global human rights régime and the speed at which the environment in which they are operating is changing, it is essential to undertake such long-term analysis at some point and it is clear that the General Assembly and the Commission on Human Rights are the bodies best situated to do so. Thus, while some of the issues raised here may not be of immediate and pressing concern, they must nevertheless be factored into any overall analysis today if the human rights régime is to be made both more effective and more efficient tomorrow.

6. The second objective of the study is to present an overview and analysis of a number of issues that are of very immediate concern and have a direct bearing on the effective functioning of the existing treaty bodies. An indication of those issues emerges very clearly from recent resolutions adopted by the General Assembly and the Commission on Human Rights as well as from the problems identified by the 1988 meeting of persons chairing the human rights treaty bodies (see A/44/98). They include the following.

(a) The persistence of financial arrangements that do not guarantee that treaty bodies can meet regularly and as scheduled;

(b) The growing burden imposed on many States by the expansion and overlapping of reporting obligations;

(c) Excessive delays by some States parties in the submission of their reports;

(d) The difficulties confronted by the treaty bodies in seeking to induce the relevant States to submit their overdue reports;

(e) The problem of inadequate reports;

(f) Insufficient resources to enable the treaty bodies to function effectively;

(g) The inability of the secretariat, for reasons of inadequate staffing levels, to provide the treaty bodies with the administrative and technical support they require;

(h) The need for more innovative procedures if the less well endowed treaty bodies in particular are to function effectively;

(i) Concern that the creation of additional treaty bodies will exacerbate existing problems.

7. It has been suggested that all of this adds up to a crisis situation and that there is an 'impending deadlock affecting international procedures for monitoring compliance with United Nations human rights conventions' (A/C. 3/43/5, p. 6). Other commentators have conceded that United Nations 'bodies dealing with human rights . . . need to be reorganized on the basis of . . . new thinking'. Similarly, a member of the Human Rights Committee has recently warned that 'there comes a critical moment in the life of successful international institutions, a moment at which they can go forward or begin to disintegrate. And among all the generous words [praising the achievements of the Human Rights Committee] I see dangers for the International Covenant on Civil and Political Right'.

8. Whatever terms may be used to characterize the present situation, however, it is generally agreed that the United Nations human rights treaty monitoring system has reached a critical crossroads. Its successful future evolution demands that the gravity of existing problems be recognized, that the vital importance of the treaty régime as a whole be reaffirmed and that the quest for creative and effective solutions be pursued with energy and commitment. By the same token, that quest must not be embarked upon without acknowledging the very considerable achievements to date and the importance of proceeding with sensitivity and sophistication in order to ensure that the fundamental integrity of the system, and particularly its ability to safeguard human rights, are not sacrificed to illusory notions of streamlining and efficiency. In other words, a time of crisis or challenge should also be seen as a time of opportunity for constructive reform and improvement. . . .

35. In the following review of some of the dimensions of the current problems it would seem appropriate to bear in mind two factors. The first is that the reporting system, for all its shortcomings or weaknesses, has developed very rapidly in less than two decades and that it has, in a number of respects, surpassed the expectations that might reasonably have been held out for it originally. Thus, the principles underlying the system remain valid. What is required is not a sweeping overhaul but a systematic endeavour to respond to changing circumstances. The second factor is that there is evidence to support the existence of a positive correlation between the efficiency and effectiveness of reporting systems and the extent to which States parties take their reporting obligations seriously. The most important implications of this proposition are that the treaty bodies themselves can play an important part in resolving some of the existing problems and that one of the best ways of doing so is to demonstrate that the results achieved by the process justify the efforts made by States parties to comply fully with their obligations. Seen from a different angle, this also implies that any measures designed to make the system more effective by being less demanding may well be counterproductive.

9.2.1.1 Other reports

Other reports by non-governmental organisations, academics and United Nations staff have also focused on the need for reform of the UN Human Rights mechanisms and offered proposals therefore. A variety of reports are available through, for example, http://www.bayefsky.com

9.2.1.2 Backlog of State reports

As Chapter 6 notes, States Parties to the various core international human rights instruments are required to submit periodic reports to the relevant committee for review. The reports are examined and the State has the opportunity to send representatives to the Committee in question. Shortly after the Committee meets, it produces (and publishes) its concluding observations on the report of the State, noting the level of compliance with the treaty and highlighting areas requiring redress. Given the remarkable increase in the membership of the United Nations and the resultant increase in parties to the main human rights treaties, it is perhaps inevitable that a backlog would accrue.

Some steps have already been taken to address this problem, notably in increases in membership of certain Committees (eg the Committee on the Elimination of All Forms of Discrimination against Women) and in increasing the frequency and duration of meetings (for example the Committee on the Rights of the Child). Moreover, many Committees now issue lists of issues for discussion in advance of their sessions—States are thus forewarned of the principal areas which will be under discussion and some can submit written observations on these before the hearing. The lists of issues allow for a targeted focus. The support provided by the Office of the High Commissioner for Human Rights is invaluable, as United Nations 'civil servants' often assist in reading State reports/communications and undertaking any necessary background research, thereby helping to maximise the use of available time by the Committee when in session. However, in some respects the system was simply not created to cope with the volume of reports and States Parties of the twenty-first century.

Fifteenth meeting of Chairpersons of the human rights treaty bodies Geneva, 23–27 June 2003, Items 4, 5 and 6 of the provisional agenda, UN Doc. HRI/MC/2003/2 5 June 2003

Consideration of reports and multiple chambers

5. At its twenty-seventh session in June 2002, the Committee on the Elimination of Discrimination against Women revised its methods of work regarding the consideration of periodic reports. Questions posed by members are clustered in accordance with the four substantive sections of the relevant Convention, and the State party is given an opportunity to respond to questions asked after each cluster. The Committee also set a time limit of five minutes per intervention per expert and a time limit for the presentation of the report by the State party (45 minutes for initial reports and 30 minutes for periodic reports). At the same session, the Committee also adopted revised guidelines on reporting by States parties which called for concise reports and set a page limit of 100 pages for initial reports and 70 pages for periodic reports (see HRI/GEN/2/Rev.1/Add.1).

6. The Human Rights Committee decided from its seventy-fifth session in July 2002 to introduce Country Report Task Forces in order to increase the effectiveness and efficiency of the Committee in preparing the written lists of issues and to improve the quality of the dialogue between the Committee and the State party under review. The Country Report Task Force consists of four to six members, who are responsible for formulating the list of issues, taking the lead in conducting the dialogue with the State party and, as necessary, assisting the Special Rapporteur on follow-up to concluding observations.

7. The Committee on the Rights of the Child, as a result of the increase in its membership (see Section V, part B), has discussed the possibility of examining State party reports in multiple chambers. The Committee of 18 members met for the first time in May 2003 at the Committee's thirty-third session. Noting that, prior to the increase of its membership, the Committee had recommended convening in two parallel chambers to review reports as a means of addressing the backlog of reports awaiting review, the Chairperson distributed a discussion paper summarizing previous discussions on working methods as a basis for further dialogue.

8. The paper focused on the feasibility of working in parallel chambers, and included specific ideas for the elaboration of procedural rules, indicating that, by meeting in two chambers for five sessions, the Committee could increase its consideration of States parties' reports from 45 to 80 during the same period. It was noted that this would be of particular significance as the submission of initial reports of States parties under the Convention's two optional protocols is expected in early 2004.

The problem is not unique to the international committees. Indeed a significant backlog of cases pending accrued before the European Court of Human Rights which prompted Protocol 11 to the European Convention on Human Rights. Even establishing a permanent court operating through chambers and committees has failed to make significant inroads into the backlog before the European Court. Further reforms are thus ongoing—see below.

9.2.2   Overlapping obligations/coexistence of monitoring systems

Backlogs accrue across the spectrum of treaty monitoring bodies. The coexistence of reporting systems has been identified as a key problem for the United Nations.

Report of Independent Expert, UN Doc. A/44/668

36. It has been suggested with increasing frequency in recent years that one of the most signifi-cant problems facing States parties is the cumulative impact of the demands placed upon them for reporting on human rights matters. While the focus of the present study is limited in scope, it should be noted that such problems of proliferation are by no means limited to the human rights field. 17/

37. The problem of proliferating requests for human rights reports is a multifaceted one. Viewed from the perspective of a specific State, requests may emanate from any or all of the following sources: (a) United Nations treaty bodies; (b) United Nations policy-making organs and most notably the Commission on Human Rights and the Sub-Commission on Prevention of Discrimin-ation and Protection of Minorities and their respective subsidiary bodies; (c) specialized agencies and in particular ILO and UNESCO; (d) regional human rights treaty bodies; and (e) regional human rights policy-making organs. A variety of other, less formally institutionalized sources of requests for information could also be cited. Some of the non-treaty-based procedures are in effect quite formal. An example is the procedures for the effective implementation of the Stand-ard Minimum Rules for the Treatment of Prisoners, adopted by the Economic and Social Council in its resolution 1984/47 and endorsed by the General Assembly in resolution 39/118 of 14 December 1984. Under those procedures, Governments are requested, *inter alia*, to respond to the Secretary-General's periodic inquiries on the implementation of the Rules and on difficulties encountered. In addition, new proposals for similar procedures relating to non-binding standards continue to be made in various contexts. An example is the drafting of a declaration on the rights of indigenous populations in connection with which the need for an effective implementation mechanism has frequently been stressed in the Working Group on Indigenous Populations.

38. The cumulative burden of these various procedures (each of which is no doubt easily justifi-able in its own right) is also greatly exacerbated by the fact that States which have ratified the International Covenants on Human Rights also tend to have a significantly higher rate of adher-ence to human rights treaties generally than do those which have not. In the present context, it need hardly be said that there is a fundamental difference between reporting obligations under-taken by virtue of treaty ratification (or accession) and requests for reports that emanate from other sources. Nevertheless, this difference might not always be uppermost in the minds of those national officials who are inundated with requests for information. Thus, one means by which to reduce the overall pressure placed upon the responsible authorities at the national level would to be seek to reduce or rationalize the number of *ad hoc* requests for information generated by the policy-making organs. In that regard, it may be that greater use should be made by the latter of information provided to the treaty bodies (assuming, of course, that States which are not parties to the relevant treaties would still be asked to provide the information required).

39. In general terms, three measures have been identified with a view to reducing the consider-able reporting burden already borne by many States. The first is to extend the periodicity of reporting. This has been done directly by the Committee on Economic, Social and Cultural Rights, which has moved from a three-year to a five-year cycle (although the five-yearly reports are to be comprehensive, whereas each of the three-yearly reports dealt only with one third of the sub-stantive articles in Part III of the Covenant). In addition, the Committee on the Elimination of Racial Discrimination has also eased the burden on States parties by introducing, in August 1988, a revised system providing for the submission of comprehensive reports every four years (instead of two years) with brief update reports to be submitted in the interval. Furthermore, at its forty-fifth session, the Commission on Human Rights approved a recommendation made by the Group of Three requesting the States parties to the Convention against *Apartheid* to submit their

periodic reports at four-year intervals, on the understanding that they may submit additional information to the Group at any time in the intervening period. As a result of these changes the periodicity under all of the instruments has become closely co-ordinated. Reporting under the two Covenants is now required at five-year intervals and under each of the other four conventions at four-year intervals.

Bayefsky recommends streamlining the treaty monitoring process.

A significant problem caused by the burgeoning number of human rights instruments and the growing pressure towards universal ratification is that States find themselves bound to the same right in several different instruments. Accordingly States can find the same conduct or law being considered by several different committees. There is obviously some potential for different results as the Committees may focus on certain issues to the partial exclusion of others. Similarly, States refraining from ratifying an instrument on account of specific rights contained in that treaty may find that they are in fact already bound to the provision through a different instrument. The most obvious example of this is the Convention on the Rights of the Child which has achieved almost universal ratification (all United Nations member States bar Somalia and the United States of America). Few rights found in other instruments are not also found in the Convention on the Rights of the Child.

Report of Independent Expert, UN Doc. A/44/668

44. The problem of overlapping competences among the various treaty bodies is an inevitable consequence of the approach adopted by the United Nations compared to that of, for example, the Council of Europe. While the latter started with a single core treaty (the European Convention on Human Rights) and has subsequently expanded its scope by adding concentric circles around the core, the United Nations chose instead to supplement its two principal Covenants with a series of independent and increasingly narrowly focused instruments dealing in more detail, or with greater specificity, with issues that, to a significant extent, are also dealt with in the Covenants. Moreover, since each instrument is designed so that a State could become a party to it without necessarily being a party to any of the other treaties and since each treaty body is entirely separate from the others, overlapping competences are effectively ensured.

45. The nature and extent of the problem are best illustrated by taking an example. Many different rights could be used for the purpose but the right to freedom of association is probably as good as any. The right is recognized in five of the six treaties covered by the present study. It is also contained in each of the draft conventions dealing with the rights of the child and of migrant workers respectively. Moreover, the two principal ILO Conventions dealing with that right have (as at 1 January 1989) been ratified by 99 States (in the case of Convention No. 87 of 1948 on Freedom of Association and Protection of the Right to Organize) and 115 States (in the case of Convention No. 98 of 1949 on the Right to Organize and Collective Bargaining). Thus any State that is a party to all or most of these treaties is obligated to submit periodic reports under each and every one of them detailing the situation with respect to, inter alia, the right to freedom of Association.

46. The principle of non-discrimination is dealt with by an even larger number of treaties and gives rise to even more complex questions relating to the overlapping competences of different treaty bodies. Some indication of the overall extent of overlapping among the six United Nations treaty bodies is provided by an analysis undertaken by the Secretary-General (E/C.12/1989/3) in response to a request by the Committee on Economic, Social and Cultural Rights, endorsed by the Economic and Social Council in its resolution 1988/4, that a report be prepared 'showing clearly the extent and nature of any overlapping of issues dealt with in the principal human rights treaties, with a view to reducing, as appropriate, duplication in the different supervisory bodies of issues raised with respect to any given State party'.

Chapter 1 contains a table of the rights in the International Bill of Rights, the Convention on the Rights of the Child and the major regional instruments. Consider the table below which draws together the obligations under all seven of the core international (United Nations) instruments. Note that absolute accuracy has given way to space considerations thus the chart is indicative and representative only. Once again those rights and freedoms in the Universal Declaration are taken as a standard tabulation of rights. The instruments are as follows:

ICERD: International Convention on the Elimination of all forms of Racial Discrimination

ICCPR: International Covenant on Civil and Political Rights

ICESCR: International Covenant on Economic, Social and Cultural Rights

CEDAW: Convention on the Elimination of All Forms of Discrimination against Women

CAT: Convention against Torture

CRC: United Nations Convention on the Rights of the Child

CMW: Convention on the Rights of Migrant Workers.

Right/freedom (UDHR)	ICERD	ICCPR	ICESCR	CEDAW	CAT	CRC	CMW
Non-discrimination	(X)	X	X	(X)		X	X
Life and liberty	X	X				X	X
Slavery		X		X			X
Torture	X	X			X	X	X
Equal before the law	X	X		X		X	X
Effective national remedy	X				X		
Arbitrary arrest and detention	(X)	X				X	X
Fair trial	(X)	X				X	X
Presumption innocence		X				X	X
Non-retrospective crimes							X
Private and family life		X		X		X	X
Freedom of movement	X	X				X	X
Asylum						X	
Nationality	X	X		X		X	(X)

Right/freedom	ICERD	ICCPR	ICESCR	CEDAW	CAT	CRC	CMW
Marriage and family	X	X	X	X			
Property	X			X			X
Thought conscience and religion	X	X				X	X
Opinion and expression	X	X				X	X
Assembly and association	X	X	X	(X)		X	X
Political participation	X	X		X		(X?)	
Social security ESCR	X		X	X		X	
Work	X		X	X		X	X
Rest and leisure		X				X	
Adequate standard of living, health, food etc.	X		X	X		X	
Education	X		X	X		X	X
Cultural life	X	X	X	X		X	X
Social and international order							

As regards more procedural aspects, only the Convention on the Elimination of All Forms of Discrimination against Women and the Convention on Migrant Workers and Their Families do not have provisions on derogations and public emergencies. Article 2(2) of the Convention against Torture explicitly excludes the possibility of derogations, this is unsurprising given the status of the prohibition on torture (see Chapter 1). All bar the Convention on Migrant Workers involve the adoption of national legislation to implement the provisions of each convention and the International Covenant on the Elimination of all forms of Racial Discrimination, the Convention on the Elimination of All Forms of Discrimination against Women and the Convention against Torture demand penal laws to enforce certain of their provisions.

There is clearly significant overlap in the treaty obligations undertaken by States. While this may reflect the universal nature of basic rights, it also gives rise to unique difficulties. As Tistounet notes, '[I]t is no surprise that those responsible for drafting subsequent [to the twin Covenants] human rights instruments found it more convenient to adopt new texts rather than face the challenge of convincing states parties to the Covenants to adhere to additional protocols' (Tistounet, E, 'The problem of overlapping among different treaty bodies', in Alston, P and Crawford, J (eds), *The Future of UN Human Rights Treaty Monitoring*, 2000, Cambridge: CUP, pp 383–401). Congruence between the seven core instruments is thus inevitable (see also, Alston UN Doc. A/44/668 at para 44).

9.2.2.1   Different treaties, different approaches

While co-existing treaty obligations may increase the reporting burden on States, it can also give rise to different regimes of rights and duties. For examples, States may enter reservations to a clause in one treaty but not to a similar clause in another treaty. This is particularly noticeable when a State has, for example, ratified the two International Covenants (neither has substantial numbers of reservations) and a treaty with many reservations (Convention on the Elimination of All Forms of Discrimination against Women, for example). Significant overlap in obligations between the three means that a victim may have additional avenues of complaint open.

9.2.2.2   Case study: overlapping United Nations obligations

This complaint was brought before the Human Rights Committee on the basis of rights under the International Covenant on Civil and Political Rights, particularly Arts 27, 2, 3, 23 and 26. There was clearly discrimination in that men and women were treated differently. Had it been open to the author, in other words, had there been an individual complaint mechanism in respect of the Convention on the Elimination of All Forms of Discrimination against Women and had Canada ratified it, then a complaint could have competently been brought before that body too. Would both have reached the same conclusion? In the instant case, probably yes. Of particular note, however, is the fact that the matter could still be raised before the treaty monitoring bodies in the absence of an individual communication procedure under the Convention on the Elimination of All Forms of Discrimination against Women.

Lovelace v Canada

The applicant was born and registered a Maliseet Indian. She lost her rights and status as an Indian when she married a non-Indian.

> 7.2 The Human Rights Committee recognized that the relevant provision of the Indian Act, although not legally restricting the right to marry as laid down in article 23 (2) of the Covenant, entails serious disadvantages on the part of the Indian woman who wants to marry a non-Indian man and may in fact cause her to live with her fiancé in an unmarried relationship. There is thus a question as to whether the obligation of the State party under article 23 of the Covenant with regard to the protection of the family is complied with. Moreover, since only Indian women and not Indian men are subject to these disadvantages under the Act, the question arises whether Canada complies with its commitment under articles 2 and 3 to secure the rights under the Covenant without discrimination as to sex. On the other hand, article 27 of the Covenant requires States parties to accord protection to ethnic and linguistic minorities and the Committee must give due weight to this obligation. To enable it to form an opinion on these issues, it would assist the Committee to have certain additional observations and information. . . .

> 7.4 Since the author of the communication is ethnically an Indian, some persisting effects of her loss of legal status as an Indian may, as from the entry into force of the Covenant for Canada, amount to a violation of rights protected by the Covenant. The Human Rights Committee has

been informed that persons in her situation are denied the right to live on an Indian reserve with resultant separation from the Indian community and members of their families. Such prohibition may affect rights which the Covenant guarantees in articles 12 (1), 17, 23 (1), 24 and 27. There may be other such effects of her loss of status. . . .

17. The case of Sandra Lovelace should be considered in the light of the fact that her marriage to a non-Indian has broken up. It is natural that in such a situation she wishes to return to the environment in which she was born, particularly as after the dissolution of her marriage her main cultural attachment again was to the Maliseet band. Whatever may be the merits of the Indian Act in other respects, it does not seem to the Committee that to deny Sandra Lovelace the right to reside on the reserve is reasonable, or necessary to preserve the identity of the tribe. The Committee therefore concludes that to prevent her recognition as belonging to the band is an unjustifiable denial of her rights under article 27 of the Covenant, read in the context of the other provisions referred to.

18. In view of this finding, the Committee does not consider it necessary to examine whether the same facts also show separate breaches of the other rights invoked. The specific rights most directly applicable to her situation are those under article 27 of the Covenant. The rights to choose one's residence (article 12), and the rights aimed at protecting family life and children (articles 17, 23 and 24) are only indirectly at stake in the present case. The facts of the case do not seem to require further examination under those articles. The Committee's finding of a lack of a reasonable justification for the interference with Sandra Lovelace's rights under article 27 of the Covenant also makes it unnecessary, as suggested above (para. 12), to examine the general provisions against discrimination (arts. 2, 3 and 26) in the context of the present case, and in particular to determine their bearing upon inequalities predating the coming into force of the Covenant for Canada.

Question

What reasons may there be for States failing to consistently lodge reservations when ratifying the various international human rights treaties? (see also Tistounet, E, 'The problem of overlapping among different treaty bodies' in Alston, P and Crawford, J (eds), The Future of UN Human Rights Treaty Monitoring, *2000, Cambridge: CUP pp 383–401, for a detailed discussion of this).*

9.2.2.3   Case study: regional and international

There can also be an overlap between regional and international systems. This is axiomatic, given the rights enshrined in the major regional instruments. However, there is thus an even greater potential for divergence between two bodies operating under the auspices of totally different organisations.

Fernández v Spain, Communication No. 1396/2005, UN Doc. CCPR/C/85/D/1396/2005 (November 2005)

2.1 On 13 June 2001, the author applied for membership in the General Council of the Judiciary (*Consejo General del Poder Judicial,* hereinafter referred to as the Council). The Council is the managing body of the Spanish judiciary. It is composed of 21 members, 12 of whom come from the Bench. These 12 members are designated by the Congress. On 28 June 2001, an amendment to the Law on the Judiciary modified the system for the appointment of the 12 members of the Council from the Bench. Before the entry into force of the amendment, judges could freely elect their candidates to be proposed to Congress as representatives of the Bench in the Council. After the amendment, up to 36 candidates have to be proposed by either an existing judges association, or by non-associated judges supported at least by 2% of all the judges in active service. Associated judges can only vote for candidates who belong to their respective association. Non-associated judges running for membership in the General Council, although obliged to be supported at least by 2% of all judges in service, can only seek such endorsement among non-associated judges. The law also set out that the total membership of any association of judges should remain unchanged as of 1 June 2001.

2.2 Until 12 June 2001, the author was a member of the Professional Association of Magistrates of Murcia, from which he resigned in order to present an independent candidacy, which was supported by 40 judges, none of whom belonged at that time to any of the existing judges' associations. On 18 July 2001, the President of the General Council dismissed the author's application, because it was not supported by the minimum number of endorsements required by the Law on the Judiciary (*Ley Orgánica del Poder Judicial*).

2.3 On 31 July 2001, the author appealed (*recurso contencioso-administrativo*) to the Seventh Section of the Third Chamber of the Supreme Court. On 27 September 2001, the Third Chamber dismissed the author's appeal. It considered that the General Council's prerogative to communicate to Congress a list with the names of 36 candidates for membership in the Council was preparatory in nature, and that the final decision nominating the 12 candidates to the King belonged to Congress. This prerogative of the Congress, not being a definite administrative act, could not be challenged through an appeal (*recurso contencioso-administrativo*). On 9 October 2001, the author asked the Court to reconsider its decision. He alleged violations of fair trial guarantees and that he had been discriminated. On 15 November 2001, the Chamber dismissed the appeal for reconsideration. On 27 November 2001, the author appealed (*amparo*) to the Constitutional Court. While this appeal was pending, the author withdrew the allegations related to fair trial guarantees and discrimination. On 14 November 2002, the Court dismissed the appeal.

2.4 On 19 March 2003, the author applied to the European Court of Human Rights, alleging violations of article 11 (1) (freedom of association), in conjunction with article 14 (prohibition of discrimination), article 6(1) (right to fair trial), and article 13 (right to an effective remedy), of the European Convention on Human Rights. On 11 May 2004, the Court declared the application inadmissible, since it did not reveal the appearance of any violation of any of the rights enshrined in the Convention. . . .

6.2 With regard to the alleged violation of article 22 (freedom of association), the Committee recalls its jurisprudence that article 11, paragraph 1, of the European Convention as interpreted by the European Court of Human Rights, is sufficiently proximate to article 22, paragraph 1, of the Covenant; that when the European Court based a declaration of inadmissibility not solely on procedural grounds but on reasons that include a certain consideration of the merits of the case, then the same matter should be deemed to have been 'examined' within the meaning of the respective reservations to article 5, paragraph 2 (a), of the Optional Protocol; and that the European Court should be considered to have gone beyond the examination of purely procedural admissibility criteria when declaring the application inadmissible, because it does 'not disclose any appearance of a violation of the rights and freedoms set out in the Convention or its Protocols'. The same criteria apply to the present case. The fact that article 26 of the Covenant differs from article 14 of the European Convention appears to be of no relevance in this case, because the author invoked these provisions before the respective competent bodies in relation to the right to freedom of association, which is regulated similarly under both treaties. Consequently, the Committee concludes that this part of the communication is inadmissible under article 5, paragraph 2 (a), of the Optional Protocol and the reservation of Spain to the said provision.

6.3 With regard to the alleged violations of article 14, paragraph 1, the Committee recalls it jurisprudence that a claim related to the election of members of the High Council of Justice is not related to the determination of rights and obligations in a suit at law, within the meaning of article 14, paragraph 1, and concludes that author's allegations concerning article 14 are incompatible *ratione materiae* with that provision and thus inadmissible under article 3 of the Optional Protocol.

6.4 The Human Rights Committee therefore decides:

(a) That the communication is inadmissible under articles 3 and 5, paragraph 2 (a), of the Optional Protocol;

See also *Sanders v Netherlands*, Communication No. 1193/2003 UN Doc. CCPR/C/84/D/1193/2003 (2005) and *Irschik v Austria*, Communication No. 990/2001, UN Doc. CCPR/C/80/D/990/2001 (2004). It is clear that the Human Rights Committee is not willing to encroach on the jurisdiction of the European Court of Human Rights and thus will not permit the use of the Committee as an 'appeal' from the regional court.

Question

To what extent would a hierarchy of rights' systems, with the United Nations at the apex and the regional systems thereunder be a) workable, b) realistic and c) a solution to such problems?

As noted in previous chapters, when contemplating raising a complaint, it is essential to explore all viable options, as frequently rights being protected under two or more instruments open up additional avenues to the victims of a violation.

A further issue, and of potentially greater concern, is the possibility of conflicting interpretations of a particular right by different treaty monitoring bodies! Obviously, there is a considerable degree of consistency of approach between the different bodies. Surveying the periodic reports and concluding observations of any given State to the various bodies reveals certain discrepancies, even if only in the emphasis accorded to different rights.

Question

Having regard to common rights and freedoms contained in the core instruments, in what circumstances may committees offer different advice to States?

Of course, it must be remembered that the same rights can have different meanings in different treaties. The right to self-determination is a key example. According to the Human Rights Committee, self-determination has an impact in an economic and social context which may differ from the effect in a civil and political sense. Thus the two international covenants are perhaps less mutually exclusive than consistent. To reiterate Chapter 2, human rights are indivisible and universal, thus inevitably there is some overlap and complementariness.

General Comments issued by the treaty monitoring bodies hold the same latent potential for problems. However, clearly as these are all freely available, there is less potential for conflict. Moreover, it is not so likely that the same issue will be debated and a comment issued simultaneously by two Committees.

9.2.2.4   Reform initiatives

A number of initiatives seek to address these problems. Most important has been the greater interaction between the treaty monitoring bodies. The chairs now meet regularly and consider common issues.

**Fifteenth meeting of Chairpersons of the human rights treaty bodies
Geneva, 23–27 June 2003, Items 4, 5 and 6 of the provisional agenda UN Doc.
HRI/MC/2003/2, 5 June 2003**

Collaboration between treaty bodies

16. In 2002, as a follow-up to discussions held at the preceding sessions of both Committees, and in accordance with the recommendations of the first Inter-Committee meeting, the Chairperson of the Committee on Economic, Social and Cultural Rights was invited by the Committee on the

Elimination of Discrimination against Women (CEDAW) to have consultations on issues of common concern. At its twenty-ninth session, the Committee on Economic, Social and Cultural Rights requested its Chairperson to explore CEDAW, the possibility of adopting a first joint general comment on article 3 of the Covenant on Economic, Social and Cultural Rights and article 3 of the Convention on the Elimination of all Forms of Discrimination against Women. A draft general comment was prepared by the Chairperson, taking into account relevant provisions of both treaties and submitted for consideration to CEDAW.

17. In January 2003, the Chairperson met with CEDAW during its twenty-eighth session. While welcoming efforts to foster cooperation between the two Committees, CEDAW indicated that there was a need for more careful consideration before a joint general comment was adopted. At the same time, CEDAW expressed its willingness to take advantage of other opportunities for joint work, such as in the area of technical assistance.

18. With respect to its draft General Comment on article 2 on the Nature of the General Legal Obligation imposed on States Parties to the Covenant, the Human Rights Committee has circulated the draft to other treaty bodies for comment, as has been the practice of the Committee on the Rights of the Child and the Committee on Economic, Social and Cultural rights. The draft General Comment has also been posted on the homepage of the Office of the United Nations High Commissioner for Human Rights and comments have been solicited.

19. In a letter dated 14 March 2003, the Committee against Torture has solicited suggestions from the Committee on the Rights of the Child about possible future joint general comments.

Furthermore, with greater technological capacity, it becomes ever easier for Committees to consider the reports of other bodies when determining rights and obligations of States under the various treaties.

Note the views of the Committee on Elimination of Racial Discrimination in respect of Guyana's non-submission of its periodic report (above).

Question

How helpful would it be for the Committee on the Elimination of Racial Discrimination to use the reports of a State to the Human Rights Committee and Committee on the Rights of the Child when determining compliance with the Convention by a State which has consistently failed to submit reports to the Committee on the Elimination of Racial Discrimination?

The issue of consolidating reports has also been considered in detail.

Review of the efficiency of the administrative and financial functioning of the United Nations Report of the Secretary-General on the activities of the Office of Internal Oversight Services, UN Doc. A/57/488 Agenda items 111 and 122

Management review of the Office of the United Nations High Commissioner for Human Rights

XI. Recommendations

62. The High Commissioner should pursue further the consolidation of reporting to different organs on similar or closely related topics, with oral updates on recently issued reports, as necessary, and propose enabling actions for such arrangements to the General Assembly (paras. 7–9).

63. The High Commissioner should consistently pursue consultations with the treaty bodies on the modalities for consolidating reporting under various treaty obligations into a single national report with a view to achieving a steady progress towards this goal (para. 10)

The new guidelines for consolidated State reports are considered below.

9.2.3   Delays/non-submission of reports

Obviously, State delays in submitting reports compound the problem of backlog. Moreover, States occasionally claim that the coexistence of the reporting systems (and overlapping rights) is the reason for non-submission of reports. In his final report, Alston comments that non-reporting has reached chronic proportions (UN Doc. E/CN.4/1997/74 at para 112), clearly not an improvement on the steady deterioration in recent years he noted in 1993 (UN Doc. A/CONF.157/PC/62/Add.11/Rev.1 at para 104).

Interim Report of Independent Expert, UN Doc. A/CONF.157/PC/62/Add.11/Rev.1

109. The consequences of non-reporting and of significantly overdue reports are immense. Failure to provide an initial report is particularly disturbing since it constitutes prima facie evidence that the State concerned has failed to undertake the initial comprehensive review of law, policy and practice that should enable it to identify the panoply of measures required to bring the situation into conformity with the treaty. As noted above, there are currently some 108 such initial reports overdue a good many of which are well beyond the stage of merely being delayed. Failure to produce subsequent periodic reports is also very troubling because such failure may well reflect the fact that major problems do indeed exist and that Governments are anxious to avoid a dialogue with the relevant treaty body.

110. All parties concerned suffer from a failure to report. For the treaty body the price is relatively mild, although in the longer term its credibility is inevitably diminished. In the short-term it may well be receiving a somewhat distorted picture of the situation in the world. For the State party itself, the price is much higher. Government officials may justifiably come to assume that ratification or accession to a human rights treaty is an act that brings much sought after kudos but is otherwise of little consequence. The standards contained in the treaty are unlikely to be taken seriously in the context of domestic law and policy-making if the obligation to report to the treaty body, which in many respects is one of the less onerous implications of becoming a party, is ignored. Finally, any fears on the part of non-governmental organizations or of political and other interest groups that the treaty system is toothless and even irrelevant are reinforced.

111. But perhaps the highest price is extracted from the system itself. The treaty régime must inevitably lose some of its precious credibility if a State can ostentatiously signal its acceptance of a significant range of obligations and then thumb its nose at the committee. Acceptance of such a situation also leads to a system of double standards whereby some States parties regularly subject themselves to monitoring and to the probing of the treaty bodies while others are not subjected to any such scrutiny, even though their records may be far less satisfactory. This concern led the fourth meeting of chairpersons to note 'that a persistent and long-term failure to report should not result in the State party concerned being immune from supervision while others, which had reported, were subject to careful monitoring' (A/47/628, para. 71). In effect, the failure of the treaty bodies to insist upon carrying out their monitoring responsibilities can only encourage other States parties to delay, or entirely neglect, their own reporting obligations.

Bayefsky also comments on the problem of delays in reporting, problems that are inevitable in an expanding system. Her recommendations are as follows:

Bayefsky, A, The UN Human Rights Treaty System: University at the Crossroads, 2001

The Committee should introduce a rule of procedure which requires it to deal with applications in the order in which they become ready for examination. Decisions to give priority to a particular application should be made on an exceptional basis.

Delays resulting from state party efforts to avoid prompt consideration of a case (including unjustified requests for time extensions, for separating the consideration of admissibility from the merits, repetitive submissions) should not be tolerated by committee practices. The author should be kept fully informed of all state party communications with the committee, including all efforts to delay the prompt consideration of a case.

Time limits should be more rigorously enforced. A clear timetable should be articulated for reminders for different stages of the proceedings. Consequences should be identified for failures, by either the state party or complainant, to adhere to time limits. Reminders should be sent as required. The treaty bodies should regularly be kept up-to-date on the timetable and status of each case – incorporating a 'consequence/bring forward' methodology.

The reasons for non-reporting are varied but the independent expert suggests they fall into two categories:

Final report of Independent Expert, UN Doc. E/CN.4/1997/74

43. Broadly stated, there are two reasons why States do not report: administrative incapacity including a lack of specialist expertise or lack of political will, or a combination of both. In the first situation, repeated appeals are, almost by definition, unlikely to bear fruit. Instead, the solution lies in a more serious, more expert and more carefully targeted advisory services programme in relation to reporting. This is discussed briefly below.

44. In the second situation, a lack of political will translates essentially into a calculation by the State concerned that the consequences, both domestic and international, of a failure to report are less important than the costs, administrative and political, of complying with reporting obligations. In that case, the only viable approach on the part of the treaty bodies and/or the political organs is to seek to raise the 'costs' of non-compliance. A failure to devise appropriate responses of this nature has ramifications which extend well beyond the consequences for any individual State party. Large scale non-reporting makes a mockery of the reporting system as a whole. It leads to a situation in which many States are effectively rewarded for violating their obligations while others are penalized for complying (in the sense of subjecting themselves to scrutiny by the treaty bodies), and it will lead to a situation in which a diminishing number of States will report very regularly and others will almost never do so.

To the World Conference on Human Rights, Alston suggested four steps to address the problem (UN Doc. A/CONF.157/PC/62/Add.11/Rev.1 at paras 113–122):

(1) Providing advisory services to States parties whose reports are more than two years overdue

(2) States must be examined by the Committees even if they fail to submit reports

(3) Naming and shaming of States Parties whose reports are long overdue

(4) Provision of a positive incentive for States to report by virtue of additional technical services.

Note, however, Alston's comments on the impact of non-submissions and its relevance to the issue of backlog.

Alston Final Report, UN Doc. E/CN.4/1997/74

48. The present supervisory system can function only because of the large scale delinquency of States which either do not report at all, or report long after the due date. This is hardly a satisfactory foundation upon which to build an effective and efficient monitoring system. Thus, for example, the Committee on the Elimination of Discrimination against Women noted in its 1994 annual report (A/49/38, para. 12) that if States parties reported on schedule it would need to consider 30 reports per session.

9.2.3.1 Responding to the situation

Many of these issues have already been addressed. The following extract demonstrates some of the advancements made.

Fifteenth meeting of Chairpersons of the human rights treaty bodies Geneva, 23–27 June 2003, Items 4, 5 and 6 of the provisional agenda UN Doc. HRI/MC/2003/2, 5 June 2003

Measures to encourage reporting

13. In May 2002, the Committee on the Rights of the Child began applying a procedure for dealing with long overdue reports. In cases where an initial report is nine years overdue, the Committee sends a letter of reminder to the State party requesting the submission of its report within the following year, indicating that if this report is not submitted, the country situation will be considered on the basis of available information and in the absence of a report. Six letters of reminder have been sent out, and in three cases the report has been submitted. Three States parties have been scheduled for examination in the absence of a report, during the thirty-seventh session of the Committee in September 2004.

14. At its twenty-seventh session in June 2002, the Committee on the Elimination of Discrimination against Women adopted recommendations regarding incremental measures to encourage reporting. These include, *inter alia*, systematic reporting reminders, informal meetings between the Bureau and non-reporting States parties either individually or on a regional basis, and closed meetings between the Committee and representatives of individual non-reporting States parties.

15. In addition, as part of its strategy to encourage States parties to report, the Committee has requested the Division for the Advancement of Women to prepare for its twenty-ninth session in July 2003 an analysis of non-reporting States parties in order to facilitate the Committee's consideration of the root causes of non-reporting. The issue of non-reporting was also raised during the Committee's informal meeting with States parties in June 2002.

Question

Refer back to Chapter 6 which provides some examples of the Committees considering State situations in the absence of a report. Consult the relevant parts of the www.ohchr.org website and note how frequently (or otherwise) States submit reports following the threat of consideration of a State situation in absentia.

9.2.4   Follow-up mechanisms to ensure compliance

Clearly, the benefits of the reporting mechanism and even the individual communications procedure (where applicable) are undermined when there is little or no follow-up. Within Europe (see below) the most recent reforms propose to strengthen the follow-up mechanisms for judgments of the European Court of Human Rights. Note, however, the concerns expressed by Australia in response to the Secretary-General's review of the report on enhancing the long-term effectiveness of the human rights system (p 24, E/CN.4/1998/85).

Alston noted in 1993 that the treaty monitoring bodies require access to information from intergovernmental organisations, NGOs and the creation of country files in order to ensure that compliance with the main treaties can be accurately and adequately monitored (see UN Doc. A/CONF.157/PC/62/Add.11/Rev.1 at paras 207–244).

Some improvements took place during the review period.

Final report of Independent Expert, UN Doc. E/CN.4/1997/74 at para 109

109. In 1990, the Committee on Economic, Social and Cultural Rights pioneered the practice of adopting concluding observations which reflected the views of the Committee as a whole, were structured in a systematic fashion and sought to be as specific as possible. Although it was the Human Rights Committee which, in 1984, had first made use of the phrase 'concluding observations', it was not until 1992 that that Committee began to adopt collective evaluations of the report of each State. The Committee on the Elimination of Racial Discrimination followed the example in 1993. Prior to this development all of the effort required on the part of the relevant Government, the United Nations, the treaty body and other interested parties culminated in little more than a few disparate, sometimes inconsistent, observations made in the name of individual members of the committees. While the present approach thus constitutes a major step forward there is still considerable room for improvement in the quality of concluding observations, especially in terms of their clarity, degree of detail, level of accuracy and specificity. This will require, *inter alia*, a more sustained expert contribution to the process by the Secretariat. A marked improvement in the level of sophistication of concluding observations is indispensable if the reporting process is ultimately going to justify the expense and effort involved.

Bayefsky also comments on the need for improved concluding observations to provide greater guidance to States.

Bayefsky, A, *Universality at the Crossroads*, 2001

Concluding observations should be adopted in closed-session, with members uninhibited by observers.

The committee member charged with the development of an initial draft and with the incorporation of members' comments into subsequent drafts, must be willing and able to undertake the task.

Concluding observations should be released as soon as they are adopted, which may be prior to the end of the session. All the treaty bodies, including CEDAW, should release concluding observations no later than the last day of the session.

The introductory remarks of governments should not be included in concluding observations (CEDAW).

The portions of concluding observations entitled 'Positive Aspects' and 'Factors and difficulties impeding implementation' have already been highly attenuated, are generally not useful, and should be discontinued.

Concluding observations should include the following information:

(a) introductory information

- due date of the report
- submission date of the report (and symbol number)
- dates and meetings at which the report was considered
- the kind of report (additional information, special, initial, more than one report)
- names and positions of the members of the delegation which presented it
- committee's views about the composition of the delegates in terms of their positions and expertise
- whether written replies to the list of issues were submitted (symbol number)
- (if so) when written replies were submitted (as compared to the consideration of the report)
- the level of cooperation of the delegation in responding to oral questions; whether questions were left unanswered
- promises made about the future submission of information
- how the report was prepared (by whom, over what period of time, consultations held)

(b) concerns and recommendations

- the concluding observations should then proceed directly to a consideration of concerns and recommendations
- concerns should be clearly connected to recommendations
- recommendations should concentrate on concrete proposals; they should be practical and as precise as possible
- recommendations should clarify whether they relate to policies, practices, or legislation and identify them
- recommendations should be grouped thematically and provide some indication of priorities
- recommendations based on concerns about human rights violations caused by third parties should clearly indicate the treaty bodies' expectations of government action and responsibility, and the foundation of these expectations
- references to any kind of external documentation required to understand the content of recommendations should be avoided; necessary references or substantive documentation referred to should be footnoted; the recommendations should be self-explanatory

(c) concluding information

- additional information promised and/or requested
- deadlines for the submission of additional information
- plans for the dissemination of the concluding observations
- processes the state should have for the dissemination of the concluding observations
- languages into which concluding observations should be translated
- processes or structures the state party should institute for follow-up to the concluding observations; concrete proposals can be made about best practices for ongoing monitoring of the treaty's implementation (including the preparation of the next report)

All interested parties should be given the concluding observations at the same time.

Government comments or responses on concluding observations should be posted on the web and published as separate documents at the discretion of the Committee. All such submissions received should be noted in the Annual Report.

Concluding observations finalized in the absence of the participation of a state party must be preceded by a careful compilation and analysis of information from a wide variety of sources. It will sometimes be preferable in the absence of the participation of a state party to identify only 'preliminary' concluding observations, to be revisited upon full participation. (See *supra* section 3, The Consideration of a State Party's Record in the Absence of a Report.)

Note also the concerted effort of the chairs of the various United Nations human rights treaty monitoring bodies to ensure a coordinated approach to follow-up procedures.

Fifteenth meeting of Chairpersons of the human rights treaty bodies Geneva, 23–27 June 2003, Items 4, 5 and 6 of the provisional agenda UN Doc. HRI/MC/2003/2, 5 June 2003

Follow-up procedures

9. The Human Rights Committee began applying a systematic procedure to follow up concluding observations from March 2001. According to this procedure, the Committee identifies a number of priority recommendations and requests the State party to provide additional information on their implementation. Using this information and any additional information from other sources, the Committee's Special Rapporteur on follow-up to concluding observations and the country rapporteur recommend whether further action, including possible adjustment to the date on which the next report is due, is warranted.

10. Deadlines for the provision of such additional information in accordance with this procedure have fallen due for 17 States parties. Of those 17 States parties, 11 provided complete replies, 3 provided partial replies and 3 did not provide the requested information. With regards to those States that submitted partial replies, the Committee has sought a full reply before considering whether further action is warranted. Where no reply was received from the State party, action is being taken to solicit the provision of the information sought. At the conclusion of its seventy-seventh session in March 2003, the Committee had considered full replies of eight of the States parties. In each case, the Committee decided to take no further action, and thus the date provisionally set in the concluding observations for the provision of the next report became definitive.

11. At its twenty-ninth session in November 2002, the Committee on Economic, Social and Cultural Rights recalled its follow-up procedures adopted at its twenty-first session whereby the Committee may invite the State party to provide additional information on the implementation of certain recommendations prior to the date on which the next periodic report is due. The additional information is considered at the next meeting of the pre-sessional working group and based on the information provided, the Committee may choose to take note of the information, adopt supplementary concluding observations on the issues concerned, request further information or authorize the Chairperson to take up the issue at the next session with a delegation of the State party. If the additional information is not provided by the State party, the Chairperson, in consultation with the Bureau, may choose to take up the question directly with the State party. In cases where the information provided is insufficient, the Committee may also request the State party to accept a technical assistance mission by one or two members. These procedures were applied in one case during the twenty-ninth session.

12. At its thirtieth session in May 2003, the Committee against Torture initiated a practice to follow up concluding observations, similar to the follow-up procedure of the Human Rights Committee. The Committee selects, as appropriate, a number of priority concerns, and requests further information from the State party, within one year, on measures taken by the Government to implement these priority recommendations. . . .

Technical assistance

20. The Office of the High Commissioner for Human Rights (OHCHR), in cooperation with the Government of Ecuador, held the first Pilot Workshop for Dialogue on the Concluding Observations of the Human Rights Committee from 27 to 29 August 2002 in Quito. The workshop was attended by representatives of the Governments of Argentina, Costa Rica, Ecuador, Guatemala, Mexico, Peru, the Dominican Republic and Venezuela, as well as by representatives of national human rights institutions, the Inter-American Commission on Human Rights, United Nations agencies and non-governmental organizations (NGOs). The OHCHR Regional Advisor for Latin America, several members of the Human Rights Committee and members of the secretariat acted as resource persons.

21. The purpose of the workshop was to analyse the concluding observations of the Human Rights Committee with a view to strengthening follow-up measures at the national level. Issues such as obstacles to implementation, institutional arrangements and the role of civil society and national human rights institutions in following up concluding observations were discussed. Participants adopted a broad set of recommendations aimed at States parties, the Human Rights Committee, OHCHR, international bodies, national human rights institutions and NGOs. More detailed information and the conclusions of the workshop can be found in its report (HRI/TB/FU/1).

22. A similar workshop on the follow-up to concluding observations of the Committee on the Rights of the Child for three countries in the Arab region will be held in collaboration with the Government of Syria in September 2003.

In April 2003, the Division for the Advancement of Women provided technical input at a regional training workshop, held in Samoa, on reporting under the Convention on the Elimination of All

Forms of Discrimination against Women, in which nine countries participated. One CEDAW expert and one staff member from the Division for the Advancement of Women acted as resource persons.

9.2.5   Progress towards addressing these issues

Progress has been made on these original recommendations, and, indeed on some of the final recommendations. Before the submission of the final report by Alston, work was already being carried out on overlapping obligation under the different treaties and the potential for cross-referencing in both the reports and conclusions. The issue of a budget for the CAT and CERD was also examined. However, funding continues to be a problem for the United Nations and its human rights bodies. This position is unlikely to radically change in the future. To improve the actual process of examining the State reports, maximising the short time available at committee meetings, committees now prepare lists of key issues in advance, thereby providing States with an indication of areas of concern and/or interest and proposing a framework for the discussion. Committees are also more receptive to information provided by third parties—most notably NGOs. Accepting a wider range of materials can inevitably offer a more complete snapshot of the human rights situations in any given State.

One of the most significant reforms which has been undertaken, however, relates to the content and quantity of State periodic reports. Alston mooted the idea of reduced State reports.

Alston Final Report, UN Doc. E/CN.4/1997/74 at paras 53–54

53. As noted at the beginning of this report, it has been proposed by conference servicing officials in Geneva, in addressing both the seventh meeting of chairpersons and individual committees in the course of 1996, that a limit of an average of 50 pages be imposed on the length of State party reports to be processed and translated. To the extent that such a limitation would apply to processing (copy-editing, clean typing and reproduction) as well as translating, it would even eliminate the option for a committee to be prepared to consider a longer report in the original language in which it is submitted. This proposal has yet to be fully implemented but its effects are already being felt in various ways. Although it is beyond the scope of this report to address the possible implications of the proposal, two procedural matters are worthy of note since they bear on the modalities of future treaty body-related reform processes. The first is that both the chairpersons' meeting and the treaty bodies themselves have been provided with very little solid statistical information to substantiate the need for draconian measures of the type proposed. Indeed the message has, for the most part, been conveyed orally rather than in the form of a detailed written analysis which would provide a basis for careful consideration of alternative responses. The second is that the Centre for Human Rights has not provided any analysis of the alternatives that might be considered. Given the difficulty of obtaining information about the functioning of the system and the costs involved, the absence of such an analysis, or briefing paper, would seem to increase considerably the prospects for ill-informed and uncreative responses.

54. The incongruity of the proposed limitation is perhaps best illustrated by the fact that the general guidelines for the submission of periodic reports (CRC/C/58), adopted by the Committee on the Rights of the Child in October 1996, are 49 pages long. In other words, States parties would be asked to respond to 49 pages of questions and of lists of issues in relation to which information is required in the course of a report of precisely the same length. This is clearly impossible, and it is doubly so in the case of federal States which must report on the situation in relation to the different laws and practices applying in each of their constituent territories. Moreover, the suggestion that reports could be confined to 50 pages is entirely at odds with the

trend in most of the committees to request ever more precise and detailed information in order to enable the experts to obtain a clearer picture of the situation. On the other hand, two committees (the Committee against Torture and the Committee on the Elimination of Racial Discrimination) have generally managed with comparatively brief reports. This is, however, primarily a function of the more restricted nature of their focus rather than of their greater frugality.

The Chairs of the Treaty Monitoring Bodies have now agreed core guidelines for reports. The emphasis is on a single core document, common to all the treaties substantiated by a more focussed report on the treaty in question. The following is an extract therefrom.

Draft guidelines, UN Doc. HRI/GEN.2/Rev.2 (2004)

General legal framework within which human rights are protected

3. This section should contain information on:

(a) Which judicial, administrative or other competent authorities have jurisdiction affecting human rights;

(b) What remedies are available to an individual who claims that any of his rights have been violated; and what systems of compensation and rehabilitation exist for victims;

(c) Whether any of the rights referred to in the various human rights instruments are protected either in the constitution or by a separate bill of rights and, if so, what provisions are made in the constitution or bill of rights for derogations and in what circumstances;

(d) How human rights instruments are made part of the national legal system;

(e) Whether the provisions of the various human rights instruments can be invoked before, or directly enforced by, the courts, other tribunals or administrative authorities or whether they must be transformed into internal laws or administrative regulations in order to be enforced by the authorities concerned;

(f) Whether there exist any institutions or national machinery with responsibility for overseeing the implementation of human rights.

Information and publicity

4. This section should indicate whether any special efforts have been made to promote awareness among the public and the relevant authorities of the rights contained in the various human rights instruments. The topics to be addressed should include the manner and extent to which the texts of the various human rights instruments have been disseminated, whether such texts have been translated into the local language or languages, what government agencies have responsibility for preparing reports and whether they normally receive information or other inputs from external sources, and whether the contents of the reports are the subject of public debate.

Question

Are the above guidelines sufficient to address the problems discussed above?

9.3   TOWARDS UNIVERSAL RATIFICATION OF KEY INSTRUMENTS

Universal ratification of all major human rights instruments was one of the key objectives highlighted in the Vienna Programme of Action (see also Chapter 2). In theory the target year was 2003. Obviously, this deadline has passed without the achievement of universal ratification of the core instruments although there have been many notable improvements. The following table notes the number of States Parties to the major human rights instruments as of 4 September 2006.

ICCPR	ICESCR	ICERD	CEDAW	CAT	CRC	CMW
156	153	170	183	141	192	34

Note that in the case of the Convention on the Rights of the Child, additional States Parties are not members of the United Nations. This explains why there are two United Nations members (USA and Somalia) who are not parties and yet the total number of States parties exceeds the membership of the United Nations!

Given the success of the Convention on the Rights of the Child in attracting almost universal ratification, the Independent Expert on enhancing the long-term effectiveness of the United Nations human rights treaties made the following comments.

Final Report of Independent Expert, UN Doc. E.CN.4/1997/74

15. Since the Vienna Conference there has been a very significant improvement in the ratification rate of the principal treaties. On 1 January 1993 there were 678 States parties to the six treaties. By 30 June 1996 this figure had risen to 853, an increase of 175 or 26 per cent. This constitutes an impressive achievement but there is also another side to the coin which is illustrated by the fact that 31 per cent of States (59 out of 193) have not become a party to either of the two International Covenants on Human Rights, despite their centrality to the overall human rights regime.

16. Equally surprising is the fact that almost 50 per cent of States (95 out of 193) have not become parties to the Convention against Torture. When it is recalled that the Convention on the Rights of the Child contains a comprehensive prohibition against torture in the case of all persons covered by that treaty (in essence, all persons below the age of 18), it is not clear why so many States can accept that obligation but not the equivalent obligation in the Convention against Torture. Similarly, there are 36 States which have accepted the obligation not to torture under the International Covenant on Civil and Political Rights but have not yet ratified the Convention against Torture.

17. The increase in the total number of ratifications also needs to be viewed in the light of three important factors which partly account for the success. The first is that a number of new States succeeded to the treaties during this period, thus expanding the number of total ratifications but not thereby reducing the number of States which had not become parties to the various treaties by the time of the Vienna Conference. The second factor is the impact of the Fourth World Conference on Women, both before and after the event, in terms of encouraging States to ratify the Convention on the Elimination of All Forms of Discrimination against Women. Ratifications of the Convention went from 114 on 1 January 1993 to 153 on 30 June 1996, an increase of 39 States parties, or 34 per cent. The Beijing Platform for Action called for universal ratification of the Convention by the year 2000.

18. The third factor is the extraordinary success of efforts to promote ratification of the Convention on the Rights of the Child. As a result, 30 per cent of the overall increase in ratifications during this three and a half year period (53 ratifications) was attributable exclusively to that Convention, the number of States parties to which went from 134 to 187. Taken together those two conventions accounted for 92 of the new ratifications, or some 53 per cent.

19. There are some important lessons to be learned from the successes achieved in relation to the two conventions which have attracted so many new ratifications in recent years. The first concerns the importance of political will, whether expressed through the holding of international conferences which place appropriate emphasis upon the convention in question or through consistent efforts by international organizations. In contrast, the lead-up to international conferences focusing on social development (Copenhagen) and human settlements (Istanbul) saw no attention at all to efforts to promote ratification of the relevant human rights treaties. The second

lesson concerns the importance of mobilizing domestic constituencies (in this case, women's and children's non-governmental organizations) in support of the goals and mechanisms reflected in the treaty, thus making it easier for Governments to undertake ratification.

20. The third lesson, and in the case of the Convention on the Rights of the Child the most important, concerns the provision of assistance and advice by an international agency, which in this instance was the United Nations Children's Fund. Such agencies can, whenever requested, assist Governments and the principal social partners in various ways, including: by explaining the significance of the treaty as a whole and of its specific provisions; by promoting an awareness of the treaty which facilitates domestic consultations and discussions; by shedding light upon the requirements of the treaty in the event of ratification; by providing assistance to enable any necessary pre ratification measures to be identified and implemented; by assisting in relation to the preparation of reports, both indirectly through the agency's own situation analyses, and directly through the provision of expert assistance where appropriate; and by reassuring developing countries in particular that ratification should bring with it enhanced access to at least some of the expert or financial resources needed to implement key provisions of the treaty.

21. In this respect the success of the effort to promote ratification of the Convention on the Rights of the Child indicates that there is no (or at least no longer) deep-rooted resistance to the principle of participation in human rights supervisory arrangements. Given the relative comprehensiveness of the Convention, along with the integral links between respect for children's rights and those of the rest of the community, it might be thought that the reasons which had previously led various States not to ratify all six of the core human rights treaties are no longer compelling and that there will be a new openness to increased participation in the overall treaty regime. Indeed, there is something odd about a situation in which all States but four have become parties to such a far-reaching Convention while almost one State in every three has not become a party to either of the two International Covenants.

In an attempt to improve ratification levels, target dates have been adopted for several instruments. The effect of the Beijing Conference in 1995 on ratifications of the CEDAW was marked. Similar advances on CERD and MWC following Durban were aspired to. Obviously, the MWC succeeded in securing the requisite minimum number of ratifications and entered into force in July 2003.

Finally, on the matter of dissemination of materials, advances in technology have promulgated an explosion in internet sources. Not only has the OUNHCHR developed and promoted its website, a number of other bodies have established comprehensive documentation centres online.

9.4   REGIONAL REFORMS

9.4.1   Europe

The European human rights system, under the auspices of the Council of Europe, has long suffered from a backlog of caselaw, and, in many respects, the system is a victim of its own success. The following diagram demonstrates the increase in applications lodged before the court (and earlier, the Commission) (Statistics from the 2004 Council of Europe Survey of Activities). Note that the first column is the combined number of applications from 1955 until 1989!

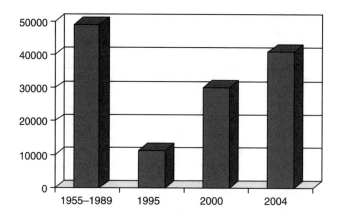

Protocol 11 altered the original two tier (Commission and Court) structure into a single permanent court with rapporteurs, committees and chambers of judges. An increase in member States, in concert with increased awareness of the Council of Europe machinery and human rights in general, has resulted in ever-escalating numbers of cases. That something had to be done was self-evident, as the increasing backlog and ensuing delays were continually undermining the efficacy of the court. The Committee of Ministers was thus charged with reviewing reform options following the 50th anniversary commemorations of the European Convention. The result is Protocol 14 (ETS 194) which was opened for signature in May 2004. It aims at ensuring the court can 'continue to play its pre-eminent role in protecting human rights in Europe' (Preamble). Only one State (Russia) has yet to ratify the protocol.

9.4.1.1   Limiting individual petitions

Article 12 of the protocol proposes an amendment to Art 35 ECHR:

Article 12

Paragraph 3 of Article 35 of the Convention shall be amended to read as follows:

'3. The Court shall declare inadmissible any individual application submitted under Article 34 if it considers that :

a. the application is incompatible with the provisions of the Convention or the Protocols thereto, manifestly ill-founded, or an abuse of the right of individual application; or

b. the applicant has not suffered a significant disadvantage, unless respect for human rights as defined in the Convention and the Protocols thereto requires an examination of the application on the merits and provided that no case may be rejected on this ground which has not been duly considered by a domestic tribunal.'

The Court exercises a supervisory function monitoring State compliance with norms of human rights. Primary responsibility for the enforcement of human rights lies with the States themselves, subject to the guidance and advice of the court.

However, this provision has proved controversial as some commentators consider it to restrict the right to individual petition, thereby undermining the very success story of the Council of Europe.

9.4.1.2 Reforming the court structure

Article 7 seeks to accelerate the decision-making process. Rather than preliminary decisions being taken by a committee of three judges, a single judge will now have jurisdiction to determine admissibility

Article 7

After the new Article 26, a new Article 27 shall be inserted into the Convention, which shall read as follows:

'Article 27—Competence of single judges
1. A single judge may declare inadmissible or strike out of the Court's list of cases an application submitted under Article 34, where such a decision can be taken without further examination.
2. The decision shall be final.
3. If the single judge does not declare an application inadmissible or strike it out, that judge shall forward it to a committee or to a Chamber for further examination.'

Logistically a court of some 45 judges, with the capacity for a number of them to sit singly, should be able to efficiently process many manifestly inadmissible applications thereby alleviating a considerable time burden otherwise imposed on the existing court formations. This could free up judicial time for addressing the backlog of cases pending.

Article 13

A new paragraph 3 shall be added at the end of Article 36 of the Convention, which shall read as follows:

'3. In all cases before a Chamber or the Grand Chamber, the Council of Europe Commissioner for Human Rights may submit written comments and take part in hearings.'

Formalising the role of the Commissioner in this respect has potentially positive repercussions.

9.4.1.3 Enforceability of judgments

Article 10 of the amending protocol gives jurisdiction to the Grand Chamber of the Court to determine, on application by the Committee of Ministers, whether a State has failed to comply with a judgment.

FURTHER READING

Alston, P, and Crawford, J (eds), *The Future of UN Human Rights Treaty Monitoring*, 2000, Cambridge: CUP

Bayefsky, A, *The UN Human Rights Treaty System: Universality at the Crossroads*, 2001, New York: Transnational (pbk)/the Hague: Kluwer (hbk), online from www.bayefsky.com/tree.php/id/9250

Douzinas, C, *The End of Human Rights*, 2000, Oxford: Hart Publishing

Eden, P, and O'Donnell, T (eds), *September 11, 2001: A Turning Point in International and Domestic Law?*, 2005, Ardsley, NY: Transnational

Symonides, J (ed), *Human Rights: International Protection, Monitoring, Enforcement*, 2003, Aldershot: Ashgate/UNESCO

Wilson, R (ed), *Human Rights in the War on Terror*, 2005, Cambridge: CUP

Websites

www.un.org/reform/—UN Reform website

www.un.org/secureworld/—Secretary-General's High Level Panel on Threats, Challenges and Change

www.un.org/millennium/—Millennium Summit

www.un.org/largerfreedom/—Secretary-General's 'In larger Freedom' reform proposals

www.un.org/summit2005/—High Level Plenary session of the General Assembly, September 2005

www.un.org/millenniumgoals/—UN Millennium goals website

www.africa-union.org—the African Union

www.echr.coe.int—the European Court of Human Rights

CHAPTER 10

PROTECTING CHILDREN

Vienna Declaration and Programme of Action Art 21

The World Conference on Human Rights, welcoming the early ratification of the Convention on the Rights of the Child by a large number of States and noting the recognition of the human rights of children in the World Declaration on the Survival, Protection and Development of Children and Plan of Action adopted by the World Summit for Children, urges universal ratification of the Convention by 1995 and its effective implementation by States Parties through the adoption of all the necessary legislative, administrative and other measures and the allocation to the maximum extent of the available resources. In all actions concerning children, non-discrimination and the best interest of the child should be primary considerations and the views of the child given due weight. National and international mechanisms and programmes should be strengthened for the defense and protection of children, in particular, the girl-child, abandoned children, street children, economically and sexually exploited children, including through child pornography, child prostitution or sale of organs, children victims of diseases including acquired immunodeficiency syndrome, refugee and displaced children, children in detention, children in armed conflict, as well as children victims of famine and drought and other emergencies. International cooperation and solidarity should be promoted to support the implementation of the Convention and the rights of the child should be a priority in the United Nations system-wide action on human rights.

The World Conference on Human Rights also stresses that the child for the full and harmonious development of his or her personality should grow up in a family environment which accordingly merits broader protection.

In the words of the 1924 Geneva Declaration on the Rights of the Child, mankind owes to the child the best it has to give. Eighty years later, the sentiment articulated by the Assembly of the League of Nations still echoes true. This chapter examines the rights of children, tracing the reasoning behind developing a distinct set of rights for them, then considers the nature and scope of those rights.

10.1   CHILDREN AS HUMANS

For children, recognition of their human rights is a two part process: first recognition that children are entitled to human rights in their own independent right (not as the property of their guardians) and second recognition that children require additional protection, protection which the international community has now developed. The first stage of this process was the adoption of the Geneva Declaration on the Rights of the Child which acknowledged the need for protection of children but stopped short of granting them rights. As a declaration, there was of course no issue of enforcement against the State. Many States still viewed children as part of their parents—there was little recognition of children enjoying their own legal, political and personal status.

The Geneva Declaration is perhaps best viewed as a statement of principle. As the chapter progresses, more rights are added to this list and the rights themselves are further elaborated.

Geneva Declaration of the Rights of the Child of 1924, adopted 26 September 1924, League of Nations OJ Spec. Supp. 21 at 43 (1924)

By the present Declaration of the Rights of the Child, commonly known as 'Declaration of Geneva', men and women of all nations, recognizing that mankind owes to the Child the best that it has to give, declare and accept it as their duty that, beyond and above all considerations of race, nationality or creed:

(1) The child must be given the means requisite for its normal development, both materially and spiritually;

(2) The child that is hungry must be fed; the child that is sick must be nursed; the child that is backward must be helped; the delinquent child must be reclaimed; and the orphan and the waif must be sheltered and succored;

(3) The child must be the first to receive relief in times of distress;

(4) The child must be put in a position to earn a livelihood, and must be protected against every form of exploitation;

(5) The child must be brought up in the consciousness that its talents must be devoted to the service of fellow men.

Question

To what extent were these obligations realisable by States in the inter-war period? To what extent does the declaration recognise that children are entitled to 'rights'?

The Declaration was subsequently endorsed by the United Nations and eventually children were accorded their own charter of rights in the form of the United Nations Convention on the Rights of the Child. Under the auspices of the International Labour Organisation, further protection for children was developed with conventions concerning night work and types of employment to which children could be subjected. Internationally there was no comparable statement (to the Declaration) on human rights. This was possibly a step too far for the international community.

Question

To what extent has the content of the Declaration lasted the test of time? Are similar rights found in the United Nations Convention on the Rights of the Child? Contrast each progressive statement of children's rights as they are discussed.

Children are entitled of course to the full range of international human rights and fundamental freedoms which are the birthright of all. Age is not a barrier to enjoyment of human rights. They are, as Chapter 2 indicated, inalienable. However, children are deemed particularly deserving of additional support and, unlike some of the groups discussed in subsequent chapters, there is almost universal corroboration of this. Even from the pre-existing human rights monitoring bodies, jurisprudence on children's issues and thus rights has emerged. The issue of corporal punishment is discussed *supra* in Chapter 1. Other examples relate to education and legal status. The European Court of Human Rights and, for example, the Human Rights Committee of the United Nations have been proactive in advancing the rights of children.

10.1.1   Why separate rights?

Inherently vulnerable for physiological reasons, children depend on others for their survival in a manner not matched by any other groups which have been accorded discrete protection (refugees, women, migrant workers, prisoners etc.). Young infants, for example, are unable to feed themselves and thus depend on others for essential nourishment and thus their survival. According to Piaget (a Swiss child development expert), children are unable to see things beyond their own perspective up until the age of five when they start to decentre. Therefore, children have no concept of the autonomy of others and thus they depend on others to protect them. Their sense of right and wrong develops from around seven years (according to Freud) and thus children require guidance up to and indeed through this stage.

Much of the international rhetoric focuses on the fact that children are the adults of the future. A somewhat idealistic and altruistic stance thus permeates international children's rights as the following preambular statements demonstrate.

Declaration of the Rights of the Child, GA Res. 1386 (XIV), 14 UN GAOR Supp. (No. 16) at 19, UN Doc. A/4354 (1959)

Whereas the peoples of the United Nations have, in the Charter, reaffirmed their faith in fundamental human rights and in the dignity and worth of the human person, and have determined to promote social progress and better standards of life in larger freedom,

Whereas the United Nations has, in the Universal Declaration of Human Rights, proclaimed that everyone is entitled to all the rights and freedoms set forth therein, without distinction of any kind, such as race, colour, sex, language, religion, political or other opinion, national or social origin, property, birth or other status,

Whereas the child, by reason of his physical and mental immaturity, needs special safeguards and care, including appropriate legal protection, before as well as after birth,

Whereas the need for such special safeguards has been stated in the Geneva Declaration of the Rights of the Child of 1924, and recognized in the Universal Declaration of Human Rights and in the statutes of specialized agencies and international organizations concerned with the welfare of children,

Whereas mankind owes to the child the best it has to give.

United Nations Convention on the Rights of the Child 1989, Preamble

The States Parties to the present Convention,

Considering that, in accordance with the principles proclaimed in the Charter of the United Nations, recognition of the inherent dignity and of the equal and inalienable rights of all members of the human family is the foundation of freedom, justice and peace in the world, . . .

Recalling that, in the Universal Declaration of Human Rights, the United Nations has proclaimed that childhood is entitled to special care and assistance,

Convinced that the family, as the fundamental group of society and the natural environment for the growth and well-being of all its members and particularly children, should be afforded the necessary protection and assistance so that it can fully assume its responsibilities within the community,

Recognizing that the child, for the full and harmonious development of his or her personality, should grow up in a family environment, in an atmosphere of happiness, love and understanding,

Considering that the child should be fully prepared to live an individual life in society, and brought up in the spirit of the ideals proclaimed in the Charter of the United Nations, and in particular in the spirit of peace, dignity, tolerance, freedom, equality and solidarity,

Bearing in mind that the need to extend particular care to the child has been stated in the Geneva Declaration of the Rights of the Child of 1924 and in the Declaration of the Rights of the Child adopted by the General Assembly on 20 November 1959 and recognized in the Universal Declaration of Human Rights, in the International Covenant on Civil and Political Rights (in particular in articles 23 and 24), in the International Covenant on Economic, Social and Cultural Rights (in particular in article 10) and in the statutes and relevant instruments of specialized agencies and international organizations concerned with the welfare of children,

Bearing in mind that, as indicated in the Declaration of the Rights of the Child, 'the child, by reason of his physical and mental immaturity, needs special safeguards and care, including appropriate legal protection, before as well as after birth',

Recalling the provisions of the Declaration on Social and Legal Principles relating to the Protection and Welfare of Children, with Special Reference to Foster Placement and Adoption Nationally and Internationally; the United Nations Standard Minimum Rules for the Administration of Juvenile Justice (The Beijing Rules); and the Declaration on the Protection of Women and Children in Emergency and Armed Conflict,

Recognizing that, in all countries in the world, there are children living in exceptionally difficult conditions, and that such children need special consideration,

Taking due account of the importance of the traditions and cultural values of each people for the protection and harmonious development of the child,

Recognizing the importance of international co-operation for improving the living conditions of children in every country, in particular in the developing countries.

African Charter on the Rights and Welfare of the Child, OAU Doc. CAB/ LEG/24.9/49 (1990)

PREAMBLE

The African Member States of the Organization of African Unity, Parties to the present Charter entitled 'African Charter on the Rights and Welfare of the Child',

CONSIDERING that the Charter of the Organization of African Unity recognizes the paramountcy of Human Rights and the African Charter on Human and People's Rights proclaimed and agreed that everyone is entitled to all the rights and freedoms recognized and guaranteed therein, without distinction of any kind such as race, ethnic group, colour, sex, language, religion, political or any other opinion, national and social origin, fortune, birth or other status,

RECALLING the Declaration on the Rights and Welfare of the African Child (AHG/ST.4 Rev.l) adopted by the Assembly of Heads of State and Government of the Organization of African Unity, at its Sixteenth Ordinary Session in Monrovia, Liberia from 17 to 20 July 1979, recognized the need to take appropriate measures to promote and protect the rights and welfare of the African Child,

NOTING WITH CONCERN that the situation of most African children, remains critical due to the unique factors of their socio-economic, cultural, traditional and developmental circumstances, natural disasters, armed conflicts, exploitation and hunger, and on account of the child's physical and mental immaturity he/she needs special safeguards and care,

RECOGNIZING that the child occupies a unique and privileged position in the African society and that for the full and harmonious development of his personality the child should grow up in a family environment in an atmosphere of happiness, love and understanding,

RECOGNIZING that the child, due to the needs of his physical and mental development requires particular care with regard to health, physical, mental, moral and social development, and requires legal protection in conditions of freedom, dignity and security,

TAKING INTO CONSIDERATION the virtues of their cultural heritage, historical background and the values of the African civilization which should inspire and characterize their reflection on the concept of the rights and welfare of the child,

CONSIDERING that the promotion and protection of the rights and welfare of the child also implies the performance of duties on the part of everyone,

REAFFIRMING ADHERENCE to the principles of the rights and welfare of the child contained in the declaration, conventions and other instruments of the Organization of African Unity and in the United Nations and in particular the United Nations Convention on the Rights of the Child; and the OAU Heads of State and Government's Declaration on the Rights and Welfare of the African Child.

Question

How compelling is this rhetoric? Consider what reasons there may be for emphasising the vulnerability of children. Does the preamble of the African Charter suggest that a uniquely African tabulation of rights is required or desired?

There is little dispute over the vulnerability of children.

The following table contains information drawn from UNICEF's official statistics. The statistics are accurate (to the nearest thousand) as of 2 August 2004, and are taken from UNICEF's annual report.

State of the World's Children 2005 (from www.unicef.org)
Basic Indicators, Summary indicators

Region	Total Population	Annual no. of births	Annual no. under-5 deaths	Life expectancy at birth (years)
World	6,286,228,000	133,043,000	10,643,000	63
Sub-Saharan Africa	665,496,000	26,882,000	4,704	46
Middle East and North Africa	362,498,000	9,790,000	548,000	67
South Asia	1,436,478,000	37,099,000	3,413,000	63
East Asia and Pacific	1,928,182,000	31,621,000	1,265,000	69
Latin America and Caribbean	537,825,000	11,572,000	370,000	70
CEE/CIS	406,157,000	5,250,000	215,000	70
Industrialised Countries	949,593,000	10,829,000	65,000	78
Developing countries	5,083,370,000	119,986,000	10,439,000	62
Least developed countries	718,858,000	27,821,000	4,312,000	49

The lowest life expectancy at birth is 34 years in Sierra Leone and, while a number of countries record 79 years, the highest life expectancy is 80 years in Iceland. In many parts of the world, 40 or 50 is the maximum life expectancy. Childhood, adopting the United Nations definition of under 18 years, is almost half the lifespan of many people. The highest ranked under-5 mortality rates are in Afghanistan, Angola, Liberia, Niger and Sierra Leone. Surviving to school age is a not insignificant achievement in these States. Such statistics evidence that children are vulnerable and that the plight of their carers is indelibly linked to their own fate. In November 2005, UNICEF launched a major campaign to address the issue of children suffering from the ravages of HIV/AIDS, many afflicted children have become primary carers for their siblings and family members. Their 2006 State of the World's Children report focuses on the 'invisible' children.

Question

Consider what factors make children particularly vulnerable, in law as well as in reality. Is it feasible to expect law (in this case human rights) to be successful as a vehicle in championing the rights of children?

## 10.1.2	Secondary violations of rights

'A World Fit for Children', UN Doc. A/RES/S–27/2

#### 1.	Promoting healthy lives

35.	Owing to poverty and lack of access to basic social services, more than 10 million children under five years of age, nearly half of them in their neonatal period, die every year of preventable diseases and malnutrition. Complications related to pregnancy and childbirth and maternal anaemia and malnutrition kill more than half a million women and adolescents each year, and injure and disable many more. More than one billion people cannot obtain safe drinking water, 150 million children under five years of age are malnourished, and more than two billion people lack access to adequate sanitation.

36.	We are determined to break the intergenerational cycle of malnutrition and poor health by providing a safe and healthy start in life for all children; providing access to effective, equitable, sustained and sustainable primary health-care systems in all communities, ensuring access to information and referral services; providing adequate water and sanitation services; and promoting a healthy lifestyle among children and adolescents. Accordingly, we resolve to achieve the following goals in conformity with the outcomes of recent United Nations conferences, summits and special sessions of the General Assembly, as reflected in their respective reports:

(a)	Reduction in the infant and under-five mortality rate by at least one third, in pursuit of the goal of reducing it by two thirds by 2015;

(b)	Reduction in the maternal mortality ratio by at least one third, in pursuit of the goal of reducing it by three quarters by 2015;

(c)	Reduction of child malnutrition among children under five years of age by at least one third, with special attention to children under two years of age, and reduction in the rate of low birth weight by at least one third of the current rate;

(d)	Reduction in the proportion of households without access to hygienic sanitation facilities and affordable and safe drinking water by at least one third;

(e)	Development and implementation of national early childhood development policies and programmes to ensure the enhancement of children's physical, social, emotional, spiritual and cognitive development;

(f)	Development and implementation of national health policies and programmes for adolescents, including goals and indicators, to promote their physical and mental health;

(g)	Access through the primary health-care system to reproductive health for all individuals of appropriate age as soon as possible, and no later than 2015.

As indicated by the statistics above, children also can suffer from 'secondary violations' of human rights. When the rights of their primary carer are infringed, the child can suffer too. Obvious examples include children born to homeless parents lacking adequate housing and children born to malnourished women being deprived of milk or milk of suitable quality thereby compounding the suffering from lack of food. Children can indirectly be denied an adequate standard of living and appropriate health care in much of the world due to poverty. With pandemics such as HIV/AIDS in sub-Saharan Africa the right to life of the child is threatened by the lack of appropriate anti-viral drugs or pre/post-birth diagnostic tests and medical treatment. Securing respect for universal rights must therefore remain a priority as the rights of children and the rights of their carers are often interdependent to a degree which defies separation, especially during the formative years of the child's development.

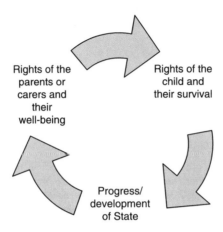

The rights of the child clearly link into the progressive development of the State in so far as factors such as life expectancy, literacy and the poverty cycle have an impact. The development of the State obviously has an impact on the rights and freedoms of the parents/carers and thereafter a direct impact on the child.

Note Art 25(2) of the Universal Declaration of Human Rights. Article 25 provides a general right to a standard of living adequate for the health and well-being of each and every person.

Universal Declaration of Human Rights Art 25(2)

Motherhood and childhood are entitled to special care and assistance. All children, whether born in or out of wedlock, shall enjoy the same social protection.

Question

To what extent are the rights of other identified vulnerable people interdependent? Are children in a unique position in this respect? What characteristics single out children for particular attention? Can any instrument on children's rights thus be successful, when the related rights of their carers are not explicitly mentioned?

10.2 TABULATING CHILDREN'S RIGHTS

Progress towards universal agreement on children's rights took time. Taking up the mantle of children's rights from the League of Nations, the United Nations General Assembly proclaimed its own Declaration on the Rights of the Child in 1959.

Declaration of the Rights of the Child, GA Res. 1386 (XIV), UN Doc. A/4354 (1959)

The General Assembly

Proclaims this Declaration of the Rights of the Child to the end that he may have a happy childhood and enjoy for his own good and for the good of society the rights and freedoms herein set forth, and calls upon parents, upon men and women as individuals, and upon voluntary organizations, local authorities and national Governments to recognize these rights and strive for their observance by legislative and other measures progressively taken in accordance with the following principles:

Principle 1

The child shall enjoy all the rights set forth in this Declaration. Every child, without any exception whatsoever, shall be entitled to these rights, without distinction or discrimination on account of race, colour, sex, language, religion, political or other opinion, national or social origin, property, birth or other status, whether of himself or of his family.

Principle 2

The child shall enjoy special protection, and shall be given opportunities and facilities, by law and by other means, to enable him to develop physically, mentally, morally, spiritually and socially in a healthy and normal manner and in conditions of freedom and dignity. In the enactment of laws for this purpose, the best interests of the child shall be the paramount consideration.

Principle 3

The child shall be entitled from his birth to a name and a nationality.

Principle 4

The child shall enjoy the benefits of social security. He shall be entitled to grow and develop in health; to this end, special care and protection shall be provided both to him and to his mother, including adequate pre-natal and post-natal care. The child shall have the right to adequate nutrition, housing, recreation and medical services.

Principle 5

The child who is physically, mentally or socially handicapped shall be given the special treatment, education and care required by his particular condition.

Principle 6

The child, for the full and harmonious development of his personality, needs love and understanding. He shall, wherever possible, grow up in the care and under the responsibility of his parents, and, in any case, in an atmosphere of affection and of moral and material security; a child of tender years shall not, save in exceptional circumstances, be separated from his mother. Society and the public authorities shall have the duty to extend particular care to children without a family and to those without adequate means of support. Payment of State and other assistance towards the maintenance of children of large families is desirable.

Principle 7

The child is entitled to receive education, which shall be free and compulsory, at least in the elementary stages. He shall be given an education which will promote his general culture and enable him, on a basis of equal opportunity, to develop his abilities, his individual judgement, and his sense of moral and social responsibility, and to become a useful member of society.

The best interests of the child shall be the guiding principle of those responsible for his education and guidance; that responsibility lies in the first place with his parents.

The child shall have full opportunity for play and recreation, which should be directed to the same purposes as education; society and the public authorities shall endeavour to promote the enjoyment of this right.

Principle 8

The child shall in all circumstances be among the first to receive protection and relief.

Principle 9

The child shall be protected against all forms of neglect, cruelty and exploitation. He shall not be the subject of traffic, in any form.

The child shall not be admitted to employment before an appropriate minimum age; he shall in no case be caused or permitted to engage in any occupation or employment which would prejudice his health or education, or interfere with his physical, mental or moral development.

Principle 10

The child shall be protected from practices which may foster racial, religious and any other form of discrimination. He shall be brought up in a spirit of understanding, tolerance, friendship among peoples, peace and universal brotherhood, and in full consciousness that his energy and talents should be devoted to the service of his fellow men.

Although not *per se* a list of rights, these ten principles retain applicability today. Note that the standard of the best interest of the child (Principle 2) still governs legislation on children today and finds legal expression in the United Nations Convention on the Rights of the Child (below). Arguably Principle 5 is an early indication of the now more evolved recognition of the rights of disabled peoples. The General Assembly has clearly acknowledged that some children are more vulnerable than others. That the situation may be acute in humanitarian situations is evident from Principle 8 and the sobering statistics produced in wake of recent humanitarian crises in Africa and the Indian Ocean rim. Children do indeed require an early call on aid given their increased vulnerability in survival situations.

Token recognition of the special status of children appears in the International Covenant on Civil and Political Rights, as well as the American Convention on Human Rights.

International Covenant on Civil and Political Rights 1966 Art 24

1. Every child shall have, without any discrimination as to race, colour, sex, language, religion, national or social origin, property or birth, the right to such measures of protection as are required by his status as a minor, on the part of his family, society and the State.

2. Every child shall be registered immediately after birth and shall have a name.

3. Every child has the right to acquire a nationality.

Shortly thereafter, the Organisation of American States acknowledged the special status of children with a short provision within the American Convention on Human Rights. In addition, Art 17(5) provides for legal equality between children born in and out of wedlock while Art 18 encapsulates the right to a name.

American Convention on Human Rights 1969 Art 19

Every minor child has the right to the measures of protection required by his condition as a minor on the part of his family, society, and the state.

Note that the Convention on Elimination of All Forms of Discrimination against Women 1979 makes specific reference to prevention of discrimination against girl children. A lot of details are provided in the Convention and this still constitutes a considerable contribution to children's rights.

1979 was the International Year of the Child with the goal of advancing the United Nations Declaration, spurring the international community into further action to prepare a binding charter of children's rights. As will be seen, such a dedicated year (or decade) is a common precursor to international tabulations of rights: the year serves to focus international attention on the predicament at issue, raising awareness, galvanising concern at grass-roots level.

General Assembly Resolution 31/169 (1976)

1. *Proclaims* the year 1979 International Year of the Child;

2. *Decides* that the International Year of the Child should have the following general objectives:

   (a) To provide a framework for advocacy on behalf of children and for enhancing the awareness of the special needs of children on the part of decision-makers and the public;

   (b) To promote recognition of the fact that programmes for children should be an integral part of economic and social development plans with a view to achieving, in both the long term and the short term, sustained activities for the benefit of children at the national and international levels.

A decade later, the international community agreed the final text of a comprehensive convention on children's rights. In September 1990, a World Summit for Children was held in New York. A World Declaration on the Survival, Protection and Development of Children and a Plan of Action was adopted.

World Declaration on the Survival, Protection and Development of Children 1990

1. We have gathered at the World Summit for Children to undertake a joint commitment and to make an urgent universal appeal—to give every child a better future.

2. The children of the world are innocent, vulnerable and dependent. They are also curious, active and full of hope. Their time should be one of joy and peace, of playing, learning and growing. Their future should be shaped in harmony and co-operation. Their lives should mature, as they broaden their perspectives and gain new experiences.

3. But for many children, the reality of childhood is altogether different.

The challenge

4. Each day, countless children around the world are exposed to dangers that hamper their growth and development. They suffer immensely as casualties of war and violence; as victims of racial discrimination, apartheid, aggression, foreign occupation and annexation; as refugees and displaced children, forced to abandon their homes and their roots; as disabled; or as victims of neglect, cruelty and exploitation.

5. Each day, millions of children suffer from the scourges of poverty and economic crisis—from hunger and homelessness, from epidemics and illiteracy, from degradation of the environment. They suffer from the grave effects of the problems of external indebtedness and also from the lack of sustained and sustainable growth in many developing countries, particularly the least developed ones.

6. Each day, 40,000 children die from malnutrition and disease, including acquired immuno-deficiency syndrome (AIDS), from the lack of clean water and inadequate sanitation and from the effects of the drug problem.

7. These are challenges that we, as political leaders, must meet. . . .

The task

10. Enhancement of children's health and nutrition is a first duty, and also a task for which

solutions are now within reach. The lives of tens of thousands of boys and girls can be saved every day, because the causes of their death are readily preventable. Child and infant mortality is unacceptably high in many parts of the world, but can be lowered dramatically with means that are already known and easily accessible.

11. Further attention, care and support should be accorded to disabled children, as well as to other children in very difficult circumstances

12. Strengthening the role of women in general and ensuring their equal rights will be to the advantage of the world's children. Girls must be given equal treatment and opportunities from the very beginning.

13. At present, over 100 million children are without basic schooling, and two-thirds of them are girls. The provision of basic education and literacy for all are among the most important contributions that can be made to the development of the world's children.

14. Half a million mothers die each year from causes related to childbirth. Safe motherhood must be promoted in all possible ways. Emphasis must be placed on responsible planning of family size and on child spacing. The family, as a fundamental group and natural environment for the growth and well-being of children, should be given all necessary protection and assistance.

15. All children must be given the chance to find their identity and realize their worth in a safe and supportive environment, through families and other care-givers committed to their welfare. They must be prepared for responsible life in a free society. They should, from their early years, be encouraged to participate in the cultural life of their societies.

16. Economic conditions will continue to influence greatly the fate of children, especially in developing nations. For the sake of the future of all children, it is urgently necessary to ensure or reactivate sustained and sustainable economic growth and development in all countries and also to continue to give urgent attention to an early, broad and durable solution to the external debt problems facing developing debtor countries.

17. These tasks require a continued and concerted effort by all nations, through national action and international co-operation.

Note the view of Hammarberg commenting on the summit.

Hammarberg, T, 'Children', Chapter 19 in Eide, Krause and Rosas (eds) *Economic, Social and Cultural Rights—a Textbook*, the Hague: Martinus Nijhoff

Never before had so many world leaders assembled to discuss the situation of children. With its focus on health and education, the Summit also became a major meeting on economic and social rights. All decisions were taken unanimously. In fact, it appeared as if the draft texts were non-controversial in spite of the heavy burdens they placed on governments. Clearly one reason for this sense of unanimity was that the subject matter was children.

Question

Why do children and children's interests generate such a consensual international response? Consider the approach of various international fundraising bodies—to what extent do they capitalise on this?

10.3   THE UNITED NATIONS CONVENTION ON THE RIGHTS OF THE CHILD

Now the principal instrument on international children's rights, the United Nations Convention on the Rights of the Child represents not only the apex of international children's rights, but also, some would argue, the pinnacle of achievement for the contemporary international human rights movement. Note the range and breadth of the various rights and freedoms as well as the detail therein. The terms of the Convention are unparalleled in scope and have attracted unprecedented support. The Convention on the Rights of the Child is the most comprehensive instrument in force under any international or regional human rights regime. This perhaps renders all the more surprising the number of ratifications it has attracted. Indeed all members of the United Nations, bar Somalia and the United States of America, have ratified it. (See for example, Kilbourne, S, 'The wayward Americans—why the USA has not ratified the UN convention on the rights of the child' (1998) 10 Child and Family Law Quarterly 243.)

Question

Evaluate the potential arguments for and against ratification by the United States of America. What can be gained (legally, politically or diplomatically) by remaining outwith the treaty system?

However, as with so many instruments, the operation of the Convention is plagued by reservations (for information on reservations, see Chapter 3). Some reservations are broad, protecting constitutional rights or Shari'a law against any contrary provisions or application of the United Nations Convention. See also, para 46 of the Vienna World Conference urging States to withdraw their reservations.

The Convention has been augmented by two optional protocols, both adopted in 2000, one on the involvement of children in armed conflict, the other on the sale of children, child prostitution and child pornography. These instruments were controversial, both topics are addressed in the principal treaty and some commentators felt that the drafting of distinct instruments on them undermined the base provisions in the Convention. However, for others, just as international human rights are frequently rewritten and extended, so too children's rights. Adding protocols is thus viewed as a logical process in the progressive realisation of children's rights.

10.3.1   What is the applicable definition of a child?

First, however, scope of application: who benefits from the Convention?

Convention on the Rights of the Child, GA res. 44/25, annex, 44 UN GAOR Supp. (No. 49) at 167, UN Doc. A/44/49 (1989)

Article 1

For the purposes of the present Convention, a child means every human being below the age of eighteen years unless under the law applicable to the child, majority is attained earlier.

Article 2

1. States Parties shall respect and ensure the rights set forth in the present Convention to each child within their jurisdiction without discrimination of any kind, irrespective of the child's or his or her parent's or legal guardian's race, colour, sex, language, religion, political or other opinion, national, ethnic or social origin, property, disability, birth or other status.

2. States Parties shall take all appropriate measures to ensure that the child is protected against all forms of discrimination or punishment on the basis of the status, activities, expressed opinions, or beliefs of the child's parents, legal guardians, or family members.

In general, everyone under the age of 18 is covered. This issue proved contentious during the drafting process and in true United Nations fashion, a compromise was reached: 18 was finalised as the age limit with a caveat that national law may make provision for a lower limit. Some States use 16 as an age of legal capacity, other States have a lower age for marriage. Irrespective of this, the Committee on the Rights of the Child consistently advocates the raising of the national age limit to 18. Obviously the Committee expresses concern if a State has discriminatory age limits— often in marriage, for example. Such practices should be eradicated and equality introduced, whatever the actual age limit. Should a State permit the early attainment of majority, then such a young adult is not right-less. He or she is entitled to all human rights and fundamental freedoms and indeed remains within the scope of some children-orientated instruments. For example, discrete instruments make provisions on child labour and include the prohibition on the death penalty for those under 18 years of age. The upper limit of 18 remains aspirational for many States but is worthwhile nonetheless. Extending protection to those under 18 has clear benefits when it comes to social and economic protection.

Note that the optional protocol on the involvement of children in armed conflict has 18 as the age limit for compulsory recruitment into the armed forces (Art 2). This contrasts with Art 38(3) of the Convention which has 15 as the minimum age for recruitment.

Contrast this with the African Charter.

African Charter of the Rights and Welfare of the Child Art 2
For the purposes of this Charter, a child means every human being below the age of 18 years.

Question
Investigate the various age limits applicable in your, or any other, State. If below 18 in any respect, is it unduly detrimental to children and young people? (You can find the primary information in the State reports to the Committee on the Rights of the Child.)

10.4   GOVERNING PRINCIPLES

There are four guiding principles which govern the operation of the United Nations Convention: non-discrimination (Art 2); the best interests of the child (Art 3); rights to life, survival and development of the child (Art 6); and the view of the child (Art 12). The principle of non-discrimination is deeply ingrained in international human rights, as of course is the necessity for the right to life and survival. Obviously, for a child these rights bring their own unique challenges. As mentioned above, the survival of a child depends to a large extent (at least in the formative years) on their carer/parent. The other two principles: participation of children in matters affecting them and the welfare principle (best interest of the child), are more progressive.

Van Beuren categorised the principles as the four Ps: protection of children from harm, prevention of discrimination, participation in decisions and provision of essentials for survival and development (1995, reference below). To facilitate as broad a discussion of children's rights as possible within the confines of this text, a generous interpretation will be taken of each of these principles to enable a large swathe of convention rights to be considered.

The convention includes civil, political, economic, social and cultural rights. Many rights are similar to those contained in other instruments although there remain some unusual elements.

10.4.1 'The best interests of the child'

The governing principle which underpins the entire Convention and associated juris-prudence is the best interests of the child. Given the universality of the Convention and the wide acceptance of its principles by all States, with credence being taken of the best interests of the child even when the Convention is not incorporated into the laws of the State concerned, it is possible to argue that the 'best interests of the child' has now crystallised into customary international law. (Customary international law is discussed in Chapter 1.)

Convention on the Rights of the Child

Article 3

1. In all actions concerning children, whether undertaken by public or private social welfare institutions, courts of law, administrative authorities or legislative bodies, the best interests of the child shall be a primary consideration.

2. States Parties undertake to ensure the child such protection and care as is necessary for his or her well-being, taking into account the rights and duties of his or her parents, legal guardians, or other individuals legally responsible for him or her, and, to this end, shall take all appropriate legislative and administrative measures.

3. States Parties shall ensure that the institutions, services and facilities responsible for the care or protection of children shall conform with the standards established by competent authorities, particularly in the areas of safety, health, in the number and suitability of their staff, as well as competent supervision.

Article 4

States Parties shall undertake all appropriate legislative, administrative, and other measures for the implementation of the rights recognized in the present Convention. With regard to economic, social and cultural rights, States Parties shall undertake such measures to the maximum extent of their available resources and, where needed, within the framework of international co-operation.

Article 4 of the African Charter on the Rights and Welfare of the Child makes similar provision. Article 21 explicitly protects children against harmful social and cultural practices. This would appear based on respect for the best interests of the child. As mentioned in Chapter 2, practices such as female circumcision are potentially very injurious to girls, even although the practice may be in conformity with cultural tradition. Interestingly Art 21 explicitly mentions discriminatory traditional practices.

African Charter on the Rights and Welfare of the Child Art 21

1. States Parties to the present Charter shall take all appropriate measures to eliminate harmful social and cultural practices affecting the welfare, dignity, normal growth and development of the child and in particular:

(a) those customs and practices prejudicial to the health or life of the child; and

(b) those customs and practices discriminatory to the child on the grounds of sex or other status.

2. Child marriage and the betrothal of girls and boys shall be prohibited and effective action, including legislation, shall be taken to specify the minimum age of marriage to be 18 years and make registration of all marriages in an official registry compulsory.

Many States now include reference to the best interests of the child in statutes concerning children. In other instances, practice dictates that courts consider it when addressing family matters and related issues. In terms of Article 4, States Parties should ensure that all the rights in the treaty are recognised at the national level. This includes the adoption of provisions giving effect to the prevailing principle of the best interests of the child. Many States responded to this by incorporating the principle into national law. The breadth of States doing so adds credence to the argument that the 'best interests of the child' is actually transformed into customary law. Obviously this applies to the principle in general rather than specifically as there is considerable State variation as regards issues such as education and juvenile justice.

See for example, the Children (Scotland) Act 1995, c 36 or s 28(2) of the Constitution of the Republic of South Africa 1996.

10.4.2 'Participation' of the child in decisions affecting him or her

These provisions go to the root of children's rights. In some theories, children's rights exist to prepare the child for adulthood. This certainly is the underlying theory behind the provisions on participation in the United Nations Convention. It is perhaps unreasonable to expect children, overnight on their eighteenth birthday, to suddenly have all the necessary lifeskills for adulthood and the necessary knowledge and ability to acquit themselves in all situations. Consequently, the Convention makes provision for children to progressively develop the skills needed for adulthood. Children thus also enjoy freedom of expression, religion and association.

Hammarberg (Hammarberg, T, 'The U.N. Convention on the Rights of the Child—and How to Make it Work' (1990) 12 Human Rights Quarterly 97) considers the Convention weakest on participation. There are a number of reasons for this. An independent right of a child to form and express opinions and have them taken into account in relevant decisions clearly reflects not only an evolving capacity of the child but also the evolving transfer of some parental rights to the child. Religious freedom is an obvious example of this.

Convention on the Rights of the Child

Article 12

1. States Parties shall assure to the child who is capable of forming his or her own views the right to express those views freely in all matters affecting the child, the views of the child being given due weight in accordance with the age and maturity of the child.

2. For this purpose, the child shall in particular be provided the opportunity to be heard in any judicial and administrative proceedings affecting the child, either directly, or through a representative or an appropriate body, in a manner consistent with the procedural rules of national law.

Article 13

1. The child shall have the right to freedom of expression; this right shall include freedom to seek, receive and impart information and ideas of all kinds, regardless of frontiers, either orally, in writing or in print, in the form of art, or through any other media of the child's choice.

2. The exercise of this right may be subject to certain restrictions, but these shall only be such as are provided by law and are necessary:

(a) For respect of the rights or reputations of others; or

(b) For the protection of national security or of public order (ordre public), or of public health or morals.

Article 14

1. States Parties shall respect the right of the child to freedom of thought, conscience and religion.

2. States Parties shall respect the rights and duties of the parents and, when applicable, legal guardians, to provide direction to the child in the exercise of his or her right in a manner consistent with the evolving capacities of the child.

3. Freedom to manifest one's religion or beliefs may be subject only to such limitations as are prescribed by law and are necessary to protect public safety, order, health or morals, or the fundamental rights and freedoms of others.

Article 15

1. States Parties recognize the rights of the child to freedom of association and to freedom of peaceful assembly.

2. No restrictions may be placed on the exercise of these rights other than those imposed in conformity with the law and which are necessary in a democratic society in the interests of national security or public safety, public order (ordre public), the protection of public health or morals or the protection of the rights and freedoms of others.

Article 16

1. No child shall be subjected to arbitrary or unlawful interference with his or her privacy, family, home or correspondence, nor to unlawful attacks on his or her honour and reputation.

2. The child has the right to the protection of the law against such interference or attacks.

Article 17

States Parties recognize the important function performed by the mass media and shall ensure that the child has access to information and material from a diversity of national and international sources, especially those aimed at the promotion of his or her social, spiritual and moral well-being and physical and mental health. To this end, States Parties shall:

(a) Encourage the mass media to disseminate information and material of social and cultural benefit to the child and in accordance with the spirit of article 29;

(b) Encourage international co-operation in the production, exchange and dissemination of such information and material from a diversity of cultural, national and international sources;

(c) Encourage the production and dissemination of children's books;

(d) Encourage the mass media to have particular regard to the linguistic needs of the child who belongs to a minority group or who is indigenous;

(e) Encourage the development of appropriate guidelines for the protection of the child from information and material injurious to his or her well-being, bearing in mind the provisions of articles 13 and 18.

Question

Does Article 14 make adequate and appropriate provision for the balance between a parent's right to bring his/her child up in a particular religious belief system and the right of a child to determine to follow a different system?

Reconciling the rights of parents with those of their children runs as an undercurrent throughout the convention and is particularly obvious in the foregoing articles. No similar conflict arises consistently in respect of other identified vulnerable groups. Children are unique in their evolving capacity. This links in to elements of human rights education and the need for children to learn about civic society and form their own independent views thereon in preparation for assuming the full raft of civic obligations which should be extended to adults. Accordingly, children require Art 17 access to information in order to develop and form their own opinions, which they can then express in terms of Art 13. Article 17 also relates to educational development—note the provisions encouraging the production and dissemination of children's books and associated material. There are clear links to the right to education (Art 29) and to the rights of minorities. Article 17 notes the linguistic needs of minority and indigenous children. This echoes regional provisions found in the Council of Europe's European Charter for Regional and Minority Languages 1992 and the Framework Convention for the Protection of National Minorities 1995 as well as the OSCE's Oslo Recommendations Regarding the Linguistic Rights of National Minorities 1998 and their Hague Recommendations Regarding the Education Rights of National Minorities 1996.

Question

Can adult and children's rights ever be reconciled?

Note that the African Charter encapsulates responsibilities for the child, though not a corresponding right *per se* of participation.

African Charter on the Rights and Welfare of the Child Art 31

Every child shall have responsibilities towards his family and society, the State and other legally recognized communities and the international community. The child, subject to his age and ability, and such limitations as may be contained in the present Charter, shall have the duty;

(a) to work for the cohesion of the family, to respect his parents, superiors and elders at all times and to assist them in case of need;

(b) to serve his national community by placing his physical and intellectual abilities at its service;

(c) to preserve and strengthen social and national solidarity;

(d) to preserve and strengthen African cultural values in his relations with other members of the society, in the spirit of tolerance, dialogue and consultation and to contribute to the moral well-being of society;

(e) to preserve and strengthen the independence and the integrity of his country;

(f) to contribute to the best of his abilities, at all times and at all levels, to the promotion and achievement of African Unity.

For many States, involving children in decision-making processes is inherently problematic. Quite clearly, not all children of all ages will have appropriate opinions to feed into the salient processes. There is room for involvement in judicial processes, for example concerning child care arrangements ensuing from a divorce or separation. Children's views are not the sole deciding factor but are clearly a relevant consideration. Schools in, for example, Australia often include children on the school governing body. Such children can hold some power in influencing events. Again, their power is not absolute, but their opinions can be a valuable contribution. More controversial is the role of children in the political decision-making process. (The role of children's commissioners is considered in Chapter 7.) Youth parliaments and similar fora have an important role to play in this respect.

In 2005, Australia and the Commonwealth Parliamentary Association organised and hosted a youth parliament with participants from across the commonwealth (see www.parliament.qld.gov.au/cpaYouthParliament2005/overview.htm). There is also a Scottish Youth Parliament (www.scottishyouthparliament.org.uk/). There are many other national, regional and international examples.

10.4.3   Provision of a safe environment and basic needs

Given the aforementioned interdependence of children, the State is also obliged to respect the rights of the child's parents and guardians. This can cause problems as a judgment must be made as to when a child ceases to be subject to parental control and should be recognised as having an evolving autonomy over their own life. This links in to Art 12.

Convention on the Rights of the Child

Article 5

States Parties shall respect the responsibilities, rights and duties of parents or, where applicable, the members of the extended family or community as provided for by local custom, legal guardians or other persons legally responsible for the child, to provide, in a manner consistent with the evolving capacities of the child, appropriate direction and guidance in the exercise by the child of the rights recognized in the present Convention.

Parental responsibilities, and when they are transferred to the child or indeed the State, remains a highly charged political issue. Recognising a child as an autonomous individual, distinct from his or her parents/guardians, is contrary to the paternalistic approach of some States.

African Charter on the Rights and Welfare of the Child Art 20

1. Parents or other persons responsible for the child shall have the primary responsibility of the upbringing and development the child and shall have the duty:

(a) to ensure that the best interests of the child are their basic concern at all times;

(b) to secure, within their abilities and financial capacities, conditions of living necessary to the child's development; and

(c) to ensure that domestic discipline is administered with humanity and in a manner consistent with the inherent dignity of the child.

2. States Parties to the present Charter shall in accordance with their means and national conditions the all appropriate measures;

(a) to assist parents and other persons responsible for the child and in case of need provide material assistance and support programmes particularly with regard to nutrition, health, education, clothing and housing;

(b) to assist parents and others responsible for the child in the performance of child-rearing and ensure the development of institutions responsible for providing care of children; and

(c) to ensure that the children of working parents are provided with care services and facilities.

Note the emphasis on the best interests of the child as a guiding principle influencing parents.

The convention deals chronologically with the life of the child from birth. Note however, that birth is the determining factor—in contrast see the American Convention on Human Rights, Art 4. Children have the right to life and the right to a name. This right also appears as a human right in the American Convention and African Charter. Without a name and an identity, children can remain commodities and lack the legal status necessary to be attributed independent rights and freedoms. Traumatic problems were encountered in January 2005 in Indonesia and other affected countries when trying to create registers of all children found and saved in the wake of the tsunami. Once registered, it was easier to trace family and the children were also 'safe' from predatory paedophiles as the State and non-governmental organisations were better able to monitor their geographical location.

Convention on the Rights of the Child

Article 6

1. States Parties recognize that every child has the inherent right to life.

2. States Parties shall ensure to the maximum extent possible the survival and development of the child. . . .

Article 24

1. States Parties recognize the right of the child to the enjoyment of the highest attainable standard of health and to facilities for the treatment of illness and rehabilitation of health. States Parties shall strive to ensure that no child is deprived of his or her right of access to such health care services.

2. States Parties shall pursue full implementation of this right and, in particular, shall take appropriate measures:

(a) To diminish infant and child mortality;

(b) To ensure the provision of necessary medical assistance and health care to all children with emphasis on the development of primary health care;

(c) To combat disease and malnutrition, including within the framework of primary health care, through, *inter alia*, the application of readily available technology and through the provision of adequate nutritious foods and clean drinking-water, taking into consideration the dangers and risks of environmental pollution;

(d) To ensure appropriate pre-natal and post-natal health care for mothers;

(e) To ensure that all segments of society, in particular parents and children, are informed, have access to education and are supported in the use of basic knowledge of child health and nutrition, the advantages of breastfeeding, hygiene and environmental sanitation and the prevention of accidents;

(f) To develop preventive health care, guidance for parents and family planning education and services.

3. States Parties shall take all effective and appropriate measures with a view to abolishing traditional practices prejudicial to the health of children.

4. States Parties undertake to promote and encourage international co-operation with a view to achieving progressively the full realization of the right recognized in the present article. In this regard, particular account shall be taken of the needs of developing countries. . . .

Article 7

1. The child shall be registered immediately after birth and shall have the right from birth to a name, the right to acquire a nationality and, as far as possible, the right to know and be cared for by his or her parents.

2. States Parties shall ensure the implementation of these rights in accordance with their national law and their obligations under the relevant international instruments in this field, in particular where the child would otherwise be stateless.

Article 8

1. States Parties undertake to respect the right of the child to preserve his or her identity, including nationality, name and family relations as recognized by law without unlawful interference.

2. Where a child is illegally deprived of some or all of the elements of his or her identity, States Parties shall provide appropriate assistance and protection, with a view to re-establishing speedily his or her identity.

Healthcare impacts on the right to life and development. Note that Art 24 also emphasises the need for maternal pre- and post-natal care, identifying the unique interrelationship between the rights of the child and the mother.

10.4.3.1   Family rights

The family is viewed traditionally with the family recognised as the natural unit within which a child should be raised and in the convention there is a corresponding emphasis on family rights. However, the scope of 'family' is broad, encompassing a variety of cultural practices and societal traditions. Adoption and fostering are also addressed. Overriding all permutations is the need for stability for the child. Accordingly, no child should be unnecessarily separated from his or her parents and any arrangements for alternative care/custody should be dealt with swiftly to minimise the disruption to the child.

Convention on the Rights of the Child

Article 9

1. States Parties shall ensure that a child shall not be separated from his or her parents against their will, except when competent authorities subject to judicial review determine, in accordance with applicable law and procedures, that such separation is necessary for the best interests of the child. Such determination may be necessary in a particular case such as one involving abuse or neglect of the child by the parents, or one where the parents are living separately and a decision must be made as to the child's place of residence.

2. In any proceedings pursuant to paragraph 1 of the present article, all interested parties shall be given an opportunity to participate in the proceedings and make their views known.

3. States Parties shall respect the right of the child who is separated from one or both parents to maintain personal relations and direct contact with both parents on a regular basis, except if it is contrary to the child's best interests.

4. Where such separation results from any action initiated by a State Party, such as the detention, imprisonment, exile, deportation or death (including death arising from any cause while the person is in the custody of the State) of one or both parents or of the child, that State Party shall, upon request, provide the parents, the child or, if appropriate, another member of the family with the essential information concerning the whereabouts of the absent member(s) of the family unless the provision of the information would be detrimental to the well-being of the child. States Parties shall further ensure that the submission of such a request shall of itself entail no adverse consequences for the person(s) concerned.

Article 10

1. In accordance with the obligation of States Parties under article 9, paragraph 1, applications by a child or his or her parents to enter or leave a State Party for the purpose of family reunification shall be dealt with by States Parties in a positive, humane and expeditious manner. States Parties shall further ensure that the submission of such a request shall entail no adverse consequences for the applicants and for the members of their family.

2. A child whose parents reside in different States shall have the right to maintain on a regular basis, save in exceptional circumstances personal relations and direct contacts with both parents. Towards that end and in accordance with the obligation of States Parties under article 9, paragraph 1, States Parties shall respect the right of the child and his or her parents to leave any

country, including their own, and to enter their own country. The right to leave any country shall be subject only to such restrictions as are prescribed by law and which are necessary to protect the national security, public order (ordre public), public health or morals or the rights and freedoms of others and are consistent with the other rights recognized in the present Convention. . . .

Article 18

1. States Parties shall use their best efforts to ensure recognition of the principle that both parents have common responsibilities for the upbringing and development of the child. Parents or, as the case may be, legal guardians, have the primary responsibility for the upbringing and development of the child. The best interests of the child will be their basic concern.

2. For the purpose of guaranteeing and promoting the rights set forth in the present Convention, States Parties shall render appropriate assistance to parents and legal guardians in the performance of their child-rearing responsibilities and shall ensure the development of institutions, facilities and services for the care of children.

3. States Parties shall take all appropriate measures to ensure that children of working parents have the right to benefit from child-care services and facilities for which they are eligible. . . .

Article 20

1. A child temporarily or permanently deprived of his or her family environment, or in whose own best interests cannot be allowed to remain in that environment, shall be entitled to special protection and assistance provided by the State.

2. States Parties shall in accordance with their national laws ensure alternative care for such a child.

3. Such care could include, *inter alia*, foster placement, *kafalah* of Islamic law, adoption or if necessary placement in suitable institutions for the care of children. When considering solutions, due regard shall be paid to the desirability of continuity in a child's upbringing and to the child's ethnic, religious, cultural and linguistic background.

See also the equivalent provisions in the African Charter on the Rights and Welfare of the Child.

Article 18 emphasises the commonality of interests of both parents in the upbringing of children. It is the States Parties who have the secondary role of supporting parents in fulfilling the rights of children guaranteed by the Convention. Some States have fully embraced this. Indeed Art 44(6) obliges States to make their periodic reports available to their citizens. Therefore the State must ensure that parents know the relevant provisions. This links in to the positive obligation on States as regards human rights (see Chapter 2). States must ensure that parents comply with the guarantees and protection in the Convention or fail in their own obligation to ensure the State's rights are discharged.

United Nations Convention on the Rights of the Child

Article 21

States Parties that recognize and/or permit the system of adoption shall ensure that the best interests of the child shall be the paramount consideration and they shall:

(a) Ensure that the adoption of a child is authorized only by competent authorities who determine, in accordance with applicable law and procedures and on the basis of all pertinent and reliable information, that the adoption is permissible in view of the child's status concerning parents, relatives and legal guardians and that, if required, the persons concerned have given their informed consent to the adoption on the basis of such counselling as may be necessary;

(b) Recognize that inter-country adoption may be considered as an alternative means of child's care, if the child cannot be placed in a foster or an adoptive family or cannot in any suitable manner be cared for in the child's country of origin;

(c) Ensure that the child concerned by inter-country adoption enjoys safeguards and standards equivalent to those existing in the case of national adoption;

(d) Take all appropriate measures to ensure that, in inter-country adoption, the placement does not result in improper financial gain for those involved in it;

(e) Promote, where appropriate, the objectives of the present article by concluding bilateral or multilateral arrangements or agreements, and endeavour, within this framework, to ensure that the placement of the child in another country is carried out by competent authorities or organs.

Question

Consider the application of these articles to issues such as inter-country adoption from China to the Netherlands; the special protection afforded to children when endangered within the family situation and with respect to Article 18, the scope for parental-State interaction and guidance.

Inter-country adoption is addressed in more detail in the Hague Convention on Protection of Children and Co-operation in Respect of Intercountry Adoption 1993. A discussion of this instrument is outwith the scope of the present work. Article 24 of the African Charter also addresses this topic in some detail.

10.4.3.2 Child abduction

Convention on the Rights of the Child

Article 11

1. States Parties shall take measures to combat the illicit transfer and non-return of children abroad.

2. To this end, States Parties shall promote the conclusion of bilateral or multilateral agreements or accession to existing agreements.

See also Arts 9 and 10, excerpted above. This issue is dealt with at length in Private International law. International child abduction is a major problem and distinct from the issue of child trafficking. Child abduction is particularly problematic when it occurs as a result of a breakdown in family relations with one parent taking a child to a second or third country thereby illegally terminating the parental rights of the other parent. As the sad cases reported in the media indicate, problems can occur in enforcing national court orders for the return of a child when the child is in a different State. For children and parents the situation can become barely tolerably, very traumatic and have long-term effects. The Hague Convention on the Civil Aspects of International Child Abduction 1980 has attracted accessions by around half the membership of the United Nations. Essentially the Convention creates judicial mechanisms for redressing the removal of a child from his or her 'habitual residence'.

Hague Convention on the Civil Aspects of International Child Abduction 1980

Article 1

The objects of the present Convention are—

a) to secure the prompt return of children wrongfully removed to or retained in any Contracting State; and

b) to ensure that rights of custody and of access under the law of one Contracting State are effectively respected in the other Contracting States.

Article 2

Contracting States shall take all appropriate measures to secure within their territories the implementation of the objects of the Convention. For this purpose they shall use the most expeditious procedures available.

Article 3

The removal or the retention of a child is to be considered wrongful where—

a) it is in breach of rights of custody attributed to a person, an institution or any other body, either jointly or alone, under the law of the State in which the child was habitually resident immediately before the removal or retention; and

b) at the time of removal or retention those rights were actually exercised, either jointly or alone, or would have been so exercised but for the removal or retention.

The rights of custody mentioned in sub-paragraph a) above, may arise in particular by operation of law or by reason of a judicial or administrative decision, or by reason of an agreement having legal effect under the law of that State.

Article 4

The Convention shall apply to any child who was habitually resident in a Contracting State immediately before any breach of custody or access rights. The Convention shall cease to apply when the child attains the age of 16 years.

A European Convention on Recognition and Enforcement of Decisions Concerning Custody of Children and on the Restoration of Custody of Children 1980 can be invoked to enforce existing custody orders/decisions by competent courts.

The principal problems with these mechanisms is lack of participation. Universal compliance and universal acceptance of third State judicial decisions concerning child custody would be essential, if unlikely, to ensure the system functions. For more information, specialist texts should be consulted and/or relevant websites such as those listed below. A full discussion is outwith the scope of the current text.

- www.reunite.org—for helping families of abducted children
- hcch.e-vision.nl—Hague Conference on Private International Law with access to relevant source material

10.4.4 Protecting the child from harm

To facilitate their development, children should be protected from all forms of harm. Both the optional protocols to the United Nations Convention aimed at strengthening these provisions. In the African Charter on the Rights and Welfare of the Child, many of the threats to children are addressed in individual articles. For example, Art 23 on refugee children, Art 21 on harmful social and cultural practices and Art 22 on armed conflict.

Many of the rights are similar to those in other international instruments. The following are some examples.

United Nations Convention on the Rights of the Child

Article 19

1. States Parties shall take all appropriate legislative, administrative, social and educational measures to protect the child from all forms of physical or mental violence, injury or abuse, neglect or

negligent treatment, maltreatment or exploitation, including sexual abuse, while in the care of parent(s), legal guardian(s) or any other person who has the care of the child.

2. Such protective measures should, as appropriate, include effective procedures for the establishment of social programmes to provide necessary support for the child and for those who have the care of the child, as well as for other forms of prevention and for identification, reporting, referral, investigation, treatment and follow-up of instances of child maltreatment described heretofore, and, as appropriate, for judicial involvement. . . .

Article 25

States Parties recognize the right of a child who has been placed by the competent authorities for the purposes of care, protection or treatment of his or her physical or mental health, to a periodic review of the treatment provided to the child and all other circumstances relevant to his or her placement.

Article 26

1. States Parties shall recognize for every child the right to benefit from social security, including social insurance, and shall take the necessary measures to achieve the full realization of this right in accordance with their national law.

2. The benefits should, where appropriate, be granted, taking into account the resources and the circumstances of the child and persons having responsibility for the maintenance of the child, as well as any other consideration relevant to an application for benefits made by or on behalf of the child.

Article 27

1. States Parties recognize the right of every child to a standard of living adequate for the child's physical, mental, spiritual, moral and social development.

2. The parent(s) or others responsible for the child have the primary responsibility to secure, within their abilities and financial capacities, the conditions of living necessary for the child's development.

3. States Parties, in accordance with national conditions and within their means, shall take appropriate measures to assist parents and others responsible for the child to implement this right and shall in case of need provide material assistance and support programmes, particularly with regard to nutrition, clothing and housing.

4. States Parties shall take all appropriate measures to secure the recovery of maintenance for the child from the parents or other persons having financial responsibility for the child, both within the State Party and from abroad. In particular, where the person having financial responsibility for the child lives in a State different from that of the child, States Parties shall promote the accession to international agreements or the conclusion of such agreements, as well as the making of other appropriate arrangements. . . .

Article 37

States Parties shall ensure that:

(a) No child shall be subjected to torture or other cruel, inhuman or degrading treatment or punishment. Neither capital punishment nor life imprisonment without possibility of release shall be imposed for offences committed by persons below eighteen years of age;

(b) No child shall be deprived of his or her liberty unlawfully or arbitrarily. The arrest, detention or imprisonment of a child shall be in conformity with the law and shall be used only as a measure of last resort and for the shortest appropriate period of time;

(c) Every child deprived of liberty shall be treated with humanity and respect for the inherent dignity of the human person, and in a manner which takes into account the needs of persons of his or her age. In particular, every child deprived of liberty shall be separated from adults unless it is considered in the child's best interest not to do so and shall have the right to maintain contact with his or her family through correspondence and visits, save in exceptional circumstances;

(d) Every child deprived of his or her liberty shall have the right to prompt access to legal and other appropriate assistance, as well as the right to challenge the legality of the deprivation of his or her liberty before a court or other competent, independent and impartial authority, and to a prompt decision on any such action.

Other provisions address particular issues which are tabulated in specific instruments (convention or declarations). The provisions on refugee children obviously overlap with the provisions in the Convention Relating to the Status of Refugees (see Chapter 13), cultural rights are found in the International Covenant on Civil and Political Rights as well as in the instruments on indigenous peoples (see Chapter 12) and child civilians in conflict situations of course fall within the provisions of the Geneva Conventions (see Chapter 15). Of perhaps more interest is the provision on respecting the rights of mentally and physically disabled children. The African Charter makes similar provision. This despite the fact that the United Nations has not yet succeeded in agreeing the text of a framework of rights and freedoms for such people. (Note that the text of a Draft Convention on the Rights of Persons with Disabilities and Protocol was agreed in August 2006.)

United Nations Convention on the Rights of the Child

Article 22

1. States Parties shall take appropriate measures to ensure that a child who is seeking refugee status or who is considered a refugee in accordance with applicable international or domestic law and procedures shall, whether unaccompanied or accompanied by his or her parents or by any other person, receive appropriate protection and humanitarian assistance in the enjoyment of applicable rights set forth in the present Convention and in other international human rights or humanitarian instruments to which the said States are Parties.

2. For this purpose, States Parties shall provide, as they consider appropriate, co-operation in any efforts by the United Nations and other competent intergovernmental organizations or non-governmental organizations co-operating with the United Nations to protect and assist such a child and to trace the parents or other members of the family of any refugee child in order to obtain information necessary for reunification with his or her family. In cases where no parents or other members of the family can be found, the child shall be accorded the same protection as any other child permanently or temporarily deprived of his or her family environment for any reason, as set forth in the present Convention.

Article 23

1. States Parties recognize that a mentally or physically disabled child should enjoy a full and decent life, in conditions which ensure dignity, promote self-reliance and facilitate the child's active participation in the community.

2. States Parties recognize the right of the disabled child to special care and shall encourage and ensure the extension, subject to available resources, to the eligible child and those responsible for his or her care, of assistance for which application is made and which is appropriate to the child's condition and to the circumstances of the parents or others caring for the child.

3. Recognizing the special needs of a disabled child, assistance extended in accordance with paragraph 2 of the present article shall be provided free of charge, whenever possible, taking into account the financial resources of the parents or others caring for the child, and shall be designed to ensure that the disabled child has effective access to and receives education, training, health care services, rehabilitation services, preparation for employment and recreation opportunities in

a manner conducive to the child's achieving the fullest possible social integration and individual development, including his or her cultural and spiritual development

4. States Parties shall promote, in the spirit of international cooperation, the exchange of appropriate information in the field of preventive health care and of medical, psychological and functional treatment of disabled children, including dissemination of and access to information concerning methods of rehabilitation, education and vocational services, with the aim of enabling States Parties to improve their capabilities and skills and to widen their experience in these areas. In this regard, particular account shall be taken of the needs of developing countries. . . .

Article 30

In those States in which ethnic, religious or linguistic minorities or persons of indigenous origin exist, a child belonging to such a minority or who is indigenous shall not be denied the right, in community with other members of his or her group, to enjoy his or her own culture, to profess and practise his or her own religion, or to use his or her own language.

Article 38

1. States Parties undertake to respect and to ensure respect for rules of international humanitarian law applicable to them in armed conflicts which are relevant to the child.

2. States Parties shall take all feasible measures to ensure that persons who have not attained the age of fifteen years do not take a direct part in hostilities.

3. States Parties shall refrain from recruiting any person who has not attained the age of fifteen years into their armed forces. In recruiting among those persons who have attained the age of fifteen years but who have not attained the age of eighteen years, States Parties shall endeavour to give priority to those who are oldest.

4. In accordance with their obligations under international humanitarian law to protect the civilian population in armed conflicts, States Parties shall take all feasible measures to ensure protection and care of children who are affected by an armed conflict.

Protecting children from the illicit use of narcotic and psychotropic substances is an interesting addition. The drafters probably had in mind not only the extensive use of 'recreational drugs' by children, but also the role such substances play in recruiting and maintaining child participation in armed conflicts and the sex trade. As Art 33 notes, children are also often used to traffic drugs. Employing children in drug smuggling can range from using their prams and toys to hide the substances through to using children to actually carry (externally or internally) large volumes of drugs. If caught, such children are often abandoned by the gang of smugglers at the border.

United Nations Convention on the Rights of the Child Art 33

States Parties shall take all appropriate measures, including legislative, administrative, social and educational measures, to protect children from the illicit use of narcotic drugs and psychotropic substances as defined in the relevant international treaties, and to prevent the use of children in the illicit production and trafficking of such substances.

Children are also entitled to special protection when facing the criminal justice system in a State (see also Chapter 11). The minimum age for criminal responsibility varies from State to State and thus the Convention focuses on ensuring the rights of the child are adequately protected during the criminal proceedings. (For a detailed analysis of associated rights by the European Court of Justice, see *T & V v United Kingdom* (Chapter 11).)

United Nations Convention on the Rights of the Child Art 40

1. States Parties recognize the right of every child alleged as, accused of, or recognized as having infringed the penal law to be treated in a manner consistent with the promotion of the child's

sense of dignity and worth, which reinforces the child's respect for the human rights and funda-mental freedoms of others and which takes into account the child's age and the desirability of promoting the child's reintegration and the child's assuming a constructive role in society.

2. To this end, and having regard to the relevant provisions of international instruments, States Parties shall, in particular, ensure that:

(a) No child shall be alleged as, be accused of, or recognized as having infringed the penal law by reason of acts or omissions that were not prohibited by national or international law at the time they were committed;

(b) Every child alleged as or accused of having infringed the penal law has at least the following guarantees:

(i) To be presumed innocent until proven guilty according to law;

(ii) To be informed promptly and directly of the charges against him or her, and, if appropri-ate, through his or her parents or legal guardians, and to have legal or other appropriate assistance in the preparation and presentation of his or her defence;

(iii) To have the matter determined without delay by a competent, independent and impartial authority or judicial body in a fair hearing according to law, in the presence of legal or other appropriate assistance and, unless it is considered not to be in the best interest of the child, in particular, taking into account his or her age or situation, his or her parents or legal guardians;

(iv) Not to be compelled to give testimony or to confess guilt; to examine or have examined adverse witnesses and to obtain the participation and examination of witnesses on his or her behalf under conditions of equality;

(v) If considered to have infringed the penal law, to have this decision and any measures imposed in consequence thereof reviewed by a higher competent, independent and impartial authority or judicial body according to law;

(vi) To have the free assistance of an interpreter if the child cannot understand or speak the language used;

(vii) To have his or her privacy fully respected at all stages of the proceedings.

3. States Parties shall seek to promote the establishment of laws, procedures, authorities and institutions specifically applicable to children alleged as, accused of, or recognized as having infringed the penal law, and, in particular:

(a) The establishment of a minimum age below which children shall be presumed not to have the capacity to infringe the penal law;

(b) Whenever appropriate and desirable, measures for dealing with such children without resort-ing to judicial proceedings, providing that human rights and legal safeguards are fully respected.

4. A variety of dispositions, such as care, guidance and supervision orders; counselling; probation; foster care; education and vocational training programmes and other alternatives to institutional care shall be available to ensure that children are dealt with in a manner appropriate to their well-being and proportionate both to their circumstances and the offence.

Children are, as is apparent, particularly vulnerable during armed conflict. Child soldiers, whether drawn into international or civil insurgency, are protected by the United Nations Convention and its 2000 Protocol. The International Committee of the Red Cross/Red Crescent and the International Labour Organisation (Convention No. 182) both condemn the use of children in armed conflict while the Statute of the International Criminal Court lists 'conscripting or enlisting children under the age of fifteen years into armed forces or groups or using them to participate actively in the hostilities' as a war crime (Art 8(2)(e)(vii)).

Naturally all children should be fully supported when recovering from any form of neglect and exploitation and every attempt should be made to help reintegrate them into society. Consider the work done in orphanages in Sierra Leone and Angola with former child soldiers—a perfect example of this provision in practice. This provision may have significant resource implications for States. However, to ensure the child at issue a future with as few limitations and hindrances as possible, it is imperative that recovery and reintegration are assisted.

United Nations Convention on the Rights of the Child

Article 39

States Parties shall take all appropriate measures to promote physical and psychological recovery and social reintegration of a child victim of: any form of neglect, exploitation, or abuse; torture or any other form of cruel, inhuman or degrading treatment or punishment; or armed conflicts. Such recovery and reintegration shall take place in an environment which fosters the health, self-respect and dignity of the child.

Question

Compare and contrast the range of rights and freedoms in this Convention with those in the Universal Declaration/ the International Covenants.

Note Art 21(2) of the African Charter and its impact on sexual exploitation:

African Charter on the Rights and Welfare of the Child

Article 21(2) Child marriage and the betrothal of girls and boys shall be prohibited and effective action, including legislation, shall be taken to specify the minimum age of marriage to be 18 years and make registration of all marriages in an official registry compulsory.

Article 27 States Parties to the present Charter shall undertake to protect the child from all forms of sexual exploitation and sexual abuse and shall in particular take measures to prevent:

(a) the inducement, coercion or encouragement of a child to engage in any sexual activity;

(b) the use of children in prostitution or other sexual practices;

(c) the use of children in pornographic activities, performances and materials.

Question

To what extent does specifying a relatively high age for marriage extend the protection of children against exploitation?

10.4.4.1   Child labour

The International Labour Organisation has, since inception, campaigned against the worst forms of child labour. Naturally some work, within and even outwith the home, can be beneficial for young people. What the international community is seeking to regulate is the abusive impact of child labour. Many reports of the ILO focus on negative aspects of child labour, including its effect on education and health. See, generally, www.ilo.org/public/english/standards/ipec/index.htm—the International Programme on the Elimination of Child Labour.

Child labour is inevitably linked to poverty. The International Labour Office has further linked this to education. Indeed the economic and social developmental progress of a State can be indicated by its child labour statistics (see www.ilo.org).

African Charter on the Rights and Welfare of the Child Art 15

1. Every child shall be protected from all forms of economic exploitation and from performing any work that is likely to be hazardous or to interfere with the child's physical, mental, spiritual, moral, or social development.

2. States Parties to the present Charter take all appropriate legislative and administrative measures to ensure the full implementation of this Article which covers both the formal and informal sectors of employment and having regard to the relevant provisions of the International Labour Organization's instruments relating to children, States Parties shall in particular:

(a) provide through legislation, minimum wages for admission to every employment;

(b) provide for appropriate regulation of hours and conditions of employment;

(c) provide for appropriate penalties or other sanctions to ensure the effective enforcement of this Article;

(d) promote the dissemination of information on the hazards of child labour to all sectors of the community.

Poverty, social exclusion, hunger and homelessness inevitably impact on children. In many households, children are the healthiest and strongest members thus inevitably they can be made to work. The International Labour Organisation has been concerned with limiting working hours and restricting abusive working conditions for children since its inception following the Treaty of Versailles. Many of its conventions impact on the rights of children, seeking to prevent economic exploitation. These range from Convention No. 5 Minimum Age (Industry) and Convention No. 6 Night Work of Young Persons (industry) Convention, both 1919 through to two more recent instruments adopted under the auspices of the International Labour Organisation. These are highlighted in its capsule list of eight fundamental instruments: Convention No. 138 (1973) on minimum age and the 1999 Convention No. 182 on the elimination of the worst forms of child labour. In many instances, children are sold into practices analogous to slavery or are trafficked to work in exploitative industries and the sex trade. The 2000 Protocol to the United Nations Convention on the Rights of the Child addresses this issue in more detail. A number of international conferences and initiatives also seek to internationalise protection of children from such treatment. For example, the Organisation of American States adopted a resolution on child trafficking (OAS Doc. AG/RES.1948 (XXXIII-O/03)).

ILO Convention No. 138 Minimum Age 1973

Article 1

Each Member for which this Convention is in force undertakes to pursue a national policy designed to ensure the effective abolition of child labour and to raise progressively the minimum age for admission to employment or work to a level consistent with the fullest physical and mental development of young persons.

Article 2

1. Each Member which ratifies this Convention shall specify, in a declaration appended to its ratification, a minimum age for admission to employment or work within its territory and on means of transport registered in its territory; subject to Articles 4 to 8 of this Convention, no one under that age shall be admitted to employment or work in any occupation.

2. Each Member which has ratified this Convention may subsequently notify the Director-General of the International Labour Office, by further declarations, that it specifies a minimum age higher than that previously specified.

3. The minimum age specified in pursuance of paragraph 1 of this Article shall not be less than the age of completion of compulsory schooling and, in any case, shall not be less than 15 years.

4. Notwithstanding the provisions of paragraph 3 of this Article, a Member whose economy and educational facilities are insufficiently developed may, after consultation with the organisations of employers and workers concerned, where such exist, initially specify a minimum age of 14 years.

5. Each Member which has specified a minimum age of 14 years in pursuance of the provisions of the preceding paragraph shall include in its reports on the application of this Convention submitted under article 22 of the Constitution of the International Labour Organisation a statement—

(a) that its reason for doing so subsists; or

(b) that it renounces its right to avail itself of the provisions in question as from a stated date.

Article 3

1. The minimum age for admission to any type of employment or work which by its nature or the circumstances in which it is carried out is likely to jeopardise the health, safety or morals of young persons shall not be less than 18 years.

2. The types of employment or work to which paragraph 1 of this Article applies shall be determined by national laws or regulations or by the competent authority, after consultation with the organisations of employers and workers concerned, where such exist.

3. Notwithstanding the provisions of paragraph 1 of this Article, national laws or regulations or the competent authority may, after consultation with the organisations of employers and workers concerned, where such exist, authorise employment or work as from the age of 16 years on condition that the health, safety and morals of the young persons concerned are fully protected and that the young persons have received adequate specific instruction or vocational training in the relevant branch of activity.

Question

To what extent is this instrument standard-setting? Note the flexibility in the age limits.

While there may be some flexibility in the instrument as regards age, the position changes with respect to the worst forms of child labour. Here there is an absolute prohibition.

ILO Convention No. 182 on the worst forms of child labour 1999
Article 2

For the purposes of this Convention, the term **child** shall apply to all persons under the age of 18.

Article 3

For the purposes of this Convention, the term **the worst forms of child labour** comprises:

(a) all forms of slavery or practices similar to slavery, such as the sale and trafficking of children, debt bondage and serfdom and forced or compulsory labour, including forced or compulsory recruitment of children for use in armed conflict;

(b) the use, procuring or offering of a child for prostitution, for the production of pornography or for pornographic performances;

(c) the use, procuring or offering of a child for illicit activities, in particular for the production and trafficking of drugs as defined in the relevant international treaties;

(d) work which, by its nature or the circumstances in which it is carried out, is likely to harm the health, safety or morals of children. . . .

Article 7

1. Each Member shall take all necessary measures to ensure the effective implementation and

enforcement of the provisions giving effect to this Convention including the provision and application of penal sanctions or, as appropriate, other sanctions.

2. Each Member shall, taking into account the importance of education in eliminating child labour, take effective and time-bound measures to:

(a) prevent the engagement of children in the worst forms of child labour;

(b) provide the necessary and appropriate direct assistance for the removal of children from the worst forms of child labour and for their rehabilitation and social integration;

(c) ensure access to free basic education, and, wherever possible and appropriate, vocational training, for all children removed from the worst forms of child labour;

(d) identify and reach out to children at special risk; and

(e) take account of the special situation of girls.

Several provisions of the United Nations Convention are also relevant for child labour. Note that Art 31 further guarantees children the right to rest and leisure, the right to be a child. This applies on top of existing employment provisions on rest and leisure time

United Nations Convention on the Rights of the Child

Article 32

1. States Parties recognize the right of the child to be protected from economic exploitation and from performing any work that is likely to be hazardous or to interfere with the child's education, or to be harmful to the child's health or physical, mental, spiritual, moral or social development.

2. States Parties shall take legislative, administrative, social and educational measures to ensure the implementation of the present article. To this end, and having regard to the relevant provisions of other international instruments, States Parties shall in particular:

(a) Provide for a minimum age or minimum ages for admission to employment;

(b) Provide for appropriate regulation of the hours and conditions of employment;

(c) Provide for appropriate penalties or other sanctions to ensure the effective enforcement of the present article.

Article 31

1. States Parties recognize the right of the child to rest and leisure, to engage in play and recreational activities appropriate to the age of the child and to participate freely in cultural life and the arts.

2. States Parties shall respect and promote the right of the child to participate fully in cultural and artistic life and shall encourage the provision of appropriate and equal opportunities for cultural, artistic, recreational and leisure activity. . . .

Article 34

States Parties undertake to protect the child from all forms of sexual exploitation and sexual abuse. For these purposes, States Parties shall in particular take all appropriate national, bilateral and multilateral measures to prevent:

(a) The inducement or coercion of a child to engage in any unlawful sexual activity;

(b) The exploitative use of children in prostitution or other unlawful sexual practices;

(c) The exploitative use of children in pornographic performances and materials.

Article 35

States Parties shall take all appropriate national, bilateral and multilateral measures to prevent the abduction of, the sale of or traffic in children for any purpose or in any form.

Article 36

States Parties shall protect the child against all other forms of exploitation prejudicial to any aspects of the child's welfare.

UNICEF and UNESCO are both heavily involved in promoting the rights of children. One of the key areas in which these organisations are active is education. In many respects education and human rights education is the key to the future of the human rights movement (see Chapter 9). Compulsory (and focussed) education of children has been shown to protect against accidental injury by landmines and the transmission of disease through poor personal hygiene. A number of similar educational schemes are currently being funded globally. Educating children can also have a positive effect on the parents and carers of the child. From a human rights perspective, much has been done to generate an awareness of children's rights among children.

10.5   REGIONAL INSTRUMENTS

Within the main regions, little attention has been paid to discrete children's rights. Africa is the sole exception as discussed below. The Council of Europe restricted themselves to encouraging national mechanisms for enforcing the United Nations Convention on the Rights of the Child (European Convention on the Exercise of Children's Rights 1996, ETS 160). Perhaps part of the reason is the fast and almost universal ratification of the United Nations Convention. Obviously, the United Nations has a comparatively new instrument to which States have proven remarkably receptive. Perhaps there is little that regional systems could add to the United Nations Convention.

Question

Revisit and consider the arguments for and against regional systems creating and protecting the range of human rights. Is the 'success' of the United Nations Conventions sufficient justification for the lack of regional instruments?

10.5.1   African Charter on the Rights and Welfare of the Child

Within the regions, only Africa has adopted a substantial tabulation of children's rights. In Africa, over half the population of many countries are children hence the situation is often acute. In 1990, the African Charter on the Rights and Welfare of the Child was adopted by the then OAU. It applies to all human beings below the age of 18 and is reminiscent of the UN Convention, for example the principle of the best interest of the child (Art 4). Children enjoy a variety of rights including the right to life, survival and development, the right to a name and nationality, freedom of expression, association, thought, conscience and religion, privacy, education and healthcare. Children are to be protected from abuse, economic and sexual exploitation, harmful traditional practices, torture, armed conflict, apartheid and trafficking. Refugees and mentally and handicapped children are singled out for particular care. All children are also entitled to have their opinions heard in matters concerning them in specified situations (Art 4(2)). In keeping with the ethos of the African Charter on Human and Peoples' Rights, children are also the incumbents of a series of duties. These include respecting their parents, serving the national community, preserving African cultural values and contributing towards African unity (Art 31).

Question

In a region such as Africa, how feasible is the realisation of these rights? Consequently, what is the value of the African Charter?

Given that children are owed the best the world has to give, what must be asked is whether the current range of children's rights realise that standard.

FURTHER READING

Ackers, L and Stalford, H, *A Community for Children? Children, Citizenship and Internal Migration in the EU*, 2004, London: Ashgate

Alston, P, Parker, S, and Seymour, J (eds), *Children, Rights and the Law*, 1992, Oxford: Clarendon

Bonthuys, E, 'The Best Interest of Children in the South African Constitution' (2005) 20(1) International Journal of Law, Policy and the Family 23

Buck, T, *International Child Law*, 2005, London: Cavendish

Detrick, S, *A Commentary on the United Nations Convention on the Rights of the Child*, 1999, the Hague: Martinus Nijhoff

Eekelaar, J, 'The emergence of children's rights' (1986) 6 Oxford Journal of Legal Studies 161

Fenwick, H, 'Clashing rights, the Welfare of the Child and the Human Rights Act' (2004) 76 Modern Law Review 889

Fortin, J, 'Rights Brought Home for Children' (1999) 62 Modern Law Review 359

Fottrell, D, *Revisiting Children's Rights—10 years of the UN Convention on the Rights of the Child*, 2001, Leiden: Kluwer

Freeman, M (ed), *Children's Rights—a comparative perspective*, 1996, Aldershot: Dartmouth

Goodwin-Gill, G and Cohen, I, *Child Soldiers: The Role of Children in Armed Conflict—A Study for the Henry Dunant Institute, Geneva*, 1994, Oxford: Clarendon Press

Hammarberg, T, 'Children' in Eide, A, Krause, C, and Rosas, A (eds), *Economic, Social and Cultural Rights—A Textbook*, the Hague: Martinus Nijhoff

Hammarberg, T, 'The U.N. Convention on the Rights of the Child—and How to Make it Work' (1990) 12 Human Rights Quarterly 97

Happold, M, *Child Soldiers in International Law*, 2005, Manchester: Manchester University Press

Kilkelly, U, *The Child and the European Convention on Human Rights*, 1999, Aldershot: Ashgate

Kilkelly, U, 'The best of both worlds for children's rights: Interpreting the European Convention on Human Rights in the light of the United Nations Convention on the Rights of the Child' (2001) 23 Human Rights Quarterly 308

Kuper, J, *International Law Concerning Child Civilians in Armed Conflict*, 1997, Oxford: OUP

Lansdown, G, 'The Reporting Process under the Convention on the Rights of the Child' in Alston, P, and Crawford, J (eds), *The Future of the UN Human Rights Treaty Monitoring* (2001), Cambridge: CUP 113

Smolin, D, 'Strategic choices in the international campaign against child labour' (2000) 22 Human Rights Quarterly 942

UNICEF, *The State of the World's Children 2005: Childhood under threat*, 2005, New York: UNICEF (also available online)

United Nations, *Fact Sheet No. 10 (Rev.1), The Rights of the Child*, Office of the High Commissioner for Human Rights: Geneva

Van Beuren, G, *The International Law on the Rights of the Child*, 1994, Dordrecht: Martinus Nijhoff

Websites

www.unicef.org—United Nations Children's Fund

www.unesco.org—United Nations Education, Science and Cultural Organisation

www.savethechildren.org—Save the Children International

www.ohchr.org/english/bodies/crc/index.htm—United Nations Committee of the Rights of the Child

www.ilo.org—the International Labour Organisation

www.europeanchildrensnetwork.org—euronet on children

www.unicef-icdc.org/—Innocenti Research Centre homepage

www.unicef.org/specialsession/wffc/—a World Fit for Children—the United Nations Special Session 2002

CHAPTER 11

DETAINEES, PRISONERS AND CONVICTS

In few situations is conflict between the State and individuals more apparent than when considering the application of criminal law. The arrest, detention and trial of an individual brings to the fore a plethora of human rights. For many, the invocation of rights in such circumstances emphasises the importance of human rights. This is particularly so in societies strongly advocating civil liberties. Encompassing political prisoners, disappeared detainees, State use of force and the notion of a fair trial, the rights of detainees, prisoners and convicts demonstrate the reality of human rights.

Crucially, irrespective of how heinous the alleged or actual crimes, individuals are still entitled to respect for their basic rights and freedoms. Whether implicated in mass murders (Saddam Hussein under domestic Iraqi law in 2005/2006), torture (Zardad, convicted in July 2005 London for crimes in Afghanistan) or a series of war crimes and crimes against humanity, the same basic principles apply. Human rights cannot be denied to alleged terrorists, murderers or rapists or even those convicted of such crimes.

The pre-eminence and importance of this area may be gauged by the array of provisions relating to the issues under the various international and regional systems which are augmented by a series of recommendations and principles drafted by the international community.

As the subject is vast, only selected elements will be discussed in detail here. It should be noted that prisoners of war are addressed in Chapter 15 in the context of the Geneva Conventions.

11.1 EQUALITY BEFORE THE LAW

Given that the international human rights regime is based on the principle of equal treatment and non-discrimination, it is not surprising that States must ensure equal treatment before the courts and under the law. Equality before the law stems from respect for human dignity and indeed from the rule of law itself.

Given the importance of the law and the judicial system in ensuring respect for fundamental rights and freedoms, the issue of equality before the law has been rigorously examined in jurisprudence.

11.1.1 Recognition as a person before the law

Once recognised as a person under national law (usually upon birth, although see the potential impact of Arts 3 and 4 of the American Convention on Human Rights) elements of equality before the law apply. There is potential for national and regional differences in equality before the law.

Smith, R, *Textbook on International Human Rights,* **2nd edn, 2005, p 250**
The first and certainly most crucial aspect of those rights associated with a fair trial is the right to be recognized as a person before the law, Clearly non-recognition presents severe challenges to the individual wishing to enforce rights before, or even appear before, a court or tribunal. . . . The

right to recognition as a person before the law is embedded in the concept of the right to an existence. It enables the individual to enter into certain legal obligations including contracts and facilitates the exercise and enforcement of rights before the courts. Every person is thus entitled [prima facie] to bear legal rights and obligations. It is not open to a State to subject a citizen to a 'civil death', that is to deprive an individual of legal personality.

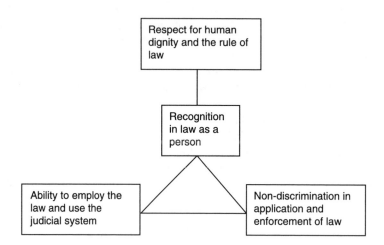

Obviously certain categories of persons do not enjoy full rights and responsibilities—minors and those deemed legally impaired through senility or mental illness are examples.

11.1.2   Non-discrimination/equality before the law

The concept of equality before the law has comparatively early origins. It is alluded to in instruments dating from the French Revolution, as well as even earlier religious texts. The French Declaration is more unequivocal about the extension of equality to all. (In some religious texts, the concept of equality was riddled with caveats.)

French Declaration of the Rights of Man and the Citizen 1789 Art 7 (obtained in translation from www.diplomatie.gouv.fr/france/14juillet/gb/decldroits.html)

No man may be accused, arrested or detained except in the cases determined by the Law, and following the procedure that it has prescribed. Those who solicit, expedite, carry out, or cause to be carried out arbitrary orders must be punished; but any citizen summoned or apprehended by virtue of the Law, must give instant obedience; resistance makes him guilty.

General Comment 18 (1989) of the Human Rights Committee elaborates on the principle of non-discrimination and the concept of equality before the law. The principle of non-discrimination is fundamental to the international human rights system. Equality before the law is a slightly different matter. Without equality before the law, some individuals will be denied access to the legal system. Accordingly they will be unable to enforce their rights at the national level and thus will encounter problems at the international level.

11.1.3   Case study: women

In some societies, women do not enjoy equal access to the legal system with men. This is often especially so with respect to matrimonial matters. Consider the following complaints raised before the international mechanisms. *Ato del Avellanal v Peru* and *Broeks v Netherlands*. Both authors raised issues before the Human Rights Committee alleging violations of the International Covenant on Civil and Political Rights. *Ato del Avellanal* is extracted in Chapter 14 on women.

Broeks v Netherlands, Communication 172/1984, Human Rights Committee UN Doc. CCPR/C/29/D/172/1984

The author was dismissed from employment due to disability. She was then entitled to social security benefits from the Dutch authorities. Her unemployment (but not disability) payments were terminated in terms of the relevant Netherlands' law. She contended that this would not have occurred if she had been a man, irrespective of marital status.

> 12.4 Although article 26 requires that legislation should prohibit discrimination, it does not of itself contain any obligation with respect to the matters that may be provided for by legislation. Thus it does not, for example, require any State to enact legislation to provide for social security. However, when such legislation is adopted in the exercise of a State's sovereign power, then such legislation must comply with article 26 of the Covenant.

> 12.5 The Committee observes in this connection that what is at issue is not whether or not social security should be progressively established in the Netherlands but whether the legislation providing for social security violates the prohibition against discrimination contained in article 26 of the International Covenant on Civil and Political Rights and the guarantee given therein to all persons regarding equal and effective protection against discrimination.

> 13. The right to equality before the law and to equal protection of the law without any discrimination does not make all differences of treatment discriminatory. A differentiation based on reasonable and objective criteria does not amount to prohibited discrimination within the meaning of article 26.

> 14. It therefore remains for the Committee to determine whether the differentiation in Netherlands law at the time in question and as applied to Mrs. Broeks constituted discrimination within the meaning of article 26. The Committee notes that in Netherlands law the provisions of articles 84 and 85 of the Netherlands Civil Code impose equal rights and obligations on both spouses with regard to their joint income. Under section 13, subsection 1 (1), of the Unemployment Benefits Act (WWV), a married woman, in order to receive WWV benefits, had to prove that she was a 'breadwinner'—a condition that did not apply to married men. Thus a differentiation which appears on one level to be one of status is in fact one of sex, placing married women at a disadvantage compared with married men. Such a differentiation is not reasonable; and this seems to have been effectively acknowledged even by the State party by the enactment of a change in the law on 29 April 1985, with retroactive effect to 23 December 1984 (see para. 4.5 above).

> 15. The circumstances in which Mrs. Broeks found herself at the material time and the application of the then valid Netherlands law made her a victim of a violation, based on sex, of article 26 of the International Covenant on Civil and Political Rights, because she was denied a social security benefit on an equal footing with men.

Note that the need for equality before the law involves equal access to the courts and the legal process for all. States must have regard to the special need of young people (discussed below) and the needs for other special groups who may not be able to invoke the protection of the legal system (those with mental health issues, for example).

11.2 ARREST

The lawful exercise of the power of arrest is an important aspect of respecting the right to liberty. In what circumstances can an individual be arrested?

European Convention for the Protection of Human Rights and Fundamental Freedoms Art 5

1 Everyone has the right to liberty and security of person. No one shall be deprived of his liberty save in the following cases and in accordance with a procedure prescribed by law:

a   the lawful detention of a person after conviction by a competent court;

b   the lawful arrest or detention of a person for non-compliance with the lawful order of a court or in order to secure the fulfilment of any obligation prescribed by law;

c   the lawful arrest or detention of a person effected for the purpose of bringing him before the competent legal authority on reasonable suspicion of having committed an offence or when it is reasonably considered necessary to prevent his committing an offence or fleeing after having done so;

d   the detention of a minor by lawful order for the purpose of educational supervision or his lawful detention for the purpose of bringing him before the competent legal authority;

e   the lawful detention of persons for the prevention of the spreading of infectious diseases, of persons of unsound mind, alcoholics or drug addicts or vagrants;

f   the lawful arrest or detention of a person to prevent his effecting an unauthorised entry into the country or of a person against whom action is being taken with a view to deportation or extradition.

2 Everyone who is arrested shall be informed promptly, in a language which he understands, of the reasons for his arrest and of any charge against him.

3 Everyone arrested or detained in accordance with the provisions of paragraph 1.c of this article shall be brought promptly before a judge or other officer authorised by law to exercise judicial power and shall be entitled to trial within a reasonable time or to release pending trial. Release may be conditioned by guarantees to appear for trial.

4 Everyone who is deprived of his liberty by arrest or detention shall be entitled to take proceedings by which the lawfulness of his detention shall be decided speedily by a court and his release ordered if the detention is not lawful.

5 Everyone who has been the victim of arrest or detention in contravention of the provisions of this article shall have an enforceable right to compensation.

International Covenant on Civil and Political Rights Art 10

1. All persons deprived of their liberty shall be treated with humanity and with respect for the inherent dignity of the human person.

2. (a) Accused persons shall, save in exceptional circumstances, be segregated from convicted persons and shall be subject to separate treatment appropriate to their status as unconvicted persons;

(b) Accused juvenile persons shall be separated from adults and brought as speedily as possible for adjudication.

3. The penitentiary system shall comprise treatment of prisoners the essential aim of which shall be their reformation and social rehabilitation. Juvenile offenders shall be segregated from adults and be accorded treatment appropriate to their age and legal status.

The arresting officials must ensure they comply with a concept of fairness to the suspect and the presumption of innocence. Arrests must not be arbitrary. When State officials arrest and detain an individual, there is a clear invocation of human rights. However, arrest and detention is lawful if in accordance with the principles prescribed in the various human rights treaties. Of particular importance in preventing arbitrary detention is ensuring that arrests are only carried out by authorised officials and for authorised reasons. These matters are addressed within national law of most States—regulations governing the police, requirements for arrest warrants and summons etc.

There is an evident need for an established legal basis for an arrest. Of course, this relates in part to a fundamental element of the rule of law. A prohibition on retroactive penal legislation and the need for fairness demands that an individual is informed of his arrest, and the reason for it.

Borisenco v Hungary, Communication 852/1999, Human Rights Committee, UN Doc. CCPR/C/76/D/852/1999

2.1 On 29 April 1996, the author and his friend, Mr. Kuspish arrived in Budapest . . . Because they were late for their train, they ran to the metro station. At this point, they were stopped by three policemen in civilian clothing. The police suspected them of pick-pocketing. They ill-treated the author and his friend by 'tightening handcuffs and striking our heads against metal booths when we attempted to speak'. They were interrogated for three hours at the police station.

2.2 On 30 April 1996, the author and his friend were charged with theft. Although the charge was not translated from Hungarian they were provided with an interpreter. Mr. Kuspish signed the investigation report but the author refused to do so without the presence of a lawyer and without including his version of the facts of the incident. The author and his friend lodged complaints against their arrest and interrogation. On 1 May 1996, in a written decision, the public prosecutor rejected these complaints, having reviewed the legality of the arrest and detention.

2.3 On 2 May 1996 the author and his friend were brought before the Pescht Central District Court for the purpose of deciding whether they should be remanded in custody. The court decided to detain them due to the risk of flight. During the police interrogation, the hearing on detention and the detention itself, the author and his friend were not allowed to contact their Embassy, families, lawyers or sports organization. On 7 May 1996, the police authorities completed the investigation and referred the case to the public prosecutor's office. . . .

3.1 The author complains that his rights were violated as he was arrested and charged without any proof of being involved in criminal activity and was ill-treated by police on arrest. He claims that he did not understand what he was being charged with and that the charge itself was not translated. He also claims a violation of the Covenant, for having been detained for over two weeks without trial. . . .

7.3 With respect to the author's claim that the State party violated article 9, paragraph 2, of the Covenant as he did not understand the reasons for his arrest or the charges against him, the Committee notes the State party's argument that the author was provided with an interpreter who explained to him the reasons for his arrest and the charge against him and finds that in the circumstances, the Committee is unable to find a violation of the Covenant in this regard (see para. 3.1).

This point has been reiterated by the Human Rights Committee and by the various regional bodies.

11.2.1   Recording detainees

The United Nations has offered guidelines to be adhered to during detention. This is particularly important with respect to ensuring that individuals subject to detention are not deprived of their rights to a legal existence. In November 2005, Iraqi and US forces uncovered a large number of detainees in secret confinement who showed evidence of torture and ill-treatment. Had strict official records of all detainees been kept, then this situation would (should) not have arisen. In conflict situations, recording of detainees and monitoring their condition is a task frequently undertaken by independent and neutral humanitarian bodies such as the International Committee of the Red Cross.

General Assembly Declaration on the Protection of all Persons from Enforced Disappearances, Resolution 47/133, 1992

Article 10

1. Any person deprived of liberty shall be held in an officially recognized place of detention and, in conformity with national law, be brought before a judicial authority promptly after detention.

2. Accurate information on the detention of such persons and their place or places of detention, including transfers, shall be made promptly available to their family members, their counsel or to any other persons having a legitimate interest in the information unless a wish to the contrary has been manifested by the persons concerned.

3. An official up-to-date register of all persons deprived of their liberty shall be maintained in every place of detention. Additionally, each State shall take steps to maintain similar centralized registers. The information contained in these registers shall be made available to the persons mentioned in the preceding paragraph, to any judicial or other competent and independent national authority and to any other competent authority entitled under the law of the State concerned or any international legal instrument to which a State concerned is a party, seeking to trace the whereabouts of a detained person.

Article 11

All persons deprived of liberty must be released in a manner permitting reliable verification that they have actually been released and, further, have been released in conditions in which their physical integrity and ability fully to exercise their rights are assured.

11.3 DISAPPEARANCES

An area of significant concern to the international community is the issue of disappearances of individuals. In terms of international law, enforced disappearances are deemed to violate the principle of respect for human dignity. Consequently, the practice is condemned and contrary to international law.

11.3.1 The international prohibition

The international prohibition is grounded in respect for the inviolability of human dignity and also those provisions concerning rights to liberty and security of the person. Accordingly there is no legally binding international instrument on the subject, although various instruments and 'soft law' can be used to substantiate the ban. In June 2006, the Human Rights Council adopted the International Convention for the Protection of All Persons from Enforced Disappearances. The text is now awaiting adoption by the General Assembly. Much of the text reflects the Declaration extracted here. The Americas, as is discussed below, have a specific international instrument.

General Assembly Declaration on the Protection of all Persons from Enforced Disappearances, Resolution 47/133, 1992

Article 1

1. Any act of enforced disappearance is an offence to human dignity. It is condemned as a denial of the purposes of the Charter of the United Nations and as a grave and flagrant violation of the human rights and fundamental freedoms proclaimed in the Universal Declaration of Human Rights and reaffirmed and developed in international instruments in this field.

2. Any act of enforced disappearance places the persons subjected thereto outside the protection of the law and inflicts severe suffering on them and their families. It constitutes a violation of the rules of international law guaranteeing, *inter alia*, the right to recognition as a person before the law, the right to liberty and security of the person and the right not to be subjected to torture and other cruel, inhuman or degrading treatment or punishment. It also violates or constitutes a grave threat to the right to life.

Article 2

1. No State shall practise, permit or tolerate enforced disappearances.

2. States shall act at the national and regional levels and in cooperation with the United Nations to contribute by all means to the prevention and eradication of enforced disappearance. . . .

Article 7

No circumstances whatsoever, whether a threat of war, a state of war, internal political instability or any other public emergency, may be invoked to justify enforced disappearances.

11.3.2 Duty to investigate disappearances

As would be expected, the laws concerning disappearances involve positive obligations on States. Just as with the right to life and the prohibition on torture (both of which are often invoked in cases of enforced disappearances), States are under a duty to properly investigate enforced disappearances and prosecute the perpetrators.

General Assembly Declaration on the Protection of all Persons from Enforced Disappearances, Resolution 47/133, 1992

Article 3

Each State shall take effective legislative, administrative, judicial or other measures to prevent and terminate acts of enforced disappearance in any territory under its jurisdiction.

Article 4

1. All acts of enforced disappearance shall be offences under criminal law punishable by appropriate penalties which shall take into account their extreme seriousness.

2. Mitigating circumstances may be established in national legislation for persons who, having participated in enforced disappearances, are instrumental in bringing the victims forward alive or in providing voluntarily information which would contribute to clarifying cases of enforced disappearance.

Article 13 *et seq.* of the General Assembly Declaration addresses in more detail the process of investigation and the mechanisms for ensuring due process is followed. This was confirmed shortly thereafter by the wider world community at the Vienna Global Conference on Human Rights.

Vienna Declaration of the World Conference on Human Rights 1993, para 62

The World Conference on Human Rights, welcoming the adoption by the General Assembly of the Declaration on the Protection of All Persons from Enforced Disappearances, calls upon all

States to take effective legislative, administrative, judicial or other measures to prevent, terminate and punish acts of enforced disappearances. The World Conference on Human Rights reaffirms that it is the duty of all State, under any circumstances, to make investigations whenever there is reason to believe that an enforced disappearance has taken place on a territory under their jurisdiction and, if allegations are confirmed, to prosecute the perpetrators.

11.3.3   The Americas

Within the Americas, thousands of people disappeared in the 1970s and 1980s. For many who have lost family and friends, the unresolved nature of disappearances is particularly difficult to come to terms with. Indeed, part of the truth and reconciliation process in some States has involved recognition of disappearances, if not reparation and apologies. Thus it is unsurprising that the Americas has produced not only the first instruments solely concerned with forced disappearances, but also the seminal case—*Velásquez Rodriguez*. The Parties to the Inter-American Convention note in the preamble that enforced disappearances violate numerous human rights and the forced disappearance of persons is an affront to the conscience of the Hemisphere and a grave and abominable offence against the inherent dignity of the human being, and one that contradicts the principles and purposes enshrined in the Charter of the Organisation of American States.

Inter-American Convention on the Forced Disappearances of Persons 1994
Article I

The States Parties to this Convention undertake:

a. Not to practice, permit, or tolerate the forced disappearance of persons, even in states of emergency or suspension of individual guarantees;

b. To punish within their jurisdictions, those persons who commit or attempt to commit the crime of forced disappearance of persons and their accomplices and accessories;

c. To cooperate with one another in helping to prevent, punish, and eliminate the forced disappearance of persons;

d. To take legislative, administrative, judicial, and any other measures necessary to comply with the commitments undertaken in this Convention.

Article II

For the purposes of this Convention, forced disappearance is considered to be the act of depriving a person or persons of his or their freedom, in whatever way, perpetrated by agents of the state or by persons or groups of persons acting with the authorization, support, or acquiescence of the state, followed by an absence of information or a refusal to acknowledge that deprivation of freedom or to give information on the whereabouts of that person, thereby impeding his or her recourse to the applicable legal remedies and procedural guarantees.

Article III

The States Parties undertake to adopt, in accordance with their constitutional procedures, the legislative measures that may be needed to define the forced disappearance of persons as an offense and to impose an appropriate punishment commensurate with its extreme gravity. This offense shall be deemed continuous or permanent as long as the fate or whereabouts of the victim has not been determined.

The States Parties may establish mitigating circumstances for persons who have participated in acts constituting forced disappearance when they help to cause the victim to reappear alive or provide information that sheds light on the forced disappearance of a person. . . .

Article VII

Criminal prosecution for the forced disappearance of persons and the penalty judicially imposed on its perpetrator shall not be subject to statutes of limitations.

However, if there should be a norm of a fundamental character preventing application of the stipulation contained in the previous paragraph, the period of limitation shall be equal to that which applies to the gravest crime in the domestic laws of the corresponding State Party.

Article VIII

The defense of due obedience to superior orders or instructions that stipulate, authorize, or encourage forced disappearance shall not be admitted. All persons who receive such orders have the right and duty not to obey them.

The States Parties shall ensure that the training of public law-enforcement personnel or officials includes the necessary education on the offense of forced disappearance of persons.

Article IX

Persons alleged to be responsible for the acts constituting the offense of forced disappearance of persons may be tried only in the competent jurisdictions of ordinary law in each state, to the exclusion of all other special jurisdictions, particularly military jurisdictions.

The acts constituting forced disappearance shall not be deemed to have been committed in the course of military duties.

Privileges, immunities, or special dispensations shall not be admitted in such trials, without prejudice to the provisions set forth in the Vienna Convention on Diplomatic Relations.

Article X

In no case may exceptional circumstances such as a state of war, the threat of war, internal political instability, or any other public emergency be invoked to justify the forced disappearance of persons. In such cases, the right to expeditious and effective judicial procedures and recourse shall be retained as a means of determining the whereabouts or state of health of a person who has been deprived of freedom, or of identifying the official who ordered or carried out such deprivation of freedom.

In pursuing such procedures or recourse, and in keeping with applicable domestic law, the competent judicial authorities shall have free and immediate access to all detention centers and to each of their units, and to all places where there is reason to believe the disappeared person might be found including places that are subject to military jurisdiction.

Article XI

Every person deprived of liberty shall be held in an officially recognized place of detention and be brought before a competent judicial authority without delay, in accordance with applicable domestic law.

The States Parties shall establish and maintain official up-to-date registries of their detainees and, in accordance with their domestic law, shall make them available to relatives, judges, attorneys, any other person having a legitimate interest, and other authorities.

Article XII

The States Parties shall give each other mutual assistance in the search for, identification, location, and return of minors who have been removed to another state or detained therein as a consequence of the forced disappearance of their parents or guardians.

Question

Consider the extent to which the provisions of this convention go beyond the provisions on deprivation of liberty and detention which are enshrined in the Inter-American Convention on Human Rights and the International Covenant on Civil and Political Rights.

11.3.4   Case study: *Velásquez Rodriguez*, Inter-American Court of Human Rights 1988, Series C, No. 4

Facts: a complaint was received on behalf of Velásquez Rodriguez who had disappeared following an 'arrest' in Tegucigalpa, Honduras. It was alleged that the State was responsible as Rodriguez had been arrested by State security forces although this was consistently officially denied. The complaint also alleged that he had been subjected to interrogation and ill-treatment/torture. As a consequence, violations of numerous rights protected by the American Convention were claimed. The Inter-American Commission referred the matter to the Court which found violations of the Convention. It should be noted that Honduras repeatedly failed to reply to communications from the Inter-American Commission concerning the facts and disputed the Commission's finding of fact.

174. The State has a legal duty to take reasonable steps to prevent human rights violations and to use the means at its disposal to carry out a serious investigation of violations committed within its jurisdiction, to identify those responsible, to impose the appropriate punishment and to ensure the victim adequate compensation.

175. This duty to prevent includes all those means of a legal, political, administrative and cultural nature that promote the protection of human rights and ensure that any violations are considered and treated as illegal acts, which, as such, may lead to the punishment of those responsible and the obligation to indemnify the victims for damages. It is not possible to make a detailed list of all such measures, since they vary with the law and the conditions of each State Party. Of course, while the State is obligated to prevent human rights abuses, the existence of a particular violation does not, in itself, prove the failure to take preventive measures. On the other hand, subjecting a person to official, repressive bodies that practice torture and assassination with impunity is itself a breach of the duty to prevent violations of the rights to life and physical integrity of the person, even if that particular person is not tortured or assassinated, or if those facts cannot be proven in a concrete case.

176. The State is obligated to investigate every situation involving a violation of the rights protected by the Convention. If the State apparatus acts in such a way that the violation goes unpunished and the victim's full enjoyment of such rights is not restored as soon as possible, the State has failed to comply with its duty to ensure the free and full exercise of those rights to the persons within its jurisdiction. The same is true when the State allows private persons or groups to act freely and with impunity to the detriment of the rights recognized by the Convention.

177. In certain circumstances, it may be difficult to investigate acts that violate an individual's rights. The duty to investigate, like the duty to prevent, is not breached merely because the investigation does not produce a satisfactory result. Nevertheless, it must be undertaken in a serious manner and not as a mere formality preordained to be ineffective. An investigation must have an objective and be assumed by the State as its own legal duty, not as a step taken by private interests that depends upon the initiative of the victim or his family or upon their offer of proof, without an effective search for the truth by the government. This is true regardless of what agent is eventually found responsible for the violation. Where the acts of private parties that violate the Convention are not seriously investigated, those parties are aided in a sense by the government, thereby making the State responsible on the international plane.

178. In the instant case, the evidence shows a complete inability of the procedures of the State of Honduras, which were theoretically adequate, to carry out an investigation into the disappearance of Manfredo Velásquez, and of the fulfillment of its duties to pay compensation and punish those responsible, as set out in Article 1 (1) of the Convention.

179 As the Court has verified above, the failure of the judicial system to act upon the writs brought before various tribunals in the instant case has been proven. Not one writ of habeas

corpus was processed. No judge has access to the places where Manfredo Velásquez might have been detained. The criminal complaint was dismissed.

180. Nor did the organs of the Executive Branch carry out a serious investigation to establish the fate of Manfredo Velásquez. There was no investigation of public allegations of a practice of disappearances nor a determination of whether Manfredo Velásquez had been a victim of that practice. The Commission's requests for information were ignored to the point that the Commission had to presume, under Article 42 of its Regulations, that the allegations were true. The offer of an investigation in accord with Resolution 30/83 of the Commission resulted in an investigation by the Armed Forces, the same body accused of direct responsibility for the disappearances. This raises grave questions regarding the seriousness of the investigation. The Government often resorted to asking relatives of the victims to present conclusive proof of their allegations even though those allegations, because they involved crimes against the person, should have been investigated on the Government's own initiative in fulfillment of the State's duty to ensure public order. This is especially true when the allegations refer to a practice carried out within the Armed Forces, which, because of its nature, is not subject to private investigations. No proceeding was initiated to establish responsibility for the disappearance of Manfredo Velásquez and apply punishment under internal law. All of the above leads to the conclusion that the Honduran authorities did not take effective action to ensure respect for human rights within the jurisdiction of that State as required by Article 1 (1) of the Convention.

181. The duty to investigate facts of this type continues as long as there is uncertainty about the fate of the person who has disappeared. Even in the hypothetical case that those individually responsible for crimes of this type cannot be legally punished under certain circumstances, the State is obligated to use the means at its disposal to inform the relatives of the fate of the victims and, if they have been killed, the location of their remains.

182. The Court is convinced, and has so found, that the disappearance of Manfredo Velásquez was carried out by agents who acted under cover of public authority. However, even had that fact not been proven, the failure of the State apparatus to act, which is clearly proven, is a failure on the part of Honduras to fulfill the duties it assumed under Article 1 (1) of the Convention, which obligated it to ensure Manfredo Velásquez the free and full exercise of his human rights.

183. The Court notes that the legal order of Honduras does not authorize such acts and that internal law defines them as crimes. The Court also recognizes that not all levels of the Government of Honduras were necessarily aware of those acts, nor is there any evidence that such acts were the result of official orders. Nevertheless, those circumstances are irrelevant for the purposes of establishing whether Honduras is responsible under international law for the violations of human rights perpetrated within the practice of disappearances.

184. According to the principle of the continuity of the State in international law, responsibility exists both independently of changes of government over a period of time and continuously from the time of the act that creates responsibility to the time when the act is declared illegal. The foregoing is also valid in the area of human rights although, from an ethical or political point of view, the attitude of the new government may be much more respectful of those rights than that of the government in power when the violations occurred.

185. The Court, therefore, concludes that the facts found in this proceeding show that the State of Honduras is responsible for the involuntary disappearance of Angel Manfredo Velásquez Rodríguez. Thus, Honduras has violated Articles 7, 5 and 4 of the Convention.

186. As a result of the disappearance, Manfredo Velásquez was the victim of an arbitrary detention, which deprived him of his physical liberty without legal cause and without a determination of the lawfulness of his detention by a judge or competent tribunal. Those acts directly violate the right to personal liberty recognized by Article 7 of the Convention and are a violation imputable to Honduras of the duties to respect and ensure that right under Article 1 (1).

187. The disappearance of Manfredo Velásquez violates the right to personal integrity recognized by Article 5 of the Convention. First, the mere subjection of an individual to prolonged isolation

and deprivation of communication is in itself cruel and inhuman treatment which harms the psychological and moral integrity of the person, and violates the right of every detainee under Article 5 (1) and 5 (2) to treatment respectful of his dignity. Second, although it has not been directly shown that Manfredo Velásquez was physically tortured, his kidnapping and imprisonment by governmental authorities, who have been shown to subject detainees to indignities, cruelty and torture, constitute a failure of Honduras to fulfill the duty imposed by Article 1 (1) to ensure the rights under Article 5 (1) and 5 (2) of the Convention. The guarantee of physical integrity and the right of detainees to treatment respectful of their human dignity require States Parties to take reasonable steps to prevent situations which are truly harmful to the rights protected.

188. The above reasoning is applicable to the right to life recognized by Article 4 of the Convention. The context in which the disappearance of Manfredo Velásquez occurred and the lack of knowledge seven years later about his fate create a reasonable presumption that he was killed. Even if there is a minimal margin of doubt in this respect, it must be presumed that his fate was decided by authorities who systematically executed detainees without trial and concealed their bodies in order to avoid punishment. This, together with the failure to investigate, is a violation by Honduras of a legal duty under Article 1 (1) of the Convention to ensure the rights recognized by Article 4 (1). That duty is to ensure every person subject to its jurisdiction the inviolability of the right to life and the right not to have one's life taken arbitrarily. These rights imply an obligation on the part of States Parties to take reasonable steps to prevent situations that could result in the violation of that right.

This case remains one of the most influential as regards state detention and enforced disappearances. Other regional and national courts have considered and applied it.

11.3.5   Other examples

The Americas are not the only region within which enforced disappearances have occurred. The following case was heard by a Grand Chamber of the European Court of Human Rights. It is unusual insofar as it is an inter-State complaint. As noted in Chapters 4 and 5, these are not common in international and regional law. Due to the contentious nature of the division of Cyprus, several inter-State applications have been made. The following case is the most recent and concerns, *inter alia*, the matter of disappearances. It is the first of the complaints to have been referred to the Court.

Cyprus v Turkey, Application no. 25781/94, judgment, 10 May 2001

Cyprus is currently a divided island with the northern Turkish part and the southern Greek part. The island (south) is now a member State of the European Union and is recognised as being Cyprus. Turkish armed forces occupy the northern part of the island. Cyprus claimed that about 1,491 Greek Cypriots were still missing twenty years after the cessation of hostilities. They were last seen alive in Turkish custody and their fate has never been accounted for by the respondent State. Turkey noted a lack of proof that any of the missing persons were still alive or were being kept in custody. In their principal submission, the issues raised by the applicant Government should continue to be pursued within the framework of the United Nations Committee on Missing Persons rather than under the Convention. Note that in 1981 the United Nations Committee on Missing Persons (CMP) was set up to 'look into cases of persons reported missing in the inter-communal fighting as well as in the events of July 1974 and afterwards' and 'to draw up comprehensive lists of missing persons of both communities, specifying as appropriate whether they are still alive or dead, and in the latter case approximate times of death'.

132. The Court recalls that there is no proof that any of the missing persons have been unlawfully killed. However, in its opinion, and of relevance to the instant case, the above-mentioned procedural obligation also arises upon proof of an arguable claim that an individual, who was last seen in the custody of agents of the State, subsequently disappeared in a context which may be considered life-threatening.

133. Against this background, the Court observes that the evidence bears out the applicant Government's claim that many persons now missing were detained either by Turkish or Turkish-Cypriot forces. Their detention occurred at a time when the conduct of military operations was accompanied by arrests and killings on a large scale. The Commission correctly described the situation as life-threatening. The above-mentioned broadcast statement of Mr Denktaş and the later report of Professor Küçük, if not conclusive of the respondent State's liability for the death of missing persons are, at the very least, clear indications of the climate of risk and fear obtaining at the material time and of the real dangers to which detainees were exposed. . . .

136. Having regard to the above considerations, the Court concludes that there has been a continuing violation of Article 2 on account of the failure of the authorities of the respondent State to conduct an effective investigation aimed at clarifying the whereabouts and fate of Greek-Cypriot missing persons who disappeared in life threatening circumstances. . . .

148. The Court refers to the irrefutable evidence that Greek Cypriots were held by Turkish or Turkish-Cypriot forces. There is no indication of any records having been kept of either the identities of those detained or the dates or location of their detention. From a humanitarian point of view, this failing cannot be excused with reference either to the fighting which took place at the relevant time or to the overall confused and tense state of affairs. Seen in terms of Article 5 of the Convention, the absence of such information has made it impossible to allay the concerns of the relatives of the missing persons about the latter's fate. Notwithstanding the impossibility of naming those who were taken into custody, the respondent State should have made other inquiries with a view to accounting for the disappearances. As noted earlier, there has been no official reaction to new evidence that Greek-Cypriot missing persons were taken into Turkish custody (see paragraph 134 above).

149. The Court has addressed this allegation from the angle of the procedural requirements of Article 5 of the Convention and the obligations devolving on the respondent State as a Contracting Party to the Convention. Like the Commission, and without questioning the value of the humanitarian work being undertaken by the CMP, the Court reiterates that those obligations cannot be discharged with reference to the nature of the CMP's investigation (see paragraph 135 above).

150. The Court concludes that, during the period under consideration, there has been a continuing violation of Article 5 of the Convention by virtue of the failure of the authorities of the respondent State to conduct an effective investigation into the whereabouts and fate of the missing Greek-Cypriot persons in respect of whom there is an arguable claim that they were in custody at the time they disappeared. . . .

157. The Court observes that the authorities of the respondent State have failed to undertake any investigation into the circumstances surrounding the disappearance of the missing persons. In the absence of any information about their fate, the relatives of persons who went missing during the events of July and August 1974 were condemned to live in a prolonged state of acute anxiety which cannot be said to have been erased with the passage of time. The Court does not consider, in the circumstances of this case, that the fact that certain relatives may not have actually witnessed the detention of family members or complained about such to the authorities of the respondent State deprives them of victim status under Article 3. It recalls that the military operation resulted in a considerable loss of life, large-scale arrests and detentions and enforced separation of families. The overall context must still be vivid in the minds of the relatives of persons whose fate has never been accounted for by the authorities. They endure the agony of not knowing whether family members were killed in the conflict or are still in detention or, if

detained, have since died. The fact that a very substantial number of Greek Cypriots had to seek refuge in the south coupled with the continuing division of Cyprus must be considered to constitute very serious obstacles to their quest for information. The provision of such information is the responsibility of the authorities of the respondent State. This responsibility has not been discharged. For the Court, the silence of the authorities of the respondent State in the face of the real concerns of the relatives of the missing persons attains a level of severity which can only be categorised as inhuman treatment within the meaning of Article 3.

158. For the above reasons, the Court concludes that, during the period under consideration, there has been a continuing violation of Article 3 of the Convention in respect of the relatives of the Greek-Cypriot missing persons.

11.4 DETENTION PENDING TRIAL

While it is feasible to detain suspects pending trial, care must be taken to ensure that detention is actually necessary and that the period of it is reasonable. States should not detain people while undertaking investigation unless they have a reasonable suspicion that an offence has been committed and release could encourage flight or tampering with evidence. As to the reasonableness of length of detention, this varies from State to State and case to case. The circumstances of the case dictate how long is acceptable. Note, however, that the need for a judge to approve and authorise pro-longed periods of pre-trial detention remains.

Aside from issues of length of detention, care must also be taken to treat pre-trial detainees as innocent. Ideally they should be kept separate from convicts. The pre-sumption of innocence operates in their favour. This is, of course, problematic for many States. Lack of resources and appropriate detention facilities can give rise to complaints. In light of this, a balance must be achieved between the need to detain an individual pending trial (for whatever legitimate reason) and the need to treat detainees with the respect due to the presumed innocent during custody.

Wilson v Philippines, Communication 868/1999, Human Rights Committee, UN Doc. CCPR/C/79/D/868/1999

2.1 On 16 September 1996, the author was forcibly arrested without warrant as a result of a complaint of rape filed by the biological father of the author's twelve year old step-daughter and transferred to a police station. He was not advised of his rights, and, not speaking the local language, was unaware as to the reasons for what was occurring. At the police station, he was held in a 4 × 4 ft cage with three others, and charged on the second day with attempted rape of his stepdaughter. He was then transferred to Valenzuela municipal jail, where the charge was changed to rape. There he was beaten and ill-treated in a 'concrete coffin'. This 16 × 16 ft cell held 40 prisoners with a 6 inch air gap some 10 ft from the floor. One inmate was shot by a drunken guard, and the author had a gun placed to his head on several occasions by guards. The bottoms of his feet were struck by a guard's baton, and other inmates struck him on the guards' orders. He was ordered to strike other prisoners and was beaten when he refused to do so. He was also constantly subjected to extortion by other inmates with the acquiescence and in some instances on the direct instruction of the prison authorities, and beaten when he refused to pay or perform the directed act(s). There was no running water, insufficient sanitary conditions (a single non-flush bowl in the cell for all detainees), no visiting facility, and severe food rationing. Nor was he segregated from convicted prisoners. . . .

2.4 The author was then placed on death row in Muntinlupa prison, where 1,000 death row prisoners were kept in three dormitories. Foreign inmates were continually extorted by other inmates with the acquiescence, and sometimes at the direction of, prison authorities. The author refers to media reports that the prison was controlled by gangs and corrupt officials, at whose mercy the author remained throughout his confinement on death row. Several high-ranking prison officials were sentenced for extortion of prisoners, and large amounts of weapons were found in cells. The author was pressured and tortured to provide gangs and officials with money. There were no guards in the dormitory or cells, which contained over 200 inmates and remained unlocked at all times. His money and personal effects had been removed from him en route to the prison, and for three weeks he had no visitors, and therefore no basic necessities such as soap or bedding. Food comprised unwashed rice and other inappropriate substances. Sanitation consisted of two non-flushing toilet bowls in an area which was also a 200-person communal shower.

2.5 The author was forced to pay for the 8×8 ft area in which he slept and financially to support the eight others with him. He was forced to sleep alongside drug-deranged individuals and persons who deliberately and constantly deprived him of sleep. He was forcibly tattooed with a permanent gang mark. Inmates were stretched out on a bench on public display and beaten with wood across the thighs, or otherwise 'taught a lesson'. The author states he lived in constant fear coming close to death and suicidal depression, watching six inmates walk to their execution while five others died violent deaths. Fearing death after a 'brutally unfair and biased' trial, he suffered severe physical and psychological distress and felt 'total helplessness and hopelessness'. As a result, he is 'destroyed both financially and in many ways emotionally'.

Following submission of this communication, the national Supreme Court released Wilson, dismissing the allegations against him.

7.3 As to the author's claims under articles 7 and 10 regarding his treatment in detention and the conditions of detention, both before and after conviction, the Committee observes that the State party, rather than responding to the specific allegations made, has indicated that they require further investigation. In the circumstances, therefore, the Committee is obliged to give due weight to the author's allegations, which are detailed and particularized. The Committee considers that the conditions of detention described, as well as the violent and abusive behaviour both of certain prison guards and of other inmates, as apparently acquiesced in by the prison authorities, are seriously in violation of the author's right, as a prisoner, to be treated with humanity and in with respect for his inherent dignity, in violation of article 10, paragraph 1. As at least some of the acts of violence against the author were committed either by the prison guards, upon their instigation or with their acquiescence, there was also a violation of article 7. There is also a specific violation of article 10, paragraph 2, arising from the failure to segregate the author, pre-trial, from convicted prisoners.

7.4 As to the claims concerning the author's mental suffering and anguish as a consequence of being sentenced to death, the Committee observes that the authors' mental condition was exacerbated by his treatment in, as well as the conditions of, his detention, and resulted in documented long-term psychological damage to him. In view of these aggravating factors consti-tuting further compelling circumstances beyond the mere length of time spent by the author in imprisonment under a sentence of death, the Committee concludes that the author's suffering under a sentence of death amounted to an additional violation of article 7. None of these violations were remedied by the Supreme Court's decision to annul the author's conviction and death sentence after he had spent almost months of imprisonment under a sentence of death.

7.5 As to the author's claims under article 9 the Committee notes that the State party has not contested the factual submissions of the author. Hence, due weight must be given to the informa-tion submitted by the author. The Committee concludes that the author was not informed, at the time of arrest, of the reasons for his arrest and was not promptly informed of the charges against him; that the author was arrested without a warrant and hence in violation of domestic law; and that after the arrest the author was not brought promptly before a judge. Consequently, there was a violation of article 9, paragraphs 1, 2 and 3, of the Covenant.

Question

Identify the various provisions of the code of conduct for law enforcement officials which have been breached.

11.4.1　Terrorism and derogations

In the current political climate, detention of terrorism suspects is increasingly common. For a variety of reasons, the individuals are not brought to trial but rather detained without trial and often for long periods of time. This has resulted in derogations from the provisions on detention. In other instances, legalistic devices have been used in an attempt to obviate the international requirements.

11.4.1.1　United States of America detainees in Guantanamo Bay, Cuba/Bagram, Afghanistan/Kandahar, Afghanistan/Charleston, USA

The United States of America has a number of detainees at the above locations, detained under the 'war on terror'. In addition, others are detained at undisclosed locations. Note that a major issue in the United States, that of the use of subversive techniques to extract information was addressed in a bill before the houses in December 2005 which prohibits the use of torture and related techniques for the purpose of obtaining information. Following the Supreme Court's rejection of the tribunal system for trying detainees, a new draft measure (August 2006) allegedly seeks to ensure detention of enemy combatants until the cessation of hostilities. Note also the issues arising from George W. Bush's confirmation in September 2006 of CIA detention centres (no longer in use) for terror suspects. These were based outwith the US but all suspects are now in Guantanamo.

11.4.1.2　Case study: United Kingdom

The United Kingdom provides a good case study of extended periods of detention.

Prevention of Terrorism (Temporary Provisions) Act 1974, c56

7. (1) A constable may arrest without warrant a person whom he reasonably suspects to be—

a)　a person guilty of an offence under section 1 or 3, of this Act;

b)　a person concerned in the commission, preparation or instigation of acts of terrorism;

c)　a person subject to an exclusion order.

(2) A person arrested under this section shall not be detained in right of the arrest for more than 48 hours after his arrest:

Provided that the Secretary of State may, in any particular case, extend the period of 48 hours by a further period not exceeding 5 days.

This act was intended to be a temporary measure, as the name suggests, adopted in response to rising tensions in Northern Ireland. Controversially, it was renewed annually. The United Kingdom entered a derogation to Art 5 of the European Convention on Human Rights to permit detention of terrorist suspects. Note in particular the caveat that the Secretary of State may authorise an extension of the period of detention. This appeared in subsequent versions of the Prevention of Terrorism Act. The derogation was withdrawn eventually but, following the finding of an infringement of the treaty by the court in *Brogan v United Kingdom*, Series A, No. 145 (1988), a new derogation was inserted and upheld in *Brannigan & McBride v United Kingdom*, Series A, No. 258B (1993).

Note the Provisions of the Prevention of Terrorism Act 2005, an act adopted in response to the perceived change in the threat to the United Kingdom (that is, from beyond Northern Ireland).

Prevention of Terrorism Act 2005, c2

Arrest and detention pending derogating control order

5. (1) A constable may arrest and detain an individual if—

(a) the Secretary of State has made an application to the court for a derogating control order to be made against that individual; and

(b) the constable considers that the individual's arrest and detention is necessary to ensure that he is available to be given notice of the order if it is made.

(2) A constable who has arrested an individual under this section must take him to the designated place that the constable considers most appropriate as soon as practicable after the arrest.

(3) An individual taken to a designated place under this section may be detained there until the end of 48 hours from the time of his arrest.

(4) If the court considers that it is necessary to do so to ensure that the individual in question is available to be given notice of any derogating control order that is made against him, it may, during the 48 hours following his arrest, extend the period for which the individual may be detained under this section by a period of no more than 48 hours. . . .

(7) An individual detained under this section—

(a) shall be deemed to be in legal custody throughout the period of his detention; and

(b) after having been taken to a designated place shall be deemed—

(i) in England and Wales, to be in police detention for the purposes of the Police and Criminal Evidence Act 1984 (c. 60); and

(ii) in Northern Ireland, to be in police detention for the purposes of the Police and Criminal Evidence (Northern Ireland) Order 1989 (S.I. 1989/1341 (N.I. 12));

but paragraph (b) has effect subject to subsection (8). . . .

(9) The power to detain an individual under this section includes power to detain him in a manner that is incompatible with his right to liberty under Article 5 of the Human Rights Convention if, and only if—

(a) there is a designated derogation in respect of the detention of individuals under this section in connection with the making of applications for derogating control orders; and

(b) that derogation and the designated derogation relating to the power to make the orders applied for are designated in respect of the same public emergency.

Given the involvement of the courts in the process, the derogation of the United Kingdom was finally withdrawn.

Late in 2005, the Terrorism Bill 2005 was introduced to Parliament. The Home Secretary declared it to be compatible with the European Convention (such a declaration being a requirement of the Human Rights Act 1998, s 19). Clause 23 of the Bill, as presented initially to Parliament, permitted detention for up to three months with judicial consent (this would be a revision to the Terrorism Act 2000, the current statute which replaced the various temporary provisions statutes of the 1970s and 1990s). Famously this was rejected by the House of Commons. Ultimately s 23 of the Terrorism Act 2006 does permit an extended period of detention (28 days) but the section itself must be renewed by Parliament after a year's operation.

11.5   TORTURE AND THE USE OF FORCE

Abuse of prisoners can arise at various stages of the detention and trial process. Obviously, international human rights law includes an absolute prohibition on torture. However, as history regularly attests, there are regular allegations of torture and/or excessive use of force against detainees. More commonly, complaints of confessions extracted under duress are raised. Although miscarriages of justice are a major risk, not all systems in all countries provide appropriate and available remedies. However, as arrest, detention and incarceration all involve the State impacting dramatically and overtly on the rights and liberties of the individual, there is a clear and pressing need for international guidelines to be adhered to. Detainees are clearly incredibly vulnerable in these circumstances.

11.5.1   At arrest

The first instance (to be examined here) in which force may be encountered is at the time of arrest. Although due force can be used to effect an arrest, the level of force should be reasonable in the circumstances of the case.

Basic Principles on the Use of Force and Firearms by Law Enforcement Officials Adopted by the Eighth United Nations Congress on the Prevention of Crime and the Treatment of Offenders, Havana, Cuba, 27 August to 7 September 1990

3. The development and deployment of non-lethal incapacitating weapons should be carefully evaluated in order to minimize the risk of endangering uninvolved persons, and the use of such weapons should be carefully controlled.

4. Law enforcement officials, in carrying out their duty, shall, as far as possible, apply non-violent means before resorting to the use of force and firearms. They may use force and firearms only if other means remain ineffective or without any promise of achieving the intended result.

5. Whenever the lawful use of force and firearms is unavoidable, law enforcement officials shall:

(a) Exercise restraint in such use and act in proportion to the seriousness of the offence and the legitimate objective to be achieved;

(b) Minimize damage and injury, and respect and preserve human life;

(c) Ensure that assistance and medical aid are rendered to any injured or affected persons at the earliest possible moment;

(d) Ensure that relatives or close friends of the injured or affected person are notified at the earliest possible moment.

6. Where injury or death is caused by the use of force and firearms by law enforcement officials, they shall report the incident promptly to their superiors, in accordance with principle 22.

7. Governments shall ensure that arbitrary or abusive use of force and firearms by law enforcement officials is punished as a criminal offence under their law.

8. Exceptional circumstances such as internal political instability or any other public emergency may not be invoked to justify any departure from these basic principles.

9. Law enforcement officials shall not use firearms against persons except in self-defence or defence of others against the imminent threat of death or serious injury, to prevent the perpetration of a particularly serious crime involving grave threat to life, to arrest a person presenting such a danger and resisting their authority, or to prevent his or her escape, and only when less extreme means are insufficient to achieve these objectives. In any event, intentional lethal use of firearms may only be made when strictly unavoidable in order to protect life.

10. In the circumstances provided for under principle 9, law enforcement officials shall identify themselves as such and give a clear warning of their intent to use firearms, with sufficient time for the warning to be observed, unless to do so would unduly place the law enforcement officials at risk or would create a risk of death or serious harm to other persons, or would be clearly inappropriate or pointless in the circumstances of the incident.

Force is not proscribed but must be reasonable in the circumstances. Without a doubt, State practice varies as regards arming regular police and law enforcement officials. Countries such as the United Kingdom which normally operate a consensual policing system refrain from arming police officers in ordinary situations. Only when responding to certain events, including terrorism, are officers armed.

Question

Note the problems which arose in summer 2005 when Jean Charles de Menezes, a Brazilian, was mistakenly shot and killed by armed officers pursuing alleged terrorist bombing suspects in London. Can the actions of the police be justified (in human rights terms) given the heightened security in place at the time?

11.5.2 Effective investigation of allegations of torture

While the provisions governing arrest and detention have been addressed, a further issue of concern is allegations of torture, inhuman or degrading treatment made by a detainee or prisoner against his or her captors. As is noted in Chapter 3, some rights and freedoms are non-derogable. The prohibition on torture is a prime example. Moreover, as Chapter 1 notes, it may even be regarded as jus cogens. To discharge their obligations, States have to ensure that systems are put in place to ensure that infringing treatment does not occur. In the worst scenario, if it does, it has to be investigated fully and expeditiously with appropriate steps taken to ensure no repeat.

Principles on the Effective Investigation and Documentation of Torture and other Cruel Inhuman or Degrading Treatment or Punishment, General Assembly Resolution 55/89 of 4 December 2000

2. States shall ensure that complaints and reports of torture or ill-treatment are promptly and effectively investigated. Even in the absence of an express complaint, an investigation shall be undertaken if there are other indications that torture or ill-treatment might have occurred. The investigators, who shall be independent of the suspected perpetrators and the agency they serve, shall be competent and impartial. They shall have access to, or be empowered to commission investigations by, impartial medical or other experts. The methods used to carry out such investigations shall meet the highest professional standards and the findings shall be made public.

3. (a) The investigative authority shall have the power and obligation to obtain all the information necessary to the inquiry. The persons conducting the investigation shall have at their disposal all the necessary budgetary and technical resources for effective investigation. They shall also have the authority to oblige all those acting in an official capacity allegedly involved in torture or ill-treatment to appear and testify. The same shall apply to any witness. To this end, the investigative authority shall be entitled to issue summonses to witnesses, including any officials allegedly involved, and to demand the production of evidence.

   (b) Alleged victims of torture or ill-treatment, witnesses, those conducting the investigation and their families shall be protected from violence, threats of violence or any other form of intimidation that may arise pursuant to the investigation. Those potentially implicated in torture or ill-treatment shall be removed from any position of control or power, whether direct or indirect, over complainants, witnesses and their families, as well as those conducting the investigation.

4. Alleged victims of torture or ill-treatment and their legal representatives shall be informed of, and have access to, any hearing, as well as to all information relevant to the investigation, and shall be entitled to present other evidence.

Note also the role of the Committee against Torture in monitoring detention centres through visits though bear in mind that the State must consent to such visits—see Chapter 6—noting the provisions of the Optional Protocol.

11.5.3   Deaths in custody—Australia and aboriginal deaths in custody

Deaths in custody require particularly careful investigation to ensure that the action or indeed inaction of State officials did not contribute to the death. In 1987, a Royal Commission was established in Australia to investigate the prevalence of aboriginal deaths in custody. The Commission was set up jointly by the Commonwealth (of Australia), the various States and the Northern Territory. It was precipitated by growing public awareness of the large number of Aboriginal and Torres Strait Islander peoples dying in custody. The Commission examined 99 incidences (deaths in custody, prison or juvenile detention) which occurred between 1 January 1980 and 31 May 1989. Cognisance was taken of the circumstances of the death, action taken by the appropriate authorities at the time and any relevant underlying causes (social, cultural, legal factors).

Royal Commission Report into Aboriginal Deaths in Custody, 1991, Canberra: Commonwealth Publishers (5 volumes)
Average personal profiles of the deceased

Age: young, average age 32 at time of death

Education: only two had completed secondary education

Health: poor

Family: almost half had been separated from their birth families as children (the so-called stolen generation policies)

Work: 83 were unemployed at the date of detention

Criminal record: 74 had previously been charged with offences when they were under 19 years and 43 of that group had been taken into custody for alcohol-related offences.

The Commissioners did not consider any of the deaths attributable to violence or brutality on the part of police or prison officers. There was, however, an allegation of a lack of proper care for detainees. Aboriginal and Torres Strait Islanders were not statistically more likely to die in custody than other Australians, however that statistic is tempered by the fact that they are twenty-nine times more likely to end up in custody in the first place! The recommendations of the Commission were wide-ranging, covering all aspects of Australian life and aboriginal society.

The resulting report was not only lengthy, but a uniquely comprehensive review of the status of indigenous peoples within Australia. Three hundred and thirty-nine recommendations were made, encompassing all aspects of Aboriginal life, including education, health, housing and land.

11.6 FAIR TRIAL

The right to a fair trial is one of the most heavily litigated human rights. Within the Council of Europe, the majority of cases before the Court involve Art 6, the right to a fair trial. For many, particularly in democratic liberal traditions, this is one of the more fundamental of rights. It finds expression in all the major instruments.

International Covenant on Civil and Political Rights 1966

Article 14

1. All persons shall be equal before the courts and tribunals. In the determination of any criminal charge against him, or of his rights and obligations in a suit at law, everyone shall be entitled to a fair and public hearing by a competent, independent and impartial tribunal established by law. The press and the public may be excluded from all or part of a trial for reasons of morals, public order (ordre public) or national security in a democratic society, or when the interest of the private lives of the parties so requires, or to the extent strictly necessary in the opinion of the court in special circumstances where publicity would prejudice the interests of justice; but any judgement rendered in a criminal case or in a suit at law shall be made public except where the interest of juvenile persons otherwise requires or the proceedings concern matrimonial disputes or the guardianship of children.

2. Everyone charged with a criminal offence shall have the right to be presumed innocent until proved guilty according to law.

3. In the determination of any criminal charge against him, everyone shall be entitled to the following minimum guarantees, in full equality:

(a) To be informed promptly and in detail in a language which he understands of the nature and cause of the charge against him;

(b) To have adequate time and facilities for the preparation of his defence and to communicate with counsel of his own choosing;

(c) To be tried without undue delay;

(d) To be tried in his presence, and to defend himself in person or through legal assistance of his own choosing; to be informed, if he does not have legal assistance, of this right; and to have legal assistance assigned to him, in any case where the interests of justice so require, and without payment by him in any such case if he does not have sufficient means to pay for it;

(e) To examine, or have examined, the witnesses against him and to obtain the attendance and examination of witnesses on his behalf under the same conditions as witnesses against him;

(f) To have the free assistance of an interpreter if he cannot understand or speak the language used in court;

(g) Not to be compelled to testify against himself or to confess guilt.

4. In the case of juvenile persons, the procedure shall be such as will take account of their age and the desirability of promoting their rehabilitation.

5. Everyone convicted of a crime shall have the right to his conviction and sentence being reviewed by a higher tribunal according to law.

6. When a person has by a final decision been convicted of a criminal offence and when subsequently his conviction has been reversed or he has been pardoned on the ground that a new or newly discovered fact shows conclusively that there has been a miscarriage of justice, the person who has suffered punishment as a result of such conviction shall be compensated according to law, unless it is proved that the non-disclosure of the unknown fact in time is wholly or partly attributable to him.

7. No one shall be liable to be tried or punished again for an offence for which he has already been finally convicted or acquitted in accordance with the law and penal procedure of each country.

Article 15

1. No one shall be held guilty of any criminal offence on account of any act or omission which did not constitute a criminal offence, under national or international law, at the time when it was committed. Nor shall a heavier penalty be imposed than the one that was applicable at the time when the criminal offence was committed. If, subsequent to the commission of the offence, provision is made by law for the imposition of the lighter penalty, the offender shall benefit thereby.

2. Nothing in this article shall prejudice the trial and punishment of any person for any act or omission which, at the time when it was committed, was criminal according to the general principles of law recognized by the community of nations.

Among civil and political rights and for many people, the right to a fair trial is a fundamental human right. The right to a fair trial and the right to equality before the law has roots deep in modern concepts of justice and fairness. Many proponents trace it back to the rule of law. For citizens, the right to liberty and the right to a fair trial represent obvious examples of when the State and the individual interact. As a fair trial is an important aspect of determining the legitimacy of any detention and as lawful detention is often a consequence of a trial, this chapter will consider the law concerning a fair trial.

The modern definition of a fair trial also finds expression in the Statute of the International Criminal Court which indeed provides one of the most detailed tabulations of the right to be found in international human rights law.

Rome Statute of the International Criminal Court Art 20(1)

Except as provided in this Statute, no person shall be tried before the Court with respect to conduct which formed the basis of crimes for which the person has been convicted or acquitted by the Court.

The same applies to people tried for genocide, crimes against humanity or war crimes in other courts. They cannot also be tried in the International Criminal Court unless there are significant queries over the purpose of the initial trial or the independence or impartiality of proceedings.

Rome Statute of the International Criminal Court

Art 22(1)

A person shall not be criminally responsible under this Statute unless the conduct in question constitutes, at the time it takes place, a crime within the jurisdiction of the Court.

Art 23

A person convicted by the Court may be punished only in accordance with this Statute.

Article 24

No person shall be criminally responsible under this Statute for conduct prior to the entry into force of the Statute.

Art 40

The judges shall be independent in the performance of their functions.

Art 42

The Office of the Prosecutor shall act independently as a separate organ of the Court.

Art 55

1. In respect of an investigation under this Statute, a person:

(a) Shall not be compelled to incriminate himself or herself or to confess guilt;

(b) Shall not be subjected to any form of coercion, duress or threat, to torture or to any form of cruel, inhuman or degrading treatment or punishment;

(c) Shall, if questioned in a language other than a language the person fully understands and speaks, have, free of cost, the assistance of a competent interpreter and such translations as are necessary to meet the requirement of fairness; and

(d) Shall not be subjected to arbitrary arrest or detention, and shall not be deprived of his or her liberty except on such grounds and in accordance with such procedures as are established in this Statute.

2. Where there are grounds to believe that a person has committed a crime within the jurisdiction of the Court and that person is about to be questioned . . . that person shall also have the following rights of which he or she shall be informed prior to being questioned:

(a) To be informed, prior to being questioned, that there are grounds to believe that he or she has committed a crime within the jurisdiction of the Court;

(b) To remain silent without such silence being a consideration in the determination of guilt or innocence;

(c) To have legal assistance of the person's choosing, or, if the person does not have legal assistance, to have legal assistance assigned to him or her, in any case where the interests of justice so require, and without payment by the person in any case if the person does not have sufficient means to pay for it; and

(d) To be questioned in the presence of counsel unless the person has voluntarily waived his or her right to counsel.

Art 63 (1)

The accused shall be present during the trial.

Art 66

1. Everyone shall be presumed innocent until proved guilty before the Court in accordance with the applicable law.

2. The onus is on the Prosecutor to prove the guilt of the accused.

3. In order to convict the accused, the Court must be convinced of the guilt of the accused beyond reasonable doubt.

Question

Read Article 6 of the European Convention for the Protection of Human Rights and Fundamental Freedoms. Compare and contrast its provisions with those of the Statute of the International Criminal Court.

11.6.1 Access to a court

The European Court of Human Rights created an early precedent by articulating the actual right of access to a court.

Golder v UK, European Court of Human Rights, Ser A, No. 12 (1975)

Facts: the applicant in this complaint before the European Commission and then Court of Human Rights was allegedly involved in serious disturbances in Parkhurst Prison on the Isle of Wight. He had been convicted in the United Kingdom of robbery with violence and was sentenced to 15 years' imprisonment. Following the disturbances, he was placed in solitary confinement pending disciplinary action and refused access to a solicitor. He wished to consult a solicitor but the Home Secretary rejected this. The Commission and Court found violations of Art 6 of the European Convention.

34. As stated in Article 31 para. 2 of the Vienna Convention, the preamble to a treaty forms an integral part of the context. Furthermore, the preamble is generally very useful for the determination of the 'object' and 'purpose' of the instrument to be construed.

In the present case, the most significant passage in the Preamble to the European Convention is the signatory Governments declaring that they are 'resolved, as the Governments of European countries which are like-minded and have a common heritage of political traditions, ideals, freedom and the rule of law, to take the first steps for the collective enforcement of certain of the Rights stated in the Universal Declaration' of 10 December 1948.

In the Government's view, that recital illustrates the 'selective process' adopted by the draftsmen: that the Convention does not seek to protect Human Rights in general but merely 'certain of the Rights stated in the Universal Declaration'. Articles 1 and 19 (art. 1, art. 19) are, in their submission, directed to the same end.

The Commission, for their part, attach great importance to the expression 'rule of law' which, in their view, elucidates Article 6 para. 1 (art. 6–1).

The 'selective' nature of the Convention cannot be put in question. It may also be accepted, as the Government have submitted, that the Preamble does not include the rule of law in the object and purpose of the Convention, but points to it as being one of the features of the common spiritual heritage of the member States of the Council of Europe. The Court however considers, like the Commission, that it would be a mistake to see in this reference a merely 'more or less rhetorical reference', devoid of relevance for those interpreting the Convention. One reason why the signatory Governments decided to 'take the first steps for the collective enforcement of certain of the Rights stated in the Universal Declaration' was their profound belief in the rule of law. It seems both natural and in conformity with the principle of good faith (Article 31 para. 1 of the Vienna Convention) to bear in mind this widely proclaimed consideration when interpreting the terms of Article 6 para. 1 (art. 6–1) according to their context and in the light of the object and purpose of the Convention.

This is all the more so since the Statute of the Council of Europe, an organisation of which each of the States Parties to the Convention is a Member (Article 66 of the Convention) (art. 66), refers in two places to the rule of law: first in the Preamble, where the signatory Governments affirm their devotion to this principle, and secondly in Article 3 (art. 3) which provides that 'every Member of the Council of Europe must accept the principle of the rule of law ...'

And in civil matters one can scarcely conceive of the rule of law without there being a possibility of having access to the courts.

35. Article 31 para. 3 (c) of the Vienna Convention indicates that account is to be taken, together with the context, of 'any relevant rules of international law applicable in the relations between the parties'. Among those rules are general principles of law and especially 'general principles of law recognized by civilized nations' (Article 38 para. 1 (c) of the Statute of the International Court of Justice). Incidentally, the Legal Committee of the Consultative Assembly of the Council of Europe foresaw in August 1950 that 'the Commission and the Court must necessarily apply such principles' in the execution of their duties and thus considered it to be 'unnecessary' to insert a specific clause to this effect in the Convention (Documents of the Consultative Assembly, working papers of the 1950 session, Vol. III, no. 93, p. 982, para. 5).

The principle whereby a civil claim must be capable of being submitted to a judge ranks as one of the universally 'recognised' fundamental principles of law; the same is true of the principle of international law which forbids the denial of justice. Article 6 para. 1 (art. 6–1) must be read in the light of these principles.

Were Article 6 para. 1 (art. 6–1) to be understood as concerning exclusively the conduct of an action which had already been initiated before a court, a Contracting State could, without acting in breach of that text, do away with its courts, or take away their jurisdiction to determine certain classes of civil actions and entrust it to organs dependent on the Government. Such assumptions, indissociable from a danger of arbitrary power, would have serious consequences which are repugnant to the aforementioned principles and which the Court cannot overlook (Lawless judgment of 1 July 1961, Series A no. 3, p. 52, and Delcourt judgment of 17 January 1970, Series A no. 11, pp. 14–15).

It would be inconceivable, in the opinion of the Court, that Article 6 para. 1 (art. 6–1) should describe in detail the procedural guarantees afforded to parties in a pending lawsuit and should not first protect that which alone makes it in fact possible to benefit from such guarantees, that is, access to a court. The fair, public and expeditious characteristics of judicial proceedings are of no value at all if there are no judicial proceedings.

36. Taking all the preceding considerations together, it follows that the right of access constitutes an element which is inherent in the right stated by Article 6 para. 1 (art. 6–1). This is not an extensive interpretation forcing new obligations on the Contracting States: it is based on the very terms of the first sentence of Article 6 para. 1 (art. 6–1) read in its context and having regard to the object and purpose of the Convention, a lawmaking treaty (see the Wemhoff judgment of 27 June 1968, Series A no. 7, p. 23, para. 8), and to general principles of law.

The Court thus reaches the conclusion, without needing to resort to 'supplementary means of interpretation' as envisaged at Article 32 of the Vienna Convention, that Article 6 para. 1 (art. 6–1) secures to everyone the right to have any claim relating to his civil rights and obligations brought before a court or tribunal. In this way the Article embodies the 'right to a court', of which the right of access, that is the right to institute proceedings before courts in civil matters, constitutes one aspect only. To this are added the guarantees laid down by Article 6 para. 1 (art. 6–1) as regards both the organisation and composition of the court, and the conduct of the proceedings. In sum, the whole makes up the right to a fair hearing.

Thus although the Convention makes no explicit mention of the right to access a court, it appears that this is an integral part of the right to a fair trial. A related issue is that of legal advice and indeed, State-funded assistance to permit a detainee to properly present a defence. On the issue of access to legal advice, the international bodies are of the opinion that this may be necessary, most particularly in criminal proceedings.

Borisenco v Hungary, Communication 852/1999, Human Rights Committee, outlined above

2.3 On 2 May 1996 the author and his friend were brought before the Pescht Central District Court for the purpose of deciding whether they should be remanded in custody. The court decided to detain them due to the risk of flight. During the police interrogation, the hearing on detention and the detention itself, the author and his friend were not allowed to contact their Embassy, families, lawyers or sports organization. On 7 May 1996, the police authorities completed the investigation and referred the case to the public prosecutor's office. . . .

7.5 With respect to the author's claim that he was not provided with legal representation from the time of his arrest to his release from detention, which included a hearing on detention at which he had to represent himself, the Committee notes that the State party has confirmed that although it assigned a lawyer to the author, the lawyer failed to appear at the interrogation or at the detention hearing. In its previous jurisprudence, the Committee has made it clear that it is incumbent upon the State party to ensure that legal representation provided by the State guarantees effective representation. It recalls its prior jurisprudence that legal assistance should be available at all stages of criminal proceedings. Consequently the Committee finds that the facts before it reveal a violation of article 14, paragraph 3 (d) of the Covenant.

Most of the other fair trial communications raised before the international bodies are drawn from a rash of complaints against Uruguay in the early 80s or relate to capital murder trials and associated proceedings in Trinidad, Tobago and Jamaica.

Note that access to legal advice is a requirement where the interests of fairness so dictate, see *inter alia Artico v Italy*, Series A, No. 47 (1980) European Court of Human Rights, or *Airey v Ireland*, Series A, No. 32 (1979) European Court of Human Rights.

Aliev v Ukraine, Communication 781/1997, Human Rights Committee, UN Doc. CCPR/C/78/D/781/1997

2.1 On 8 June 1996, in the town of Makeevka, Ukraine, having consumed a large quantity of alcohol, the author, Mr. Kroutovertsev and Mr. Kot had an altercation in an apartment. The altercation degenerated into a fight. A fourth person, Mr. Goncharenko, witnessed the incident. According to the author, Mr. Kot and Mr. Kroutovertsev beat him severely. Mr. Kroutovertsev also struck him with an empty bottle. While defending himself, the author seriously wounded Mr. Kot and Mr. Kroutovertsev with a knife, whereupon he fled . . .

7.2 First, the author alleges that he did not have the services of a counsel during his first five months of detention. The Committee notes that the State party is silent in this regard; it also notes that the copies of the relevant judicial decisions do not address the author's allegation that he was not represented for five months, even though the author had mentioned this allegation in his complaint to the Supreme Court dated 29 April 1997. Considering the nature of the case and questions dealt with during this period, particularly the author's interrogation by police officers and the reconstruction of the crime, in which the author was not invited to participate, the Committee is of the view that the author should have had the possibility of consulting and being represented by a lawyer. Consequently, and in the absence of any relevant information from the State party, the Committee is of the view that the facts before it constitute a violation of article 14, paragraph 1, of the Covenant.

7.3 Secondly, the author alleges that, subsequently, on 17 July 1997, the Supreme Court heard his case in his absence and in the absence of his counsel. The Committee notes that the State party has not challenged this allegation and has not provided any reason for this absence. The Committee finds that the decision of 17 July 1997 does not mention that the author or his counsel was present, but mentions the presence of a procurator. Moreover it is uncontested that the author had no legal representation in the early stages of the investigations. Bearing in mind the facts before it, and in the absence of any relevant observation by the State party, the Committee considers that due weight must be given to the author's allegations. The Committee recalls its jurisprudence that legal representation must be available at all stages of criminal proceedings, particularly in cases in which the accused incurs capital punishment. Consequently, the Committee is of the view that the facts before it disclose a violation of article 14, paragraph 1, as well as a separate violation of article 14, paragraph 3 (d), of the Covenant.

Question

To what extent is such an inference acceptable? Are there circumstances in which some charges/complaints may not be resolvable by recourse to a court? What role is there for alternative forms of dispute resolution?

Related to this is the vexed issue of legal aid as one of the main limitations on court access in practice may be the lack of funds to employ legal expertise. As is noted above, legal counsel is required for determination of criminal charges, most importantly when liberty is threatened. Those facing serious charges should have legal assistance provided free of charge, if their circumstances prevent an adequate defence being provided. Note the comments of the Committee, above, with respect to what constitutes appropriate, unbiased, legal assistance.

11.6.2   Independent and fair judiciary

Fundamental to the concept of the rule of law and to the principle of separation of powers between the three principal organs of the State (executive, judiciary and legislature) is the need for a fair and independent judiciary. Independence is required from political, economic and other external influences. Judges should remain influenced only by the application of the law to the facts arising in the case before them.

International Covenant on Civil and Political Rights 1966 Art 14(1)

Everyone shall be entitled to a fair and public hearing by a competent, independent and impartial tribunal established by law.

Question

Note that Art 6(1) of the European Convention on Human Rights does not include a reference to the competence of the judiciary. Article 8 of the American Convention includes competence as a requirement while Art 7 of the African Charter mentions only impartiality and competence. Consider whether competence is implied by Art 6 of the European Convention, the oldest of all these instruments.

More detailed provisions can be found in the Statute of the International Criminal Court, which though obviously restricted to the International Court in application, provides an indication of the prevailing international standard.

Rome Statute of the International Criminal Court 1998

Article 40
Independence of the judges

1. The judges shall be independent in the performance of their functions.

2. Judges shall not engage in any activity which is likely to interfere with their judicial functions or to affect confidence in their independence.

3. Judges required to serve on a full-time basis at the seat of the Court shall not engage in any other occupation of a professional nature.

4. Any question regarding the application of paragraphs 2 and 3 shall be decided by an absolute majority of the judges. Where any such question concerns an individual judge, that judge shall not take part in the decision.

Article 41
Excusing and disqualification of judges

1. The Presidency may, at the request of a judge, excuse that judge from the exercise of a function under this Statute, in accordance with the Rules of Procedure and Evidence.

2. (a) A judge shall not participate in any case in which his or her impartiality might reasonably be doubted on any ground. A judge shall be disqualified from a case in accordance with this paragraph if, *inter alia*, that judge has previously been involved in any capacity in that case before the Court or in a related criminal case at the national level involving the person being investigated or prosecuted. A judge shall also be disqualified on such other grounds as may be provided for in the Rules of Procedure and Evidence.

(b) The Prosecutor or the person being investigated or prosecuted may request the disqualification of a judge under this paragraph.

(c) Any question as to the disqualification of a judge shall be decided by an absolute majority of the judges. The challenged judge shall be entitled to present his or her comments on the matter, but shall not take part in the decision.

Similar provisions are made under Art 42 to guarantee the independence of the prosecutors in the International Criminal Court.

Naturally judges may not judge a case in which they were previously involved as prosecutor or investigator. This is particularly important with regard to appeal cases as, of course, a judge may be a recent appointment to the bench.

Question

Look at the procedures in place in systems such as the European Court of Human Rights when a judge rapporteur is appointed at the preliminary stages. Contrast this with the role of Advocates General in the European Court of Justice.

There are many complaints before the European Court of Human Rights concerning such issues. As the concept is so fundamental to a human rights concept of a fair trial, many states comply and thus there have been comparatively few violations, at least violations brought to the attention of the international bodies. The principles of bias are very well established.

General Comment 13 (1984), Human Rights Committee

5. The second sentence of article 14, paragraph 1, provides that 'everyone shall be entitled to a fair and public hearing'. Paragraph 3 of the article elaborates on the requirements of a 'fair hearing' in regard to the determination of criminal charges. However, the requirements of paragraph 3 are minimum guarantees, the observance of which is not always sufficient to ensure the fairness of a hearing as required by paragraph 1.

6. The publicity of hearings is an important safeguard in the interest of the individual and of society at large. At the same time article 14, paragraph 1, acknowledges that courts have the power to exclude all or part of the public for reasons spelt out in that paragraph. It should be noted that, apart from such exceptional circumstances, the Committee considers that a hearing must be open to the public in general, including members of the press, and must not, for instance, be limited only to a particular category of persons. It should be noted that, even in cases in which the public is excluded from the trial, the judgement must, with certain strictly defined exceptions, be made public.

Bahamonde v Equatorial Guinea, Communication 468/1991, Human Rights Committee, UN Doc. CCPR/C/49/D/468/1991

9.4 The author has contended that despite several attempts to obtain judicial redress before the courts of Equatorial Guinea, all of his *démarches* have been unsuccessful. This claim has been refuted summarily by the State party, which argued that the author could have invoked specific legislation before the courts, without however linking its argument to the circumstances of the case. The Committee observes that the notion of equality before the courts and tribunals encompasses the very access to the courts and that a situation in which an individual's attempts to seize the competent jurisdictions of his/her grievances are systematically frustrated runs counter to the guarantees of article 14, paragraph 1. In this context, the Committee has also noted the author's contention that the State party's president controls the judiciary in Equatorial Guinea. The Committee considers that a situation where the functions and competences of the judiciary and the executive are not clearly distinguishable or where the latter is able to control or direct the former is incompatible with the notion of an independent and impartial tribunal within the meaning of article 14, paragraph 1, of the Covenant.

Consider also the guarantees as to independence found in the Statute of the International Court of Justice.

Statute of the International Court of Justice 1945

Article 14. Vacancies shall be filled by the same method as that laid down for the first election, subject to the following provision: the Secretary-General shall, within one month of the occurrence of the vacancy, proceed to issue the invitations provided for in Article 5, and the date of the election shall be fixed by the Security Council.

Article 15. A member of the Court elected to replace a member whose term of office has not expired shall hold office for the remainder of his predecessor's term.

Article 16. (1) No member of the Court may exercise any political or administrative function, or engage in any other occupation of a professional nature.

(2) Any doubt on this point shall be settled by the decision of the Court.

Article 17. (1) No member of the Court may act as agent, counsel, or advocate in any case.

(2) No member may participate in the decision of any case in which he has previously taken part as agent, counsel or advocate for one of the parties, or as a member of a national or international court, or of a commission of enquiry, or in any other capacity.

(3) Any doubt on this point shall be settled by the decision of the Court.

Article 18. (1) No member of the Court can be dismissed unless, in the unanimous opinion of the other members, be has ceased to fulfil the required conditions.

(2) Formal notification thereof shall be made to the Secretary-General by the Registrar

(3) This notification makes the place vacant.

Article 19. The members of the Court, when engaged in the business of the Court, shall enjoy diplomatic privileges and immunities.

Article 20. Every member of the Court shall, before taking up his duties, make a solemn declaration in open court that he will exercise his powers impartially and conscientiously.

The United Nations Congress on the Prevention of Crime and the Treatment of Offenders adopted a series of principles on the independence of the judiciary. These were subsequently endorsed by the United Nations General Assembly and thus now form part of the body of 'soft law' in the area. According to the preamble, the principles were 'formulated to assist Member States in their task of securing and promoting the independence of the judiciary . . . [and] principally with professional judges in mind, but they apply equally, as appropriate, to lay judges, where they exist'.

Basic Principles on the Independence of the Judiciary, endorsed by General Assembly Resolution 40/32 (1985) and 40/146 (1985)

Independence of the judiciary

1. The independence of the judiciary shall be guaranteed by the State and enshrined in the Constitution or the law of the country. It is the duty of all governmental and other institutions to respect and observe the independence of the judiciary.

2. The judiciary shall decide matters before them impartially, on the basis of facts and in accordance with the law, without any restrictions, improper influences, inducements, pressures, threats or interferences, direct or indirect, from any quarter or for any reason. . . .

4. There shall not be any inappropriate or unwarranted interference with the judicial process, nor shall judicial decisions by the courts be subject to revision. This principle is without prejudice to judicial review or to mitigation or commutation by competent authorities of sentences imposed by the judiciary, in accordance with the law. . . .

6. The principle of the independence of the judiciary entitles and requires the judiciary to ensure that judicial proceedings are conducted fairly and that the rights of the parties are respected.

7. It is the duty of each Member State to provide adequate resources to enable the judiciary to properly perform its functions.

Other matters addressed include conditions of service and tenure, and qualifications,

selection and training. The provision of adequate resources imposes a positive obligation on States and is a clear example of a civil and political right the realisation of
which entails financial outlay.

11.6.2.1 Judicial appointments

In some States judges are elected, while in others, they are appointed through panels
or by recommendations to the legislature or executive.

Question

*Choose any State, what safeguards apply to the appointment process to ensure independence of
the judiciary?*

11.6.2.2 Termination of judicial appointment

While obviously provisions on judicial selection and the conduct of the case are
important to demonstrating impartiality, so too is the need to ensure that the judiciary
is not subjected to external pressures stemming from the duration of their appointment and the conditions governing the termination of their service. Temporary judges
who are subject to potential reappointment are a potential problem, especially if the
executive or legislature is involved in the appointment process.

Consider the international guidelines on disciplining, suspending and removing
judiciary.

**Basic Principles on the Independence of the Judiciary, endorsed by General
Assembly Resolution 40/32 (1985) and 40/146 (1985)**
Discipline, suspension and removal

17. A charge or complaint made against a judge in his/her judicial and professional capacity shall
be processed expeditiously and fairly under an appropriate procedure. The judge shall have the
right to a fair hearing. The examination of the matter at its initial stage shall be kept confidential,
unless otherwise requested by the judge.

18. Judges shall be subject to suspension or removal only for reasons of incapacity or behaviour
that renders them unfit to discharge their duties.

19. All disciplinary, suspension or removal proceedings shall be determined in accordance with
established standards of judicial conduct.

20. Decisions in disciplinary, suspension or removal proceedings should be subject to an
independent review. This principle may not apply to the decisions of the highest court and those
of the legislature in impeachment or similar proceedings.

Question

*In what circumstances can judges be dismissed from the African Court on Human Rights? Is
this compliant with the international norms?*

11.6.3 Trial in absentia

Generally, the accused should be present at the trial and thus in a position to ensure
the conduct of his or her defence. However, not all trials are conducted in person. This
is not problematic at all stages of proceedings as long as the principles of fairness and
equality are complied with.

Mbenge v Republic of Congo, Communication 16/1977, Human Rights Committee, UN Doc. CCPR/C/18/D/16/1977 (1983)

13. Daniel Monguya Mbenge, a Zairian citizen and former Governor of the province of Shaba, who had left Zaire in 1974 and is at present living in Brussels, was twice sentenced to capital punishment by Zairian tribunals. The first death sentence was pronounced against him by judgement of 17 August 1977, in particular for his alleged involvement in the invasion of the province of Shaba by the so-called Katangan gendarmes in March 1977. The second judgement is dated 16 March 1978. It pronounces the death sentence for 'treason' and 'conspiracy' without providing facts to establish these charges. Daniel Monguya Mbenge learned about the trials through the press. He had not been duly summoned at his residence in Belgium to appear before the tribunals. An amnesty decree of 28 June 1978 (Act 78–023 of 29 December 1978) covering offences 'against the external or internal security of the State or any other offence against the laws and regulations of the Republic of Zaire', committed by Zairians having sought refuge abroad, was restricted to persons returning to Zaire before 30 June 1979.

14.1 In the first place, the Human Rights Committee has to examine whether the proceedings on the basis of which the author of the communication has been twice sentenced to death disclose any breach of rights protected under the International Covenant on Civil and Political Rights. According to article 14 (3) of the Covenant, everyone is entitled to be tried in his presence and to defend himself in person or through legal assistance. This provision and other requirements of due process enshrined in article 14 cannot be construed as invariably rendering proceedings *in absentia* inadmissible irrespective of the reasons for the accused person's absence. Indeed, proceedings *in absentia* are in some circumstances (for instance, when the accused person, although informed of the proceedings sufficiently in advance, declines to exercise his right to be present) permissible in the interest of the proper administration of justice. Nevertheless, the effective exercise of the rights under article 14 presupposes that the necessary steps should be taken to inform the accused beforehand about the proceedings against him (art. 14 (3) (a)). Judgement *in absentia* requires that, notwithstanding the absence of the accused, all due notification has been made to inform him of the date and place of his trial and to request his attendance. Otherwise, the accused, in particular, is not given adequate time and facilities for the preparation of his defence (art. 14 (3) (b)), cannot defend himself through legal assistance of his own choosing (art. 14 (3) (d)) nor does he have the opportunity to examine, or have examined, the witnesses against him and to obtain the attendance and examination of witnesses on his behalf (art. 14 (3) (e)).

14.2 The Committee acknowledges that there must be certain limits to the efforts which can duly be expected of the responsible authorities of establishing contact with the accused. With regard to the present communication, however, those limits need not be specified. The State party has not challenged the author's contention that he had known of the trials only through press reports after they had taken place. It is true that both judgements state explicitly that summonses to appear had been issued by the clerk of the court. However, no indication is given of any steps actually taken by the State party in order to transmit the summonses to the author, whose address in Belgium is correctly reproduced in the judgement of 17 August 1977 and which was therefore known to the judicial authorities. The fact that, according to the judgement in the second trial of March 1978, the summons had been issued only three days before the beginning of the hearings before the court, confirms the Committee in its conclusion that the State party failed to make sufficient efforts with a view to informing the author about the impending court proceedings, thus enabling him to prepare his defence. In the view of the Committee, therefore, the State party has not respected D. Monguya Mbenge's rights under article 14 (3) (a), (b), (d) and (e) of the Covenant.

11.7 DETENTION AFTER CONVICTION

Generally, imprisonment is one of the appropriate sentences following conviction by a competent court. However, note that not all offences justify imprisonment.

International Covenant on Civil and Political Rights

Article 11

No one shall be imprisoned merely on the ground of inability to fulfil a contractual obligation.

American Convention on Human Rights Art 7(7)

7. No one shall be detained for debt. This principle shall not limit the orders of a competent judicial authority issued for nonfulfillment of duties of support.

Article 1, Protocol 4 to the European Convention on Human Rights makes similar provision.

Those who are sentenced to detention following trial should be housed separately from those detained pending trial. Although those incarcerated for violations of national (and indeed international) law may forfeit some civic rights, they are still entitled to the protection accorded by inalienable human rights.

Basic Principles for the Treatment of Prisoners, General Assembly Resolution 45/111 (1990)

1. All prisoners shall be treated with the respect due to their inherent dignity and value as human beings. . . .

5. Except for those limitations that are demonstrably necessitated by the fact of incarceration, all prisoners shall retain the human rights and fundamental freedoms set out in the Universal Declaration of Human Rights, and, where the State concerned is a party, the International Covenant on Economic, Social and Cultural Rights, and the International Covenant on Civil and Political Rights and the Optional Protocol thereto, as well as such other rights as are set out in other United Nations covenants.

6. All prisoners shall have the right to take part in cultural activities and education aimed at the full development of the human personality.

7. Efforts addressed to the abolition of solitary confinement as a punishment, or to the restriction of its use, should be undertaken and encouraged.

8. Conditions shall be created enabling prisoners to undertake meaningful remunerated employment which will facilitate their reintegration into the country's labour market and permit them to contribute to their own financial support and to that of their families.

9. Prisoners shall have access to the health services available in the country without discrimination on the grounds of their legal situation.

10. With the participation and help of the community and social institutions, and with due regard to the interests of victims, favourable conditions shall be created for the reintegration of the ex-prisoner into society under the best possible conditions.

Question

Compare and contrast the rights of prisoners, as expressed in this resolution of the General Assembly, with the general rights and freedom expressed in the principal human rights instruments (the Bill of Rights, for example).

Standard Minimum Rules for the Treatment of Prisoners Adopted by the First United Nations Congress on the Prevention of Crime and the Treatment of Offenders, held at Geneva in 1955, and approved by the Economic and Social Council by its Resolutions 663 C (XXIV) of 31 July 1957 and 2076 (LXII) of 13 May 1977

Basic principle

6. (1) The following rules shall be applied impartially. There shall be no discrimination on

grounds of race, colour, sex, language, religion, political or other opinion, national or social origin, property, birth or other status.

(2) On the other hand, it is necessary to respect the religious beliefs and moral precepts of the group to which a prisoner belongs.

Register

7. (1) In every place where persons are imprisoned there shall be kept a bound registration book with numbered pages in which shall be entered in respect of each prisoner received:

(a) Information concerning his identity;

(b) The reasons for his commitment and the authority therefor;

(c) The day and hour of his admission and release.

(2) No person shall be received in an institution without a valid commitment order of which the details shall have been previously entered in the register.

Separation of categories

8. The different categories of prisoners shall be kept in separate institutions or parts of institutions taking account of their sex, age, criminal record, the legal reason for their detention and the necessities of their treatment. Thus,

(a) Men and women shall so far as possible be detained in separate institutions; in an institution which receives both men and women the whole of the premises allocated to women shall be entirely separate;

(b) Untried prisoners shall be kept separate from convicted prisoners;

(c) Persons imprisoned for debt and other civil prisoners shall be kept separate from persons imprisoned by reason of a criminal offence;

(d) Young prisoners shall be kept separate from adults.

Accommodation

9. (1) Where sleeping accommodation is in individual cells or rooms, each prisoner shall occupy by night a cell or room by himself. If for special reasons, such as temporary overcrowding, it becomes necessary for the central prison administration to make an exception to this rule, it is not desirable to have two prisoners in a cell or room.

(2) Where dormitories are used, they shall be occupied by prisoners carefully selected as being suitable to associate with one another in those conditions. There shall be regular supervision by night, in keeping with the nature of the institution.

10. All accommodation provided for the use of prisoners and in particular all sleeping accommodation shall meet all requirements of health, due regard being paid to climatic conditions and particularly to cubic content of air, minimum floor space, lighting, heating and ventilation.

11. In all places where prisoners are required to live or work,

(a) The windows shall be large enough to enable the prisoners to read or work by natural light, and shall be so constructed that they can allow the entrance of fresh air whether or not there is artificial ventilation;

(b) Artificial light shall be provided sufficient for the prisoners to read or work without injury to eyesight.

12. The sanitary installations shall be adequate to enable every prisoner to comply with the needs of nature when necessary and in a clean and decent manner.

13. Adequate bathing and shower installations shall be provided so that every prisoner may be enabled and required to have a bath or shower, at a temperature suitable to the climate, as frequently as necessary for general hygiene according to season and geographical region, but at least once a week in a temperate climate.

14. All parts of an institution regularly used by prisoners shall be properly maintained and kept scrupulously clean at all times.

Personal hygiene

15. Prisoners shall be required to keep their persons clean, and to this end they shall be provided with water and with such toilet articles as are necessary for health and cleanliness.

16. In order that prisoners may maintain a good appearance compatible with their self-respect, facilities shall be provided for the proper care of the hair and beard, and men shall be enabled to shave regularly.

Clothing and bedding

17. (1) Every prisoner who is not allowed to wear his own clothing shall be provided with an outfit of clothing suitable for the climate and adequate to keep him in good health. Such clothing shall in no manner be degrading or humiliating.

(2) All clothing shall be clean and kept in proper condition. Underclothing shall be changed and washed as often as necessary for the maintenance of hygiene.

(3) In exceptional circumstances, whenever a prisoner is removed outside the institution for an authorized purpose, he shall be allowed to wear his own clothing or other inconspicuous clothing.

18. If prisoners are allowed to wear their own clothing, arrangements shall be made on their admission to the institution to ensure that it shall be clean and fit for use.

19. Every prisoner shall, in accordance with local or national standards, be provided with a separate bed, and with separate and sufficient bedding which shall be clean when issued, kept in good order and changed often enough to ensure its cleanliness.

Food

20. (1) Every prisoner shall be provided by the administration at the usual hours with food of nutritional value adequate for health and strength, of wholesome quality and well prepared and served.

(2) Drinking water shall be available to every prisoner whenever he needs it.

Exercise and sport

21. (1) Every prisoner who is not employed in outdoor work shall have at least one hour of suitable exercise in the open air daily if the weather permits.

(2) Young prisoners, and others of suitable age and physique, shall receive physical and recreational training during the period of exercise. To this end space, installations and equipment should be provided.

Medical services

22. (1) At every institution there shall be available the services of at least one qualified medical officer who should have some knowledge of psychiatry. The medical services should be organized in close relationship to the general health administration of the community or nation. They shall include a psychiatric service for the diagnosis and, in proper cases, the treatment of states of mental abnormality.

(2) Sick prisoners who require specialist treatment shall be transferred to specialized institutions or to civil hospitals. Where hospital facilities are provided in an institution, their equipment, furnishings and pharmaceutical supplies shall be proper for the medical care and treatment of sick prisoners, and there shall be a staff of suitable trained officers.

(3) The services of a qualified dental officer shall be available to every prisoner.

23. (1) In women's institutions there shall be special accommodation for all necessary pre-natal and post-natal care and treatment. Arrangements shall be made wherever practicable for children

to be born in a hospital outside the institution. If a child is born in prison, this fact shall not be mentioned in the birth certificate.

(2) Where nursing infants are allowed to remain in the institution with their mothers, provision shall be made for a nursery staffed by qualified persons, where the infants shall be placed when they are not in the care of their mothers.

24. The medical officer shall see and examine every prisoner as soon as possible after his admission and thereafter as necessary, with a view particularly to the discovery of physical or mental illness and the taking of all necessary measures; the segregation of prisoners suspected of infectious or contagious conditions; the noting of physical or mental defects which might hamper rehabilitation, and the determination of the physical capacity of every prisoner for work.

25. (1) The medical officer shall have the care of the physical and mental health of the prisoners and should daily see all sick prisoners, all who complain of illness, and any prisoner to whom his attention is specially directed.

(2) The medical officer shall report to the director whenever he considers that a prisoner's physical or mental health has been or will be injuriously affected by continued imprisonment or by any condition of imprisonment.

26. (1) The medical officer shall regularly inspect and advise the director upon:

(a) The quantity, quality, preparation and service of food;

(b) The hygiene and cleanliness of the institution and the prisoners;

(c) The sanitation, heating, lighting and ventilation of the institution;

(d) The suitability and cleanliness of the prisoners' clothing and bedding;

(e) The observance of the rules concerning physical education and sports, in cases where there is no technical personnel in charge of these activities.

(2) The director shall take into consideration the reports and advice that the medical officer submits according to rules 25 (2) and 26 and, in case he concurs with the recommendations made, shall take immediate steps to give effect to those recommendations; if they are not within his competence or if he does not concur with them, he shall immediately submit his own report and the advice of the medical officer to higher authority.

Discipline and punishment

27. Discipline and order shall be maintained with firmness, but with no more restriction than is necessary for safe custody and well-ordered community life. . . .

33. Instruments of restraint, such as handcuffs, chains, irons and strait-jackets, shall never be applied as a punishment. Furthermore, chains or irons shall not be used as restraints. Other instruments of restraint shall not be used except in the following circumstances:

(a) As a precaution against escape during a transfer, provided that they shall be removed when the prisoner appears before a judicial or administrative authority;

(b) On medical grounds by direction of the medical officer;

(c) By order of the director, if other methods of control fail, in order to prevent a prisoner from injuring himself or others or from damaging property; in such instances the director shall at once consult the medical officer and report to the higher administrative authority.

34. The patterns and manner of use of instruments of restraint shall be decided by the central prison administration. Such instruments must not be applied for any longer time than is strictly necessary.

Information to and complaints by prisoners

35. (1) Every prisoner on admission shall be provided with written information about the

regulations governing the treatment of prisoners of his category, the disciplinary requirements of the institution, the authorized methods of seeking information and making complaints, and all such other matters as are necessary to enable him to understand both his rights and his obligations and to adapt himself to the life of the institution.

(2) If a prisoner is illiterate, the aforesaid information shall be conveyed to him orally.

36. (1) Every prisoner shall have the opportunity each week day of making requests or complaints to the director of the institution or the officer authorized to represent him.

(2) It shall be possible to make requests or complaints to the inspector of prisons during his inspection. The prisoner shall have the opportunity to talk to the inspector or to any other inspecting officer without the director or other members of the staff being present.

(3) Every prisoner shall be allowed to make a request or complaint, without censorship as to substance but in proper form, to the central prison administration, the judicial authority or other proper authorities through approved channels.

(4) Unless it is evidently frivolous or groundless, every request or complaint shall be promptly dealt with and replied to without undue delay.

Contact with the outside world

37. Prisoners shall be allowed under necessary supervision to communicate with their family and reputable friends at regular intervals, both by correspondence and by receiving visits.

38. (1) Prisoners who are foreign nationals shall be allowed reasonable facilities to communicate with the diplomatic and consular representatives of the State to which they belong.

(2) Prisoners who are nationals of States without diplomatic or consular representation in the country and refugees or stateless persons shall be allowed similar facilities to communicate with the diplomatic representative of the State which takes charge of their interests or any national or international authority whose task it is to protect such persons.

39. Prisoners shall be kept informed regularly of the more important items of news by the reading of newspapers, periodicals or special institutional publications, by hearing wireless transmissions, by lectures or by any similar means as authorized or controlled by the administration.

Books

40. Every institution shall have a library for the use of all categories of prisoners, adequately stocked with both recreational and instructional books, and prisoners shall be encouraged to make full use of it.

Religion

41. (1) If the institution contains a sufficient number of prisoners of the same religion, a qualified representative of that religion shall be appointed or approved. If the number of prisoners justifies it and conditions permit, the arrangement should be on a full-time basis.

(2) A qualified representative appointed or approved under paragraph (1) shall be allowed to hold regular services and to pay pastoral visits in private to prisoners of his religion at proper times.

(3) Access to a qualified representative of any religion shall not be refused to any prisoner. On the other hand, if any prisoner should object to a visit of any religious representative, his attitude shall be fully respected.

42. So far as practicable, every prisoner shall be allowed to satisfy the needs of his religious life by attending the services provided in the institution and having in his possession the books of religious observance and instruction of his denomination.

Retention of prisoners' property

43. (1) All money, valuables, clothing and other effects belonging to a prisoner which under the regulations of the institution he is not allowed to retain shall on his admission to the institution be placed in safe custody. An inventory thereof shall be signed by the prisoner. Steps shall be taken to keep them in good condition.

(2) On the release of the prisoner all such articles and money shall be returned to him except in so far as he has been authorized to spend money or send any such property out of the institution, or it has been found necessary on hygienic grounds to destroy any article of clothing. The prisoner shall sign a receipt for the articles and money returned to him.

(3) Any money or effects received for a prisoner from outside shall be treated in the same way.

(4) If a prisoner brings in any drugs or medicine, the medical officer shall decide what use shall be made of them.

Notification of death, illness, transfer, etc.

44. (1) Upon the death or serious illness of, or serious injury to a prisoner, or his removal to an institution for the treatment of mental affections, the director shall at once inform the spouse, if the prisoner is married, or the nearest relative and shall in any event inform any other person previously designated by the prisoner.

(2) A prisoner shall be informed at once of the death or serious illness of any near relative. In case of the critical illness of a near relative, the prisoner should be authorized, whenever circumstances allow, to go to his bedside either under escort or alone.

(3) Every prisoner shall have the right to inform at once his family of his imprisonment or his transfer to another institution.

Removal of prisoners

45. (1) When the prisoners are being removed to or from an institution, they shall be exposed to public view as little as possible, and proper safeguards shall be adopted to protect them from insult, curiosity and publicity in any form.

(2) The transport of prisoners in conveyances with inadequate ventilation or light, or in any way which would subject them to unnecessary physical hardship, shall be prohibited.

(3) The transport of prisoners shall be carried out at the expense of the administration and equal conditions shall obtain for all of them. . . .

53. (1) In an institution for both men and women, the part of the institution set aside for women shall be under the authority of a responsible woman officer who shall have the custody of the keys of all that part of the institution.

(2) No male member of the staff shall enter the part of the institution set aside for women unless accompanied by a woman officer.

(3) Women prisoners shall be attended and supervised only by women officers. This does not, however, preclude male members of the staff, particularly doctors and teachers, from carrying out their professional duties in institutions or parts of institutions set aside for women.

54. (1) Officers of the institutions shall not, in their relations with the prisoners, use force except in self-defence or in cases of attempted escape, or active or passive physical resistance to an order based on law or regulations. Officers who have recourse to force must use no more than is strictly necessary and must report the incident immediately to the director of the institution.

(2) Prison officers shall be given special physical training to enable them to restrain aggressive prisoners.

(3) Except in special circumstances, staff performing duties which bring them into direct contact with prisoners should not be armed. Furthermore, staff should in no circumstances be provided with arms unless they have been trained in their use.

Inspection

55. There shall be a regular inspection of penal institutions and services by qualified and experienced inspectors appointed by a competent authority. Their task shall be in particular to ensure that these institutions are administered in accordance with existing laws and regulations and with a view to bringing about the objectives of penal and correctional services.

11.8   JUVENILES IN CAPTIVITY AND COURT

While human rights are indeed universal, careful consideration must be given to the rights of vulnerable people subjected to incarceration and brought before the judicial process. A body of rules has emerged on juveniles and the protection of those suffering from mental health complaints.

With respect to children, the first point to note is that not all juveniles fall within the criminal justice system. A minimum age of criminal responsibility is specified. This should reflect the age at which a child is capable of distinguishing right from wrong and thus understanding the consequences of his or her actions and taking responsibility for them. However, note the text of the United Nations Convention on the Rights of the Child 1989.

United Nations Convention on the Rights of the Child 1989 Art 40

1. States Parties recognize the right of every child alleged as, accused of, or recognized as having infringed the penal law to be treated in a manner consistent with the promotion of the child's sense of dignity and worth, which reinforces the child's respect for the human rights and fundamental freedoms of others and which takes into account the child's age and the desirability of promoting the child's reintegration and the child's assuming a constructive role in society.

2. To this end, and having regard to the relevant provisions of international instruments, States Parties shall, in particular, ensure that:

(a) No child shall be alleged as, be accused of, or recognized as having infringed the penal law by reason of acts or omissions that were not prohibited by national or international law at the time they were committed; . . .

3. States Parties shall seek to promote the establishment of laws, procedures, authorities and institutions specifically applicable to children alleged as, accused of, or recognized as having infringed the penal law, and, in particular:

(a) The establishment of a minimum age below which children shall be presumed not to have the capacity to infringe the penal law;

(b) Whenever appropriate and desirable, measures for dealing with such children without resorting to judicial proceedings, providing that human rights and legal safeguards are fully respected.

4. A variety of dispositions, such as care, guidance and supervision orders; counselling; probation; foster care; education and vocational training programmes and other alternatives to institutional care shall be available to ensure that children are dealt with in a manner appropriate to their well-being and proportionate both to their circumstances and the offence.

Question

Why is no minimum age specified in the Convention? Research the minimum ages which apply in different countries—is there any consistency? Should there be?

The following extract is taken from the General Principles contained in the Beijing rules.

United Nations Standard Minimum Rules for the Administration of Juvenile Justice (Beijing rules)

4.1 In those legal systems recognizing the concept of the age of criminal responsibility for juveniles, the beginning of that age shall not be fixed at too low an age level, bearing in mind the facts of emotional, mental and intellectual maturity.

5.1 The juvenile justice system shall emphasize the well-being of the juvenile and shall ensure that any reaction to juvenile offenders shall always be in proportion to the circumstances of both the offenders and the offence.

6.1 In view of the varying special needs of juveniles as well as the variety of measures available, appropriate scope for discretion shall be allowed at all stages of proceedings and at the different levels of juvenile justice administration, including investigation, prosecution, adjudication and the follow-up of dispositions.

6.2 Efforts shall be made, however, to ensure sufficient accountability at all stages and levels in the exercise of any such discretion.

6.3 Those who exercise discretion shall be specially qualified or trained to exercise it judiciously and in accordance with their functions and mandates. . . .

8.1 The juvenile's right to privacy shall be respected at all stages in order to avoid harm being caused to her or him by undue publicity or by the process of labelling.

8.2 In principle, no information that may lead to the identification of a juvenile offender shall be published.

The following guidelines seek to ensure the full implementation of the United Nations Convention on the Rights of the Child.

Guidelines for Action on Children in the Criminal Justice System Recommended by Economic and Social Council Resolution 1997/30 of 21 July 1997

13. Notwithstanding the age of criminal responsibility, civil majority and the age of consent as defined by national legislation, States should ensure that children benefit from all their rights, as guaranteed to them by international law, specifically in this context those set forth in articles 3, 37 and 40 of the Convention.

14. Particular attention should be given to the following points:

(a) There should be a comprehensive child-centred juvenile justice process;

(b) Independent expert or other types of panels should review existing and proposed juvenile justice laws and their impact on children;

(c) No child who is under the legal age of criminal responsibility should be subject to criminal charges;

(d) States should establish juvenile courts with primary jurisdiction over juveniles who commit criminal acts and special procedures should be designed to take into account the specific needs of children. As an alternative, regular courts should incorporate such procedures, as appropriate. Wherever necessary, national legislative and other measures should be considered to accord all the rights of and protection for the child, where the child is brought before a court other than a juvenile court, in accordance with articles 3, 37 and 40 of the Convention.

15. A review of existing procedures should be undertaken and, where possible, diversion or other alternative initiatives to the classical criminal justice systems should be developed to avoid recourse to the criminal justice systems for young persons accused of an offence. Appropriate steps should be taken to make available throughout the State a broad range of alternative and

educative measures at the pre-arrest, pre-trial, trial and post-trial stages, in order to prevent recidivism and promote the social rehabilitation of child offenders. Whenever appropriate, mechanisms for the informal resolution of disputes in cases involving a child offender should be utilized, including mediation and restorative justice practices, particularly processes involving victims. In the various measures to be adopted, the family should be involved, to the extent that it operates in favour of the good of the child offender. States should ensure that alternative measures comply with the Convention, the United Nations standards and norms in juvenile justice, as well as other existing standards and norms in crime prevention and criminal justice, such as the United Nations Standard Minimum Rules for Non-custodial Measures (The Tokyo Rules), with special regard to ensuring respect for due process rules in applying such measures and for the principle of minimum intervention.

11.8.1   Case study: 'child killers'

T and V v United Kingdom, European Court of Human Rights, Applications 24724/94 and 24888/94

The applicants (Thomson and Venables) were convicted of killing a two year old boy, Jamie Bulger, whom they had abducted from a shopping centre in England. They were just over the age set for criminal responsibility in England (10 years). There was extensive media coverage of the event and the trial within the United Kingdom. The names of the two boys were released.

27. Pursuant to section 50 of the Children and Young Persons Act 1933 as amended by section 16(1) of the Children and Young Persons Act 1963 ('the 1933 Act'), the age of criminal responsibility in England and Wales is ten years, below which no child can be found guilty of a criminal offence. The age of ten was endorsed by the Home Affairs Select Committee (composed of Members of Parliament) in October 1993 (*Juvenile Offenders*, Sixth Report of the Session 1992–93, Her Majesty's Stationary (*sic*) Office). At the time of the applicant's trial, a child between the ages of ten and fourteen was subject to a presumption that he did not know that what he was doing was wrong (*doli incapax*). This presumption had to be rebutted by the prosecution proving beyond reasonable doubt that, at the time of the offence, the child knew that the act was wrong as distinct from merely naughty or childish mischief (*C. (a minor) v. the Director of Public Prosecutions* [1996] Appeal Cases 1).

The *doli incapax* presumption has since been abolished with effect from 30 September 1998 (section 34 of the Crime and Disorder Act 1998). . . .

48. The age of criminal responsibility is seven in Cyprus, Ireland, Switzerland and Liechtenstein; eight in Scotland; thirteen in France; fourteen in Germany, Austria, Italy and many Eastern European countries; fifteen in the Scandinavian countries; sixteen in Portugal, Poland and Andorra; and eighteen in Spain, Belgium and Luxembourg. . . .

82. The Commission expressed the view that where a child was faced with a criminal charge and the domestic system required a fact-finding procedure with a view to establishing guilt, it was essential that the child's age, level of maturity and intellectual and emotional capacities be taken into account in the procedures followed. It considered that the public trial process in an adult court with attendant publicity must be regarded in the case of an eleven-year-old child as a severely intimidating procedure and concluded that, having regard to the applicant's age, the application of the full rigours of an adult, public trial deprived him of the opportunity to participate effectively in the determination of the criminal charges against him, in breach of Article 6 § 1.

83. The Court notes that Article 6, read as a whole, guarantees the right of an accused to participate effectively in his criminal trial.

It has not until the present time been called upon to consider how this Article 6 § 1 guarantee applies to criminal proceedings against children, and in particular whether procedures which are generally considered to safeguard the rights of adults on trial, such as publicity, should be abrogated in respect of children in order to promote their understanding and participation (but see the Nortier v. the Netherlands judgment of 24 August 1993, Series A no. 267, and particularly the separate opinions thereto).

84. The Court recalls its above findings that there is not at this stage any clear common standard amongst the member States of the Council of Europe as to the minimum age of criminal responsibility and that the attribution of criminal responsibility to the applicant does not in itself give rise to a breach of Article 3 of the Convention. Likewise, it cannot be said that the trial on criminal charges of a child, even one as young as eleven, as such violates the fair trial guarantee under Article 6 § 1. The Court does, however, agree with the Commission that it is essential that a child charged with an offence is dealt with in a manner which takes full account of his age, level of maturity and intellectual and emotional capacities, and that steps are taken to promote his ability to understand and participate in the proceedings.

85. It follows that, in respect of a young child charged with a grave offence attracting high levels of media and public interest, it would be necessary to conduct the hearing in such a way as to reduce as far as possible his or her feelings of intimidation and inhibition. In this connection it is noteworthy that in England and Wales children charged with less serious crimes are dealt with in special Youth Courts, from which the general public is excluded and in relation to which there are imposed automatic reporting restrictions on the media (see paragraphs 28 and 29 above). Moreover, the Court has already referred to the international tendency towards the protection of the privacy of child defendants. It has considered carefully the Government's argument that public trials serve the general interest in the open administration of justice, and observes that, where appropriate in view of the age and other characteristics of the child and the circumstances surrounding the criminal proceedings, this general interest could be satisfied by a modified procedure providing for selected attendance rights and judicious reporting.

86. The Court notes that the applicant's trial took place over three weeks in public in the Crown Court. Special measures were taken in view of the applicant's young age and to promote his understanding of the proceedings: for example, he had the trial procedure explained to him and was taken to see the courtroom in advance, and the hearing times were shortened so as not to tire the defendants excessively. Nonetheless, the formality and ritual of the Crown Court must at times have seemed incomprehensible and intimidating for a child of eleven, and there is evidence that certain of the modifications to the courtroom, in particular the raised dock which was designed to enable the defendants to see what was going on, had the effect of increasing the applicant's sense of discomfort during the trial, since he felt exposed to the scrutiny of the press and public. The trial generated extremely high levels of press and public interest, both inside and outside the courtroom, to the extent that the judge in his summing-up referred to the problems caused to witnesses by the blaze of publicity and asked the jury to take this into account when assessing their evidence.

87. As previously mentioned, there is limited psychiatric evidence in relation to this applicant. However, it is noteworthy that Dr Vizard found in her report of 5 November 1993 that the post-traumatic stress disorder suffered by the applicant, combined with the lack of any therapeutic work since the offence, had limited his ability to instruct his lawyers and testify adequately in his own defence. Moreover, the applicant in his memorial states that due to the conditions in which he was put on trial, he was unable to follow the trial or take decisions in his own best interests.

88. In such circumstances the Court does not consider that it was sufficient for the purposes of Article 6 § 1 that the applicant was represented by skilled and experienced lawyers. This case is different from that of Stanford, where the Court found no violation arising from the fact that the accused could not hear some of the evidence given at trial, in view of the fact that his counsel, who

could hear all that was said and was able to take his client's instructions at all times, chose for tactical reasons not to request that the accused be seated closer to the witnesses. Here, although the applicant's legal representatives were seated, as the Government put it, 'within whispering distance', it is highly unlikely that the applicant would have felt sufficiently uninhibited, in the tense courtroom and under public scrutiny, to have consulted with them during the trial or, indeed, that, given his immaturity and his disturbed emotional state, he would have been capable outside the courtroom of cooperating with his lawyers and giving them information for the purposes of his defence.

89. In conclusion, the Court considers that the applicant was unable to participate effectively in the criminal proceedings against him and was, in consequence, denied a fair hearing in breach of Article 6 § 1.

Question

To what extent has a general consensus on the age of criminal responsibility emerged since this time? Does the Convention on the Rights of the Child exert any influence over law and practice in this area?

11.9 CAPITAL PUNISHMENT

At the time of drafting many of the international instruments, capital punishment was still accepted practice. Today, the situation is rather different and it is proscribed in many States. However, many of the international instruments still make reference to the death penalty as an acceptable exception to the right to life.

International Covenant on Civil and Political Rights 1966 Art 6 (2, 4, 5 and 6)

2. In countries which have not abolished the death penalty, sentence of death may be imposed only for the most serious crimes in accordance with the law in force at the time of the commission of the crime and not contrary to the provisions of the present Covenant and to the Convention on the Prevention and Punishment of the Crime of Genocide. This penalty can only be carried out pursuant to a final judgement rendered by a competent court.

4. Anyone sentenced to death shall have the right to seek pardon or commutation of the sentence. Amnesty, pardon or commutation of the sentence of death may be granted in all cases.

5. Sentence of death shall not be imposed for crimes committed by persons below eighteen years of age and shall not be carried out on pregnant women.

6. Nothing in this article shall be invoked to delay or to prevent the abolition of capital punishment by any State Party to the present Covenant.

See also Art 2(1) of the European Convention on Human Rights 1950.

American Convention on Human Rights 1969 Art 4 (2, 3, 4, 5 and 6)

2. In countries that have not abolished the death penalty, it may be imposed only for the most serious crimes and pursuant to a final judgment rendered by a competent court and in accordance with a law establishing such punishment, enacted prior to the commission of the crime. The application of such punishment shall not be extended to crimes to which it does not presently apply.

3. The death penalty shall not be reestablished in states that have abolished it.

4. In no case shall capital punishment be inflicted for political offenses or related common crimes.

5. Capital punishment shall not be imposed upon persons who, at the time the crime was

committed, were under 18 years of age or over 70 years of age; nor shall it be applied to pregnant women.

6. Every person condemned to death shall have the right to apply for amnesty, pardon, or commutation of sentence, which may be granted in all cases. Capital punishment shall not be imposed while such a petition is pending decision by the competent authority.

Perhaps indicative of the prevalence of the death penalty in some member States and their reluctance to condemn it, the League of Arab States extends provisions on the death penalty over several articles, thereby effectively giving the matter greater prominence than the other regional systems.

Arab Charter on Human Rights 1994

Article 10

The death penalty may be imposed only for the most serious crimes and anyone sentenced to death shall have the right to seek pardon or commutation of the sentence.

Article 11

The death penalty shall under no circumstances be imposed for a political offence.

Article 12

The death penalty shall not be inflicted on a person under 18 years of age, on a pregnant woman prior to her delivery or on a nursing mother within two years from the date on which she gave birth.

Obviously for those States in which the death penalty is a legitimate penalty, careful safeguards need to be built into the judicial process to ensure that no error exists. Moreover, there is a need for certain standards to be reached in the trial process.

Most importantly, the full legal process has to be complied with before the ultimate sanction can be imposed. Failure to do so will infringe international law and may infringe the Principles on the Effective Prevention and Investigation of Extra-legal, Arbitrary and Summary Executions (ECOSOC Resolution 1989/65, 1989).

Safeguards guaranteeing protection of the rights of those facing the death penalty, ECOSOC Resolution 1984/50 (1984)

1. In countries which have not abolished the death penalty, capital punishment may be imposed only for the most serious crimes, it being understood that their scope should not go beyond intentional crimes with lethal or other extremely grave consequences.

4. Capital punishment may be imposed only when the guilt of the person charged is based upon clear and convincing evidence leaving no room for an alternative explanation of the facts.

5. Capital punishment may only be carried out pursuant to a final judgement rendered by a competent court after legal process which gives all possible safeguards to ensure a fair trial, at least equal to those contained in article 14 of the International Covenant on Civil and Political Rights, including the right of anyone suspected of or charged with a crime for which capital punishment may be imposed to adequate legal assistance at all stages of the proceedings.

6. Anyone sentenced to death shall have the right to appeal to a court of higher jurisdiction, and steps should be taken to ensure that such appeals shall become mandatory.

7. Anyone sentenced to death shall have the right to seek pardon, or commutation of sentence; pardon or commutation of sentence may be granted in all cases of capital punishment.

8. Capital punishment shall not be carried out pending any appeal or other recourse procedure or other proceeding relating to pardon or commutation of the sentence.

Inevitably, reflecting some of the exclusion clauses contained in the instruments extracted above, not everyone may be subjected to the death penalty.

Safeguards guaranteeing protection of the rights of those facing the death penalty, ECOSOC Resolution 1984/50 (1984)

2. Capital punishment may be imposed only for a crime for which the death penalty is prescribed by law at the time of its commission, it being understood that if, subsequent to the commission of the crime, provision is made by law for the imposition of a lighter penalty, the offender shall benefit thereby.

3. Persons below 18 years of age at the time of the commission of the crime shall not be sentenced to death, nor shall the death sentence be carried out on pregnant women, or on new mothers, or on persons who have become insane.

Finally, should all appropriate procedures be followed and the death penalty imposed, then care must be taken to ensure that it is administered in as fair and humane a manner as possible.

Safeguards guaranteeing protection of the rights of those facing the death penalty, ECOSOC Resolution 1984/50 (1984)

9. Where capital punishment occurs, it shall be carried out so as to inflict the minimum possible suffering.

Question

Would a public execution be justified for a mass murderer (consider retributive justice balanced against the standard for human treatment)?

11.9.1　Case study: 'death row'

Soering v United Kingdom is discussed in Chapter 2. The European Court opined that States were under a positive obligation to ensure their action did not give rise to a violation of the European Convention on Human Rights. Extradicting Soering to the United States of America for almost certain capital punishment was contrary to the prohibition on inhuman and degrading treatment or punishment due to the prolonged length of time an individual could spend on death row.

Pratt and Morgan v Jamaica, Communications 210/1986 and 225/1987, Human Rights Committee, UN Doc. CCPR/C/35/D/210/1986

The authors of the communication were convicted of murder and sentenced to death, with execution scheduled for February 1987. A stay of proceedings was notified to them 45 minutes before the scheduled time of execution.

13.4 The State party has contended that the time span of three years and nine months between the dismissal of the authors' appeal and the delivery of the Court of Appeal's written judgement was attributable to an oversight and that the authors should have asserted their right to receive earlier the written judgement. The Committee considers that the responsibility for the delay of 45 months lies with the judicial authorities of Jamaica. This responsibility is neither dependent on a request for production by the accused in a trial nor is non-fulfillment of this responsibility excused by the absence of a request from the accused. The Committee further observes that the Privy Council itself described the delay as inexcusable.

13.5 In the absence of a written judgement of the Court of Appeal, the authors were not able to proceed to appeal before the Privy Council, thus entailing a violation of article 14, paragraph 3 (c), and article 14, paragraph 5. In reaching this conclusion it matters not that in the event the Privy

Council affirmed the conviction of the authors. The Committee notes that in all cases, and especially in capital cases, accused persons are entitled to trial and appeal without undue delay, whatever the outcome of those judicial proceedings turns out to be.

13.6 There are two issues concerning article 7 before the Committee: the first is whether the excessive delays in judicial proceedings constituted not only a violation of article 14, but 'cruel, inhuman and degrading treatment'. The possibility that such a delay as occurred in this case could constitute cruel and inhuman treatment was referred to by the Privy Council. In principle pro-longed judicial proceedings do not per se constitute cruel, inhuman or degrading treatment even if they can be a source of mental strain for the convicted prisoners. However, the situation could be otherwise in cases involving capital punishment and an assessment of the circumstances of each case would be necessary. In the present cases the Committee does not find that the authors have sufficiently substantiated their claim that delay in judicial proceedings constituted for them cruel, inhuman and degrading treatment under article 7.

In Iraq, the American-led coalition forces removed the death penalty, only for the incoming Iraqi regime to re-impose it in advance of the trial of Saddam Hussein. Hussein was sentenced to death by hanging in November 2006, though may appeal. This remains an exception to the growing tendency of States to abolish the death penalty or at least cease to invoke it. (Of course, certain parts of the USA have recently returned to the death penalty as the ultimate sanction.)

11.9.2   Moves towards abolition of the death penalty

The formal calls for abolition first found legal expression in the Sixth Protocol to the European Convention on Human Rights 1983. However, the international community followed in 1990—Second Optional Protocol to the International Covenant on Civil and Political Rights, Aimed at abolishing the Death Penalty 1990—and the Americas (Protocol to the American Convention on Human Rights to Abolish the Death Penalty 1990). Note also that even for those States ratifying the relevant protocols, the aboli-tion is not necessarily absolute, and some derogations are occasionally permitted.

Second Optional Protocol to the International Covenant on Civil and Political Rights, aiming at the abolition of the death penalty, General Assembly Resolution 44/128 (1989)

Article 1

1. No one within the jurisdiction of a State Party to the present Protocol shall be executed.

2. Each State Party shall take all necessary measures to abolish the death penalty within its jurisdiction.

Article 2

1. No reservation is admissible to the present Protocol, except for a reservation made at the time of ratification or accession that provides for the application of the death penalty in time of war pursuant to a conviction for a most serious crime of a military nature committed during wartime.

Compare to Arts 1–4 of Protocol 6 to the European Convention on Human Rights and Fundamental Freedoms and Arts 1–2 of the Protocol to the American Convention on Human Rights to Abolish the Death Penalty.

Question

What elements of international law permit such a reservation and for what crimes may the death penalty thus be preserved?

FURTHER READING

Lehtimaja, L, and Pellonpaa, M, 'Article 10' in Alfredsson, G, and Eide, A (eds), *The Universal Declaration of Human Rights—a common standrd of achievement*, 1999, the Hague: Martinus Nijhof

Morgan, R, and Evans, M, *Protecting Prisoners—the standards of the European Committee for the Prevention of Torture in Context*, 1999, Oxford: OUP

Rodley, N, *The Treatment of Prisoners in International Law*, 2nd edn, 1999, Oxford: Clarendon Press

Weissbrodt, D, *The Right to a fair trial under the Universal Declaration of Human Rights and the International Covenant on Civil and Political Rights—background, development and interpretation*, 2001, the Hague: Kluwer

Websites

www.icc-cpi.int—International Criminal Court
www.icj-cij.org—International Court of Justice
www.echr.coe.int—European Court of Human Rights
www.corteidh.or.cr—Inter-American Court of Human Rights
www.ohchr.org/english/bodies/cat/index.htm—United Nations Committee against Torture
www.cpt.coe.int—European Convention/Committee on Torture

CHAPTER 12

INDIGENOUS PEOPLES AND THEIR RIGHTS

The rights of indigenous peoples were initially linked to minority rights. However, many commentators, the peoples themselves and indeed the international and regional bodies now appear to recognise indigenous people as a distinct group. Indeed indigenous peoples require redress for many problems not faced by other minority groups. Many of the claims of indigenous peoples are particular to the historic situations leading to their alienation. They reflect colonisation, assimilation and alienation of traditional ways of living.

This chapter will include materials drawn from the international and regional bodies on the rights of indigenous peoples, and some minorities, focusing on the following key areas: self-determination/autonomy; land rights and restitution; reconciliation and culture.

12.1 TOWARDS RECOGNITION OF INDIGENOUS RIGHTS

Many indigenous peoples suffered from non-recognition by the conquering forces invading their lands. Land was claimed in the name of the relevant sovereign and the indigenous peoples were either ignored or persecuted although in many instances their skills and produce were bartered for. The traditional approach was one of removal and/or assimilation.

The International Labour Organisation (ILO) was one of the first international bodies to address the rights of indigenous peoples (see, for example, Charles, 'Tribal Society and Labour Legislation' 65 International Labour Review (1952) 423). This in many ways was a strange development as it may be viewed as tangential to the object and purpose of the International Labour Organisation. However, issues such as forced labour, addressed in ILO Convention No. 35 (1930), are particularly relevant for indigenous people. In 1936, the ILO considered the Recruiting of Indigenous Workers in Convention No. 50 (1936), following this with Convention No. 64 Contracts of Employment (Indigenous Workers) and Convention No. 65 Penal Sanctions (Indigenous Workers), both in 1939. Note the definition of beneficiaries of these initiatives.

Convention No. 50, Recruiting of Indigenous Workers 1936 Art 2(b)

For the purposes of this Convention—

(b) the term *indigenous workers* includes workers belonging to or assimilated to the indigenous populations of the dependent territories of Members of the Organisation and workers belonging to or assimilated to the dependent indigenous populations of the home territories of Members of the Organisation.

(Note that this Convention is no longer operational)

A Committee of Experts on Indigenous Labour was created to examine the problems of indigenous populations, problems seen as being social and economic in character. This was followed by a global survey which prompted the tabulation of more detailed rights in two principal instruments on the rights of tribal and indigenous peoples.

Consider the differences in the preambles to both conventions:

Convention 107, Indigenous and Tribal Populations Convention 1957

The General Conference of the International Labour Organisation, . . .

Having decided upon the adoption of certain proposals with regard to the protection and integration of indigenous and other tribal and semi-tribal populations in independent countries, which is the sixth item on the agenda of the session, and

Having determined that these proposals shall take the form of an international Convention, and . . .

Considering that there exist in various independent countries indigenous and other tribal and semi-tribal populations which are not yet integrated into the national community and whose social, economic or cultural situation hinders them from benefiting fully from the rights and advantages enjoyed by other elements of the population, and

Considering it desirable both for humanitarian reasons and in the interest of the countries concerned to promote continued action to improve the living and working conditions of these populations by simultaneous action in respect of all the factors which have hitherto prevented them from sharing fully in the progress of the national community of which they form part, and

Considering that the adoption of general international standards on the subject will facilitate action to assure the protection of the populations concerned, their progressive integration into their respective national communities, and the improvement of their living and working conditions.

Question

What aspects of the preambular paragraphs may be deemed objectionable by indigenous peoples, both at adoption and, indeed now?

Convention 169, Indigenous and Tribal Peoples Convention 1989

The General Conference of the International Labour Organisation, . . .

Noting the international standards contained in the Indigenous and Tribal Populations Convention and Recommendation, 1957, and

Recalling the terms of the Universal Declaration of Human Rights, the International Covenant on Economic, Social and Cultural Rights, the International Covenant on Civil and Political Rights, and the many international instruments on the prevention of discrimination, and

Considering that the developments which have taken place in international law since 1957, as well as developments in the situation of indigenous and tribal peoples in all regions of the world, have made it appropriate to adopt new international standards on the subject with a view to removing the assimilationist orientation of the earlier standards, and

Recognising the aspirations of these peoples to exercise control over their own institutions, ways of life and economic development and to maintain and develop their identities, languages and religions, within the framework of the States in which they live, and

Noting that in many parts of the world these peoples are unable to enjoy their fundamental human rights to the same degree as the rest of the population of the States within which they live, and that their laws, values, customs and perspectives have often been eroded, and

Calling attention to the distinctive contributions of indigenous and tribal peoples to the cultural diversity and social and ecological harmony of humankind and to international co-operation and understanding, and . . .

Having decided upon the adoption of certain proposals with regard to the partial revision of the Indigenous and Tribal Populations Convention, 1957 (No. 107), which is the fourth item on the agenda of the session, and

Having determined that these proposals shall take the form of an international Convention revising the Indigenous and Tribal Populations Convention, 1957.

The preamble to the second ILO Convention clearly indicates an intention that the problems identified in the first Convention have been addressed.

Question

Read both conventions and ascertain the extent to which the assimilationist approach is removed in Convention 169.

Ascertaining the scope of the term 'indigenous' has, and indeed remains, problematic. Although there are many indigenous peoples in the world, they do not all wish to be treated differently from their co-citizens in a State. No uniform definition has been agreed upon. The following guidelines were adopted by the International Labour Organisation and retain currency today.

Indigenous Peoples: Living and Working Conditions of Aboriginal Populations in Independent Countries, Studies and Reports, Series 35, 1953 International Labour Office: Geneva, para 25–6

Indigenous persons are descendants of the aboriginal population living in a given country at the time of settlement or conquest (or of successive waves of conquest) by some of the ancestors of the non-indigenous groups in whose hand political and economic power at present lies. In general, these descendants tend to live more in conformity with the social, economic and cultural institutions which existed before colonisation or conquest . . . than with the culture of the nation to which they belong; they do not fully share in the national economy and culture owing to barriers of language, customs, creed, prejudice, and often out-of-date and unjust systems of worker-employer relationship and other social and political factors. When their full participation in national life is not hindered by one of the obstacles mentioned above, it is restricted by historical influences producing in them an attitude of overriding loyalty to their position as members of a given tribe; in the case of marginal indigenous persons or groups, the problem arises from the fact that they are not accepted into, or cannot or will not participate in, the organised life of either the nation or the indigenous society.

Many indigenous peoples fall outwith this working definition, or at least do not fully fall within it. Indigenous peoples often occupy border territories and may move freely between States (for example, the Kurds and Druze). The definition also appears inconsistent with the initial paternalistic assimilationist approach of the International Labour Organisation. The ILO continued its 'monopoly' of indigenous rights after its affiliation to the new United Nations, '[i]n effect, the United Nations system assigned responsibility for this subject to the ILO' (Lee Swepston, 'Indigenous and tribal populations: a return to centre stage' 126 International Labour Review (1987) 447).

12.1.1 ILO successes in evincing indigenous rights

The ILO had a number of successes in promulgating indigenous peoples' rights:

(1) The creation of the Andean Indian Programme—an inter-agency programme coordinated by the ILO which aimed at improving the living and working conditions of the indigenous Andean communities. It commenced in 1954 in Bolivia, Ecuador and Peru though subsequently was expanded to Argentina, Chile, Columbia and Venezuela (see Rens, J, 'The Andean Programme', International Labour Review (1961) 423).

(2) A comprehensive study on indigenous peoples and their rights: *Indigenous Peoples: Living and Working Conditions of Aboriginal Populations in Independent Countries*, Studies and Reports, Series 35, 1953, International Labour Office: Geneva. It represented a culmination of the work undertaken as part of the Andean Indian

Programme and laid the groundwork for the subsequent instruments on indigenous rights.

(3) The adoption of the first Convention on indigenous peoples in 1957 (Convention No. 107 concerning the Protection and Integration of Indigenous and other Tribal and Semi-Tribal Populations in Independent Countries) and a Recommendation (No. 104) on the same heralded recognition of the unique status and needs of indigenous peoples.

Both these treaties were unusual in that they addressed indigenous and tribal peoples directly. Initially, as indicated, much of their protection for indigenous peoples was grounded in protection of minorities. Depending on the definition adopted for 'minority' (this in itself is controversial in international law) many indigenous peoples do indeed fall within the scope of these provisions. However, the concept of minority was viewed as patronising, implying inferiority.

Minority rights have nevertheless achieved greater international acceptance and recognition than the rights of indigenous peoples. Accordingly, for some indigenous people, there may be considerable advantage in accepting minority rights and benefiting from them.

12.2   INVOKING MINORITY RIGHTS

In contemporary international human rights law, Art 27 of the International Covenant on Civil and Political Rights contains the principal provision on minority rights.

International Covenant on Civil and Political Rights Art 27

In those States in which ethnic, religious or linguistic minorities exist, persons belonging to such minorities shall not be denied the right, in community with the other members of their group, to enjoy their own culture, to profess and practise their own religion, or to use their own language.

Many groups have indeed been able to employ Art 27 successfully submitting complaints to the Human Rights Committee. Minority rights may be utilised by indigenous peoples to secure their traditional practices.

General Comment No. 23 (1994), Human Rights Committee (see also Chapter 5)

6.1. Although article 27 is expressed in negative terms, that article, nevertheless, does recognize the existence of a 'right' and requires that it shall not be denied. Consequently, a State party is under an obligation to ensure that the existence and the exercise of this right are protected against their denial or violation. Positive measures of protection are, therefore, required not only against the acts of the State party itself, whether through its legislative, judicial or administrative authorities, but also against the acts of other persons within the State party.

6.2. Although the rights protected under article 27 are individual rights, they depend in turn on the ability of the minority group to maintain its culture, language or religion. Accordingly, positive measures by States may also be necessary to protect the identity of a minority and the rights of its members to enjoy and develop their culture and language and to practise their religion, in community with the other members of the group. In this connection, it has to be observed that such positive measures must respect the provisions of articles 2.1 and 26 of the Covenant both as regards the treatment between different minorities and the treatment between the persons belonging to them and the remaining part of the population. However, as long as those measures are aimed at correcting conditions which prevent or impair the enjoyment of the rights guaranteed under article 27, they may constitute a legitimate differentiation under the Covenant, provided that they are based on reasonable and objective criteria. . . .

9. The Committee concludes that article 27 relates to rights whose protection imposes specific obligations on States parties. The protection of these rights is directed towards ensuring the survival and continued development of the cultural, religious and social identity of the minorities concerned, thus enriching the fabric of society as a whole. Accordingly, the Committee observes that these rights must be protected as such and should not be confused with other personal rights conferred on one and all under the Covenant. States parties, therefore, have an obligation to ensure that the exercise of these rights is fully protected and they should indicate in their reports the measures they have adopted to this end.

The relevance of elements of minority rights is obvious. So too the benefit—minority rights are enforceable in international law. Few instruments on the rights of indigenous people are. Naturally some problems emerge as many States have not ratified the optional protocol to the Covenant and thus have no right to submit communications to the Human Rights Committee (the salient treaty monitoring body). There are, however, a number of instances of indigenous people successfully invoking Article 27 to protect elements of their cultural identity.

Lovelace v Canada, Communication No. 24/1977 (1) and (2), UN Doc. CCPR/ C/13/D/24/1977

The author of the communication, Sandra Lovelace, was born and registered a Maliseet Indian but lost her rights and status as an Indian when she married a non-Indian as, in accordance with domestic law, she ceased to be a member of the Tobique band at that time. The same restriction did not apply to Indian men marrying non-Indian women. Possession of Indian status carries with it, *inter alia*, rights of residency on reserve land. Following her divorce, the author wished to return to live on a reserve. As she was prohibited from so doing, she claimed a violation of Arts 2(1), 3, 23(1) and (4), 26 and 27 of the International Covenant on Civil and Political Rights. The Human Rights Committee noted the Canadian Government's intention to change to relevant laws (which has been done). Lovelace was ultimately permitted to return to her reserve and engage in a full cultural Maliseet life.

13.1 The Committee considers that the essence of the present complaint concerns the continuing effect of the Indian Act, in denying Sandra Lovelace legal status as an Indian, in particular because she cannot for this reason claim a legal right to reside where she wishes to, on the Tobique Reserve. This fact persists after the entry into force of the Covenant, and its effects have to be examined, without regard to their original cause. Among the effects referred to on behalf of the author (see para. 9.9, above), the greater number, ((1) to (8)), relate to the Indian Act and other Canadian rules in fields which do not necessarily adversely affect the enjoyment of rights protected by the Covenant. In this respect the significant matter is her last claim, that 'the major loss to a person ceasing to be an Indian is the loss of the cultural benefits of living in an Indian community, the emotional ties to home, family, friends and neighhours, and the loss of identity'. . . .

14. The rights under article 27 of the Covenant have to be secured to 'persons belonging' to the minority. At present Sandra Lovelace does not qualify as an Indian under Canadian legislation. However, the Indian Act deals primarily with a number of privileges which, as stated above, do not as such come within the scope of the Covenant. Protection under the Indian Act and protection under article 27 of the Covenant therefore have to be distinguished. Persons who are born and brought up on a reserve, who have kept ties with their community and wish to maintain these ties must normally be considered as belonging to that minority within the meaning of the Covenant. Since Sandra Lovelace is ethnically a Maliseet Indian and has only been absent from her home reserve for a few years during the existence of her marriage, she is, in the opinion of the Committee, entitled to be regarded as 'belonging' to this minority and to claim the benefits of

article 27 of the Covenant. The question whether these benefits have been denied to her depends on how far they extend.

15. The right to live on a reserve is not as such guaranteed by article 27 of the Covenant. Moreover, the Indian Act does not interfere directly with the functions which are expressly mentioned in that article. However, in the opinion of the Committee the right of Sandra Lovelace to access to her native culture and language 'in community with the other members' of her group, has in fact been, and continues to be interfered with, because there is no place outside the Tobique Reserve where such a community exists. On the other hand, not every interference can be regarded as a denial of rights within the meaning of article 27. Restrictions on the right to residence, by way of national legislation, cannot be ruled out under article 27 of the Covenant. This also follows from the restrictions to article 12 (l) of the Covenant set out in article 12 (3). The Committee recognizes the need to define the category of persons entitled to live on a reserve, for such purposes as those explained by the Government regarding protection of its resources and preservation of the identity of its people. However, the obligations which the Government has since undertaken under the Covenant must also be taken into account.

16. In this respect, the Committee is of the view that statutory restrictions affecting the right to residence on a reserve of a person belonging to the minority concerned, must have both a reasonable and objective justification and be consistent with the other provisions of the Covenant, read as a whole. Article 27 must be construed and applied in the light of the other provisions mentioned above, such as articles 12, 17 and 23 in so far as they may be relevant to the particular case, and also the provisions against discrimination, such as articles 2, 3 and 26, as the case may be. It is not necessary, however, to determine in any general manner which restrictions may be justified under the Covenant, in particular as a result of marriage, because the circumstances are special in the present case.

17. The case of Sandra Lovelace should be considered in the light of the fact that her marriage to a non-Indian has broken up. It is natural that in such a situation she wishes to return to the environment in which she was born, particularly as after the dissolution of her marriage her main cultural attachment again was to the Maliseet band. Whatever may be the merits of the Indian Act in other respects, it does not seem to the Committee that to deny Sandra Lovelace the right to reside on the reserve is reasonable, or necessary to preserve the identity of the tribe. The Committee therefore concludes that to prevent her recognition as belonging to the band is an unjustifiable denial of her rights under article 27 of the Covenant, read in the context of the other provisions referred to.

18. In view of this finding, the Committee does not consider it necessary to examine whether the same facts also show separate breaches of the other rights invoked. The specific rights most directly applicable to her situation are those under article 27 of the Covenant. The rights to choose one's residence (article 12), and the rights aimed at protecting family life and children (articles 17, 23 and 24) are only indirectly at stake in the present case. The facts of the case do not seem to require further examination under those articles. The Committee's finding of a lack of a reasonable justification for the interference with Sandra Lovelace's rights under article 27 of the Covenant also makes it unnecessary, as suggested above (para. 12), to examine the general provisions against discrimination (arts. 2, 3 and 26) in the context of the present case, and in particular to determine their bearing upon inequalities predating the coming into force of the Covenant for Canada.

19. Accordingly, the Human Rights Committee, acting under article 5 (4) of the Optional Protocol to the International Covenant on Civil and Political Rights, is of the view that the facts of the present case, which establish that Sandra Lovelace has been denied the legal right to reside on the Tobique Reserve, disclose a breach by Canada of article 27 of the Covenant.

The element of sex discrimination was crucial in the determination of this case. (See also, Bayefsky, A.F, 'The Human Rights Committee and the case of Sandra Lovelace' 20 Canadian Yearbook of International Law (1982), pp 244–266.)

Question

To what extent did the cultural arguments influence the Committee? Is it possible that the Committee would have concluded there was a violation of Art 27 had discrimination not occurred?

In neither Lovelace nor the following case, Lubicon Lake Band, did the Human Rights Committee express an opinion on whether the author of the complaint belonged to what could be termed a minority. Thus it appears that it was accepted that indigenous people could be included within the protective ambit of Art 27 without requiring them to overtly embrace designation as a minority. Given that most indigenous groups are reluctant to accept minority status, this is an important point.

Lubicon Lake Band v Canada, Communication 167/1984, UN Doc. CCPR/C/ 38/D/167/1984

Chief Bernard Ominayak of the Lubicon Lake Band primarily complained about a violation of Art 1 of the International Covenant on Civil and Political Rights though aspects of the case were resolved with reference to Art 27. The Lubicon Lake Band are a Cree Indian band who speak Cree and inhabit their traditional lands in northern Alberta, maintaining their traditional culture, religion, political structure and subsistence economy. The Canadian government expropriated the territory for the benefit of private corporate interests—leases for oil and gas exploration among others. It was alleged that the very existence of the group was threatened by the government's actions. Article 1 was dismissed by the Committee as falling outwith their jurisdiction, not being an individual right. Article 27 was considered although the Committee accepted that the proposed remedial actions of the government sufficiently met the standard of the Covenant.

32.1 The question has arisen of whether any claim under article 1 of the Covenant remains, the Committee's decision on admissibility notwithstanding. While all peoples have the right of self-determination and the right freely to determine their political status, pursue their economic, social and cultural development and dispose of their natural wealth and resources, as stipulated in article 1 of the Covenant, the question whether the Lubicon Lake Band constitutes a 'people' is not an issue for the Committee to address under the Optional Protocol to the Covenant. The Optional Protocol provides a procedure under which individuals can claim that their individual rights have been violated. These rights are set out in part III of the Covenant, articles 6 to 27, inclusive. There is, however, no objection to a group of individuals, who claim to be similarly affected, collectively to submit a communication about alleged breaches of their rights.

32.2 Although initially couched in terms of alleged breaches of the provisions of article 1 of the Covenant, there is no doubt that many of the claims presented raise issues under article 27. The Committee recognizes that the rights protected by article 27, include the right of persons, in community with others, to engage in economic and social activities which are part of the culture of the community to which they belong. Sweeping allegations concerning extremely serious breaches of other articles of the Covenant (6, 7, 14, para. 1, and 26), made after the communication was declared admissible, have not been substantiated to the extent that they would deserve serious consideration. The allegations concerning breaches of articles 17 and 23, paragraph 1, are similarly of a sweeping nature and will not be taken into account except in so far as they may be considered subsumed under the allegations which, generally, raise issues under article 27.

32.3 The most recent allegations that the State party has conspired to create an artificial band, the Woodland Cree Band, said to have competing claims to traditional Lubicon land, are dismissed as an abuse of the right of submission within the meaning of article 3 of the Optional Protocol.

33. Historical inequities, to which the State party refers, and certain more recent developments

threaten the way of life and culture of the Lubicon Lake Band, and constitute a violation of article 27 so long as they continue. The State party proposes to rectify the situation by a remedy that the Committee deems appropriate within the meaning of article 2 of the Covenant.

The opinion of the Committee was not unanimous. Nisuke Ando submitted an individual opinion on the application of Art 27. He concluded that only culture was affected, there being no issue of religion or language denied to the band. He accepted that culture may be closely tied to the land but expressed reservation at the Committee's conclusion:

> The communication in its present form essentially concerns the authors' rights to freely dispose of their natural wealth and resources, and to retain their own means of subsistence, such as hunting and fishing. In its decision of 22 July 1987, the Human Rights Committee decided that the communication was admissible in so far as it could have raised issues under article 27 or other articles of the Covenant. With respect to provisions other than article 27 the authors' allegations have remained, however, of such a sweeping nature that the Committee has not been able to take them into account except in so far as they may be subsumed under the claims which, generally, raise issues under article 27. That is the basis of my individual opinion.

> Since the Committee adopted its decision on admissibility, discussions seeking a resolution of the matter have taken place between the Federal Government, the Province of Alberta and the authors. As no progress was made towards a settlement, the Federal Government initiated legal proceedings against the Province of Alberta and the Lubicon Lake Band on 17 May 1988, in order to enable Canada to meet its legal obligations vis-a-vis the authors under Treaty 8. The Statement of Claim, initiating the legal action, seeks from the Court of the Queen's Bench of Alberta (a) a declaration that the Lubicon Lake Band is entitled to a reserve and (b) a determination of the size of that reserve.

> On 9 June 1988, the Lubicon Lake Band filed a Statement of Defence and Counterclaim. In this connection, the State party has submitted that the issue forming the basis of the domestic dispute as well as the basis of the communication before the Human Rights Committee concerns the extent of the territory to be set aside as a reserve, and related issues. It is not altogether clear that all issues which may be raised under article 27 of the Covenant are issues to be considered by the Court of Queen's Bench of Alberta in the case still pending before it. At the same time, it does appear that issues under article 27 of the Covenant are inextricably linked with the extent of the territory to be set aside as a reserve, and questions related to those issues.

> The rationale behind the general rule of international law that domestic remedies should be exhausted before a claim is submitted to an instance of international investigation or settlement is primarily to give a respondent State an opportunity to redress, by its own means within the framework of its domestic legal system, the wrongs alleged to have been suffered by the individual. In my opinion, this rationale implies that, in a case such as the present one, an international instance shall not examine a matter pending before a court of the respondent State. To my mind, it is not compatible with international law that an international instance consider issues which, concurrently, are pending before a national court. An instance of international investigation or settlement must, in my opinion, refrain from considering any issue pending before a national court until such time as the matter has been adjudicated upon by the national courts. As that is not the case here, I find the communication inadmissible at this point in time.

Ando's opinion gains further credence when considered along with the opinion of the Committee in the case of *Mahuika v New Zealand* (below). The cultural elements are discussed in detail in Dominic McGoldrick, 'Canadian Indians, Cultural Rights and the Human Rights Committee' (1991) 40 International and Comparative Law Quarterly, pp 658–669.

This communication illustrates a potential use of Art 27 with respect to the right to self-determination as obviously a group wishing to claim self-determination may articulate their claim in terms of cultural, linguistic or religious rights under Art 27 rather than Art 1. The same result may be achieved although obviously full self-determination is unlikely to result in the case of most indigenous peoples for the reasons stated above.

Moreover, these two communications are of note as the concept of Art 27 comprising a series of individual rights was promulgated and accepted by the Committee. Thus, although the rights are only exercisable in community with others, the rights clearly can attach to individuals rather than groups, thereby obviating the problems encountered in claiming under Art 1 (self-determination).

Kitok v Sweden, Communication 197/1985, UN Doc. CCPR/C/33/D/197/1985

Ivan Kitok was a member of a Sami family which had been actively involved in reindeer husbandry for a hundred years. The author of the communication claimed that he had inherited rights to reindeer breeding territory and water in Sorkaitum Sami village. However, under Swedish law, membership of a Sami village (in terms of exercising reindeer breeding rights) is lost by a Sami person who engages in any other profession for a minimum period of three years. Such legislation had the sole purpose of protecting those who practise reindeer husbandry as their primary source of income. Indeed few Sami people retain their traditional rights. Violations of Arts 1 and 27 were alleged. Article 1 was deemed inapplicable for the reasons later elaborated on in *Lubicon Lake Band v Canada*—that is, it is a group not individual right.

Article 27 was considered in context. Preserving the traditional livelihood of the Sami people was considered a reasonable aim of the Swedish legislation. Kitok's continued links with his Sami community were noted and it was suggested that the application of the Swedish law to him may have been disproportionate to these aims not least because he was permitted to graze and farm reindeer, albeit he did not enjoy an inalienable right to do so.

9.7 It can thus be seen that the Act provides certain criteria for participation in the life of an ethnic minority whereby a person who is ethnically a Sami can be held not to be a Sami for the purposes of the Act. The Committee has been concerned that the ignoring of objective ethnic criteria in determining membership of a minority, and the application to Mr. Kitok of the designated rules, may have been disproportionate to the legitimate ends sought by the legislation. It has further noted that Mr. Kitok has always retained some links with the Sami community, always living on Sami lands and seeking to return to full-time reindeer farming as soon as it became financially possible, in his particular circumstances, for him to do so.

9.8 In resolving this problem, in which there is an apparent conflict between the legislation, which seems to protect the rights of the minority as a whole, and its application to a single member of that minority, the Committee has been guided by the ratio decidendi in the Lovelace case (No. 24/ 1977, *Lovelace v. Canada*), namely, that a restriction upon the right of an individual member of a minority must be shown to have a reasonable and objective justification and to be necessary for the continued viability and welfare of the minority as a whole. After a careful review of all the elements involved in this case, the Committee is of the view that there is no violation of article 27 by the State party. In this context, the Committee notes that Mr. Kitok is permitted, albeit not as of right, to graze and farm his reindeer, to hunt and to fish.

The Swedish legislation took no account of the economic reality of reindeer breeding and thus the fact that many Sami wished to pursue a second more economically viable profession contemporaneous to reindeer husbandry. Moreover, the right to breed reindeer was effectively a once-only right, renunciation thereof (through alternative employment) being irreversible thereby excluding the majority of the Sami population from the ambit of the legislation.

No violation was found of Art 27.

Mahuika v New Zealand, Communication 547/1993, UN Doc. CCPR/C/70/D/547/1993

6.1 The authors claim that the Treaty of Waitangi (Fisheries Claims) Settlement Act confiscates their fishing resources, denies them their right to freely determine their political status and interferes with their right to freely pursue their economic, social and cultural development. It is submitted that the Treaty of Waitangi (Fisheries Claims) Settlement Act 1992 is in breach of the State party's obligations under the Treaty of Waitangi. In this context, the authors claim that the right to self-determination under article 1 of the Covenant is only effective when people have access to and control over their resources.

6.2 The authors claim that the Government's actions are threatening their way of life and the culture of their tribes, in violation of article 27 of the Covenant. They submit that fishing is one of the main elements of their traditional culture, that they have present-day fishing interests and the strong desire to manifest their culture through fishing to the fullest extent of their traditional territories. They further submit that their traditional culture comprises commercial elements and does not distinguish clearly between commercial and other fishing. They claim that the new legislation removes their right to pursue traditional fishing other than in the limited sense preserved by the law and that the commercial aspect of fishing is being denied to them in exchange for a share in fishing quota. In this connection, the authors refer to the Committee's Views in communication No. 167/1984 (*Ominayak v. Canada*), where it was recognised that 'the rights protected by article 27 include the right of persons, in community with others, to engage in economic and social activities which are part of the culture of the community to which they belong.' . . .

9.4 The right to enjoy one's culture cannot be determined *in abstracto* but has to be placed in context. In particular, article 27 does not only protect traditional means of livelihood of minorities, but allows also for adaptation of those means to the modern way of life and ensuing technology. In this case the legislation introduced by the State affects, in various ways, the possibilities for Maori to engage in commercial and non-commercial fishing. The question is whether this constitutes a denial of rights. . . .

9.6 The Committee notes that the State party undertook a complicated process of consultation in order to secure broad Maori support to a nation-wide settlement and regulation of fishing activities. Maori communities and national Maori organizations were consulted and their proposals did affect the design of the arrangement. The Settlement was enacted only following the Maori representatives' report that substantial Maori support for the Settlement existed. For many Maori, the Act was an acceptable settlement of their claims. The Committee has noted the authors' claims that they and the majority of members of their tribes did not agree with the Settlement and that they claim that their rights as members of the Maori minority have been overridden. In such circumstances, where the right of individuals to enjoy their own culture is in conflict with the exercise of parallel rights by other members of the minority group, or of the minority as a whole, the Committee may consider whether the limitation in issue is in the interests of all members of the minority and whether there is reasonable and objective justification for its application to the individuals who claim to be adversely affected. . . .

10. The Human Rights Committee, acting under article 5, paragraph 4, of the Optional Protocol to the International Covenant on Civil and Political Rights, is of the view that the facts before it do not reveal a breach of any of the articles of the Covenant.

12.2.1   Language rights

The following cases involve issues concerning language rights. Language is another distinctive characteristic of many indigenous groups. Moreover, it is of crucial importance to cultural rights in respect of the continuation of literature, myths and legends.

Diergaardt v Namibia, Communication 760/1997, UN Doc. CCPR/C/69/D/760/1996

10.2 The Committee regrets that the State party has not provided any information with regard to the substance of the authors' claims. It recalls that it is implicit in the Optional Protocol that States parties make available to the Committee all information at its disposal. In the absence of a reply from the State party, due weight must be given to the authors' allegations to the extent that they are substantiated. . . .

10.4 The authors have made available to the Committee the judgement which the Supreme Court gave on 14 May 1996 on appeal from the High Court which had pronounced on the claim of the Baster community to communal property. Those courts made a number of findings of fact in the light of the evidence which they assessed and gave certain interpretations of the applicable domestic law. The authors have alleged that the land of their community has been expropriated and that, as a consequence, their rights as a minority are being violated since their culture is bound up with the use of communal land exclusive to members of their community. This is said to constitute a violation of Article 27 of the Covenant.

10.5 The authors state that, although the land passed to the Rehoboth Government before 20 March 1976, that land reverted to the community by operation of law after that date. According to the judgement, initially the Basters acquired for and on behalf of the community land from the Wartbooi Tribe but there evolved a custom of issuing papers (*papieren*) to evidence the granting of land to private owners and much of the land passed into private ownership. However, the remainder of the land remained communal land until the passing of the Rehoboth Self-Government Act No. 56 of 1976 by virtue of which ownership or control of the land passed from the community and became vested in the Rehoboth Government. The Baster Community had asked for it. Self-Government was granted on the basis of proposals made by the Baster Advisory Council of Rehoboth. Elections were held under this Act and the Rehoboth area was governed in terms of the Act until 1989 when the powers granted under the Act were transferred by law to the Administrator General of Namibia in anticipation and in preparation for the independence of Namibia which followed on 21 March 1990. And in terms of the Constitution of Namibia, all property or control over property by various public institutions, including the Government of South West Africa, became vested in, or came under the control, of the Government of Namibia. The Court further stated:

> 'In 1976 the Baster Community, through its leaders, made a decision opting for Self-Government. The community freely decided to transfer its communal land to the new Government. Clearly it saw advantage in doing so. Then in 1989, the community, through the political party to which its leaders were affiliated, subscribed to the Constitution of an independent Namibia. No doubt, once again, the Community saw advantage in doing so. It wished to be part of the new unified nation which the Constitution created. . . . One aim of the Constitution was to unify a nation previously divided under the system of apartheid. Fragmented self-governments had no place in the new constitutional scheme. The years of divide and rule were over.'

10.6 To conclude on this aspect of the complaint, the Committee observes that it is for the domestic courts to find the facts in the context of, and in accordance with, the interpretation of domestic laws. On the facts found, if 'expropriation' there was, it took place in 1976, or in any event before the entry into force of the Covenant and the Optional Protocol for Namibia on 28 February 1995. As to the related issue of the use of land, the authors have claimed a violation of article 27 in that a part of the lands traditionally used by members of the Rehoboth community for the grazing of cattle no longer is in the de facto exclusive use of the members of the community. Cattle raising is said to be an essential element in the culture of the community. As the earlier case law by the Committee illustrates, the right of members of a minority to enjoy their culture under article 27 includes protection to a particular way of life associated with the use of land resources through economic activities, such as hunting and fishing, especially in the case of indigenous peoples. However, in the present case the Committee is unable to find that the authors can rely on article 27 to support their claim for exclusive use of the pastoral lands in question. This conclusion is based on the Committee's assessment of the relationship between the authors' way of life and the lands covered by their claims. Although the link of the Rehoboth community to the lands in question dates back some 125 years, it is not the result of a relationship that would have given rise to a distinctive culture. Furthermore, although the Rehoboth community bears distinctive properties as to the historical forms of self-government, the authors have failed to demonstrate how these factors would be based on their way of raising cattle. The Committee therefore finds that there has been no violation of article 27 of the Covenant in the present case.

10.7 The Committee further considers that the authors have not substantiated any claim under article 17 that would raise separate issues from their claim under article 27 with regard to their exclusion from the lands that their community used to own. . . .

10.10 The authors have also claimed that the lack of language legislation in Namibia has had as a consequence that they have been denied the use of their mother tongue in administration, justice, education and public life. The Committee notes that the authors have shown that the State party has instructed civil servants not to reply to the authors' written or oral communications with the authorities in the Afrikaans language, even when they are perfectly capable of doing so. These instructions barring the use of Afrikaans do not relate merely to the issuing of public documents but even to telephone conversations. In the absence of any response from the State party the Committee must give due weight to the allegation of the authors that the circular in question is intentionally targeted against the possibility to use Afrikaans when dealing with public authorities. Consequently, the Committee finds that the authors, as Afrikaans speakers, are victims of a violation of article 26 of the Covenant.

11. The Human Rights Committee, acting under article 5, paragraph 4, of the Optional Protocol to the International Covenant on Civil and Political Rights, is of the view that the facts before it disclose a violation of article 26 of the Covenant.

See also *Guedson v France*, UN Doc. CCPR/C/39/D/219/1986, extracted in Chapter 3.

12.2.2   Religious rights

Many indigenous peoples are also distinguishable from the rest of the population by their religious beliefs.

1994/45, Draft United Nations declaration on the rights of indigenous peoples (Now before General Assembly)

Article 13

Indigenous peoples have the right to manifest, practise, develop and teach their spiritual and religious traditions, customs and ceremonies; the right to maintain, protect, and have access in privacy to their religious and cultural sites; the right to the use and control of ceremonial objects; and the right to the repatriation of human remains.

States shall take effective measures, in conjunction with the indigenous peoples concerned, to ensure that indigenous sacred places, including burial sites, be preserved, respected and protected.

However, indigenous groups may also use existing human rights to prevent discrimination on religious grounds. Religious practices may also benefit from the various provisions on freedom of religion.

International Covenant on Civil and Political Rights 1966
Article 18

1. Everyone shall have the right to freedom of thought, conscience and religion. This right shall include freedom to have or to adopt a religion or belief of his choice, and freedom, either individually or in community with others and in public or private, to manifest his religion or belief in worship, observance, practice and teaching.

2. No one shall be subject to coercion which would impair his freedom to have or to adopt a religion or belief of his choice.

3. Freedom to manifest one's religion or beliefs may be subject only to such limitations as are prescribed by law and are necessary to protect public safety, order, health, or morals or the fundamental rights and freedoms of others.

4. The States Parties to the present Covenant undertake to have respect for the liberty of parents and, when applicable, legal guardians to ensure the religious and moral education of their children in conformity with their own convictions.

Article 26

All persons are equal before the law and are entitled without any discrimination to the equal protection of the law. In this respect, the law shall prohibit any discrimination and guarantee to all persons equal and effective protection against discrimination on any ground such as race, colour, sex, language, religion, political or other opinion, national or social origin, property, birth or other status.

Singh Bhinder v Canada, Communication 208/1986, UN Doc. CCPR/C/37/D/208/1986

The author lost his job as a maintenance electrician with the Canadian Railway Company because of his refusal to wear the mandatory hard hat. As a Sikh, he argued that he should be permitted solely to wear his turban. Health and safety issues were accepted as overruling respect for religious beliefs in the instant case.

6.1 The Committee notes that in the case under consideration legislation which, on the face of it, is neutral in that it applies to all persons without distinction, is said to operate in fact in a way which discriminates against persons of the Sikh religion. The author has claimed a violation of article 18 of the Covenant. The Committee has also examined the issue in relation to article 26 of the Covenant.

6.2 Whether one approaches the issue from the perspective of article 18 or article 26, in the view of the Committee the same conclusion must be reached. If the requirement that a hard hat be worn is regarded as raising issues under article 18, then it is a limitation that is justified by reference to the grounds laid down in article 18, paragraph 3. If the requirement that a hard hat be worn is seen as a discrimination *de facto* against persons of the Sikh religion under article 26, then, applying criteria now well established in the jurisprudence of the Committee, the legislation requiring that workers in federal employment be protected from injury and electric shock by the wearing of hard hats is to be regarded as reasonable and directed towards objective purposes that are compatible with the Covenant.

7. The Human Rights Committee, acting under article 5, paragraph 4, of the Optional Protocol to the International Covenant on Civil and Political Rights, is of the view that the facts which have been placed before it do not disclose a violation of any provision of the International Covenant on Civil and Political Rights.

Obviously this case represents a success for common sense. However, the dicta of the Committee indicates the potential for invoking the International Covenant in respect of minority religious beliefs. This provides some potential for indigenous peoples if they can phrase their claim in terms of rights under their belief systems. This communication also suggests possibilities for land claims given the close spiritual ties enjoyed by many indigenous people towards their traditional lands.

12.2.3   Other

Other overt manifestations of culture may be protected under a diverse range of pre-existing rights. As with all groups it should be remembered that indigenous people are also entitled to the full range of human rights articulated in all relevant regional and international instruments.

Moreover, minority rights are also an emergent characteristic of the European regional system. The Council of Europe adopted the European Charter for Regional or Minority Languages 1992 and the Framework Convention for the Protection of National Minorities 1994. This is the first ever legally binding multilateral instrument on minority rights. It is open for accession by any State and subject to national implementation. Reports are used to evaluate compliance with the standards. Both these instruments represent a response to increasing ethnic tensions and unrest in parts of Europe.

12.2.4   International Decade of the World's Indigenous People, towards legal rights

Within the United Nations, securement of an international declaration on the rights of indigenous peoples was one of the principal objectives of the International Decade on the World's Indigenous Peoples. The current instrument remains the draft presented in 1994 in the inaugural year of the international decade. These preambular paragraphs precede the United Nations Draft Declaration. A final text was not adopted during the UN Decade which concluded in December 2004. It is still anticipated that a declaration will eventually be concluded. Indeed at its first session in June 2006, the new Human Rights Council adopted the text of the Declaration. It is now before the General Assembly for approval. Obstacles to be overcome include the opposition of Canada, Australia, the United Kingdom and the United States of America. These countries all host considerable numbers of indigenous peoples and have adopted various approaches towards them over the centuries and decades including persecution, assimilation, alienation and devolution. By Resolution 59/174, 20/12/04, the General Assembly proclaimed a second International Decade commencing 1 January 2005.

Draft United Nations Declaration on the Rights of Indigenous Peoples, Resn 1994/45, Annex (Now awaiting General Assembly approval)

Affirming that indigenous peoples are equal in dignity and rights to all other peoples, while recognizing the right of all peoples to be different, to consider themselves different, and to be respected as such,

Affirming also that all peoples contribute to the diversity and richness of civilizations and cultures, which constitute the common heritage of humankind,

Affirming further that all doctrines, policies and practices based on or advocating superiority of peoples or individuals on the basis of national origin, racial, religious, ethnic or cultural differences are racist, scientifically false, legally invalid, morally condemnable and socially unjust,

Reaffirming also that indigenous peoples, in the exercise of their rights, should be free from discrimination of any kind,

Concerned that indigenous peoples have been deprived of their human rights and fundamental freedoms, resulting, inter alia, in their colonization and dispossession of their lands, territories and resources, thus preventing them from exercising, in particular, their right to development in accordance with their own needs and interests,

Recognizing the urgent need to respect and promote the inherent rights and characteristics of indigenous peoples, especially their rights to their lands, territories and resources, which derive from their political, economic and social structures and from their cultures, spiritual traditions, histories and philosophies,

Welcoming the fact that indigenous peoples are organizing themselves for political, economic, social and cultural enhancement and in order to bring an end to all forms of discrimination and oppression wherever they occur,

Convinced that control by indigenous peoples over developments affecting them and their lands, territories and resources will enable them to maintain and strengthen their institutions, cultures and traditions, and to promote their development in accordance with their aspirations and needs,

Recognizing also that respect for indigenous knowledge, cultures and traditional practices contributes to sustainable and equitable development and proper management of the environment,

Emphasizing the need for demilitarization of the lands and territories of indigenous peoples, which will contribute to peace, economic and social progress and development, understanding and friendly relations among nations and peoples of the world,

Recognizing in particular the right of indigenous families and communities to retain shared responsibility for the upbringing, training, education and well-being of their children,

Recognizing also that indigenous peoples have the right freely to determine their relationships with States in a spirit of coexistence, mutual benefit and full respect,

Considering that treaties, agreements and other arrangements between States and indigenous peoples are properly matters of international concern and responsibility,

Acknowledging that the Charter of the United Nations, the International Covenant on Economic, Social and Cultural Rights and the International Covenant on Civil and Political Rights affirm the fundamental importance of the right of self-determination of all peoples, by virtue of which they freely determine their political status and freely pursue their economic, social and cultural development,

Bearing in mind that nothing in this Declaration may be used to deny any peoples their right of self-determination,

Encouraging States to comply with and effectively implement all international instruments, in particular those related to human rights, as they apply to indigenous peoples, in consultation and cooperation with the peoples concerned,

Emphasizing that the United Nations has an important and continuing role to play in promoting and protecting the rights of indigenous peoples,

Believing that this Declaration is a further important step forward for the recognition, promotion and protection of the rights and freedoms of indigenous peoples and in the development of relevant activities of the United Nations system in this field.

Question

Consider the preambular paragraphs to the United Nations Draft Declaration. Do they indicate a difference in approach to that of the ILO, even in its revised Convention 169?

The United Nations Draft Declaration was compiled in consultation with indigenous peoples. Related to this, the creation of the United Nations Forum for Indigenous Peoples was a major success of the International Decade. This body comprises a number of indigenous peoples and has been heavily involved in the process of revising the draft declaration.

Economic and Social Council Resolution 2000/22, Establishment of a Permanent Forum on Indigenous Issues

1. *Decides* to establish as a subsidiary organ of the Council a permanent forum on indigenous issues, consisting of sixteen members, eight members to be nominated by Governments and elected by the Council, and eight members to be appointed by the President of the Council following formal consultation with the Bureau and the regional groups through their coordinators, on the basis of broad consultations with indigenous organizations, taking into account the diversity and geographical distribution of the indigenous people of the world as well as the principles of transparency, representativity and equal opportunity for all indigenous people, including internal processes, when appropriate, and local indigenous consultation processes, with all members serving in their personal capacity as independent experts on indigenous issues for a period of three years with the possibility of re-election or reappointment for one further period; States, United Nations bodies and organs, intergovernmental organizations and non-governmental organizations in consultative status with the Council may participate as observers; organizations of indigenous people may equally participate as observers in accordance with the procedures which have been applied in the Working Group on Indigenous Populations of the Subcommission on the Promotion and Protection of Human Rights;

2. *Also decides* that the Permanent Forum on Indigenous Issues shall serve as an advisory body to the Council with a mandate to discuss indigenous issues within the mandate of the Council relating to economic and social development, culture, the environment, education, health and human rights; in so doing the Permanent Forum shall:

(a) Provide expert advice and recommendations on indigenous issues to the Council, as well as to programmes, funds and agencies of the United Nations, through the Council;

(b) Raise awareness and promote the integration and coordination of activities relating to indigenous issues within the United Nations system;

(c) Prepare and disseminate information on indigenous issues;

12.2.5   Regional Initiatives

To date only one regional body has addressed in detail specific rights of indigenous peoples. That is the Organisation of American States. It should be noted, however, that considerable progress towards articulating minority rights and instruments aimed at protecting cultural heritage including indigenous languages has been made in Europe, under the auspices of the Council of Europe and the Organisation of Security and Cooperation in Europe.

The American Declaration appears set for a speedy adoption and thus it will most probably predate the United Nations Declaration as a finalised text. Lengthy preambular paragraphs follow the introductory paragraphs below and, as before, indicate the position underpinning the text which follows. This allows contrast with the approaches of the ILO and UN. Obviously the full text of the salient instruments should be consulted to facilitate a determination as to whether the instruments follow the approach indicated in the preambular paragraphs.

Consolidated Text of the Proposed American Declaration on the Rights of Indigenous Peoples, OEA/Ser.K/XVI GT/DADIN/doc.139/03, 17 June 2003

The Member States of the Organization of American States (hereinafter 'the States'),

RECOGNIZING that the rights of indigenous peoples constitute a fundamental and historically significant issue for the present and future of the Americas;

RECOGNIZING, moreover, the importance for humankind of preserving the indigenous cultures of the Americas.

Mention perhaps should also be made of the Council of Europe's Framework Convention on the Protection of National Minorities. Although focused on national minorities, it has clear relevance to indigenous peoples within a State.

Preamble to Framework Convention on National Minorities

Being resolved to protect within their respective territories the existence of national minorities;

Considering that the upheavals of European history have shown that the protection of national minorities is essential to stability, democratic security and peace in this continent;

Considering that a pluralist and genuinely democratic society should not only respect the ethnic, cultural, linguistic and religious identity of each person belonging to a national minority, but also create appropriate conditions enabling them to express, preserve and develop this identity;

Considering that the creation of a climate of tolerance and dialogue is necessary to enable cultural diversity to be a source and a factor, not of division, but of enrichment for each society;

Considering that the realisation of a tolerant and prosperous Europe does not depend solely on co-operation between States but also requires transfrontier co-operation between local and regional authorities without prejudice to the constitution and territorial integrity of each State.

The first issue when dealing with any group right is to determine the membership of the group in question, or the parameters thereof. As with minorities, self-identification is the key for determining whether a person is indeed indigenous.

12.3   THE SCOPE OF 'INDIGENOUS PEOPLE'

Of the groups discussed in the present text, indigenous peoples are the most problematic from a definitional perspective. It is easier to determine who are women, children, detainees or even, arguably refugees, than indigenous people. Plurality of cultures, languages and religions in States heighten cross-culturalisation, inter-racial marriages produce offspring who are not necessarily biologically 100 per cent indigenous. There is no general rule as to whether or not such people wish to be considered indigenous. National assimilation policies and issues like the 'stolen generation' in Australia (mid-twentieth century) may result in indigenous peoples denying their heritage and claiming non-indigenous practices. The issue of definition has also been mentioned above in connection with the ILO.

Consider the scope of application of the following instruments.

Organization of American States Draft Declaration on the Rights of Indigenous Peoples

Article I.

1. This Declaration applies to the indigenous peoples of the Americas and their members, who within the national States descend from a native culture that predates European colonization and who conserve their fundamental distinctive features, such as their language, normative systems,

usages and customs, artistic expressions, beliefs, and social, economic, cultural, and political institutions.

2. Self-identification as indigenous peoples will be a fundamental criterion for determining to whom this Declaration applies. The States shall ensure respect for self-identification as indigenous, individually and collectively, in keeping with the institutions of each indigenous people.

As Gordon Bennett notes, '[g]iven the lack of unanimity among Member States as to the criteria to be applied in identifying indigenous groups, a rambling definition of indigenous peoples was perhaps inevitable' (Bennett, G, *Aboriginal Rights in International Law*, 1978, London: Royal Anthropological Institute, p 17).

ILO Convention No. 169 (1989) Art 1

1. This Convention applies to:

(a) tribal peoples in independent countries whose social, cultural and economic conditions distinguish them from other sections of the national community, and whose status is regulated wholly or partially by their own customs or traditions or by special laws or regulations;

(b) peoples in independent countries who are regarded as indigenous on account of their descent from the populations which inhabited the country, or a geographical region to which the country belongs, at the time of conquest or colonisation or the establishment of present state boundaries and who, irrespective of their legal status, retain some or all of their own social, economic, cultural and political institutions.

2. Self-identification as indigenous or tribal shall be regarded as a fundamental criterion for determining the groups to which the provisions of this Convention apply.

3. The use of the term *peoples* in this Convention shall not be construed as having any implications as regards the rights which may attach to the term under international law.

The provision of ILO Convention 169 can be contrasted with its predecessor, Art 1 of Convention 107:

ILO Convention No. 107 (1957) Art 1

1. This Convention applies to—

(a) members of tribal or semi-tribal populations in independent countries whose social and economic conditions are at a less advanced stage than the stage reached by the other sections of the national community, and whose status is regulated wholly or partially by their own customs or traditions or by special laws or regulations;

(b) members of tribal or semi-tribal populations in independent countries which are regarded as indigenous on account of their descent from the populations which inhabited the country, or a geographical region to which the country belongs, at the time of conquest or colonisation and which, irrespective of their legal status, live more in conformity with the social, economic and cultural institutions of that time than with the institutions of the nation to which they belong.

2. For the purposes of this Convention, the term *semi-tribal* includes groups and persons who, although they are in the process of losing their tribal characteristics, are not yet integrated into the national community.

3. The indigenous and other tribal or semi-tribal populations mentioned in paragraphs 1 and 2 of this Article are referred to hereinafter as 'the populations concerned'.

From a definitional perspective, the element of self-identification is important. Not all indigenous peoples wish to avail themselves of the rights and opportunities open to indigenous peoples, many prefer assimilation and the progressive modernisation of society rather than respect and protection for their traditional values and ways of life. Some of the communications discussed above, e.g. *Kitok v Sweden*, demonstrate this.

Note also that the definition clause of the ILO 169 convention contains a caveat excluding implications as regards rights attaching to the term under international law—that is, excluding potential implications for self-determination.

A more general (working) definition, with enumerated criteria can be found in the work of the Special Rapporteur, Jose Martinez-Cobo in his seminal report E/CN.4/Sub.2/1986/7/Add.4, 1986 at paras 378–380.

Question

To what extent do the definitions above include or exclude members of indigenous groups? Do the definitions facilitate an appropriate distinction between minority groups and indigenous groups?

While aspects of indigenous peoples' rights are inevitably mired in controversy, the definitional issues are of central importance. Many States wish to limit the rights evinced by indigenous people and an easy way of achieving such a limitation is to apply a narrow definition.

Question

Is there any element of consensus in the various definitions espoused to date?

Question

Before proceeding further, consider what rights indigenous peoples claim or may claim and identify the potential political, legal and economic problems therewith.

The International Labour Organisation Convention 169 addresses Land (Part II), Recruitment and Conditions of Employment (Part III), Vocational Training, handicrafts and rural industry (Part IV), social security (Part V) and education (Part VI). A full range of rights and freedoms are extended to indigenous peoples in one of the most comprehensive instruments yet concluded.

12.4   RIGHTS CLAIMED BY INDIGENOUS PEOPLE

Inevitably the rights of indigenous peoples attract considerable controversy in certain States. The right to self-determination, land and cultural rights are examples.

12.5   THE RIGHT TO SELF-DETERMINATION

Self-determination, though a right enshrined prominently in both international covenants, is somewhat elusive in many respects. There is little agreement on the scope of the right or the intended beneficiaries. Although it is accepted that the right applied primarily to colonised peoples seeking to divest themselves of colonial power and secure independence, the question now is to what further purpose can self-determination extend? Are indigenous peoples entitled to self-determination or some version thereof?

Self-determination is always a vexed question in international law, not least as it cohabits uncomfortably with the proclaimed UN principle of respect for the territorial integrity of a State. Respect for territorial integrity can be found in various texts.

Art 2 of the UN Charter

The Organization and its Members, in pursuit of the Purposes stated in Article 1, shall act in accordance with the following Principles.

(1) The Organization is based on the principle of the sovereign equality of all its Members. . . .

(4) All Members shall refrain in their international relations from the threat or use of force against the territorial integrity or political independence of any state, or in any other manner inconsistent with the Purposes of the United Nations.

General Assembly Resolution 1514 (XV) on the granting of independence to colonial countries and peoples (1960)

1. The subjection of peoples to alien subjugation, domination and exploitation constitutes a denial of fundamental human rights, is contrary to the Charter of the United Nations and is an impediment to the promotion of world peace and co-operation.

2. All peoples have the right to self-determination; by virtue of that right they freely determine their political status and freely pursue their economic, social and cultural development. . . .

6. Any attempt aimed at the partial or total disruption of the national unity and the territorial integrity of a country is incompatible with the purposes and principles of the Charter of the United Nations.

7. All States shall observe faithfully and strictly the provision of the Charter of the United Nations, the Universal Declaration of Human Rights and the present Declaration on the basis of equality, non-interference in the internal affairs of all States, and respect for the sovereign rights of all peoples and their territorial integrity.

To promote self-determination within the confines of territorial integrity, the whole population of the State must opt for the change and the change must apply to the peoples of a given territory as a whole. The application of this to decolonisation is obvious. So too is its application to the democratic process by which a State undergoes a change in constitutional process or government. It is not possible for a section of the community to opt for self-determination independent of the rest of the population of the State. This paradox has serious repercussions for indigenous and minority peoples as there are few such groups whose independence would not result in the break-up of the State, or, at the very least, an infringement of its territorial integrity. The spectre of secession looms over the freedom of self-determination for all peoples. 'The principle of self-determination has been one of the most vigorous and vigorously disputed collective or group rights in modern international law' (Crawford, J (ed), *The Rights of Peoples*, 1988, Oxford: Clarendon Press, p 58).

The first problem faced is one of definition. Defining the scope of indigenous peoples is a vexed issue, as discussed above. For the purpose of self-determination, the problem is magnified. Can indigenous peoples and minorities be differentiated? How do these definitions fit in with 'peoples' for self-determination. If all peoples are entitled to self-determination, who decides who the 'peoples' are?

Jennings, Sir Ivor, *The Approach to Self-Government*, 1956, Cambridge: CUP, pp 55–56

Nearly forty years ago, a Professor of Political Science, who was also President of the United States, President Wilson, enunciated a doctrine which was ridiculous, but which was widely accepted as a sensible proposition, the doctrine of self-determination. On the surface, it seemed reasonable: let the people decide. In fact it was ridiculous, because the people cannot decide until someone decides who are the people.

Perhaps the reason the definition of what constitutes a people is so controversial in law is that 'all peoples have the right of self determination' (Art 1, International Covenants on Civil and Political Rights and on Economic, Social and Cultural Rights). Thus there are potential repercussions which would flow from the automatic inclusion of indigenous peoples in the term 'people', at least insofar as self-determination could involve independence in any form. Are indigenous peoples 'peoples' for the purpose of self-determination, or is 'peoples' narrower in scope than indigenous peoples?

As noted above, inclusion in the scope of indigenous people is normally a question for self-identification. If this principle also applies as regards who is entitled to self-determination then there are surely serious implications for territorial integrity.

United Nations Draft Declaration on Indigenous Peoples' Rights 1994/45

Article 3

Indigenous peoples have the right of self-determination. By virtue of that right they freely determine their political status and freely pursue their economic, social and cultural development.

Article 4

Indigenous peoples have the right to maintain and strengthen their distinct political, economic, social and cultural characteristics, as well as their legal systems, while retaining their rights to participate fully, if they so choose, in the political, economic, social and cultural life of the State. . . .

Article 45

Nothing in this Declaration may be interpreted as implying for any State, group or person any right to engage in any activity or to perform any act contrary to the Charter of the United Nations.

Note the caveat in Art 45 which can be interpreted as including provisions on respect for territorial integrity. Contrast this with Art IV of the OAS Draft Declaration.

OAS Draft Declaration on the Rights of Indigenous Peoples

Article III.

Within the States, the right to self-determination of the indigenous peoples is recognized, pursuant to which they can define their forms of organization and promote their economic, social, and cultural development.

Article IV.

Nothing in this Declaration shall be construed so as to authorize or foster any action aimed at breaking up or diminishing, fully or in part, the territorial integrity, sovereignty, and political independence of the States, or other principles contained in the Charter of the Organization of American States.

Here the provisions on respect for territorial integrity are more explicit. Full self-determination would clearly be problematic if granted to all indigenous peoples. Given that few States are homogenous and monocultural, the issue of territorial integrity is of fundamental importance.

Advisory Opinion on Western Sahara, International Court of Justice Reps 1975, 39

Judge Dillard: it hardly seems necessary to make more explicit the cardinal restraints which the legal right of self-determination imposes. That restraint may be captured in a single sentence. It is for the people to determine the destiny of the territory and not the territory the destiny of the people.

12.5.1   Towards autonomy for indigenous peoples

One solution for indigenous people has been the evolution of land rights and of grants of autonomy to groups. Self-autonomy is perhaps the variation of self-determination best suited to addressing the needs of indigenous peoples. An element of self-determination is almost synonymous with self-preservation for indigenous people (Turpel, M, 'Indigenous Peoples' Rights of Political Self-Determination: recent international legal developments and the continuing struggle for recognition, 25 Cornell International Law Journal 579 at 593). It is essential not only that they participate in decisions affecting their destiny, but also that they can decide the direction of that destiny. Given that full self-determination is frequently mired in controversy and problems, perhaps internal autonomy represents an acceptable compromise. It would enable indigenous peoples who so desire to preserve their culture and live in accordance with traditional practices, customs and laws, while others may elect to advance and develop those traditional practices in response to the evolving society in which they find themselves. Indigenous peoples should be entitled to live their lives as they choose, in an atmosphere of respect for their heritage.

Question

Re-read the two excerpts from the draft declarations: to what extent do they achieve a balance between encouraging self-determination of indigenous people and maintaining respect for territorial integrity? Is there any potential that such a balance could be maintained effectively in practice? (Consider the disparate land claims of indigenous peoples.)

Note that the Draft Declaration explicitly includes autonomy as an option.

United Nations Draft Declaration on the Rights of Indigenous Peoples, Art 31

Indigenous peoples, as a specific form of exercising their right to self-determination, have the right to autonomy or self-government in matters relating to their internal and local affairs, including culture, religion, education, information, media, health, housing, employment, social welfare, economic activities, land and resources management, environment and entry by non-members, as well as ways and means for financing these autonomous functions.

Indigenous peoples are also accorded the right to determine their own citizenship in accordance with their traditions (Art 32). They are also encouraged to promote, develop and maintain their institutional structures and their own juridical customs and practices which are in accordance with international human rights law (Art 33). Increasingly, indigenous peoples are enjoying degrees of autonomy.

12.5.2   Models for autonomy

There are numerous models of autonomy which illustrate the potential for invoking a modified version of self-determination peacefully and successfully.

12.5.2.1   Australia

A number of different models exist in Australia. In general they are related to claims for land rights. Calls for self-determination by aboriginal peoples have been more vocal than those of the Torres Strait Islanders. Obviously, the Torres Strait Islanders are geographically separated from the mainland and enjoy greater autonomy *per se*. In contrast, land rights in Australia were highlighted by the Torres Strait islanders, as is discussed below.

ATSIC—the Aboriginal and Torres Strait Islander Commission was created in March 1990 as a focal point for the Government's policy of encouraging self-management by the first Australians. The Final Report of the Royal Commission on

Aboriginal Deaths in Custody 1991 highlighted the problem and the need for urgent action.

Established by the Aboriginal and Torres Strait Islander Commission Act 1989, the Commission and its agency was abolished by the ATSIC Amendment Act 2005 which repeals the provisions of the ATSIC Act thereby terminating ATSIC.

ATSIC was decentralised, operating independently of the Government and functioning almost as an Ombudsperson for Aboriginal and Torres Strait Islander affairs, playing a positive role in achieving equality for all Australians (ombudspersons and their role is discussed in more detail in Chapter 7 on National Institutions). Now the Office of Indigenous Policy Coordination oversees aboriginal affairs within Australia (www.oipc.gov.au).

The Aboriginal Provisional Government was created to represent Aboriginal interests in Australia. Michael Mansell, Secretary, considered its creation the first step towards 'real self-determination' ('It's Now or Never: Building an Aboriginal Government', *APG Papers*, Vol 2, December 1992, extract from a speech of Michael Mansell in Hobart 27 August 1992). The APG issues Aboriginal passports which are not officially recognised by all States. However, of greater importance, it also represents a powerful political presence, campaigning for Aboriginal peoples in Canberra (see generally www.apg.org.au/).

Land management—several Aboriginal peoples in Australia now enjoy full or partial autonomy over their lands. Examples include Arnhem Land in the Northern Territory, Uluru (Ayer's Rock) and Katu Tinggu (the Olgas) also in the Northern Territory. See the early Pitjantjatjara Land Rights Act 1981. This Act was discussed in relation to the Race Discrimination Act in *Gerhardy v Brown* (1985) 59 Australian Law Reports 311. The following is an example of land management:

Aboriginal Land Rights (Northern Territory) Act 1976
Establishment of Land Councils

S21 (1) The Minister shall, on the commencement of this section, by notice published in the *Gazette*, divide the Northern Territory into at least 2 areas and establish an Aboriginal Land Council for each area.

(2) A notice published under subsection (1) shall, in respect of each Aboriginal Land Council, set out:

    (a) the name of the Council; and

    (b) the boundaries of the area for which the Council is established.

(3) Where the Minister is satisfied that:

    (a) a substantial majority of adult Aboriginals living in an area that:

        (i) is wholly included in the area of a Land Council; or

        (ii) is partly included in the area of one Land Council and partly included in the area of another Land Council or in the areas of other Land Councils;

        is in favour of the setting up of a new Land Council for that first-mentioned area only; and

    (b) that first-mentioned area is an appropriate area for the operation of a new Land Council;

    the Minister may, by notice published in the *Gazette*, establish an Aboriginal Land Council for that first-mentioned area.

(4) A notice published under subsection (3) shall:

   (a) specify the name of the new Land Council; and

   (b) set out the boundaries of the area for which the new Land Council is established.

(5) On the publication of a notice under subsection (3), the area specified in the notice ceases by force of this subsection to be part of the area of the Land Council, or of the areas of the Land Councils, in which it was included immediately before that publication.

(6) On the establishment of a Land Council under this section, the Minister shall take whatever steps he or she considers necessary and practicable to inform the adult Aboriginals living in the area of the Land Council of the existence of the Land Council.

Grants of exploration licences

S40 An exploration licence shall not be granted to a person in respect of Aboriginal land (including Aboriginal land in a conservation zone) unless:

(a) both the Minister and the Land Council for the area in which the land is situated have consented, in writing, to the grant of the licence; or

(b) the Governor-General has, by Proclamation, declared that the national interest requires that the licence be granted;

and the Land Council and the person have entered into an agreement under this Part as to the terms and conditions to which the grant of the licence will be subject.

12.5.2.2   Canada

In Canada, certain groups have been given autonomy; consider the position of Nunuvut. However, claims for full secession have been rejected. The following extract addresses claims for secession of Quebec from Canada.

Reference re secession Quebec [1998] 2 SCR 217

83 Secession is the effort of a group or section of a state to withdraw itself from the political and constitutional authority of that state, with a view to achieving statehood for a new territorial unit on the international plane. In a federal state, secession typically takes the form of a territorial unit seeking to withdraw from the federation. Secession is a legal act as much as a political one. By the terms of Question 1 of this Reference, we are asked to rule on the legality of unilateral secession '[u]nder the Constitution of Canada'. This is an appropriate question, as the legality of unilateral secession must be evaluated, at least in the first instance, from the perspective of the domestic legal order of the state from which the unit seeks to withdraw. As we shall see below, it is also argued that international law is a relevant standard by which the legality of a purported act of secession may be measured.

84 The secession of a province from Canada must be considered, in legal terms, to require an amendment to the Constitution, which perforce requires negotiation. The amendments necessary to achieve a secession could be radical and extensive. Some commentators have suggested that secession could be a change of such a magnitude that it could not be considered to be merely an amendment to the Constitution. We are not persuaded by this contention. It is of course true that the Constitution is silent as to the ability of a province to secede from Confederation but, although the Constitution neither expressly authorizes nor prohibits secession, an act of secession would purport to alter the governance of Canadian territory in a manner which undoubtedly is inconsistent with our current constitutional arrangements. The fact that those changes would be profound, or that they would purport to have a significance with respect to international law, does not negate their nature as amendments to the Constitution of Canada.

85 The Constitution is the expression of the sovereignty of the people of Canada. It lies within the power of the people of Canada, acting through their various governments duly elected and recognized under the Constitution, to effect whatever constitutional arrangements are desired

within Canadian territory, including, should it be so desired, the secession of Quebec from Canada. As this Court held in the *Manitoba Language Rights Reference, supra*, at p. 745, '[t]he Constitution of a country is a statement of the will of the people to be governed in accordance with certain principles held as fundamental and certain prescriptions restrictive of the powers of the legislature and government'. The manner in which such a political will could be formed and mobilized is a somewhat speculative exercise, though we are asked to assume the existence of such a political will for the purpose of answering the question before us. By the terms of this Reference, we have been asked to consider whether it would be constitutional in such a circumstance for the National Assembly, legislature or government of Quebec to effect the secession of Quebec from Canada unilaterally.

86 The 'unilateral' nature of the act is of cardinal importance and we must be clear as to what is understood by this term. In one sense, any step towards a constitutional amendment initiated by a single actor on the constitutional stage is 'unilateral'. We do not believe that this is the meaning contemplated by Question 1, nor is this the sense in which the term has been used in argument before us. Rather, what is claimed by a right to secede 'unilaterally' is the right to effectuate secession without prior negotiations with the other provinces and the federal government. At issue is not the legality of the first step but the legality of the final act of purported unilateral secession. The supposed juridical basis for such an act is said to be a clear expression of democratic will in a referendum in the province of Quebec. This claim requires us to examine the possible juridical impact, if any, of such a referendum on the functioning of our Constitution, and on the claimed legality of a unilateral act of secession. . . .

92 However, we are equally unable to accept the reverse proposition, that a clear expression of self-determination by the people of Quebec would impose *no* obligations upon the other provinces or the federal government. The continued existence and operation of the Canadian constitutional order cannot remain indifferent to the clear expression of a clear majority of Quebecers that they no longer wish to remain in Canada. This would amount to the assertion that other constitutionally recognized principles necessarily trump the clearly expressed democratic will of the people of Quebec. Such a proposition fails to give sufficient weight to the underlying constitutional principles that must inform the amendment process, including the principles of democracy and federalism. The rights of other provinces and the federal government cannot deny the right of the government of Quebec to pursue secession, should a clear majority of the people of Quebec choose that goal, so long as in doing so, Quebec respects the rights of others. Negotiations would be necessary to address the interests of the federal government, of Quebec and the other provinces, and other participants, as well as the rights of all Canadians both within and outside Quebec.

93 Is the rejection of both of these propositions reconcilable? Yes, once it is realized that none of the rights or principles under discussion is absolute to the exclusion of the others. This observation suggests that other parties cannot exercise their rights in such a way as to amount to an absolute denial of Quebec's rights, and similarly, that so long as Quebec exercises its rights while respecting the rights of others, it may propose secession and seek to achieve it through negotiation. The negotiation process precipitated by a decision of a clear majority of the population of Quebec on a clear question to pursue secession would require the reconciliation of various rights and obligations by the representatives of two legitimate majorities, namely, the clear majority of the population of Quebec, and the clear majority of Canada as a whole, whatever that may be. There can be no suggestion that either of these majorities 'trumps' the other. A political majority that does not act in accordance with the underlying constitutional principles we have identified puts at risk the legitimacy of the exercise of its rights.

94 In such circumstances, the conduct of the parties assumes primary constitutional significance. The negotiation process must be conducted with an eye to the constitutional principles we have outlined, which must inform the actions of *all* the participants in the negotiation process.

95 Refusal of a party to conduct negotiations in a manner consistent with constitutional principles and values would seriously put at risk the legitimacy of that party's assertion of its rights,

and perhaps the negotiation process as a whole. Those who quite legitimately insist upon the importance of upholding the rule of law cannot at the same time be oblivious to the need to act in conformity with constitutional principles and values, and so do their part to contribute to the maintenance and promotion of an environment in which the rule of law may flourish. . . .

104 Accordingly, the secession of Quebec from Canada cannot be accomplished by the National Assembly, the legislature or government of Quebec unilaterally, that is to say, without principled negotiations, and be considered a lawful act. Any attempt to effect the secession of a province from Canada must be undertaken pursuant to the Constitution of Canada, or else violate the Canadian legal order. However, the continued existence and operation of the Canadian constitutional order cannot remain unaffected by the unambiguous expression of a clear majority of Quebecers that they no longer wish to remain in Canada. The primary means by which that expression is given effect is the constitutional duty to negotiate in accordance with the constitutional principles that we have described herein. In the event secession negotiations are initiated, our Constitution, no less than our history, would call on the participants to work to reconcile the rights, obligations and legitimate aspirations of all Canadians within a framework that emphasizes constitutional responsibilities as much as it does constitutional rights. . . .

138 In summary, the international law right to self-determination only generates, at best, a right to external self-determination in situations of former colonies; where a people is oppressed, as for example under foreign military occupation; or where a definable group is denied meaningful access to government to pursue their political, economic, social and cultural development. In all three situations, the people in question are entitled to a right to external self-determination because they have been denied the ability to exert internally their right to self-determination. Such exceptional circumstances are manifestly inapplicable to Quebec under existing conditions. Accordingly, neither the population of the province of Quebec, even if characterized in terms of 'people' or 'peoples', nor its representative institutions, the National Assembly, the legislature or government of Quebec, possess a right, under international law, to secede unilaterally from Canada.

Question

Do the arguments advanced by the Canadian Supreme Court conform to the international standards? Would the situation be different if native peoples had claimed secession?

12.5.3 Recognising cultural autonomy and rights

It is often easier to recognise aspects of indigenous culture and respect that, rather than according full or even partial autonomy. This can involve removing the indigenous peoples from the ambit of national law. For example, whale hunting, reindeer husbandry, and a variety of other usufructory rights may be extended to indigenous peoples to the exclusion of others. In instances such as whale hunting, indigenous peoples are permitted to hunt and kill animals which are otherwise protected. Such an exception to the general rule recognises cultural rights.

An element of self-determination is almost synonymous with self-preservation for indigenous people (Turpel see Further Reading at p 593). It is essential not only that they participate in decisions affecting their destiny, but also that they can decide the direction of that destiny. Given that full self-determination is frequently mired in controversy and problems, perhaps full internal autonomy represents a compromise. It would enable indigenous peoples who so desire to preserve their culture and live in accordance with traditional practices, customs and laws, or to advance and develop those traditional practices in response to the evolving society in which they find themselves. Indigenous peoples need not be preserved, somewhat paternalistically, as a living museum-piece. Rather they should be entitled to live their lives as they choose, in an atmosphere of respect for their heritage.

Equally vexatious and closely related to the issue of self-determination is the question of land rights.

12.6 LAND RIGHTS

As history attests, many indigenous peoples were dispossessed of their lands upon initial colonisation. Few indigenous peoples still live on and have full responsibility over their traditional lands. The lack of identifiable (to the colonisers) systems of land ownership caused further problems. Some indigenous peoples were forcibly removed from their lands, others ceded land under pressure. For example, some of the Maori peoples of Aotorea/New Zealand signed the Treaty of Waitangi, granting land rights to the 'invaders' while in Australia and the Americas, the land was regarded as 'terra nullius', literally empty land which was 'discovered' and occupied by Europeans.

For many indigenous peoples, land rights are crucial for several reasons. Not least land is often strongly related to cultural beliefs as the following two quotes from indigenous people aptly demonstrate.

Narritjin Maymuru, Yirrkala, Australia quoted in Isaacs, J (ed), *Australian Dreaming: 40,000 years of Aboriginal History*, 1984, Sydney: Ure Smith Press, p 99

We belong to the ground

It is our power and we must stay

Close to it or maybe

We will get lost

Elder brothers, Kogi peoples, Sierra Nevada, Columbia, interviewed in Ereira, A, *The Heart of the World*, 1990, London: Jonathan Cape, p 58

The Elder Brother was there to protect the earth

Because the earth

It is our Mother, earth

Without earth we cannot live

Similar sentiments are found in the artistic works of other indigenous peoples.

Australian Aboriginal Dreamtime ascribes cultural and moral tales to the landscape of Australia.

Question

Consider what myths and other legends explain the geological and geographical features of the landscape around you? What are their origins?

There is evidence that the special relationship between indigenous peoples and their land has been recognised.

United Nations Draft Declaration on the Rights of Indigenous Peoples
Article 7

Indigenous peoples have the collective and individual right not to be subjected to ethnocide and cultural genocide, including prevention of and redress for:

. . . (b) Any action which has the aim or effect of dispossessing them of their lands, territories or resources;

Preamble to the Draft Organization of American States Declaration on the Rights of Indigenous Peoples

4. Lands, territories, and resources

Recognizing the special relationship that the indigenous peoples maintain with their lands, territories, and resources.

Recognizing, that for the indigenous peoples their traditional collective forms of ownership and use of lands, territories, resources, waters, and coastal zones are a necessary condition for their survival, social organization, development, spirituality, and individual and collective well-being.

More detailed provisions are found in the provisions of Convention No. 169 (1989) of the International Labour Organisation, part II of which addresses land rights.

ILO Convention No. 169

Article 13

1. In applying the provisions of this Part of the Convention governments shall respect the special importance for the cultures and spiritual values of the peoples concerned of their relationship with the lands or territories, or both as applicable, which they occupy or otherwise use, and in particular the collective aspects of this relationship.

2. The use of the term *lands* in Articles 15 and 16 shall include the concept of territories, which covers the total environment of the areas which the peoples concerned occupy or otherwise use.

Article 14

1. The rights of ownership and possession of the peoples concerned over the lands which they traditionally occupy shall be recognised. In addition, measures shall be taken in appropriate cases to safeguard the right of the peoples concerned to use lands not exclusively occupied by them, but to which they have traditionally had access for their subsistence and traditional activities. Particular attention shall be paid to the situation of nomadic peoples and shifting cultivators in this respect.

2. Governments shall take steps as necessary to identify the lands which the peoples concerned traditionally occupy, and to guarantee effective protection of their rights of ownership and possession.

3. Adequate procedures shall be established within the national legal system to resolve land claims by the peoples concerned.

Article 15

1. The rights of the peoples concerned to the natural resources pertaining to their lands shall be specially safeguarded. These rights include the right of these peoples to participate in the use, management and conservation of these resources.

2. In cases in which the State retains the ownership of mineral or sub-surface resources or rights to other resources pertaining to lands, governments shall establish or maintain procedures through which they shall consult these peoples, with a view to ascertaining whether and to what degree their interests would be prejudiced, before undertaking or permitting any programmes for the exploration or exploitation of such resources pertaining to their lands. The peoples concerned shall wherever possible participate in the benefits of such activities, and shall receive fair compensation for any damages which they may sustain as a result of such activities.

Article 16

1. Subject to the following paragraphs of this Article, the peoples concerned shall not be removed from the lands which they occupy.

2. Where the relocation of these peoples is considered necessary as an exceptional measure, such relocation shall take place only with their free and informed consent. Where their consent cannot be obtained, such relocation shall take place only following appropriate procedures established by national laws and regulations, including public inquiries where appropriate, which provide the opportunity for effective representation of the peoples concerned.

3. Whenever possible, these peoples shall have the right to return to their traditional lands, as soon as the grounds for relocation cease to exist.

4. When such return is not possible, as determined by agreement or, in the absence of such agreement, through appropriate procedures, these peoples shall be provided in all possible cases with lands of quality and legal status at least equal to that of the lands previously occupied by them, suitable to provide for their present needs and future development. Where the peoples concerned express a preference for compensation in money or in kind, they shall be so compensated under appropriate guarantees.

5. Persons thus relocated shall be fully compensated for any resulting loss or injury.

Article 17

1. Procedures established by the peoples concerned for the transmission of land rights among members of these peoples shall be respected.

2. The peoples concerned shall be consulted whenever consideration is being given to their capacity to alienate their lands or otherwise transmit their rights outside their own community.

3. Persons not belonging to these peoples shall be prevented from taking advantage of their customs or of lack of understanding of the laws on the part of their members to secure the ownership, possession or use of land belonging to them.

Article 18

Adequate penalties shall be established by law for unauthorised intrusion upon, or use of, the lands of the peoples concerned, and governments shall take measures to prevent such offences.

Article 19

National agrarian programmes shall secure to the peoples concerned treatment equivalent to that accorded to other sectors of the population with regard to:

(a) the provision of more land for these peoples when they have not the area necessary for providing the essentials of a normal existence, or for any possible increase in their numbers;

(b) the provision of the means required to promote the development of the lands which these peoples already possess.

12.6.1   Conflicting land rights: pre-existing and new

Land was claimed by 'invaders' without due consideration to the pre-existing rights of the indigenous population. Frequently land deemed subject to 'discovery' in terms of international law was regarded in law as 'terra nullius', literally empty land. For examples of statements to this effect in Australia see, for example, *Attorney-General for New South Wales v Brown* (1847) 1 Legge 312 at 316 or *New South Wales v Commonwealth* (1975) 135 Commonwealth Law Reports 337 at 438. Prior proprietal rights of the indigenous population were not recognised although it was usually acknowledged that there were indigenous inhabitants. Moreover, prior rights of indigenous peoples were frequently not viewed by the peoples themselves as 'rights' to the land. This concept was alien to many indigenous people as due to their inalienable spiritual ties to the land, the concept of titular ownership of land did not exist in traditional societies.

UN Doc. E/CN.4/Sub.2/AC.4/1990/1/Add.1, p 5 (Australian submission to Working Group on Indigenous Populations)

There would be fundamental difficulties in attempting to transfer Aboriginal land systems, including concepts of ownership, custodianship and inheritance, into a legally enforceable system of rights and obligations.

Similar sentiments are expressed by other States with significant dispossessed indigenous populations. Obviously the passage of time makes the dispossession which characterised the centuries of colonisation unacceptable today. As the draft UN Declaration makes clear.

UN Draft Declaration on the Rights of Indigenous Peoples

Article 10

Indigenous peoples shall not be forcibly removed from their lands or territories. No relocation shall take place without the free and informed consent of the indigenous peoples concerned and after agreement on just and fair compensation and, where possible, with the option of return.

In some instances, land rights were transferred by the indigenous population by legal deeds. It has long since been argued that the implication of such a transfer was not necessarily apparent to the indigenous people.

12.6.2   Case study: New Zealand, Māori and the Treaty of Waitangi

In New Zealand, too, the indigenous people signed instruments concerning land rights following the arrival of the colonising powers. The Treaty of Waitangi was signed on 6 February 1840, at Waitangi in the Bay of Islands by Lieutenant General Hobson on behalf of the British Empire, several English residents, and approximately 45 Māori rangatira, Hone Heke being the first. The Māori text of the Treaty was then sent around the rest of the country for signing. In contrast the English text was signed in only two further locations by a total of 39 rangatira. In the course of 1840, over 500 Māori had signed the Treaty.

Many issues have arisen subsequently concerning the Treaty. Some of these arise due to perceived differences between the English and Māori versions. The following extracts are from the official English text and an official translation into English of the actual Māori version of the treaty which was signed by the majority of Māori rangatira.

Treaty of Waitangi, official English version

Preamble

HER MAJESTY VICTORIA Queen of the United Kingdom of Great Britain and Ireland regarding with Her Royal favour the Native Chiefs and Tribes of New Zealand and anxious to protect their just Rights and Property and to secure to them the enjoyment of Peace and Good Order has deemed it necessary in consequence of the great number of Her Majesty's Subjects who have already settled in New Zealand and the rapid extension of Emigration both from Europe and Australia which is still in progress to constitute and appoint a functionary properly authorised to treat with the Aborigines of New Zealand for the recognition of Her Majesty's Sovereign authority over the whole or any part of those islands—Her Majesty therefore being desirous to establish a settled form of Civil Government with a view to avert the evil consequences which must result from the absence of the necessary Laws and Institutions alike to the native population and to Her subjects has been graciously pleased to empower and to authorise me William Hobson a Captain in Her Majesty's Royal Navy Consul and Lieutenant Governor of such parts of New Zealand as may be or hereafter shall be ceded to her Majesty to invite the confederated and independent Chiefs of New Zealand to concur in the following Articles and Conditions.

Article the First

The Chiefs of the Confederation of the United Tribes of New Zealand and the separate and independent Chiefs who have not become members of the Confederation cede to Her Majesty the Queen of England absolutely and without reservation all the rights and powers of Sovereignty which the said Confederation or Individual Chiefs respectively exercise or possess, or may be supposed to exercise or to possess over their respective Territories as the sole Sovereigns thereof.

Article the Second

Her Majesty the Queen of England confirms and guarantees to the Chiefs and Tribes of New Zealand and to the respective families and individuals thereof the full exclusive and undisturbed possession of their Lands and Estates Forests Fisheries and other properties which they may collectively or individually possess so long as it is their wish and desire to retain the same in their possession; but the Chiefs of the United Tribes and the individual Chiefs yield to Her Majesty the exclusive right of Preemption over such lands as the proprietors thereof may be disposed to alienate at such prices as may be agreed upon between the respective Proprietors and persons appointed by Her Majesty to treat with them in that behalf.

Article the Third

In consideration thereof Her Majesty the Queen of England extends to the Natives of New Zealand Her royal protection and imparts to them all the Rights and Privileges of British Subjects.

Translation of the Māori Version of the Treaty by Professor Sir Hugh Kawharu (taken from www.waitangi-tribunal.gov.nz)

Article the First

The Chiefs of the Confederation and all the Chiefs who have not joined that Confederation give absolutely to the Queen of England for ever the complete government over their land.

Article the Second

The Queen of England agrees to protect the Chiefs, the Subtribes and all the people of New Zealand in the unqualified exercise of their chieftainship over their lands, villages and all their treasures. But on the other hand the Chiefs of the Confederation and all the Chiefs will sell land to the Queen at a price agreed to by the person owning it and by the person buying it (the latter being) appointed by the Queen as her purchase agent.

Article the Third

For this agreed arrangement therefore concerning the Government of the Queen, the Queen of England will protect all the ordinary people of New Zealand (ie the Māori) and will give them the same rights and duties of citizenship as the people of England.

Given the controversy which the Treaty of Waitangi continued to evoke, not least in relation to land rights, the 1975 Treaty of Waitangi Act established the Waitangi Tribunal which had as its primary objective of adjudicating on claims. By the end of 2003, there had been 18 settlements of historical Treaty claims, with a total value of about $580 million (from www.treatyofwaitangi.govt.nz/settlements/).

It was set up to inquire into claims by Māori against any Crown act, policy, action, or omission that prejudicially affects them. A claim lodged with the Tribunal is checked against s 6 of the Treaty of Waitangi Act 1975 to ascertain whether it is one that the Tribunal may look into. If it is, the claim is then registered, heard, and reported on to the Minister of Māori Affairs. Deciding whether the claim is well founded is a key issue for the Tribunal. If it sees fit, the Tribunal may make recommendations about the claim to the Government.

Note that new bills are under discussion to place a time limit on claims and to explain the principles of the Treaty of Waitangi.

12.6.3 Establishing native title

The pre-existence of native title is slowly being recognised. Cases in Australia and South Africa, *inter alia*, elucidate a change in opinion. Historic wrongs are being righted once again.

Mabo and Others v the State of Queensland [No.2], 175 Commonwealth Law Reports (1991–1992) 1

The Torres Strait Islands lie off the northeast tip of Australia. Certain islands including the Murray Islands (Mer, Dauar and Waier) were annexed to Queensland in terms of the Queensland Coast Islands Act 1879. Some parts of the islands were transferred to missionaries, others leased by the British Crown. The sovereignty of the British Crown was not questioned. However, in 1982, Eddie Mabo, a native Meriam, joined with others seeking judicial confirmation of their traditional land rights on the island. They sought a declaration they were entitled to the islands as owners, possessors, occupiers or as persons entitled to use and to enjoy the islands, that the islands were not and had never been Crown land and that the State of Queensland was not entitled to extinguish the title of the Meriam people. A decade later, the case arrived before the High Court of Australia by which time Eddie Mabo and some of the other initial plaintiffs had died though the case continued and its constitutional significance is undiminished.

Brennan, J: 54. Once it is accepted that indigenous inhabitants in occupation of a territory when sovereignty is acquired by the Crown are capable of enjoying—whether in community, as a group or as individuals—proprietary interests in land, the rights and interests in the land which they had theretofore enjoyed under the customs of their community are seen to be a burden on the radical title which the Crown acquires. The notion that feudal principle dictates that the land in a settled colony be taken to be a royal demesne upon the Crown's acquisition of sovereignty is mistaken. However, that was not the only basis advanced to establish the proposition of absolute Crown ownership and the alternative bases must next be considered.

60. In *Calder v. Attorney-General of British Columbia*(124) (1973) SCR, at p 416; *contra per* Judson J. at pp 328–330; (1973) 34 DLR (3d), at p 218; *contra per* Judson J. at pp 156, 157 Hall J. rejected as 'wholly wrong' 'the proposition that after conquest or discovery the native peoples have no rights at all except those subsequently granted or recognized by the conqueror or discoverer'.

61. The preferable rule, supported by the authorities cited, is that a mere change in sovereignty does not extinguish native title to land. (The term 'native title' conveniently describes the interests and rights of indigenous inhabitants in land, whether communal, group or individual, possessed under the traditional laws acknowledged by and the traditional customs observed by the indigenous inhabitants.) The preferable rule equates the indigenous inhabitants of a settled colony with the inhabitants of a conquered colony in respect of their rights and interests in land and recognizes in the indigenous inhabitants of a settled colony the rights and interests recognized by the Privy Council in *In re Southern Rhodesia* as surviving to the benefit of the residents of a conquered colony.

62. If native title survives the Crown's acquisition of sovereignty as, in my view, it does, it is unnecessary to examine the alternative arguments advanced to support the rights and interests of the Meriam people to their traditional land. One argument raised the presumption of a Crown grant arising from the Meriam people's possession of the Murray Islands from a time before annexation; another was the existence of a title arising after annexation in accordance with a supposed local legal custom under the common law whereby the Meriam people were said to be entitled to possess the Murray Islands. There are substantial difficulties in the way of accepting either of these arguments, but it is unnecessary to pursue them. It is sufficient to state that, in my opinion, the common law of Australia rejects the notion that, when the Crown acquired sovereignty over territory which is now part of Australia it thereby acquired the absolute beneficial ownership of the land therein, and accepts that the antecedent rights and interests in land possessed by the indigenous inhabitants of the territory survived the change in sovereignty. Those antecedent rights and interests thus constitute a burden on the radical title of the Crown.

64. Native title has its origin in and is given its content by the traditional laws acknowledged by and the traditional customs observed by the indigenous inhabitants of a territory. The nature and incidents of native title must be ascertained as a matter of fact by reference to those laws and customs. The ascertainment may present a problem of considerable difficulty, as Moynihan J. perceived in the present case. It is a problem that did not arise in the case of a settled colony so long as the fictions were maintained that customary rights could not be reconciled 'with the institutions or the legal ideas of civilized society' In re Southern Rhodesia (1919) AC, at p 233, that there was no law before the arrival of the British colonists in a settled colony and that there was no sovereign law-maker in the territory of a settled colony before sovereignty was acquired by the Crown. These fictions denied the possibility of a native title recognized by our laws. But once it is acknowledged that an inhabited territory which became a settled colony was no more a legal desert than it was 'desert uninhabited' in fact, it is necessary to ascertain by evidence the nature and incidents of native title. Though these are matters of fact, some general propositions about native title can be stated without reference to evidence.

65. First, unless there are pre-existing laws of a territory over which the Crown acquires sovereignty which provide for the alienation of interests in land to strangers, the rights and interests which constitute a native title can be possessed only by the indigenous inhabitants and their descendants. Native title, though recognized by the common law, is not an institution of the common law and is not alienable by the common law. Its alienability is dependent on the laws from which it is derived. If alienation of a right or interest in land is a mere matter of the custom observed by the indigenous inhabitants, not provided for by law enforced by a sovereign power, there is no machinery which can enforce the rights of the alienee. The common law cannot enforce as a proprietary interest the rights of a putative alienee whose title is not created either under a law which was enforceable against the putative alienor at the time of the alienation and thereafter until the change of sovereignty or under the common law. And, subject to an important qualification, the only title dependent on custom which the common law will recognize is one which is consistent with the common law. Thus, in The Case of Tanistry, the Irish custom of tanistry was held to be void because it was founded in violence and because the vesting of title under the custom was uncertain (1608) Davis (80 ER); 4th ed. Dublin (1762) English translation, at pp 94–99. The inconsistency that the court perceived between the custom of tanistry known to the Brehon law of Ireland and the common law precluded the recognition of the custom by the common law. At that stage in its development, the common law was too rigid to admit recognition of a native title based on other laws or customs, but that rigidity has been relaxed, at least since the decision of the Privy Council in Amodu Tijani. The general principle that the common law will recognize a customary title only if it be consistent with the common law is subject to an exception in favour of traditional native title.

66. Of course, since European settlement of Australia, many clans or groups of indigenous people have been physically separated from their traditional land and have lost their connexion with it. But that is not the universal position. It is clearly not the position of the Meriam people. Where a

clan or group has continued to acknowledge the laws and (so far as practicable) to observe the customs based on the traditions of that clan or group, whereby their traditional connexion with the land has been substantially maintained, the traditional community title of that clan or group can be said to remain in existence. The common law can, by reference to the traditional laws and customs of an indigenous people, identify and protect the native rights and interests to which they give rise. However, when the tide of history has washed away any real acknowledgment of traditional law and any real observance of traditional customs, the foundation of native title has disappeared. A native title which has ceased with the abandoning of laws and customs based on tradition cannot be revived for contemporary recognition. Australian law can protect the interests of members of an indigenous clan or group, whether communally or individually, only in conformity with the traditional laws and customs of the people to whom the clan or group belongs and only where members of the clan or group acknowledge those laws and observe those customs (so far as it is practicable to do so). Once traditional native title expires, the Crown's radical title expands to a full beneficial title, for then there is no other proprietor than the Crown.

67. It follows that a right or interest possessed as a native title cannot be acquired from an indigenous people by one who, not being a member of the indigenous people, does not acknowledge their laws and observe their customs; nor can such a right or interest be acquired by a clan, group or member of the indigenous people unless the acquisition is consistent with the laws and customs of that people. Such a right or interest can be acquired outside those laws and customs only by the Crown. This result has been reached in other jurisdictions, though for different reasons: see *Reg. v. Symonds* (1847) NZPCC, at p 390; *Johnson v. McIntosh* (1823) 8 wheat, at p 586 (21 US, at p 259); *St. Catherine's Milling and Lumber Co. v. The Queen* (1887) 13 SCR 577, at p 599. Once the Crown acquires sovereignty and the common law becomes the law of the territory, the Crown's sovereignty over all land in the territory carries the capacity to accept a surrender of native title. The native title may be surrendered on purchase or surrendered voluntarily, whereupon the Crown's radical title is expanded to absolute ownership, a plenum dominium, for there is then no other owner. *St. Catherine's Milling and Lumber Co. v. The Queen* (1888) 14 App Cas, at p 55. If native title were surrendered to the Crown in expectation of a grant of a tenure to the indigenous title holders, there may be a fiduciary duty on the Crown to exercise its discretionary power to grant a tenure in land so as to satisfy the expectation. See *Guerin v. The Queen* (1984) 13 DLR (4th) 321, at pp 334, 339, 342–343, 356–357, 360–361, but it is unnecessary to consider the existence or extent of such a fiduciary duty in this case. Here, the fact is that strangers were not allowed to settle on the Murray Islands and, even after annexation in 1879, strangers who were living on the Islands were deported. The Meriam people asserted an exclusive right to occupy the Murray Islands and, as a community, held a proprietary interest in the Islands. They have maintained their identity as a people and they observe customs which are traditionally based. There was a possible alienation of some kind of interest in 2 acres to the London Missionary Society prior to annexation but it is unnecessary to consider whether that land was alienated by Meriam law or whether the alienation was sanctioned by custom alone. As we shall see, native title to that land was lost to the Meriam people in any event on the grant of a lease by the Crown in 1882 or by its subsequent renewal.

68. Secondly, native title, being recognized by the common law (though not as a common law tenure), may be protected by such legal or equitable remedies as are appropriate to the particular rights and interests established by the evidence, whether proprietary or personal and usufructuary in nature and whether possessed by a community, a group or an individual. The incidents of a particular native title relating to inheritance, the transmission or acquisition of rights and interests on death or marriage, the transfer of rights and interests in land and the grouping of persons to possess rights and interests in land are matters to be determined by the laws and customs of the indigenous inhabitants, provided those laws and customs are not so repugnant to natural justice, equity and good conscience that judicial sanctions under the new regime must be withheld: *Idewu Inasa v. Oshodi* (1934) AC 99, at p 105. Of course in time the laws and customs of any people

will change and the rights and interests of the members of the people among themselves will change too. But so long as the people remain as an identifiable community, the members of whom are identified by one another as members of that community living under its laws and customs, the communal native title survives to be enjoyed by the members according to the rights and interests to which they are respectively entitled under the traditionally based laws and customs, as currently acknowledged and observed. Here, the Meriam people have maintained their own identity and their own customs. The Murray Islands clearly remain their home country. Their land disputes have been dealt with over the years by the Island Court in accordance with the customs of the Meriam people.

69. Thirdly, where an indigenous people (including a clan or group), as a community, are in possession or are entitled to possession of land under a proprietary native title, their possession may be protected or their entitlement to possession may be enforced by a representative action brought on behalf of the people or by a sub-group or individual who sues to protect or enforce rights or interests which are dependent on the communal native title. Those rights and interests are, so to speak, carved out of the communal native title. A sub-group or individual asserting a native title dependent on a communal native title has a sufficient interest to sue to enforce or protect the communal title *Australian Conservation Foundation v. The Commonwealth* (1980) *146 CLR 493*, at pp 530–531, 537–539, 547–548; *Onus v. Alcoa of Australia Ltd.* (1981) *149 CLR 27*, at pp 35–36, 41–42, 46, 51, 62, 74–75. A communal native title enures for the benefit of the community as a whole and for the sub-groups and individuals within it who have particular rights and interests in the community's lands.

73. Sovereignty carries the power to create and to extinguish private rights and interests in land within the Sovereign's territory *Joint Tribal Council of the Passamaquoddy Tribe v. Morton* (1975) 528 Fed 2d 370, at p 376 n.6. It follows that, on a change of sovereignty, rights and interests in land that may have been indefeasible under the old regime become liable to extinction by exercise of the new sovereign power. The sovereign power may or may not be exercised with solicitude for the welfare of indigenous inhabitants but, in the case of common law countries, the courts cannot review the merits, as distinct from the legality, of the exercise of sovereign power *United States v. Santa Fe Pacific Railroad Company* (1941) 314 US 339, at p 347; *Tee-Hit-Ton Indians v. United States* (1954) 348 US 272, at pp 281–285. However, under the constitutional law of this country, the legality (and hence the validity) of an exercise of a sovereign power depends on the authority vested in the organ of government purporting to exercise it: municipal constitutional law determines the scope of authority to exercise a sovereign power over matters governed by municipal law, including rights and interests in land.

Calder v Attorney-General of British Columbia (1973) 34 Dominion Law Reports (3rd) 145

Traditional authorities and precedents led the Provincial Courts to uphold the lawful extinction of the Nishga Indian's native title by the Crown. The Supreme Court of Canada overturned it declaring that native title once established continued unless there was specific legislation to the contrary or the land had been ceded to the Crown.

Hall, J, dissenting, pp 173–174: When asked to state the nature of the right being asserted and for which a declaration was being sought, counsel for the appellants described it as 'an interest which is a burden on the title of the Crown; an interest which is usufructuary in nature; a tribal interest inalienable except to the Crown and extinguishable only by legislative enactment of the Parliament of Canada'. The exact nature and extent of the Indian right or title does not need to be precisely stated in this litigation. The issue here is whether any right or title the Indians possess as occupants of the land from time immemorial has been extinguished. They ask for a declaration that there has been no extinguishment. The precise nature and value of that right or title would, of course, be most relevant in any litigation that might follow extinguishment in the future because in such an event, according to common law, the expropriation of private rights by the Government under the prerogative necessitates the payment of compensation: *Newcastle Breweries Ltd. v.*

The King, [1920] 1 K.B. 854. Only express words to that effect in an enactment would authorize a taking without compensation. This proposition has been extended to Canada in *City of Montreal v. Montreal Harbour Com'rs*, [1926] 1 D.L.R. 840, 47 Que. K.B. 163, [1926] A.C. 299. The principle is so much part of the common law that it even exists in time of war as was made clear in *Attorney-General v. DeKeyser's Royal Hotel, Ltd.*, [1920] A.C. 508, and *Burmah Oil Co. (Burmah Trading) Ltd. v. Lord Advocate*, [1965] A.C. 75. This is not a claim to title in *fee* but is in the nature of an equitable title or interest (see *Cherokee Nation v. State of Georgia* (1831), 5 Peters 1, 30 U.S. 1), a usufructuary right and a right to occupy the lands and to enjoy the fruits of the soil, the forest and of the rivers and streams which does not in any way deny the Crown's paramount title as it is recognized by the law of nations. Nor does the Nishga claim challenge the federal Crown's right to extinguish that title. Their position is that they possess a right of occupation against the world except the Crown and that the Crown has not to date lawfully extinguished that right. The essence of the action is that such rights as the Nishgas possessed in 1858 continue to this date. Accordingly, the declaratory judgment asked for implies that the *status quo* continues and this means that if the right is to be extinguished it must be done by specific legislation in accordance with the law.

The right to possession claimed is not prescriptive in origin because a prescriptive right presupposes a prior right in some other person or authority. Since it is admitted that the Nishgas have been in possession since time immemorial, that fact negatives that anyone ever had or claimed prior possession.

The Nishgas do not claim to be able to sell or alienate their right to possession except to the Crown. They claim the right to remain in possession themselves and to enjoy the fruits of that possession. They do not deny the right of the Crown to dispossess them but say the Crown has not done so. There is no claim for compensation in this action. The action is for a declaration without a claim for consequential relief as contemplated by British Columbia O. 25, r. 5 (M.R. 285) quoted later. However, it must be recognized that if the Nishgas succeed in establishing a right to possession, the question of compensation would remain for future determination as and when proceedings to dispossess them should be taken. British Columbia's position has been that there never was any right or title to extinguish, and alternatively, that if any such right or title did exist it was extinguished in the period between 1858 and Confederation in 1871. The respondent admits that nothing has been done since Confederation to extinguish the right or title.

12.6.4 Land, natural resources and development

Land may contain valuable resources which are exploited by others contrary to the cultural and spiritual ties of the indigenous peoples or to the detriment of elements of their right to development. More recent and ongoing challenges to indigenous peoples are the exploitation of land and natural resources. Mining and oil and mineral exploration impact heavily on traditional lands in large swathes of Africa. Note that general human rights also impact on this. Consider certain 'peoples' rights' in the African Charter.

African Charter on Human and Peoples' Rights Art 21

1. All peoples shall freely dispose of their wealth and natural resources. This right shall be exercised in the exclusive interest of the people. In no case shall a people be deprived of it.

2. In case of spoliation the dispossessed people shall have the right to the lawful recovery of its property as well as to an adequate compensation.

3. The free disposal of wealth and natural resources shall be exercised without prejudice to the obligation of promoting international economic cooperation based on mutual respect, equitable exchange and the principles of international law.

4. States parties to the present Charter shall individually and collectively exercise the right to

free disposal of their wealth and natural resources with a view to strengthening African unity and solidarity.

5. States parties to the present Charter shall undertake to eliminate all forms of foreign economic exploitations particularly that practiced by international monopolies so as to enable their peoples to fully benefit from the advantages derived form their national resources.

Chapter 8 includes the practical application of such provisions when considering cases brought before African and American courts/commissions arising from the exploitation of the Niger delta and the impact on, *inter alia*, the Ogoni peoples.

Question

Noting the Treaty of Waitangi, above, what problems may there be for indigenous peoples in the Amazon basin or Papua New Guinea when faced with incomers wishing to draft instruments for transferring mineral rights to traditional lands?

12.6.5 Restitution or compensation

Neither restitution nor compensation is habitually offered to all affected peoples. Inevitably business and politics intervene. When natural resources are exploited, the potential for compensation is greater. In Alaska, the Alaskan Native Settlement Claim Act 1971 was the largest Indian settlement in history, giving Alaska's indigenous people clear title to 40 million acres and cash of USD962.5 million. This settlement paved the way for the trans-Alaskan pipeline which impacted heavily on traditional Inuit lands and affected natural migration routes of many indigenous species. Consider the salient extracts from the Act.

Alaskan Native Settlement Claims Act 1971, Title 43, Chapter 33

S 1601. Congressional findings and declaration of policy

Congress finds and declares that—

(a) there is an immediate need for a fair and just settlement of all claims by Natives and Native groups of Alaska, based on aboriginal land claims;

(b) the settlement should be accomplished rapidly, with certainty, in conformity with the real economic and social needs of Natives, without litigation, with maximum participation by Natives in decisions affecting their rights and property, without establishing any permanent racially defined institutions, rights, privileges, or obligations, without creating a reservation system or lengthy wardship or trusteeship, and without adding to the categories of property and institutions enjoying special tax privileges or to the legislation establishing special relationships between the United States Government and the State of Alaska;

(c) no provision of this chapter shall replace or diminish any right, privilege, or obligation of Natives as citizens of the United States or of Alaska, or relieve, replace, or diminish any obligation of the United States or of the State or Alaska to protect and promote the rights or welfare of Natives as citizens of the United States or of Alaska; the Secretary is authorized and directed, together with other appropriate agencies of the United States Government, to make a study of all Federal programs primarily designed to benefit Native people and to report back to the Congress with his recommendations for the future management and operation of these programs within three years of December 18, 1971;

(d) no provision of this chapter shall constitute a precedent for reopening, renegotiating, or legislating upon any past settlement involving land claims or other matters with any Native organizations, or any tribe, band, or identifiable group of American Indians;

(e) no provision of this chapter shall effect a change or changes in the petroleum reserve policy reflected in sections 7421 through 7438 of title 10 except as specifically provided in this chapter;

(f) no provision of this chapter shall be construed to constitute a jurisdictional act, to confer jurisdiction to sue, nor to grant implied consent to Natives to sue the United States or any of its officers with respect to the claims extinguished by the operation of this chapter; and

(g) no provision of this chapter shall be construed to terminate or otherwise curtail the activities of the Economic Development Administration or other Federal agencies conducting loan or loan and grant programs in Alaska. For this purpose only, the terms 'Indian reservation' and 'trust or restricted Indian-owned land areas' in Public Law 89–136, the Public Works and Economic Development Act of 1965, as amended [42 U.S.C. 3121 *et seq.*], shall be interpreted to include lands granted to Natives under this chapter as long as such lands remain in the ownership of the Native villages or the Regional Corporations.

S 1602. Definitions

(b) 'Native' means a citizen of the United States who is a person of one-fourth degree or more Alaska Indian (including Tsimshian Indians not enrolled in the Metlaktla Indian Community) Eskimo, or Aleut blood, or combination thereof. The term includes any Native as so defined either or both of whose adoptive parents are not Natives. It also includes, in the absence of proof of a minimum blood quantum, any citizen of the United States who is regarded as an Alaska Native by the Native village or Native group of which he claims to be a member and whose father or mother is (or, if deceased, was) regarded as Native by any village or group. Any decision of the Secretary regarding eligibility for enrollment shall be final;

(c) 'Native village' means any tribe, band, clan, group, village, community, or association in Alaska listed in sections 1610 and 1615 of this title, or which meets the requirements of this chapter, and which the Secretary determines was, on the 1970 census enumeration date (as shown by the census or other evidence satisfactory to the Secretary, who shall make findings of fact in each instance), composed of twenty-five or more Natives;

(d) 'Native group' means any tribe, band, clan, village, community, or village association of Natives in Alaska composed of less than twenty-five Natives, who comprise a majority of the residents of the locality.

S 1605. Alaska Native Fund.
(a) Establishment in Treasury; deposits into Fund of general fund, interest, and revenue sharing moneys

There is hereby established in the United States Treasury an Alaska Native Fund into which the following moneys shall be deposited:

(1) $462,500,000 from the general fund of the Treasury, which are authorized to be appropriated according to the following schedule:

(A) $12,500,000 during the fiscal year in which this chapter becomes effective;

(B) $50,000,000 during the second fiscal year;

(C) $70,000,000 during each of the third, fourth, and fifth fiscal years;

(D) $40,000,000 during the period beginning July 1, 1976, and ending September 30, 1976; and

(E) $30,000,000 during each of the next five fiscal years, for transfer to the Alaska Native Fund in the fourth quarter of each fiscal year.

(2) Four percent interest per annum, which is authorized to be appropriated, on any amount authorized to be appropriated by this paragraph that is not appropriated within six months after the fiscal year in which payable.

(3) $500,000,000 pursuant to the revenue sharing provisions of section 1608 of this title.

(b) Prohibition of expenditures for propaganda or political campaigns; misdemeanor; penalty

None of the funds paid or distributed pursuant to this section to any of the Regional and Village Corporations established pursuant to this chapter shall be expended, donated, or otherwise used for the purpose of carrying on propaganda, or intervening in (including the publishing and distributing of statements) any political campaign on behalf of any candidate for public office. Any person who willfully violates the foregoing provision shall be guilty of a misdemeanor and, upon conviction thereof, shall be fined not more than 1,000 or imprisoned not more than twelve months, or both.

(c) Distribution of Fund moneys among organized Regional Corporations; basis as relative number of Native enrollees in each region; reserve for payment of attorney and other fees; retention of share in Fund until organization of corporation

After completion of the roll prepared pursuant to section 1604 of this title, all money in the Fund, except money reserved as provided in section 1619 of this title for the payment of attorney and other fees, shall be distributed at the end of each three months of the fiscal year among the Regional Corporations organized pursuant to section 1606 of this title on the basis of the relative numbers of Natives enrolled in each region. The share of a Regional Corporation that has not been organized shall be retained in the Fund until the Regional Corporation is organized.

The African Charter, see above, also makes provision for compensation in the event of loss of natural resources.

Question

Consider the scope of traditional lands in, for example, Australia or Canada. Why is full restitution impossible?

Once the existence of native title is established, restitution/compensation can be discussed. The criteria for establishing native title vary from state to state. For examples, see the *Mabo* case above or *Hamlet of Baker Lake v Minister of Indian Affairs and Northern Development* (1980) 107 Dominion Law Reports (3rd) 513 at 542.

In New Zealand too, it is recognised that native title cannot be extinguished other than by the free consent of the native peoples—Judge Chapman in *Regina v Symonds* (1847) NZPCC 387 at 390

In some areas, restitution of traditional lands, or at least restoration of traditional custodianship has been effected.

12.7 CULTURAL RIGHTS

Of considerable concern to indigenous people worldwide is the erosion of their cultural identity. Inevitably eroding elements of cultural identity, whether in furtherance of assimilationist policies or as voluntary integration/development, impacts on the rights of indigenous peoples and the continuation of their traditional way of life.

Question

'You can provide rights to protect and promote cultural diversity but you cannot force anyone to retain a traditional way of life.' Consider this view of the perennial debate between preserving and protecting indigenous culture.

Like so many terms, culture has no universally accepted meaning. Most recognise it if they encounter it, but definitions can so easily exclude important aspects of cultural identity.

Michael Leiris, Race and Culture, Paris UNESCO, 1951 (p 21)

As culture, then, comprehends all that is inherited or transmitted through society, it follows that its individual elements are proportionately diverse. They include not only beliefs, knowledge, sentiments and literature (and illiterate peoples often have an immensely rich oral tradition), but the language or other systems of symbols which are their vehicles. Other elements are the rules of kinship, methods of education, forms of Government and all the fashions followed in social relations. Gestures, bodily attitudes and even facial expressions are also included, since they are in large measure acquired by the community through education or imitation; and so, among the material elements, are fashions in housing and clothing and ranges of tools, manufactures and artistic production, all of which are to some extent traditional.

12.7.1   Cultural genocide?

Clearly genocidal practices aimed at an indigenous group would fall within the ambit of the Genocide Convention and the perpetrators could be prosecuted in accordance with the prevailing international criminal law (see Chapter 15). However, what if only the culture and traditional life of the indigenous peoples are affected? Some commentators have argued for recognition of cultural genocide (see for example, Dunn, J, 'East Timor: A Case of Cultural Genocide?' in Andreopoulos, GJ (ed), *Genocide: Conceptual and Historical Dimensions*, 1994, Philadelphia: Pennsylvania Press, pp 171–190). Early drafts of the Genocide Convention included cultural genocide: the brutal destruction of the specific characteristics of a group. With opposition from States such as the USA and France, the clause was dropped. The emphasis in the Convention is thus on political genocide. Cultural genocide remains an academic discussion point. However, some elements overlap. It is difficult to reconcile the policy in Australia of removing mixed race children to be brought up by white families etc with contemporary international law. The 'stolen generation' remains a black spot in Australia's recent history.

Draft United Nations Genocide Convention, UN Doc E/794 (1948)

In this Convention genocide also means any deliberate act committed with the intent to destroy the language, religion or culture of a national, racial or religious group on grounds of the national or racial origin or religious belief of its members such as:

(1) prohibiting the use of language of the group in daily intercourse or in schools, or the printing and circulation or publications in the language of the group;

(2) destroying or preventing the use of libraries, museums, schools, historical monuments, places of worship or other cultural institutions and objects of the group.

Of course, this clause did not reach the final version of the Convention. Rather, cultural genocide was excluded.

Question

What reasons are there for the exclusion of cultural genocide from an international convention on the punishment and prevention of genocide? Is cultural genocide less important?

Some elements of traditional practices are proscribed when deemed unacceptably injurious. Female genital mutilation is probably one of the best known examples of this. The erosion of its acceptability is discussed in Chapter 2.

Most elements of cultural rights can be preserved by deploying the protection in Art 27 of the International Covenant on Civil and Political Rights. Relevant communications brought before the Human Rights Committee of the United Nations are discussed above.

FURTHER READING

Brownlie, I, *Treaties and Indigenous Peoples*, 1992, Oxford: Clarendon

Cassesse, A, *Self-Determination of Peoples: a Legal Reappraisal*, 1995, Cambridge: Cambridge University Press

Gayim, E, 'The United Nations Law on Self-Determination of Indigenous Peoples' (1982) 51 Nordic Journal of International Law 53

Gudmundur, A, 'International Law, International Organisations and Indigenous Peoples' (1982) 36 Journal of International Affairs 113

Hannum, H, *Autonomy, Sovereignty and Self-Determination: The Accommodation of Conflicting Rights*, 1990, Philadelphia: University of Pennsylvania Press

Hocking, B (ed), *International Law and Aboriginal Human Rights*, 1988, Sydney: Law Book Company

McCorquodale, R, 'Self-determination: A Human Rights Approach' (1994) 43 International and Comparative Law Quarterly 857

Nettheim, G, ' "Peoples" and "Populations": Indigenous Peoples and the Rights of Peoples' in Crawford, J (ed), *The Rights of Peoples*, 1980, Oxford: Clarendon, p 118

Pritchard, S (ed), *Indigenous Peoples, the United Nations and Human Rights*, 1998, Annandale: Federation Press

Prott, L, 'Cultural Rights as Peoples' Rights in International Law' in Crawford, J (ed), *The Rights of Peoples*, 1980, Oxford, Clarendon, pp 93–106

Rigo-Sureda, A, *The Evolution of the Right of Self-determination: A Study of UN Practice*, 1973, Leiden: Sitjhoff

Sanders, W, 'The UN Working Group on Indigenous Populations', 11 Human Rights Quarterly 429

Tomuschat, C (ed), *Modern Law of Self-Determination*, 1993, the Netherlands: Martinus Nijhoff

Turpel, M, 'Indigenous Peoples' Rights of Political Self-Determination: recent international legal developments and the continuing struggle for recognition', 25 Cornell International Law Journal 579

Thornberry, P, *Indigenous Peoples and Human Rights*, 2002, Manchester: Manchester University Press

United Nations Office of the High Commissioner for Human Rights, *The Rights of Indigenous Peoples*, Factsheet No. 9 Rev.1, Geneva: OHCHR

Websites

www.un.org/hr/indigenousforum—United Nations Permanent Forum on Indigenous Issues

www.ohchr.english/issues/indigenous/index.htm—OHCHR Indigenous peoples website

www.coe.int/T/E/human_rights/minorities/—C of E framework

CHAPTER 13

THE PROTECTION OF REFUGEES, STATELESS PERSONS AND INTERNALLY DISPLACED PEOPLE

An increasingly high media profile is accorded to refugees, asylum seekers and internally displaced people. Whether as a result of natural disasters, famine, political persecution or conflict, millions of people seek refuge outwith their homeland. This chapter focuses on the rights of refugees and the legal regime which has evolved to protect them.

The Office of the High Commissioner for Refugees estimates that at the end of 2005, some 20.8 million people were of concern. This figure is consonant with previous years, since the UNHCHR has published 'total population of concern' figures; the number has been around 20,000,000 each year. Only 2002 evidenced a significant drop. Of those of concern, some 8,394,500 are refugees. (Note that the number of refugees is a 2005 year end figure, thus this does not reflect those becoming refugees as a result of natural disasters and other events thereafter.) The total number of refugees dropped for the 5th consecutive year in 2005. This can partly be explained by significant numbers of refugees returning to Afghanistan, Iraq, Angola and Liberia. Perhaps the most dramatic increase is in internally displaced people, Columbia and Sudan being two of the principal countries with increasing numbers of internally displaced persons.

The following graph represents the origin of the major refugee populations in 2005 (figures and statistics from www.unhcr.ch).

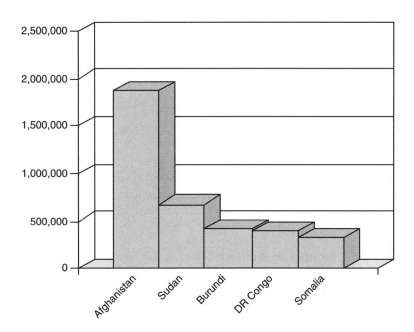

Unlike some of the other groups addressed in this text, refugees are by definition an international matter. Refugees cross borders in search of sanctuary and so unlike women, children or even indigenous peoples, the need for an international solution and transnational approach is beyond question. When the United Nations was founded, in the wake of war in Europe and Asia-Pacific, millions of displaced persons had to be considered in plans for rebuilding shattered economies and newly created States. The fundamental human rights instruments make some provision.

Universal Declaration on Human Rights 1948

Article 13

1. Everyone has the right to freedom of movement and residence within the borders of each State.

2. Everyone has the right to leave any country, including his own, and return to his country.

Article 14

1. Everyone has the right to seek and to enjoy in other countries asylum from persecution.

2. This right may not be invoked in the case of prosecutions genuinely arising from non-political crimes or from acts contrary to the purposes and principles of the United Nations.

Article 12 of the International Covenant on Civil and Political Rights 1966 reflects this.

13.1 WHO IS A REFUGEE?

The principal instrument addressing issues relating to refugees is the United Nations Convention Relating to the Status of Refugees 1951. This applies only to individuals who became refugees as a result of events occurring in Europe before 1 January 1951 and was designed to assist in the resettlement of persons displaced as a result of the Second World War. Today some 143 States are party to the Convention.

Given the continual growth in refugee populations around the world, the international community adopted a 1967 Protocol to the Convention which extended its ambit to all persons coming within the definition adopted by the original Convention without reference to the date of the events generating refugee status. There are at present 143 States Parties to the Protocol, who thus agree to the international system of protection for refugees.

13.1.1 Definition of refugee

The definition of a refugee for the purpose of international law is stated in the Convention. Read it carefully, noting the exceptions incorporated into the convention. It was created to address a particular problem, focused in Europe in the post-war period.

United Nations Convention relating to the Status of Refugees
Article 1.—Definition of the term 'refugee'

A. For the purposes of the present Convention, the term 'refugee' shall apply to any person who:

(1) Has been considered a refugee under the Arrangements of 12 May 1926 and 30 June 1928 or under the Conventions of 28 October 1933 and 10 February 1938, the Protocol of 14 September 1939 or the Constitution of the International Refugee Organization;

Decisions of non-eligibility taken by the International Refugee Organization during the period of its activities shall not prevent the status of refugee being accorded to persons who fulfil the conditions of paragraph 2 of this section;

(2) As a result of events occurring before 1 January 1951 and owing to well-founded fear of being persecuted for reasons of race, religion, nationality, membership of a particular social group or political opinion, is outside the country of his nationality and is unable or, owing to such fear, is unwilling to avail himself of the protection of that country; or who, not having a nationality and being outside the country of his former habitual residence as a result of such events, is unable or, owing to such fear, is unwilling to return to it.

In the case of a person who has more than one nationality, the term 'the country of his nationality' shall mean each of the countries of which he is a national, and a person shall not be deemed to be lacking the protection of the country of his nationality if, without any valid reason based on well-founded fear, he has not availed himself of the protection of one of the countries of which he is a national.

B. (1) For the purposes of this Convention, the words 'events occurring before 1 January 1951' in article 1, section A, shall be understood to mean either (a) 'events occurring in Europe before 1 January 1951'; or (b) 'events occurring in Europe or elsewhere before 1 January 1951'; and each Contracting State shall make a declaration at the time of signature, ratification or accession, specifying which of these meanings it applies for the purpose of its obligations under this Convention.

(2) Any Contracting State which has adopted alternative (a) may at any time extend its obligations by adopting alternative (b) by means of a notification addressed to the Secretary-General of the United Nations. . . .

D. This Convention shall not apply to persons who are at present receiving from organs or agencies of the United Nations other than the United Nations High Commissioner for Refugees protection or assistance.

When such protection or assistance has ceased for any reason, without the position of such persons being definitively settled in accordance with the relevant resolutions adopted by the General Assembly of the United Nations, these persons shall ipso facto be entitled to the benefits of this Convention.

E. This Convention shall not apply to a person who is recognized by the competent authorities of the country in which he has taken residence as having the rights and obligations which are attached to the possession of the nationality of that country.

F. The provisions of this Convention shall not apply to any person with respect to whom there are serious reasons for considering that:

(a) He has committed a crime against peace, a war crime, or a crime against humanity, as defined in the international instruments drawn up to make provision in respect of such crimes;

(b) He has committed a serious non-political crime outside the country of refuge prior to his admission to that country as a refugee;

(c) He has been guilty of acts contrary to the purposes and principles of the United Nations.

Question

Was it realistic to create such a restrictive instrument in 1951?

Governments desired the original time limitation of events before 1951 in order primarily to limit their obligations to known situations and refugees. However, as Europe did not prove the only source of refugees and, as more refugee situations emerged, the need to extend the ambit of the Convention was accepted. The scope of the Convention was therefore augmented to include all other and subsequent refugees facilitating the evolution of the Convention into the seminal global instrument addressing the plight of refugees.

Protocol Relating to the Status of Refugees 1967

The States Parties to the present Protocol,

Considering that the Convention relating to the Status of Refugees done at Geneva on 28 July 1951 (hereinafter referred to as the Convention) covers only those persons who have become refugees as a result of events occurring before 1 January 1951,

Considering that new refugee situations have arisen since the Convention was adopted and that the refugees concerned may therefore not fall within the scope of the Convention,

Considering that it is desirable that equal status should be enjoyed by all refugees covered by the definition in the Convention irrespective of the dateline 1 January 1951,

Have agreed as follows:

Article 1. General provision

1. The States Parties to the present Protocol undertake to apply articles 2 to 34 inclusive of the Convention to refugees as hereinafter defined.

2. For the purpose of the present Protocol, the term 'refugee' shall, except as regards the application of paragraph 3 of this article, mean any person within the definition of article 1 of the Convention as if the words 'As a result of events occurring before 1 January 1951 and . . .' and the words '. . . as a result of such events', in article 1 A (2) were omitted.

3. The present Protocol shall be applied by the States Parties hereto without any geographic limitation, save that existing declarations made by States already Parties to the Convention in accordance with article 1 B (1) (a) of the Convention, shall, unless extended under article 1 B (2) thereof, apply also under the present Protocol.

It is important to note that both the Convention and Protocol are self-standing. Therefore, some States are party only to the original Convention with obligations limited to refugees created by circumstances before 1951 while other States only sign up to the Protocol and thus their obligations are without the time limit. Many States Parties to the original Convention obviously subsequently extended their obligations in terms of the Protocol.

Question

To what extent does the Convention, as revised, have the potential for application to 'economic migrant workers'?

For a detailed exposition and guide to the definition of refugee, see the *Handbook of Procedures and Criteria for Determining Refugee Status* under the 1951 Convention and the 1967 Protocol relating to the Status of Refugees, HCR/IP/4/Eng/REV.1 Re-edited, Geneva, January 1992, UNHCR 1979, paras 37–105. This is available online. It is a manual aimed at guiding governments through the application of the Convention. It consolidates the accumulated experience of the Office of the High Commissioner with the practical contemporary situation. Although not part of the Convention, the Handbook is viewed authoritatively by many national governments and, indeed, courts. The purpose of the Handbook is to assist governments and other interested parties. The explanation of the definition is, according to paragraph V of the foreword, based on the knowledge accumulated by the High Commissioner's Office since the entry into force of the Convention: 'The practice of States is [also] taken into account as are exchanges of views between the Office [of the High Commissioner] and the competent authorities of Contracting States, and the literature devoted to the subject' (ibid).

A major problem which States encounter when legislating for refugees is the fact that many arrive illegally and/or are smuggled in to the country.

Bakhtiyari v Australia, Communication 1069/2002, Human Rights Committee, UN Doc. CCPR/C/79/D/1069/2002

The author of the communication left Afghanistan for Pakistan. He was joined by his wife and children. Mr. Bakhtiyari was then smuggled into Australia via Indonesia, arriving unlawfully in Australia. He lost contact with his wife and children although apparently unbeknown to him they were also smuggled into Australia over a year later. Mr. Bakhtiyari was detained on arrival in Australia (October 1999) though subsequently lodged an application for a protection visa based on his Afghan nationality and Hazara ethnicity. His wife and children had their applications for a protection visa refused in early 2001, shortly after their arrival and detention in Australia. Essentially Mrs. Bakhtiyari's testimony was found implausible and it appeared she was actually from Pakistan. A year later, subsequent evidence suggested that Mr. Bakhtiyari was from Quetta, Pakistan, not Afghanistan as originally claimed. He was notified that his visa status was being reviewed and, moreover, Mrs. Bakhtiyari's status could not be reviewed on the basis of her husband's protection visa. An application to have the children released from detention was made. In December 2002, Mr. Bakhtiyari's protection visa was cancelled and he was taken into custody. Various appeals were made against this decision.

2.14 On 19 June 2003, the Full Bench of the Family Court held, by a majority, that the Court did have jurisdiction to make orders against the Minister, including release from detention, if that was in the best interests of the child. The case was accordingly remitted for hearing as a matter of urgency as to what orders would be appropriate in the particular circumstances of the children. On 8 July 2003, the Full Bench of the Family Court granted the Minister leave to appeal to the High Court, but rejected the Minister's application for a stay on the order for rehearing as a matter of urgency. On 5 August 2003, the Family Court (Strickland J) dismissed an application for interlocutory relief, that is, that the children be released in advance of the trial of the question of what final orders would be in their best interests. On 25 August 2003, the Full Bench of the Family Court allowed an appeal and ordered the release of all of the children forthwith, pending resolution of the final application. They were released the same day and have resided with carers in Adelaide since. . . .

8.4 Referring to the arguments that Mrs. Bakhtiyari and her children, if removed to Afghanistan, would be in fear of being subjected to treatment contrary to article 7 of the Covenant, the Committee observes that as the authors have not been removed from Australia, the issue before the Committee is whether such removal if implemented at the present time would entail a real risk of treatment contrary to article 7 as a consequence. The Committee also observes that the State party's authorities, in the proceedings to date, have determined, as a matter of fact, that the authors are not from Afghanistan, and hence they do not stand in fear of being returned to that country by the State party. The authors on the other hand have failed to demonstrate that if returned to any other country, such as Pakistan, they would be liable to be sent to Afghanistan, where they would be in fear of treatment contrary to article 7. Much less have the authors substantiated that even if returned to Afghanistan, directly or indirectly, they would face, as a necessary and foreseeable consequence, treatment contrary to article 7. The Committee accordingly takes the view that the claim that, if the State party returns them at the present time, Mrs. Bakhtiyari and her children would have to face treatment contrary to article 7, has not been substantiated before the Committee, for purposes of admissibility, and is inadmissible under article 2 of the Optional Protocol. . . .

9.2 As to the claims of arbitrary detention, contrary to article 9, paragraph 1, the Committee recalls its jurisprudence that, in order to avoid any characterization of arbitrariness, detention should not continue beyond the period for which a State party can provide appropriate justification. In the present case, Mr. Bakhtiyari arrived by boat, without dependents (*sic*), with his identity in doubt and claiming to be from a State suffering serious internal disorder. In light of these factors and the fact that he was granted a protection visa and released two months after he had filed an application (some seven months after his arrival), the Committee is unable to conclude that, while the length of his first detention may have been undesirable, it was also arbitrary and in breach of article 9, paragraph 1. In the light of this conclusion, the Committee need not examine the claim under article 9, paragraph 4, with respect to Mr. Bakhtiyari. The Committee observes that Mr. Bakhtiyari's second period of detention, which has continued from his arrest for purposes of deportation on 5 December 2002 until the present may raise similar issues under article 9, but does not express a further view thereon in the absence of argument from either party.

9.3 Concerning Mrs. Bakhtiyari and her children, the Committee observes that Mrs. Bakhtiyari has been detained in immigration detention for two years and ten months, and continues to be detained, while the children remained in immigration detention for two years and eight months until their release on interim orders of the Family Court. Whatever justification there may have been for an initial detention for the purposes of ascertaining identity and other issues, the State party has not, in the Committee's view, demonstrated that their detention was justified for such an extended period. Taking into account in particular the composition of the Bakhtiyari family, the State party has not demonstrated that other, less intrusive, measures could not have achieved the same end of compliance with the State party's immigration policies by, for example, imposition of reporting obligations, sureties or other conditions which would take into account the family's particular circumstances. As a result, the continuation of immigration detention for Mrs. Bakhti-yari and her children for length of time described above, without appropriate justification, was arbitrary and contrary to article 9, paragraph 1, of the Covenant.

9.4 As to the claim under article 9, paragraph 4, related to this period of detention, the Commit-tee refers to its discussion of admissibility above and observes that the court review available to Mrs. Bakhtiyari would be confined purely to a formal assessment of whether she was a 'non-citizen' without an entry permit. The Committee observes that there was no discretion for a domestic court to review the justification of her detention in substantive terms. The Committee considers that the inability judicially to challenge a detention that was, or had become, contrary to article 9, paragraph 1, constitutes a violation of article 9, paragraph 4.

9.5 As to the children, the Committee observes that until the decision of the Full Bench of the Family Court on 19 June 2003, which held that it had jurisdiction under child welfare legislation to order the release of children from immigration detention, the children were in the same position as their mother, and suffered a violation of their rights under article 9, paragraph 4, up to that moment on the same basis. The Committee considers that the ability for a court to order a child's release if considered in its best interests, which subsequently occurred (albeit on an interim basis), is sufficient review of the substantive justification of detention to satisfy the requirements of article 9, paragraph 4, of the Covenant. Accordingly, the violation of article 9, paragraph 4, with respect to the children came to an end with the Family Court's finding of jurisdiction to make such orders.

9.6 As to the claim under articles 17 and 23, paragraph 1, the Committee observes that to separate a spouse and children arriving in a State from a spouse validly resident in a State may give rise to issues under articles 17 and 23 of the Covenant. In the present case, however, the State party contends that, at the time Mrs. Bakhtiyari made her application to the Minister under section 417 of the *Migration* Act, there was already information on Mr. Bakhtiyari's alleged visa fraud before it. As it remains unclear whether the attention of the State party's authorities was drawn to the existence of the relationship prior to that point, the Committee cannot regard it as arbitrary that the State party considered it inappropriate to unite the family at that stage. The Committee observes, however, that the State party intends at present to remove Mrs. Bakhtiyari and her children as soon as 'reasonably practicable', while it has no current plans to do so in respect of Mr. Bakhtiyari, who is currently pursuing domestic proceedings. Taking into account the specific circumstances of the case, namely the number and age of the children, including a new-born, the traumatic experiences of Mrs. Bakhtiyari and the children in long-term immigration detention in breach of article 9 of the Covenant, the difficulties that Mrs. Bakhtiyari and her children would face if returned to Pakistan without Mr. Bakhtiyari and the absence of arguments by the State party to justify removal in these circumstances, the Committee takes the view that removing Mrs. Bakhtiyari and her children without awaiting the final determination of Mr. Bakhtiyari's proceedings would constitute arbitrary interference in the family of the authors, in violation of articles 17, paragraph 1, and 23, paragraph 1, of the Covenant.

9.7 Concerning the claim under article 24, the Committee considers that the principle that in all decisions affecting a child, its best interests shall be a primary consideration, forms an integral part of every child's right to such measures of protection as required by his or her status as a minor, on the part of his or her family, society and the State, as required by article 24, paragraph 1, of the Covenant. The Committee observes that in this case children have suffered demonstrable, documented and on-going adverse effects of detention suffered by the children, and in particular the two eldest sons, up until the point of release on 25 August 2003, in circumstances where that detention was arbitrary and in violation of article 9, paragraph 1, of the Covenant. As a result, the Committee considers that the measures taken by the State party had not, until the Full Bench of the Family Court determined it had welfare jurisdiction with respect to the children, been guided by the best interests of the children, and thus revealed a violation of article 24, paragraph 1, of the Covenant, that is, of the children's right to such measures of protection as required by their status as minors up that point in time.

10. The Human Rights Committee . . . is of the view that the facts as found by the Committee reveal violations by Australia of articles 9, paragraphs 1 and 4, and 24, paragraph 1, and, potentially, of articles 17, paragraph 1, and 23, paragraph 1, of the Covenant.

11. In accordance with article 2, paragraph 3 (a), of the Covenant, the State party is under an obligation to provide the authors with an effective remedy. As to the violation of article 9, paragraphs 1 and 4, continuing up to the present time with respect to Mrs. Bakhtiyari, the State party should release her and pay her appropriate compensation. So far as concerns the violations of articles 9 and 24 suffered in the past by the children, which came to an end with their release on 25 August 2003, the State party is under an obligation to pay appropriate compensation to the children. The State party should also refrain from deporting Mrs. Bakhtiyari and her children while Mr. Bakhtiyari is pursuing domestic proccedings, as any such action on the part of the State party would result in violations of articles 17, paragraph 1, and 23, paragraph 1, of the Covenant.

Question

Is this decision appropriate? What implications does it have for States implementing a policy of detention pending verification of facts stated in an application for recognition of refugee status?

13.2 PROCEDURES FOR DETERMINING REFUGEE STATUS

While identification of members of other groups and categories may be self-evident or a matter of self-identification, refugee status is formally recognised by others, primarily the government of the State concerned. State practice varies considerably. In terms of the 1951 Convention, a person is a refugee as soon as s/he fulfils the definition in Art 1. States Parties merely recognise this pre-existing status. States do not decide whether fulfilling the criteria is or is not a refugee. Thus, the Office of the High Commissioner has specified minimum criteria to be followed in developing appropriate policies for declaring refugee status.

United Nations High Commission for Refugees 'Determination of refugee status', Document ExCOM No. 8 (XXVIII) 1977

(e) Recommended that procedures for the determination of refugee status should satisfy the following basic requirements:

(i) The competent official (e.g. immigration officer or border police officer) to whom the applicant addresses himself at the border or in the territory of a Contracting State, should have clear instructions for dealing with cases which might be within the purview of the relevant international instruments. He should be required to act in accordance with the principle of non-refoulement and to refer such cases to a higher authority.

(ii) The applicant should receive the necessary guidance as to the procedure to be followed.

(iii) There should be a clearly identified authority—wherever possible a single central authority—with responsibility for examining requests for refugee status and taking a decision in the first instance.

(iv) The applicant should be given the necessary facilities, including the services of a competent interpreter, for submitting his case to the authorities concerned. Applicants should also be given the opportunity, of which they should be duly informed, to contact a representative of UNHCR.

(v) If the applicant is recognized as a refugee, he should be informed accordingly and issued with documentation certifying his refugee status.

(vi) If the applicant is not recognized, he should be given a reasonable time to appeal for a formal reconsideration of the decision, either to the same or to a different authority, whether administrative or judicial, according to the prevailing system.

(vii) The applicant should be permitted to remain in the country pending a decision on his initial request by the competent authority referred to in paragraph (iii) above unless it has been established by that authority that his request is clearly abusive.

He should also be permitted to remain in the country while an appeal to a higher administrative authority or to the courts is pending.

The issue of determining the status of asylum seekers has produced further guidelines in Europe. The European Union, as a single internal market without frontiers, presents particular challenges to asylum and refugee laws. Once legally within the Union, in effect an asylum seeker may move freely within the larger geographical jurisdiction of the Union. Problems have arisen when asylum seekers travel through the Union then seek recognition as a refugee. The refugee camps in the north of France in the 1990s are an obvious example. Within the Union, the focus has thus been on substantiating the external borders to ensure a concerted and consistent approach to asylum seekers. The application of the freedom of movement provisions will thus present no further obstacle to asylum seekers and no further burden to States. The following guidelines determine which State should consider an application for asylum.

Council Regulation (EC) No 343/2003 of 18 February 2003 on establishing the criteria and mechanisms for determining the Member State responsible for examining an asylum application lodged in one of the Member States by a third-country national

Article 2

For the purposes of this Regulation:

(a) 'third-country national' means anyone who is not a citizen of the Union within the meaning of Article 17(1) of the Treaty establishing the European Community;

(b) 'Geneva Convention' means the Convention of 28 July 1951 relating to the status of refugees, as amended by the New York Protocol of 31 January 1967;

(c) 'application for asylum' means the application made by a third-country national which can be understood as a request for international protection from a Member State, under the Geneva Convention. Any application for international protection is presumed to be an application for asylum, unless a third-country national explicitly requests another kind of protection that can be applied for separately;

(d) 'applicant' or 'asylum seeker' means a third country national who has made an application for asylum in respect of which a final decision has not yet been taken;

(e) 'examination of an asylum application' means any examination of, or decision or ruling concerning, an application for asylum by the competent authorities in accordance with national law except for procedures for determining the Member State responsible in accordance with this Regulation;

(f) 'withdrawal of the asylum application' means the actions by which the applicant for asylum terminates the procedures initiated by the submission of his application for asylum, in accordance with national law, either explicitly or tacitly;

(g) 'refugee' means any third-country national qualifying for the status defined by the Geneva Convention and authorised to reside as such on the territory of a Member State;

(h) 'unaccompanied minor' means unmarried persons below the age of eighteen who arrive in the territory of the Member States unaccompanied by an adult responsible for them whether by law or by custom, and for as long as they are not effectively taken into the care of such a person; it includes minors who are left unaccompanied after they have entered the territory of the Member States;

(i) 'family members' means insofar as the family already existed in the country of origin, the following members of the applicant's family who are present in the territory of the Member States:

(i) the spouse of the asylum seeker or his or her unmarried partner in a stable relationship, where the legislation or practice of the Member State concerned treats unmarried couples in a way comparable to married couples under its law relating to aliens;

(ii) the minor children of couples referred to in point (i) or of the applicant, on condition that they are unmarried and dependent and regardless of whether they were born in or out of wedlock or adopted as defined under the national law;

(iii) the father, mother or guardian when the applicant or refugee is a minor and unmarried;

(j) 'residence document' means any authorisation issued by the authorities of a Member State authorising a third-country national to stay in its territory, including the documents substantiating the authorisation to remain in the territory under temporary protection arrangements or until the circumstances preventing a removal order from being carried out no longer apply, with the exception of visas and residence authorisations issued during the period required to determine the responsible Member State as established in this Regulation or during examination of an application for asylum or an application for a residence permit;

(k) 'visa' means the authorisation or decision of a Member State required for transit or entry for an intended stay in that Member State or in several Member States. The nature of the visa shall be determined in accordance with the following definitions:

(i) 'long-stay visa' means the authorisation or decision of a Member State required for entry for an intended stay in that Member State of more than three months;

(ii) 'short-stay visa' means the authorisation or decision of a Member State required for entry for an intended stay in that State or in several Member States for a period whose total duration does not exceed three months;

(iii) 'transit visa' means the authorisation or decision of a Member State for entry for transit through the territory of that Member State or several Member States, except for transit at an airport;

(iv) 'airport transit visa' means the authorisation or decision allowing a third-country national specifically subject to this requirement to pass through the transit zone of an airport, without gaining access to the national territory of the Member State concerned, during a stopover or a transfer between two sections of an international flight.

Article 3

1. Member States shall examine the application of any third-country national who applies at the border or in their territory to any one of them for asylum. The application shall be examined by a single Member State, which shall be the one which the criteria set out in Chapter III indicate is responsible.

2. By way of derogation from paragraph 1, each Member State may examine an application for asylum lodged with it by a third-country national, even if such examination is not its responsibility under the criteria laid down in this Regulation. In such an event, that Member State shall become the Member State responsible within the meaning of this Regulation and shall assume the obligations associated with that responsibility. Where appropriate, it shall inform the Member State previously responsible, the Member State conducting a procedure for determining the Member State responsible or the Member State which has been requested to take charge of or take back the applicant.

3. Any Member State shall retain the right, pursuant to its national laws, to send an asylum seeker to a third country, in compliance with the provisions of the Geneva Convention.

4. The asylum seeker shall be informed in writing in a language that he or she may reasonably be expected to understand regarding the application of this Regulation, its time limits and its effects.

Article 4

1. The process of determining the Member State responsible under this Regulation shall start as soon as an application for asylum is first lodged with a Member State.

2. An application for asylum shall be deemed to have been lodged once a form submitted by the applicant for asylum or a report prepared by the authorities has reached the competent authorities of the Member State concerned. Where an application is not made in writing, the time elapsing between the statement of intention and the preparation of a report should be as short as possible.

3. For the purposes of this Regulation, the situation of a minor who is accompanying the asylum seeker and meets the definition of a family member set out in Article 2, point (i), shall be indissociable from that of his parent or guardian and shall be a matter for the Member State responsible for examining the application for asylum of that parent or guardian, even if the minor is not individually an asylum seeker. The same treatment shall be applied to children born after the asylum seeker arrives in the territory of the Member States, without the need to initiate a new procedure for taking charge of them.

4. Where an application for asylum is lodged with the competent authorities of a Member State by an applicant who is in the territory of another Member State, the determination of the Member State responsible shall be made by the Member State in whose territory the applicant is present. The latter Member State shall be informed without delay by the Member State which received the application and shall then, for the purposes of this Regulation, be regarded as the Member State with which the application for asylum was lodged.

The applicant shall be informed in writing of this transfer and of the date on which it took place.

5. An asylum seeker who is present in another Member State and there lodges an application for

asylum after withdrawing his application during the process of determining the Member State responsible shall be taken back, under the conditions laid down in Article 20, by the Member State with which that application for asylum was lodged, with a view to completing the process of determining the Member State responsible for examining the application for asylum.

This obligation shall cease, if the asylum seeker has in the meantime left the territories of the Member States for a period of at least three months or has obtained a residence document from a Member State.

Article 5

1. The criteria for determining the Member State responsible shall be applied in the order in which they are set out in this Chapter.

2. The Member State responsible in accordance with the criteria shall be determined on the basis of the situation obtaining when the asylum seeker first lodged his application with a Member State.

Article 6

Where the applicant for asylum is an unaccompanied minor, the Member State responsible for examining the application shall be that where a member of his or her family is legally present, provided that this is in the best interest of the minor.

In the absence of a family member, the Member State responsible for examining the application shall be that where the minor has lodged his or her application for asylum.

Article 7

Where the asylum seeker has a family member, regardless of whether the family was previously formed in the country of origin, who has been allowed to reside as a refugee in a Member State, that Member State shall be responsible for examining the application for asylum, provided that the persons concerned so desire.

Article 8

If the asylum seeker has a family member in a Member State whose application has not yet been the subject of a first decision regarding the substance, that Member State shall be responsible for examining the application for asylum, provided that the persons concerned so desire.

Article 9

1. Where the asylum seeker is in possession of a valid residence document, the Member State which issued the document shall be responsible for examining the application for asylum.

2. Where the asylum seeker is in possession of a valid visa, the Member State which issued the visa shall be responsible for examining the application for asylum, unless the visa was issued when acting for or on the written authorisation of another Member State. In such a case, the latter Member State shall be responsible for examining the application for asylum. Where a Member State first consults the central authority of another Member State, in particular for security reasons, the latter's reply to the consultation shall not constitute written authorisation within the meaning of this provision.

3. Where the asylum seeker is in possession of more than one valid residence document or visa issued by different Member States, the responsibility for examining the application for asylum shall be assumed by the Member States in the following order:

(a) the Member State which issued the residence document conferring the right to the longest period of residency or, where the periods of validity are identical, the Member State which issued the residence document having the latest expiry date;

(b) the Member State which issued the visa having the latest expiry date where the various visas are of the same type;

(c) where visas are of different kinds, the Member State which issued the visa having the longest period of validity, or, where the periods of validity are identical, the Member State which issued the visa having the latest expiry date.

4. Where the asylum seeker is in possession only of one or more residence documents which have expired less than two years previously or one or more visas which have expired less than six months previously and which enabled him actually to enter the territory of a Member State, paragraphs 1, 2 and 3 shall apply for such time as the applicant has not left the territories of the Member States.

Where the asylum seeker is in possession of one or more residence documents which have expired more than two years previously or one or more visas which have expired more than six months previously and enabled him actually to enter the territory of a Member State and where he has not left the territories of the Member States, the Member State in which the application is lodged shall be responsible.

5. The fact that the residence document or visa was issued on the basis of a false or assumed identity or on submission of forged, counterfeit or invalid documents shall not prevent responsibility being allocated to the Member State which issued it. However, the Member State issuing the residence document or visa shall not be responsible if it can establish that a fraud was committed after the document or visa had been issued.

Article 10

1. Where it is established, on the basis of proof or circumstantial evidence as described in the two lists mentioned in Article 18(3), including the data referred to in Chapter III of Regulation (EC) No 2725/2000, that an asylum seeker has irregularly crossed the border into a Member State by land, sea or air having come from a third country, the Member State thus entered shall be responsible for examining the application for asylum. This responsibility shall cease 12 months after the date on which the irregular border crossing took place.

2. When a Member State cannot or can no longer be held responsible in accordance with paragraph 1, and where it is established, on the basis of proof or circumstantial evidence as described in the two lists mentioned in Article 18(3), that the asylum seeker—who has entered the territories of the Member States irregularly or whose circumstances of entry cannot be established—at the time of lodging the application has been previously living for a continuous period of at least five months in a Member State, that Member State shall be responsible for examining the application for asylum.

If the applicant has been living for periods of time of at least five months in several Member States, the Member State where this has been most recently the case shall be responsible for examining the application.

Article 11

1. If a third-country national enters into the territory of a Member State in which the need for him or her to have a visa is waived, that Member State shall be responsible for examining his or her application for asylum.

2. The principle set out in paragraph 1 does not apply, if the third-country national lodges his or her application for asylum in another Member State, in which the need for him or her to have a visa for entry into the territory is also waived. In this case, the latter Member State shall be responsible for examining the application for asylum.

Article 12

Where the application for asylum is made in an international transit area of an airport of a Member State by a third-country national, that Member State shall be responsible for examining the application.

Article 13

Where no Member State responsible for examining the application for asylum can be designated on the basis of the criteria listed in this Regulation, the first Member State with which the application for asylum was lodged shall be responsible for examining it.

Article 14

Where several members of a family submit applications for asylum in the same Member State simultaneously, or on dates close enough for the procedures for determining the Member State responsible to be conducted together, and where the application of the criteria set out in this Regulation would lead to them being separated, the Member State responsible shall be determined on the basis of the following provisions:

(a) responsibility for examining the applications for asylum of all the members of the family shall lie with the Member State which the criteria indicate is responsible for taking charge of the largest number of family members;

(b) failing this, responsibility shall lie with the Member State which the criteria indicate is responsible for examining the application of the oldest of them.

The following graph indicates the new asylum applications submitted in selected countries during 2005 (figures from www.unhcr.ch).

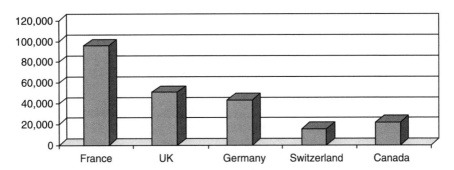

13.2.1   Children

Children may arrive with their parents/guardians or unaccompanied seeking refuge. As Chapter 10 indicates, children are often particularly vulnerable. Unsurprisingly, therefore, particular regard must be had to the rights of children of refugees and refugee children. The European Regulation above indicates this, as does the United Nations Convention on the Rights of the Child.

United Nations Convention on the Rights of the Child Art 22

1. States Parties shall take appropriate measures to ensure that a child who is seeking refugee status or who is considered a refugee in accordance with applicable international or domestic law and procedures shall, whether unaccompanied or accompanied by his or her parents or by any other person, receive appropriate protection and humanitarian assistance in the enjoyment of applicable rights set forth in the present Convention and in other international human rights or humanitarian instruments to which the said States are Parties.

2. For this purpose, States Parties shall provide, as they consider appropriate, co-operation in any efforts by the United Nations and other competent intergovernmental organizations or non-governmental organizations co-operating with the United Nations to protect and assist such a child and to trace the parents or other members of the family of any refugee child in order to

obtain information necessary for reunification with his or her family. In cases where no parents or other members of the family can be found, the child shall be accorded the same protection as any other child permanently or temporarily deprived of his or her family environment for any reason, as set forth in the present Convention.

13.2.2   Procedural safeguards

Determination of status is clearly a legal evaluation and thus the process must be in accordance with the prescribed law. Appropriate safeguards such as appeals and reconsiderations of initial denials of status are an integral part of the process. This can take time. Some States detain asylum seekers or at least restrict their freedom of movement and access to full rights and liberties pending determination of status. In such instances, the relevant procedures must be undertaken promptly and fairly to minimise further trauma for the refugee. Inevitably, problems arise when the alacrity of the decision-making process is lacking. Detaining asylum seekers for long periods of time while investigations are undertaken is problematic as the following case demonstrates. In spite of this, States are entitled to verify the details in the application of the refugee to determine the validity of their claims and thus the appropriateness of recognising refugee status.

A. v *Australia*, Communication 560/1993, Human Rights Committee. UN Doc. CCPR/C/59/D/560/1993

A Cambodian national arrived in Australia with his family by boat and shortly thereafter sought recognition of refugee status. His application was formally rejected. Various appeals were lodged.

3.3 It is contended that the State party's policy of detaining boat people is inappropriate, unjustified and arbitrary, as its principal purpose is to deter other boat people from coming to Australia, and to deter those already in the country from continuing with applications for refugee status. The application of the new legislation is said to amount to 'human deterrence', based on the practice of rigidly detaining asylum-seekers under such conditions and for periods so prolonged that prospective asylum-seekers are deterred from even applying for refugee status, and current asylum-seekers lose all hope and return home. . . .

9.1 The Human Rights Committee has examined the present communication in the light of all the information placed before it by the parties, as it is required to do under article 5, paragraph 1, of the Optional Protocol to the Covenant. Three questions are to be determined on their merits:

(a) whether the prolonged detention of the author, pending determination of his entitlement to refugee status, was 'arbitrary' within the meaning of article 9, paragraph 1;

(b) whether the alleged impossibility to challenge the lawfulness of the author's detention and his alleged lack of access to legal advice was in violation of article 9, paragraph 4 . . .

9.2 On the first question, the Committee recalls that the notion of 'arbitrariness' must not be equated with 'against the law' but be interpreted more broadly to include such elements as inappropriateness and injustice. Furthermore, remand in custody could be considered arbitrary if it is not necessary in all the circumstances of the case, for example to prevent flight or interference with evidence: the element of proportionality becomes relevant in this context. The State party however, seeks to justify the author's detention by the fact that he entered Australia unlawfully and by the perceived incentive for the applicant to abscond if left in liberty. The question for the Committee is whether these grounds are sufficient to justify indefinite and prolonged detention.

9.3 The Committee agrees that there is no basis for the author's claim that it is *per se* arbitrary to detain individuals requesting asylum. Nor can it find any support for the contention that there is a rule of customary international law which would render all such detention arbitrary.

9.4 The Committee observes however, that every decision to keep a person in detention should be open to review periodically so that the grounds justifying the detention can be assessed. In any event, detention should not continue beyond the period for which the State can provide appropriate justification. For example, the fact of illegal entry may indicate a need for investigation and there may be other factors particular to the individuals, such as the likelihood of absconding and lack of cooperation, which may justify detention for a period. Without such factors detention may be considered arbitrary, even if entry was illegal. In the instant case, the State party has not advanced any grounds particular to the author's case, which would justify his continued detention for a period of four years, during which he was shifted around between different detention centres. The Committee therefore concludes that the author's detention for a period of over four years was arbitrary within the meaning of article 9, paragraph 1.

9.5 The Committee observes that the author could, in principle, have applied to the court for review of the grounds of his detention before the enactment of the Migration Amendment Act of 5 May 1992; after that date, the domestic courts retained that power with a view to ordering the release of a person if they found the detention to be unlawful under Australian law. In effect, however, the courts' control and power to order the release of an individual was limited to an assessment of whether this individual was a 'designated person' within the meaning of the Migration Amendment Act. If the criteria for such determination were met, the courts had no power to review the continued detention of an individual and to order his/her release. In the Committee's opinion, court review of the lawfulness of detention under article 9, paragraph 4, which must include the possibility of ordering release, is not limited to mere compliance of the detention with domestic law. While domestic legal systems may institute differing methods for ensuring court review of administrative detention, what is decisive for the purposes of article 9, paragraph 4, is that such review is, in its effects, real and not merely formal. By stipulating that the court must have the power to order release 'if the detention is not lawful', article 9, paragraph 4, requires that the court be empowered to order release, if the detention is incompatible with the requirements in article 9, paragraph 1, or in other provisions of the Covenant. This conclusion is supported by article 9, paragraph 5, which obviously governs the granting of compensation for detention that is 'unlawful' either under the terms of domestic law or within the meaning of the Covenant. As the State party's submissions in the instant case show that court review available to A was, in fact, limited to a formal assessment of the self-evident fact that he was indeed a 'designated person' within the meaning of the Migration Amendment Act, the Committee concludes that the author's right, under article 9, paragraph 4, to have his detention reviewed by a court, was violated.

9.6 As regards the author's claim that article 9, paragraph 4, encompasses a right to legal assistance in order to have access to the courts, the Committee notes from the material before it that the author was entitled to legal assistance from the day he requested asylum and would have had access to it, had he requested it. Indeed, the author was informed on 9 December 1989, in the attachment to the form he signed on that day, of his right to legal assistance. This form was read in its entirety to him in Kampuchean, his own language, by a certified interpreter. That the author did not avail himself of this possibility at that point in time cannot be held against the State party. Subsequently (as of 13 September 1990), the author sought legal advice and received legal assistance whenever requesting it. That A was moved repeatedly between detention centres and was obliged to change his legal representatives cannot detract from the fact that he retained access to legal advisers; that this access was inconvenient, notably because of the remote location of Port Hedland, does not, in the Committee's opinion, raise an issue under article 9, paragraph 4.

Question

To what extent do the proposed process guidelines adequately guarantee the rights of potential refugees? Do Australian practicalities comply with the guidelines?

Note also that refugees enjoy the same rights as nationals of a State with respect to administrative and legal matters. Therefore, they are entitled to fair access to courts and equality of treatment in legal affairs.

United Nations Convention relating to the Status of Refugees 1951

Article 15—Right of association

As regards non-political and non-profit-making associations and trade unions the Contracting States shall accord to refugees lawfully staying in their territory the most favourable treatment accorded to nationals of a foreign country, in the same circumstances.

Article 16—Access to courts

1. A refugee shall have free access to the courts of law on the territory of all Contracting States.

2. A refugee shall enjoy in the Contracting State in which he has his habitual residence the same treatment as a national in matters pertaining to access to the courts, including legal assistance and exemption from *cautio judicatum solvi*.

3. A refugee shall be accorded in the matters referred to in paragraph 2 in countries other than that in which he has his habitual residence the treatment granted to a national of the country of his habitual residence. . . .

Article 29—Fiscal charges

1. The Contracting States shall not impose upon refugees duties, charges or taxes, of any description whatsoever, other or higher than those which are or may be levied on their nationals in similar situations.

2. Nothing in the above paragraph shall prevent the application to refugees of the laws and regulations concerning charges in respect of the issue to aliens of administrative documents including identity papers.

13.3   TERMINATION OF REFUGEE STATUS

Refugee status is not indefinite. The United Nations Convention itself addresses the circumstances in which refugee status ceases to be applicable in Art 1 C(1)–(6), frequently referred to as the cessation clauses.

United Nations Convention relating to the Status of Refugees 1951 Art 1

C. This Convention shall cease to apply to any person falling under the terms of section A if:

(1) He has voluntarily re-availed himself of the protection of the country of his nationality; or

(2) Having lost his nationality, he has voluntarily reacquired it; or

(3) He has acquired a new nationality, and enjoys the protection of the country of his new nationality; or

(4) He has voluntarily re-established himself in the country which he left or outside which he remained owing to fear of persecution; or

(5) He can no longer, because the circumstances in connection with which he has been recognized as a refugee have ceased to exist, continue to refuse to avail himself of the protection of the country of his nationality;

Provided that this paragraph shall not apply to a refugee falling under section A (1) of this article who is able to invoke compelling reasons arising out of previous persecution for refusing to avail himself of the protection of the country of nationality;

(6) Being a person who has no nationality he is, because the circumstances in connection with which he has been recognized as a refugee have ceased to exist, able to return to the country of his former habitual residence;

> Provided that this paragraph shall not apply to a refugee falling under section A (1) of this article who is able to invoke compelling reasons arising out of previous persecution for refusing to return to the country of his former habitual residence.

Essentially once refugee status is declared, the individual is protected unless, and until, one of the above clauses is invoked. The purpose of this is to offer protection to the individual and a guarantee that affirmed status as a refugee will not be constantly subject to re-evaluation thereby creating fear and uncertainty. Further elaboration on the scope of the clauses can be found in paras 111–139 of the *UNHCR's Handbook on Procedures and Criteria for Determining Refugee Status*.

See also the provisions of the Convention concerning removing refugee status.

United Nations Convention relating to the Status of Refugees 1951
Article 31—Refugees unlawfully in the country of refuge

1. The Contracting States shall not impose penalties, on account of their illegal entry or presence, on refugees who, coming directly from a territory where their life or freedom was threatened in the sense of article 1, enter or are present in their territory without authorization, provided they present themselves without delay to the authorities and show good cause for their illegal entry or presence.

2. The Contracting States shall not apply to the movements of such refugees restrictions other than those which are necessary and such restrictions shall only be applied until their status in the country is regularized or they obtain admission into another country. The Contracting States shall allow such refugees a reasonable period and all the necessary facilities to obtain admission into another country.

Article 32—Expulsion

1. The Contracting States shall not expel a refugee lawfully in their territory save on grounds of national security or public order.

2. The expulsion of such a refugee shall be only in pursuance of a decision reached in accordance with due process of law. Except where compelling reasons of national security otherwise require, the refugee shall be allowed to submit evidence to clear himself, and to appeal to and be represented for the purpose before competent authority or a person or persons specially designated by the competent authority.

3. The Contracting States shall allow such a refugee a reasonable period within which to seek legal admission into another country. The Contracting States reserve the right to apply during that period such internal measures as they may deem necessary.

Article 33—Prohibition of expulsion or return ('refoulement')

1. No Contracting State shall expel or return ('refouler') a refugee in any manner whatsoever to the frontiers of territories where his life or freedom would be threatened on account of his race, religion, nationality, membership of a particular social group or political opinion.

2. The benefit of the present provision may not, however, be claimed by a refugee whom there are reasonable grounds for regarding as a danger to the security of the country in which he is, or who, having been convicted by a final judgement of a particularly serious crime, constitutes a danger to the community of that country.

Article 34—Naturalization

The Contracting States shall as far as possible facilitate the assimilation and naturalization of refugees. They shall in particular make every effort to expedite naturalization proceedings and to reduce as far as possible the charges and costs of such proceedings.

Question

Do the provisions of the Convention adequately balance the rights of refugees with the right of the State to ensure protection of its territorial integrity, and preserve its national security?

Note that States cannot forcibly return refugees to a State in which they will face torture and other treatment prohibited by international human rights treaties. This is linked to the positive obligations which States undertake when accepting human rights treaties—this positive obligation is discussed in relation to extradition and deportation in Chapter 2.

Additional provisions on torture and other inhuman and degrading treatment or punishment are also of relevance in this regard:

United Nations Convention against Torture Art 3

1. No State Party shall expel, return ('*refouler*') or extradite a person to another State where there are substantial grounds for believing that he would be in danger of being subjected to torture.

2. For the purpose of determining whether there are such grounds, the competent authorities shall take into account all relevant considerations including, where applicable, the existence in the State concerned of a consistent pattern of gross, flagrant or mass violations of human rights.

This is corroborated by the United Nations Human Rights Committee in its general recommendations on Torture.

General Comment 20 (1992): UN Doc. A/47/40 (1992) 193 at para 9

9. In the view of the Committee, States parties must not expose individuals to the danger of torture or cruel, inhuman or degrading treatment or punishment upon return to another country by way of their extradition, expulsion or *refoulement*. States parties should indicate in their reports what measures they have adopted to that end.

Employing provisions on torture offers a further avenue for complaint for asylum seekers. If seeking refuge in a State which has ratified the provisions, there is the potential for an individual communication or complaint to the relevant international or regional bodies. These support and consolidate the provisions of the 1951 Refugee Convention. Given that the prohibition on torture is arguably *Jus cogens* (see Chapter 1) then of course arguably every State should refrain from torture and the issue should not arise. More pertinently, no State should send an individual back to a territory in which they may suffer from torture. As regards the use of the communications and complaints provisions, the following case provides an illustration.

Mutombo v Switzerland, Communication 13/1993, Committee Against Torture UN Doc. CAT/C/12/D/13/1993

The author of the communication had entered Italy using a friend's passport, then illegally entered Switzerland and applied for recognition of refugee status in Switzerland. He claimed that a real risk of torture would ensue if he was deported to Zaire following rejection of his application. The reasons for this are explained in the complaint.

2.1 The author states that he has been a member of the Zairian Armed Forces since 1982. In 1988, he clandestinely became a member of the political movement Union pour la démocratie et le progrès social (UDPS), as he felt discriminated against because of his ethnic background (Luba). His father had been a member of the movement since its launch in 1982 and was allegedly forced to retire as a magistrate at the Kinshasa Magistrate's Court (Tribunal de Grande Instance) because of that affiliation. The author participated in several demonstrations and attended illegal meetings.

2.2 On 20 June 1989, the author was arrested by three members of the Division Spéciale Présidentielle, when he was about to deliver a letter from his father to Mr. Etienne Tshisekedi, a founding member and leader of UDPS. He was detained in the military camp of Tshatsi, where he was locked up in a cell of one square metre. During the four days that followed, he was tortured by his interrogators, whom he mentions by name. He was subjected to electric shocks, beaten with a rifle, and his testicles were bruised until he lost consciousness. On 24 June 1989, he was brought before a military tribunal, found guilty of conspiracy against the State and sentenced to 15 years' imprisonment. He was transferred to the military prison of Ndolo, where he was detained for seven months. Although the author had lost part of his eyesight and suffered a head injury caused by the torture, he was not given any medical treatment. On 20 January 1990, he was released under the condition that he present himself twice a week at the Auditorat militaire of Mantete. In February 1990, he sought medical treatment for his eye injury at the General Hospital Mama Yemo. . . .

3.1 The author claims that a real risk exists that he would be subjected to torture or that his security would be endangered if he were to be returned to his country. It is submitted that evidence exists that there is a consistent pattern of gross and massive violations of human rights in Zaire, which, according to article 3, paragraph 2, of the Convention against Torture, are circumstances which a State party should take into account when deciding on expulsion. The author contends that on this basis alone the Swiss authorities should refrain from expelling him. . . .

9.1 . . . The issue before the Committee is whether the expulsion or return of the author of the communication to Zaire would violate the obligation of Switzerland under article 3 of the Convention not to expel or return a person to another State where there are substantial grounds for believing that he would be in danger of being subjected to torture.

9.2 The Committee is aware of the concerns of the State party that the implementation of article 3 of the Convention might be abused by asylum seekers. The Committee considers that, even if there are doubts about the facts adduced by the author, it must ensure that his security is not endangered.

9.3 . . . The Committee must decide, pursuant to paragraph 1 of article 3, whether there are substantial grounds for believing that Mr. Mutombo would be in danger of being subjected to torture. In reaching this conclusion, the Committee must take into account all relevant considerations, pursuant to paragraph 2 of article 3, including the existence of a consistent pattern of gross, flagrant or mass violations of human rights. The aim of the determination, however, is to establish whether the individual concerned would be personally at risk of being subjected to torture in the country to which he would return. It follows that the existence of a consistent pattern of gross, flagrant or mass violations of human rights in a country does not as such constitute a sufficient ground for determining that a person would be in danger of being subjected to torture upon his return to that country; additional grounds must exist that indicate that the individual concerned would be personally at risk. Similarly, the absence of a consistent pattern of gross violations of human rights does not mean that a person cannot be considered to be in danger of being subjected to torture in his specific circumstances.

9.4 The Committee considers that in the present case substantial grounds exist for believing that the author would be in danger of being subjected to torture. The Committee has noted the author's ethnic background, alleged political affiliation and detention history as well as the fact, which has not been disputed by the State party, that he appears to have deserted from the army and to have left Zaire in a clandestine manner and, when formulating an application for asylum, to have adduced arguments which may be considered defamatory towards Zaire. The Committee considers that, in the present circumstances, his return to Zaire would have the foreseeable and necessary consequence of exposing him to a real risk of being detained and tortured. Moreover, the belief that 'substantial grounds' exist within the meaning of article 3, paragraph 1, is strengthened by 'the existence in the State concerned of a consistent pattern of gross, flagrant or mass violations of human rights', within the meaning of article 3, paragraph 2. . . .

9.6 Moreover, the Committee considers that, in view of the fact that Zaire is not a party to the Convention, the author would be in danger, in the event of expulsion to Zaire, not only of being subjected to torture but of no longer having the legal possibility of applying to the Committee for protection.

9.7 The Committee therefore concludes that the expulsion or return of the author to Zaire in the prevailing circumstances would constitute a violation of article 3 of the Convention against Torture and Other Cruel, Inhuman or Degrading Treatment or Punishment.

Previously, the special position of children of refugees and refugee children has been mentioned. Special consideration must be given to children when termination of status as a refugee may affect the family relationship.

United Nations Convention on the Rights of the Child Art 9

1. States Parties shall ensure that a child shall not be separated from his or her parents against their will, except when competent authorities subject to judicial review determine, in accordance with applicable law and procedures, that such separation is necessary for the best interests of the child. Such determination may be necessary in a particular case such as one involving abuse or neglect of the child by the parents, or one where the parents are living separately and a decision must be made as to the child's place of residence.

2. In any proceedings pursuant to paragraph 1 of the present article, all interested parties shall be given an opportunity to participate in the proceedings and make their views known.

3. States Parties shall respect the right of the child who is separated from one or both parents to maintain personal relations and direct contact with both parents on a regular basis, except if it is contrary to the child's best interests.

4. Where such separation results from any action initiated by a State Party, such as the detention, imprisonment, exile, deportation or death (including death arising from any cause while the person is in the custody of the State) of one or both parents or of the child, that State Party shall, upon request, provide the parents, the child or, if appropriate, another member of the family with the essential information concerning the whereabouts of the absent member(s) of the family unless the provision of the information would be detrimental to the well-being of the child. States Parties shall further ensure that the submission of such a request shall of itself entail no adverse consequences for the person(s) concerned.

However, note that although children are a relevant consideration, they are not the sole determinative factor. The mere presence of a child cannot automatically mean that refugee status cannot be terminated.

Karker v France, Communication 833/1998, Human Rights Committee UN Doc. CCPR/C/70/D/833/1998

The salient facts are explained by the Human Rights Committee in their opinion:

2.1 In 1987, Mr. Karker, who is co-founder of the political movement Ennahdha, fled Tunisia, where he had been sentenced to death by trial *in absentia*. In 1988, the French authorities recognized him as a political refugee. On 11 October 1993, under suspicion that he actively supported a terrorist movement, the Minister of the Interior ordered him expelled from French territory as a matter of urgency. The expulsion order was not, however, enforced, and instead Mr. Karker was ordered to compulsory residence in the department of Finistère. On 6 November 1993, Mr. Karker appealed the orders to the Administrative Tribunal of Paris. The Tribunal rejected his appeals on 16 December 1994, considering that the orders were lawful. The Tribunal considered that from the information before it, it appeared that the Ministry of the Interior was in possession of information showing that Mr. Karker maintained close links with Islamic organizations which use violent methods, and that in the light of the situation in France the Minister could have concluded legally that Mr. Karker's expulsion was imperative for reasons of public security. It also considered that the resulting interference with Mr. Karker's family life was justifiable for reasons of *ordre public*. The Tribunal considered that the compulsory residence order, issued by the Minister in order to allow Mr. Karker to find a third country willing to receive him, was lawful . . . in view of the fact that Mr. Karker was a recognized political refugee and could not be returned to Tunisia. On 29 December 1997, the Council of State rejected Mr. Karker's further appeal.

2.2 Following the orders, Mr. Karker was placed in a hotel in the department of Finistère, then he was transferred to Brest. Allegedly because of media pressure, he was then transferred to St. Julien in the Loire area, and from there to Cayres, and subsequently to the South East of France. Lastly, in October 1995, he was assigned to Digne-les-Bains (Alpes de Haute Provence), where he has resided since. According to the order fixing the conditions of his residence in Digne-les-Bains, Mr. Karker is required to report to the police once a day. The author emphasizes that her husband has not been brought before the courts in connection with the suspicions against him.

2.3 The author states that she lives in Paris with her six children, a thousand kilometres away from her husband. She states that it is difficult to maintain personal contact with her husband. On 3 April 1998, Mr. Karker was sentenced to a suspended sentence of six months' imprisonment for having breached the compulsory residence order by staying with his family during three weeks. . . .

9.2. The Committee notes that Mr. Karker's expulsion was ordered in October 1993, but that his expulsion could not be enforced, following which his residence in France was subjected to restrictions of his freedom of movement. The State party has argued that the restrictions to which the author is subjected are necessary for reasons of national security. In this respect, the State party produced evidence to the domestic courts that Mr. Karker was an active supporter of a movement which advocates violent action. It should also be noted that the restrictions of movement on Mr. Karker allowed him to reside in a comparatively wide area. Moreover, the restrictions on Mr. Karker's freedom of movement were examined by the domestic courts which, after reviewing all the evidence, held them to be necessary for reasons of national security. Mr. Karker has only challenged the courts' original decision on this question and chose not to challenge the necessity of subsequent restriction orders before the domestic courts. In these circumstances, the Committee is of the view that the materials before it do not allow it to conclude that the State party has misapplied the restrictions in article 12, paragraph 3.

9.3 The Committee observes that article 13 of the Covenant provides procedural guarantees in case of expulsion. The Committee notes that Mr. Karker's expulsion was decided by the Minister of the Interior for urgent reasons of public security, and that Mr. Karker was therefore not allowed to submit reasons against his expulsion before the order was issued. He did, however, have the opportunity to have his case reviewed by the Administrative Tribunal and the Council of State, and at both procedures he was represented by counsel. The Committee concludes that the facts before it do not show that article 13 has been violated in the present case.

Question

What practical options are open to a State which considers a refugee a threat to national security but realises that returning the refugee to his or her State of origin is not compatible with obligations under international human rights?

13.4 REGIONAL INSTRUMENTS AND CRITERIA FOR DETERMINING REFUGEE STATUS AND ADDRESSING REFUGEE RIGHTS

Much of the criteria enshrined in the various regional instruments on refugees reflect that of the 1951 Refugee Convention. Elements of the European Union's provisions have been discussed above. However, Africa and the Americas have also addressed issues concerning refugees, Africa in a binding treaty which entered into force in 1974. Regional instruments generally post-date the United Nations Convention.

13.4.1 The Americas

Within the Americas, the first regional instrument on asylum was adopted in 1889 (the Montevideo Treaty on International Criminal Law which addressed issue of asylum). A Caracas Convention on Territorial Asylum followed in 1954.

Organization of American States Convention on Territorial Asylum 1954

The governments of the Member States of the Organization of American States, desirous of concluding a Convention regarding Territorial Asylum, have agreed to the following articles:

Article I

Every State has the right, in the exercise of its sovereignty, to admit into its territory such persons as it deems advisable, without, through the exercise of this right, giving rise to complaint by any other State.

Article II

The respect which, according to international law, is due the Jurisdictional right of each State over the inhabitants in its territory, is equally due, without any restriction whatsoever, to that which it has over persons who enter it proceeding from a State in which they are persecuted for their beliefs, opinions, or political affiliations, or for acts which may be considered as political offenses. Any violation of sovereignty that consists of acts committed by a government or its agents in another State against the life or security of an individual, carried out on the territory of another State, may not be considered attenuated because the persecution began outside its boundaries or is due to political considerations or reasons of state.

Article III

No State is under the obligation to surrender to another State, or to expel from its own territory, persons persecuted for political reasons or offenses.

Article IV

The right of extradition is not applicable in connection with persons who, in accordance with the qualifications of the solicited State, are sought for political offenses, or for common offenses committed for political ends, or when extradition is solicited for predominantly political motives.

Article V

The fact that a person has entered into the territorial Jurisdiction of a State surreptitiously or irregularly does not affect the provisions of this Convention.

Article VI

Without prejudice to the provisions of the following articles, no State is under the obligation to establish any distinction in its legislation, or in its regulations or administrative acts applicable to aliens, solely because of the fact that they are political asylees or refugees.

Article VII

Freedom of expression of thought, recognized by domestic law for all inhabitants of a State, may not be ground of complaint by a third State on the basis of opinions expressed publicly against it or its government by asylees or refugees, except when these concepts constitute systematic propaganda through which they incite to the use of force or violence against the government of the complaining State.

Article VIII

No State has the right to request that another State restrict for the political asylees or refugees the freedom of assembly or association which the latter State's internal legislation grants to all aliens within its territory, unless such assembly or association has as its purpose fomenting the use of force or violence against the government of the soliciting State.

Article IX

At the request of the interested State, the State that has granted refuge or asylum shall take steps to keep watch over, or to intern at a reasonable distance from its border, those political refugees or asylees who are notorious leaders of a subversive movement, as well as those against whom there is evidence that they are disposed to join it.

Determination of the reasonable distance from the border, for the purpose of internment, shall depend upon the judgment of the authorities of the State of refuge.

All expenses incurred as a result of the internment of political asylees and refugees shall be chargeable to the State that makes the request.

Article X

The political internees referred to in the preceding article shall advise the government of the host State whenever they wish to leave its territory. Departure therefrom will be granted, under the condition that they are not to go to the country from which they came; and the interested government is to be notified.

Article XI

In all cases in which a complaint or request is permissible in accordance with this Convention, the admissibility of evidence presented by the demanding State shall depend on the judgment of the solicited State.

The current Central American text is the 1984 Cartagena Declaration. Note this is not legally binding.

Cartagena Declaration on Refugees, Colloquium on the International Protection of Refugees in Central America, Mexico and Panama 1984

3. To reiterate that, in view of the experience gained from the massive flows of refugees in the Central American area, it is necessary to consider enlarging the concept of a refugee, bearing in mind, as far as appropriate and in the light of the situation prevailing in the region, the precedent of the OAU Convention (article 1, paragraph 2) and the doctrine employed in the reports of the Inter-American Commission on Human Rights. Hence the definition or concept of a refugee to be recommended for use in the region is one which, in addition to containing the elements of the 1951 Convention and the 1967 Protocol, includes among refugees persons who have fled their country because their lives, safety or freedom have been threatened by generalized violence, foreign aggression, internal conflicts, massive violation of human rights or other circumstances which have seriously disturbed public order. . . .

9. To express its concern at the situation of displaced persons within their own countries. In this connection, the Colloquium calls on national authorities and the competent international organizations to offer protection and assistance to those persons and to help relieve the hardship which many of them face.

10. To call on States parties to the 1969 American Convention on Human Rights to apply this instrument in dealing with *asilados* and refugees who are in their territories.

13.4.2   Africa

An African Convention was specifically adopted to address the growing issue of refugees in Africa. As the preamble notes, there were increasing numbers of refugees in Africa and there was growing unease about those abusing the concept of refugee status by deploying its protection for subversive reasons. Given the number of civil conflicts in this region and the presence of trans-frontier guerrilla groups in some areas, this concern is founded. See also the Khartoum Declaration on Africa's Refugee Crisis, OAU Doc. BR/COM/XV/55.90 (1990).

OAU Convention Governing the Specific Aspects of Refugee Problems in Africa 1969

Article I

Definition of the term 'Refugee'

1. For the purposes of this Convention, the term 'refugee' shall mean every person who, owing to well-founded fear of being persecuted for reasons of race, religion, nationality, membership of a particular social group or political opinion, is outside the country of his nationality and is unable or, owing to such fear, is unwilling to avail himself of the protection of that country, or who, not having a nationality and being outside the country of his former habitual residence as a result of such events is unable or, owing to such fear, is unwilling to return to it.

2. The term 'refugee' shall also apply to every person who, owing to external aggression, occupation, foreign domination or events seriously disturbing public order in either part or the whole of his country of origin or nationality, is compelled to leave his place of habitual residence in order to seek refuge in another place outside his country of origin or nationality.

3. In the case of a person who has several nationalities, the term 'a country of which he is a national' shall mean each of the countries of which he is a national, and a person shall not be deemed to be lacking the protection of the country of which he is a national if, without any valid reason based on well-founded fear, he has not availed himself of the protection of one of the countries of which he is a national.

4. This Convention shall cease to apply to any refugee if: (a) he has voluntarily re-availed himself of the protection of the country of his nationality, or, (b) having lost his nationality, he has voluntarily reacquired it, or, (c) he has acquired a new nationality, and enjoys the protection of the country of his new nationality, or, (d) he has voluntarily re-established himself in the country which he left or outside which he remained owing to fear of persecution, or, (e) he can no longer, because the circumstances in connection with which he was recognized as a refugee have ceased to exist, continue to refuse to avail himself of the protection of the country of his nationality, or, (f) he has committed a serious non-political crime outside his country of refuge after his admission to that country as a refugee, or, (g) he has seriously infringed the purposes and objectives of this Convention.

5. The provisions of this Convention shall not apply to any person with respect to whom the country of asylum has serious reasons for considering that: (a) he has committed a crime against peace, a war crime, or a crime against humanity, as defined in the international instruments drawn up to make provision in respect of such crimes; (b) he committed a serious non-political crime outside the country of refuge prior to his admission to that country as a refugee; (c) he has been guilty of acts contrary to the purposes and principles of the Organization of African Unity; (d) he has been guilty of acts contrary to the purposes and principles of the United Nations.

6. For the purposes of this Convention, the Contracting State of Asylum shall determine whether an applicant is a refugee.

Article 2

Asylum

1. Member States of the OAU shall use their best endeavours consistent with their respective legislations to receive refugees and to secure the settlement of those refugees who, for well-founded reasons, are unable or unwilling to return to their country of origin or nationality.

2. The grant of asylum to refugees is a peaceful and humanitarian act and shall not be regarded as an unfriendly act by any Member State.

3. No person shall be subjected by a Member State to measures such as rejection at the frontier, return or expulsion, which would compel him to return to or remain in a territory where his life, physical integrity or liberty would be threatened for the reasons set out in Article I, paragraphs I and 2.

4. Where a Member State finds difficulty in continuing to grant asylum to refugees, such Member State may appeal directly to other Member States and through the OAU, and such other Member States shall in the spirit of African solidarity and international co-operation take appropriate measures to lighten the burden of the Member State granting asylum.

5. Where a refugee has not received the right to reside in any country of asylum, he may be granted temporary residence in any country of asylum in which he first presented himself as a refugee pending arrangement for his resettlement in accordance with the preceding paragraph.

6. For reasons of security, countries of asylum shall, as far as possible, settle refugees at a reasonable distance from the frontier of their country of origin.

Question

Are there any differences between the 1951 UN Convention and the regional criteria and approaches outlined above?

13.5 RIGHTS OF REFUGEES

Once refugee status is established, a range of rights are guaranteed to the refugee. In general, these rights reflect those basic rights ascribed to all individuals. In particular, the rights are similar to those guaranteed as a minimum standard of treatment to aliens. The current international law on the standard of treatment to be accorded to aliens is found in the 'Declaration on the Human Rights of Individuals Who are not Nationals of the Country in which They Live', which was adopted by General Assembly Resolution 40/144 of 13 December 1985. The rights therein codify elements of existing customary international law.

United Nations General Assembly Declaration on the Human Rights of Individuals Who are not Nationals of the Country in which They Live 1985

Article 1

For the purposes of this Declaration, the term 'alien' shall apply, with due regard to qualifications made in subsequent articles, to any individual who is not a national of the State in which he or she is present. . . .

Article 5

1. Aliens shall enjoy, in accordance with domestic law and subject to the relevant international obligations of the State in which they are present, in particular the following rights:

(a) The right to life and security of person; no alien shall be subjected to arbitrary arrest or detention; no alien shall be deprived of his or her liberty except on such grounds and in accordance with such procedures as are established by law;

(b) The right to protection against arbitrary or unlawful interference with privacy, family, home or correspondence;

(c) The right to be equal before the courts, tribunals and all other organs and authorities administering justice and, when necessary, to free assistance of an interpreter in criminal proceedings and, when prescribed by law, other proceedings;

(d) The right to choose a spouse, to marry, to found a family;

(e) The right to freedom of thought, opinion, conscience and religion; the right to manifest their religion or beliefs, subject only to such limitations as are prescribed by law and are necessary to protect public safety, order, health or morals or the fundamental rights and freedoms of others;

(f) The right to retain their own language, culture and tradition;

(g) The right to transfer abroad earnings, savings or other personal monetary assets, subject to domestic currency regulations.

2. Subject to such restrictions as are prescribed by law and which are necessary in a democratic society to protect national security, public safety, public order, public health or morals or the rights and freedoms of others, and which are consistent with the other rights recognized in the relevant international instruments and those set forth in this Declaration, aliens shall enjoy the following rights:

(a) The right to leave the country;

(b) The right to freedom of expression;

(c) The right to peaceful assembly;

(d) The right to own property alone as well as in association with others, subject to domestic law.

3. Subject to the provisions referred to in paragraph 2, aliens lawfully in the territory of a State shall enjoy the right to liberty of movement and freedom to choose their residence within the borders of the State.

4. Subject to national legislation and due authorization, the spouse and minor or dependent children of an alien lawfully residing in the territory of a State shall be admitted to accompany, join and stay with the alien.

Article 6

No alien shall be subjected to torture or to cruel, inhuman or degrading treatment or punishment and, in particular, no alien shall be subjected without his or her free consent to medical or scientific experimentation.

Article 7

An alien lawfully in the territory of a State may be expelled therefrom only in pursuance of a decision reached in accordance with law and shall, except where compelling reasons of national security otherwise require, be allowed to submit the reasons why he or she should not be expelled and to have the case reviewed by, and be represented for the purpose before, the competent authority or a person or persons specially designated by the competent authority. Individual or collective expulsion of such aliens on grounds of race, colour, religion, culture, descent or national or ethnic origin is prohibited.

Article 8

1. Aliens lawfully residing in the territory of a State shall also enjoy, in accordance with the national laws, the following rights, subject to their obligations under article 4:

(a) The right to safe and healthy working conditions, to fair wages and equal remuneration for work of equal value without distinction of any kind, in particular, women being guaranteed conditions of work not inferior to those enjoyed by men, with equal pay for equal work;

(b) The right to join trade unions and other organizations or associations of their choice and to participate in their activities. No restrictions may be placed on the exercise of this right other than those prescribed by law and which are necessary, in a democratic society, in the interests of national security or public order or for the protection of the rights and freedoms of others;

(c) The right to health protection, medical care, social security, social services, education, rest and leisure, provided that they fulfil the requirements under the relevant regulations for participation and that undue strain is not placed on the resources of the State.

2. With a view to protecting the rights of aliens carrying on lawful paid activities in the country in which they are present, such rights may be specified by the Governments concerned in multi-lateral or bilateral conventions.

Article 9

No alien shall be arbitrarily deprived of his or her lawfully acquired assets. . . .

13.5.1 Refugees as aliens

As is apparent, aliens are entitled to civil, political, economic, social and cultural rights. These are arguably the range of rights which are most fundamental to all. So to the rights accorded to refugees. Unsurprisingly, refugees are entitled to a similar range of civil, political, economic and social rights—see the text of the 1951 Convention for details.

United Nations Convention relating to the Status of Refugees 1951
Article 12.—Personal status

1. The personal status of a refugee shall be governed by the law of the country of his domicile or, if he has no domicile, by the law of the country of his residence.

2. Rights previously acquired by a refugee and dependent on personal status, more particularly rights attaching to marriage, shall be respected by a Contracting State, subject to compliance, if this be necessary, with the formalities required by the law of that State, provided that the right in question is one which would have been recognized by the law of that State had he not become a refugee.

Article 13.—Movable and immovable property

The Contracting States shall accord to a refugee treatment as favourable as possible and, in any event, not less favourable than that accorded to aliens generally in the same circumstances, as regards the acquisition of movable and immovable property and other rights pertaining thereto, and to leases and other contracts relating to movable and immovable property.

Article 14.—Artistic rights and industrial property

In respect of the protection of industrial property, such as inventions, designs or models, trade marks, trade names, and of rights in literary, artistic and scientific works, a refugee shall be accorded in the country in which he has his habitual residence the same protection as is accorded to nationals of that country. In the territory of any other Contracting States, he shall be accorded the same protection as is accorded in that territory to nationals of the country in which he has his habitual residence.

Note the references to refugees being treated in a manner similar to aliens.

Question

Given that refugees may influx in greater numbers than aliens, what impact do the rights enshrined in the Refugee Convention have on the resources of States?

13.5.2   Equality of treatment and towards subsistence

In other matters, refugees are entitled to the same treatment as nationals of the host member State. When considering the following elements of the United Nations Convention, consider in particular the extent to which these rights provide measured relief for a State inundated with refugees.

United Nations Convention relating to the Status of Refugees 1951
Article 17.—Wage-earning employment

1. The Contracting States shall accord to refugees lawfully staying in their territory the most favourable treatment accorded to nationals of a foreign country in the same circumstances, as regards the right to engage in wage-earning employment.

2. In any case, restrictive measures imposed on aliens or the employment of aliens for the protection of the national labour market shall not be applied to a refugee who was already exempt from them at the date of entry into force of this Convention for the Contracting State concerned, or who fulfils one of the following conditions:

(a) He has completed three years' residence in the country;

(b) He has a spouse possessing the nationality of the country of residence. A refugee may not invoke the benefit of this provision if he has abandoned his spouse;

(c) He has one or more children possessing the nationality of the country of residence.

3. The Contracting States shall give sympathetic consideration to assimilating the rights of all refugees with regard to wage-earning employment to those of nationals, and in particular of those refugees who have entered their territory pursuant to programmes of labour recruitment or under immigration schemes.

Article 18.—Self-employment

The Contracting States shall accord to a refugee lawfully in their territory treatment as favourable as possible and, in any event, not less favourable than that accorded to aliens generally in the same circumstances, as regards the right to engage on his own account in agriculture, industry, handicrafts and commerce and to establish commercial and industrial companies.

Article 19.—Liberal professions

1. Each Contracting State shall accord to refugees lawfully staying in their territory who hold diplomas recognized by the competent authorities of that State, and who are desirous of practising a liberal profession, treatment as favourable as possible and, in any event, not less favourable than that accorded to aliens generally in the same circumstances.

2. The Contracting States shall use their best endeavours consistently with their laws and constitutions to secure the settlement of such refugees in the territories, other than the metropolitan territory, for whose international relations they are responsible.

In general, the Convention focuses on non-discrimination. Given that refugees are already vulnerable, the tenor of the Convention is to prevent further disadvantages by ensuring that refugees are treated in a manner similar to nationals with respect to basic necessities.

United Nations Convention relating to the Status of Refugees 1951

Article 20.—Rationing

Where a rationing system exists, which applies to the population at large and regulates the general distribution of products in short supply, refugees shall be accorded the same treatment as nationals.

Article 21.—Housing

As regards housing, the Contracting States, in so far as the matter is regulated by laws or regulations or is subject to the control of public authorities, shall accord to refugees lawfully staying in their territory treatment as favourable as possible and, in any event, not less favourable than that accorded to aliens generally in the same circumstances.

Article 22.—Public education

1. The Contracting States shall accord to refugees the same treatment as is accorded to nationals with respect to elementary education.

2. The Contracting States shall accord to refugees treatment as favourable as possible, and, in any event, not less favourable than that accorded to aliens generally in the same circumstances, with respect to education other than elementary education and, in particular, as regards access to studies, the recognition of foreign school certificates, diplomas and degrees, the remission of fees and charges and the award of scholarships.

Article 23.—Public relief

The Contracting States shall accord to refugees lawfully staying in their territory the same treatment with respect to public relief and assistance as is accorded to their nationals.

Article 24.—Labour legislation and social security

1. The Contracting States shall accord to refugees lawfully staying in their territory the same treatment as is accorded to nationals in respect of the following matters;

(a) In so far as such matters are governed by laws or regulations or are subject to the control of administrative authorities: remuneration, including family allowances where these form part of remuneration, hours of work, overtime arrangements, holidays with pay, restrictions on home work, minimum age of employment, apprenticeship and training, women's work and the work of young persons, and the enjoyment of the benefits of collective bargaining;

(b) Social security (legal provisions in respect of employment injury, occupational diseases, maternity, sickness, disability, old age, death, unemployment, family responsibilities and any other contingency which, according to national laws or regulations, is covered by a social security scheme), subject to the following limitations:

(i) There may be appropriate arrangements for the maintenance of acquired rights and rights in course of acquisition;

(ii) National laws or regulations of the country of residence may prescribe special arrangements concerning benefits or portions of benefits which are payable wholly out of public funds, and concerning allowances paid to persons who do not fulfil the contribution conditions prescribed for the award of a normal pension.

2. The right to compensation for the death of a refugee resulting from employment injury or from occupational disease shall not be affected by the fact that the residence of the beneficiary is outside the territory of the Contracting State.

3. The Contracting States shall extend to refugees the benefits of agreements concluded between them, or which may be concluded between them in the future, concerning the maintenance of acquired rights and rights in the process of acquisition in regard to social security, subject only to the conditions which apply to nationals of the States signatory to the agreements in question.

4. The Contracting States will give sympathetic consideration to extending to refugees so far as possible the benefits of similar agreements which may at any time be in force between such Contracting States and non-contracting States.

Refugees are also entitled to freedom of movement and to necessary identity and travel documentation to facilitate this (Arts 26–28). Obviously, not all refugees will be in a position to flee with full documentation. In the current political climate, this is obviously quite problematic. Article 28(2) provides an exception: States are permitted to not issue travel documentation if national security and public order so dictate.

13.5.3   Increasing vulnerability—conflict situations

Refugees are inherently vulnerable, being inevitably dependent on receiving States for their survival. This can be problematic in, for example, Sub-Saharan Africa when the receiving State lacks the financial and other resources necessary to guarantee the safety and survival of the refugee population. Some 80 percent of refugees are women and children, each recognised vulnerable groups in themselves. While many refugees flee from natural disasters, famine and drought, many seek refuge from conflict. The origins of contemporary provisions on refugees date to the Second World War and thus the plight of those displaced by conflict.

Fourth Geneva Convention relative to the Protection of Civilian Persons in Time of War

Art. 35. All protected persons who may desire to leave the territory at the outset of, or during a conflict, shall be entitled to do so, unless their departure is contrary to the national interests of the State. The applications of such persons to leave shall be decided in accordance with regularly established procedures and the decision shall be taken as rapidly as possible. Those persons permitted to leave may provide themselves with the necessary funds for their journey and take with them a reasonable amount of their effects and articles of personal use.

If any such person is refused permission to leave the territory, he shall be entitled to have refusal reconsidered, as soon as possible by an appropriate court or administrative board designated by the Detaining Power for that purpose.

Upon request, representatives of the Protecting Power shall, unless reasons of security prevent it, or the persons concerned object, be furnished with the reasons for refusal of any request for permission to leave the territory and be given, as expeditiously as possible, the names of all persons who have been denied permission to leave.

Art. 36. Departures permitted under the foregoing Article shall be carried out in satisfactory conditions as regards safety, hygiene, sanitation and food. All costs in connection therewith, from the point of exit in the territory of the Detaining Power, shall be borne by the country of destination, or, in the case of accommodation in a neutral country, by the Power whose nationals are benefited. The practical details of such movements may, if necessary, be settled by special agreements between the Powers concerned.

The foregoing shall not prejudice such special agreements as may be concluded between Parties to the conflict concerning the exchange and repatriation of their nationals in enemy hands.

Art. 37. Protected persons who are confined pending proceedings or serving a sentence involving loss of liberty, shall during their confinement be humanely treated.

As soon as they are released, they may ask to leave the territory in conformity with the foregoing Articles.

Art. 38. With the exception of special measures authorized by the present Convention, in particularly by Article 27 and 41 thereof, the situation of protected persons shall continue to be regulated, in principle, by the provisions concerning aliens in time of peace. In any case, the following rights shall be granted to them:

(1) they shall be enabled to receive the individual or collective relief that may be sent to them.

(2) they shall, if their state of health so requires, receive medical attention and hospital treatment to the same extent as the nationals of the State concerned.

(3) they shall be allowed to practise their religion and to receive spiritual assistance from ministers of their faith.

(4) if they reside in an area particularly exposed to the dangers of war, they shall be authorized to move from that area to the same extent as the nationals of the State concerned.

(5) children under fifteen years, pregnant women and mothers of children under seven years shall benefit by any preferential treatment to the same extent as the nationals of the State concerned.

Art. 39. Protected persons who, as a result of the war, have lost their gainful employment, shall be granted the opportunity to find paid employment. That opportunity shall, subject to security considerations and to the provisions of Article 40, be equal to that enjoyed by the nationals of the Power in whose territory they are.

Where a Party to the conflict applies to a protected person methods of control which result in his being unable to support himself, and especially if such a person is prevented for reasons of security from finding paid employment on reasonable conditions, the said Party shall ensure his support and that of his dependents.

Protected persons may in any case receive allowances from their home country, the Protecting Power, or the relief societies referred to in Article 30.

Art. 40. Protected persons may be compelled to work only to the same extent as nationals of the Party to the conflict in whose territory they are.

If protected persons are of enemy nationality, they may only be compelled to do work which is normally necessary to ensure the feeding, sheltering, clothing, transport and health of human beings and which is not directly related to the conduct of military operations.

In the cases mentioned in the two preceding paragraphs, protected persons compelled to work shall have the benefit of the same working conditions and of the same safeguards as national workers in particular as regards wages, hours of labour, clothing and equipment, previous training and compensation for occupational accidents and diseases.

If the above provisions are infringed, protected persons shall be allowed to exercise their right of complaint in accordance with Article 30.

Art. 41. Should the Power, in whose hands protected persons may be, consider the measures of control mentioned in the present Convention to be inadequate, it may not have recourse to any other measure of control more severe than that of assigned residence or internment, in accordance with the provisions of Articles 42 and 43.

In applying the provisions of Article 39, second paragraph, to the cases of persons required to leave their usual places of residence by virtue of a decision placing them in assigned residence, by virtue of a decision placing them in assigned residence, elsewhere, the Detaining Power shall be guided as closely as possible by the standards of welfare set forth in Part III, Section IV of this Convention.

Art. 42. The internment or placing in assigned residence of protected persons may be ordered only if the security of the Detaining Power makes it absolutely necessary.

If any person, acting through the representatives of the Protecting Power, voluntarily demands internment, and if his situation renders this step necessary, he shall be interned by the Power in whose hands he may be.

Art. 43. Any protected person who has been interned or placed in assigned residence shall be entitled to have such action reconsidered as soon as possible by an appropriate court or administrative board designated by the Detaining Power for that purpose. If the internment or placing in assigned residence is maintained, the court or administrative board shall periodically, and at least twice yearly, give consideration to his or her case, with a view to the favourable amendment of the initial decision, if circumstances permit.

Unless the protected persons concerned object, the Detaining Power shall, as rapidly as possible, give the Protecting Power the names of any protected persons who have been interned or subjected to assigned residence, or who have been released from internment or assigned residence. The decisions of the courts or boards mentioned in the first paragraph of the present Article shall also, subject to the same conditions, be notified as rapidly as possible to the Protecting Power.

Art. 44. In applying the measures of control mentioned in the present Convention, the Detaining Power shall not treat as enemy aliens exclusively on the basis of their nationality de jure of an enemy State, refugees who do not, in fact, enjoy the protection of any government.

Art. 45. Protected persons shall not be transferred to a Power which is not a party to the Convention.

This provision shall in no way constitute an obstacle to the repatriation of protected persons, or to their return to their country of residence after the cessation of hostilities.

Protected persons may be transferred by the Detaining Power only to a Power which is a party to the present Convention and after the Detaining Power has satisfied itself of the willingness and ability of such transferee Power to apply the present Convention. If protected persons are transferred under such circumstances, responsibility for the application of the present Convention rests on the Power accepting them, while they are in its custody. Nevertheless, if that Power fails to carry out the provisions of the present Convention in any important respect, the Power by which the protected persons were transferred shall, upon being so notified by the Protecting Power, take effective measures to correct the situation or shall request the return of the protected persons. Such request must be complied with.

In no circumstances shall a protected person be transferred to a country where he or she may have reason to fear persecution for his or her political opinions or religious beliefs.

The provisions of this Article do not constitute an obstacle to the extradition, in pursuance of extradition treaties concluded before the outbreak of hostilities, of protected persons accused of offences against ordinary criminal law.

Art. 46. In so far as they have not been previously withdrawn, restrictive measures taken regarding protected persons shall be cancelled as soon as possible after the close of hostilities.

Restrictive measures affecting their property shall be cancelled, in accordance with the law of the Detaining Power, as soon as possible after the close of hostilities.

The Geneva Convention clearly includes protection for refugees and other displaced persons. The Geneva Conventions and humanitarian law are discussed in more detail in Chapter 15.

13.6   GRANTING ASYLUM TO REFUGEES AND OTHERS

While there is nothing in the United Nations Convention on the granting of asylum to refugees, the matter has been considered by the General Assembly of the United

Nations, regional bodies such as the European Union, and naturally has been addressed by the High Commissioner for Refugees.

The spirit of the Universal Declaration on Human Rights suggests that asylum policies adopted by States should be construed generously, to ensure respect for human dignity. This is further corroborated by the preambular paragraphs preceding the Convention relating to the Status of Refugees.

United Nations Convention relating to the Status of Refugees 1951, Preamble

The High Contracting Parties,

Considering that the Charter of the United Nations and the Universal Declaration of Human Rights approved on 10 December 1948 by the General Assembly have affirmed the principle that human beings shall enjoy fundamental rights and freedoms without discrimination,

Considering that the United Nations has, on various occasions, manifested its profound concern for refugees and endeavoured to assure refugees the widest possible exercise of these fundamental rights and freedoms,

Considering that it is desirable to revise and consolidate previous international agreements relating to the status of refugees and to extend the scope of and the protection accorded by such instruments by means of a new agreement,

Considering that the grant of asylum may place unduly heavy burdens on certain countries, and that a satisfactory solution of a problem of which the United Nations has recognized the international scope and nature cannot therefore be achieved without international co-operation,

Expressing the wish that all States, recognizing the social and humanitarian nature of the problem of refugees, will do everything within their power to prevent this problem from becoming a cause of tension between States, . . .

Question

Consider the scope of the Refugee Convention 1951 and the 1967 Protocol. What reasons could explain the omission of asylum guidelines from these instruments?

United Nations Declaration on Territorial Asylum, General Assembly Resolution 2312 (XXII) (1967)

Article 1

1. Asylum granted by a State, in the exercise of its sovereignty, to persons entitled to invoke article 14 of the Universal Declaration of Human Rights, including persons struggling against colonialism, shall be respected by all other States.

2. The right to seek and to enjoy asylum may not be invoked by any person with respect to whom there are serious reasons for considering that he has committed a crime against peace, a war crime or a crime against humanity, as defined in the international instruments drawn up to make provision in respect of such crimes.

3. It shall rest with the State granting asylum to evaluate the grounds for the grant of asylum.

Article 2

1. The situation of persons referred to in article 1, paragraph 1, is, without prejudice to the sovereignty of States and the purposes and principles of the United Nations, of concern to the international community.

2. Where a State finds difficulty in granting or continuing to grant asylum, States individually or jointly or through the United Nations shall consider, in a spirit of international solidarity, appropriate measures to lighten the burden on that State.

Article 3

1. No person referred to in article 1, paragraph 1, shall be subjected to measures such as rejection at the frontier or, if he has already entered the territory in which he seeks asylum, expulsion or compulsory return to any State where he may be subjected to persecution.

2. Exception may be made to the foregoing principle only for overriding reasons of national security or in order to safeguard the population, as in the case of a mass influx of persons.

3. Should a State decide in any case that exception to the principle stated in paragraph 1 of this article would be justified, it shall consider the possibility of granting to the persons concerned, under such conditions as it may deem appropriate, an opportunity, whether by way of provisional asylum or otherwise, of going to another State.

Article 4

States granting asylum shall not permit persons who have received asylum to engage in activities contrary to the purposes and principles of the United Nations.

13.7   INTERNALLY DISPLACED

A more recent phenomenon has been the rise in internally displaced people, those who are forced to leave their homes but remain in the same country. The following graph represents the major populations of internally displaced persons of concern to the United Nations Refugee Agency (figures extracted from www.unhcr.ch).

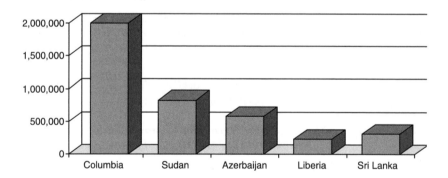

This is a growing area of concern for the High Commission and indeed for many States. Arguably, internally displaced persons should benefit from the protection of the complete range of internationally recognised human rights and fundamental freedoms. In emergency situations, certain provisions of the Geneva Conventions (humanitarian law) may apply. The prevalence of civil conflicts and natural disasters increases the likelihood of internally displaced persons. Unfortunately, space prohibits a more comprehensive discussion of the law in this area at present.

13.8   HIGH COMMISSIONER FOR REFUGEES

The work of the United Nations protecting refugees is undertaken under the auspices of the United Nations High Commissioner for Refugees. The present incumbent of the post is Mr. António Guterres, the 10th High Commissioner. More information can be found on the website of the Office of the High Commissioner. General Assembly

Resolution 319 A (IV) of 3 December 1949, established the office of High Commissioner, Resolution 428 (V) 1950 adopted the Statute of the Office. This resolution calls for international cooperation in specified areas.

General Assembly Resolution 428(V) 2

2 *Calls upon* governments to co-operate with the United Nations High Commissioner for Refugees in the performance of his functions concerning refugees falling under the competence of his Office, especially by:

(a) Becoming parties to international conventions providing for the protection of refugees, and taking the necessary steps of implementation under such conventions;

(b) Entering into special agreements with the High Commissioner for the execution of measures calculated to improve the situation of refugees and to reduce the number requiring protection;

(c) Admitting refugees to their territories, not excluding those in the most destitute categories;

(d) Assisting the High Commissioner in his efforts to promote the voluntary repatriation of refugees;

(e) Promoting the assimilation of refugees, especially by facilitating their naturalization;

(f) Providing refugees with travel and other documents such as would normally be provided to other aliens by their national authorities, especially documents which would facilitate their resettlement;

(g) Permitting refugees to transfer their assets and especially those necessary for their resettlement;

(h) Providing the High Commissioner with information concerning the number and condition of refugees, and laws and regulations concerning them.

Statute of the Office of United Nations High Commissioner for Refugees

6. The competence of the High Commissioner shall extend to:

A. (i) Any person who has been considered a refugee under the Arrangements of 12 May 1926 and 30 June 1928 or under the Conventions of 28 October 1933 and 10 February 1938, the Protocol of 14 September 1939 or the Constitution of the International Refugee Organization;

(ii) Any person who, as a result of events occurring before 1 January 1951 and owing to well-founded fear of being persecuted for reasons of race, religion, nationality or political opinion, is outside the country of his nationality and is unable or, owing to such fear or for reasons other than personal convenience, is unwilling to avail himself of the protection of that country; or who, not having a nationality and being outside the country of his former habitual residence, is unable or, owing to such fear or for reasons other than personal convenience, is unwilling to return to it.

Decisions as to eligibility taken by the International Refugee Organization during the period of its activities shall not prevent the status of refugee being accorded to persons who fulfil the conditions of the present paragraph.

The competence of the High Commissioner shall cease to apply to any person defined in section A above if:

(a) He has voluntarily re-availed himself of the protection of the country of his nationality; or

(b) Having lost his nationality, he has voluntarily re-acquired it; or

(c) He has acquired a new nationality, and enjoys the protection of the country of his new nationality; or

(d) He has voluntarily re-established himself in the country which he left or outside which he remained owing to fear of persecution; or

(e) He can no longer, because the circumstances in connection with which he has been recognized as a refugee have ceased to exist, claim grounds other than those of personal convenience, for continuing to refuse to avail himself of the protection of the country of his nationality. Reasons of a purely economic character may not be invoked; or

(f) Being a person who has no nationality, he can no longer, because the circumstances in connection with which he has been recognized as a refugee have ceased to exist and he is able to return to the country of his former habitual residence, claim grounds other than those of personal convenience for continuing to refuse to return to that country.

> B. Any other person who is outside the country of his nationality or, if he has no nationality, the country of his former habitual residence, because he has or had well-founded fear of persecution by reason of his race, religion, nationality or political opinion and is unable or, because of such fear, is unwilling to avail himself of the protection of the government of the country of his nationality, or, if he has no nationality, to return to the country of his former habitual residence.

7. Provided that the competence of the High Commissioner as defined in paragraph 6 above shall not extend to a person:

(a) Who is a national of more than one country unless he satisfies the provisions of the preceding paragraph in relation to each of the countries of which he is a national; or

(b) Who is recognized by the competent authorities of the country in which he has taken residence as having the rights and obligations which are attached to the possession of the nationality of that country; or

(c) Who continues to receive from other organs or agencies of the United Nations protection or assistance; or

(d) In respect of whom there are serious reasons for considering that he has committed a crime covered by the provisions of treaties of extradition or a crime mentioned in article 6 of the London Charter of the International Military Tribunal or by the provisions of article 14, paragraph 2, of the Universal Declaration of Human Rights.

8. The High Commissioner shall provide for the protection of refugees falling under the competence of his Office by:

(a) Promoting the conclusion and ratification of international conventions for the protection of refugees, supervising their application and proposing amendments thereto;

(b) Promoting through special agreements with governments the execution of any measures calculated to improve the situation of refugees and to reduce the number requiring protection;

(c) Assisting governmental and private efforts to promote voluntary repatriation or assimilation within new national communities;

(d) Promoting the admission of refugees, not excluding those in the most destitute categories, to the territories of States;

(e) Endeavouring to obtain permission for refugees to transfer their assets and especially those necessary for their resettlement;

(f) Obtaining from governments information concerning the number and conditions of refugees in their territories and the laws and regulations concerning them;

(g) Keeping in close touch with the governments and inter-governmental organizations concerned;

(h) Establishing contact in such manner as he may think best with private organizations dealing with refugee questions;

(i) Facilitating the co-ordination of the efforts of private organizations concerned with the welfare of refugees.

13.9 STATELESS PERSONS

Related to issues surrounding refugees and those seeking asylum is the problem of stateless persons. Clearly, people without nationality are at a severe disadvantage when it comes to human rights. Their legal status is compromised. In many respects the right to a nationality is a fundamental element of the right to identity. Early indications of the importance of the right to a nationality can be deduced from the care taken by the relevant authorities in determining the appropriate nationality, in many examples of re-delineation of borders in inter-war and post-war Europe. Nationality was a key factor in determining the composition of new States: Yugoslavia comprised the Southern Slavs, for example.

Within the new world order, the Universal Declaration itself identifies the right to a nationality as a key human right.

Universal Declaration of Human Rights 1948
Article 15

1. Everyone has the right to a nationality.

2. No one shall be arbitrarily deprived of his nationality nor denied the right to change his nationality.

United Nations Convention on the Rights of the Child 1989
Article 8

1. The child shall be registered immediately after birth and shall have the right from birth to a name, the right to acquire nationality and, as far as possible, the right to know and be cared for by his or her parents.

The 1954 Convention relating to the Status of Stateless Persons applies to those not considered to be a national by any State. Its *raison d'etre* is to grant stateless people the security of legitimising certain aspects of their residency thereby giving them a legitimate basis for living in a host State. The Convention recognises that not all stateless persons are covered by the provisions of the 1951 Convention relating to the Status of Refugees. Consequently, it was deemed desirable to create an international instrument to regulate and hopefully improve the status of stateless persons.

There are many similarities between the provisions of the Convention relating to the Status of Refugees and the Convention relating to the Status of Stateless Persons as will be seen. First note the applicable definition and relevant exceptions.

Convention relating to the Status of Stateless Persons 1954
Article 1.—Definition of the term 'stateless person'

1. For the purpose of this Convention, the term 'stateless person' means a person who is not considered as a national by any State under the operation of its law.

2. This Convention shall not apply:

(i) To persons who are at present receiving from organs or agencies of the United Nations other than the United Nations High Commissioner for Refugees protection or assistance so long as they are receiving such protection or assistance;

(ii) To persons who are recognized by the competent authorities of the country in which they have taken residence as having the rights and obligations which are attached to the possession of the nationality of that country;

(iii) To persons with respect to whom there are serious reasons for considering that:

(a) They have committed a crime against peace, a war crime, or a crime against humanity, as defined in the international instruments drawn up to make provisions in respect of such crimes;

(b) They have committed a serious non-political crime outside the country of their residence prior to their admission to that country;

(c) They have been guilty of acts contrary to the purposes and principles of the United Nations.

The general provisions relating to stateless persons and the emphasis on the guarantee of basic rights reflects the 1951 Refugee Convention.

Convention relating to the Status of Stateless Persons 1954
Article 2.—General obligations

Every stateless person has duties to the country in which he finds himself, which require in particular that he conform to its laws and regulations as well as to measures taken for the maintenance of public order.

Article 3.—Non-discrimination

The Contracting States shall apply the provisions of this Convention to stateless persons without discrimination as to race, religion or country of origin.

Article 4.—Religion

The Contracting States shall accord to stateless persons within their territories treatment at least as favourable as that accorded to their nationals with respect to freedom to practise their religion and freedom as regards the religious education of their children.

Article 5.—Rights granted apart from this Convention

Nothing in this Convention shall be deemed to impair any rights and benefits granted by a Contracting State to stateless persons apart from this Convention.

Article 6.—The term 'in the same circumstances'

For the purpose of this Convention, the term 'in the same circumstances' implies that any requirements (including requirements as to length and conditions of sojourn or residence) which the particular individual would have to fulfil for the enjoyment of the right in question, if he were not a stateless person, must be fulfilled by him, with the exception of requirements which by their nature a stateless person is incapable of fulfilling.

Article 7.—Exemption from reciprocity

1. Except where this Convention contains more favourable provisions, a Contracting State shall accord to stateless persons the same treatment as is accorded to aliens generally.

2. After a period of three years' residence, all stateless persons shall enjoy exemption from legislative reciprocity in the territory of the Contracting States.

3. Each Contracting State shall continue to accord to stateless persons the rights and benefits to which they were already entitled, in the absence of reciprocity, at the date of entry into force of this Convention for that State.

4. The Contracting States shall consider favourably the possibility of according to stateless persons, in the absence of reciprocity, rights and benefits beyond those to which they are entitled according to paragraphs 2 and 3, and to extending exemption from reciprocity to stateless persons who do not fulfil the conditions provided for in paragraphs 2 and 3.

5. The provisions of paragraphs 2 and 3 apply both to the rights and benefits referred to in articles 13, 18, 19, 21 and 22 of this Convention and to rights and benefits for which this Convention does not provide.

Article 8.—Exemption from exceptional measures

With regard to exceptional measures which may be taken against the person, property or interests of nationals or former nationals of a foreign State, the Contracting States shall not apply such measures to a stateless person solely on account of his having previously possessed the nationality of the foreign State in question. Contracting States which, under their legislation, are prevented from applying the general principle expressed in this article shall, in appropriate cases, grant exemptions in favour of such stateless persons.

Article 9.—Provisional measures

Nothing in this Convention shall prevent a Contracting State, in time of war or other grave and exceptional circumstances, from taking provisionally measures which it considers to be essential to the national security in the case of a particular person, pending a determination by the Contracting State that that person is in fact a stateless person and that the continuance of such measures is necessary in his case in the interests of national security.

Article 10.—Continuity of residence

1. Where a stateless person has been forcibly displaced during the Second World War and removed to the territory of a Contracting State, and is resident there, the period of such enforced sojourn shall be considered to have been lawful residence within that territory.

2. Where a stateless person has been forcibly displaced during the Second World War from the territory of a Contracting State and has, prior to the date of entry into force of this Convention, returned there for the purpose of taking up residence, the period of residence before and after such enforced displacement shall be regarded as one uninterrupted period for any purposes for which uninterrupted residence is required.

Article 11.—Stateless seamen

In the case of stateless persons regularly serving as crew members on board a ship flying the flag of a Contracting State, that State shall give sympathetic consideration to their establishment on its territory and the issue of travel documents to them or their temporary admission to its territory particularly with a view to facilitating their establishment in another country.

A full range of rights and freedoms is ascribed to stateless persons in terms of the convention. As with refugees, the standard of care commences at the level of that to be accorded to aliens. A full range of juridical and administrative rights ensue to ensure that the stateless person may be protected in the same manner as a national. These rights are very similar to those relating to refugees—discussed above—hence are not reproduced in full.

Convention relating to the Status of Stateless Persons 1954

Article 12.—Personal status

1. The personal status of a stateless person shall be governed by the law of the country of his domicile or, if he has no domicile, by the law of the country of his residence.

2. Rights previously acquired by a stateless person and dependent on personal status, more particularly rights attaching to marriage, shall be respected by a Contracting State, subject to

compliance, if this be necessary, with the formalities required by the law of that State, provided that the right in question is one which would have been recognized by the law of that State had he not become stateless.

Article 13.—Movable and immovable property
Article 14.—Artistic rights and industrial property
Article 15.—Right of association

Economic, social and cultural rights are also ascribed to stateless persons. Again the requisite standard is that accorded to aliens. States must clearly attempt to help state-less persons enjoy a spectrum of fundamental rights and contribute to their own existence and that of the State in which they find themselves. These are again similar to the rights in the Convention on refugees (see above). They are to be treated on a basis of non-discrimination *vis-a-vis* aliens and nationals, as appropriate.

Convention relating to the Status of Stateless Persons 1954

Article 17.—Wage-earning employment
Article 18.—Self-employment
Article 19.—Liberal professions
Article 20.—Rationing
Article 21.—Housing
Article 22.—Public education
Article 23.—Public relief
Article 24.—Labour legislation and social security

Stateless persons obviously may encounter problems leaving the State in which they find themselves and thereafter entering other States. Accordingly, provision had to be made in the convention to facilitate freedom of movement. A means of establishing identity is a clear precursor to international travel. During the 1993 International Year of Indigenous People, and the ensuing decade, the issue of establishing identity and nationality for indigenous peoples was acute. Itinerant, nomadic and border peoples frequently had no clear nationality and no identity papers, thus precluding inter-national travel and participation in the global and even regional events scheduled for their benefit. Travel documents are a particular issue for stateless persons as, without nationality, there is no potential for legal trans-frontier travel in most of the world.

The following provisions address administrative matters, providing for acquisition of identity and travel papers, and, ultimately, nationality.

Convention relating to the Status of Stateless Persons 1954
Article 26.—Freedom of movement

Each Contracting State shall accord to stateless persons lawfully in its territory the right to choose their place of residence and to move freely within its territory, subject to any regulations applicable to aliens generally in the same circumstances.

Article 27.—Identity papers

The Contracting States shall issue identity papers to any stateless person in their territory who does not possess a valid travel document.

Article 28.—Travel documents

The Contracting States shall issue to stateless persons lawfully staying in their territory travel documents for the purpose of travel outside their territory, unless compelling reasons of national security or public order otherwise require, and the provisions of the schedule to this Convention shall apply with respect to such documents. The Contracting States may issue such a travel document to any other stateless person in their territory; they shall in particular give sympathetic consideration to the issue of such a travel document to stateless persons in their territory who are unable to obtain a travel document from the country of their lawful residence.

Similar provisions to that of refugees apply to expulsion. However, with respect to stateless persons, there is a further issue to consider: those who are stateless may have no State with which they have an affiliation and thus their removal will effectively have to be to another State in which they will also be stateless.

Convention relating to the Status of Stateless Persons 1954

Article 31.—Expulsion

1. The Contracting States shall not expel a stateless person lawfully in their territory save on grounds of national security or public order.

2. The expulsion of such a stateless person shall be only in pursuance of a decision reached in accordance with due process of law. Except where compelling reasons of national security otherwise require, the stateless person shall be allowed to submit evidence to clear himself, and to appeal to and be represented for the purpose before competent authority or a person or persons specially designated by the competent authority.

3. The Contracting States shall allow such a stateless person a reasonable period within which to seek legal admission into another country. The Contracting States reserve the right to apply during that period such internal measures as they may deem necessary.

Article 32.—Naturalization

The Contracting States shall as far as possible facilitate the assimilation and naturalization of stateless persons. They shall in particular make every effort to expedite naturalization proceedings and to reduce as far as possible the charges and costs of such proceedings.

Having established the parameters of treatment for stateless persons, the United Nations then focused on attempts to effect a cultural change by reducing statelessness—General Assembly Resolution 896 (IX) of 4 December 1954. The 1961 Convention on the Reduction of Statelessness aims at ensuring a nationality to all those born within a contracting State. Moreover, the convention seeks to establish a framework for regulating the circumstances in which a State may remove nationality, thereby rendering a person stateless.

Convention on the Reduction of Statelessness 1961

Article 1

1. A Contracting State shall grant its nationality to a person born in its territory who would otherwise be stateless. Such nationality shall be granted:

(a) At birth, by operation of law, or

(b) Upon an application being lodged with the appropriate authority, by or on behalf of the person concerned, in the manner prescribed by the national law. Subject to the provisions of paragraph 2 of this article, no such application may be rejected.

A Contracting State which provides for the grant of its nationality in accordance with subparagraph (b) of this paragraph may also provide for the grant of its nationality by operation of law at such age and subject to such conditions as may be prescribed by the national law.

2. A Contracting State may make the grant of its nationality in accordance with subparagraph (b) of paragraph 1 of this article subject to one or more of the following conditions:

(a) That the application is lodged during a period, fixed by the Contracting State, beginning not later than at the age of eighteen years and ending not earlier than at the age of twenty-one years, so, however, that the person concerned shall be allowed at least one year during which he may himself make the application without having to obtain legal authorization to do so;

(b) That the person concerned has habitually resided in the territory of the Contracting State for such period as may be fixed by that State, not exceeding five years immediately preceding the lodging of the application nor ten years in all;

(c) That the person concerned has neither been convicted of an offence against national security nor has been sentenced to imprisonment for a term of five years or more on a criminal charge;

(d) That the person concerned has always been stateless.

3. Notwithstanding the provisions of paragraphs 1(b) and 2 of this article, a child born in wedlock in the territory of a Contracting State, whose mother has the nationality of that State, shall acquire at birth that nationality if it otherwise would be stateless.

4. A Contracting State shall grant its nationality to a person who would otherwise be stateless and who is unable to acquire the nationality of the Contracting State in whose territory he was born because he has passed the age for lodging his application or has not fulfilled the required residence conditions, if the nationality of one of his parents at the time of the person's birth was that of the Contracting State first above-mentioned. If his parents did not possess the same nationality at the time of his birth, the question whether the nationality of the person concerned should follow that of the father or that of the mother shall be determined by the national law of such Contracting State. If application for such nationality is required, the application shall be made to the appropriate authority by or on behalf of the applicant in the manner prescribed by the national law. Subject to the provisions of paragraph 5 of this article, such application shall not be refused.

5. The Contracting State may make the grant of its nationality in accordance with the provisions of paragraph 4 of this article subject to one or more of the following conditions:

(a) That the application is lodged before the applicant reaches an age, being not less than twenty-three years, fixed by the Contracting State;

(b) That the person concerned has habitually resided in the territory of the Contracting State for such period immediately preceding the lodging of the application, not exceeding three years, as may be fixed by that State;

(c) That the person concerned has always been stateless.

Article 2

A foundling found in the territory of a Contracting State shall, in the absence of proof to the contrary, be considered to have been born within that territory of parents possessing the nationality of that State.

Article 3

For the purpose of determining the obligations of Contracting States under this Convention, birth on a ship or in an aircraft shall be deemed to have taken place in the territory of the State whose flag the ship flies or in the territory of the State in which the aircraft is registered, as the case may be.

Article 4

1. A Contracting State shall grant its nationality to a person, not born in the territory of a Contracting State, who would otherwise be stateless, if the nationality of one of his parents at the time of the person's birth was that of that State. If his parents did not possess the same nationality at the time of his birth, the question whether the nationality of the person concerned should follow that of the father or that of the mother shall be determined by the national law of such Contracting State. Nationality granted in accordance with the provisions of this paragraph shall be granted:

(a) At birth, by operation of law, or

(b) Upon an application being lodged with the appropriate authority, by or on behalf of the person concerned, in the manner prescribed by the national law. Subject to the provisions of paragraph 2 of this article, no such application may be rejected.

2. A Contracting State may make the grant of its nationality in accordance with the provisions of paragraph 1 of this article subject to one or more of the following conditions:

(a) That the application is lodged before the applicant reaches an age, being not less than twenty-three years, fixed by the Contracting State;

(b) That the person concerned has habitually resided in the territory of the Contracting State for such period immediately preceding the lodging of the application, not exceeding three years, as may be fixed by that State;

(c) That the person concerned has not been convicted of an offence against national security;

(d) That the person concerned has always been stateless.

Article 5

1. If the law of a Contracting State entails loss of nationality as a consequence of any change in the personal status of a person such as marriage, termination of marriage, legitimation, recognition or adoption, such loss shall be conditional upon possession or acquisition of another nationality.

2. If, under the law of a Contracting State, a child born out of wedlock loses the nationality of that State in consequence of a recognition of affiliation, he shall be given an opportunity to recover that nationality by written application to the appropriate authority, and the conditions governing such application shall not be more rigorous than those laid down in paragraph 2 of article 1 of this Convention.

Article 6

If the law of a Contracting State provides for loss of its nationality by a person's spouse or children as a consequence of that person losing or being deprived of that nationality, such loss shall be conditional upon their possession or acquisition of another nationality.

Article 7

1. (a) If the law of a Contracting State entails loss or renunciation of nationality, such renunciation shall not result in loss of nationality unless the person concerned possesses or acquires another nationality;

(b) The provisions of subparagraph (a) of this paragraph shall not apply where their application would be inconsistent with the principles stated in articles 13 and 14 of the Universal Declaration of Human Rights approved on 10 December 1948 by the General Assembly of the United Nations.

2. A national of a Contracting State who seeks naturalization in a foreign country shall not lose his nationality unless he acquires or has been accorded assurance of acquiring the nationality of that foreign country.

3. Subject to the provisions of paragraphs 4 and 5 of this article, a national of a Contracting State shall not lose his nationality, so as to become stateless, on the ground of departure, residence abroad, failure to register or on any similar ground.

4. A naturalized person may lose his nationality on account of residence abroad for a period, not less than seven consecutive years, specified by the law of the Contracting State concerned if he fails to declare to the appropriate authority his intention to retain his nationality.

5. In the case of a national of a Contracting State, born outside its territory, the law of that State may make the retention of its nationality after the expiry of one year from his attaining his

majority conditional upon residence at that time in the territory of the State or registration with the appropriate authority.

6. Except in the circumstances mentioned in this article, a person shall not lose the nationality of a Contracting State, if such loss would render him stateless, notwithstanding that such loss is not expressly prohibited by any other provision of this Convention.

Article 8

1. A Contracting State shall not deprive a person of his nationality if such deprivation would render him stateless.

2. Notwithstanding the provisions of paragraph 1 of this article, a person may be deprived of the nationality of a Contracting State:

(a) In the circumstances in which, under paragraphs 4 and 5 of article 7, it is permissible that a person should lose his nationality;

(b) Where the nationality has been obtained by misrepresentation or fraud.

3. Notwithstanding the provisions of paragraph 1 of this article, a Contracting State may retain the right to deprive a person of his nationality, if at the time of signature, ratification or accession it specifies its retention of such right on one or more of the following grounds, being grounds existing in its national law at that time:

(a) That, inconsistently with his duty of loyalty to the Contracting State, the person:

    (i) Has, in disregard of an express prohibition by the Contracting State rendered or continued to render services to, or received or continued to receive emoluments from, another State, or

    (ii) Has conducted himself in a manner seriously prejudicial to the vital interests of the State;

(b) That the person has taken an oath, or made a formal declaration, of allegiance to another State, or given definite evidence of his determination to repudiate his allegiance to the Contracting State.

4. A Contracting State shall not exercise a power of deprivation permitted by paragraphs 2 or 3 of this article except in accordance with law, which shall provide for the person concerned the right to a fair hearing by a court or other independent body.

Article 9

A Contracting State may not deprive any person or group of persons of their nationality on racial, ethnic, religious or political grounds.

Article 10

1. Every treaty between Contracting States providing for the transfer of territory shall include provisions designed to secure that no person shall become stateless as a result of the transfer. A Contracting State shall use its best endeavours to secure that any such treaty made by it with a State which is not a Party to this Convention includes such provisions.

2. In the absence of such provisions a Contracting State to which territory is transferred or which otherwise acquires territory shall confer its nationality on such persons as would otherwise become stateless as a result of the transfer or acquisition.

Article 11

The Contracting States shall promote the establishment within the framework of the United Nations, as soon as may be after the deposit of the sixth instrument of ratification or accession, of a body to which a person claiming the benefit of this Convention may apply for the examination of his claim and for assistance in presenting it to the appropriate authority.

Article 12

1. In relation to a Contracting State which does not, in accordance with the provisions of paragraph 1 of article 1 or of article 4 of this Convention, grant its nationality at birth by operation of law, the provisions of paragraph 1 of article 1 or of article 4, as the case may be, shall apply to persons born before as well as to persons born after the entry into force of this Convention.

2. The provisions of paragraph 4 of article 1 of this Convention shall apply to persons born before as well as to persons born after its entry into force.

3. The provisions of article 2 of this Convention shall apply only to foundlings found in the territory of a Contracting State after the entry into force of the Convention for that State.

Question

What differences are there, in terms of legal status and entitlements, between stateless persons, refugees and internally displaced persons?

FURTHER READING

Byrne, R, Noll, G, and Vedsted-Hansen, J (eds), *New Asylum Countries? Migration Control and Refugee Protection in an Enlarged European Union*, 2002, the Hague: Kluwer

Chimni, B (ed), *International Refugee Law: A Reader*, 2000, New Delhi: Sage

Feller, E, Türk, V, and Nicholson, F (eds), *Refugee Protection in International Law: UNHCR's Global Consultations on International Protection*, 2003, Oxford: OUP

Goodwin-Gill, G, *The Refugee in International Law*, 1996, Oxford: OUP

Kneebone, S (ed), *The Refugee Convention 50 years on*, 2003, Aldershot: Ashgate

Newman, E, and van Selm, J (eds), *Refugees and Forced Displacement*, 2003, Tokyo: UN University Press

Office of the UN High Commissioner for Refugees, *The State of the World's Refugees – human displacement in the new millenium*, 2006, Oxford: OUP

Phuong, C, *The International protection of Internally Displaced Persons*, 2005, Cambridge: CUP

United Nations Office of the High Commissioner for Human Rights, *Human Rights and refugees*, Factsheet No. 20. Geneva: OHCHR

Websites

www.unhcr.ch—Office of the High Commissioner for Refugees

CHAPTER 14

PROTECTING AND PROMOTING THE RIGHTS OF WOMEN

Although a major group in terms of numbers, the plight of women has long been identified as an area of concern for the international community. Statistically women are in a strong position, however a closer perusal of the statistics reveal that more women than men are illiterate, have low earnings, are affected by reproductive health issues, do not participate in the political process etc.

Third of the Millennium Development Goals is promoting gender equality and empowering women. As a first stage, gender disparities in primary and secondary education is to be eliminated by 2005 if possible, and at all levels by 2015. Clearly the target for 2005 has not universally been achieved. Two-thirds of all illiterates are women, according to the United Nations Development Programme statistics.

Vienna World Conference on Human Rights Declaration, para 18

The human rights of women and of the girl-child are an inalienable, integral and indivisible part of universal human rights. The full and equal participation of women in political, civil, economic, social and cultural life, at the national, regional and international levels, and the eradication of all forms of discrimination on grounds of sex are priority objectives of the international community.

Gender-based violence and all forms of sexual harassment and exploitation, including those resulting from cultural prejudice and international trafficking, are incompatible with the dignity and worth of the human person, and must be eliminated. This can be achieved by legal measures and through national action and international cooperation in such fields as economic and social development, education, safe maternity and health care, and social support.

The human rights of women should form an integral part of the United Nations human rights activities, including the promotion of all human rights instruments relating to women.

The World Conference on Human Rights urges Governments, institutions, intergovernmental and non-governmental organizations to intensify their efforts for the protection and promotion of human rights of women and the girl-child.

Women seem rarely to enjoy all the rights and freedoms articulated in international human rights instruments on a true parity with men. The materials in this section seek to focus on women's rights: their needs, the specific legal regimes which have evolved to address these needs and the progress to date. To better provide a flavour of the rights of women, gender equality, trafficking, violence against women and family rights will be considered. These allow many of the problems with women's rights to be addressed. There have been notable contributions to the tabulation of women's rights in all three major regions. Such developments will also be considered.

14.1 LEADING THE WAY: THE INTERNATIONAL LABOUR ORGANISATION

The evolution of women's rights has been mired in controversy. 'Chivalry', in the form of protectionist, patronising legal measures did little to herald women's rights in the early days. Even today, one of the biggest problems faced by proponents of women's rights is promoting gender mainstreaming.

The International Labour Organisation was an early advocate of women's rights. It recognised that women required protection, particularly in vulnerable employment situations such as during maternity periods and in hazardous working environments. Even now, almost a century later, the International Labour Organisation has been instrumental in creating the global framework of women's rights. In 1919 it adopted Convention No. 3 on Maternity Protection and Convention No. 4 on Night Work of Women.

Compare and contrast the provisions on maternity protection in these two International Labour Organisation conventions.

ILO Convention No. 3, Maternity Protection 1919

Article 3

In any public or private industrial or commercial undertaking, or in any branch thereof, other than an undertaking in which only members of the same family are employed, a woman—

(a) shall not be permitted to work during the six weeks following her confinement;

(b) shall have the right to leave her work if she produces a medical certificate stating that her confinement will probably take place within six weeks;

(c) shall, while she is absent from her work in pursuance of paragraphs (a) and (b), be paid benefits sufficient for the full and healthy maintenance of herself and her child, provided either out of public funds or by means of a system of insurance, the exact amount of which shall be determined by the competent authority in each country, and as an additional benefit shall be entitled to free attendance by a doctor or certified midwife; no mistake of the medical adviser in estimating the date of confinement shall preclude a woman from receiving these benefits from the date of the medical certificate up to the date on which the confinement actually takes place;

(d) shall in any case, if she is nursing her child, be allowed half an hour twice a day during her working hours for this purpose.

Article 4

Where a woman is absent from her work in accordance with paragraph (a) or (b) of Article 3 of this Convention, or remains absent from her work for a longer period as a result of illness medically certified to arise out of pregnancy or confinement and rendering her unfit for work, it shall not be lawful, until her absence shall have exceeded a maximum period to be fixed by the competent authority in each country, for her employer to give her notice of dismissal during such absence, nor to give her notice of dismissal at such a time that the notice would expire during such absence.

ILO Convention No. 103, Maternity Protection (revised) 1952

Article 3

1. A woman to whom this Convention applies shall, on the production of a medical certificate stating the presumed date of her confinement, be entitled to a period of maternity leave.

2. The period of maternity leave shall be at least twelve weeks, and shall include a period of compulsory leave after confinement.

3. The period of compulsory leave after confinement shall be prescribed by national laws or regulations, but shall in no case be less than six weeks; the remainder of the total period of maternity leave may be provided before the presumed date of confinement or following expiration of the compulsory leave period or partly before the presumed date of confinement and partly following the expiration of the compulsory leave period as may be prescribed by national laws or regulations.

4. The leave before the presumed date of confinement shall be extended by any period elapsing

between the presumed date of confinement and the actual date of confinement and the period of compulsory leave to be taken after confinement shall not be reduced on that account.

5. In case of illness medically certified arising out of pregnancy, national laws or regulations shall provide for additional leave before confinement, the maximum duration of which may be fixed by the competent authority.

6. In case of illness medically certified arising out of confinement, the woman shall be entitled to an extension of the leave after confinement, the maximum duration of which may be fixed by the competent authority.

Article 4

1. While absent from work on maternity leave in accordance with the provisions of Article 3, the woman shall be entitled to receive cash and medical benefits.

2. The rates of cash benefit shall be fixed by national laws or regulations so as to ensure benefits sufficient for the full and healthy maintenance of herself and her child in accordance with a suitable standard of living.

3. Medical benefits shall include pre-natal, confinement and post-natal care by qualified midwives or medical practitioners as well as hospitalisation care where necessary; freedom of choice of doctor and freedom of choice between a public and private hospital shall be respected.

4. The cash and medical benefits shall be provided either by means of compulsory social insurance or by means of public funds; in either case they shall be provided as a matter of right to all women who comply with the prescribed conditions.

5. Women who fail to qualify for benefits provided as a matter of right shall be entitled, subject to the means test required for social assistance, to adequate benefits out of social assistance funds.

Question

What reasons are there for the differences between the two instruments?

Employment law has produced possibly the most substantive advance in women's rights. While the International Labour Organisation forged ahead with tabulating women's rights in the workplace, the European Economic Community (now subsumed by the European Union) made similar dramatic inroads within its small territorial jurisdiction in Europe. In all instances the balance between promotion of equality and protection of rights has proven tricky to achieve.

Question

Should women be protected in a manner which implies they need special protection solely on account of being female?

These issues are explored further in the measures prescribing equality of men and women and equal protection before the courts.

14.2 EQUALITY

Equality is clearly a lynchpin of the United Nations itself. From the tentative statements in the Charter to its reiteration over the intervening six decades, it is clear that equality between men and women is meant to be a cornerstone of the new world order.

Preamble to the United Nations Charter 1945

WE THE PEOPLES OF THE UNITED NATIONS DETERMINED

to save succeeding generations from the scourge of war, which twice in our lifetime has brought untold sorrow to mankind, and

to reaffirm faith in fundamental human rights, in the dignity and worth of the human person, in the equal rights of men and women and of nations large and small.

Gender mainstreaming is now fundamental to the ongoing development of the United Nations. For the working definition, see ECOSOC's viewpoint.

Economic and Social Council Agreed Conclusions 1997/2 (1997)

. . . the process of assessing the implications for women and men of any planned action, including legislation, policies or programmes, in all areas and at all levels. It is a strategy for making women's as well as men's concerns and experiences an integral dimension of the design, implementation, monitoring and evaluation of policies and programmes in all political, economic and societal spheres so that women and men benefit equally and inequality is not perpetuated. The ultimate goal is to achieve gender equality.

Salient policies characterise the work of the United Nations Development Programme, UNESCO, the European Union, UNIFEM and indeed the United Nations as a whole. Gender mainstreaming is viewed as an essential element of securing the objectives of the Beijing Platform for Action.

Question

Throughout this chapter, consider whether women's rights in general represent simply a re-tabulation of human rights articulated in the Universal Declaration, albeit with a focus on their application to women.

Equality between men and women, rooted as it is in the United Nations Charter is a major foundation for women's rights. As the preamble to the Convention on the Elimination of Discrimination against Women notes, a change in the traditional role of men as well as the role of women in society and in the family is needed to achieve full equality between men and women.

Irrespective of changes in attitude, there can perhaps never be true equality between the sexes, at least not in the sense of absolute similarity of treatment. What is required is recognition of the entitlement of women to equal enjoyment of all rights and freedoms. This was encapsulated in the preamble to the Charter of the United Nations, extracted above.

Men and women should thus be able to benefit from their rights and freedoms as enshrined in the various tabulations of rights without differentiation. Equality of enjoyment of all rights and freedoms, however, also demands recognition of equality of status before the law. For many women realisation of this has been a major issue impeding the progress of equality between the sexes. In extreme situations, it can also impede the progressive development of women's rights.

14.2.1   Non-discrimination

A related concept is that of non-discrimination. Non-discrimination in the exercise of rights is a common theme which pervades most instruments. Although the grounds may expand (see Chapter 2), the prohibition on discrimination on gender is a constant. The United Nations adopted an instrument specifically to reinforce the prohibition on discrimination against women: the Convention on the Elimination of All Forms of Discrimination against Women 1979. Article 1 provides a definition.

Convention on the Elimination of All Forms of Discrimination against Women Art 1

For the purposes of the present Convention, the term 'discrimination against women' shall mean any distinction, exclusion or restriction made on the basis of sex which has the effect or purpose of impairing or nullifying the recognition, enjoyment or exercise by women, irrespective of their marital status, on a basis of equality of men and women, of human rights and fundamental freedoms in the political, economic, social, cultural, civil or any other field.

Note three important aspects of this definition: discrimination may be intentional or unintentional; women may be directly or indirectly disadvantaged and the convention applies to rights in public and private spheres. The effect of the measure, not its prescribed aim is thus the important element to discern. This broadens the potential impact of the Convention but is clearly crucial: distinguishing appropriate and inappropriate legislative measures solely on account of the prescribed aim of the law would permit too wide a discretion to States and totally negate the aim of the Convention. Furthermore, the extension of the prohibition to public and private spheres implies a positive obligation on the part of States to protect women from certain actions, even where the proscribed act is undertaken by a private body. This is particularly apparent with respect to employment law.

Convention on the Elimination of All Forms of Discrimination against Women Art 2(e) and (f)

States Parties condemn discrimination against women in all its forms, agree to pursue by all appropriate means and without delay a policy of eliminating discrimination against women and, to this end, undertake: . . .

(e) To take all appropriate measures to eliminate discrimination against women by any person, organization or enterprise;

(f) To take all appropriate measures, including legislation, to modify or abolish existing laws, regulations, customs and practices which constitute discrimination against women.

Question

What problems may there be for States in ensuring that individuals conform to the standards of national law? What impact may this have on States when the issue of ratification/accession to the Convention is under discussion?

Much of the Convention on the Elimination of All Forms of Discrimination against Women reaffirms the rights of women to enjoy universal rights and freedoms on the basis of equality with men. There is little in the way of novel rights. The emphasis is firmly on non-discrimination against women in the exercise of universal rights.

14.2.2 Equality in law—Litigating the right

Individual (and group) communications can be lodged with the Committee on the Elimination of Discrimination against Women against those States which have ratified the Optional Protocol to the Convention on the Elimination of All Forms of Discrimination against Women 1999. As a remedy, this suffers from the deficiencies noted in Chapter 6. However, as a method of generating awareness and prompting a State to rethink its policies and laws, the individual petition system has considerable merit. Petitions under the Convention are still in their infancy, the Protocol only entered into force in late December 2000 although only a couple of communications have been considered. Note also that the Protocol permits the Committee to investigate incidences of systematic violations of the Convention.

Optional Protocol on the Elimination of All Forms of Discrimination against Women 1999 Art 8

1. If the Committee receives reliable information indicating grave or systematic violations by a State Party of rights set forth in the Convention, the Committee shall invite that State Party to cooperate in the examination of the information and to this end to submit observations with regard to the information concerned.

2. Taking into account any observations that may have been submitted by the State Party concerned as well as any other reliable information available to it, the Committee may designate one or more of its members to conduct an inquiry and to report urgently to the Committee. Where warranted and with the consent of the State Party, the inquiry may include a visit to its territory.

3. After examining the findings of such an inquiry, the Committee shall transmit these findings to the State Party concerned together with any comments and recommendations.

4. The State Party concerned shall, within six months of receiving the findings, comments and recommendations transmitted by the Committee, submit its observations to the Committee.

5. Such an inquiry shall be conducted confidentially and the cooperation of the State Party shall be sought at all stages of the proceedings.

The first communication, *Ms B-J v Germany*, Communication 1/2003 was declared inadmissible in July 2004 on account of non-exhaustion of domestic remedies and the fact that the events complained of occurred before the entry into force of the Optional Protocol. The second communication proceeded to merits (*Ms A-T v Hungary*, Communication 2/2003, decision January 2005, discussed below *re* violence against women).

Note particularly that complaints concerning discriminatory treatment can be brought before a variety of treaty monitoring bodies. This is an inevitable consequence of the evolution of the concept of equality between men and women under the auspices of the United Nations, and indeed, of the interdependence and indivisibility of universal human rights. For the victims, it is a positive development as many women thus have avenues of complaint open to them at the regional and international level, irrespective of whether their State has ratified the Convention on the Elimination of all Forms of Discrimination against Women and its Optional Protocol. The following list details the principal non-discrimination on gender provisions which the main treaty bodies consider. Note that additional rights may be engaged, these suggestions are not summative.

Human Rights Committee—Articles 2, 3 + 26 International Covenant on Civil and Political Rights prohibit discrimination in enjoyment of civil and political rights
European Court of Human Rights—Article 14 European Convention on Human Rights in conjunction with another right
European Court of Justice—Article 141 Consolidated Version of the Treaty of Rome Establishing the European Community and related directives, also actionable under national laws of European Union member States.
Inter-American Court of Human Rights—Articles 1, 24 American Convention on Human Rights.
African Court/Commission on Human and Peoples' Rights—African Charter and Protocol

To illustrate the potential for bringing complaints concerning inequality before alternative bodies, consider the following communications.

14.2.2.1 Human Rights Committee—Communications

Ato del Avellanal v Peru, Communication 202/1986, Human Rights Committee, 1988 UN Doc. CCPR/C/34/D/202/1986 (1988)

Under Art 168 of the Peruvian Civil Code law, married women wishing to enforce or action proceedings in respect of matrimonial property must be represented by the husband in court. Ms Ato del Avellanal was wishing to reclaim unpaid rent from apartment blocks which she owned. The decision of the court that the property issues must be represented by the husband was upheld by the Supreme Court despite a provision of the Peruvian Constitution requiring equality of rights. Article 14 of the International Covenant on Civil and Political Rights makes the following guarantee.

International Covenant on Civil and Political Rights Art 14(1)

All persons shall be equal before the courts and tribunals. In the determination of any criminal charge against him, or of his rights and obligations in a suit at law, everyone shall be entitled to a fair and public hearing by a competent, independent and impartial tribunal established by law. The press and the public may be excluded from all or part of a trial for reasons of morals, public order (ordre public) or national security in a democratic society, or when the interest of the private lives of the parties so requires, or to the extent strictly necessary in the opinion of the court in special circumstances where publicity would prejudice the interests of justice; but any judgement rendered in a criminal case or in a suit at law shall be made public except where the interest of juvenile persons otherwise requires or the proceedings concern matrimonial disputes or the guardianship of children.

Peruvian Law permits appeals to the Human Rights Committee of the United Nations for citizens who have exhausted domestic remedies and feel their constitutional rights have been infringed.

9.2 In formulating its views, the Committee takes into account the failure of the State party to furnish certain information and clarifications, in particular with regard to the allegations of discrimination of which the author has complained. It is not sufficient to forward the text of the relevant laws and decisions, without specifically addressing the issues raised in the communication. It is implicit in article 4, paragraph 2, of the Optional Protocol that the State party has the duty to investigate in good faith all allegations of violation of the Covenant made against it and its authorities, and to furnish to the Committee all relevant information. In the circumstances, due weight must be given to the author's allegations.

10.1 With respect to the requirement set forth in article 14, paragraph 1, of the Covenant that 'all persons shall be equal before the courts and tribunals', the committee notes that the court of first instance decided in favour of the author, but the Superior Court reversed that decision on the sole ground that according to article 168 of the Peruvian Civil Code only the husband is entitled to represent matrimonial property, i.e. that the wife was not equal to her husband for purposes of suing in Court.

10.2 With regard to discrimination on the ground of sex the Committee notes further that under article 3 of the Covenant State parties undertake 'to ensure the equal right of men and women to the enjoyment of all civil and political rights set forth in the present Covenant' and that article 26 provides that all persons are equal before the law and are entitled to the equal protection of the law. The Committee finds that the facts before it reveal that the application of article 168 of the Peruvian Civil Code to the author resulted in denying her equality before the courts and constituted discrimination on the ground of sex.

11. The Human Rights Committee, acting under article 5, paragraph 4, of the Optional Protocol to the International Covenant on Civil and Political Rights, is of the view that the events of this case, in so far as they continued or occurred after 3 January 1981 (the date of entry into force of the Optional Protocol for Peru), disclose violations of articles 3, 14, paragraph 1, and 26 of the Covenant.

Similar issues were raised before the Inter-American Commission on Human Rights in *Morales de Sierra v Guatemala*, Case 11.625 (2001) Report No. 4/01 (2001). The Guatemalan Civil Code conferred the primary power to represent the marital union, the children and marital property, on the husband. Moreover, the Code provided that wives had special obligations to care for children and the home and could not work outside the home if such work was prejudicial to her role as mother and housewife. The Commission considered the equality and marriage provisions of the Convention infringed.

Aumeeruddy-Cziffra and others v Mauritius, Communication 35/1978, Human Rights Committee 1981, UN Doc. CCPR/C/12/D/35/1978 (1981)

Twenty Mauritian women complained of discrimination with respect to immigration and deportation practices. Under new Mauritian laws (of 1977), the alien (that is, non-Mauritian) husband of a Mauritian woman must apply for a residence permit and may be subjected to deportation. Alien women married to Mauritian men retain their right to residency. The women claimed infringements of Arts 2–4, 17, 23, 25 and 26 of the Covenant on Civil and Political Rights. Clearly the application of the right had the potential to impact on their right to a home life and to found a family in Mauritius. For example, over three years had elapsed since Mrs Aumeeruddy-Cziffra's husband had applied to the Mauritian authorities for a residence permit without any formal decision.

9.2 (b) 2 (i) 2 The Committee takes the view that the common residence of husband and wife has to be considered as the normal behaviour of a family. Hence, and as the State party has admitted, the exclusion of a person from a country where close members of his family are living can amount to an interference within the meaning of article 17. In principle, article 17 (1) applies also when one of the spouses is an alien. Whether the existence and application of immigration laws affecting the residence of a family member is compatible with the Covenant depends on whether such interference is either 'arbitrary or unlawful' as stated in article 17 (1), or conflicts in any other way with the State party's obligations under the Covenant.

9.2 (b) 2 (i) 3 In the present cases, not only the future possibility of deportation, but the existing precarious residence situation of foreign husbands in Mauritius represents, in the opinion of the Committee, an interference by the authorities of the State party with the family life of the Mauritian wives and their husbands. The statutes in question have rendered it uncertain for the families concerned whether and for how long it will be possible for them to continue their family life by residing together in Mauritius. Moreover, as described above (para. 7.4) in one of the cases, even the delay for years, and the absence of a positive decision granting a residence permit, must be seen as a considerable inconvenience, among other reasons because the granting of a work permit, and hence the possibility of the husband to contribute to supporting the family, depends on the residence permit, and because deportation without judicial review is possible at any time.

9.2 (b) 2 (i) 4 Since, however, this situation results from the legislation itself, there can be no question of regarding this interference as 'unlawful' within the meaning of article 17 (1) in the present cases. It remains to be considered whether it is 'arbitrary' or conflicts in any other way with the Covenant.

9.2 (b) 2 (i) 5 The protection owed to individuals in this respect is subject to the principle of equal treatment of the sexes which follows from several provisions of the Covenant. It is an obligation of the State parties under article 2 (1) generally to respect and ensure the rights of the Covenant 'without distinction of any kind, such as . . . (inter alia) sex', and more particularly under article 3 'to ensure the equal right of men and women to the enjoyment' of all these rights, as well as under article 26 to provide 'without any discrimination' for 'the equal protection of the law'.

9.2 (b) 2 (i) 6 The authors who are married to foreign nationals are suffering from the adverse consequences of the statutes discussed above only because they are women. The precarious residence status of their husbands, affecting their family life as described, results from the 1977 laws which do not apply the same measures of control to foreign wives. In this connection the Committee has noted that under section 16 of the Constitution of Mauritius sex is not one of the grounds on which discrimination is prohibited.

9.2 (b) 2 (i) 7 In these circumstances, it is not necessary for the Committee to decide in the present cases how far such or other restrictions on the residence of foreign spouses might conflict with the Covenant if applied without discrimination of any kind.

9.2 (b) 2 (i) 8 The Committee considers that it is also unnecessary to say whether the existing discrimination should be called an 'arbitrary' interference with the family within the meaning of article 17. Whether or not the particular interference could as such be justified if it were applied without discrimination does not matter here. Whenever restrictions are placed on a right guaranteed by the Covenant, this has to be done without discrimination on the ground of sex. Whether the restriction in itself would be in breach of that right regarded in isolation, is not decisive in this respect. It is the enjoyment of the rights which must be secured without discrimination. Here it is sufficient, therefore, to note that in the present position an adverse distinction based on sex is made, affecting the alleged victims in their enjoyment of one of their rights. No sufficient justification for this difference has been given. The Committee must then find that there is a violation of articles 2 (1) and 3 of the Covenant, in conjunction with article 17 (1).

The issues in this case are comparable to *Abdulaziz, Cabales and Balkandali v United Kingdom*, Series A, No. 94 (1985). The European Court of Human Rights considered that the applicants' rights under Art 8 of the European Convention (right to private and family life, home and correspondence) in conjunction with the prohibition on discrimination on grounds of gender (Art 14) had been infringed.

However, compare *Broeks v Netherlands*, Communication 172/1984 with *Vos v Netherlands*, Communication 218/1986, both opinions of the Human Rights Committee applying the International Covenant on Civil and Political Rights. Discrimination was only found in the former.

Question

Can women ever be equal in law with men? To what extent can the concept of equality of rights truly make a difference to the plight of women?

14.2.2.2 European Court of Justice—preliminary ruling

Obviously, child-birth and breast-feeding are restricted to women. This has caused problems with respect to discrimination and equality law as there is no male equivalent. The European Court of Justice (an organ of the European Union) has regularly considered the issue of maternity rights and discrimination. *Brown v Rentokil* is a Scottish case which illustrates its approach. The House of Lords (highest UK Civil Court) referred various questions concerning dismissal of a woman for illness during pregnancy to the European Court of Justice under its preliminary ruling system (now

Art 234 of the Consolidated Version of the Treaty Establishing the European Union).
The final application of the law, in light of the view of the European Court, to the facts,
is left to the national court.

Case C–394/96, *Brown v Rentokil* [1998] ECR I–4185

Brown's employment contract specified that prolonged absence (26 weeks continuous illness) would justify dismissal. She became pregnant and endured various complications which caused her to be off work. Her employer notified her that 13 weeks
had elapsed and if she did not return to work by the end of the 26 week period
(following an independent medical examination) then her employment would be
terminated. Her contract was terminated and her baby born a few weeks later.
Brown's prolonged absence meant that she fell outwith the provisions of the national
Employment Protection (Consolidation) Act 1978 as she was not in work for two
years prior to the 11th week before the expected period of confinement.

16 According to settled case-law of the Court of Justice, the dismissal of a female worker on
account of pregnancy, or essentially on account of pregnancy, can affect only women and therefore constitutes direct discrimination on grounds of sex (see Case C–177/88 *Dekker v Stichting
Vormingscentrum voor Jong Volwassenen (VJV-Centrum) Plus* 1990 ECR I–3941, paragraph 12; Hertz,
paragraph 13; Case C–421/92 *Habermann-Beltermann v Arbeiterwohlfahrt Bezirksverband* 1994 ECR
I–1657, paragraph 15; and Case C–32/93 *Webb v EMO Air Cargo* 1994 ECR I–3567, paragraph 19).

17 As the Court pointed out in paragraph 20 of its judgment in *Webb*, 'by reserving to Member
States the right to retain or introduce provisions which are intended to protect women
in connection with pregnancy and maternity', Article 2(3) of Directive 76/207 recognises the
legitimacy, in terms of the principle of equal treatment, first, of protecting a woman's biological
condition during and after pregnancy and, second, of protecting the special relationship between a
woman and her child over the period which follows pregnancy and childbirth.

18 It was precisely in view of the harmful effects which the risk of dismissal may have on the
physical and mental state of women who are pregnant, women who have recently given birth or
women who are breastfeeding, including the particularly serious risk that pregnant women may
be prompted voluntarily to terminate their pregnancy, that the Community legislature, pursuant
to Article 10 of Council Directive 92/85/EEC of 19 October 1992 on the introduction of measures to encourage improvements in the safety and health at work of pregnant workers and
workers who have recently given birth or are breastfeeding (tenth individual Directive adopted
within the meaning of Article 16(1) of Directive 89/391/EEC) (OJ 1992 L 348, p. 1), which was to
be transposed into the laws of the Member States no later than two years after its adoption,
provided for special protection to be given to women, by prohibiting dismissal during the period
from the beginning of their pregnancy to the end of their maternity leave. Article 10 of Directive
92/85 provides that there is to be no exception to, or derogation from, the prohibition of
dismissal of pregnant women during that period, save in exceptional cases not connected with
their condition (see, in this regard, paragraphs 21 and 22 of the judgment in *Webb*).

Pregnancy has been variously treated as equivalent to a male illness and a disability.
The view of the European Court appears to be that any measure affecting only pregnant women constitutes direct discrimination by reason of the fact it only affects
women.

14.2.3   Towards equality of rights between men and women

Achieving equality is an ongoing process and clearly a goal for the United Nations. The Beijing Fourth World Conference on Women notes equality and non-discrimination in practice and fact as one of its strategic objectives. The following recommendations were made.

Beijing Platform for Action Strategic objective I.2. Ensure equality and non-discrimination under the law and in practice

Actions to be taken

232. By Governments:

(a) Give priority to promoting and protecting the full and equal enjoyment by women and men of all human rights and fundamental freedoms without distinction of any kind as to race, colour, sex, language, religion, political or other opinions, national or social origins, property, birth or other status;

(b) Provide constitutional guarantees and/or enact appropriate legislation to prohibit discrimination on the basis of sex for all women and girls of all ages and assure women of all ages equal rights and their full enjoyment;

(c) Embody the principle of the equality of men and women in their legislation and ensure, through law and other appropriate means, the practical realization of this principle;

(d) Review national laws, including customary laws and legal practices in the areas of family, civil, penal, labour and commercial law in order to ensure the implementation of the principles and procedures of all relevant international human rights instruments by means of national legislation, revoke any remaining laws that discriminate on the basis of sex and remove gender bias in the administration of justice;

(e) Strengthen and encourage the development of programmes to protect the human rights of women in the national institutions on human rights that carry out programmes, such as human rights commissions or ombudspersons, according them appropriate status, resources and access to the Government to assist individuals, in particular women, and ensure that these institutions pay adequate attention to problems involving the violation of the human rights of women;

(f) Take action to ensure that the human rights of women, including the rights referred to in paragraphs 94 to 96 above, are fully respected and protected;

(g) Take urgent action to combat and eliminate violence against women, which is a human rights violation, resulting from harmful traditional or customary practices, cultural prejudices and extremism;

(h) Prohibit female genital mutilation wherever it exists and give vigorous support to efforts among non-governmental and community organizations and religious institutions to eliminate such practices;

(i) Provide gender-sensitive human rights education and training to public officials, including, *inter alia*, police and military personnel, corrections officers, health and medical personnel, and social workers, including people who deal with migration and refugee issues, and teachers at all levels of the educational system, and make available such education and training also to the judiciary and members of parliament in order to enable them to better exercise their public responsibilities;

(j) Promote the equal right of women to be members of trade unions and other professional and social organizations;

(k) Establish effective mechanisms for investigating violations of the human rights of women perpetrated by any public official and take the necessary punitive legal measures in accordance with national laws;

(l) Review and amend criminal laws and procedures, as necessary, to eliminate any discrimination against women in order to ensure that criminal law and procedures guarantee women effective protection against, and prosecution of, crimes directed at or disproportionately affecting women, regardless of the relationship between the perpetrator and the victim, and ensure that women defendants, victims and/or witnesses are not revictimized or discriminated against in the investigation and prosecution of crimes;

(m) Ensure that women have the same right as men to be judges, advocates or other officers of the court, as well as police officers and prison and detention officers, among other things;

(n) Strengthen existing or establish readily available and free or affordable alternative administrative mechanisms and legal aid programmes to assist disadvantaged women seeking redress for violations of their rights;

(o) Ensure that all women and non-governmental organizations and their members in the field of protection and promotion of all human rights—civil, cultural, economic, political and social rights, including the right to development—enjoy fully all human rights and freedoms in accordance with the Universal Declaration of Human Rights and all other human rights instruments and the protection of national laws;

(p) Strengthen and encourage the implementation of the recommendations contained in the Standard Rules on the Equalization of Opportunities for Persons with Disabilities, paying special attention to ensure non-discrimination and equal enjoyment of all human rights and fundamental freedoms by women and girls with disabilities, including their access to information and services in the field of violence against women, as well as their active participation in and economic contribution to all aspects of society;

(q) Encourage the development of gender-sensitive human rights programmes.

Much remains to be done: more women than men suffer from a lack of educational opportunities; more women than men suffer from the effects of famine, pandemic diseases etc. Interestingly, the Beijing Platform for Action also mentions achieving legal literacy as a strategic objective.

Beijing Platform for Action, para 227

While women are increasingly using the legal system to exercise their rights, in many countries lack of awareness of the existence of these rights is an obstacle that prevents women from fully enjoying their human rights and attaining equality. Experience in many countries has shown that women can be empowered and motivated to assert their rights, regardless of their level of education or socio-economic status. Legal literacy programmes and media strategies have been effective in helping women to understand the link between their rights and other aspects of their lives and in demonstrating that cost-effective initiatives can be undertaken to help women obtain those rights. Provision of human rights education is essential for promoting an understanding of the human rights of women, including knowledge of recourse mechanisms to redress violations of their rights. It is necessary for all individuals, especially women in vulnerable circumstances, to have full knowledge of their rights and access to legal recourse against violations of their rights.

14.2.4 Affirmative action/positive discrimination

Note, however, that equality of treatment does not necessarily denote equality in fact. If a woman and a man were in inequal positions to begin with then treating them with total equality will simply perpetuate the difference between them. Consider the following hypothetical example. A man and woman are employed in the same law firm. Each has identical experience and qualifications and both commence work at the same time.

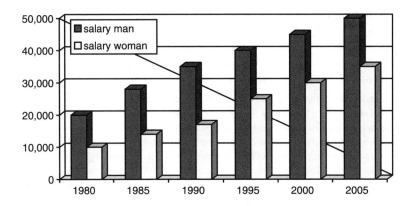

This diagram demonstrates the perpetuation of a difference in salary between a man and woman. The male salary increases more than that of the female in the first ten years. Obviously the gulf between the salaries increases. In 1990 equality legislation is enacted in the State so, thereafter, remedial action is taken to redress the imbalance and both the male and female salaries increase by the same amount each year. Note however, that the gap between the two remains constant. Salaries increase by the same amount each year for both the sexes and thus there is actual equality. This problem has given rise to demands for affirmative action/positive discrimination/ special temporary measures to redress this imbalance.

Positive discrimination means that measures intended to redress the gender imbalance are permissible even although the result may technically be discrimination against men.

Convention on the Elimination of all forms of Discrimination against Women Art 4

1. Adoption by States Parties of temporary special measures aimed at accelerating de facto equality between men and women shall not be considered discrimination as defined in the present Convention, but shall in no way entail as a consequence the maintenance of unequal or separate standards; these measures shall be discontinued when the objectives of equality of opportunity and treatment have been achieved.

2. Adoption by States Parties of special measures, including those measures contained in the present Convention, aimed at protecting maternity shall not be considered discriminatory.

Question

Consider the circumstances in which such measures may be justified. Note that similar issues arise with respect to indigenous peoples.

14.2.4.1   European Court of Justice—caselaw

Case C–450/93, *Kalanke v Freie Hansestadt Bremen* [1995] ECR I–3051

A male and female employee worked for the city of Bremen as gardeners. Both were shortlisted for a promoted position. As the applicants were equally well qualified for the position, preference was given to the woman in accordance with the positive action provisions of the local law on equal treatment of men and women in public service. Herr Kalanke brought proceedings in the national courts which upheld his rejection for the post. However, as the Federal Labour Court considered there may be a conflict with the European Community (now Union) provisions on equal treatment (Directive 76/207/EEC, 'the Equal Treatment Directive'), reference was made to the European Court of Justice. (Note that such preliminary rulings on issues of EU law are permissible in accordance with the now Art 234 of the Consolidated Version of the Treaty Establishing the European Community.)

14 In its order for reference, the national court points out that a quota system such as that in issue may help to overcome in the future the disadvantages which women currently face and which perpetuate past inequalities, inasmuch as it accustoms people to seeing women also filling certain more senior posts. The traditional assignment of certain tasks to women and the concentration of women at the lower end of the scale are contrary to the equal rights criteria applicable today. In that connection, the national court cites figures illustrating the low proportion of women in the higher career brackets among city employees in Bremen, particularly if sectors, such as education, where the presence of women in higher posts is now established are excluded.

15 The purpose of the Directive is, as stated in Article 1(1), to put into effect in the Member States the principle of equal treatment for men and women as regards, *inter alia*, access to employment, including promotion. Article 2(1) states that the principle of equal treatment means that 'there shall be no discrimination whatsoever on grounds of sex either directly or indirectly'.

16 A national rule that, where men and women who are candidates for the same promotion are equally qualified, women are automatically to be given priority in sectors where they are under-represented, involves discrimination on grounds of sex.

17 It must, however, be considered whether such a national rule is permissible under Article 2(4), which provides that the Directive 'shall be without prejudice to measures to promote equal opportunity for men and women, in particular by removing existing inequalities which affect women's opportunities'.

18 That provision is specifically and exclusively designed to allow measures which, although discriminatory in appearance, are in fact intended to eliminate or reduce actual instances of inequality which may exist in the reality of social life (see Case 312/86 *Commission v France* 1988 ECR 6315, paragraph 15).

19 It thus permits national measures relating to access to employment, including promotion, which give a specific advantage to women with a view to improving their ability to compete on the labour market and to pursue a career on an equal footing with men. . . .

21 Nevertheless, as a derogation from an individual right laid down in the Directive, Article 2(4) must be interpreted strictly (see Case 222/84 *Johnston v Chief Constable of the Royal Ulster Constabulary* 1986 ECR 1651, paragraph 36).

22 National rules which guarantee women absolute and unconditional priority for appointment or promotion go beyond promoting equal opportunities and overstep the limits of the exception in Article 2(4) of the Directive. . . .

On those grounds,

THE COURT,

in answer to the questions referred to it by the Bundesarbeitsgericht by order of 22 June 1993, hereby rules:

> Article 2(1) and (4) of Council Directive 76/207/EEC of 9 February 1976 on the implementation of the principle of equal treatment for men and women as regards access to employment, vocational training and promotion, and working conditions precludes national rules such as those in the present case which, where candidates of different sexes shortlisted for promotion are equally qualified, automatically give priority to women in sectors where they are under-represented, under-representation being deemed to exist when women do not make up at least half of the staff in the individual pay brackets in the relevant personnel group or in the function levels provided for in the organization chart.

In accordance with the European Community Law system, each case is considered before an Advocate General who renders a detailed opinion on the legal issues prior to the Court's deliberations. The opinion of the Advocate General is not binding on the Court but may prove influential. In the instant case, the Advocate General provides a detailed discussion of the concept of affirmative action/positive discrimination.

Opinion of Mr Advocate General Tesauro delivered on 6 April 1995

13 Next, in order to establish what positive actions are authorized by Article 2(4), it is necessary to define the concept of equal opportunities, more specifically in order to clarify whether that expression means equality with respect to starting points or with respect to points of arrival. To my mind, giving equal opportunities can only mean putting people in a position to attain equal results and hence restoring conditions of equality as between members of the two sexes as regards starting points. In order to achieve such a result, it is obviously necessary to removing the existing barriers standing in the way of the attainment of equal opportunities as between men and women in the field of employment: it will therefore be necessary first to identify the barriers and then remove them, using the most suitable instruments for the purpose.

It seems to me to be all too obvious that the national legislation at issue in this case is not designed to guarantee equality as regards starting points. The very fact that two candidates of different sex have equivalent qualifications implies in fact by definition that the two candidates have had and continue to have equal opportunities: they are therefore on an equal footing at the starting block. By giving priority to women, the national legislation at issue therefore aims to achieve equality as regards the result or, better, fair job distribution simply in numerical terms between men and women. This does not seem to me to fall within either the scope or the rationale of Article 2(4) of the directive.

14 That having been said, it should not be overlooked that the ultimate objective of equal opportunities is to promote the employment of women and attain substantive equality, and that equality as regards starting points alone will not in itself guarantee equal results, which, apart from depending on the merits of the persons concerned and the individual efforts which they make, (12) may also be influenced by a particular social structure which penalizes women, in particular because of their dual role, on account of past discrimination, which causes their presence in some sectors, particularly at management level, to be marginal.

Accordingly, it remains to be considered whether Article 2(4) of the directive can be interpreted in such a way as to encompass also actions entailing the predetermination of 'results' through the imposition of quotas, be they strict or, as in this case, dependent on the fulfilment of specific conditions.

15 On the only occasion on which the Court has ruled on the interpretation of Article 2(4), it held that the exception provided for in that provision is 'specifically and exclusively designed to allow measures which, although discriminatory in appearance, are in fact intended to eliminate or reduce actual instances of inequality which may exist in the reality of social life'. (13) As a result, the Court held that the derogating provision contained in Article 2(4) did not cover special rights for women, such as shortening of working hours, advancement of the retirement age, obtaining leave when a child is ill, granting additional days of annual leave in respect of each child, payment of an allowance to mothers who have to meet the cost of nurseries and the like, and so on.

The Court therefore considered that Article 2(4) authorizes treatment which is only discriminatory in appearance but designed in practice to remove existing obstacles standing in the way of equal opportunities for women. (14) This confirms that the objective is substantive equality; but, in my view, it also confirms that that objective may be pursued only through measures designed to achieve an actual situation of equal opportunities, with the result that the only inequalities authorized are those necessary to eliminate the obstacles or inequalities which prevent women from pursuing the same results as men on equal terms. Indeed, it is from that point of view that the measures specifically intended for women are only discriminatory in appearance; and it is only in this way that real and effective substantive equality will be achieved.

16 The principle of substantive equality necessitates taking account of the existing inequalities which arise because a person belongs to a particular class of persons or to a particular social group; it enables and requires the unequal, detrimental effects which those inequalities have on the members of the group in question to be eliminated or, in any event, neutralized by means of specific measures.

Unlike the principle of formal equality, which precludes basing unequal treatment of individuals on certain differentiating factors, such as sex, the principle of substantive equality refers to a positive concept by basing itself precisely on the relevance of those different factors themselves in order to legitimize an unequal right, which is to be used in order to achieve equality as between persons who are regarded not as neutral but having regard to their differences. In the final analysis, the principal of substantive equality complements the principle of formal equality and authorizes only such deviations from that principle as are justified by the end which they seek to achieve, that of securing actual equality. The ultimate objective is therefore the same: securing equality as between persons.

Question

Balance positive discrimination and ascertain whether the advantage (achieving true equality) outweighs the discrimination against men which is a necessary consequence.

14.2.5   Case study: women and political participation

In November 2005, the first female political leaders were appointed in Germany and Liberia (Chancellor and President, respectively). Women's right to political participation was established early in the evolution of the United Nations.

Convention on the Political Rights of Women 1952

Article I

Women shall be entitled to vote in all elections on equal terms with men, without any discrimination.

Article II

Women shall be eligible for election to all publicly elected bodies, established by national law, on equal terms with men, without any discrimination.

Article III

Women shall be entitled to hold public office and to exercise all public functions, established by national law, on equal terms with men, without any discrimination.

Note also Arts 7 and 8 of the Convention on the Elimination of All Forms of Discrimination against Women.

Convention on the Elimination of All Forms of Discrimination against Women

Article 7

States Parties shall take all appropriate measures to eliminate discrimination against women in the political and public life of the country and, in particular, shall ensure to women, on equal terms with men, the right:

(a) To vote in all elections and public referenda and to be eligible for election to all publicly elected bodies;

(b) To participate in the formulation of government policy and the implementation thereof and to hold public office and perform all public functions at all levels of government;

(c) To participate in non-governmental organizations and associations concerned with the public and political life of the country.

Article 8

States Parties shall take all appropriate measures to ensure to women, on equal terms with men and without any discrimination, the opportunity to represent their Governments at the international level and to participate in the work of international organizations.

Consider the following statistics on women in high political decision-making positions.

The following graph illustrates the percentage of women involved in national political organisations in the world's regions. Figures are taken from the website of the Inter-Parliamentary Union (www.ipu.org/english/home.htm).

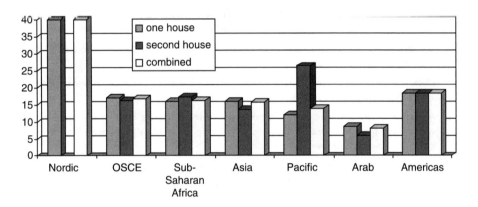

The Nordic countries have long had a positive record of women in Parliament. Note, however, that many other countries (in autumn 2005 Liberia joined the list) have had female presidents/heads of State/heads of government. However, the rest of the Parliamentary body has not necessarily reflected equal representation.

The Labour government which assumed political dominance in the British General Election in 1997 boasted a record number of female Members of Parliament. Late in 2005, a new opposition (conservative) leader was elected—one of his first statements was a call for more women in Parliament.

Question

To remedy the imbalance, can States reform electoral procedures to ensure more women are appointed to political office?

14.3   TABULATING WOMEN'S RIGHTS

Some commentators contend that rather than be accorded distinctive rights, the emphasis in the international community should be in ensuring that women enjoy the full range of universal human rights on a parity with men.

Question

Is there merit in this argument?

Despite universal human rights, women appear still to be more vulnerable than men. They suffer more from infringements of their rights and are more commonly discriminated against than for. Perhaps at least partially the answer should lie in strengthening the existing mechanisms for enforcing human rights and ensuring that women are in a position to advance their rights. That women required additional protection became increasingly apparent. The international community has to date convened four major international conferences on women. The first was in Mexico 1975, the second in Denmark (Copenhagen) 1980, a third in Kenya (Nairobi) 1985 and most recently the Fourth World Conference on Women was held in China (Beijing) in 1995.

The Fourth World Conference on Women represented a watershed for women's rights and indeed for international human rights. It adopted a Declaration and a Programme of Action for achieving the goals in the declaration. Enhancing and promoting women's rights is the principal goal.

Fourth World Conference on Women Beijing Declaration

1. We, the Governments participating in the Fourth World Conference on Women,

2. Gathered here in Beijing in September 1995, the year of the fiftieth anniversary of the founding of the United Nations,

3. Determined to advance the goals of equality, development and peace for all women everywhere in the interest of all humanity,

4. Acknowledging the voices of all women everywhere and taking note of the diversity of women and their roles and circumstances, honoring the women who paved the way and inspired by the hope present in the world's youth,

5. Recognize that the status of women has advanced in some important respects in the past decade but that progress has been uneven, inequalities between women and men have persisted and major obstacles remain, with serious consequences for the well-being of all people,

6. Also recognize that this situation is exacerbated by the increasing poverty that is affecting the lives of the majority of the world's people, in particular women and children, with origins in both the national and international domains,

7. Dedicate ourselves unreservedly to addressing these constraints and obstacles and thus enhancing further the advancement and empowerment of women all over the world, and agree that this requires urgent action in the spirit of determination, hope, cooperation and solidarity, now and to carry us forward into the next century.

We reaffirm our commitment to:

8. The equal rights and inherent human dignity of women and men and other purposes and principles enshrined in the Charter of the United Nations, to the Universal Declaration of Human Rights and other international human rights instruments, in particular the Convention on the Elimination of All Forms of Discrimination against Women and the Convention on the Rights of the Child, as well as the Declaration on the Elimination of Violence against Women and the Declaration on the Right to Development;

9. Ensure the full implementation of the human rights of women and of the girl child as an inalienable, integral and indivisible part of all human rights and fundamental freedoms;

10. Build on consensus and progress made at previous United Nations conferences and summits—on women in Nairobi in 1985, on children in New York in 1990, on environment and development in Rio de Janeiro in 1992, on human rights in Vienna in 1993, on population and development in Cairo in 1994 and on social development in Copenhagen in 1995 with the objective of achieving equality, development and peace;

11.   Achieve the full and effective implementation of the Nairobi Forward-looking Strategies for the Advancement of Women;

12.   The empowerment and advancement of women, including the right to freedom of thought, conscience, religion and belief, thus contributing to the moral, ethical, spiritual and intellectual needs of women and men, individually or in community with others and thereby guaranteeing them the possibility of realizing their full potential in society and shaping their lives in accordance with their own aspirations.

We are convinced that:

13.   Women's empowerment and their full participation on the basis of equality in all spheres of society, including participation in the decision-making process and access to power, are fundamental for the achievement of equality, development and peace;

14.   Women's rights are human rights;

15.   Equal rights, opportunities and access to resources, equal sharing of responsibilities for the family by men and women, and a harmonious partnership between them are critical to their well-being and that of their families as well as to the consolidation of democracy;

16.   Eradication of poverty based on sustained economic growth, social development, environmental protection and social justice requires the involvement of women in economic and social development, equal opportunities and the full and equal participation of women and men as agents and beneficiaries of people-centred sustainable development;

17.   The explicit recognition and reaffirmation of the right of all women to control all aspects of their health, in particular their own fertility, is basic to their empowerment;

18.   Local, national, regional and global peace is attainable and is inextricably linked with the advancement of women, who are a fundamental force for leadership, conflict resolution and the promotion of lasting peace at all levels;

19.   It is essential to design, implement and monitor, with the full participation of women, effective, efficient and mutually reinforcing gender-sensitive policies and programmes, including development policies and programmes, at all levels that will foster the empowerment and advancement of women;

20.   The participation and contribution of all actors of civil society, particularly women's groups and networks and other non-governmental organizations and community-based organizations, with full respect for their autonomy, in cooperation with Governments, are important to the effective implementation and follow-up of the Platform for Action;

21.   The implementation of the Platform for Action requires commitment from Governments and the international community. By making national and international commitments for action, including those made at the Conference, Governments and the international community recognize the need to take priority action for the empowerment and advancement of women.

We are determined to:

22.   Intensify efforts and actions to achieve the goals of the Nairobi Forward-looking Strategies for the Advancement of Women by the end of this century;

23.   Ensure the full enjoyment by women and the girl child of all human rights and fundamental freedoms and take effective action against violations of these rights and freedoms;

24.   Take all necessary measures to eliminate all forms of discrimination against women and the girl child and remove all obstacles to gender equality and the advancement and empowerment of women;

25.   Encourage men to participate fully in all actions towards equality;

26.   Promote women's economic independence, including employment, and eradicate the persistent and increasing burden of poverty on women by addressing the structural causes of

poverty through changes uneconomic, ensuring equal access for all women, including those in rural areas, as vital development agents, to productive resources, opportunities and public services;

27. Promote people-centred sustainable development, including sustained economic growth, through the provision of basic education, life-long education, literacy and training, and primary health care for girls and women;

28. Take positive steps to ensure peace for the advancement of women and, recognizing the leading role that women have played in the peace movement, work actively towards general and complete disarmament under strict and effective international control, and support negotiations on the conclusion, without delay, of a universal and multilaterally and effectively verifiable comprehensive nuclear-test-ban treaty which contributes to nuclear disarmament and the prevention of the proliferation of nuclear weapons in all its aspects;

29. Prevent and eliminate all forms of violence against women and girls;

30. Ensure equal access to and equal treatment of women and men in education and health care and enhance women's sexual and reproductive health as well as education;

31. Promote and protect all human rights of women and girls;

32. Intensify efforts to ensure equal enjoyment of all human rights and fundamental freedoms for all women and girls who face multiple barriers to their empowerment and advancement because of such factors as their race, age, language, ethnicity, culture, religion, or disability, or because they are indigenous people;

33. Ensure respect for international law, including humanitarian law, in order to protect women and girls in particular;

34. Develop the fullest potential of girls and women of all ages, ensure their full and equal participation in building a better world for all and enhance their role in the development process.

We are determined to:

35. Ensure women's equal access to economic resources, including land, credit, science and technology, vocational training, information, communication and markets, as a means to further the advancement and empowerment of women and girls, including through the enhancement of their capacities to enjoy the benefits of equal access to these resources, *inter alia*, by means of international cooperation;

36. Ensure the success of the Platform for Action, which will require a strong commitment on the part of Governments, international organizations and institutions at all levels. We are deeply convinced that economic development, social development and environmental protection are interdependent and mutually reinforcing components of sustainable development, which is the framework for our efforts to achieve a higher quality of life for all people. Equitable social development that recognizes empowering the poor, particularly women living in poverty, to utilize environmental resources sustainably is a necessary foundation for sustainable development. We also recognize that broad-based and sustained economic growth in the context of sustainable development is necessary to sustain social development and social justice. The success of the Platform for Action will also require adequate mobilization of resources at the national and international levels as well as new and additional resources to the developing countries from all available funding mechanisms, including multilateral, bilateral and private sources for the advancement of women; financial resources to strengthen the capacity of national, sub-regional, regional and international institutions; a commitment to equal rights, equal responsibilities and equal opportunities and to the equal participation of women and men in all national, regional and international bodies and policy-making processes; and the establishment or strengthening of mechanisms at all levels for accountability to the world's women;

37.   Ensure also the success of the Platform for Action in countries with economies in transition, which will require continued international cooperation and assistance;

38.   We hereby adopt and commit ourselves as Governments to implement the following Platform for Action, ensuring that a gender perspectives (*sic*) reflected in all our policies and programmes. We urge the United Nations system, regional and international financial institutions, other relevant regional and international institutions and all women and men, as well as non-governmental organizations, with full respect for their autonomy, and all sectors of civil society, in cooperation with Governments, to fully commit themselves and contribute to the implementation of this Platform for Action.

A Platform for Action was concluded to provide a blueprint to advancing women's rights towards the twenty-first century. Extracts have already been considered.

Twelve areas of critical concern were identified: Women and Poverty; Education and Training of Women; Women and Health; Violence against Women; Women and Armed Conflict; Women and the Economy; Women in Power and Decision-Making; Institutional Mechanisms for the Advancement of Women; Human Rights of Women; Women and the Media; Women and the Environment; the Girl Child. The process and plan is as follows:

Fourth World Conference on Women's Rights Platform for Action

45.   In each critical area of concern, the problem is diagnosed and strategic objectives are proposed with concrete actions to be taken by various actors in order to achieve those objectives. The strategic objectives are derived from the critical areas of concern and specific actions to be taken to achieve them cut across the boundaries of equality, development and peace—the goals of the Nairobi Forward-looking Strategies for the Advancement of Women—and reflect their interdependence. The objectives and actions are interlinked, of high priority and mutually reinforcing. The Platform for Action is intended to improve the situation of all women, without exception, who often face similar barriers, while special attention should be given to groups that are the most disadvantaged.

46.   The Platform for Action recognizes that women face barriers to full equality and advancement because of such factors as their race, age, language, ethnicity, culture, religion or disability, because they are indigenous women or because of other status. Many women encounter specific obstacles related to their family status, particularly as single parents; and to their socio-economic status, including their living conditions in rural, isolated or impoverished areas. Additional barriers also exist for refugee women, other displaced women, including internally displaced women as well as for immigrant women and migrant women, including women migrant workers. Many women are also particularly affected by environmental disasters, serious and infectious diseases and various forms of violence against women.

14.3.1   Women and health: an example from the Beijing platform for action

Initially the Platform for Action identifies the problems arising in respect of women and health.

Beijing Platform for Action part C. Women and Health

89.   Women have the right to the enjoyment of the highest attainable standard of physical and mental health. The enjoyment of this right is vital to their life and well-being and their ability to participate in all areas of public and private life. Health is a state of complete physical, mental and social well-being and not merely the absence of disease or infirmity. Women's

health involves their emotional, social and physical well-being and is determined by the social, political and economic context of their lives, as well as by biology. However, health and well-being elude the majority of women. A major barrier for women to the achievement of the highest attainable standard of health is inequality, both between men and women and among women in different geographical regions, social classes and indigenous and ethnic groups. In national and international forums, women have emphasized that to attain optimal health throughout the life cycle, equality, including the sharing of family responsibilities, development and peace are necessary conditions.

90.   Women have different and unequal access to and use of basic health resources, including primary health services for the prevention and treatment of childhood diseases, malnutrition, anaemia, diarrhoeal diseases, communicable diseases, malaria and other tropical diseases and tuberculosis, among others. Women also have different and unequal opportunities for the protection, promotion and maintenance of their health. In many developing countries, the lack of emergency obstetric services is also of particular concern. Health policies and programmes often perpetuate gender stereotypes and fail to consider socioeconomic disparities and other differences among women and may not fully take account of the lack of autonomy of women regarding their health. Women's health is also affected by gender bias in the health system and by the provision of inadequate and inappropriate medical services to women.

91.   In many countries, especially developing countries, in particular the least developed countries, a decrease in public health spending and, in some cases, structural adjustment, contribute to the deterioration of public health systems. In addition, privatization of health-care systems without appropriate guarantees of universal access to affordable health care further reduces health-care availability. This situation not only directly affects the health of girls and women, but also places disproportionate responsibilities on women, whose multiple roles, including their roles within the family and the community, are often not acknowledged; hence they do not receive the necessary social, psychological and economic support.

92.   Women's right to the enjoyment of the highest standard of health must be secured throughout the whole life cycle in equality with men. Women are affected by many of the same health conditions as men, but women experience them differently. The prevalence among women of poverty and economic dependence, their experience of violence, negative attitudes towards women and girls, racial and other forms of discrimination, the limited power many women have over their sexual and reproductive lives and lack of influence in decision-making are social realities which have an adverse impact on their health. Lack of food and inequitable distribution of food for girls and women in the household, inadequate access to safe water, sanitation facilities and fuel supplies, particularly in rural and poor urban areas, and deficient housing conditions, all overburden women and their families and have a negative effect on their health. Good health is essential to leading a productive and fulfilling life, and the right of all women to control all aspects of their health, in particular their own fertility, is basic to their empowerment.

93.   Discrimination against girls, often resulting from son preference, in access to nutrition and health-care services endangers their current and future health and well-being. Conditions that force girls into early marriage, pregnancy and child-bearing and subject them to harmful practices, such as female genital mutilation, pose grave health risks. Adolescent girls need, but too often do not have, access to necessary health and nutrition services as they mature. Counselling and access to sexual and reproductive health information and services for adolescents are still inadequate or lacking completely, and a young woman's right to privacy, confidentiality, respect and informed consent is often not considered. Adolescent girls are both biologically and psychosocially more vulnerable than boys to sexual abuse, violence and prostitution, and to the consequences of unprotected and premature sexual relations. The trend towards early sexual experience, combined with a lack of information

and services, increases the risk of unwanted and too early pregnancy, HIV infection and other sexually transmitted diseases, as well as unsafe abortions. Early child-bearing continues to be an impediment to improvements in the educational, economic and social status of women in all parts of the world. Overall, for young women early marriage and early motherhood can severely curtail educational and employment opportunities and are likely to have a long-term, adverse impact on the quality of their lives and the lives of their children. Young men are often not educated to respect women's self-determination and to share responsibility with women in matters of sexuality and reproduction.

94.   Reproductive health is a state of complete physical, mental and social well-being and not merely the absence of disease or infirmity, in all matters relating to the reproductive system and to its functions and processes. Reproductive health therefore implies that people are able to have a satisfying and safe sex life and that they have the capability to reproduce and the freedom to decide if, when and how often to do so. Implicit in this last condition are the right of men and women to be informed and to have access to safe, effective, affordable and acceptable methods of family planning of their choice, as well as other methods of their choice for regulation of fertility which are not against the law, and the right of access to appropriate health-care services that will enable women to go safely through pregnancy and childbirth and provide couples with the best chance of having a healthy infant. In line with the above definition of reproductive health, reproductive health care is defined as the constellation of methods, techniques and services that contribute to reproductive health and well-being by preventing and solving reproductive health problems. It also includes sexual health, the purpose of which is the enhancement of life and personal relations, and not merely counselling and care related to reproduction and sexually trans-mitted diseases.

95.   Bearing in mind the above definition, reproductive rights embrace certain human rights that are already recognized in national laws, international human rights documents and other consensus documents. These rights rest on the recognition of the basic right of all couples and individuals to decide freely and responsibly the number, spacing and timing of their children and to have the information and means to do so, and the right to attain the highest standard of sexual and reproductive health. It also includes their right to make decisions concerning reproduction free of discrimination, coercion and violence, as expressed in human rights documents. In the exercise of this right, they should take into account the needs of their living and future children and their responsibilities towards the community. The promotion of the responsible exercise of these rights for all people should be the fundamental basis for government- and community-supported policies and pro-grammes in the area of reproductive health, including family planning. As part of their commitment, full attention should be given to the promotion of mutually respectful and equitable gender relations and particularly to meeting the educational and service needs of adolescents to enable them to deal in a positive and responsible way with their sexuality. Reproductive health eludes many of the world's people because of such factors as: inadequate levels of knowledge about human sexuality and inappropriate or poor-quality reproductive health information and services; the prevalence of high-risk sexual behaviour; discriminatory social practices; negative attitudes towards women and girls; and the limited power many women and girls have over their sexual and reproductive lives. Adolescents are particularly vulnerable because of their lack of information and access to relevant services in most countries. Older women and men have distinct reproductive and sexual health issues which are often inadequately addressed.

96.   The human rights of women include their right to have control over and decide freely and responsibly on matters related to their sexuality, including sexual and reproductive health, free of coercion, discrimination and violence. Equal relationships between women and men in matters of sexual relations and reproduction, including full respect for the integrity of the

person, require mutual respect, consent and shared responsibility for sexual behaviour and its consequences.

97.   Further, women are subject to particular health risks due to inadequate responsiveness and lack of services to meet health needs related to sexuality and reproduction. Complications related to pregnancy and childbirth are among the leading causes of mortality and morbidity of women of reproductive age in many parts of the developing world. Similar problems exist to a certain degree in some countries with economies in transition. Unsafe abortions threaten the lives of a large number of women, representing a grave public health problem as it is primarily the poorest and youngest who take the highest risk. Most of these deaths, health problems and injuries are preventable through improved access to adequate health-care services, including safe and effective family planning methods and emergency obstetric care, recognizing the right of women and men to be informed and to have access to safe, effective, affordable and acceptable methods of family planning of their choice, as well as other methods of their choice for regulation of fertility which are not against the law, and the right of access to appropriate health-care services that will enable women to go safely through pregnancy and childbirth and provide couples with the best chance of having a healthy infant. These problems and means should be addressed on the basis of the report of the International Conference on Population and Development, with particular reference to relevant paragraphs of the Programme of Action of the Conference. In most countries, the neglect of women's reproductive rights severely limits their opportunities in public and private life, including opportunities for education and economic and political empowerment. The ability of women to control their own fertility forms an important basis for the enjoyment of other rights. Shared responsibility between women and men in matters related to sexual and reproductive behaviour is also essential to improving women's health.

98.   HIV/AIDS and other sexually transmitted diseases, the transmission of which is sometimes a consequence of sexual violence, are having a devastating effect on women's health, particularly the health of adolescent girls and young women. They often do not have the power to insist on safe and responsible sex practices and have little access to information and services for prevention and treatment. Women, who represent half of all adults newly infected with HIV/AIDS and other sexually transmitted diseases, have emphasized that social vulnerability and the unequal power relationships between women and men are obstacles to safe sex, in their efforts to control the spread of sexually transmitted diseases. The consequences of HIV/AIDS reach beyond women's health to their role as mothers and caregivers and their contribution to the economic support of their families. The social, developmental and health consequences of HIV/AIDS and other sexually transmitted diseases need to be seen from a gender perspective.

99.   Sexual and gender-based violence, including physical and psychological abuse, trafficking in women and girls, and other forms of abuse and sexual exploitation place girls and women at high risk of physical and mental trauma, disease and unwanted pregnancy. Such situations often deter women from using health and other services.

100. Mental disorders related to marginalization, powerlessness and poverty, along with overwork and stress and the growing incidence of domestic violence as well as substance abuse, are among other health issues of growing concern to women. Women throughout the world, especially young women, are increasing their use of tobacco with serious effects on their health and that of their children. Occupational health issues are also growing in importance, as a large number of women work in low-paid jobs in either the formal or the informal labour market under tedious and unhealthy conditions, and the number is rising. Cancers of the breast and cervix and other cancers of the reproductive system, as well as infertility affect growing numbers of women and may be preventable, or curable, if detected early.

101. With the increase in life expectancy and the growing number of older women, their health concerns require particular attention. The long-term health prospects of women are influ-

enced by changes at menopause, which, in combination with life-long conditions and other factors, such as poor nutrition and lack of physical activity, may increase the risk of cardiovascular disease and osteoporosis. Other diseases of ageing and the interrelationships of ageing and disability among women also need particular attention.

102. Women, like men, particularly in rural areas and poor urban areas, are increasingly exposed to environmental health hazards owing to environmental catastrophes and degradation. Women have a different susceptibility to various environmental hazards, contaminants and substances and they suffer different consequences from exposure to them.

103. The quality of women's health care is often deficient in various ways, depending on local circumstances. Women are frequently not treated with respect, nor are they guaranteed privacy and confidentiality, nor do they always receive full information about the options and services available. Furthermore, in some countries, over-medicating of women's life events is common, leading to unnecessary surgical intervention and inappropriate medication.

104. Statistical data on health are often not systematically collected, disaggregated and analysed by age, sex and socio-economic status and by established demographic criteria used to serve the interests and solve the problems of subgroups, with particular emphasis on the vulnerable and marginalized and other relevant variables. Recent and reliable data on the mortality and morbidity of women and conditions and diseases particularly affecting women are not available in many countries. Relatively little is known about how social and economic factors affect the health of girls and women of all ages, about the provision of health services to girls and women and the patterns of their use of such services, and about the value of disease prevention and health promotion programmes for women. Subjects of importance to women's health have not been adequately researched and women's health research often lacks funding. Medical research, on heart disease, for example, and epidemiological studies in many countries are often based solely on men; they are not gender specific. Clinical trials involving women to establish basic information about dosage, side-effects and effectiveness of drugs, including contraceptives, are noticeably absent and do not always conform to ethical standards for research and testing. Many drug therapy protocols and other medical treatments and interventions administered to women are based on research on men without any investigation and adjustment for gender differences.

105. In addressing inequalities in health status and unequal access to and inadequate health-care services between women and men, Governments and other actors should promote an active and visible policy of mainstreaming a gender perspective in all policies and programmes, so that, before decisions are taken, an analysis is made of the effects for women and men, respectively.

Thereafter a number of strategic objectives are identified and actions to be taken by States (and others) are listed. For reasons of space, only one is extracted here.

Strategic Objective C.1: Increase women's access throughout the life cycle to appropriate, affordable and quality health care, information and related services.

Strategic Objective C.2: Strengthen preventive programmes that promote women's health.

Strategic Objective C.3: Undertake gender-sensitive initiatives that address sexually transmitted diseases, HIV/AIDS, and sexual and reproductive health issues.

Strategic Objective C.4: Promote research and disseminate information on women's health.

Strategic Objective C.5: Increase resources and monitor follow-up for women's health.

Strategic Objective C.5 Increase resources and monitor follow-up for women's health. Beijing Platform for Action

110. By Governments at all levels and, where appropriate, in cooperation with non-governmental organizations, especially women's and youth organizations:

(a)   Increase budgetary allocations for primary health care and social services, with adequate support for secondary and tertiary levels, and give special attention to the reproductive and sexual health of girls and women and give priority to health programmes in rural and poor urban areas;

(b)   Develop innovative approaches to funding health services through promoting community participation and local financing; increase, where necessary, budgetary allocations for community health centres and community-based programmes and services that address women's specific health needs;

(c)   Develop local health services, promoting the incorporation of gender-sensitive community-based participation and self-care and specially designed preventive health programmes;

(d)   Develop goals and time-frames, where appropriate, for improving women's health and for planning, implementing, monitoring and evaluating programmes, based on gender-impact assessments using qualitative and quantitative data disaggregated by sex, age, other established demographic criteria and socio-economic variables;

(e)   Establish, as appropriate, ministerial and inter-ministerial mechanisms for monitoring the implementation of women's health policy and programme reforms and establish, as appropriate, high-level focal points in national planning authorities responsible for monitoring to ensure that women's health concerns are mainstreamed in all relevant government agencies and programmes.

III.   By Governments, the United Nations and its specialized agencies, international financial institutions, bilateral donors and the private sector, as appropriate:

(a)   Formulate policies favourable to investment in women's health and, where appropriate, increase allocations for such investment;

(b)   Provide appropriate material, financial and logistical assistance to youth non-governmental organizations in order to strengthen them to address youth concerns in the area of health, including sexual and reproductive health;

(c)   Give higher priority to women's health and develop mechanisms for coordinating and implementing the health objectives of the Platform for Action and relevant international agreements to ensure progress.

Question

To what extent is the approach indicated conducive to advancing women's rights and realistic for States?

14.3.2.   Monitoring progress towards the Beijing goals

Progress towards the goals articulated in Beijing is monitored by the United Nations. Women 2000: Gender Equality, Development and Peace for the Twenty-first Century was the Special Session of the United Nations General Assembly in 2000. This setting is also referred to as Beijing +5. Commitment to the Beijing Platform for Action was reaffirmed by the members of the General Assembly (UN Doc. A/RES/S–23–3 (2000)). In Beijing +10 (2005), the UN Commission reviewed progress once again. While welcoming the progress to date, the Commission calls on States and the wider community to further advance the Platform for Action (UN Doc. E/CN.6/2005/L.1).

14.3.3   A positive obligation on States?

Many women's rights require positive intervention on the part of the State. (The nature of the duties on States is discussed in more detail in Chapter 2.) Protecting women from domestic and other violence, for example, may require a revision of criminal law. For example, marital rape has only recently been recognised as a crime in many States yet clearly involves violence against women and is degrading and aimed at subjugation and assertion of male power and dominance. To eradicate the practice, national legislatures are required to enact legislation which punishes the perpetrators adequately and renders prosecution effective as a remedy and a deterrent.

14.4   PROTECTION FROM PERSECUTION: TRAFFICKING, EXPLOITATION

Persecution of women may be for a variety of reasons. Cultural traditions may account for some elements. The issue of trafficking continues to affect more women and girl-children than men. Europe is one of the principal destinations of trafficked women. There they frequently enter the sex trade and can end up using drugs. The vicious cycle of poverty is rarely broken and women find themselves unable to repay the bond money and thus subjected to working for their controller. The Convention on the Elimination of All Forms of Discrimination against Women is unequivocal in its prohibition of such activities.

Convention on the Elimination of All Forms of Discrimination against Women Art 6

States Parties shall take all appropriate measures, including legislation, to suppress all forms of traffic in women and exploitation or prostitution of women.

Trafficking, by definition, is a transnational problem. As the Beijing Platform for Action notes at para 122, 'the effective suppression of trafficking in women and girls for the sex trade is a matter of pressing international concern'. A concerted global response is thus the only approach likely to succeed in eliminating trafficking.

Convention for the Suppression of the Traffic in Persons and of the Exploitation of the Prostitution of Others 1949

The Contracting parties

Hereby agree as hereinafter provided :

Article 1

The Parties to the present Convention agree to punish any person who, to gratify the passions of another:

(1) Procures, entices or leads away, for purposes of prostitution, another person, even with the consent of that person;

(2) Exploits the prostitution of another person, even with the consent of that person.

Article 2

The Parties to the present Convention further agree to punish any person who:

(1) Keeps or manages, or knowingly finances or takes part in the financing of a brothel;

(2) Knowingly lets or rents a building or other place or any part thereof for the purpose of the prostitution of others.

Article 3

To the extent permitted by domestic law, attempts to commit any of the offences referred to in articles 1 and 2, and acts preparatory to the commission thereof, shall also be punished.

Article 4

To the extent permitted by domestic law, intentional participation in the acts referred to in articles 1 and 2 above shall also be punishable.

To the extent permitted by domestic law, acts of participation shall be treated as separate offences whenever this is necessary to prevent impunity.

This Convention continues by addressing penal matters to ensure that all perpetrators can be tried and punished for engaging in such activities. Further attempts to regulate the area have been made by the General Assembly. Given that much trafficking occurs through organised crime linked activity, a Protocol to the United Nations Convention against Transnational Organised Crime has been adopted. It indicates the approach of the United Nations to the subject. According to the preamble, combating trafficking in persons, especially women and children, requires a comprehensive international approach in the countries of origin, transit and destination that includes measures to prevent such trafficking, to punish the traffickers and to protect the victims of such trafficking. Existing law was found inadequate and the lack of a single international instrument was decried, being a barrier to protection of women.

Protocol to Prevent, Suppress and Punish Trafficking in Persons Especially Women and Children, supplementing the United Nations Convention against Transnational Organized Crime 2000

Article 3
Use of terms

For the purposes of this Protocol:

(a) 'Trafficking in persons' shall mean the recruitment, transportation, transfer, harbouring or receipt of persons, by means of the threat or use of force or other forms of coercion, of abduction, of fraud, of deception, of the abuse of power or of a position of vulnerability or of the giving or receiving of payments or benefits to achieve the consent of a person having control over another person, for the purpose of exploitation. Exploitation shall include, at a minimum, the exploitation of the prostitution of others or other forms of sexual exploitation, forced labour or services, slavery or practices similar to slavery, servitude or the removal of organs;

(b) The consent of a victim of trafficking in persons to the intended exploitation set forth in subparagraph (a) of this article shall be irrelevant where any of the means set forth in subparagraph (a) have been used;

(c) The recruitment, transportation, transfer, harbouring or receipt of a child for the purpose of exploitation shall be considered 'trafficking in persons' even if this does not involve any of the means set forth in subparagraph (a) of this article;

(d) 'Child' shall mean any person under eighteen years of age.

Article 4
Scope of application

This Protocol shall apply, except as otherwise stated herein, to the prevention, investigation and prosecution of the offences established in accordance with article 5 of this Protocol, where those offences are transnational in nature and involve an organized criminal group, as well as to the protection of victims of such offences. . . .

Article 9

Prevention of trafficking in persons

1. States Parties shall establish comprehensive policies, programmes and other measures:

(a) To prevent and combat trafficking in persons; and

(b) To protect victims of trafficking in persons, especially women and children, from revictimization.

2. States Parties shall endeavour to undertake measures such as research, information and mass media campaigns and social and economic initiatives to prevent and combat trafficking in persons.

3. Policies, programmes and other measures established in accordance with this article shall, as appropriate, include cooperation with non-governmental organizations, other relevant organizations and other elements of civil society.

4. States Parties shall take or strengthen measures, including through bilateral or multilateral cooperation, to alleviate the factors that make persons, especially women and children, vulnerable to trafficking, such as poverty, underdevelopment and lack of equal opportunity.

5. States Parties shall adopt or strengthen legislative or other measures, such as educational, social or cultural measures, including through bilateral and multilateral cooperation, to discourage the demand that fosters all forms of exploitation of persons, especially women and children, that leads to trafficking.

As occurred in the principal convention, the emphasis is on creating criminal liability for traffickers. Given the transnational nature of trafficking, this can only be established by international agreement. Article 5 provides the details.

The need for protecting the victims of trafficking is also recognised.

Protocol to Prevent, Suppress and Punish Trafficking in Persons Especially Women and Children, supplementing the United Nations Convention against Transnational Organized Crime 2000

Article 6

Assistance to and protection of victims of trafficking in persons

1. In appropriate cases and to the extent possible under its domestic law, each State Party shall protect the privacy and identity of victims of trafficking in persons, including, *inter alia*, by making legal proceedings relating to such trafficking confidential.

2. Each State Party shall ensure that its domestic legal or administrative system contains measures that provide to victims of trafficking in persons, in appropriate cases:

(a) Information on relevant court and administrative proceedings;

(b) Assistance to enable their views and concerns to be presented and considered at appropriate stages of criminal proceedings against offenders, in a manner not prejudicial to the rights of the defence.

3. Each State Party shall consider implementing measures to provide for the physical, psychological and social recovery of victims of trafficking in persons, including, in appropriate cases, in cooperation with non-governmental organizations, other relevant organizations and other elements of civil society, and, in particular, the provision of:

(a) Appropriate housing;

(b) Counselling and information, in particular as regards their legal rights, in a language that the victims of trafficking in persons can understand;

(c) Medical, psychological and material assistance; and

(d) Employment, educational and training opportunities.

4. Each State Party shall take into account, in applying the provisions of this article, the age, gender and special needs of victims of trafficking in persons, in particular the special needs of children, including appropriate housing, education and care.

5. Each State Party shall endeavour to provide for the physical safety of victims of trafficking in persons while they are within its territory.

6. Each State Party shall ensure that its domestic legal system contains measures that offer victims of trafficking in persons the possibility of obtaining compensation for damage suffered.

Given the transnational nature of trafficking, it is also important that regard be had to the need to repatriate many victims. The Protocol protects individual victims by facilitating their residence in the State to which they were trafficked (Art 7) and their repatriation (Art 8).

Note also the provisions of the 2000 Protocol against the Smuggling of Migrants by Land, Sea and Air, supplementing the United Nations Convention against Transnational Organized Crime. It has relevance to the issue of trafficking as it addresses the related issue of people smuggling. Article 3(a) notes ' "Smuggling of migrants" shall mean the procurement, in order to obtain, directly or indirectly, a financial or other material benefit, of the illegal entry of a person into a State Party of which the person is not a national or a permanent resident'. There are correlations between trafficking and people smuggling. While men may often be willing migrants, women are sometimes sold to smugglers to be taken to another country for financial gain. Many of these women end up involved in prostitution and other aspects of the sex trade. They lack the financial independence to return home.

The United Nations Sub-Commission on the Promotion and Protection of Human Rights established a working group to examine contemporary forms of slavery. In the latest report (UN Doc. E/CN.4/Sub.2/2005/34 (filed by Marc Bossuyt, the Chair/ Special Rapporteur)), the working group made the following recommendations.

UN Doc. E/CN.4/Sub.2/2005/34
V. RECOMMENDATIONS ADOPTED by the working group AT its THIRTIETH SESSION

36. The Working Group adopted the following recommendations:

1. The Sub-Commission should emphasize that the sessions of the Working Group provide a unique platform for non-governmental organizations and victims of slavery and slavery-like practices to appear before an international forum, and acknowledge the value of their contributions to international awareness of and debate about slavery-related issues. Their testimonies provide important empirical evidence of the evolution of contemporary forms of slavery. . . .

15. The Working Group considers that priority thematic issues that should be addressed at upcoming sessions include trafficking in persons, the exploitation of prostitution, forced labour, the exploitation of domestic workers, forced marriage and domestic violence.

16. The Working Group decides to select as its thematic focus for its thirty-first session the human rights dimensions of prostitution, and the need to strengthen international cooperation to suppress international transfers of profits from the exploitation of the prostitution of others and trafficking in persons, and to postpone consideration of the impact of the media and the Internet on contemporary forms of slavery.

17. In addition, on the basis of the information provided at the thirtieth session, the Working Group decided to recall the recommendations adopted at previous sessions and to draw attention, in particular, to the following substantive conclusions and recommendations:

The Working Group on Contemporary Forms of Slavery:

General

(a) Recalls that slavery, in all its forms and practices, is a crime against humanity and reaffirms that every woman, man and child has a fundamental right to be free from all forms of slavery and servitude;

(b) Affirms once again that all forms of discrimination and prejudice, especially gender discrimination and violence against women, are among the many factors perpetuating slavery and slavery-like practices, and that gender inequality and low status of women and girls in society strongly increase their vulnerability to exploitation;

(c) Considers that poverty, social exclusion, illiteracy, ignorance, rapid population growth, HIV/AIDS, poor governance, corruption, irregular migration, impunity, discrimination in all its forms and armed conflicts are among the main root causes of contemporary forms of slavery, and urges the specialized agencies of the United Nations to include in their technical assistance programmes activities designed to eliminate slavery and slavery-like practices, as well as their causes. It also considers that progress towards the realization of the right to development contributes to the efforts to combat contemporary forms of slavery;

(d) Notes with concern that the treaties forbidding slavery and slavery-like practices, as well as other instruments relevant to the work of the Working Group, have not been universally ratified, and recommends that States ratify such instruments, in particular, the Slavery Conventions of 1926 and 1956, the 1949 Convention for the Suppression of the Traffic in Persons and of the Exploitation of the Prostitution of Others, the ILO Forced Labour Convention, 1930 (No. 29) and the Abolition of Forced Labour Convention, 1957 (No. 105), as well as the Worst Forms of Child Labour Convention, 1999 (No. 182), the United Nations Convention against Transnational Organized Crime and the Protocol to Prevent, Suppress and Punish Trafficking in Persons, Especially Women and Children supplementing the Convention, and the International Convention on the Protection of the Rights of All Migrant Workers and Members of Their Families;

(e) Notes with concern the impact of corruption on the continuation and spread of slavery and slavery-like practices, and urges States to adopt and enforce legislation that prohibits corruption, including that committed by public officials, as well as recommending closer international cooperation for the prevention, sanction and suppression of corruption, and of money-laundering of the profits resulting from all forms of slavery, including trafficking and sexual exploitation;

(f) Urges States to initiate prevention programmes at local, national, regional and international levels in order to educate the public about the consequences of prostitution and trafficking; . . .

(i) Reaffirms that prostitution is incompatible with the dignity and worth of the human person and constitutes a source of serious violations of human rights;

(j) Expresses grave concern at the evidence of increased trafficking in human beings, notes that it is a global phenomenon affecting every continent and stresses that countries of origin, transit and destination all have a responsibility to address this problem;

(k) Notes that some States have legalized or regulated prostitution, while others have criminalized the demand, and recognizes the need to take stock of different national approaches to analyse their human rights impact;

(l) Recalls that the demand for prostitution and all other forms of sexual exploitation plays a critical role in the growth and expansion of trafficking in women and children, and calls upon Governments to take effective measures to punish those who benefit from the sexual exploitation of others, particularly by ensuring that all those involved in trafficking in persons (for any purpose) receive adequate punishment, including sentences which are proportionate to the gravity of their offences, and by confiscating the property and assets of convicted traffickers and other perpetrators of sexual exploitation, as well as their accomplices, and using the proceeds to compensate their victims, in accordance with applicable international law standards;

(m) Calls upon all States to ensure that the protection and support of the victims are at the centre of any anti-trafficking policy and to provide protection and assistance to victims based on humanitarian considerations and not contingent on their cooperation with the prosecution of their exploiters, including the provision of free legal services to pursue compensation, reparation and other relief;

(n) Notes with concern that, regardless of positive steps taken by international, regional and local authorities and agencies in that respect, the Working Group continues to receive reports about the involvement of international personnel in sexual abuse and exploitation of local populations. It calls upon United Nations bodies and agencies to intensify their efforts to implement the administrative rules and codes of conduct adopted, as well as upon troop-contributing States to ensure that the same rules are applicable to peacekeepers;

Elimination of forced labour

(o) Notes with great concern that the 2005 ILO Global Report *A Global Alliance Against Forced Labour* estimates that 12.3 million people are victims of forced labour worldwide;

(p) Urges States to take urgent action to implement the provisions of international law and their own constitutions which prohibit the practice of forced labour, and in this regard to enact or amend legislation, accompanied by implementation mechanisms that facilitate the identification of forced labour in its various manifestations, including through surveys to identify the use of forced labourers and the number of victims involved, the design of appropriate prevention and protection programmes and monitoring of progress;

(q) Urges concerned States to ensure that forced labour is criminalized and that sanctions are commensurate with the gravity of the offences, that public information campaigns are launched, that relief and assistance to freed forced labourers are provided to facilitate their social reintegration, and that unions and NGOs that defend the rights of forced labourers receive support.

14.5   VIOLENCE AGAINST WOMEN

Women can be subject to violence, in the home or outwith. More women are at risk from assault and even death within the home at the hands of someone they know than outside. Domestic violence is prevalent in many parts of the world, and in fact, part of the ingrained culture. Latin America, Asia and the Pacific all produce evidence of cultures which condone (even passively) some domestic violence. One of the most significant problems with violence against women is the lack of public (official) awareness. Many women do not report domestic violence to the authorities and, even if they do, frequently they will not press charges. See Economic and Social Council Resolution 1990/15 (1990) *per* the last para.

Many different instruments impact on the rights of women to be protected from domestic violence and, as discussed in Chapter 15, implementing policies of systematic rape can constitute genocide. Therefore, perpetrators of systematic rape of an ethnic group will be tried in accordance with the principles of International Criminal Law. However, domestic violence was omitted from the provisions of the Convention on the Elimination of All Forms of Discrimination against Women. This was partially ameliorated by the Committee on the Elimination of Discrimination against Women which adopted a General Recommendation on the subject.

General Recommendation No. 19, 1992 (CEDAW)

Background

1. Gender-based violence is a form of discrimination that seriously inhibits women's ability to enjoy rights and freedoms on a basis of equality with men. . . .

General comments

6. The Convention in article 1 defines discrimination against women. The definition of discrimination includes gender-based violence, that is, violence that is directed against a woman because she is a woman or that affects women disproportionately. It includes acts that inflict physical, mental or sexual harm or suffering, threats of such acts, coercion and other deprivations of liberty. Gender-based violence may breach specific provisions of the Convention, regardless of whether those provisions expressly mention violence.

7. Gender-based violence, which impairs or nullifies the enjoyment by women of human rights and fundamental freedoms under general international law or under human rights conventions, is discrimination within the meaning of article 1 of the Convention. These rights and freedoms include:

(a) The right to life;

(b) The right not to be subject to torture or to cruel, inhuman or degrading treatment or punishment;

(c) The right to equal protection according to humanitarian norms in time of international or internal armed conflict;

(d) The right to liberty and security of person;

(e) The right to equal protection under the law;

(f) The right to equality in the family;

(g) The right to the highest standard attainable of physical and mental health;

(h) The right to just and favourable conditions of work. . . .

9. It is emphasized, however, that discrimination under the Convention is not restricted to action by or on behalf of Governments (see articles 2(e), 2(f) and 5). For example, under article 2(e) the Convention calls on States parties to take all appropriate measures to eliminate discrimination against women by any person, organization or enterprise. Under general international law and specific human rights covenants, States may also be responsible for private acts if they fail to act with due diligence to prevent violations of rights or to investigate and punish acts of violence, and for providing compensation.

Comments on specific articles of the Convention
Articles 2 and 3

10. Articles 2 and 3 establish a comprehensive obligation to eliminate discrimination in all its forms in addition to the specific obligations under articles 5–16.

Articles 2(f), 5 and 10(c)

11. Traditional attitudes by which women are regarded as subordinate to men or as having stereotyped roles perpetuate widespread practices involving violence or coercion, such as family violence and abuse, forced marriage, dowry deaths, acid attacks and female circumcision. Such prejudices and practices may justify gender-based violence as a form of protection or control of women. The effect of such violence on the physical and mental integrity of women is to deprive them of the equal enjoyment, exercise and knowledge of human rights and fundamental freedoms.

While this comment addresses mainly actual or threatened violence the underlying consequences of these forms of gender-based violence help to maintain women in subordinate roles and contribute to the low level of political participation and to their lower level of education, skills and work opportunities.

12. These attitudes also contribute to the propagation of pornography and the depiction and other commercial exploitation of women as sexual objects, rather than as individuals. This in turn contributes to gender-based violence.

Article 6

13. States parties are required by article 6 to take measures to suppress all forms of traffic in women and exploitation of the prostitution of women.

14. Poverty and unemployment increase opportunities for trafficking in women. In addition to established forms of trafficking there are new forms of sexual exploitation, such as sex tourism, the recruitment of domestic labour from developing countries to work in developed countries and organized marriages between women from developing countries and foreign nationals. These practices are incompatible with the equal enjoyment of rights by women and with respect for their rights and dignity. They put women at special risk of violence and abuse.

15. Poverty and unemployment force many women, including young girls, into prostitution. Prostitutes are especially vulnerable to violence because their status, which may be unlawful, tends to marginalize them. They need the equal protection of laws against rape and other forms of violence.

16. Wars, armed conflicts and the occupation of territories often lead to increased prostitution, trafficking in women and sexual assault of women, which require specific protective and punitive measures.

Article 11

17. Equality in employment can be seriously impaired when women are subjected to gender-specific violence, such as sexual harassment in the workplace.

18. Sexual harassment includes such unwelcome sexually determined behaviour as physical contact and advances, sexually coloured remarks, showing pornography and sexual demand, whether by words or actions. Such conduct can be humiliating and may constitute a health and safety problem; it is discriminatory when the woman has reasonable grounds to believe that her objection would disadvantage her in connection with her employment, including recruitment or promotion, or when it creates a hostile working environment.

Article 12

19. States parties are required by article 12 to take measures to ensure equal access to health care. Violence against women puts their health and lives at risk.

20. In some States there are traditional practices perpetuated by culture and tradition that are harmful to the health of women and children. These practices include dietary restrictions for pregnant women, preference for male children and female circumcision or genital mutilation.

Article 14

21. Rural women are at risk of gender-based violence because of traditional attitudes regarding the subordinate role of women that persist in many rural communities. Girls from rural communities are at special risk of violence and sexual exploitation when they leave the rural community to seek employment in towns.

Article 16 (and article 5)

22. Compulsory sterilization or abortion adversely affects women's physical and mental health, and infringes the right of women to decide on the number and spacing of their children.

23. Family violence is one of the most insidious forms of violence against women. It is prevalent in all societies. Within family relationships women of all ages are subjected to violence of all kinds, including battering, rape, other forms of sexual assault, mental and other forms of violence, which are perpetuated by traditional attitudes. Lack of economic independence forces many women to stay in violent relationships. The abrogation of their family responsibilities by men can be a form of violence, and coercion. These forms of violence put women's health at risk and impair their ability to participate in family life and public life on a basis of equality.

Question

Note the range of pre-existing rights which can be invoked to create a body of laws prohibiting domestic violence. Does this indicate that there is no need for a discrete instrument on violence against women?

The Committee made a number of recommendations. Following this, the General Assembly adopted a declaration on eliminating violence against women in 1993 in light of the aspirations voiced in the Vienna World Conference and the earlier recommendation of the Economic and Social Council (Resolution 1991/18) on the development of a framework for an international instrument aimed at preventing violence against women.

Declaration on the Elimination of Violence against Women, General Assembly Resolution 48/104 of 20 December 1993

Article 1

For the purposes of this Declaration, the term 'violence against women' means any act of gender-based violence that results in, or is likely to result in, physical, sexual or psychological harm or suffering to women, including threats of such acts, coercion or arbitrary deprivation of liberty, whether occurring in public or in private life.

Article 2

Violence against women shall be understood to encompass, but not be limited to, the following:

(a) Physical, sexual and psychological violence occurring in the family, including battering, sexual abuse of female children in the household, dowry-related violence, marital rape, female genital mutilation and other traditional practices harmful to women, non-spousal violence and violence related to exploitation;

(b) Physical, sexual and psychological violence occurring within the general community, including rape, sexual abuse, sexual harassment and intimidation at work, in educational institutions and elsewhere, trafficking in women and forced prostitution;

(c) Physical, sexual and psychological violence perpetrated or condoned by the State, wherever it occurs.

Article 4

States should condemn violence against women and should not invoke any custom, tradition or religious consideration to avoid their obligations with respect to its elimination. States should pursue by all appropriate means and without delay a policy of eliminating violence against women and, to this end, should:

(a) Consider, where they have not yet done so, ratifying or acceding to the Convention on the Elimination of All Forms of Discrimination against Women or withdrawing reservations to that Convention;

(b) Refrain from engaging in violence against women;

(c) Exercise due diligence to prevent, investigate and, in accordance with national legislation, punish acts of violence against women, whether those acts are perpetrated by the State or by private persons;

(d) Develop penal, civil, labour and administrative sanctions in domestic legislation to punish and redress the wrongs caused to women who are subjected to violence; women who are subjected to violence should be provided with access to the mechanisms of justice and, as provided for by national legislation, to just and effective remedies for the harm that they have suffered; States should also inform women of their rights in seeking redress through such mechanisms;

(e) Consider the possibility of developing national plans of action to promote the protection of women against any form of violence, or to include provisions for that purpose in plans already existing, taking into account, as appropriate, such cooperation as can be provided by non-governmental organizations, particularly those concerned with the issue of violence against women;

(f) Develop, in a comprehensive way, preventive approaches and all those measures of a legal, political, administrative and cultural nature that promote the protection of women against any form of violence, and ensure that the re-victimization of women does not occur because of laws insensitive to gender considerations, enforcement practices or other interventions;

(g) Work to ensure, to the maximum extent feasible in the light of their available resources and, where needed, within the framework of international cooperation, that women subjected to violence and, where appropriate, their children have specialized assistance, such as rehabilitation, assistance in child care and maintenance, treatment, counselling, and health and social services, facilities and programmes, as well as support structures, and should take all other appropriate measures to promote their safety and physical and psychological rehabilitation;

(h) Include in government budgets adequate resources for their activities related to the elimination of violence against women;

(i) Take measures to ensure that law enforcement officers and public officials responsible for implementing policies to prevent, investigate and punish violence against women receive training to sensitize them to the needs of women;

(j) Adopt all appropriate measures, especially in the field of education, to modify the social and cultural patterns of conduct of men and women and to eliminate prejudices, customary practices and all other practices based on the idea of the inferiority or superiority of either of the sexes and on stereotyped roles for men and women;

(k) Promote research, collect data and compile statistics, especially concerning domestic violence, relating to the prevalence of different forms of violence against women and encourage research on the causes, nature, seriousness and consequences of violence against women and on the effectiveness of measures implemented to prevent and redress violence against women; those statistics and findings of the research will be made public;

(l) Adopt measures directed towards the elimination of violence against women who are especially vulnerable to violence;

(m) Include, in submitting reports as required under relevant human rights instruments of the United Nations, information pertaining to violence against women and measures taken to implement the present Declaration;

(n) Encourage the development of appropriate guidelines to assist in the implementation of the principles set forth in the present Declaration;

(o) Recognize the important role of the women's movement and non-governmental organizations world wide in raising awareness and alleviating the problem of violence against women;

(p) Facilitate and enhance the work of the women's movement and non-governmental organizations and cooperate with them at local, national and regional levels;

(q) Encourage intergovernmental regional organizations of which they are members to include the elimination of violence against women in their programmes, as appropriate.

Question

Does the definition in Arts 1/2 include all permutations of domestic violence? Look carefully at Art 2(a)—there are clear implications for cultural relativity. Is the correct balance of rights reached?

Domestic violence was the subject matter of the first merits opinion of the Committee on the Elimination of Discrimination against Women (opinion issues January 2005). The communication was brought under the Optional Protocol to the Convention.

14.5.1   Committee on Elimination of Discrimination against Women—Communication

Ms A-T v Hungary, Communication 2/2003, decision January 2005

The author of the communication, Ms A-T, claimed that she had been subject to regular domestic violence and threats of violence by her common law husband. Despite threats to her and their children, she has not been able to flee to a woman's refuge as none offer the essential support for her brain-damaged child. The man in question left the family home but continued physical and 'financial' abuse. Interim measures of protection were requested and stipulated. Moreover, the State instituted a comprehensive action plan against domestic violence. Some of the facts were disputed in the case, particularly those concerning national legal proceedings. The Committee recalled its general recommendation No. 19 on domestic violence and then adopted a positive approach to the obligations imposed on the State.

> 9.3 With regard to article 2 (a), (b), and (e), the Committee notes that the State party has admitted that the remedies pursued by the author, were not capable of providing immediate protection to her against ill-treatment by her former partner and, furthermore, that legal and institutional arrangements in the State party are not yet ready to ensure the internationally expected, coordinated, comprehensive and effective protection and support for the victims of domestic violence. While appreciating the State party's efforts at instituting a comprehensive action programme against domestic violence and the legal and other measures envisaged, the Committee believes that these have yet to benefit the author and address her persistent situation of insecurity. The Committee further notes the State party's general assessment that domestic violence cases as such do not enjoy high priority in court proceedings. The Committee is of the opinion that the description provided of the proceedings resorted to in the present case, both the civil and criminal proceedings, coincides with this general assessment. Women's human rights to life and to physical and mental integrity cannot be superseded by other rights, including the right to property and the right to privacy. The Committee also takes note that the State party does not offer information as to the existence of alternative avenues that the author may have pursued that would have provided sufficient protection or security from the danger of continued violence. In this connection, the Committee recalls its concluding comments from August 2002 on the State party's combined fourth and fifth periodic report that states '. . . [T]he Committee is concerned about the prevalence of violence against women and girls, including domestic violence. It is particularly concerned that no specific legislation has been enacted to combat domestic violence and sexual harassment and that no protection or exclusion orders or shelters exist for the immediate protection of women victims of domestic violence'. Bearing this in mind, the Committee concludes that the obligations of the State party that are set out in article 2 (a), (b) and (e) of the Convention extend to the prevention of, and protection from violence against women and, in the instant case, remain unfulfilled and constitute a violation of the author's human rights and fundamental freedoms, particularly her right to security of person.

> 9.4 The Committee addressed articles 5 and 16 together in its general recommendation No. 19 in dealing with family violence. In its general recommendation No. 21, the Committee stressed

that 'the provisions of General Recommendation 19 . . . concerning violence against women have great significance for women's abilities to enjoy rights and freedoms on an equal basis with men'. It has stated on many occasions that traditional attitudes by which women are regarded as subordinate to men contribute to violence against them. The Committee recognized those very attitudes when it considered the combined fourth and fifth periodic report of Hungary in 2002, and was concerned about the 'persistence of entrenched traditional stereotypes regarding the role and responsibilities of women and men in the family . . .'. In respect of the instant case before the Committee, the facts of the communication reveal aspects of the relationships between the sexes and attitudes towards women that the Committee recognized vis-à-vis the country as a whole. For four years and continuing to the present day, the author has felt threatened by her former common law husband—the father of her two children. The author has been battered by the same man, i.e. her former common law husband. She has been unsuccessful, either through civil or criminal proceedings, to temporarily or permanently bar L.F. from the apartment where she and her children have continued to reside. The author could not have asked for a restraining or protection order since neither option currently exists in the State party. She has been unable to flee to a shelter because none are equipped to take her in together with her children, one of whom is fully disabled. None of these facts have been disputed by the State party and, considered together, they indicate that the rights of the author under articles 5 (a) and 16 of the Convention have been violated.

9.5 The Committee also notes that the lack of effective legal and other measures prevented the State party from dealing in a satisfactory manner with the Committee's request for interim measures.

9.6 Acting under article 7, paragraph 3, of the Optional Protocol to the Convention on the Elimination of All Forms of Discrimination against Women, the Committee is of the view that the State party has failed to fulfill its obligations and has thereby violated the rights of the author under article 2 (a), (b) and (e) and article 5(a) in conjunction with article 16 of the Convention on the Elimination of All Forms of Discrimination against Women, and makes the following recommendations to the State party:

I. concerning the author of the communication

i.   take immediate and effective measures to guarantee the physical and mental integrity of A.T. and her family; and

ii.   ensure that A.T. is given a safe home in which to live with her children, receives appropriate child support and legal assistance and that she receives reparation proportionate to the physical and mental harm undergone and to the gravity of the violations of her rights;

II. general

i.   respect, protect, promote and fulfill women's human rights, including their right to be free from all forms of domestic violence, including intimidation and threats of violence;

ii.   assure victims of domestic violence the maximum protection of the law by acting with due diligence to prevent and respond to such violence against women;

iii. take all necessary measures to ensure that the national strategy for the prevention and effective treatment of violence within the family is promptly implemented and evaluated;

iv.   take all necessary measures to provide regular training on the Convention on the Elimination of All Forms of Discrimination against Women and the Optional Protocol thereto to judges, lawyers and law enforcement officials;

v.   implement expeditiously and without delay the Committee's concluding comments of August 2002 on the combined fourth and fifth periodic report of Hungary in respect of violence against women and girls, in particular the Committee's recommendation that a specific law be introduced prohibiting domestic violence against women, which would provide for protection and exclusion orders as well as support services, including shelters;

vi. investigate promptly, thoroughly, impartially and seriously all allegations of domestic violence and bring the offenders to justice in accordance with international standards;

vii. provide victims of domestic violence with safe and prompt access to justice, including free legal aid where necessary, to ensure them available, effective and sufficient remedies and rehabilitation; and

viii. provide offenders with rehabilitation programmes and programmes on non-violent conflict resolution methods.

14.5.2   Regional provision in the Americas

Within the Americas, violence against women has been regarded as a particular problem. The traditional balance of power was deemed to leave women more vulnerable to violence. A specific convention was thus adopted on the topic. The instrument carefully defines the scope of its application in Art 1. Note the breadth of the definition and also the caveat 'based on gender'. Clearly the focus of this instrument is on violence against women and thus it represents a form of affirmative action, redressing the historic imbalance in power perceived to exist between men and women, the abuse of which may result in violence. Domestic violence is explicitly included in Art 2 as, it appears, is marital rape.

Inter-American Convention on the Prevention, Punishment and Eradication of Violence Against Women 1994

Article 1

For the purposes of this Convention, violence against women shall be understood as any act or conduct, based on gender, which causes death or physical, sexual or psychological harm or suffering to women, whether in the public or the private sphere.

Article 2

Violence against women shall be understood to include physical, sexual and psychological violence:

that occurs within the family or domestic unit or within any other interpersonal relationship, whether or not the perpetrator shares or has shared the same residence with the woman, including, among others, rape, battery and sexual abuse;

that occurs in the community and is perpetrated by any person, including, among others, rape, sexual abuse, torture, trafficking in persons, forced prostitution, kidnapping and sexual harassment in the workplace, as well as in educational institutions, health facilities or any other place; and

that is perpetrated or condoned by the state or its agents regardless of where it occurs.

Question

Is the Inter-American's Convention's definition similar to that advanced by the General Assembly? Are any differences important?

A list of rights of women follow in the American Convention. Note the interrelationship between the prohibition on violence and the fundamental civil and political rights of women.

Inter-American Convention on the Prevention, Punishment and Eradication of Violence Against Women

Article 3

Every woman has the right to be free from violence in both the public and private spheres.

Article 4

Every woman has the right to the recognition, enjoyment, exercise and protection of all human rights and freedoms embodied in regional and international human rights instruments. These rights include, among others:

The right to have her life respected;

The right to have her physical, mental and moral integrity respected;

The right to personal liberty and security;

The right not to be subjected to torture;

The right to have the inherent dignity of her person respected and her family protected;

The right to equal protection before the law and of the law;

The right to simple and prompt recourse to a competent court for protection against acts that violate her rights;

The right to associate freely;

The right of freedom to profess her religion and beliefs within the law; and

The right to have equal access to the public service of her country and to take part in the conduct of public affairs, including decision-making.

Article 5

Every woman is entitled to the free and full exercise of her civil, political, economic, social and cultural rights, and may rely on the full protection of those rights as embodied in regional and international instruments on human rights. The States Parties recognize that violence against women prevents and nullifies the exercise of these rights.

Article 6

The right of every woman to be free from violence includes, among others:

The right of women to be free from all forms of discrimination; and

The right of women to be valued and educated free of stereotyped patterns of behavior and social and cultural practices based on concepts of inferiority or subordination.

Perhaps of particular note is the associated duties on States. Not only are there reporting duties (Chapter IV of the Convention), but also duties in respect of ensuring appropriate penal legislation, and of particular note, duties in respect of education aimed at effecting a cultural change (Art 8). This latter is of fundamental importance to the Convention and represents a brave contemporary approach to an historic issue. As with so many areas of human rights, education is key.

Inter-American Convention on the Prevention, Punishment and Eradication of Violence Against Women

Article 7

The States Parties condemn all forms of violence against women and agree to pursue, by all appropriate means and without delay, policies to prevent, punish and eradicate such violence and undertake to:

refrain from engaging in any act or practice of violence against women and to ensure that their authorities, officials, personnel, agents, and institutions act in conformity with this obligation;

apply due diligence to prevent, investigate and impose penalties for violence against women;

include in their domestic legislation penal, civil, administrative and any other type of provisions that may be needed to prevent, punish and eradicate violence against women and to adopt appropriate administrative measures where necessary;

adopt legal measures to require the perpetrator to refrain from harassing, intimidating or threatening the woman or using any method that harms or endangers her life or integrity, or damages her property;

take all appropriate measures, including legislative measures, to amend or repeal existing laws and regulations or to modify legal or customary practices which sustain the persistence and tolerance of violence against women;

establish fair and effective legal procedures for women who have been subjected to violence which include, among others, protective measures, a timely hearing and effective access to such procedures;

establish the necessary legal and administrative mechanisms to ensure that women subjected to violence have effective access to restitution, reparations or other just and effective remedies; and

adopt such legislative or other measures as may be necessary to give effect to this Convention.

Article 8

The States Parties agree to undertake progressively specific measures, including programs:

to promote awareness and observance of the right of women to be free from violence, and the right of women to have their human rights respected and protected;

to modify social and cultural patterns of conduct of men and women, including the development of formal and informal educational programs appropriate to every level of the educational process, to counteract prejudices, customs and all other practices which are based on the idea of the inferiority or superiority of either of the sexes or on the stereotyped roles for men and women which legitimize or exacerbate violence against women;

to promote the education and training of all those involved in the administration of justice, police and other law enforcement officers as well as other personnel responsible for implementing policies for the prevention, punishment and eradication of violence against women;

to provide appropriate specialized services for women who have been subjected to violence, through public and private sector agencies, including shelters, counseling services for ail family members where appropriate, and care and custody of the affected children;

to promote and support governmental and private sector education designed to raise the awareness of the public with respect to the problems of and remedies for violence against women;

to provide women who are subjected to violence access to effective readjustment and training programs to enable them to fully participate in public, private and social life;

to encourage the communications media to develop appropriate media guidelines in order to contribute to the eradication of violence against women in all its forms, and to enhance respect for the dignity of women;

to ensure research and the gathering of statistics and other relevant information relating to the causes, consequences and frequency of violence against women, in order to assess the effectiveness of measures to prevent, punish and eradicate violence against women and to formulate and implement the necessary changes; and

to foster international cooperation for the exchange of ideas and experiences and the execution of programs aimed at protecting women who are subjected to violence.

Article 9

With respect to the adoption of the measures in this Chapter, the States Parties shall take special account of the vulnerability of women to violence by reason of, among others, their race or ethnic background or their status as migrants, refugees or displaced persons. Similar consideration shall be given to women subjected to violence while pregnant or who are disabled, of minor age, elderly, socio-economically disadvantaged, affected by armed conflict or deprived of their freedom.

No comparable binding measure exists in other jurisdictions. This convention thus is an important indicator of the potential for legislation in this area. Great potential appears in its approach to the subject with the range of duties on State Parties. Perhaps emulating this in other instruments is one way forward for the international community. However, as usual, the rhetoric may be good, but the reality depends on what approach the State adopts when giving effect to the provisions.

14.5.3 The international agenda: the Beijing Platform for Action

The Fourth World Conference on Women focused on violence against women and identified it as one of the key areas of concern. Three strategic objectives were identified: take integrated measures to prevent and eliminate violence against women; study the causes and consequences of violence against women and the effectiveness of preventive measures; eliminate trafficking in women and assist victims of violence due to prostitution and trafficking. Consider the actions to be taken by States and others in furtherance of the elimination of violence.

Beijing Platform for Action Strategic objective D.1. Take integrated measures to prevent and eliminate violence against women

Actions to be taken

124.   By Governments:

(a)   Condemn violence against women and refrain from invoking any custom, tradition or religious consideration to avoid their obligations with respect to its elimination as set out in the Declaration on the Elimination of Violence against Women;

(b)   Refrain from engaging in violence against women and exercise due diligence to prevent, investigate and, in accordance with national legislation, punish acts of violence against women, whether those acts are perpetrated by the State or by private persons;

(c)   Enact and/or reinforce penal, civil, labour and administrative sanctions in domestic legislation to punish and redress the wrongs done to women and girls who are subjected to any form of violence, whether in the home, the workplace, the community or society;

(d)   Adopt and/or implement and periodically review and analyse legislation to ensure its effectiveness in eliminating violence against women, emphasizing the prevention of violence and the prosecution of offenders; take measures to ensure the protection of women subjected to violence, access to just and effective remedies, including compensation and indemnification and healing of victims, and rehabilitation of perpetrators;

(e)   Work actively to ratify and/or implement international human rights norms and instruments as they relate to violence against women, including those contained in the Universal Declaration of Human Rights, the International Covenant on Civil and Political Rights, the International Covenant on Economic, Social and Cultural Rights, and the Convention against Torture and Other Cruel, Inhuman or Degrading Treatment or Punishment;

(f)   Implement the Convention on the Elimination of All Forms of Discrimination against Women, taking into account general recommendation 19, adopted by the Committee on the Elimination of Discrimination against Women at its eleventh session;

(g)   Promote an active and visible policy of mainstreaming a gender perspective in all policies and programmes related to violence against women; actively encourage, support and implement measures and programmes aimed at increasing the knowledge and understanding of the causes, consequences and mechanisms of violence against women among those responsible for implementing these policies, such as law enforcement officers, police personnel and judicial, medical and social workers, as well as those who deal with minority, migration and refugee issues, and develop strategies to ensure that the revictimization of women victims of violence does not occur because of gender-insensitive laws or judicial or enforcement practices;

(h) Provide women who are subjected to violence with access to the mechanisms of justice and, as provided for by national legislation, to just and effective remedies for the harm they have suffered and inform women of their rights in seeking redress through such mechanisms;

(i) Enact and enforce legislation against the perpetrators of practices and acts of violence against women, such as female genital mutilation, female infanticide, prenatal sex selection and dowry-related violence, and give vigorous support to the efforts of non-governmental and community organizations to eliminate such practices;

(j) Formulate and implement, at all appropriate levels, plans of action to eliminate violence against women;

(k) Adopt all appropriate measures, especially in the field of education, to modify the social and cultural patterns of conduct of men and women, and to eliminate prejudices, customary practices and all other practices based on the idea of the inferiority or superiority of either of the sexes and on stereotyped roles for men and women;

(l) Create or strengthen institutional mechanisms so that women and girls can report acts of violence against them in a safe and confidential environment, free from the fear of penalties or retaliation, and file charges;

(m) Ensure that women with disabilities have access to information and services in the field of violence against women;

(n) Create, improve or develop as appropriate, and fund the training programmes for judicial, legal, medical, social, educational and police and immigrant personnel, in order to avoid the abuse of power leading to violence against women and sensitize such personnel to the nature of gender-based acts and threats of violence so that fair treatment of female victims can be assured;

(o) Adopt laws, where necessary, and reinforce existing laws that punish police, security forces or any other agents of the State who engage in acts of violence against women in the course of the performance of their duties; review existing legislation and take effective measures against the perpetrators of such violence;

(p) Allocate adequate resources within the government budget and mobilize community resources for activities related to the elimination of violence against women, including resources for the implementation of plans of action at all appropriate levels;

(q) Include in reports submitted in accordance with the provisions of relevant United Nations human rights instruments, information pertaining to violence against women and measures taken to implement the Declaration on the Elimination of Violence against Women;

(r) Cooperate with and assist the Special Rapporteur of the Commission on Human Rights on violence against women in the performance of her mandate and furnish all information requested; cooperate also with other competent mechanisms, such as the Special Rapporteur of the Commission on Human Rights on torture and the Special Rapporteur of the Commission on Human Rights on summary, extrajudiciary and arbitrary executions, in relation to violence against women;

(s) Recommend that the Commission on Human Rights renew the mandate of the Special Rapporteur on violence against women when her term ends in 1997 and, if warranted, to update and strengthen it.

125. By Governments, including local governments, community organizations, non-governmental organizations, educational institutions, the public and private sectors, particularly enterprises, and the mass media, as appropriate:

   (a) Provide well-funded shelters and relief support for girls and women subjected to violence, as well as medical, psychological and other counselling services and free or low-cost legal aid, where it is needed, as well as appropriate assistance to enable them to find a means of subsistence;

   (b) Establish linguistically and culturally accessible services for migrant women and girls, including women migrant workers, who are victims of gender-based violence;

   (c) Recognize the vulnerability to violence and other forms of abuse of women migrants, including women migrant workers, whose legal status in the host country depends on employers who may exploit their situation;

   (d) Support initiatives of women's organizations and non-governmental organizations all over the world to raise awareness on the issue of violence against women and to contribute to its elimination;

   (e) Organize, support and fund community-based education and training campaigns to raise awareness about violence against women as a violation of women's enjoyment of their human rights and mobilize local communities to use appropriate gender-sensitive traditional and innovative methods of conflict resolution;

   (f) Recognize, support and promote the fundamental role of intermediate institutions, such as primary health-care centres, family-planning centres, existing school health services, mother and baby protection services, centres for migrant families and so forth in the field of information and education related to abuse;

   (g) Organize and fund information campaigns and educational and training programmes in order to sensitize girls and boys and women and men to the personal and social detrimental effects of violence in the family, community and society; teach them how to communicate without violence and promote training for victims and potential victims so that they can protect themselves and others against such violence;

   (h) Disseminate information on the assistance available to women and families who are victims of violence;

   (i) Provide, fund and encourage counselling and rehabilitation programmes for the perpetrators of violence and promote research to further efforts concerning such counselling and rehabilitation so as to prevent the recurrence of such violence;

   (j) Raise awareness of the responsibility of the media in promoting non-stereotyped images of women and men, as well as in eliminating patterns of media presentation that generate violence, and encourage those responsible for media content to establish professional guidelines and codes of conduct; also raise awareness of the important role of the media in informing and educating people about the causes and effects of violence against women and in stimulating public debate on the topic.

126. By Governments, employers, trade unions, community and youth organizations and non-governmental organizations, as appropriate:

   (a) Develop programmes and procedures to eliminate sexual harassment and other forms of violence against women in all educational institutions, workplaces and elsewhere;

   (b) Develop programmes and procedures to educate and raise awareness of acts of violence against women that constitute a crime and a violation of the human rights of women;

   (c) Develop counselling, healing and support programmes for girls, adolescents and young women who have been or are involved in abusive relationships, particularly those who live in homes or institutions where abuse occurs;

(d)   Take special measures to eliminate violence against women, particularly those in vulnerable situations, such as young women, refugee, displaced and internally displaced women, women with disabilities and women migrant workers, including enforcing any existing legislation and developing, as appropriate, new legislation for women migrant workers in both sending and receiving countries.

127.   By the Secretary-General of the United Nations:

Provide the Special Rapporteur of the Commission on Human Rights on violence against women with all necessary assistance, in particular the staff and resources required to perform all mandated functions, especially in carrying out and following up on missions undertaken either separately or jointly with other special rapporteurs and working groups, and adequate assistance for periodic consultations with the Committee on the Elimination of Discrimination against Women and all treaty bodies.

128.   By Governments, international organizations and non-governmental organizations:

Encourage the dissemination and implementation of the UNHCR Guidelines on the Protection of Refugee Women and the UNHCR Guidelines on the Prevention of and Response to Sexual Violence against Refugees.

Question

Consider the financial and political implications for States of the proposals above—what barriers may there be to their achievement? Are the proposals sufficient to redress the cultural acceptability of violence against women (particularly domestic violence) in some regions of the world?

14.5.4   Investigating the problem—recent UN developments

The Beijing Conference noted the need for a detailed study of the causes and consequences of violence against women and the effectiveness of preventive measures. Paragraphs 129 *et seq.* of the Platform for Action address this matter. A comprehensive study should enable the root causes to be identified and thus target remedial measures more effectively, indeed the general raising of awareness is in itself a positive step to changing the culture.

The General Assembly requested the Secretary-General to conduct an in-depth study on all forms of violence against women.

General Assembly Resolution 58/185

Requests the Secretary-General:

(a)   To conduct an in-depth study, from existing available resources and, if necessary, supplemented by voluntary contributions, on all forms and manifestations of violence against women, as identified in the Beijing Declaration and Platform for Action adopted at the Fourth World Conference on Women and the outcome of the twenty-third special session of the General Assembly entitled 'Women 2000: gender equality, development and peace for the twenty-first century', and relevant documents, disaggregated by type of violence, and based on research undertaken and data collected at the national, regional and international levels, in particular in the following fields:

(i)   A statistical overview on all forms of violence against women, in order to better evaluate the scale of such violence, while identifying gaps in data collection and formulating proposals for assessing the extent of the problem;

(ii)   The causes of violence against women, including its root causes and other contributing factors;

(iii) The medium and long-term consequences of violence against women;

(iv) The health, social and economic costs of violence against women;

(v) The identification of best practice examples in areas including legislation, policies, pro-grammes and effective remedies, and the efficiency of such mechanisms to the end of combating and eliminating violence against women;

(b) To cooperate closely with all relevant United Nations bodies, as well as with the Special Rapporteur of the Commission on Human Rights on violence against women, its causes and consequences, when preparing the study;

(c) To solicit information, including on strategies, policies, programmes and best practices, from Member States as well as relevant non-governmental organizations in the preparation of the study.

The objective of the report is simple: to determine the scale of violence against women and its prevalence, reinforce and raise awareness of the unacceptability of such violence and identify policies and mechanisms for better realising and implementing the rights of women thereby eradicating violence. Disseminating examples of 'good practice' may assist in the creation of societies free from violence. Work undertaken in preparation of the report complements the ongoing project on children's rights concerning violence against children.

The key rights of women which are related to the eradication of violence are represented in the following diagram. As with all individuals and groups requiring the protection of human rights, the full range of international human rights are open to victims. Therefore it is appropriate to recap the range of rights which may be of benefit to women seeking protection from domestic violence.

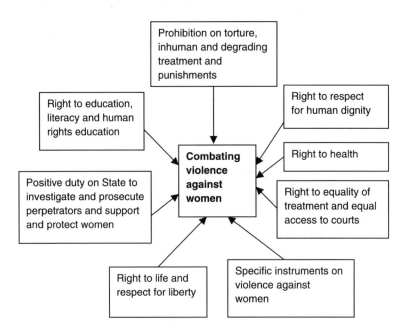

This report was scheduled for submission to the General Assembly's 60th session in December 2005. The views of member States will then be solicited to facilitate a broader discussion of the topic. More information and all documentation can be located online: www.un.org/womenwatch/daw/vaw/index.htm.

14.5.4.1   World Health Organisation Report

The World Health Organisation completed and published its first study on domestic violence towards the end of 2005. It is based on interviews with women across ten countries (Bangladesh, Brazil, Ethiopia, Japan, Namibia, Peru, Samoa, Serbia and Montenegro, Thailand and the United Republic of Tanzania). The study identified major health implications for domestic violence. The following definitions were used:

- **Physical violence**: being slapped, pushed, hit with fist or other object which could hurt, kicked, beaten up, choked, burnt on purpose, threatened with or attacked with gun, knife or other weapon or having something thrown with intent to injure.
- **Sexual violence**: being physically forced to have sexual intercourse; having intercourse out of fear of what the partner would do otherwise; being forced to engage in sexual practices the woman found degrading or humiliating.

The study found that abused women are twice as likely to have physical and mental health problems as non-abused women. Sexual and reproductive health can also be affected—the spread of sexually transmitted diseases often occurs and pregnant women were also found subject to violence.

The World Health Organisation report recommends education and violence prevention programming. Further information can be found on the website of the Organisation: www.who.int.

14.6   FAMILY RIGHTS: MARRIAGE AND CHILDREN

Inevitably, family rights affect women. In many societies, women undertake much responsibility for homemaking and childrearing (see, for example, the Guatemalan code, discussed in *Morales de Sierra v Guatemala*). However, in some instances, particularly in subsistence societies, they also have to work outwith the home. Other women may choose to work alongside undertaking family responsibilities. Marriage itself is often open to abuse; women can be exploited by being sold into marriage and treated as domestic and sex slaves.

As is indicated above, women are entitled to full equality of rights and to equal protection of the law. As a consequence, even when married, women should still retain their individual rights and legal equality. The Committee on Elimination of Discrimination against Women adopted General Recommendation 21 (1994) on Equality in Marriage and Family Relations. This was adopted in the designated Year of the Family. The following extract relates to the implications of marriage on a woman's legal status.

CEDAW General Recommendation 21 (1994), extract in respect of Art 15 of the Convention on the Elimination of All Forms of Discrimination against Women

7. When a woman cannot enter into a contract at all, or have access to financial credit, or can do so only with her husband's or a male relative's concurrence or guarantee, she is denied legal autonomy. Any such restriction prevents her from holding property as the sole owner and precludes her from the legal management of her own business or from entering into any other form of contract. Such restrictions seriously limit the woman's ability to provide for herself and her dependents (*sic*).

8. A woman's right to bring litigation is limited in some countries by law or by her access to legal advice and her ability to seek redress from the courts. In others, her status as a witness or her

evidence is accorded less respect or weight than that of a man. Such laws or customs limit the woman's right effectively to pursue or retain her equal share of property and diminish her standing as an independent, responsible and valued member of her community. When countries limit a woman's legal capacity by their laws, or permit individuals or institutions to do the same, they are denying women their rights to be equal with men and restricting women's ability to provide for themselves and their dependents (*sic*).

14.6.1   The right to enter freely into marriage

Marriage is a proclaimed right under several international and regional instruments. Note that the scope of marriage rights is under examination in several States with respect to post-operative transsexuals and, even, homosexuals. See for example, *Goodwin and I v United Kingdom*, Application 28957/95, decision 11 July 2002 before the European Court of Human Rights *re* post-operative transsexuals, and the ongoing challenges to civil partnership arrangements (as applied to same-sex partnerships) in north America and elsewhere. Note also, the Human Rights Committee in *Joslin v New Zealand*, Communication 902/1999, UN Doc. CCPR/C/75/D/902 at para 8.2 confirming the International Covenant on Civil and Political Rights being explicit *re* men and women in respect of the right to marry. A New Zealand refusal to condone a lesbian marriage was thus not an infringement of the covenant. These issues, while important, fall outwith the scope of the present text. The focus here is on marriage freely entered into by a man and a woman.

CEDAW General Recommendation 21 (1994), extract in respect of Article 16 of the Convention on the Elimination of All Forms of Discrimination against Women

13. The form and concept of the family can vary from State to State, and even between regions within a State. Whatever form it takes, and whatever the legal system, religion, custom or tradition within the country, the treatment of women in the family both at law and in private must accord with the principles of equality and justice for all people, as article 2 of the Convention requires.

14. States parties' reports also disclose that polygamy is practised in a number of countries. Polygamous marriage contravenes a woman's right to equality with men, and can have such serious emotional and financial consequences for her and her dependents (*sic*) that such marriages ought to be discouraged and prohibited. The Committee notes with concern that some States parties, whose constitutions guarantee equal rights, permit polygamous marriage in accordance with personal or customary law. This violates the constitutional rights of women, and breaches the provisions of article 5 (a) of the Convention.

15. While most countries report that national constitutions and laws comply with the Convention, custom, tradition and failure to enforce these laws in reality contravene the Convention.

16. A woman's right to choose a spouse and enter freely into marriage is central to her life and to her dignity and equality as a human being. An examination of States parties' reports discloses that there are countries which, on the basis of custom, religious beliefs or the ethnic origins of particular groups of people, permit forced marriages or remarriages. Other countries allow a woman's marriage to be arranged for payment or preferment and in others women's poverty forces them to marry foreign nationals for financial security. Subject to reasonable restrictions based for example on woman's youth or consanguinity with her partner, a woman's right to choose when, if, and whom she will marry must be protected and enforced at law.

One of the key instruments on this is the Convention on Consent to Marry, Minimum Age for Marriage and Registration for Marriages 1962.

14.6.1.1 The right to marry

The right to marry is guaranteed as a fundamental right in most major instruments

European Convention on Human Rights Art 6

Men and women of marriageable age have the right to marry and to found a family, according to the national laws governing the exercise of this right.

Contrast this with the provision in the Protocol to the African Charter.

Protocol to the African Charter on Human and Peoples' Rights on the Rights of Women in Africa 2000

Article 6

Marriage

States Parties shall ensure that women and men enjoy equal rights and are regarded as equal partners in marriage. They shall enact appropriate national legislative measures to guarantee that:

a) no marriage shall take place without the free and full consent of both parties;

b) the minimum age of marriage for women shall be 18 years;

c) monogamy is encouraged as the preferred form of marriage and that the rights of women in marriage and family, including in polygamous marital relationships, are promoted and protected;

d) every marriage shall be recorded in writing and registered in accordance with national laws, in order to be legally recognised;

e) the husband and wife shall, by mutual agreement, choose their matrimonial regime and place of residence;

f) a married woman shall have the right to retain her maiden name, to use it as she pleases, jointly or separately with her husband's surname;

g) a woman shall have the right to retain her nationality or to acquire the nationality of her husband;

h) a woman and a man shall have equal rights, with respect to the nationality of their children except where this is contrary to a provision in national legislation or is contrary to national security interests;

i) a woman and a man shall jointly contribute to safeguarding the interests of the family, protecting and educating their children;

j) during her marriage, a woman shall have the right to acquire her own property and to administer and manage it freely.

The emphasis tends to be on marriage in accordance with national laws. National laws may prescribe formalities of marriage and make specific requirements of the parties concerned. The criteria employed for determining who is a woman, and thus the plight of transsexuals and intersexuals is one example of a matter left to national law. Similarly the number of marriages a party can enter into is determined by national law. Polygamous and polygynous arrangements do not *ipso facto* infringe international human rights law.

Question

Marriage formalities and procedures may be prescribed by religious texts, cultural beliefs and/ or the State. Do the provisions on marriage reflect the need to take into account cultural differences?

The age of the individuals involved is often specified in national law and is subject to regional variations.

14.6.1.2   Minimum age for marriage

While the right to marry is widely accepted, there is greater controversy surrounding the age at which marriage is permissible.

Convention on Consent to Marry, Minimum Age for Marriage and Registration for Marriages 1962 Art 2

States Parties to the present Convention shall take legislative action to specify a minimum age for marriage. No marriage shall be legally entered into by any person under this age, except where a competent authority has granted a dispensation as to age, for serious reasons, in the interest of the intending spouses.

14.6.1.3   Consent to marriage

Convention on Consent to Marry, Minimum Age for Marriage and Registration for Marriages 1962 Art 1

1. No marriage shall be legally entered into without the full and free consent of both parties, such consent to be expressed by them in person after due publicity and in the presence of the authority competent to solemnize the marriage and of witnesses, as prescribed by law.

2. Notwithstanding anything in paragraph 1 above, it shall not be necessary for one of the parties to be present when the competent authority is satisfied that the circumstances are exceptional and that the party has, before a competent authority and in such manner as may be prescribed by law, expressed and not withdrawn consent.

A distinction must be drawn between arranged marriages and forced marriages. Where the parties freely agree to enter into a marriage, is it immaterial whether they have met in advance? Many societies advocate arranged marriages and many young people elect to opt into such schemes. When the law must intervene is if one or both parties are being coerced into agreeing to marriage or when one party has no choice.

14.6.2   A correlative right to divorce and remarry?

An interesting question which arises is whether the right to marry is a once only right and similarly whether people have the right to separate and divorce (obviously a precursor to a non-polygamous/polygynous remarriage). Note the decisions of the European Court of Human Rights in *F v Switzerland*, Series A, No. 128 (1987) concerning national prohibitions on remarriage within a specified time after divorce and *Johnston v Ireland*, Series A, No. 112 (1986) on the affect of Art 12 of the European Convention on legal separation and divorce. Most States have distinct regulations on remarriage, separation and, as noted above, marriage.

Protocol to the African Charter on Human and Peoples' Rights on the Rights of Women in Africa 2000 Art 7

Separation, Divorce and Annulment of Marriage

States Parties shall enact appropriate legislation to ensure that women and men enjoy the same rights in case of separation, divorce or annulment of marriage. In this regard, they shall ensure that:

a)   separation, divorce or annulment of a marriage shall be effected by judicial order;

b)   women and men shall have the same rights to seek separation, divorce or annulment of a marriage;

c)   in case of separation, divorce or annulment of marriage, women and men shall have reciprocal rights and responsibilities towards their children. In any case, the interests of the children shall be given paramount importance;

d)   in case of separation, divorce or annulment of marriage, women and men shall have the right to an equitable sharing of the joint property deriving from the marriage.

14.6.3   Reproductive rights

Frequently rights to marry and found a family are linked. Obviously childbearing is primarily the role of the woman, although child rearing may be shared with a partner, family and friends. Of fundamental importance is freedom of choice in reproduction and sexual health.

14.6.3.1   Children and Women—rights intertwined?

Particularly with regard to health, the rights of women and children are inter-related. A malnourished mother may produce insufficient milk for her baby and a mother with HIV/AIDS who is not offered the necessary anti-viral treatment is more likely to pass the virus on to her baby.

Protocol to the African Charter on Human and Peoples' Rights on the Rights of Women in Africa 2000 Art 14

Health and Reproductive Rights

1. States Parties shall ensure that the right to health of women, including sexual and reproductive health is respected and promoted. This includes:

a)   the right to control their fertility;

b)   the right to decide whether to have children, the number of children and the spacing of children;

c)   the right to choose any method of contraception;

d)   the right to self protection and to be protected against sexually transmitted infections, including HIV/AIDS;

e)   the right to be informed on one's health status and on the health status of one's partner, particularly if affected with sexually transmitted infections, including HIV/AIDS, in accordance with internationally recognised standards and best practices;

g)   the right to have family planning education.

2. States Parties shall take all appropriate measures to:

a)   provide adequate, affordable and accessible health services, including information, education and communication programmes to women especially those in rural areas;

b)   establish and strengthen existing pre-natal, delivery and post-natal health and nutritional services for women during pregnancy and while they are breast-feeding;

c)   protect the reproductive rights of women by authorising medical abortion in cases of sexual assault, rape, incest, and where the continued pregnancy endangers the mental and physical health of the mother or the life of the mother or the foetus.

14.6.3.2 A right to abortion?

Perhaps the topic is just too controversial, but the issue of abortion has long been avoided in international instruments. Rights to terminate a pregnancy clearly have the potential to involve the conflicting rights of the mother and the unborn child. Abortion by choice may respect the right of the mother to choose what to do with her body. Forced abortions and forced sterilisations are another issue entirely.

The issue of abortions is rarely raised before the international and regional bodies. The case of *Paton v United Kingdom* [1981] 3 EHRR 408 is one of the few examples to have reached an international body—the European Commission on Human Rights. The matter was effectively avoided, there being no breach of Art 2 (right to life). What was not discussed was whether the foetus was not entitled to a right to life or whether the prevailing consideration was the qualification in Art 8(2) in respect of the mother.

However, in the Protocol to the African Charter on Women's Rights, the pro-choice movement seems to have scored a considerable victory.

Protocol to the African Charter on Human and Peoples' Rights on the Rights of Women 2000 Art 14(c)

States Parties take all appropriate measures to protect the reproductive rights of women by authorising medical abortion in cases of sexual assault, rape, incest, and where the continued pregnancy endangers the mental and physical health of the mother or the life of the mother or the foetus.

Admittedly the right is somewhat qualified by the circumstances in which such a medical abortion is justified. It is not a freedom of reproductive choice for women. However, women do have the right to control their fertility, to choose any method of contraception and to decide on the number and spacing of any children they wish to have. These provisions are in themselves quite novel and may be viewed as significantly empowering for women.

Question

Can Art 14(c) of the African Protocol be reconciled with the rights of the child, another major issue of concern in Africa? Interestingly human rights in terms of the Inter-American instruments commences at birth (Art 4(1) American Convention on Human Rights). Can the apparent differences between these regional instruments be explained in cultural terms?

14.7 REGIONAL INSTRUMENTS AND APPROACHES TO WOMEN'S RIGHTS

Within Europe, the European Union has been most proactive in fostering an environment in which women's rights in the workplace can be protected and promoted. A number of prominent decisions of the European Court of Justice have contributed significantly to the law in this area. All European Union cases can be accessed through the website of the European Court of Justice: (www.curia.eu.int). Note also that due to the nature of the European Union and the principles of direct effect and direct applicability, a number of prominent decisions on this area have also been taken by the national courts of the various Member States. Relevant EU textbooks will provide more information.

However, in terms of tabulation of rights, the African system represents the most progressive development.

14.7.1   Africa

The most progressive instrument on women's rights is undoubtedly the most recent: the Protocol to the African Charter on Human and Peoples' Rights on the Rights of Women in Africa. The Protocol was adopted by the second ordinary session of the Assembly of the Union at Maputa in July 2003 and, as such, is one of the first human rights instruments to be adopted by the new African Union. The range of rights enshrined therein is remarkable. Given the interrelationship of economic, social, civil, political and cultural rights which characterised the African Charter on Human and Peoples' Rights, it is perhaps not surprising that the Protocol on Women's Rights is one of the most comprehensive instruments in the area. While arguably reflecting a truly African view of rights, the influence of the Beijing Platform for Action appears to permeate throughout.

Many of the rights reflect universal rights: non-discrimination, rights to life, integrity and security of person, prohibition on exploitation and cruel, inhuman or degrading treatment or punishment, access to justice and equal protection before the law, political participation, education and training, adequate housing, food, culture.

The right to a healthy and sustainable environment is also included.

The following rights of particular interest appear in the instrument:

Protocol to the African Charter on Human and Peoples' Rights on the Rights of Women in Africa 2000

Article 3
Right to Dignity

1. Every woman shall have the right to dignity inherent in a human being and to the recognition and protection of her human and legal rights;

2. Every woman shall have the right to respect as a person and to the free development of her personality;

3. States Parties shall adopt and implement appropriate measures to prohibit any exploitation or degradation of women;

4. States Parties shall adopt and implement appropriate measures to ensure the protection of every woman's right to respect for her dignity and protection of women from all forms of violence, particularly sexual and verbal violence.

Article 5
Elimination of Harmful Practices

States Parties shall prohibit and condemn all forms of harmful practices which negatively affect the human rights of women and which are contrary to recognised international standards. States Parties shall take all necessary legislative and other measures to eliminate such practices, including:

  a) creation of public awareness in all sectors of society regarding harmful practices through information, formal and informal education and outreach programmes;

  b) prohibition, through legislative measures backed by sanctions, of all forms of female genital mutilation, scarification, medicalisation and para-medicalisation of female genital mutilation and all other practices in order to eradicate them;

  c) provision of necessary support to victims of harmful practices through basic services such as health services, legal and judicial support, emotional and psychological counselling as well as vocational training to make them self-supporting;

d) protection of women who are at risk of being subjected to harmful practices or all other forms of violence, abuse and intolerance.

Article 10
Right to Peace

1. Women have the right to a peaceful existence and the right to participate in the promotion and maintenance of peace.

2. States Parties shall take all appropriate measures to ensure the increased participation of women:

a) in programmes of education for peace and a culture of peace;

b) in the structures and processes for conflict prevention, management and resolution at local, national, regional, continental and international levels;

c) in the local, national, regional, continental and international decision making structures to ensure physical, psychological, social and legal protection of asylum seekers, refugees, returnees and displaced persons, in particular women;

d) in all levels of the structures established for the management of camps and settlements for asylum seekers, refugees, returnees and displaced persons, in particular, women;

e) in all aspects of planning, formulation and implementation of post conflict reconstruction and rehabilitation.

3. States Parties shall take the necessary measures to reduce military expenditure significantly in favour of spending on social development in general, and the promotion of women in particular.

Article 13
Economic and Social Welfare Rights

States Parties shall adopt and enforce legislative and other measures to guarantee women equal opportunities in work and career advancement and other economic opportunities. In this respect, they shall:

a) promote equality of access to employment;

b) promote the right to equal remuneration for jobs of equal value for women and men;

c) ensure transparency in recruitment, promotion and dismissal of women and combat and punish sexual harassment in the workplace;

d) guarantee women the freedom to choose their occupation, and protect them from exploitation by their employers violating and exploiting their fundamental rights as recognised and guaranteed by conventions, laws and regulations in force;

e) create conditions to promote and support the occupations and economic activities of women, in particular, within the informal sector;

f) establish a system of protection and social insurance for women working in the informal sector and sensitise them to adhere to it;

g) introduce a minimum age for work and prohibit the employment of children below that age, and prohibit, combat and punish all forms of exploitation of children, especially the girl-child;

h) take the necessary measures to recognise the economic value of the work of women in the home;

i) guarantee adequate and paid pre- and post-natal maternity leave in both the private and public sectors;

j) ensure the equal application of taxation laws to women and men;

k) recognise and enforce the right of salaried women to the same allowances and entitlements as those granted to salaried men for their spouses and children;

l) recognise that both parents bear the primary responsibility for the upbringing and development of children and that this is a social function for which the State and the private sector have secondary responsibility;

m) take effective legislative and administrative measures to prevent the exploitation and abuse of women in advertising and pornography.

Another unusual feature is specific protection of certain women. Widows, the elderly, women with disabilities and women in distress are singled out—see Arts 20, 22–24.

Question

To what extent is the realisation of these rights a reasonable aspiration within the African region? What purpose does the adoption of such a wide-ranging instrument serve?

FURTHER READING

Amirthalingm, K, 'Women's Rights, International Norms, and Domestic Violence: Asian Perspective', 2005, 27 Human Rights Quarterly 653

Askin, K, and Koenig, D, *Women and International Human Rights Law*, 1999–2000, New York: Transnational Press

Bayefsky, A, 'The Principle of Equality or Non-Discrimination in International Law', 1990, 11 Human Rights Law Journal 1

Benedek, W, Kisaakye, M, and Oberleitner, G (eds), *The Human Rights of Women: International Instruments and African Experiences*, 2002, New York: Zed Books

Byrnes, A, 'The Committee on the Elimination of Discrimination Against Women' in Alston, P (ed), *The United Nations and Human Rights: A Critical Appraisal*, 1992, Oxford: Clarendon

Charlesworth, H, 'Not Waving but Drowning: Gender Mainstreaming and Human Rights in the United Nations', 2001, 18 Harvard Human Rights Journal 1

Charlesworth, H, Chinkin, C, and Wright, K, 'Feminist approaches to International Law', 1991, 85 American Journal of International Law 613

Clark, B, 'The Vienna Convention Reservations Regime and the Convention on Discrimination against Women', 1991, 85 American Journal of International Law 281

Cook, R, 'Women's International Human Rights Law: the way forward', 1993, 15 Human Rights Quarterly 230

Cook, R (ed), *Human Rights of Women, national and international perspectives*, 1994, Philadelphia: University of Pennsylvania Press

Emerton, R, Adams, K, Byrnes, A, and Connors, J, *International Women's Rights Cases*, 2005, London: Cavendish Publishing

Jalal, PI, *Law for Pacific Women: a legal rights handbook*, 1998, Suva, Fiji: Women's Rights Movement

Reanda, L, 'The Commission on the Status of Women' in Alston, P (ed), *The United Nations and Human Rights: A critical appraisal*, 1992, Oxford: OUP

Reanda, L, 'Human Rights and Women's Rights: the UN approach', 1981, 3 Human Rights Quarterly 11

Tomasevski, K, *Women and Human Rights*, 1993, London: Zed Books

Websites

www.un.org/womenwatch/—United Nations Inter-Agency Network on Women and Gender equality www.un.org/womenwatch/daw/—United Nations Division for the Advancement of Women

www.un.org/womenwatch/daw/cedaw/—website for the Convention on the Elimination of All Forms of Discrimination against Women. It also contains relevant information and associated documents on the Committee which monitors the Convention

www.un.org/womenwatch/daw/csw/—United Nations Commission on the Status of Women

www.interpol.int/Public/THB/Women/Default.asp—Interpol website on trafficking in women

www.catwinternational.org/—NGO Coalition against Trafficking in Women

www.law-lib.utoronto.ca/diana—the University of Toronto's Women's Human Rights Resources Database, part of its DIANA project

www.womenslinkworldwide.org—Women's Link Worldwide Network website

CHAPTER 15

HUMAN RIGHTS IN CONFLICT AND EMERGENCY SITUATIONS

In times of conflict and emergency situations, abuses of human rights are perhaps more likely. However, at such times, respect for human rights is ever more essential. Conflicts and civil emergencies represent perhaps the ultimate challenge for international human rights—only the most vital and universal rights may survive such a test. Human rights in extreme situations is, in effect, international humanitarian law.

This chapter will focus on examples of human rights protection in such circumstances. It will also outline briefly the legal requirements for redressing violations of these rights to be redressed: international criminal law.

15.1 UNIVERSAL RIGHTS

International human rights are, as previously noted, universal. They should apply to all peoples at all times. However, the potential for derogations (discussed in Chapter 3) raises the issue of reduced human rights protection for a population at the very time they are perhaps most vulnerable.

Generally, the prohibition on torture, the prohibition on retrospective criminal legislation, provisions on equality before the law and non-discrimination remain.

The importance of human rights in emergency situations is emphasised in the words of the Secretary-General writing in his report on reform 'In Larger Freedom':

Kofi Annan, 'In larger freedom, towards development, security and human rights for all', UN Doc. A/59/2005

Paragraph 130. But without implementation, our declarations ring hollow. Without action, promises are meaningless. Villagers huddling in fear at the sound of Government bombing raids or the appearance of murderous militias on the horizon find no solace in the unimplemented words of the Geneva Conventions, to say nothing of the international community's solemn promises of 'never again' when reflecting on the horrors of Rwanda a decade ago. Treaties prohibiting torture are cold comfort to prisoners abused by their captors, particularly if the international human rights machinery enables those responsible to hide behind friends in high places. A war-weary population infused with hope after the signing of a peace agreement quickly reverts to despair when, instead of seeing tangible progress towards a Government under the rule of law, it sees war lords and gang leaders take power and become laws unto themselves. And solemn commitments to strengthen democracy at home, which all State made in the Millennium Declaration, remain empty words to those who have never voted for their rulers and who see no sign that things are changing.

134. Nowhere is the gap between rhetoric and reality—between declarations and deeds—so stark and so deadly as in the field of international humanitarian law. It cannot be right, when the international community is faced with genocide or massive human rights abuses, for the United Nations to stand by and let them unfold to the end, with disastrous consequences for many thousands of innocent people.

15.2 INTERNATIONAL HUMANITARIAN LAW

International and civil conflicts, famine, natural disasters, terrorism . . . for many the world appears to be an increasingly dangerous place. Guaranteeing human rights when the State is in a conflict situation or when the very infrastructure of the State is under threat can be problematic. Normal laws may be suspended as well as many ordinary judicial operations. How then can human rights be ensured?

15.2.1 Non-derogable rights and freedoms

As Chapter 3 noted, States retain the power to derogate from certain human rights and fundamental freedoms. The 'life' of the State must be threatened and the derogation must be notified to the relevant international and regional bodies. Moreover, the derogation must only be as absolutely necessary in the exigencies of the situation and should be subject to regular review.

As the case of *Aksoy v Turkey* (examined in Chapter 3) demonstrated, international monitoring bodies may be willing to look beyond the actual lodging of a derogation to determine whether the action taken is justified.

Table of non-derogable rights and freedoms under the principal instruments

Right	Instrument		
	ICCPR Art 4	ECHR Art 15	Am CHR Art 27
Life	✓	✓	✓
Liberty			
Slavery	✓	✓	✓
Torture	✓	✓	✓
Fair trial			
Ex post facto laws	✓	✓	✓
Recognition in law	✓		✓
Freedom of thought, conscience and religion	✓		✓

In addition, the American Convention permits no derogation from the provisions on family rights, the rights of the child, the right to a nationality, the right to a name and rights to participation in government.

Note that the African Charter does not make provision for derogation from any of its provisions in the event of conflict or emergency situations.

Question

Look at the principal instruments which permit derogations and note the rights which can be compromised in emergency situations. Are too many rights included in the 'derogable' category? Are derogations operational necessities in time of conflict?

15.2.1.1 Religious freedom and Europe

Within Europe, freedom of thought, conscience and religion is derogable; this may be regarded as somewhat amazing given European history and religious and other beliefs' persecution. However, the European Court has strictly interpreted the scope of the relevant Art 9 of the European Convention, limiting flexibility. Despite this, States are accorded a comparatively wide margin of appreciation with respect to manifestations of religious and other beliefs.

Sahin v Turkey, Application 44774/98, judgment June 2004

The complaint concerned a ban on wearing headscarves in Turkish universities. The applicant was precluded from finishing her studies and complained about a violation of Art 9 of the European Convention. Note that this case was referred to the Grand Chamber which passed judgment in November 2005 upholding the initial decision.

104. It must first be observed that the interference was based, in particular, on two principles—secularism and equality—which reinforce and complement each other (see paragraphs 34 and 36 above).

105. In its judgment of 7 March 1989, the Constitutional Court stated that secularism in Turkey was, among other things, the guarantor of democratic values, the principle that freedom of religion is inviolable—to the extent that it stems from individual conscience—and the principle that citizens are equal before the law (see paragraph 36 above). Secularism also protected the individual from external pressure. It added that restrictions could be placed on freedom to manifest one's religion in order to defend those values and principles.

106. This notion of secularism appears to the Court to be consistent with the values underpinning the Convention and it accepts that upholding that principle may be regarded as necessary for the protection of the democratic system in Turkey.

107. The Court further notes the emphasis placed in the Turkish constitutional system on the protection of the rights of women (see paragraph 28 above). Gender equality—recognised by the European Court as one of the key principles underlying the Convention and a goal to be achieved by member States of the Council of Europe (. . . .)—was also found by the Turkish Constitutional Court to be a principle implicit in the values underlying the Constitution (see paragraph 36 above).

108. In addition, like the Constitutional Court (see paragraph 36 above), the Court considers that, when examining the question of the Islamic headscarf in the Turkish context, there must be borne in mind the impact which wearing such a symbol, which is presented or perceived as a compulsory religious duty, may have on those who choose not to wear it. As has already been noted (see *Karaduman*, decision cited above; and *Refah Partisi and Others*, cited above, § 95), the issues at stake include the protection of the 'rights and freedoms of others' and the 'maintenance of public order' in a country in which the majority of the population, while professing a strong attachment to the rights of women and a secular way of life, adhere to the Islamic faith. Imposing limitations on freedom in this sphere may, therefore, be regarded as meeting a pressing social need by seeking to achieve those two legitimate aims, especially since, as the Turkish courts stated (see paragraphs 32 and 34 above), this religious symbol has taken on political significance in Turkey in recent years.

109. The Court does not lose sight of the fact that there are extremist political movements in Turkey which seek to impose on society as a whole their religious symbols and conception of a society founded on religious precepts (see paragraphs 32 and 33 above). It has previously said that each Contracting State may, in accordance with the Convention provisions, take a stance against such political movements, based on its historical experience (*Refah Partisi and Others*, cited above, § 124). The regulations concerned have to be viewed in that context and constitute a measure intended to achieve the legitimate aims referred to above and thereby to preserve pluralism in the university.

111. The applicant has been critical of the manner in which the university authorities applied the measures (see paragraphs 86–88 above). However, the Court notes that it is undisputed that in Turkish universities, to the extent that they do not overstep the limits imposed by the

organisational requirements of State education, practising Muslim students are free to perform the religious duties that are habitually part of Muslim observance. In addition, the resolution which was adopted by Istanbul University on 9 July 1998 (see paragraph 45 above) treated all forms of dress symbolising or manifesting a religion or faith on an equal footing in barring them from the university premises.

114. In the light of the foregoing and having regard in particular to the margin of appreciation left to the Contracting States, the Court finds that the University of Istanbul's regulations imposing restrictions on the wearing of Islamic headscarves and the measures taken to implement them were justified in principle and proportionate to the aims pursued and, therefore, could be regarded as 'necessary in a democratic society'.

Of course, the very right to derogate under Art 15 of the European Convention is a matter within the discretion and arguably margin of appreciation of States. While subject to the supervisory jurisdiction of the European Court, it is difficult to conceive of the Court criticising a State wishing to derogate within the strict terms of the article.

15.2.2   Case study: liberty and terrorism

Question

Rights to liberty and the right to a fair trial may be subject to derogation. In what situations can you foresee this?

Liberty is a concept enshrined in the constitutions of many democratic states. Indeed, *liberté* was one of the original (along with *fraternité* and *égalité*) cornerstones of the French Republic in the aftermath of the revolution of 1789. However, in times of conflict, perceived enemies of the State are often detained without trial and freedom of movement within States may be limited. In the twenty-first century, conflicts have been augmented by a 'new' and more invidious threat to peace and security— terrorism.

Accordingly, many States are enacting ever more draconian measures aimed at limiting the threat from terrorism. Chechnya, the United Kingdom and the United States of America have all recently experienced significant terrorism. Within these States (and many more), many commentators are now pondering the extent to which measures to combat terrorism can and should impinge on the rights and civil liberties of the rest of the population. Should the State dramatically alter its approach to matters such as fundamental personal freedom, then arguably the terrorists may have achieved at least a partial victory.

Question

Look at the Homeland Security Act 2002 (USA) or the Prevention of Terrorism Act 2005 (UK). Balance these provisions against the threat to the United Kingdom and the United States of America posed by terrorism and evidence, inter alia, by the events of September 2001 and July 2005. Is there an emergency situation in those States?

Note the situation of those detained in Guantanamo Bay (Cuba) by the United States of America. Termed 'illegal combatants', they are removed from the ambit of the principal international human rights instruments without the legal requirement of a derogation (see below for a more detailed discussion).

15.2.3   Evolution of humanitarian law

However, international humanitarian law evolved to guarantee rights to disabled combatants and civilians alike. When in operation, it functions as the last resort, the line beyond which a State should not go.

International humanitarian law has roots deep in history. Many cultures enshrined guarantees of protection for non-combatants and similarly, many pre-scribed parameters for the conduct of hostilities. A just war, *jus in bello*, is the goal of the laws of war. (Note the full text of many historical treaties impacting on international humanitarian law can be found on the website of the Committee of the International Red Cross.)

In concept, international humanitarian law has different origins from human rights protection norms. However, it retains a place in the present text as the system operates to protect the rights of especially vulnerable people and it applies when the operation of other human rights may have been suspended by the State.

15.2.4   The Hague Conventions

International humanitarian law seeks to regulate the conduct of hostilities and protect fundamental rights and freedoms of those caught up in the hostilities. The Hague Conventions govern the former, the regulation of hostilities. They remain in force today.

Early Hague (and Geneva) Conventions on war

Convention for the Amelioration of the Condition of the Wounded in Armies in the Field, Geneva 1864

Convention with respect to the laws and customs of War on Land and its annex: Regulations concerning the laws and customs of war on land, the Hague 1899

Convention for the Adaptation to Maritime Warfare of the Principles of the Geneva Convention 1864, the Hague 1899

Convention respecting the laws and customs of war on Land and its annex: Regulations concerning the laws and customs of war on land, the Hague 1907

Convention relating to the Opening of Hostilities, the Hague 1907

Convention relating to the conversion of merchant Ships into Warships, the Hague 1907

Convention relative to the laying of automatic submarine contact mines, the Hague 1907

Convention concerning the Bombardment by Naval Forces in Times of War, the Hague 1907

Convention relative to certain restrictions with regard to the Exercise of the right to Capture Naval War, the Hague 1907

Convention respecting the rights and duties of neutral powers and persons in case of war on land, the Hague 1907

Convention respecting the rights and duties of neutral powers in naval war, the Hague 1907.

Subsequent instruments make provision for limiting the use of excessively injurious weapons: 1922 Treaty relating to the use of submarines and noxious gases in warfare and 1925 protocol for the prohibition on the use of asphyxiating, poisonous or other gases and of bacteriological methods of warfare, for example. Indeed, there has been a significant tendency in recent decades to focus on eliminating the use of weapons which have proven to have an indiscriminate application. These instruments not only contribute towards the literature on the conduct of war but also impact on the protection of civilians and other non-combatants. This further emphasises the overlap between *jus ad bellum* and *jus in bello*.

Instruments relating to weaponry

Convention on the Prohibition of the Development, Production and Stockpiling of Bacteriological (Biological) and Toxin Weapons and on their Destruction 1972

Convention on Prohibitions or Restrictions on The Use of Certain Conventional Weapons Which May Be Deemed To Be Excessively Injurious or To Have Indiscriminate Effects 1980

> Protocol on Non-Detectable Fragments 1980
>
> Protocol II on Prohibitions on the Use of Mines, Booby-Traps and Other Devices 1980
>
> Protocol III on Prohibitions or Restrictions on the use of Incendiary Weapons 1980
>
> Protocol IV on Blinding Laser Weapons 1995
>
> Protocol V on Explosive Remnants of War 2003

Convention on The Prohibition of The Development, Production, Stockpiling And Use Of Chemical Weapons And On Their Destruction 1993

Convention on The Prohibition Of The Use, Stockpiling, Production And Transfer Of Anti-Personnel Mines And On Their Destruction 1997

Statistics on deaths by landmines and evidence on the indiscriminate effect of chemical and biological weapons leave no doubt that prohibitions of such weaponry will limit civilian casualties and deaths. Note the dates and contemporary conflicts/campaigns particularly relative to the conventions on chemical weapons and landmines.

15.2.5   The Geneva Conventions

Perhaps the most famous and oft-cited examples of humanitarian law are the Geneva Conventions. These four conventions are accepted by 194 State Parties. According to the International Committee of the Red Cross, this means the conventions are almost unique in being signed by all world States. Many elements of the Geneva Conventions represent codification of existing practices. The conventions also reflect the fact that the existing law proved insufficient to protect non-combatants and indeed more involved people from the impact and effect of the Second World War. The four Geneva Conventions have been augmented by two additional protocols which ensure the extension of the principles to internal conflicts.

Geneva Conventions of 1949

> Convention for the Amelioration of the Condition of the Wounded and Sick in Armed Forces in the Field
>
> Convention for the Amelioration of the Condition of Wounded, Sick and Shipwrecked Members of the Armed Forces at Sea
>
> Convention relative to the Treatment of Prisoners of War
>
> Convention relative to the protection of Civilian Persons in Time of War
>
> Protocol Additional to the Geneva Conventions on 12 August 1949, and relating to the Protection of Victims of International Armed Conflicts 1977

Protocol Additional to the Geneva Conventions on 12 August 1949, and relating to the Protection of Victims of Non-International Armed Conflicts 1977.

Note the general provisions of the conventions.

Convention for the Amelioration of the Condition of the Wounded and Sick in Armed Forces in the Field 1949

Chapter I. General Provisions

Article 1. The High Contracting Parties undertake to respect and to ensure respect for the present Convention in all circumstances.

Article 2. In addition to the provisions which shall be implemented in peacetime, the present Convention shall apply to all cases of declared war or of any other armed conflict which may arise between two or more of the High Contracting Parties, even if the state of war is not recognized by one of them.

The Convention shall also apply to all cases of partial or total occupation of the territory of a High Contracting Party, even if the said occupation meets with no armed resistance.

Although one of the Powers in conflict may not be a party to the present Convention, the Powers who are parties thereto shall remain bound by it in their mutual relations. They shall furthermore be bound by the Convention in relation to the said Power, if the latter accepts and applies the provisions thereof.

Article 3. In the case of armed conflict not of an international character occurring in the territory of one of the High Contracting Parties, each Party to the conflict shall be bound to apply, as a minimum, the following provisions:

(1) Persons taking no active part in the hostilities, including members of armed forces who have laid down their arms and those placed *hors de combat* by sickness, wounds, detention, or any other cause, shall in all circumstances be treated humanely, without any adverse distinction founded on race, colour, religion or faith, sex, birth or wealth, or any other similar criteria.

To this end, the following acts are and shall remain prohibited at any time and in any place whatsoever with respect to the above-mentioned persons:

(a) violence to life and person, in particular murder of all kinds, mutilation, cruel treatment and torture;

(b) taking of hostages;

(c) outrages upon personal dignity, in particular humiliating and degrading treatment;

(d) the passing of sentences and the carrying out of executions without previous judgement pronounced by a regularly constituted court, affording all the judicial guarantees which are recognized as indispensable by civilized peoples.

(2) The wounded and sick shall be collected and cared for.

An impartial humanitarian body, such as the International Committee of the Red Cross, may offer its services to the Parties to the conflict.

The Parties to the conflict should further endeavour to bring into force, by means of special agreements, all or part of the other provisions of the present Convention.

The application of the preceding provisions shall not affect the legal status of the Parties to the conflict.

These provisions are common to the various Geneva Conventions. They enshrine fundamental principles of international humanitarian law, the limits of acceptable behaviour in conflict situations. Some of the subsequent provisions of the first Geneva Convention also relate directly to the general principles. They are also similar to provisions found in the other conventions.

Convention for the Amelioration of the Condition of the Wounded and Sick in Armed Forces in the Field 1949

Article. 7. Wounded and sick, as well as members of the medical personnel and chaplains, may in no circumstances renounce in part or in entirety the rights secured to them by the present Convention, and by the special agreements referred to in the foregoing Article, if such there be.

Article. 12. Members of the armed forces and other persons mentioned in the following Article, who are wounded or sick, shall be respected and protected in all circumstances.

They shall be treated humanely and cared for by the Party to the conflict in whose power they may be, without any adverse distinction founded on sex, race, nationality, religion, political opinions, or any other similar criteria. Any attempts upon their lives, or violence to their persons, shall be strictly prohibited; in particular, they shall not be murdered or exterminated, subjected to torture or to biological experiments; they shall not wilfully be left without medical assistance and care, nor shall conditions exposing them to contagion or infection be created.

Only urgent medical reasons will authorize priority in the order of treatment to be administered.

Women shall be treated with all consideration due to their sex. The Party to the conflict which is compelled to abandon wounded or sick to the enemy shall, as far as military considerations permit, leave with them a part of its medical personnel and material to assist in their care.

Article. 13. The present Convention shall apply to the wounded and sick belonging to the following categories:

(1) Members of the armed forces of a Party to the conflict, as well as members of militias or volunteer corps forming part of such armed forces.

(2) Members of other militias and members of other volunteer corps, including those of organized resistance movements, belonging to a Party to the conflict and operating in or outside their own territory, even if this territory is occupied, provided that such militias or volunteer corps, including such organized resistance movements, fulfil the following conditions:

(a) that of being commanded by a person responsible for his subordinates;

(b) that of having a fixed distinctive sign recognizable at a distance;

(c) that of carrying arms openly;

(d) that of conducting their operations in accordance with the laws and customs of war.

(3) Members of regular armed forces who profess allegiance to a Government or an authority not recognized by the Detaining Power.

(4) Persons who accompany the armed forces without actually being members thereof, such as civil members of military aircraft crews, war correspondents, supply contractors, members of labour units or of services responsible for the welfare of the armed forces, provided that they have received authorization from the armed forces which they accompany.

(5) Members of crews, including masters, pilots and apprentices, of the merchant marine and the crews of civil aircraft of the Parties to the conflict, who do not benefit by more favourable treatment under any other provisions in international law.

(6) Inhabitants of a non-occupied territory, who on the approach of the enemy, spontaneously take up arms to resist the invading forces, without having had time to form themselves into regular armed units, provided they carry arms openly and respect the laws and customs of war.

Article. 15. At all times, and particularly after an engagement, Parties to the conflict shall, without delay, take all possible measures to search for and collect the wounded and sick, to protect them against pillage and ill-treatment, to ensure their adequate care, and to search for the dead and prevent their being despoiled.

Whenever circumstances permit, an armistice or a suspension of fire shall be arranged, or local arrangements made, to permit the removal, exchange and transport of the wounded left on the battlefield.

Likewise, local arrangements may be concluded between Parties to the conflict for the removal or exchange of wounded and sick from a besieged or encircled area, and for the passage of medical and religious personnel and equipment on their way to that area.

Article 16. Parties to the conflict shall record as soon as possible, in respect of each wounded, sick or dead person of the adverse Party falling into their hands, any particulars which may assist in his identification.

These records should if possible include:

(a) designation of the Power on which he depends;

(b) army, regimental, personal or serial number;

(c) surname;

(d) first name or names;

(e) date of birth;

(f) any other particulars shown on his identity card or disc;

(g) date and place of capture or death;

(h) particulars concerning wounds or illness, or cause of death.

As soon as possible the above mentioned information shall be forwarded to the Information Bureau described in Article 122 of the Geneva Convention relative to the Treatment of Prisoners of War of 12 August 1949, which shall transmit this information to the Power on which these persons depend through the intermediary of the Protecting Power and of the Central Prisoners of War Agency.

Parties to the conflict shall prepare and forward to each other through the same bureau, certificates of death or duly authenticated lists of the dead. They shall likewise collect and forward through the same bureau one half of a double identity disc, last wills or other documents of importance to the next of kin, money and in general all articles of an intrinsic or sentimental value, which are found on the dead. These articles, together with unidentified articles, shall be sent in sealed packets, accompanied by statements giving all particulars necessary for the identification of the deceased owners, as well as by a complete list of the contents of the parcel.

Question

To what extent do these provisions reflect respect for human dignity, as enshrined in the Charter of the United Nations?

The Convention prescribes measures to protect medical units and personnel engaged in searching and caring for the sick and wounded. All members of armed forces in the countries of all contracting States are expected to be informed of the scope and nature of the conventions and act in accordance with them.

Note also elements of criminalisation of contraventions of the convention.

Geneva Convention for the Amelioration of the Condition of the Wounded and Sick in Armed Forces in the Field 1949 Arts 49–50

Article 49. The High Contracting Parties undertake to enact any legislation necessary to provide effective penal sanctions for persons committing, or ordering to be committed, any of the grave breaches of the present Convention defined in the following Article.

Each High Contracting Party shall be under the obligation to search for persons alleged to have committed, or to have ordered to be committed, such grave breaches, and shall bring such persons, regardless of their nationality, before its own courts. It may also, if it prefers, and in accordance with the provisions of its own legislation, hand such persons over for trial to another High Contracting Party concerned, provided such High Contracting Party has made out a *prima facie* case.

Each High Contracting Party shall take measures necessary for the suppression of all acts contrary to the provisions of the present Convention other than the grave breaches defined in the following Article.

In all circumstances, the accused persons shall benefit by safeguards of proper trial and defence, which shall not be less favourable than those provided by Article 105 and those following, of the Geneva Convention relative to the Treatment of Prisoners of War of 12 August 1949.

Article 50. Grave breaches to which the preceding Article relates shall be those involving any of the following acts, if committed against persons or property protected by the Convention: wilful killing, torture or inhuman treatment, including biological experiments, wilfully causing great suffering or serious injury to body or health, and extensive destruction and appropriation of property, not justified by military necessity and carried out unlawfully and wantonly.

This is reinforced by Art 2 of the Statute of the International Criminal Court.

Statute of the International Criminal Court Art 8

1. The Court shall have jurisdiction in respect of war crimes in particular when committed as part of a plan or policy or as part of a large-scale commission of such crimes.

2. For the purpose of this Statute, 'war crimes' means:

(a) Grave breaches of the Geneva Conventions of 12 August 1949, namely, any of the following acts against persons or property protected under the provisions of the relevant Geneva Convention:

   (i)   Wilful killing;

   (ii) Torture or inhuman treatment, including biological experiments;

   (iii) Wilfully causing great suffering, or serious injury to body or health;

   (iv) Extensive destruction and appropriation of property, not justified by military necessity and carried out unlawfully and wantonly;

   (v)   Compelling a prisoner of war or other protected person to serve in the forces of a hostile Power;

   (vi) Wilfully depriving a prisoner of war or other protected person of the rights of fair and regular trial;

   (vii) Unlawful deportation or transfer or unlawful confinement;

   (viii) Taking of hostages.

Note also the comment of the Trial Chamber of the International Tribunal for the Prosecution of Persons Responsible for Serious Violations of International Humanitarian Law Committed in the territory of Former Yugoslavia since 1991.

Prosecutor v Dusko Tadic, IT–94–1-T (1997), para 577

Article 2 of the Statute provides that the 'International Tribunal shall have the power to prosecute persons committing or ordering to be committed grave breaches of the Geneva Conventions of 12 August 1949', and there follows a list of the specific crimes proscribed. Implicit in the *Appeals Chamber Decision* is the conclusion that the Geneva Conventions are a part of customary international law, and as such their application in the present case does not violate the principle of *nullum crime sine lege.*

15.2.5.1   The Distinctive Emblem

Geneva Convention for the Amelioration of the Condition of the Wounded and Sick in Armed Forces in the Field 1949 Arts 38–44

Chapter VII. The Distinctive Emblem

Art. 38. As a compliment to Switzerland, the heraldic emblem of the red cross on a white ground, formed by reversing the Federal colours, is retained as the emblem and distinctive sign of the Medical Service of armed forces.

Nevertheless, in the case of countries which already use as emblem, in place of the red cross, the red crescent or the red lion and sun on a white ground, those emblems are also recognized by the terms of the present Convention.

Art. 39. Under the direction of the competent military authority, the emblem shall be displayed on the flags, armlets and on all equipment employed in the Medical Service.

Art. 40. The personnel designated in Article 24 and in Articles 26 and 27 shall wear, affixed to the left arm, a water-resistant armlet bearing the distinctive emblem, issued and stamped by the military authority.

Such personnel, in addition to wearing the identity disc mentioned in Article 16, shall also carry a special identity card bearing the distinctive emblem. This card shall be water-resistant and of such size that it can be carried in the pocket. It shall be worded in the national language, shall mention at least the surname and first names, the date of birth, the rank and the service number of the bearer, and shall state in what capacity he is entitled to the protection of the present Convention. The card shall bear the photograph of the owner and also either his signature or his finger-prints or both. It shall be embossed with the stamp of the military authority.

The identity card shall be uniform throughout the same armed forces and, as far as possible, of a similar type in the armed forces of the High Contracting Parties. The Parties to the conflict may be guided by the model which is annexed, by way of example, to the present Convention. They shall inform each other, at the outbreak of hostilities, of the model they are using. Identity cards should be made out, if possible, at least in duplicate, one copy being kept by the home country.

In no circumstances may the said personnel be deprived of their insignia or identity cards nor of the right to wear the armlet. In case of loss, they shall be entitled to receive duplicates of the cards and to have the insignia replaced.

Art. 41. The personnel designated in Article 25 shall wear, but only while carrying out medical duties, a white armlet bearing in its centre the distinctive sign in miniature; the armlet shall be issued and stamped by the military authority.

Military identity documents to be carried by this type of personnel shall specify what special training they have received, the temporary character of the duties they are engaged upon, and their authority for wearing the armlet.

Art. 42. The distinctive flag of the Convention shall be hoisted only over such medical units and establishments as are entitled to be respected under the Convention, and only with the consent of the military authorities. In mobile units, as in fixed establishments, it may be accompanied by the national flag of the Party to the conflict to which the unit or establishment belongs.

Nevertheless, medical units which have fallen into the hands of the enemy shall not fly any flag other than that of the Convention. Parties to the conflict shall take the necessary steps, in so far as military considerations permit, to make the distinctive emblems indicating medical units and establishments clearly visible to the enemy land, air or naval forces, in order to obviate the possibility of any hostile action.

Art. 43. The medical units belonging to neutral countries, which may have been authorized to lend their services to a belligerent under the conditions laid down in Article 27, shall fly, along with the flag of the Convention, the national flag of that belligerent, wherever the latter makes use of the faculty conferred on him by Article 42.

Subject to orders to the contrary by the responsible military authorities, they may on all occasions fly their national flag, even if they fall into the hands of the adverse Party.

Art. 44. With the exception of the cases mentioned in the following paragraphs of the present Article, the emblem of the red cross on a white ground and the words 'Red Cross' or 'Geneva Cross' may not be employed, either in time of peace or in time of war, except to indicate or to protect the medical units and establishments, the personnel and material protected by the present Convention and other Conventions dealing with similar matters. The same shall apply to the emblems mentioned in Article 38, second paragraph, in respect of the countries which use them. The National Red Cross Societies and other societies designated in Article 26 shall have the right to use the distinctive emblem conferring the protection of the Convention only within the framework of the present paragraph.

Furthermore, National Red Cross (Red Crescent, Red Lion and Sun) Societies may, in time of peace, in accordance with their rational legislation, make use of the name and emblem of the Red Cross for their other activities which are in conformity with the principles laid down by the International Red Cross Conferences. When those activities are carried out in time of war, the conditions for the use of the emblem shall be such that it cannot be considered as conferring the protection of the Convention; the emblem shall be comparatively small in size and may not be placed on armlets or on the roofs of buildings.

The international Red Cross organizations and their duly authorized personnel shall be permitted to make use, at all times, of the emblem of the red cross on a white ground.

As an exceptional measure, in conformity with national legislation and with the express permission of one of the National Red Cross (Red Crescent, Red Lion and Sun) Societies, the emblem of the Convention may be employed in time of peace to identify vehicles used as ambulances and to mark the position of aid stations exclusively assigned to the purpose of giving free treatment to the wounded or sick.

The red cross and red crescent are the only symbols to have been retained from this treaty.

As an international sign of neutrality, the International Committee of the Red Cross adopted the famous red cross symbol (the inverse of neutral Switzerland's flag). To placate those who felt this had Christian connotations, a red crescent on a white background was subsequently adopted as an alternative. While this proved satisfactory for work in Islamic States, problems arose with other religious-based conflicts. For example, in the former Yugoslavia, ethnic and religious tensions rendered both a cross and a crescent potentially problematic and, indeed, dangerous. After much debate, a crystal (diamond-shape) has been agreed as a third symbol. The Swiss authorities secured agreement for this in December 2005 and a third additional protocol to the Geneva Convention incorporates the red crystal as a new emblem.

15.2.6   Prisoners of war

Convention relative to the Treatment of Prisoners of War Arts 4–5 and 7

Article 4. A. Prisoners of war, in the sense of the present Convention, are persons belonging to one of the following categories, who have fallen into the power of the enemy:

(1) Members of the armed forces of a Party to the conflict, as well as members of militias or volunteer corps forming part of such armed forces.

(2) Members of other militias and members of other volunteer corps, including those of organized resistance movements, belonging to a Party to the conflict and operating in or outside

their own territory, even if this territory is occupied, provided that such militias or volunteer corps, including such organized resistance movements, fulfil the following conditions:

(a) that of being commanded by a person responsible for his subordinates;

(b) that of having a fixed distinctive sign recognizable at a distance;

(c) that of carrying arms openly;

(d) that of conducting their operations in accordance with the laws and customs of war.

(3) Members of regular armed forces who profess allegiance to a government or an authority not recognized by the Detaining Power.

(4) Persons who accompany the armed forces without actually being members thereof, such as civilian members of military aircraft crews, war correspondents, supply contractors, members of labour units or of services responsible for the welfare of the armed forces, provided that they have received authorization, from the armed forces which they accompany, who shall provide them for that purpose with an identity card similar to the annexed model.

(5) Members of crews, including masters, pilots and apprentices, of the merchant marine and the crews of civil aircraft of the Parties to the conflict, who do not benefit by more favourable treatment under any other provisions of international law.

(6) Inhabitants of a non-occupied territory, who on the approach of the enemy spontaneously take up arms to resist the invading forces, without having had time to form themselves into regular armed units, provided they carry arms openly and respect the laws and customs of war.

B. The following shall likewise be treated as prisoners of war under the present Convention:

(1) Persons belonging, or having belonged, to the armed forces of the occupied country, if the occupying Power considers it necessary by reason of such allegiance to intern them, even though it has originally liberated them while hostilities were going on outside the territory it occupies, in particular where such persons have made an unsuccessful attempt to rejoin the armed forces to which they belong and which are engaged in combat, or where they fail to comply with a summons made to them with a view to internment.

(2) The persons belonging to one of the categories enumerated in the present Article, who have been received by neutral or non-belligerent Powers on their territory and whom these Powers are required to intern under international law, without prejudice to any more favourable treatment which these Powers may choose to give and with the exception of Articles 8, 10, 15, 30, fifth paragraph, 58–67, 92, 126 and, where diplomatic relations exist between the Parties to the conflict and the neutral or non-belligerent Power concerned, those Articles concerning the Protecting Power. Where such diplomatic relations exist, the Parties to a conflict on whom these persons depend shall be allowed to perform towards them the functions of a Protecting Power as provided in the present Convention, without prejudice to the functions which these Parties normally exercise in conformity with diplomatic and consular usage and treaties.

C. This Article shall in no way affect the status of medical personnel and chaplains as provided for in Article 33 of the present Convention.

Article 5. The present Convention shall apply to the persons referred to in Article 4 from the time they fall into the power of the enemy and until their final release and repatriation.

Should any doubt arise as to whether persons, having committed a belligerent act and having fallen into the hands of the enemy, belong to any of the categories enumerated in Article 4, such persons shall enjoy the protection of the present Convention until such time as their status has been determined by a competent tribunal.

Article 7. Prisoners of war may in no circumstances renounce in part or in entirety the rights secured to them by the present Convention, and by the special agreements referred to in the foregoing Article, if such there be.

15.2.6.1   Comment on detainees in Guantanamo Bay, Cuba

Those detained by the American forces in Guantanamo Bay are deemed 'illegal combatants'. Accordingly, the United States initially sought to differentiate between prisoners of war and civilians (Geneva Convention), armed combatants (Geneva and Hague) and those involved in the 'war on terror'. Note that mercenaries fall outwith the main provisions of the Geneva and Hague Conventions. Arguably, however, those detained in Guantanamo, mainland United States, Iraq and Afghanistan are not mercenaries.

Question

With respect to the detainees, to what extent do they satisfy the criteria for prisoners of war in terms of the Geneva Convention?

Note that the American authorities have publicly stated that the detainees are being accorded all the applicable rights under the Geneva Convention.

Convention relative to the Treatment of Prisoners of War Arts 12–16
Part II. General Protection of Prisoners of War

Article 12. Prisoners of war are in the hands of the enemy Power, but not of the individuals or military units who have captured them. Irrespective of the individual responsibilities that may exist, the Detaining Power is responsible for the treatment given them.

Prisoners of war may only be transferred by the Detaining Power to a Power which is a party to the Convention and after the Detaining Power has satisfied itself of the willingness and ability of such transferee Power to apply the Convention. When prisoners of war are transferred under such circumstances, responsibility for the application of the Convention rests on the Power accepting them while they are in its custody.

Nevertheless, if that Power fails to carry out the provisions of the Convention in any important respect, the Power by whom the prisoners of war were transferred shall, upon being notified by the Protecting Power, take effective measures to correct the situation or shall request the return of the prisoners of war. Such requests must be complied with.

Article 13. Prisoners of war must at all times be humanely treated. Any unlawful act or omission by the Detaining Power causing death or seriously endangering the health of a prisoner of war in its custody is prohibited, and will be regarded as a serious breach of the present Convention. In particular, no prisoner of war may be subjected to physical mutilation or to medical or scientific experiments of any kind which are not justified by the medical, dental or hospital treatment of the prisoner concerned and carried out in his interest.

Likewise, prisoners of war must at all times be protected, particularly against acts of violence or intimidation and against insults and public curiosity.

Measures of reprisal against prisoners of war are prohibited.

Article 14. Prisoners of war are entitled in all circumstances to respect for their persons and their honour.

Women shall be treated with all the regard due to their sex and shall in all cases benefit by treatment as favourable as that granted to men.

Prisoners of war shall retain the full civil capacity which they enjoyed at the time of their capture. The Detaining Power may not restrict the exercise, either within or without its own territory, of the rights such capacity confers except in so far as the captivity requires.

Article 15. The Power detaining prisoners of war shall be bound to provide free of charge for their maintenance and for the medical attention required by their state of health.

Article 16. Taking into consideration the provisions of the present Convention relating to rank and sex, and subject to any privileged treatment which may be accorded to them by reason of their state of health, age or professional qualifications, all prisoners of war shall be treated alike by the Detaining Power, without any adverse distinction based on race, nationality, religious belief or political opinions, or any other distinction founded on similar criteria.

Note particularly Art 13 and the potential effect of it on the significant news coverage which accompanied the predominantly American and British military actions from 2003 onwards in Iraq. On several occasions 'news' pictures and video coverage showed Iraqi and allied captives. Such coverage is potentially problematic under the Geneva Convention. (Note that the rather serious situation of photos depicting alleged abuse of detainees is quite a different matter—such treatment clearly contravenes the Geneva Convention and consequently, a number of internal military tribunals and courts have been reviewing these particular cases.)

Increased internal and civil conflicts characterises international relations. War itself was renounced in 1928 by the Pact of Paris, the Kellog-Briand pact. Although now virtually superseded by the UN Charter, this treaty was accepted by almost the then entire international community. Irrespective of this, within a decade, the Second World War flouted the terms of the treaty with spectacularly destructive results. Internal conflicts remain a major source of tension today, and frequently give rise to threats to international peace and security. As a result, the second protocol to the Geneva Conventions prescribed rights for those caught up in such conflicts.

Protocol Additional to the Geneva Convention of 12 August 1949 Arts 1–18 and relating to the Protection of Victims of Non-International Armed Conflicts 1977

Part I. Scope of this Protocol

Article 1. Material field of application

1. This Protocol, which develops and supplements Article 3 common to the Geneva Conventions of 12 August 1949 without modifying its existing conditions or application, shall apply to all armed conflicts which are not covered by Article 1 of the Protocol Additional to the Geneva Conventions of 12 August 1949, and relating to the Protection of Victims of International Armed Conflicts (Protocol I) and which take place in the territory of a High Contracting Party between its armed forces and dissident armed forces or other organized armed groups which, under responsible command, exercise such control over a part of its territory as to enable them to carry out sustained and concerted military operations and to implement this Protocol.

2. This Protocol shall not apply to situations of internal disturbances and tensions, such as riots, isolated and sporadic acts of violence and other acts of a similar nature, as not being armed conflicts.

Article 2. Personal field of application

1. This Protocol shall be applied without any adverse distinction founded on race, colour, sex, language, religion or belief, political or other opinion, national or social origin, wealth, birth or other status, or on any other similar criteria (hereinafter referred to as 'adverse distinction') to all persons affected by an armed conflict as defined in Article 1.

2. At the end of the armed conflict, all the persons who have been deprived of their liberty or whose liberty has been restricted for reasons related to such conflict, as well as those deprived of

their liberty or whose liberty is restricted after the conflict for the same reasons, shall enjoy the protection of Articles 5 and 6 until the end of such deprivation or restriction of liberty.

Article 3. Non-intervention

1. Nothing in this Protocol shall be invoked for the purpose of affecting the sovereignty of a State or the responsibility of the government, by all legitimate means, to maintain or re-establish law and order in the State or to defend the national unity and territorial integrity of the State.

2. Nothing in this Protocol shall be invoked as a justification for intervening, directly or indirectly, for any reason whatever, in the armed conflict or in the internal or external affairs of the High Contracting Party in the territory of which that conflict occurs.

Part II. Humane Treatment
Article 4. Fundamental guarantees

1. All persons who do not take a direct part or who have ceased to take part in hostilities, whether or not their liberty has been restricted, are entitled to respect for their person, honour and convictions and religious practices. They shall in all circumstances be treated humanely, without any adverse distinction. It is prohibited to order that there shall be no survivors.

2. Without prejudice to the generality of the foregoing, the following acts against the persons referred to in paragraph I are and shall remain prohibited at any time and in any place whatsoever:

(a) violence to the life, health and physical or mental well-being of persons, in particular murder as well as cruel treatment such as torture, mutilation or any form of corporal punishment;

(b) collective punishments;

(c) taking of hostages;

(d) acts of terrorism;

(e) outrages upon personal dignity, in particular humiliating and degrading treatment, rape, enforced prostitution and any form of indecent assault;

(f) slavery and the slave trade in all their forms;

(g) pillage;

(h) threats to commit any or the foregoing acts.

3. Children shall be provided with the care and aid they require, and in particular:

(a) they shall receive an education, including religious and moral education, in keeping with the wishes of their parents, or in the absence of parents, of those responsible for their care;

(b) all appropriate steps shall be taken to facilitate the reunion of families temporarily separated;

(c) children who have not attained the age of fifteen years shall neither be recruited in the armed forces or groups nor allowed to take part in hostilities;

(d) the special protection provided by this Article to children who have not attained the age of fifteen years shall remain applicable to them if they take a direct part in hostilities despite the provisions of subparagraph (c) and are captured;

(e) measures shall be taken, if necessary, and whenever possible with the consent of their parents or persons who by law or custom are primarily responsible for their care, to remove children temporarily from the area in which hostilities are taking place to a safer area within the country and ensure that they are accompanied by persons responsible for their safety and well-being.

Article 5. Persons whose liberty has been restricted

1. In addition to the provisions of Article 4 the following provisions shall be respected as a minimum with regard to persons deprived of their liberty for reasons related to the armed conflict, whether they are interned or detained:

(a) the wounded and the sick shall be treated in accordance with Article 7;

(b) the persons referred to in this paragraph shall, to the same extent as the local civilian population, be provided with food and drinking water and be afforded safeguards as regards health and hygiene and protection against the rigours of the climate and the dangers of the armed conflict;

(c) they shall be allowed to receive individual or collective relief;

(d) they shall be allowed to practise their religion and, if requested and appropriate, to receive spiritual assistance from persons, such as chaplains, performing religious functions;

(e) they shall, if made to work, have the benefit of working conditions and safeguards similar to those enjoyed by the local civilian population.

2. Those who are responsible for the internment or detention of the persons referred to in paragraph 1 shall also, within the limits of their capabilities, respect the following provisions relating to such persons:

(a) except when men and women of a family are accommodated together, women shall be held in quarters separated from those of men and shall be under the immediate supervision of women;

(b) they shall be allowed to send and receive letters and cards, the number of which may be limited by competent authority if it deems necessary;

(c) places of internment and detention shall not be located close to the combat zone. The persons referred to in paragraph 1 shall be evacuated when the places where they are interned or detained become particularly exposed to danger arising out of the armed conflict, if their evacuation can be carried out under adequate conditions of safety;

(d) they shall have the benefit of medical examinations;

(e) their physical or mental health and integrity shall not be endangered by any unjustified act or omission. Accordingly, it is prohibited to subject the persons described in this Article to any medical procedure which is not indicated by the state of health of the person concerned, and which is not consistent with the generally accepted medical standards applied to free persons under similar medical circumstances.

3. Persons who are not covered by paragraph 1 but whose liberty has been restricted in any way whatsoever for reasons related to the armed conflict shall be treated humanely in accordance with Article 4 and with paragraphs 1 (a), (c) and (d), and 2 (b) of this Article.

4. If it is decided to release persons deprived of their liberty, necessary measures to ensure their safety shall be taken by those so deciding.

Article 6. Penal prosecutions

1. This Article applies to the prosecution and punishment of criminal offences related to the armed conflict.

2. No sentence shall be passed and no penalty shall be executed on a person found guilty of an offence except pursuant to a conviction pronounced by a court offering the essential guarantees of independence and impartiality.

In particular:

(a) the procedure shall provide for an accused to be informed without delay of the particulars of the offence alleged against him and shall afford the accused before and during his trial all necessary rights and means of defence;

(b) no one shall be convicted of an offence except on the basis of individual penal responsibility;

(c) no one shall be held guilty of any criminal offence on account of any act or omission which did not constitute a criminal offence, under the law, at the time when it was committed; nor shall a heavier penalty be imposed than that which was applicable at the time when the criminal offence was committed; if, after the commission of the offence, provision is made by law for the imposition of a lighter penalty, the offender shall benefit thereby;

(d) anyone charged with an offence is presumed innocent until proved guilty according to law;

(e) anyone charged with an offence shall have the right to be tried in his presence;

(f) no one shall be compelled to testify against himself or to confess guilt.

3. A convicted person shall be advised on conviction of his judicial and other remedies and of the time-limits within which they may be exercised.

4. The death penalty shall not be pronounced on persons who were under the age of eighteen years at the time of the offence and shall not be carried out on pregnant women or mothers of young children.

5. At the end of hostilities, the authorities in power shall endeavour to grant the broadest possible amnesty to persons who have participated in the armed conflict, or those deprived of their liberty for reasons related to the armed conflict, whether they are interned or detained.

Part III. Wounded, Sick and Shipwrecked
Article 7. Protection and care

1. All the wounded, sick and shipwrecked, whether or not they have taken part in the armed conflict, shall be respected and protected.

2. In all circumstances they shall be treated humanely and shall receive to the fullest extent practicable and with the least possible delay, the medical care and attention required by their condition. There shall be no distinction among them founded on any grounds other than medical ones.

Article 8. Search

Whenever circumstances permit and particularly after an engagement, all possible measures shall be taken, without delay, to search for and collect the wounded, sick and shipwrecked, to protect them against pillage and ill-treatment, to ensure their adequate care, and to search for the dead, prevent their being despoiled, and decently dispose of them.

Article 9. Protection of medical and religious personnel

1. Medical and religious personnel shall be respected and protected and shall be granted all available help for the performance of their duties. They shall not be compelled to carry out tasks which are not compatible with their humanitarian mission.

2. In the performance of their duties medical personnel may not be required to give priority to any person except on medical grounds.

Article 10. General protection of medical duties

1. Under no circumstances shall any person be punished for having carried out medical activities compatible with medical ethics, regardless of the person benefiting therefrom.

2. Persons engaged in medical activities shall neither be compelled to perform acts or to carry out work contrary to, nor be compelled to refrain from acts required by, the rules of medical ethics or other rules designed for the benefit of the wounded and sick, or this Protocol.

3. The professional obligations of persons engaged in medical activities regarding information which they may acquire concerning the wounded and sick under their care shall, subject to national law, be respected.

4. Subject to national law, no person engaged in medical activities may be penalized in any way for refusing or failing to give information concerning the wounded and sick who are, or who have been, under his care.

Article 11. Protection of medical units and transports

1. Medical units and transports shall be respected and protected at all times and shall not be the object of attack.

2. The protection to which medical units and transports are entitled shall not cease unless they are used to commit hostile acts, outside their humanitarian function. Protection may, however, cease only after a warning has been given, setting, whenever appropriate, a reasonable time-limit, and after such warning has remained unheeded.

Article 12. The distinctive emblem

Under the direction of the competent authority concerned, the distinctive emblem of the red cross, red crescent or red lion and sun on a white ground shall be displayed by medical and religious personnel and medical units, and on medical transports. It shall be respected in all circumstances. It shall not be used improperly.

Part IV. Civilian Population
Article 13. Protection of the civilian population

1. The civilian population and individual civilians shall enjoy general protection against the dangers arising from military operations. To give effect to this protection, the following rules shall be observed in all circumstances.

2. The civilian population as such, as well as individual civilians, shall not be the object of attack. Acts or threats of violence the primary purpose of which is to spread terror among the civilian population are prohibited.

3. Civilians shall enjoy the protection afforded by this part, unless and for such time as they take a direct part in hostilities.

Article 14. Protection of objects indispensable to the survival of the civilian population

Starvation of civilians as a method of combat is prohibited. It is therefore prohibited to attack, destroy, remove or render useless for that purpose, objects indispensable to the survival of the civilian population such as food-stuffs, agricultural areas for the production of food-stuffs, crops, livestock, drinking water installations and supplies and irrigation works.

Article 15. Protection of works and installations containing dangerous forces

Works or installations containing dangerous forces, namely dams, dykes and nuclear electrical generating stations, shall not be made the object of attack, even where these objects are military objectives, if such attack may cause the release of dangerous forces and consequent severe losses among the civilian population.

Article 16. Protection of cultural objects and of places of worship

Without prejudice to the provisions of the Hague Convention for the Protection of Cultural Property in the Event of Armed Conflict of 14 May 1954, it is prohibited to commit any acts of hostility directed against historic monuments, works of art or places of worship which constitute the cultural or spiritual heritage of peoples, and to use them in support of the military effort.

Article 17. Prohibition of forced movement of civilians

1. The displacement of the civilian population shall not be ordered for reasons related to the conflict unless the security of the civilians involved or imperative military reasons so demand. Should such displacements have to be carried out, all possible measures shall be taken in order that the civilian population may be received under satisfactory conditions of shelter, hygiene, health, safety and nutrition.

2. Civilians shall not be compelled to leave their own territory for reasons connected with the conflict.

Article 18. Relief societies and relief actions

1. Relief societies located in the territory of the High Contracting Party, such as Red Cross (Red Crescent, Red Lion and Sun) organizations may offer their services for the performance of their traditional functions in relation to the victims of the armed conflict. The civilian population may, even on its own initiative, offer to collect and care for the wounded, sick and shipwrecked.

2. If the civilian population is suffering undue hardship owing to a lack of the supplies essential for its survival, such as food-stuffs and medical supplies, relief actions for the civilian population which are of an exclusively humanitarian and impartial nature and which are conducted without any adverse distinction shall be undertaken subject to the consent of the High Contracting Party concerned.

Question

Compare the rights contained in the Protocol with those articulated in the Universal Declaration. Note any overlaps with derogable rights contained in the international covenants and the principal regional instruments.

15.3 INTERNATIONAL CRIMINAL LAW

International criminal law sits at a junction between international human rights law and international humanitarian law. It is of primary significance as individuals can be held to account for violations of fundamental human rights and humanitarian laws. Individuals become subject to international law and cannot hide behind the veil of the State. In extreme situations, responsibility for violations of human rights can be found and criminal sanction imposed. Crimes under international criminal law usually fall within 'universal jurisdiction', thus any and every State can exercise jurisdiction over those responsible. The origins of customary elements of international criminal law include universal jurisdiction over piracy (established in the seventeenth and eighteenth centuries) and war crimes (late nineteenth century). An early example of international criminal law appeared in the USA. The Lieber Code (Instructions for the Government of Armies of the United States in the Field, approved by President Lincoln of the United States of America) of 1863 was implemented during the American Civil War with military courts considering alleged violations thereof.

Question

Look at the terms of the War Crimes Act 1991, c13 (United Kingdom). Consider the extent to which the rules on universal jurisdiction balance allegations that this legislation incorporates retrospective criminal law and thus is contrary to norms of human rights.

15.3.1.1 Time limits

While the principles of international criminal law are well established, the international community has also considered the issue of time limitations. A Convention on the Non-Applicability of Statutory Limitations to War Crimes and Crimes against Humanity was adopted in 1968, while in Europe, the European Convention on the Non-Applicability of Statutory Limitations to Crimes against Humanity and War Crimes 1974 makes similar provisions.

R v Sawoniuk [2001] 2 Criminal Appeal Reports 220

Sawoniuk had been convicted of murder on two charges of violating the laws and custom of war. He had been involved in the deaths of two Jews in Belorussia in 1942. (Sawoniuk was a policeman in Belorussia at the time.) Sawoniuk had moved to the United Kingdom after the war and settled there. The principal evidence against him was led by two eyewitnesses, aged 13 and 20 years old at the time of the event. Given the prosecution was in 1999, clearly a considerable time had elapsed since the event. This was the first instance of a conviction under the War Crimes Act.

Lord Chief Justice: On 1 April 1999 a jury at the Central Criminal Court convicted the appellant of two counts of murder. He had earlier been acquitted of two further counts of murder on the direction of the trial judge, Potts J.

The particulars of count one, on which the appellant was unanimously convicted, were that on a day between 19 September 1942 and 27 September 1942 the appellant, 'a person resident in the United Kingdom on 8 March 1990, in Domachevo, Belorussia, a town under German occupation, murdered a Jewess in circumstances constituting a violation of the laws and customs of war'. The particulars of count three, of which the appellant was convicted by a majority of 10–1, were to similar effect, save that the murder was said to be committed between 19 September and 4 October 1942, and the victim was specified to be a person other than that specified in count one. The two counts on which acquittal was directed were to similar effect, save that each referred to a named Jewish victim and the murders were said to have been committed during different periods in 1942.

All four counts were laid by virtue of the War Crimes Act 1991 which in section 1 provides, so far as relevant:

'(1) Subject to the provisions of this section, proceedings for murder . . . may be brought against a person in the United Kingdom irrespective of his nationality at the time of the alleged offence if that offence—

(a) was committed during the period beginning with 1 September 1939 and ending with 5 June 1945 in a place which at the time was part of Germany or under German occupation; and

(b) constituted a violation of the laws and customs of war.

(2) No proceedings shall by virtue of this section be brought against any person unless he was on 8 March 1990, or has subsequently become, . . . resident in the United Kingdom . . .'.

It was not disputed at the trial that the legal conditions for application of this section were met. The proceedings were for murder. The murders were said to have been committed within the period specified in section 1(1)(a). They were said to have been committed at a place, Domachevo, which was at the time in German occupation. The victims were civilian members of the Jewish population, and their killing (if committed) was a violation of the laws and customs of war. The appellant has for many years before 8 March 1990 been a resident of the United Kingdom.

The appeal was dismissed. Sawoniuk died in the autumn of 2005.

15.3.1.2 Individual liability

In terms of the Judgment of the Nuremberg International Military Tribunal, international law was accepted as imposing duties and liabilities upon individuals as well as States, thus justifying the punishment of individuals for what was, in effect, a violation of international law and thus commonly regarded as the exclusive domain of States. 'Crimes against international law are committed by men, not by abstract entities, and only by punishing individuals who commit such crimes can the provisions of international law be enforced.'

Prosecutor v Dusko Tadic, IT–94–1-T Appeal Judgment 15 July 1999

Tadic was indicted with thirty-four counts of crimes within the jurisdiction of the International Criminal Tribunal for the Former Yugoslavia. He pled not guilty on all accounts. Eventually, the trial chamber convicted him of nine counts and in part of a further two counts.

Thus, all those who have engaged in serious violations of international humanitarian law, whatever the manner in which they may have perpetrated, or participated in the perpetration of those violations, must be brought to justice. If this is so, it is fair to conclude that the Statute does not confine itself to providing for jurisdiction over those persons who plan, instigate, order, physically perpetrate a crime or otherwise aid and abet in its planning, preparation or execution. The Statute does not stop there. It does not exclude those modes of participating in the commission of crimes which occur where several persons having a common purpose embark on criminal activity that is then carried out either jointly or by some members of this plurality of persons. Whoever contributes to the commission of crimes by the group of persons or some members of the group, in execution of a common criminal purpose, may be held to be criminally liable, subject to certain conditions, which are specified below.

191. The above interpretation is not only dictated by the object and purpose of the Statute but is also warranted by the very nature of many international crimes which are committed most commonly in wartime situations. Most of the time these crimes do not result from the criminal propensity of single individuals but constitute manifestations of collective criminality: the crimes are often carried out by groups of individuals acting in pursuance of a common criminal design. Although only some members of the group may physically perpetrate the criminal act (murder, extermination, wanton destruction of cities, towns or villages, etc.), the participation and contribution of the other members of the group is often vital in facilitating the commission of the offence in question. It follows that the moral gravity of such participation is often no less—or indeed no different—from that of those actually carrying out the acts in question.

192. Under these circumstances, to hold criminally liable as a perpetrator only the person who materially performs the criminal act would disregard the role as co-perpetrators of all those who in some way made it possible for the perpetrator physically to carry out that criminal act. At the same time, depending upon the circumstances, to hold the latter liable only as aiders and abettors might understate the degree of their criminal responsibility.

193. This interpretation, based on the Statute and the inherent characteristics of many crimes perpetrated in wartime, warrants the conclusion that international criminal responsibility embraces actions perpetrated by a collectivity of persons in furtherance of a common criminal design. It may also be noted that—as will be mentioned below—international criminal rules on common purpose are substantially rooted in, and to a large extent reflect, the position taken by many States of the world in their national legal systems.

Since the military tribunals in Tokyo and Nuremberg after the Second World War, international criminal law has become increasingly prevalent in international relations. The following extract indicates the jurisdiction of the Nuremberg Tribunal, created after the conclusion of the Second World War.

Agreement for the Prosecution and Punishment of the Major War Criminals of the European Axis, and Charter of the International Military Tribunal 1945 Art 6

The Tribunal established by the Agreement referred to in Article 1 hereof for the trial and punishment of the major war criminals of the European Axis countries shall have the power to try and punish persons who, acting in the interests of the European Axis countries, whether as individuals or as members of organizations, committed any of the following crimes. The following acts, or any of them, are crimes coming within the jurisdiction of the Tribunal for which there shall be individual responsibility:

(a) 'Crimes against peace': namely, planning, preparation, initiation or waging of a war of aggression, or a war in violation of international treaties, agreements or assurances, or participation in a common plan or conspiracy for the accomplishment of any of the foregoing;

(b) 'War crimes': namely, violations of the laws or customs of war. Such violations shall include, but not be limited to, murder, ill-treatment or deportation to slave labour or for any other purpose of civilian population of or in occupied territory, murder or ill-treatment of prisoners of war or persons on the seas, killing of hostages, plunder of public or private property, wanton destruction of cities, towns or villages, or devastation not justified by military necessity;

(c) 'Crimes against humanity': namely, murder, extermination, enslavement, deportation, and other inhumane acts committed against any civilian population, before or during the war, or persecutions on political, racial or religious grounds in execution of or in connection with any crime within the jurisdiction of the Tribunal, whether or not in violation of the domestic law of the country where perpetrated.

Leaders, organizers, instigators and accomplices participating in the formulation or execution of a common plan or conspiracy to commit any of the foregoing crimes are responsible for all acts performed by any persons in execution of such plan.

The genocide of Rwanda in 1994 and the plethora of war crimes committed during the dissolution of the former Yugoslavia in the early 1990s prompted the establishment of international military tribunals for both regions. Mixed tribunals and courts followed, hybrid bodies operating within the national system yet applying international and national laws. These were established in Sierra Leone, Cambodia and East Timor/ Indonesia. Now a permanent International Criminal Court has been established in the Hague. Its grounds of jurisdiction have been considered in Chapter 4. This section will thus focus on the emerging jurisprudence shaping international criminal law and indicating the likely scope of the law for future transgressions. Given the space constraints, a fraction of the relevant laws can be examined.

15.3.2   The crime of genocide

Genocide, although a comparatively new term, has long been recognised as a crime. Today, with universal acceptance of the principles enshrined in the Genocide Convention, widespread support for the *ad hoc* tribunals and Criminal Court and an international concession of regret on the 10th anniversary of the Rwandan genocide, the prohibition on genocide appears to be entrenched in customary international law and *jus cogens*. The Convention on the Prevention and Punishment of the Crime of Genocide was adopted in General Assembly Resolution 260II (9 December 1948) and considers genocide an odious scourge from which mankind should be liberated. Moreover, it clearly delineated genocide as a discrete crime.

Convention on the Prevention and Punishment of the Crime of Genocide, General Assembly resolution 260 A (III) of 9 December 1948

Article 1

The Contracting Parties confirm that genocide, whether committed in time of peace or in time of war, is a crime under international law which they undertake to prevent and to punish.

Article 2

In the present Convention, genocide means any of the following acts committed with intent to destroy, in whole or in part, a national, ethnical, racial or religious group, as such:

(a) Killing members of the group;

(b) Causing serious bodily or mental harm to members of the group;

(c) Deliberately inflicting on the group conditions of life calculated to bring about its physical destruction in whole or in part;

(d) Imposing measures intended to prevent births within the group;

(e) Forcibly transferring children of the group to another group.

Article 3

The following acts shall be punishable:

(a) Genocide;

(b) Conspiracy to commit genocide;

(c) Direct and public incitement to commit genocide;

(d) Attempt to commit genocide;

(e) Complicity in genocide. . . .

Article 6

Persons charged with genocide or any of the other acts enumerated in article III shall be tried by a competent tribunal of the State in the territory of which the act was committed, or by such international penal tribunal as may have jurisdiction with respect to those Contracting Parties which shall have accepted its jurisdiction.

Note particularly Art 6 given the lack of any international penal court until recently!

Question

To what extent is the definition in the convention unduly restrictive?—consider the potential for cultural genocide, which is omitted from the Convention.

Genocide has long been accepted as an international crime. The International Court of Justice was required to pronounce on its status in its advisory opinion on the Reservations to the Genocide Convention opinion.

Reservations to the Convention on the Prevention and Punishment of the Crime of Genocide, Advisory Opinion of 28 May 1951

The principles underlying the Convention are recognised by civilised nations as binding on States even without any conventional obligation. It was intended that the Convention would be universal in scope. Its purpose is purely humanitarian and civilising. The contracting States do not have any individual advantages or disadvantages nor interests of their own, but merely a common interest. This leads to the conclusion that the object and purpose of the Convention imply that it was the intention of the General Assembly and of the States which adopted it, that as many States as possible should participate.

Genocide also appears in the Statute of the International Criminal Court.

Rome Statute of the International Criminal Court Art 6

For the purpose of this Statute, 'genocide' means any of the following acts committed with intent to destroy, in whole or in part, a national, ethnical, racial or religious group, as such:

(a) Killing members of the group;

(b) Causing serious bodily or mental harm to members of the group;

(c) Deliberately inflicting on the group conditions of life calculated to bring about its physical destruction in whole or in part;

(d) Imposing measures intended to prevent births within the group;

(e) Forcibly transferring children of the group to another group.

Question

Are there any differences between the definition in the Statute of the International Criminal Court and that in the earlier Genocide Convention?

15.3.2.1   Rape as genocide

With the two *ad hoc* International Criminal Tribunals, the scope and nature of genocide has been considered in greater detail. One of the developments has been the inclusion of systematic rape in the definition of genocide. Rape is included in the list of crimes against humanity in the Statutes of the two tribunals and indeed the International Criminal Court. It is also deemed a war crime and can fall within inhuman treatment. The inclusion of it within genocide reflects its use as a tool for securing the physical destruction of an ethnic group.

Prosecutor v Jean-Paul Akayesu, ICTR–96–4–Tk, decision 2 September 1998,
Ad hoc International Tribunal for Rwanda

731. With regard, particularly, to the acts described in paragraphs 12(A) and 12(B) of the Indictment, that is, rape and sexual violence, the Chamber wishes to underscore the fact that in its opinion, they constitute genocide in the same way as any other act as long as they were committed with the specific intent to destroy, in whole or in part, a particular group, targeted as such. Indeed, rape and sexual violence certainly constitute infliction of serious bodily and mental harm on the victims and are even, according to the Chamber, one of the worst ways of inflicting harm on the victim as he or she suffers both bodily and mental harm. In light of all the evidence before it, the Chamber is satisfied that the acts of rape and sexual violence described above, were committed solely against Tutsi women, many of whom were subjected to the worst public humiliation, mutilated, and raped several times, often in public, in the Bureau Communal premises or in other public places, and often by more than one assailant. These rapes resulted in physical and psychological destruction of Tutsi women, their families and their communities. Sexual violence was an integral part of the process of destruction, specifically targeting Tutsi women and specifically contributing to their destruction and to the destruction of the Tutsi group as a whole.

732. The rape of Tutsi women was systematic and was perpetrated against all Tutsi women and solely against them. A Tutsi woman, married to a Hutu, testified before the Chamber that she was not raped because her ethnic background was unknown. As part of the propaganda campaign geared to mobilizing the Hutu against the Tutsi, the Tutsi women were presented as sexual objects. Indeed, the Chamber was told, for an example, that before being raped and killed, Alexia, who was the wife of the Professor, Ntereye, and her two nieces, were forced by the Interahamwe to undress and ordered to run and do exercises 'in order to display the thighs of Tutsi women'. The Interahamwe who raped Alexia said, as he threw her on the ground and got on top of her, 'let us now see what the vagina of a Tutsi woman takes like'. As stated above, Akayesu himself, speaking to the Interahamwe who were committing the rapes, said to them: 'don't ever ask again what a Tutsi woman tastes like'. This sexualized representation of ethnic identity graphically illustrates that tutsi women were subjected to sexual violence because they were Tutsi. Sexual violence was a step in the process of destruction of the tutsi group—destruction of the spirit, of the will to live, and of life itself.

733. On the basis of the substantial testimonies brought before it, the Chamber finds that in most cases, the rapes of Tutsi women in Taba were accompanied with the intent to kill those women. Many rapes were perpetrated near mass graves where the women were taken to be killed. A victim testified that Tutsi women caught could be taken away by peasants and men with

the promise that they would be collected later to be executed. Following an act of gang rape, a witness heard Akayesu say 'tomorrow they will be killed' and they were actually killed. In this respect, it appears clearly to the Chamber that the acts of rape and sexual violence, as other acts of serious bodily and mental harm committed against the Tutsi, reflected the determination to make Tutsi women suffer and to mutilate them even before killing them, the intent being to destroy the Tutsi group while inflicting acute suffering on its members in the process.

734. In light of the foregoing, the Chamber finds firstly that the acts described *supra* are indeed acts as enumerated in Article 2 (2) of the Statute, which constitute the factual elements of the crime of genocide, namely the killings of Tutsi or the serious bodily and mental harm inflicted on the Tutsi. The Chamber is further satisfied beyond reasonable doubt that these various acts were committed by Akayesu with the specific intent to destroy the Tutsi group, as such. Consequently, the Chamber is of the opinion that the acts alleged in paragraphs 12, 12A, 12B, 16, 18, 19, 20, 22 and 23 of the Indictment and proven above, constitute the crime of genocide, but not the crime of complicity; hence, the Chamber finds Akayesu individually criminally responsible for genocide.

Subsequent trials in both ad hoc tribunals have reinforced this argument. It is clear that systematic rape, while included in crimes against humanity, may also constitute genocide.

Question

Do you agree with the inclusion of rape in the scope of genocide? Consider carefully the arguments evinced in the tribunal.

The definition of rape is fairly broad though obviously some examples will fall within crimes against humanity/war crimes rather than genocide. See, generally, *Prosecutor v Furundzija*, IT–95–17/1, Trial Chamber decision 10 December 1998 at paras 174 et seq. In July 2000, the Appeals Court upheld the conviction and Furundzija was transferred to Finland to serve his sentence. On 29 July 2004, the President granted a request for early release filed by the Government of Finland, effective 17 August 2004.

15.3.3   Crimes against humanity

Crimes against humanity encompass a wide variety of activities which threaten human dignity and are repugnant. As mentioned above, rape (and indeed other forms of sexual violence) are included, as is torture. Elements of slavery and forced labour are also covered, though slavery constitutes an international crime in its own right.

Extreme forms of discriminatory behaviour may also fall within crimes against humanity.

International Convention on the Suppression and Punishment of the Crime of Apartheid 1973

1. The States Parties to the present Convention declare that apartheid is a crime against humanity and that inhuman acts resulting from the policies and practices of apartheid and similar policies and practices of racial segregation and discrimination, as defined in article II of the Convention, are crimes violating the principles of international law, in particular the purposes and principles of the Charter of the United Nations, and constituting a serious threat to international peace and security.

2. The States Parties to the present Convention declare criminal those organizations, institutions and individuals committing the crime of apartheid.

Crimes against humanity find expression today in Art 7 of the Rome Statute.

Rome Statute of the International Criminal Court Art 7

1. For the purpose of this Statute, 'crime against humanity' means any of the following acts when committed as part of a widespread or systematic attack directed against any civilian population, with knowledge of the attack:

(a) Murder;

(b) Extermination;

(c) Enslavement;

(d) Deportation or forcible transfer of population;

(e) Imprisonment or other severe deprivation of physical liberty in violation of fundamental rules of international law;

(f) Torture;

(g) Rape, sexual slavery, enforced prostitution, forced pregnancy, enforced sterilization, or any other form of sexual violence of comparable gravity;

(h) Persecution against any identifiable group or collectivity on political, racial, national, ethnic, cultural, religious, gender as defined in paragraph 3, or other grounds that are universally recognized as impermissible under international law, in connection with any act referred to in this paragraph or any crime within the jurisdiction of the Court;

(i) Enforced disappearance of persons;

(j) The crime of apartheid;

(k) Other inhumane acts of a similar character intentionally causing great suffering, or serious injury to body or to mental or physical health.

2. For the purpose of paragraph 1:

(a) 'Attack directed against any civilian population' means a course of conduct involving the multiple commission of acts referred to in paragraph 1 against any civilian population, pursuant to or in furtherance of a State or organizational policy to commit such attack;

(b) 'Extermination' includes the intentional infliction of conditions of life, *inter alia* the deprivation of access to food and medicine, calculated to bring about the destruction of part of a population;

(c) 'Enslavement' means the exercise of any or all of the powers attaching to the right of ownership over a person and includes the exercise of such power in the course of trafficking in persons, in particular women and children;

(d) 'Deportation or forcible transfer of population' means forced displacement of the persons concerned by expulsion or other coercive acts from the area in which they are lawfully present, without grounds permitted under international law;

(e) 'Torture' means the intentional infliction of severe pain or suffering, whether physical or mental, upon a person in the custody or under the control of the accused; except that torture shall not include pain or suffering arising only from, inherent in or incidental to, lawful sanctions;

(f) 'Forced pregnancy' means the unlawful confinement of a woman forcibly made pregnant, with the intent of affecting the ethnic composition of any population or carrying out other grave violations of international law. This definition shall not in any way be interpreted as affecting national laws relating to pregnancy;

(g) 'Persecution' means the intentional and severe deprivation of fundamental rights contrary to international law by reason of the identity of the group or collectivity;

(h) 'The crime of apartheid' means inhumane acts of a character similar to those referred to in paragraph 1, committed in the context of an institutionalized regime of systematic oppression and domination by one racial group over any other racial group or groups and committed with the intention of maintaining that regime;

(i) 'Enforced disappearance of persons' means the arrest, detention or abduction of persons by, or with the authorization, support or acquiescence of, a State or a political organization, followed by a refusal to acknowledge that deprivation of freedom or to give information on the fate or whereabouts of those persons, with the intention of removing them from the protection of the law for a prolonged period of time.

3. For the purpose of this Statute, it is understood that the term 'gender' refers to the two sexes, male and female, within the context of society. The term 'gender' does not indicate any meaning different from the above.

Crimes against humanity are, it appears, necessarily restricted to situations of armed conflict though note Saddam Hussein's conviction under Iraqi law in November 2006.

Prosecutor v Dusko Tadic, decision on the defence motion on jurisdiction, 10 August 1995, Case IT–94–1, International Criminal Tribunal for the Former Yugoslavia

The Indictment alleged that in May 1992, Serb forces attacked Bosnian Muslim and Croat population centres in the Prijedor municipality in Bosnia and Herzegovina. Thousands of Muslims and Croats were illegally detained in camps. The Indictment further alleged that between late May 1992 and 31 December 1992, Dusko Tadic participated in attacks on and the seizure, murder and maltreatment of Bosnian Muslims and Croats in the Prijedor municipality, both within and outside the camps.

77. The Defence claims that 'the Tribunal only has jurisdiction under Article 5 of the Statute if it involves crimes that have been committed in the execution of or in connection with an international armed conflict.' It purports to find authority for this proposition requiring the existence of an armed conflict of an *international* nature in the Nuremberg Charter which, in its definition of crimes against humanity, spoke of inhumane acts committed 'in execution of or in connection with any crime within the jurisdiction of the Tribunal . . .' and in the affirmation given to the principles of international law recognised by the Charter of the Nuremberg Tribunal and Judgement of the Tribunal in General Assembly resolution 95(1) of 1948. The Defence further contends that the broadening of the scope of Article 5 to crimes when committed in armed conflicts of an *internal* character offends the *nullum crimen* principle.

. . . . [The Trial Chamber does not agree . . .]

81. Finally, this view that crimes against humanity are autonomous is confirmed by the *opus classicus* on international law, *Oppenheim's International Law*, where special reference is made to the fact that crimes against humanity 'are now generally regarded as a self-contained category, without the need for any formal link with war crimes . . .' (R. Jennings and A. Watts, I *Oppenheim's International Law* 966 (1992)).

82. Even were it arguable that a nexus is required between crimes against humanity and war crimes, the element of internationality certainly forms no jurisidictional criterion because, as has been shown above, war crimes are prohibited under customary international law in armed conflicts both of an international and internal nature.

83. In conclusion, the Trial Chamber emphasises that the definition of Article 5 is in fact more restrictive than the general definition of crimes against humanity recognised by customary international law. The inclusion of the nexus with armed conflict in the article imposes a limitation on the jurisdiction of the International Tribunal and certainly can in no way offend the *nullum crimen* principle so as to bar the International Tribunal from trying the crimes enumerated therein. Because the language of Article 5 is clear, the crimes against humanity to be tried in the International Tribunal must have a nexus with an armed conflict, be it international or internal.

15.3.4   War crimes

The scope of war crimes has continued to evolve. War crimes are serious violations of customary and treaty rules governing the conduct of armed conflict. As the *ad hoc* international tribunals have clarified, the concept of war crimes may also include violations of rules governing civil (internal) conflicts. With the number of internal conflicts worldwide, this development has marked importance. The terms of the Statute of the International Criminal Court makes it clear that inter-national and internal conflicts are included within the ambit of war crimes.

Rome Statute of the International Criminal Court Art 8

1. The Court shall have jurisdiction in respect of war crimes in particular when committed as part of a plan or policy or as part of a large-scale commission of such crimes.

2. For the purpose of this Statute, 'war crimes' means:

(a) Grave breaches of the Geneva Conventions of 12 August 1949, namely, any of the following acts against persons or property protected under the provisions of the relevant Geneva Convention:

 (i) Wilful killing;

 (ii) Torture or inhuman treatment, including biological experiments;

 (iii) Wilfully causing great suffering, or serious injury to body or health;

 (iv) Extensive destruction and appropriation of property, not justified by military necessity and carried out unlawfully and wantonly;

 (v) Compelling a prisoner of war or other protected person to serve in the forces of a hostile Power;

 (vi) Wilfully depriving a prisoner of war or other protected person of the rights of fair and regular trial;

 (vii) Unlawful deportation or transfer or unlawful confinement;

 (viii) Taking of hostages.

(b) Other serious violations of the laws and customs applicable in international armed conflict, within the established framework of international law, namely, any of the following acts:

 (i) Intentionally directing attacks against the civilian population as such or against individual civilians not taking direct part in hostilities;

 (ii) Intentionally directing attacks against civilian objects, that is, objects which are not military objectives;

 (iii) Intentionally directing attacks against personnel, installations, material, units or vehicles involved in a humanitarian assistance or peacekeeping mission in accordance with the Charter of the United Nations, as long as they are entitled to the protection given to civilians or civilian objects under the international law of armed conflict;

 (iv) Intentionally launching an attack in the knowledge that such attack will cause incidental loss of life or injury to civilians or damage to civilian objects or widespread, long-term and severe damage to the natural environment which would be clearly excessive in relation to the concrete and direct overall military advantage anticipated;

 (v) Attacking or bombarding, by whatever means, towns, villages, dwellings or buildings which are undefended and which are not military objectives;

 (vi) Killing or wounding a combatant who, having laid down his arms or having no longer means of defence, has surrendered at discretion;

(vii)   Making improper use of a flag of truce, of the flag or of the military insignia and uniform of the enemy or of the United Nations, as well as of the distinctive emblems of the Geneva Conventions, resulting in death or serious personal injury;

(viii)   The transfer, directly or indirectly, by the Occupying Power of parts of its own civilian population into the territory it occupies, or the deportation or transfer of all or parts of the population of the occupied territory within or outside this territory;

(ix)   Intentionally directing attacks against buildings dedicated to religion, education, art, science or charitable purposes, historic monuments, hospitals and places where the sick and wounded are collected, provided they are not military objectives;

(x)   Subjecting persons who are in the power of an adverse party to physical mutilation or to medical or scientific experiments of any kind which are neither justified by the medical, dental or hospital treatment of the person concerned nor carried out in his or her interest, and which cause death to or seriously endanger the health of such person or persons;

(xi)   Killing or wounding treacherously individuals belonging to the hostile nation or army;

(xii)   Declaring that no quarter will be given;

(xiii)   Destroying or seizing the enemy's property unless such destruction or seizure be imperatively demanded by the necessities of war;

(xiv)   Declaring abolished, suspended or inadmissible in a court of law the rights and actions of the nationals of the hostile party;

(xv)   Compelling the nationals of the hostile party to take part in the operations of war directed against their own country, even if they were in the belligerent's service before the commencement of the war;

(xvi)   Pillaging a town or place, even when taken by assault;

(xvii)   Employing poison or poisoned weapons;

(xviii)   Employing asphyxiating, poisonous or other gases, and all analogous liquids, materials or devices;

(xix)   Employing bullets which expand or flatten easily in the human body, such as bullets with a hard envelope which does not entirely cover the core or is pierced with incisions;

(xx)   Employing weapons, projectiles and material and methods of warfare which are of a nature to cause superfluous injury or unnecessary suffering or which are inherently indiscriminate in violation of the international law of armed conflict, provided that such weapons, projectiles and material and methods of warfare are the subject of a comprehensive prohibition and are included in an annex to this Statute, by an amendment in accordance with the relevant provisions set forth in articles 121 and 123;

(xxi)   Committing outrages upon personal dignity, in particular humiliating and degrading treatment;

(xxii)   Committing rape, sexual slavery, enforced prostitution, forced pregnancy, as defined in article 7, paragraph 2 (f), enforced sterilization, or any other form of sexual violence also constituting a grave breach of the Geneva Conventions;

(xxiii)   Utilizing the presence of a civilian or other protected person to render certain points, areas or military forces immune from military operations;

(xxiv) Intentionally directing attacks against buildings, material, medical units and transport, and personnel using the distinctive emblems of the Geneva Conventions in conformity with international law;

(xxv) Intentionally using starvation of civilians as a method of warfare by depriving them of objects indispensable to their survival, including wilfully impeding relief supplies as provided for under the Geneva Conventions;

(xxvi) Conscripting or enlisting children under the age of fifteen years into the national armed forces or using them to participate actively in hostilities.

(c) In the case of an armed conflict not of an international character, serious violations of article 3 common to the four Geneva Conventions of 12 August 1949, namely, any of the following acts committed against persons taking no active part in the hostilities, including members of armed forces who have laid down their arms and those placed *hors de combat* by sickness, wounds, detention or any other cause:

(i) Violence to life and person, in particular murder of all kinds, mutilation, cruel treatment and torture;

(ii) Committing outrages upon personal dignity, in particular humiliating and degrading treatment;

(iii) Taking of hostages;

(iv) The passing of sentences and the carrying out of executions without previous judgement pronounced by a regularly constituted court, affording all judicial guarantees which are generally recognized as indispensable.

(d) Paragraph 2 (c) applies to armed conflicts not of an international character and thus does not apply to situations of internal disturbances and tensions, such as riots, isolated and sporadic acts of violence or other acts of a similar nature.

(e) Other serious violations of the laws and customs applicable in armed conflicts not of an international character, within the established framework of international law, namely, any of the following acts:

(i) Intentionally directing attacks against the civilian population as such or against individual civilians not taking direct part in hostilities;

(ii) Intentionally directing attacks against buildings, material, medical units and transport, and personnel using the distinctive emblems of the Geneva Conventions in conformity with international law;

(iii) Intentionally directing attacks against personnel, installations, material, units or vehicles involved in a humanitarian assistance or peacekeeping mission in accordance with the Charter of the United Nations, as long as they are entitled to the protection given to civilians or civilian objects under the international law of armed conflict;

(iv) Intentionally directing attacks against buildings dedicated to religion, education, art, science or charitable purposes, historic monuments, hospitals and places where the sick and wounded are collected, provided they are not military objectives;

(v) Pillaging a town or place, even when taken by assault;

(vi) Committing rape, sexual slavery, enforced prostitution, forced pregnancy, as defined in article 7, paragraph 2 (f), enforced sterilization, and any other form of sexual violence also constituting a serious violation of article 3 common to the four Geneva Conventions;

(vii) Conscripting or enlisting children under the age of fifteen years into armed forces or groups or using them to participate actively in hostilities;

(viii) Ordering the displacement of the civilian population for reasons related to the conflict, unless the security of the civilians involved or imperative military reasons so demand;

(ix) Killing or wounding treacherously a combatant adversary;

(x) Declaring that no quarter will be given;

(xi) Subjecting persons who are in the power of another party to the conflict to physical mutilation or to medical or scientific experiments of any kind which are neither justified by the medical, dental or hospital treatment of the person concerned nor carried out in his or her interest, and which cause death to or seriously endanger the health of such person or persons;

(xii) Destroying or seizing the property of an adversary unless such destruction or seizure be imperatively demanded by the necessities of the conflict;

(f) Paragraph 2 (e) applies to armed conflicts not of an international character and thus does not apply to situations of internal disturbances and tensions, such as riots, isolated and sporadic acts of violence or other acts of a similar nature. It applies to armed conflicts that take place in the territory of a State when there is protracted armed conflict between governmental authorities and organized armed groups or between such groups.

3. Nothing in paragraph 2 (c) and (e) shall affect the responsibility of a Government to maintain or re-establish law and order in the State or to defend the unity and territorial integrity of the State, by all legitimate means.

The rules of war include the Hague Conventions of 1899 and 1907 which consolidate and codify existing customary rules and practices on both the conduct of war and the treatment of those excluded from combat. The latter was elaborated on considerably by the Geneva Conventions of 1949 (and 1977 Protocols) as discussed above. Cassesse suggests that the previous distinction between the two sets of rules (Hague and Geneva) is 'fading away' (*International Criminal Law*, 2003, Oxford: OUP at p 48).

Prosecutor v Georges Anderson Nderubumwe Rutaganda, ICTR–96–3-T 6 December 1999

1. On April 6, 1994, a plane carrying President Juvenal Habyarimana of Rwanda and President Cyprien Ntaryamira of Burundi crashed at Kigali airport, killing all on board. Following the deaths of the two Presidents, widespread killings, having both political and ethnic dimensions, began in Kigali and spread to other parts of Rwanda. . . .

14. On or about April 11, 1994, immediately after the Belgians withdrew from the ETO school, members of the Rwandan armed forces, the gendarmerie and militia, including the Interahamwe, attacked the ETO school and, using machetes, grenades and guns, killed the people who had sought refuge there. The Interahamwe separated Hutus from Tutsis during the attack, killing the Tutsis. Georges RUTAGANDA participated in the attack at the ETO school, which resulted in the deaths of a large number of Tutsis.

90. . . . at the time the crimes alleged in the Indictment were perpetrated, persons were bound to respect the guarantees provided for by the 1949 Geneva Conventions and their 1977 Additional Protocols, as incorporated in Article 4 of the Statute. Violations thereof, as a matter of custom and convention, incurred individual responsibility, and could result in the prosecution of the authors of the offences.

91. The 1949 Geneva Conventions and Additional Protocol I generally apply to international armed conflicts, whereas Common Article 3 extends a minimum threshold of humanitarian protection to persons affected by non-international armed conflicts. This protection has been enhanced and developed in the 1977 Additional Protocol II. Offences alleged to be covered by Article 4 of the Statute must, as a preliminary matter, have been committed in the context of a conflict of a non-international character satisfying the requirements of Common Article 3, which

applies to 'armed conflict not of an international character' and Additional Protocol II, applicable to conflicts which 'take place in the territory of a High Contracting Party between its armed forces and dissident armed forces or other organized armed groups which, under responsible command, exercise such control over a part of its territory as to enable them to carry out sustained and concerted military operations and to implement this Protocol'.

94. In addition to armed conflicts of a non-international character, satisfying the requirements of Common Article 3, under Article 4 of the Statute, the Tribunal has the power to prosecute persons responsible for serious violations of the 1977 Additional Protocol II, a legal instrument whose overall purpose is to afford protection to persons affected by non-international armed conflicts. As aforesaid, this instrument develops and supplements the rules contained in Common Article 3, without modifying its existing conditions of applicability. Additional Protocol II reaffirms Common Article 3, which, although it objectively characterized internal armed conflicts, lacked clarity and enabled the States to have a wide area of discretion in its application. Thus the impetus behind the Conference of Government Experts and the Diplomatic Conference in this regard was to improve the protection afforded to victims in non-international armed conflicts and to develop objective criteria which would not be dependent on the subjective judgements of the parties. The result is, on the one hand, that conflicts covered by Additional Protocol II have a higher intensity threshold than Common Article 3, and on the other, that Additional Protocol II is immediately applicable once the defined material conditions have been fulfilled. If an internal armed conflict meets the material conditions of Additional Protocol II, it then also automatically satisfies the threshold requirements of the broader Common Article 3.

106. The crime committed must represent a serious violation of Common Article 3 and Additional Protocol II, as incorporated in Article 4 of the Statute. A 'serious violation' is one which breaches a rule protecting important values with grave consequences for the victim. The fundamental guarantees included in Article 4 of the Statute represent elementary considerations of humanity. Violations thereof would, by their very nature, be deemed serious.

117. Furthermore, the Chamber holds that offences covered under the Statute—genocide, crimes against humanity and violations of Article 3 common to Geneva Conventions and of Additional Protocol II—have disparate ingredients and, especially, that their punishment is aimed at protecting discrete interests. As a result, multiple offenses may be charged on the basis of the same acts, in order to capture the full extent of the crimes committed by an accused.

The trial chamber found no violation of war crimes. This was reversed on appeal and thus the first person was convicted of war crimes by the Rwandan tribunal.

Prosecutor v Georges Anderson Nderubumwe Rutaganda, ICTR–96–3–A 26 April 2003

573. The Prosecution's contention is that every reasonable trier of fact, (1) having found a general link between Rutaganda and one of the parties to the armed conflict; (2) having found a general link between killings by the Interahamwe za MRND and the armed conflict, and (3) having made several other findings about the role of the Interahamwe and Rutaganda in the particular crimes of conviction, could not help but find the required nexus between the crimes for which the respondent was convicted and the armed conflict. The Appeals Chamber notes that the error alleged by the Prosecution does not concern as such the factual conclusions reached by the Trial Chamber; rather, it concerns the Trial Chamber's refusal to make a last inference leap based on those observations.

574. The Appeals Chamber stresses that the only issue in the present appeal is whether the Trial Chamber committed an error of fact that occasioned a miscarriage of justice by finding that the Prosecutor had established beyond a reasonable doubt the existence of a nexus between the crimes for which Rutaganda was convicted and the armed conflict. Before examining the Prosecution's argument concerning the acquittals entered in respect of Counts 4 and 6, the Appeals Chamber deems it necessary to recall the applicable standard of review with respect to

allegations of factual error in an appeal against acquittal. In this instance, it is not enough for the Prosecution to show that a reasonable trier of fact could have come to a different conclusion from that reached by the Trial Chamber by making the inferential leap it urges this Chamber to make. The Prosecution must show that no reasonable trier of fact would have failed to make that leap, that is, that no reasonable trier of fact would have had any reasonable doubt that the required nexus between the crimes for which the Respondent was convicted and the armed conflict had been established.

584. For these reasons, the Appeals Chamber allows the Prosecution's appeal and, pursuant to Articles 6(1) and 4(a) of the Statute, holds that it has been established beyond reasonable doubt that Georges Rutaganda is individually responsible for the crimes of murder as violations of common Article 3 of the Geneva Conventions and, accordingly, convicts him on Counts 4 and 6 of the Indictment.

15.3.5 Torture

While the prohibition on torture is an integral aspect of contemporary human rights and non-derogable, it is also part of international humanitarian law. The two areas overlap, though this has caused little problem. Indeed, the Convention against Torture 1984 has contributed to International Humanitarian Law as a judgment of the Trial Chamber of the Yugoslav tribunal illustrates.

Prosecutor v Furundzija, IT–95–17/1, 10 December 1998 Trial Chamber

143. The prohibition of torture laid down in international humanitarian law with regard to situations of armed conflict is reinforced by the body of international treaty rules on human rights: these rules ban torture both in armed conflict and in time of peace. In addition, treaties as well as resolutions of international organisations set up mechanisms designed to ensure that the prohibition is implemented and to prevent resort to torture as much as possible.

144. It should be noted that the prohibition of torture laid down in human rights treaties enshrines an absolute right, which can never be derogated from, not even in time of emergency (on this ground the prohibition also applies to situations of armed conflicts). This is linked to the fact, discussed below, that the prohibition on torture is a peremptory norm or *jus cogens*. This prohibition is so extensive that States are even barred by international law from expelling, returning or extraditing a person to another State where there are substantial grounds for believing that the person would be in danger of being subjected to torture.

145. These treaty provisions impose upon States the obligation to prohibit and punish torture, as well as to refrain from engaging in torture through their officials. In international human rights law, which deals with State responsibility rather than individual criminal responsibility, torture is prohibited as a criminal offence to be punished under national law; in addition, all States parties to the relevant treaties have been granted, and are obliged to exercise, jurisdiction to investigate, prosecute and punish offenders. Thus, in human rights law too, the prohibition of torture extends to and has a direct bearing on the criminal liability of individuals.

146. The existence of this corpus of general and treaty rules proscribing torture shows that the international community, aware of the importance of outlawing this heinous phenomenon, has decided to suppress any manifestation of torture by operating both at the interstate level and at the level of individuals. No legal loopholes have been left.

However, a number of national courts have instituted proceedings for individuals involved in torture.

R v Bow Street Metropolitan Stipendiary Magistrates ex parte Pinochet Ugarte
[1999] 2 All ER 97

Provisional extradition warrants were issued in terms of the Extradition Act 1989 for the arrest of the former Chilean head of State. Spain had requested the extradition on charges of torture and conspiracy to commit torture. Senator Pinochet was arrested in a London hospital. He appealed against the warrants, not least on the basis of sovereign immunity. The following extracts from the House of Lords address the issue of torture under international law.

Lord Browne-Wilkinson: Moreover, the Republic of Chile accepted before your Lordships that the international law prohibiting torture has the character of *jus cogens* or a peremptory norm, i.e. one of those rules of international law which have a particular status. In *Furundzija (supra)* at para. 153, the Tribunal said:

> 'Because of the importance of the values it protects, [the prohibition of torture] has evolved into a peremptory norm or jus cogens, that is, a norm that enjoys a higher rank in the international hierarchy than treaty law and even "ordinary" customary rules. The most conspicuous consequence of this higher rank is that the principle at issue cannot be derogated from by states through international treaties or local or special customs or even general customary rules not endowed with the same normative force.... Clearly, the *jus cogens* nature of the prohibition against torture articulates the notion that the prohibition has now become one of the most fundamental standards of the international community. Furthermore, this prohibition is designed to produce a deterrent effect, in that it signals to all members of the international community and the individuals over whom they wield authority that the prohibition of torture is an absolute value from which nobody must deviate.' (See also the cases cited in Note 170 to the *Furundzija* case.)

The *jus cogens* nature of the international crime of torture justifies states in taking universal jurisdiction over torture wherever committed. International law provides that *offences jus cogens* may be punished by any state because the offenders are 'common enemies of all mankind and all nations have an equal interest in their apprehension and prosecution': *Demjanjuk v. Petrovsky* (1985) 603 F. Supp. 1468; 776 F. 2d. 571....

The Torture Convention was agreed not in order to create an international crime which had not previously existed but to provide an international system under which the international criminal—the torturer—could find no safe haven. Burgers and Danelius (respectively the chairman of the United Nations Working Group on the 1984 Torture Convention and the draftsmen of its first draft) say, at p. 131, that it was 'an essential purpose [of the Convention] to ensure that a torturer does not escape the consequences of his act by going to another country.'

I gather the following important points from the Torture Convention:

1) Torture within the meaning of the Convention can only be committed by 'a public official or other person acting in an official capacity', but these words include a head of state. A single act of official torture is 'torture' within the Convention.

2) Superior orders provide no defence.

3) If the states with the most obvious jurisdiction (the Article 5(1) states) do not seek to extradite, the state where the alleged torturer is found must prosecute or, apparently, extradite to another country, i.e. there is universal jurisdiction.

4) There is no express provision dealing with state immunity of heads of state, ambassadors or other officials.

5) Since Chile, Spain and the United Kingdom are all parties to the Convention, they are bound under treaty by its provisions whether or not such provisions would apply in the absence of treaty obligation. Chile ratified the Convention with effect from 30 October 1988 and the United Kingdom with effect from 8 December 1988....

Lord Goff of Chievely

> It is to be observed that no mention is made of state immunity in the Convention. Had it been intended to exclude state immunity, it is reasonable to assume that this would have been the subject either of a separate article, or of a separate paragraph in Article 7, introduced to provide for that particular matter. This would have been consistent with the logical framework of the Convention, under which separate provision is made for each topic, introduced in logical order.

15.3.6   Others

Non-derogable human rights (those derogable human rights a State has chosen to leave in force) and those rights which are now *jus cogens* remain in force during any conflict or emergency situation. Failing to respect the human rights of any human being whether or not caught up in conflict can clearly be a violation of international human rights law.

FURTHER READING

Ackerman, J, and O'Sullivan, E, *Practice and Procedure of the International Criminal Tribunal for the Yugoslavia with selected materials from the International Criminal Tribunal for Rwanda*, 2000, Leiden: Brill

Bantekas, I, and Nash, S, *International Criminal Law*, 2nd edn, 2003, London: Cavendish

Cassese, A, *International Criminal Law*, 2003, Oxford: Oxford University Press

De Than, C, and Shorts, E, *International Criminal Law and Human Rights*, 2003, London: Sweet and Maxwell

Destexhe, A, *Rwanda and Genocide in the Twentieth Century*, 1995, New York: New York University Press

Dormann, K, *Elements of War Crimes under the Rome Statute of the International Criminal Court: Sources and Commentary*, 2003, Cambridge: Cambridge University Press

Eden, P, and O'Donnell, T (eds), *September 11, 2001: A Turning Point in International and Domestic Law?*, 2005, Ardsley, NY: Transnational

Fitzpatrick, J, *Human Rights in Crisis. The International System for Protecting Rights during States of Emergency*, 1994, Philadelphia: University of Pennsylvania Press

Kittichaisaree, K, *International Criminal Law*, 2001, Oxford: Oxford University Press

Kunz, J, 'The UN Convention on Genocide' (1949) 43 AJIL 738

Kuper, L, *The Prevention of Genocide*, 1985, New Haven: Yale University Press

Lemkin, E, 'Genocide as a Crime under International Law' (1947) 41 American Journal of International Law 147

McGoldrick, D, *From 9–11 to the Iraq War 2003: International Law in an age of complexity*, 2004, Oxford/Portland: Hart Publishing

Meron, T, 'International Criminalisation of Internal Atrocities', 1995, 89 AJIL 554

Meron, T, 'Rape as a Crime under International Law', 1993, 87 AJIL 424

Meron, T, 'War Crimes Law Comes of Age', 1998, 92 AJIL 462

Mettraux, G, 'Crimes against Humanity in the Jurisprudence of the International Criminal Tribunals for the Former Yugoslavia and for Rwanda', 2002, 43 Harvard International Law Journal 237

Moir, L, *The Law of Internal Armed Conflict*, 2002, Cambridge: Cambridge University Press

Niarchos, C, 'Women, War and Rape Challenges facing the International Tribunal for the Former Yugoslavia', 1995, 17 Human Rights Quarterly 649

Rodley, N, *The Treatment of Prisoners under International Law*, 2nd edn, 1999, Oxford: Clarendon Press

Schabas, W, *Genocide in International Law: The Crime of Crimes*, 2000, Cambridge: Cambridge University Press

Van Schaack, B, 'The Crime of Political Genocide: Repairing the Genocide Convention's Blind Spot', 1997, 106 Yale Law Journal 2259

United Nations Office of the High Commissioner for Human Rights, *International Humanitarian Law and Human Rights*, Factsheet No. 13, Geneva: OHCHR

Wilson, R (ed), *Human Rights in the War on Terror*, 2005, Cambridge: CUP

Websites

www.icrc.org—The International Committee of the Red Cross
www.icc-cpi.org—The International Criminal Court
www.ictr.org—Ad hoc International Criminal Tribunal for Rwanda
www.un.org/icty/index.html—*Ad hoc* International Criminal Tribunal for the Former Yugoslavia